Black Jack

Volume 9

Osamu Tezuka

VERTICAL.

Translation—Maya Rosewood
Production—Glen Isip
　　　　 Akane Ishida
　　　　 Hiroko Mizuno

Copyright © 2010 by Tezuka Productions
Translation Copyright © 2010 by Vertical, Inc.

This is a work of fiction.

Published by Vertical, Inc., New York.

Originally published in Japanese as *Burakku Jakku 9*
by Akita Shoten, Tokyo, 1988.
Burakku Jakku first serialized in *Shukan Shonen Champion*,
Akita Shoten, 1973-83.

ISBN: 978-1-934287-73-6

Manufactured in the United States of America

First Edition

Vertical, Inc.
1185 Avenue of the Americas 32nd Floor
New York, NY 10036
www.vertical-inc.com

CONTENTS

TEACHER AND PUPIL

HISAO, YOU'LL BE LATE FOR SCHOOL!
I'M NOT GOING. MY HEAD HURTS.
AGAIN?
DID SOMETHING HAPPEN AGAIN AT SCHOOL?
UH, NO ... ...
THEN I'LL HAVE THE DOCTOR GIVE YOU A SHOT.
A REALLY PAINFUL SHOT.
UGH! I HATE SHOTS!
SEE? YOU'RE PERFECTLY FINE. GO WASH UP.

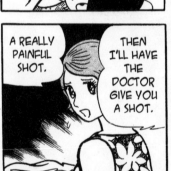

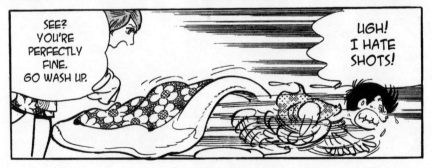

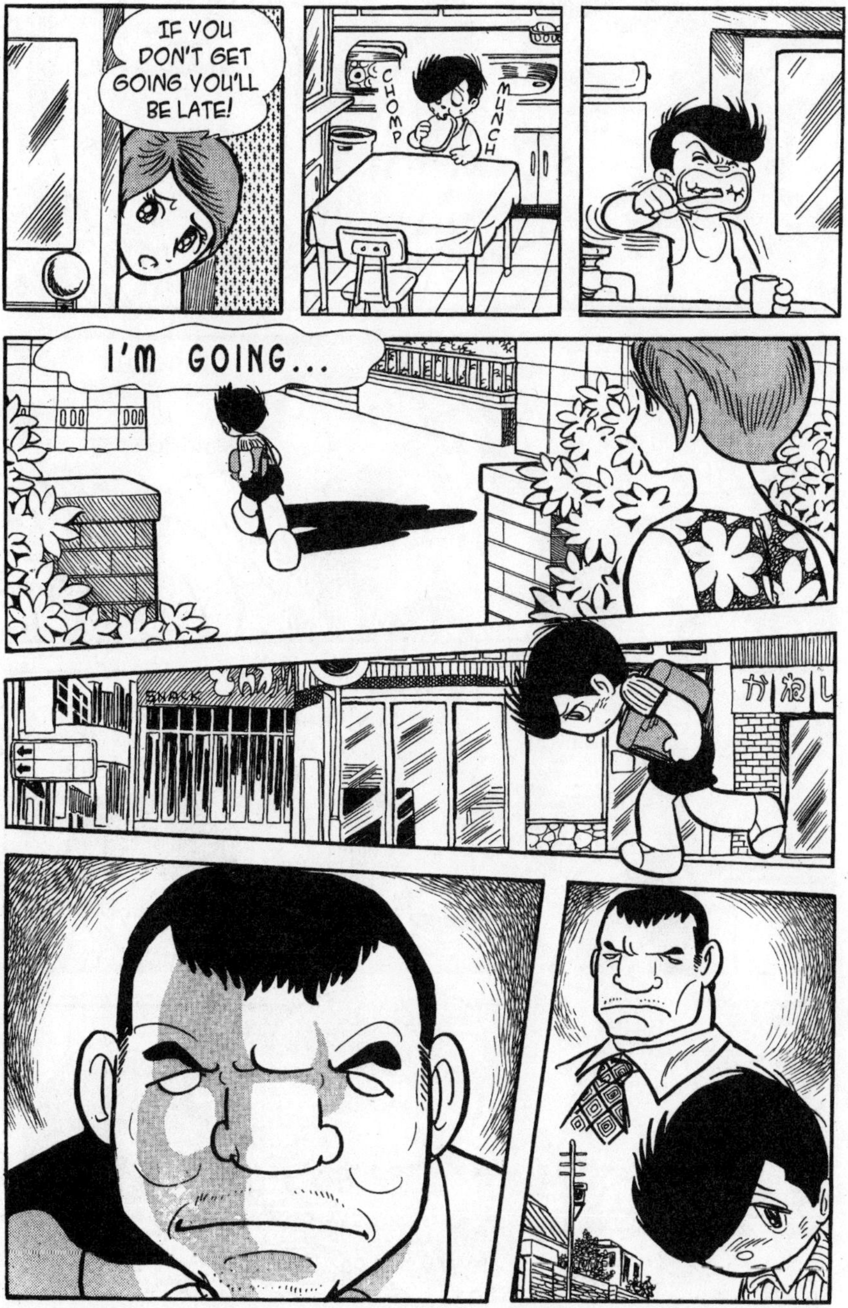
MUNCH
CHOMP
IF YOU DON'T GET GOING YOU'LL BE LATE!
I'M GOING...
SNACK

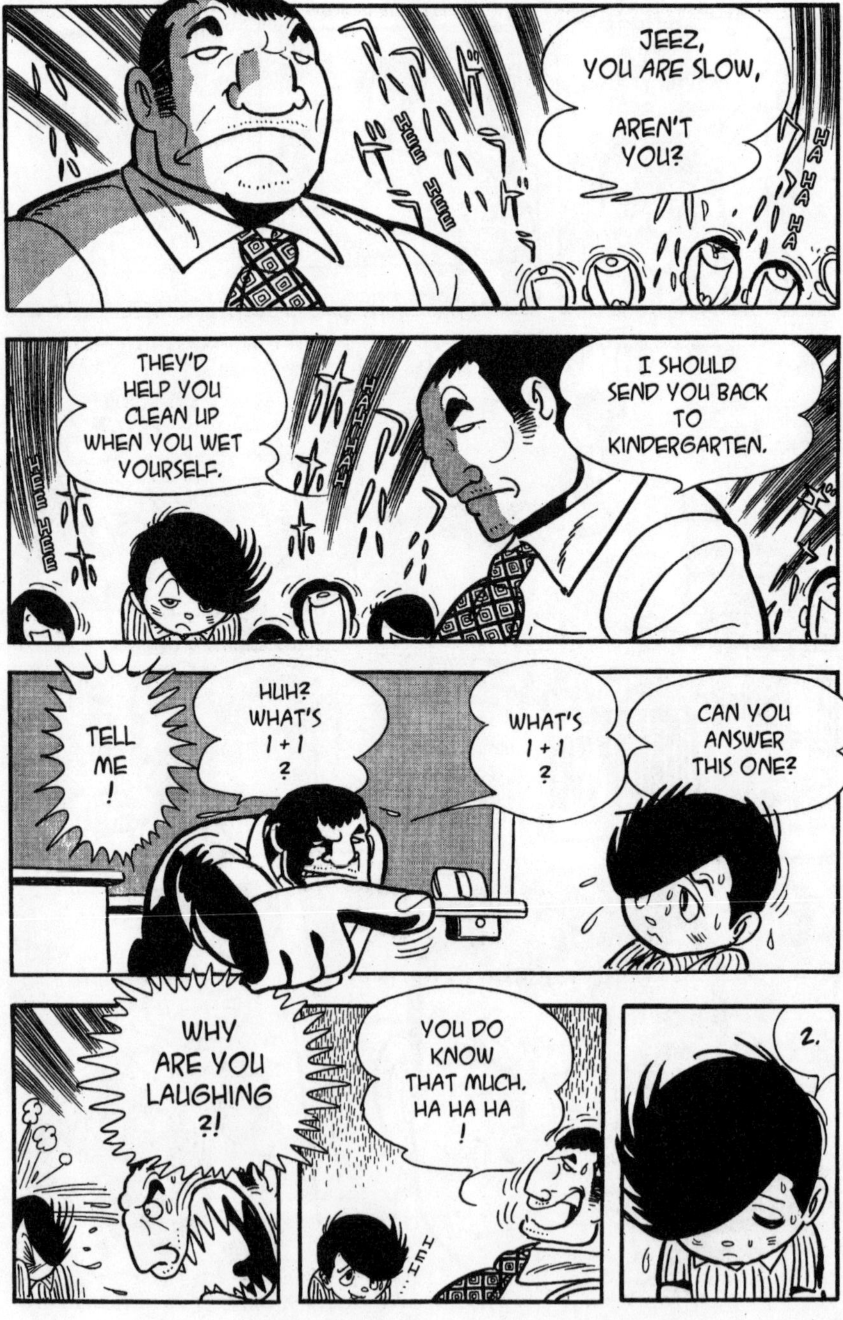
JEEZ, YOU ARE SLOW, AREN'T YOU?
HEE HEE
HA HA HA
I SHOULD SEND YOU BACK TO KINDERGARTEN.
THEY'D HELP YOU CLEAN UP WHEN YOU WET YOURSELF.
HEE HEE
CAN YOU ANSWER THIS ONE?
WHAT'S 1 + 1 ?
HUH? WHAT'S 1 + 1 ?
TELL ME !
2.
YOU DO KNOW THAT MUCH. HA HA HA !
HEH
WHY ARE YOU LAUGHING ?!

WORK ON IT TILL YOU GET IT.

IF YOU CAN'T THEN DON'T BE GRINNING!

WELL? TELL ME.

NOW... WHAT'S TWICE FIFTEEN TAKEN FROM TWICE TWENTY-FIVE?

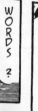

WORDS?

YEAH. I GIVE THEM A REAL TONGUE-LASHING.

I NEVER USE VIOLENCE. INSTEAD, I BEAT 'EM UP WITH WORDS.

IT MAKES ME SO MAD THAT I CAN'T.

REALLY, BAD STUDENTS MAKE YOU WANNA HIT THEM.

IT DEALS THEM THE SHOCK THEY NEED AS WELL AS ANY BLOW.

9

BUT THEY STILL HAVE TO SEE ME IN CLASS.

WELL, SURE. THERE ARE A FEW WHO PROBABLY WISH ME DEAD.

HATE ME?

WON'T THEY JUST BEGIN TO HATE YOU?

NOT ALL STUDENTS HAVE THAT SORT OF FIGHT IN THEM...

AND THEY START STUDYING TO SHOW ME.

I'M FINE AS LONG AS THEIR HATRED GETS THEM ALL FIRED UP

I CAN KEEP A SECRET.

WHAT IS IT?

ARE YOU SKIPPING SCHOOL AGAIN? WHY?

I HATE OUR TEACHER, MISTER MURAMASA!

10

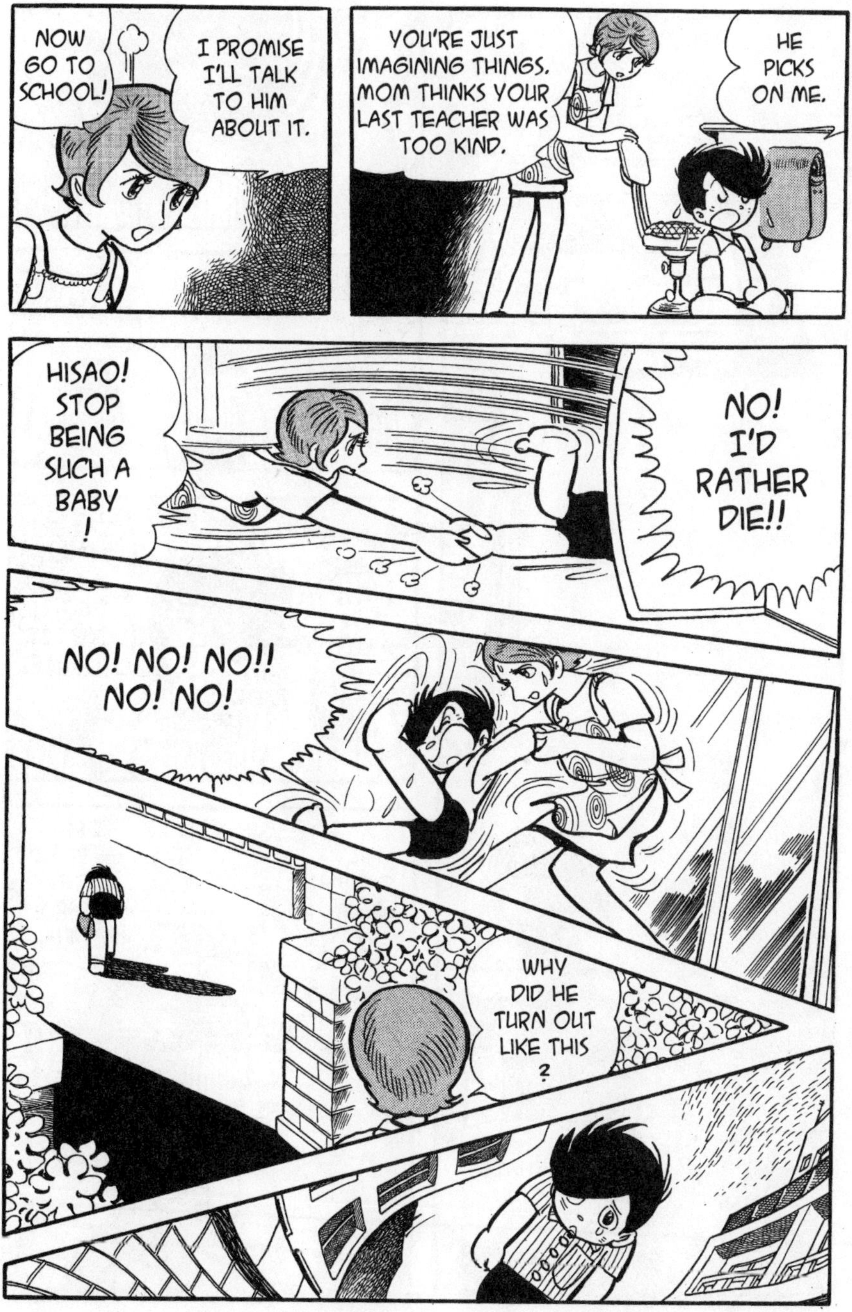
HE PICKS ON ME.
YOU'RE JUST IMAGINING THINGS. MOM THINKS YOUR LAST TEACHER WAS TOO KIND.
I PROMISE I'LL TALK TO HIM ABOUT IT.
NOW GO TO SCHOOL!
NO! I'D RATHER DIE!!
HISAO! STOP BEING SUCH A BABY!
NO! NO! NO!! NO! NO!
WHY DID HE TURN OUT LIKE THIS?

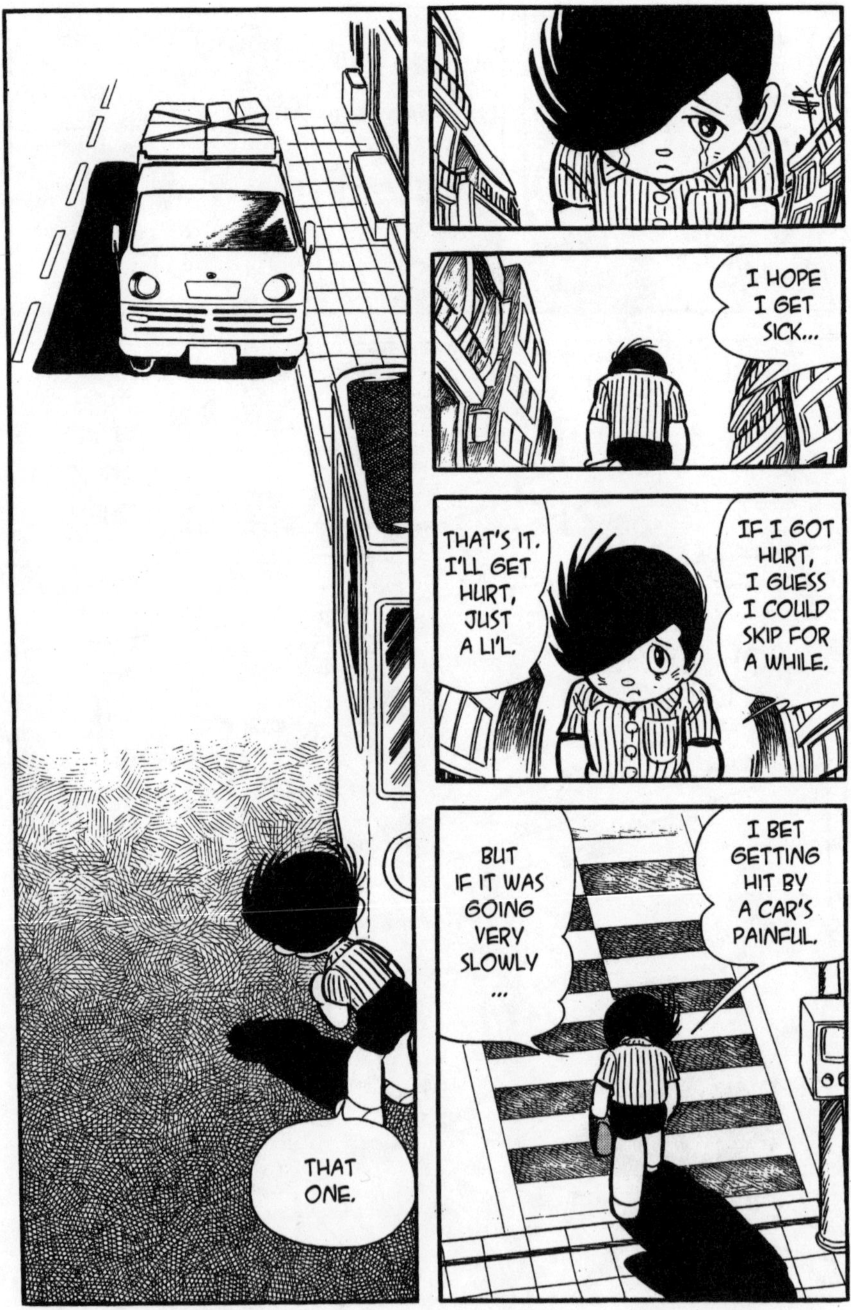
I HOPE I GET SICK...
IF I GOT HURT, I GUESS I COULD SKIP FOR A WHILE.
THAT'S IT. I'LL GET HURT, JUST A LI'L.
I BET GETTING HIT BY A CAR'S PAINFUL.
BUT IF IT WAS GOING VERY SLOWLY ...
THAT ONE.

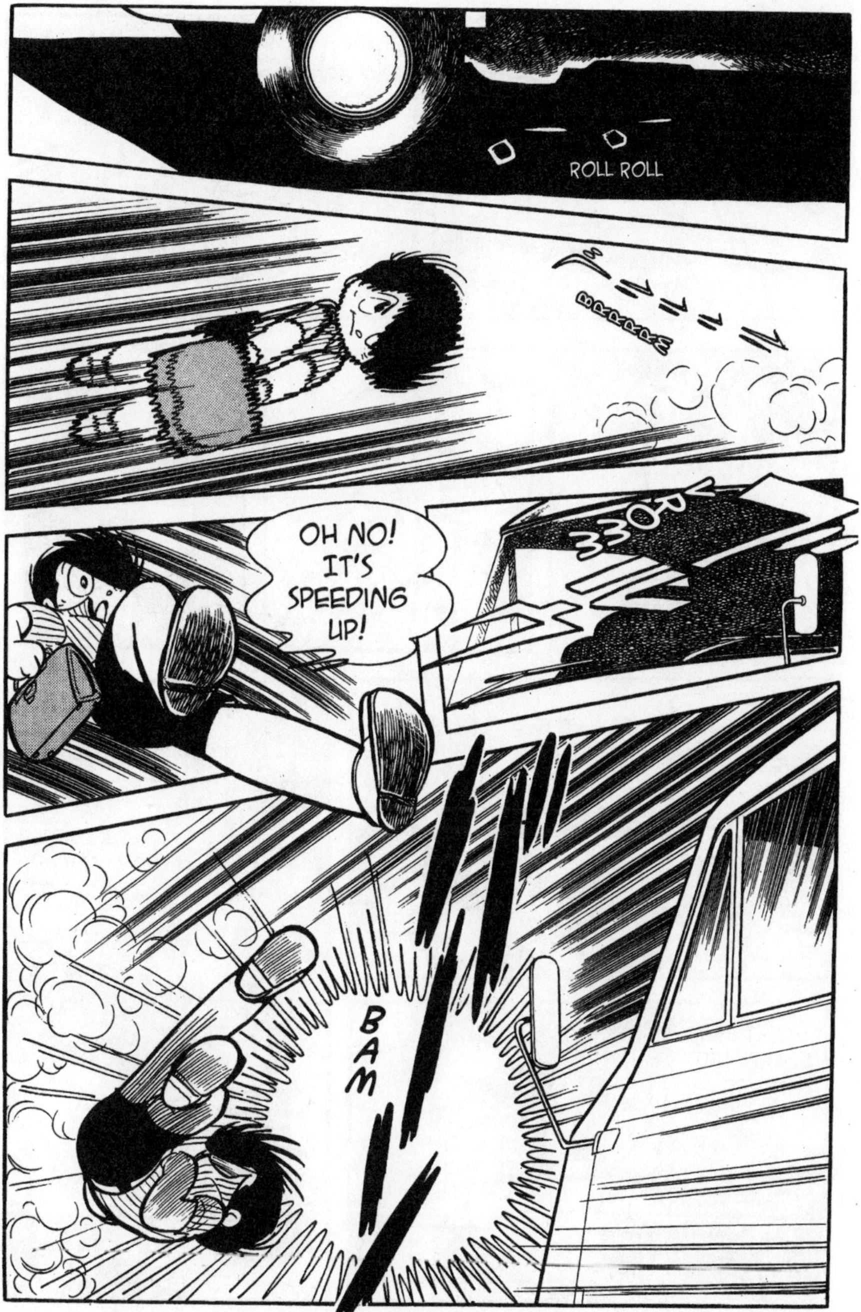
ROLL ROLL
BRRRRRM
VROOM
OH NO! IT'S SPEEDING UP!
BAM

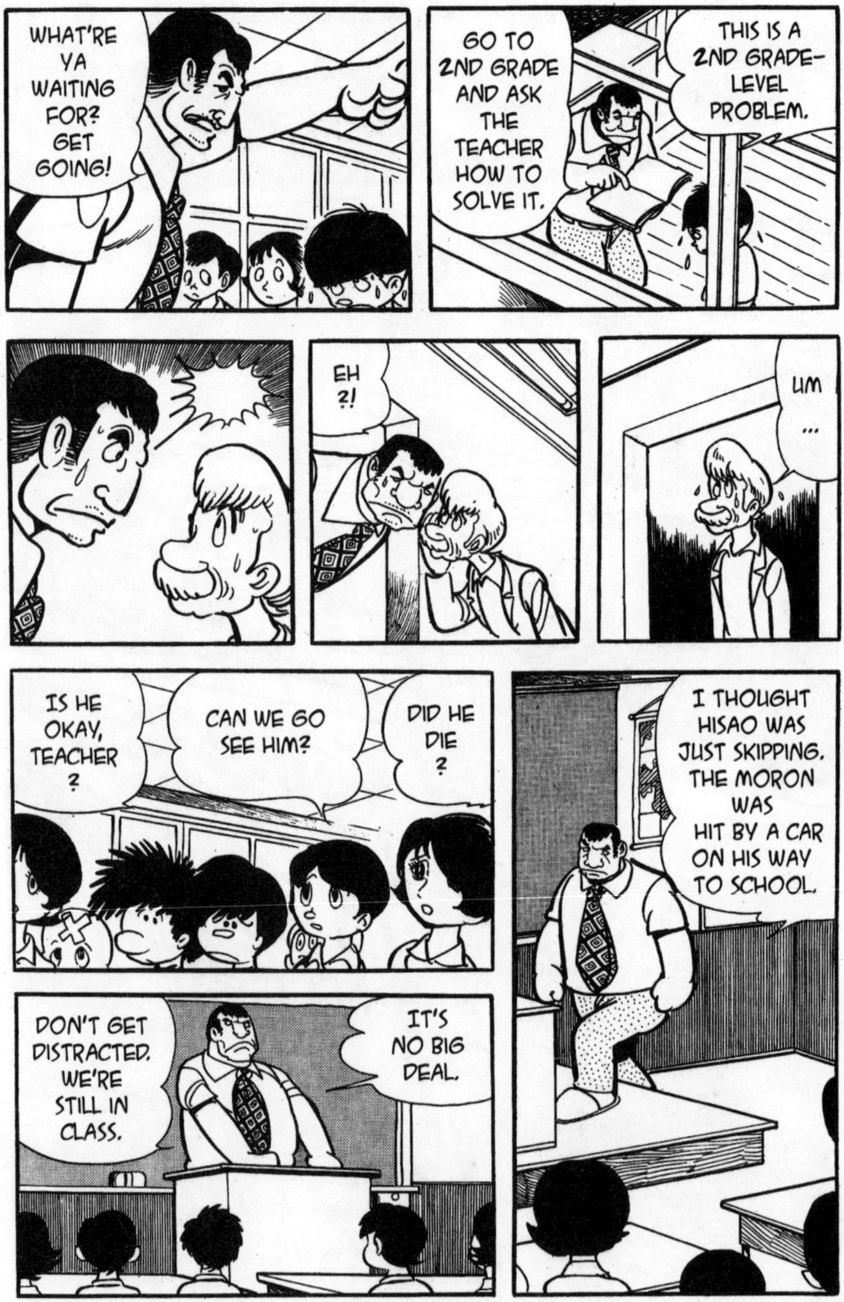
THIS IS A 2ND GRADE-LEVEL PROBLEM.
GO TO 2ND GRADE AND ASK THE TEACHER HOW TO SOLVE IT.
WHAT'RE YA WAITING FOR? GET GOING!
UM ...
EH ?!
I THOUGHT HISAO WAS JUST SKIPPING. THE MORON WAS HIT BY A CAR ON HIS WAY TO SCHOOL.
DID HE DIE ?
CAN WE GO SEE HIM?
IS HE OKAY, TEACHER ?
IT'S NO BIG DEAL.
DON'T GET DISTRACTED. WE'RE STILL IN CLASS.

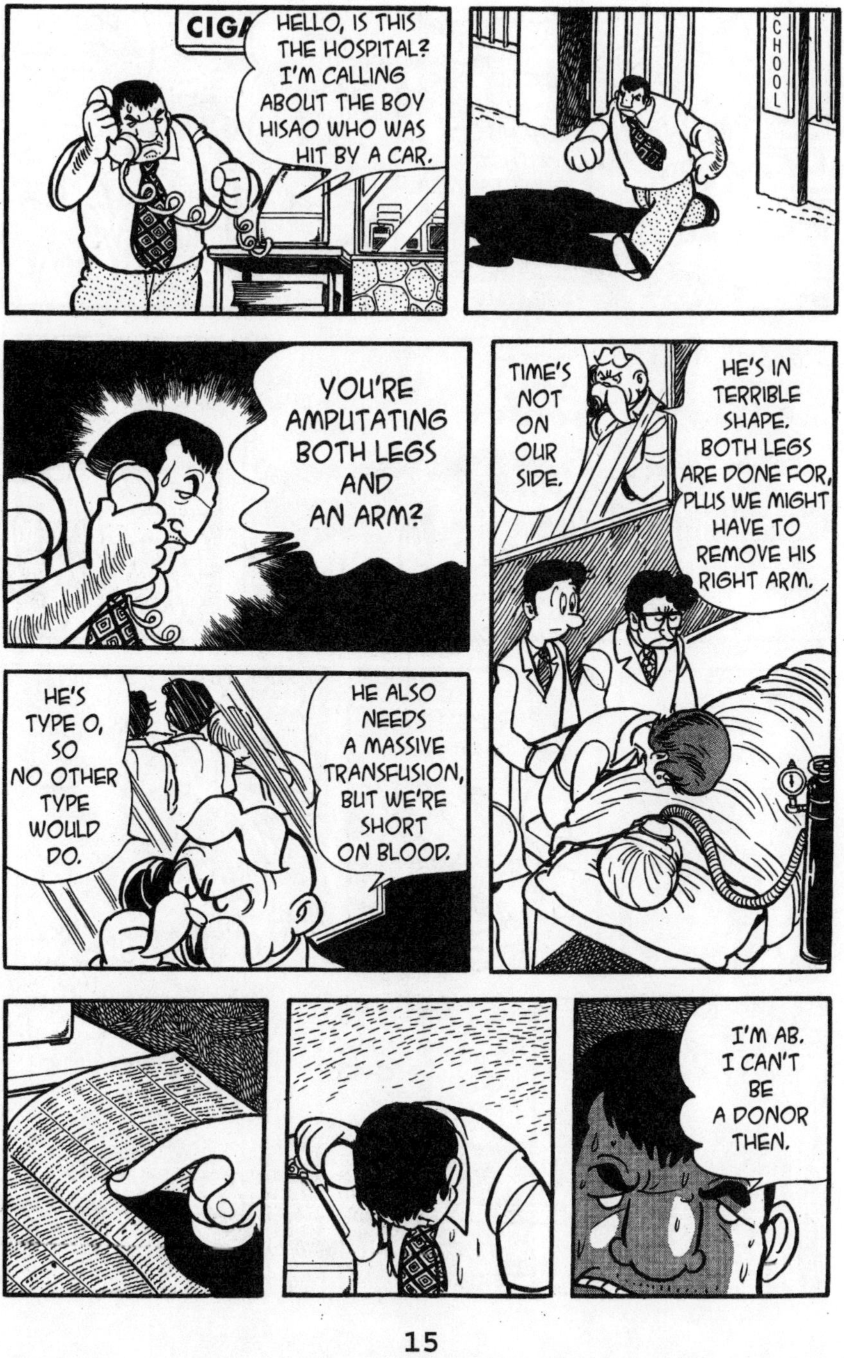
CIGA
HELLO, IS THIS THE HOSPITAL? I'M CALLING ABOUT THE BOY HISAO WHO WAS HIT BY A CAR.
HE'S IN TERRIBLE SHAPE. BOTH LEGS ARE DONE FOR, PLUS WE MIGHT HAVE TO REMOVE HIS RIGHT ARM.
TIME'S NOT ON OUR SIDE.
YOU'RE AMPUTATING BOTH LEGS AND AN ARM?
HE ALSO NEEDS A MASSIVE TRANSFUSION, BUT WE'RE SHORT ON BLOOD.
HE'S TYPE O, SO NO OTHER TYPE WOULD DO.
I'M AB. I CAN'T BE A DONOR THEN.

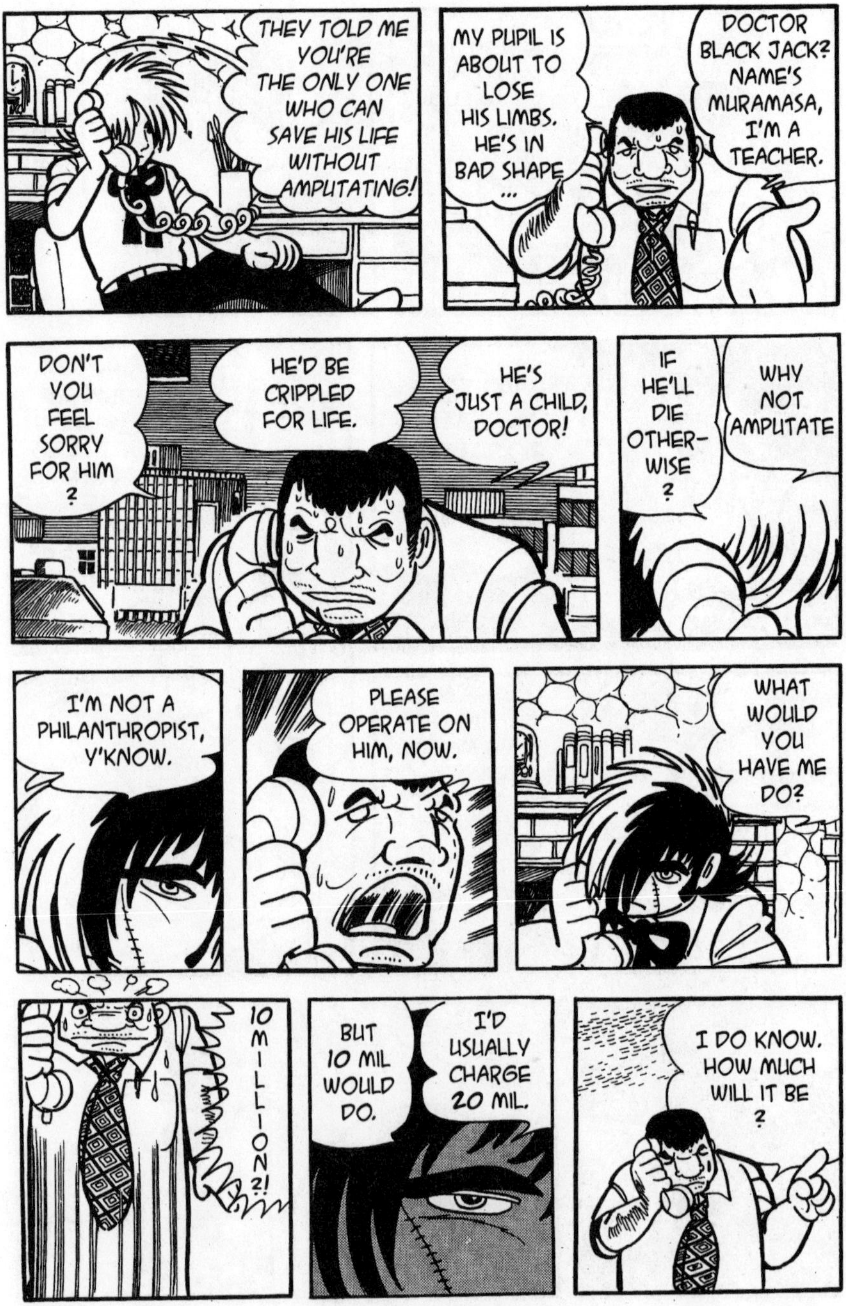
DOCTOR BLACK JACK? NAME'S MURAMASA, I'M A TEACHER.
MY PUPIL IS ABOUT TO LOSE HIS LIMBS. HE'S IN BAD SHAPE ...
THEY TOLD ME YOU'RE THE ONLY ONE WHO CAN SAVE HIS LIFE WITHOUT AMPUTATING!
WHY NOT AMPUTATE
IF HE'LL DIE OTHERWISE ?
HE'S JUST A CHILD, DOCTOR!
HE'D BE CRIPPLED FOR LIFE.
DON'T YOU FEEL SORRY FOR HIM ?
WHAT WOULD YOU HAVE ME DO?
PLEASE OPERATE ON HIM, NOW.
I'M NOT A PHILANTHROPIST, Y'KNOW.
I DO KNOW. HOW MUCH WILL IT BE ?
I'D USUALLY CHARGE 20 MIL.
BUT 10 MIL WOULD DO.
10 MILLION?!

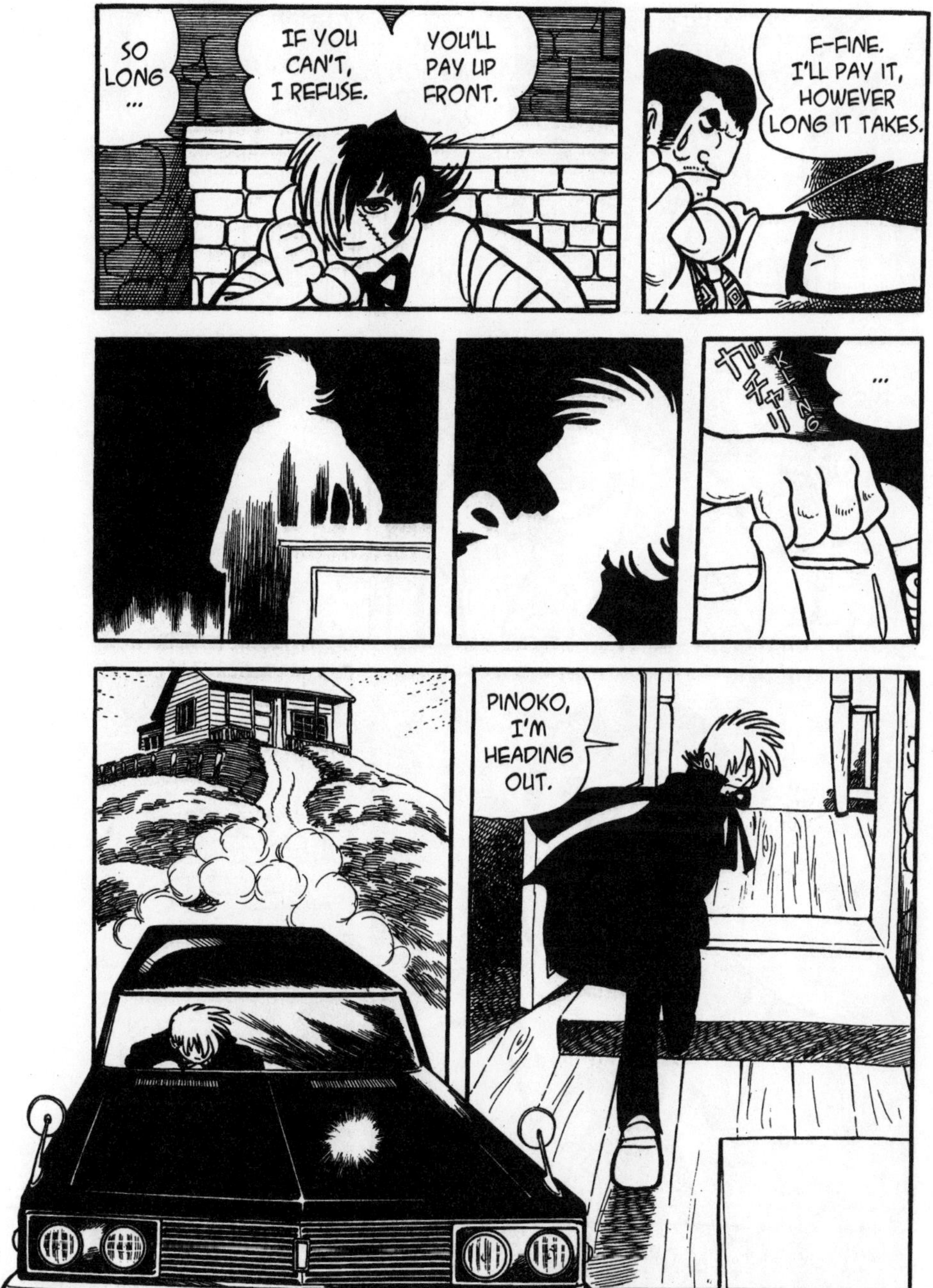
F-FINE. I'LL PAY IT, HOWEVER LONG IT TAKES.
YOU'LL PAY UP FRONT.
IF YOU CAN'T, I REFUSE.
SO LONG ...
KLING
...
PINOKO, I'M HEADING OUT.

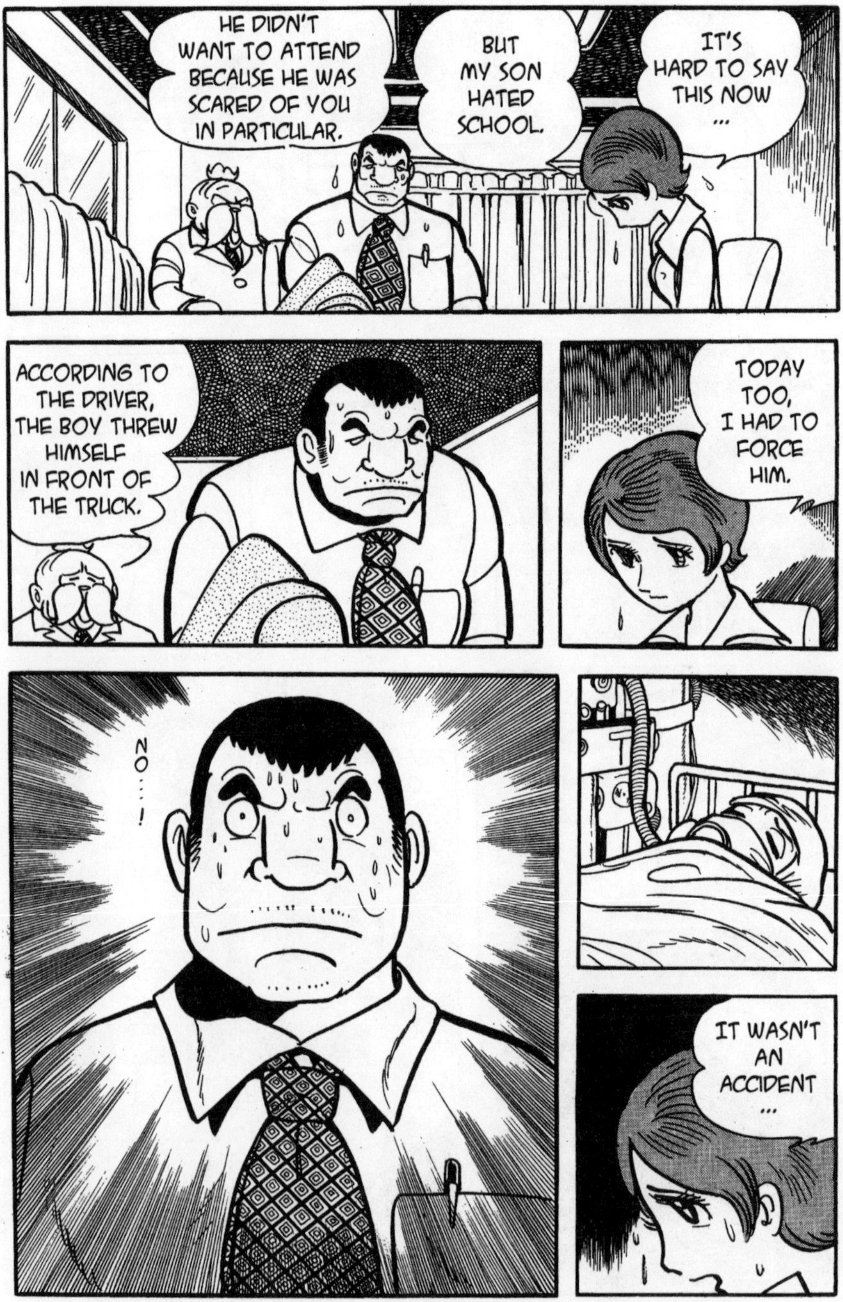
IT'S HARD TO SAY THIS NOW ...
BUT MY SON HATED SCHOOL.
HE DIDN'T WANT TO ATTEND BECAUSE HE WAS SCARED OF YOU IN PARTICULAR.
TODAY TOO, I HAD TO FORCE HIM.
ACCORDING TO THE DRIVER, THE BOY THREW HIMSELF IN FRONT OF THE TRUCK.
IT WASN'T AN ACCIDENT ...
NO...!

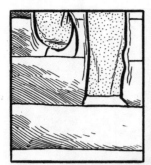

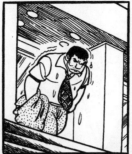

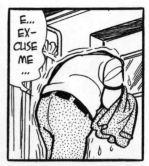

E... EX-CUSE ME ...
I'M BLACK JACK.
I... I'VE HEARD OF YOU, YES.
I'D LIKE TO WORK ON THE BOY WHO WAS RUN OVER.

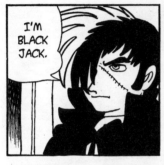

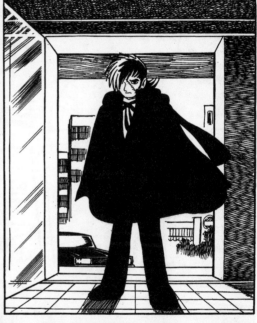

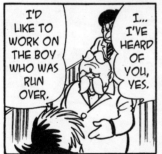

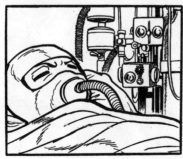

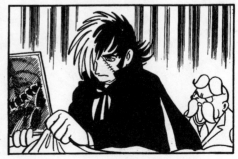

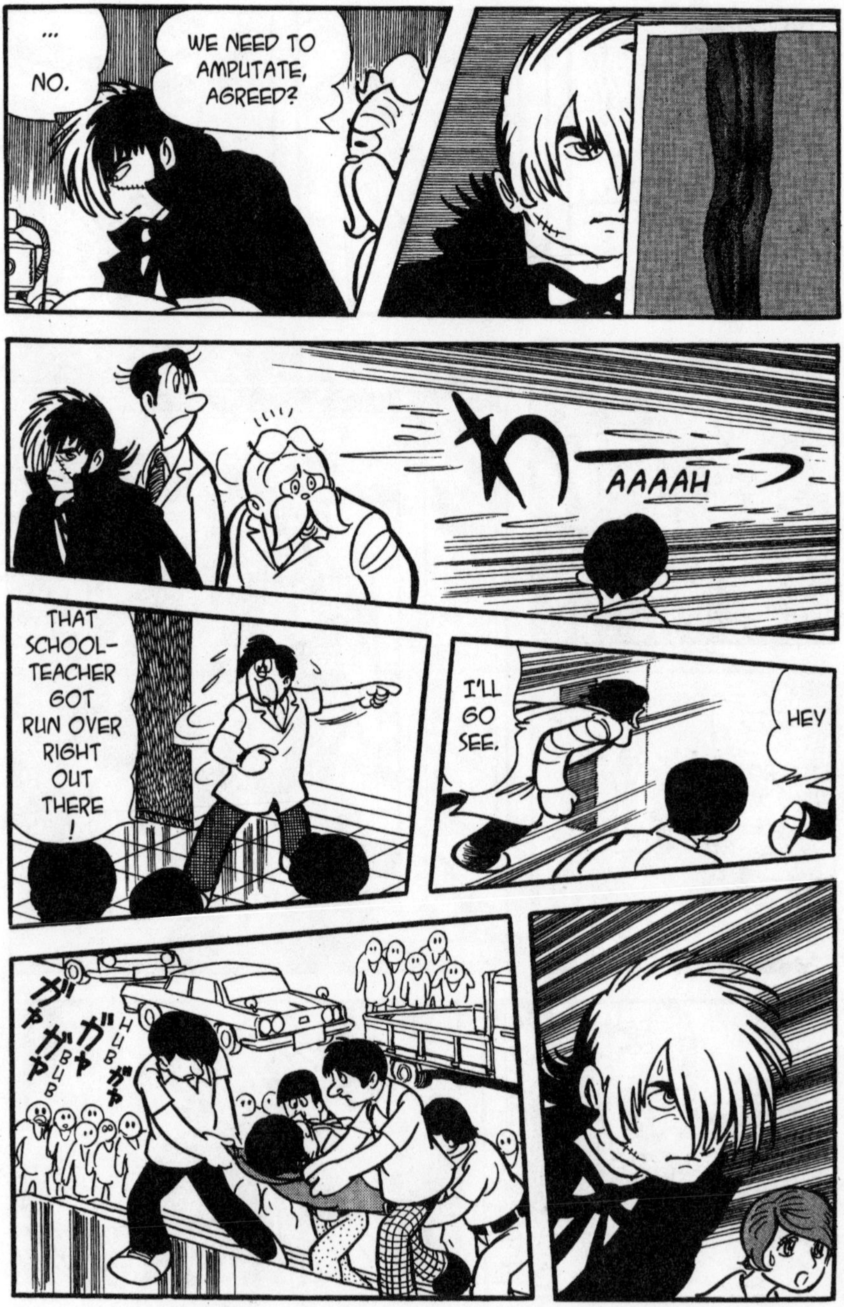
WE NEED TO AMPUTATE, AGREED?
... NO.
AAAAH
HEY
I'LL GO SEE.
THAT SCHOOL-TEACHER GOT RUN OVER RIGHT OUT THERE!
HUBBUB

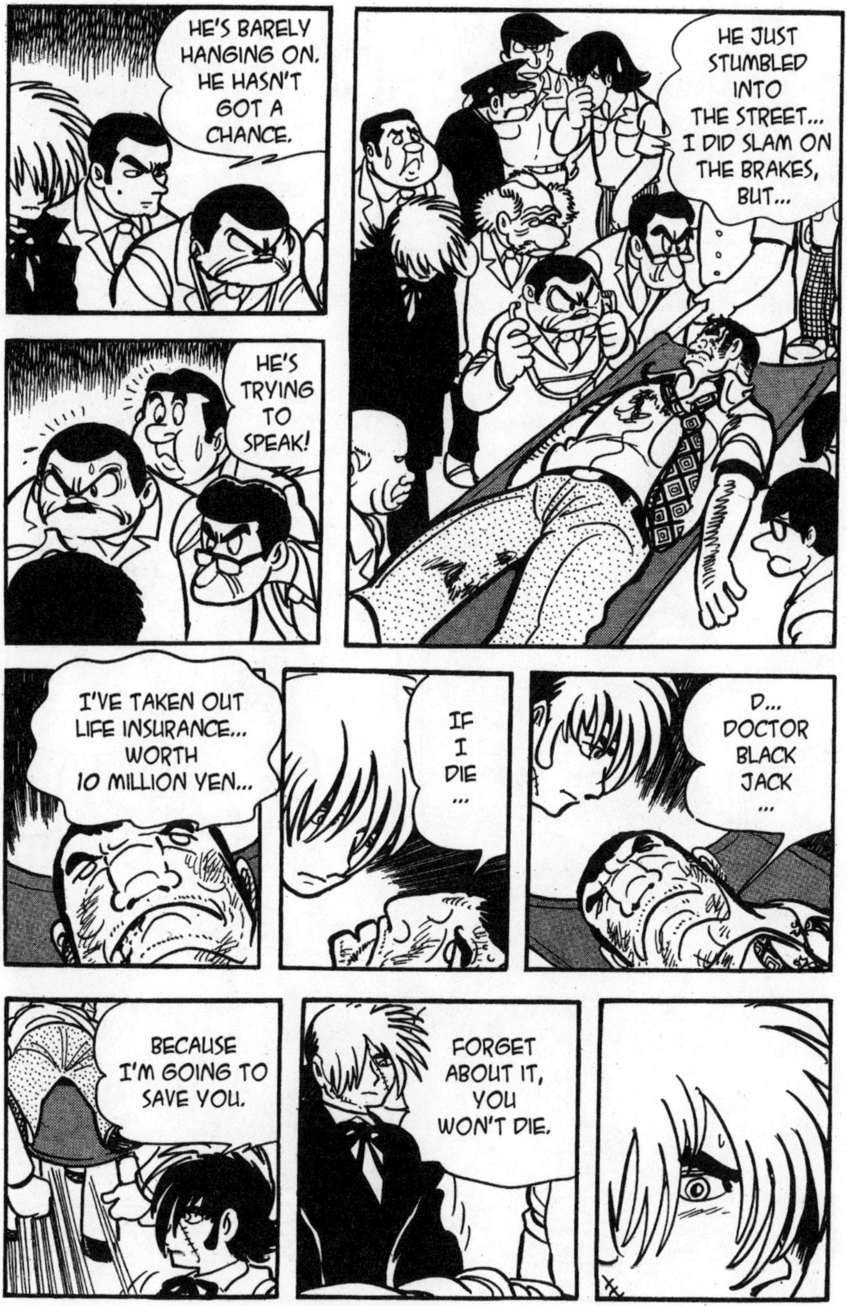
HE JUST STUMBLED INTO THE STREET... I DID SLAM ON THE BRAKES, BUT...
HE'S BARELY HANGING ON. HE HASN'T GOT A CHANCE.
HE'S TRYING TO SPEAK!
D... DOCTOR BLACK JACK ...
IF I DIE ...
I'VE TAKEN OUT LIFE INSURANCE... WORTH 10 MILLION YEN...
FORGET ABOUT IT, YOU WON'T DIE.
BECAUSE I'M GOING TO SAVE YOU.

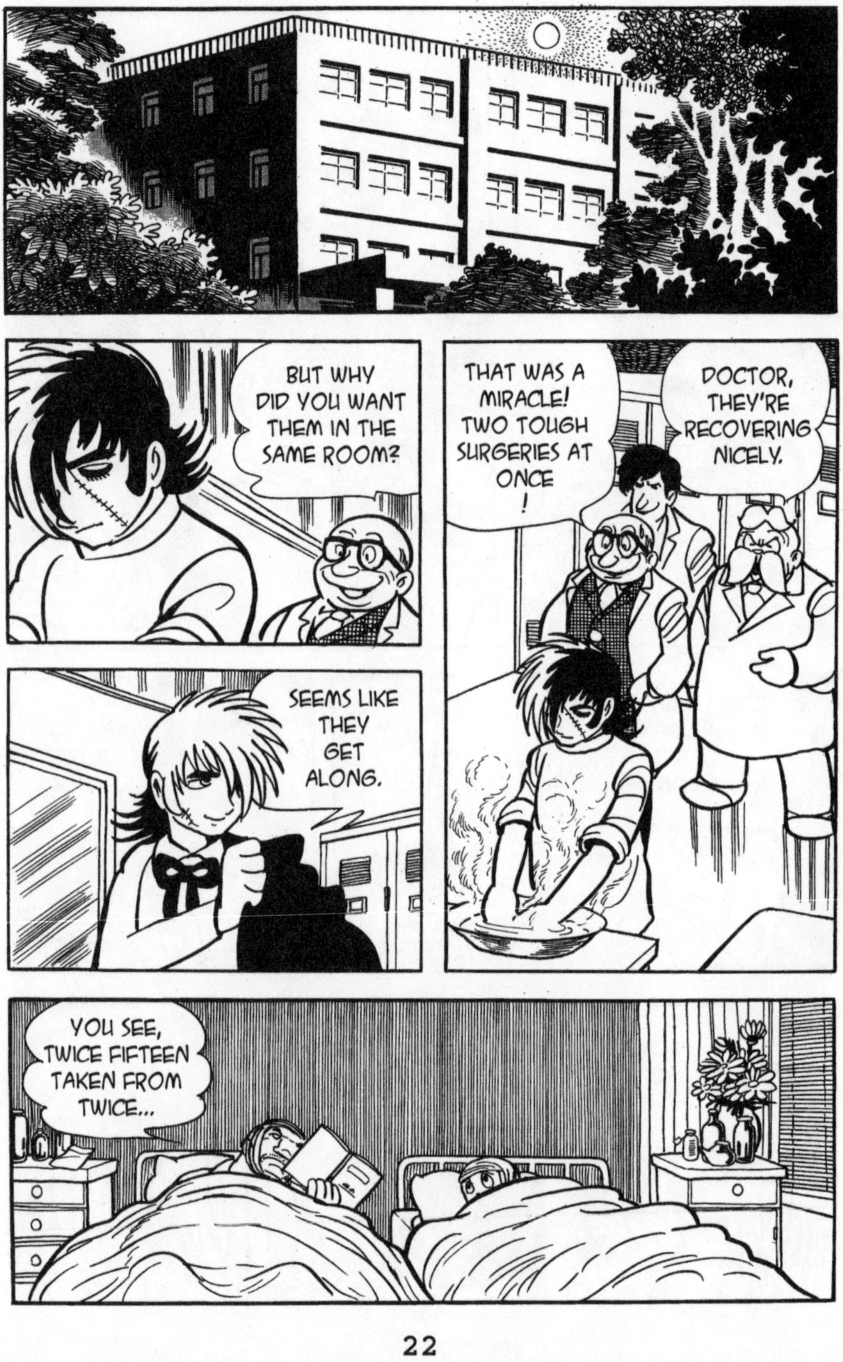
DOCTOR, THEY'RE RECOVERING NICELY.
THAT WAS A MIRACLE! TWO TOUGH SURGERIES AT ONCE!
BUT WHY DID YOU WANT THEM IN THE SAME ROOM?
SEEMS LIKE THEY GET ALONG.
YOU SEE, TWICE FIFTEEN TAKEN FROM TWICE...

PINOKO LIVES

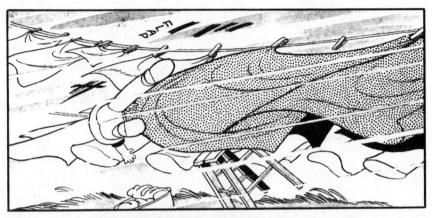

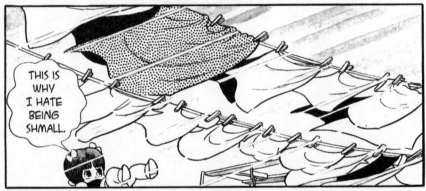

THIS IS WHY I HATE BEING SHMALL.
IF I WAJN'T, THISH'D TAKE ME ONLY HALF AS LONG!
IT'S TIME
DOCTOR MADE PINOKO BIGGER AND
QUIT TWEATING ME LIKE A LITTLE KID.

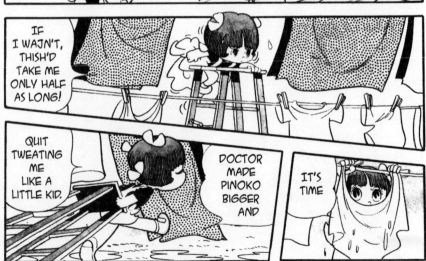

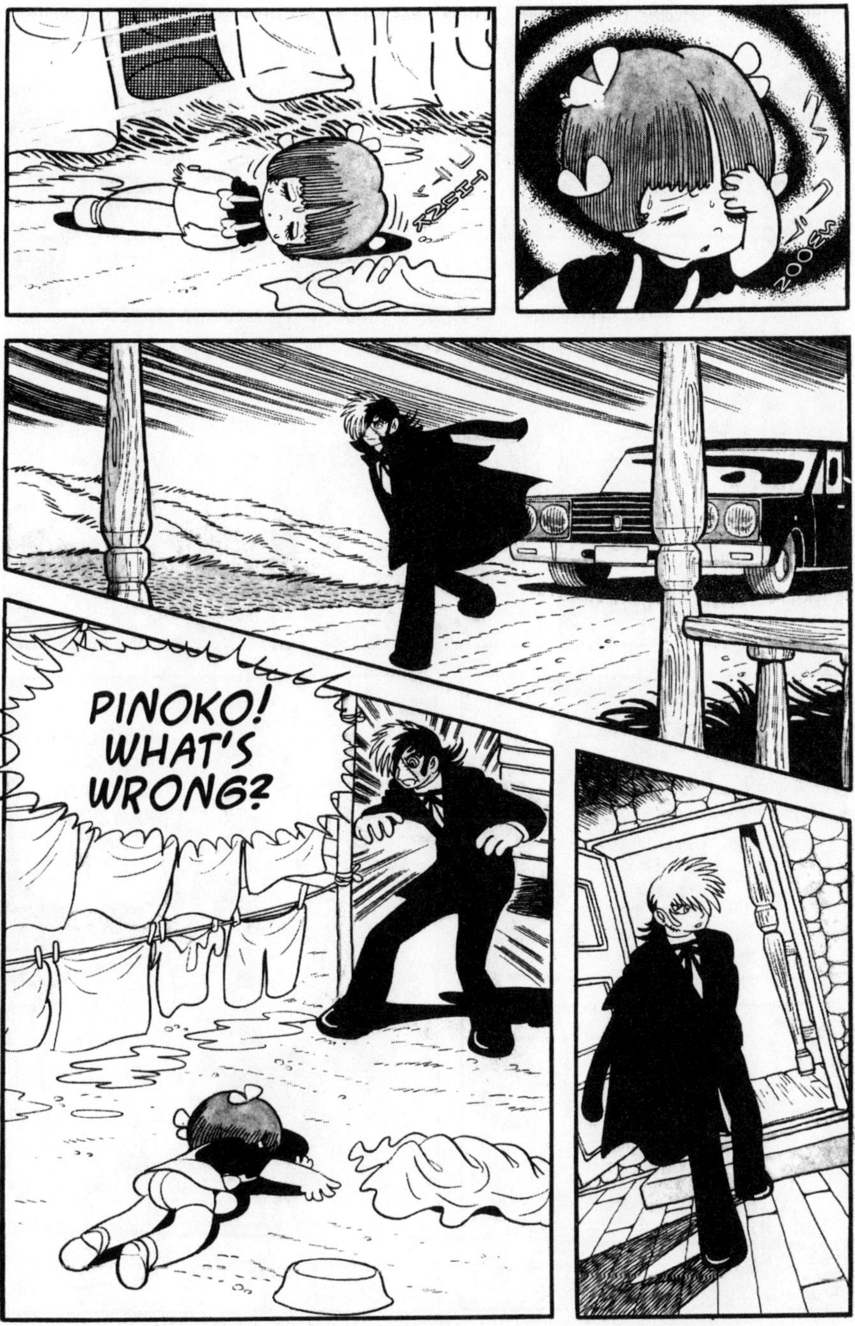
ZOOM
PINOKO! WHAT'S WRONG?

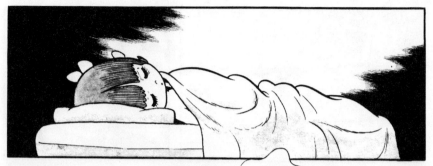

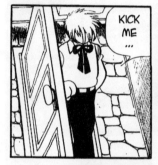

HOW DID I MISS THIS?!
KICK ME ...
SOWWY, DOCTOR. ALL OF A SHUDDEN I SHPACED OUT AND GOT ALL DIJJY.
COME TO THINK OF IT, YOU'VE LOOKED SORT OF PALE LATELY.
I WAS ALOOF.
SOWWY I CAN'T MAKE DINNER TONIGHT.
AW, IT'S FINE. IT'LL PASH IN A DAY.
DON'T WORRY ABOUT THAT.

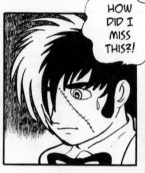

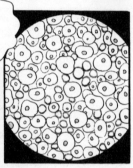

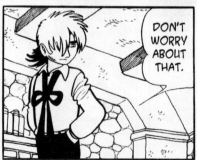

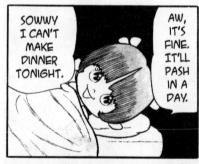

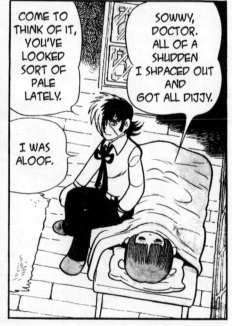

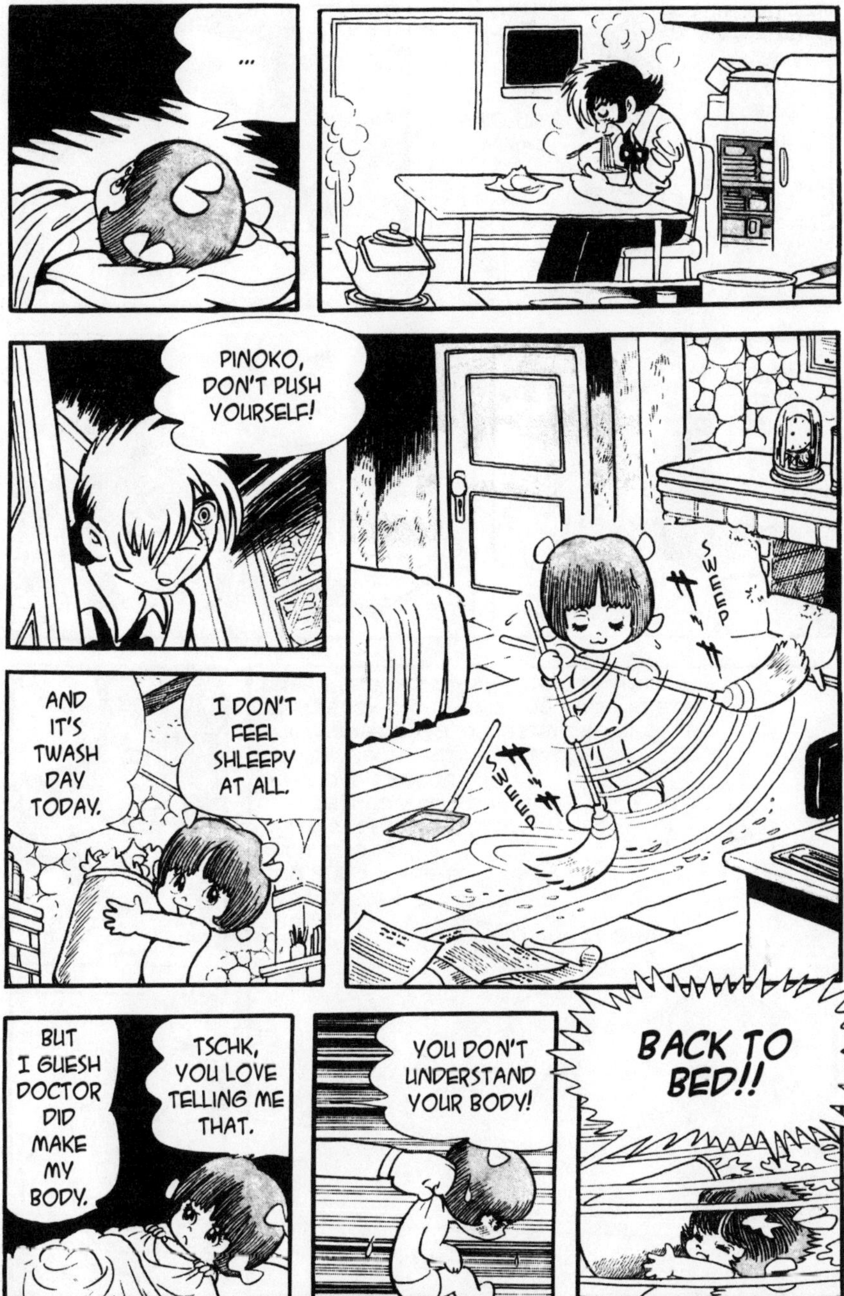
...
SWEEP
SWEEP
PINOKO, DON'T PUSH YOURSELF!
I DON'T FEEL SHLEEPY AT ALL.
AND IT'S TWASH DAY TODAY.
BACK TO BED!!
YOU DON'T UNDERSTAND YOUR BODY!
TSCHK, YOU LOVE TELLING ME THAT.
BUT I GUESH DOCTOR DID MAKE MY BODY.

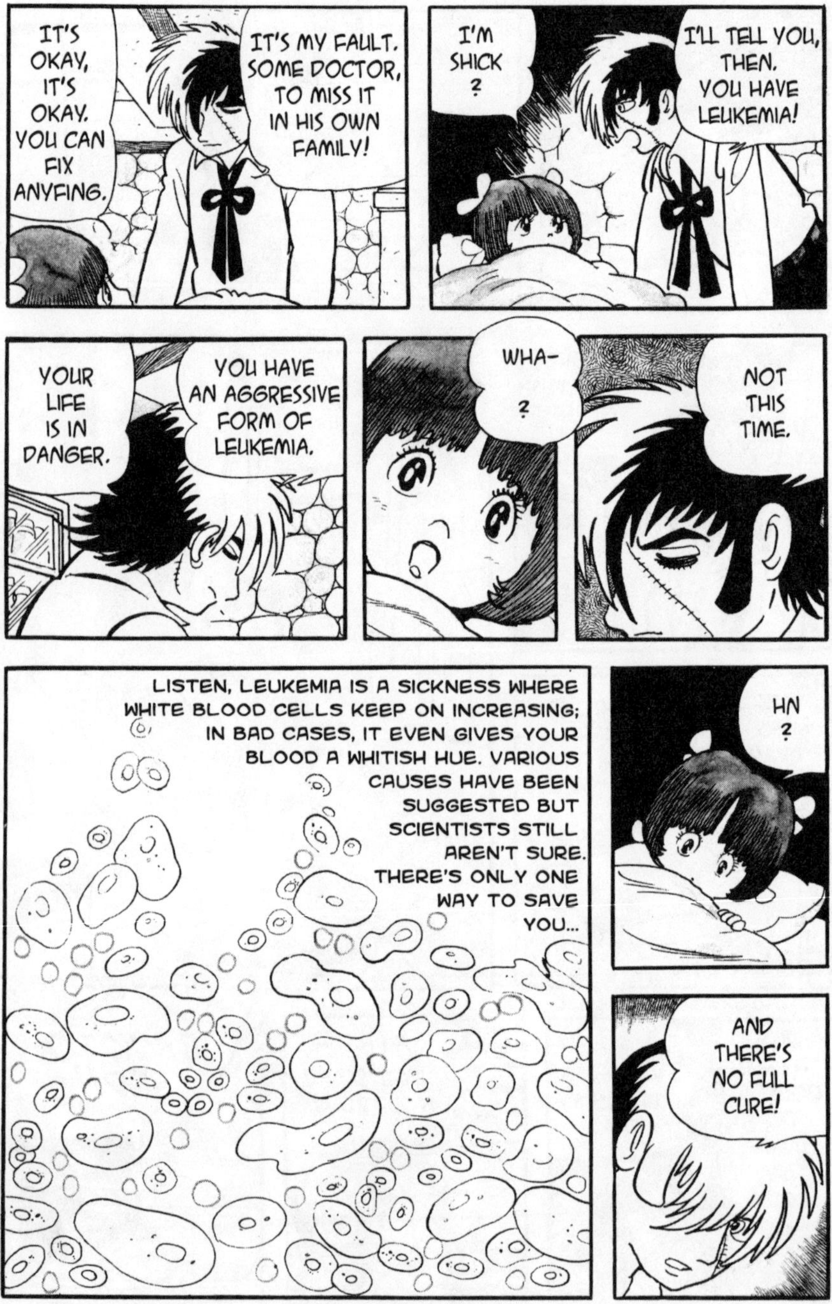
I'LL TELL YOU, THEN. YOU HAVE LEUKEMIA!
I'M SHICK ?
IT'S MY FAULT. SOME DOCTOR, TO MISS IT IN HIS OWN FAMILY!
IT'S OKAY, IT'S OKAY. YOU CAN FIX ANYFING.
NOT THIS TIME.
WHA- ?
YOU HAVE AN AGGRESSIVE FORM OF LEUKEMIA.
YOUR LIFE IS IN DANGER.
HN ?
AND THERE'S NO FULL CURE!
LISTEN, LEUKEMIA IS A SICKNESS WHERE WHITE BLOOD CELLS KEEP ON INCREASING; IN BAD CASES, IT EVEN GIVES YOUR BLOOD A WHITISH HUE. VARIOUS CAUSES HAVE BEEN SUGGESTED BUT SCIENTISTS STILL AREN'T SURE. THERE'S ONLY ONE WAY TO SAVE YOU...

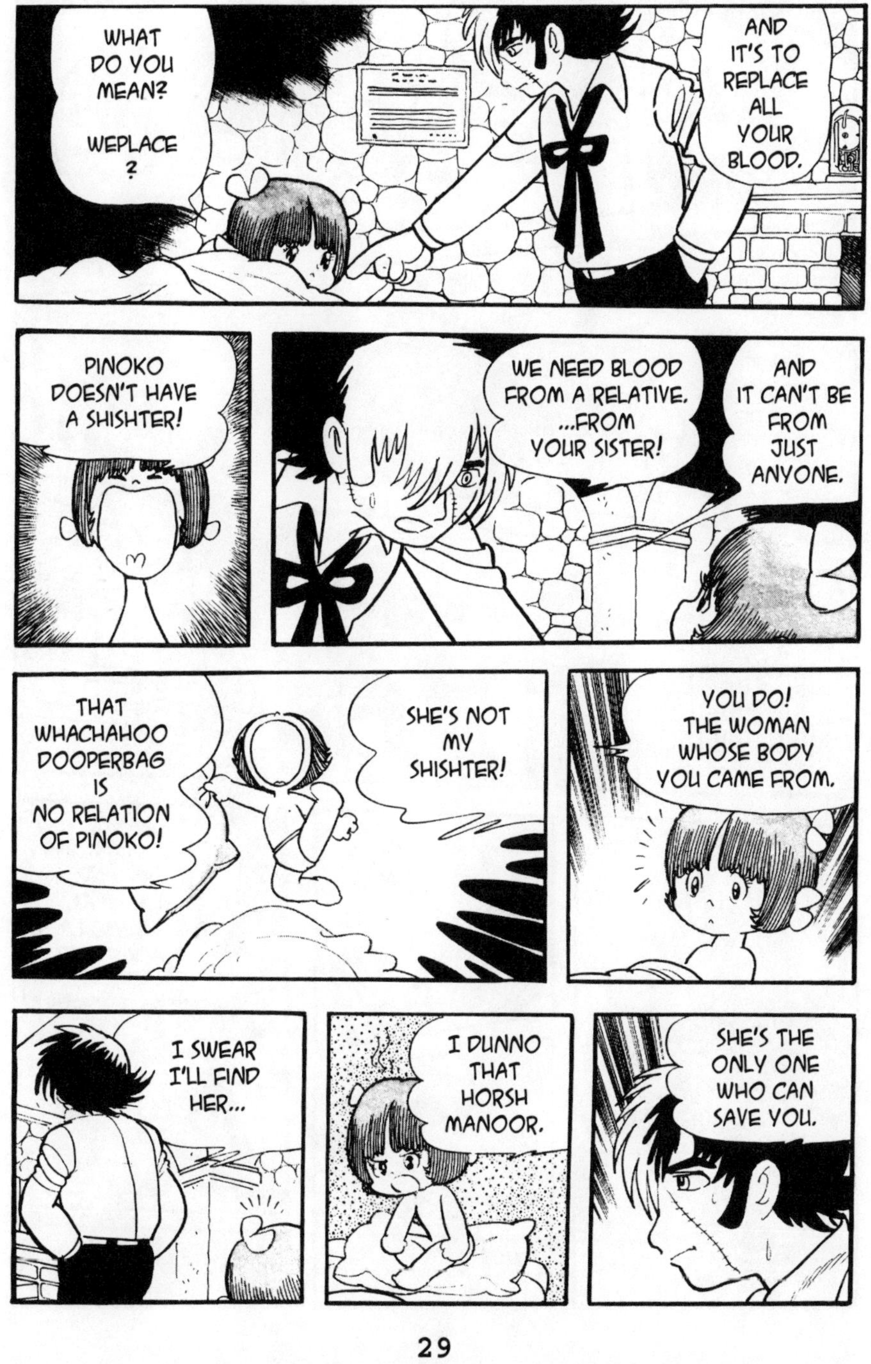
AND IT'S TO REPLACE ALL YOUR BLOOD.
WHAT DO YOU MEAN? WEPLACE?
AND IT CAN'T BE FROM JUST ANYONE.
WE NEED BLOOD FROM A RELATIVE. ...FROM YOUR SISTER!
PINOKO DOESN'T HAVE A SHISHTER!
YOU DO! THE WOMAN WHOSE BODY YOU CAME FROM.
SHE'S NOT MY SHISHTER!
THAT WHACHAHOO DOOPERBAG IS NO RELATION OF PINOKO!
SHE'S THE ONLY ONE WHO CAN SAVE YOU.
I DUNNO THAT HORSH MANOOR.
I SWEAR I'LL FIND HER...

A YOUNG LADY FROM A WEALTHY FAMILY WHO HAD A CYSTOMA? NOPE, DOESN'T RING ANY BELLS.

NO IDEA.

...

...

WHAT, ARE YA GONNA TRY AND BLACKMAIL THE YOUNG LADY, BLACK JACK?

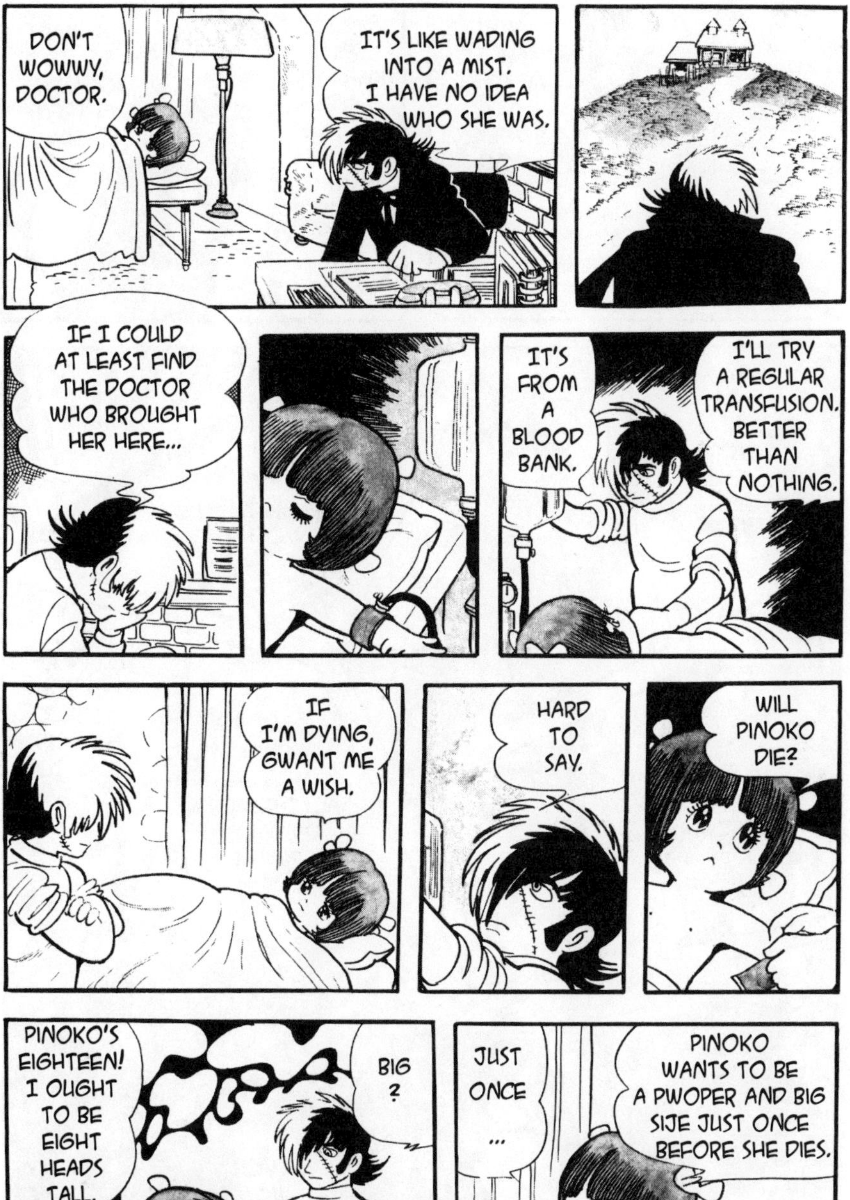
IT'S LIKE WADING INTO A MIST. I HAVE NO IDEA WHO SHE WAS.
DON'T WOWWY, DOCTOR.
I'LL TRY A REGULAR TRANSFUSION. BETTER THAN NOTHING.
IT'S FROM A BLOOD BANK.
IF I COULD AT LEAST FIND THE DOCTOR WHO BROUGHT HER HERE...
WILL PINOKO DIE?
HARD TO SAY.
IF I'M DYING, GWANT ME A WISH.
PINOKO WANTS TO BE A PWOPER AND BIG SIJE JUST ONCE BEFORE SHE DIES.
JUST ONCE ...
BIG ?
PINOKO'S EIGHTEEN! I OUGHT TO BE EIGHT HEADS TALL.

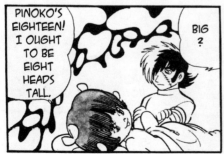

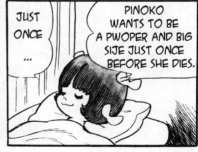

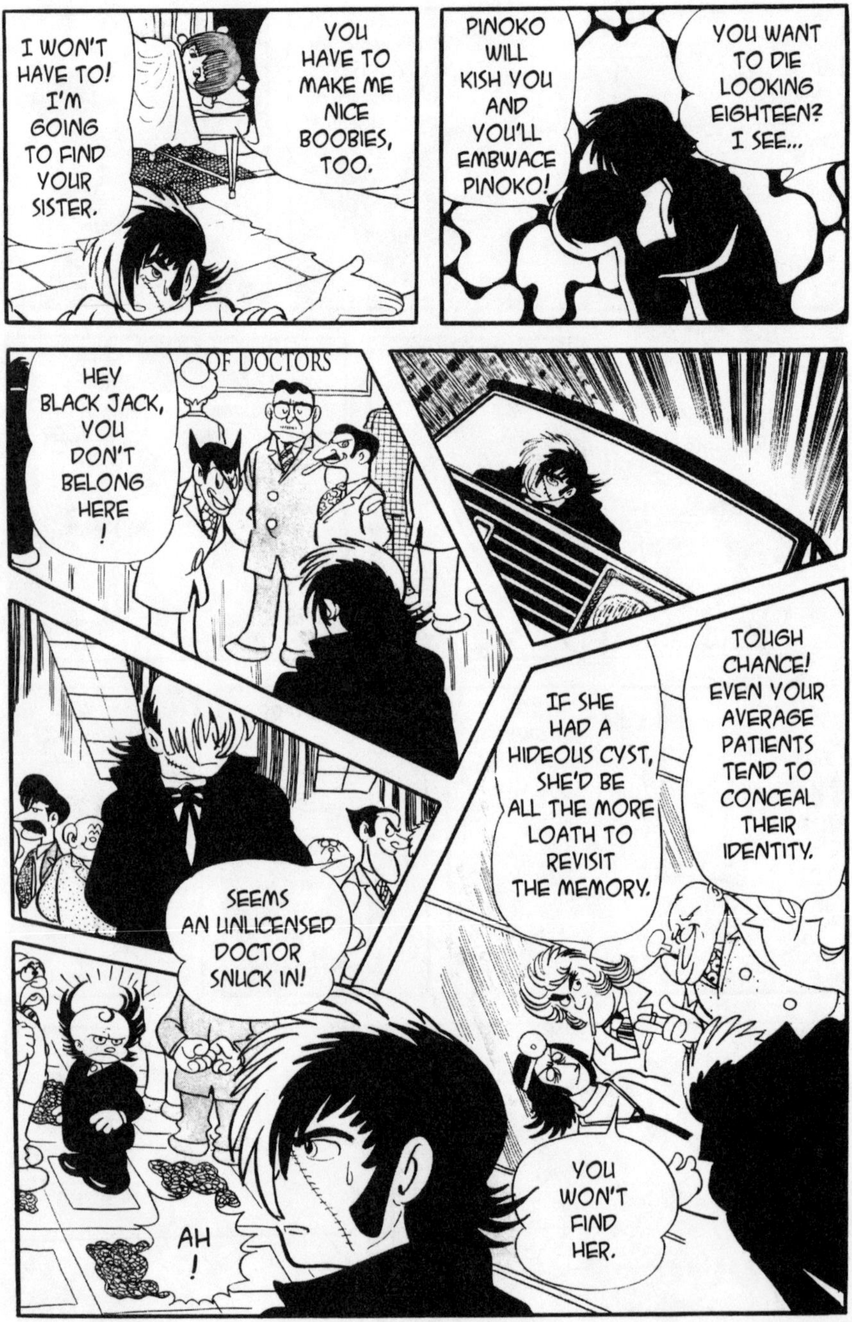
YOU WANT TO DIE LOOKING EIGHTEEN? I SEE...
PINOKO WILL KISH YOU AND YOU'LL EMBWACE PINOKO!
YOU HAVE TO MAKE ME NICE BOOBIES, TOO.
I WON'T HAVE TO! I'M GOING TO FIND YOUR SISTER.
OF DOCTORS
HEY BLACK JACK, YOU DON'T BELONG HERE!
TOUGH CHANCE! EVEN YOUR AVERAGE PATIENTS TEND TO CONCEAL THEIR IDENTITY.
IF SHE HAD A HIDEOUS CYST, SHE'D BE ALL THE MORE LOATH TO REVISIT THE MEMORY.
SEEMS AN UNLICENSED DOCTOR SNUCK IN!
YOU WON'T FIND HER.
AH!

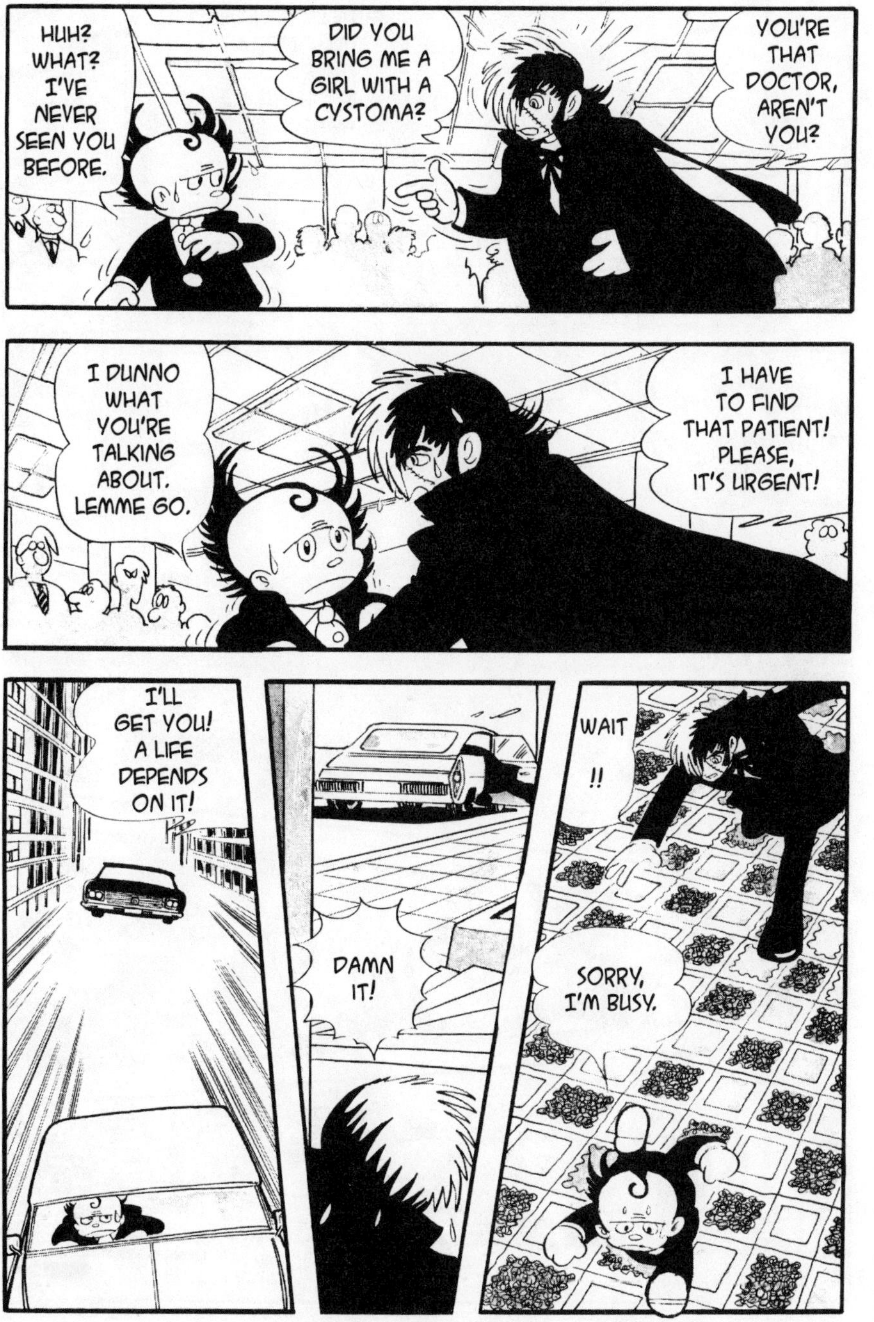
YOU'RE THAT DOCTOR, AREN'T YOU?
DID YOU BRING ME A GIRL WITH A CYSTOMA?
HUH? WHAT? I'VE NEVER SEEN YOU BEFORE.
I HAVE TO FIND THAT PATIENT! PLEASE, IT'S URGENT!
I DUNNO WHAT YOU'RE TALKING ABOUT. LEMME GO.
WAIT !!
SORRY, I'M BUSY.
DAMN IT!
I'LL GET YOU! A LIFE DEPENDS ON IT!

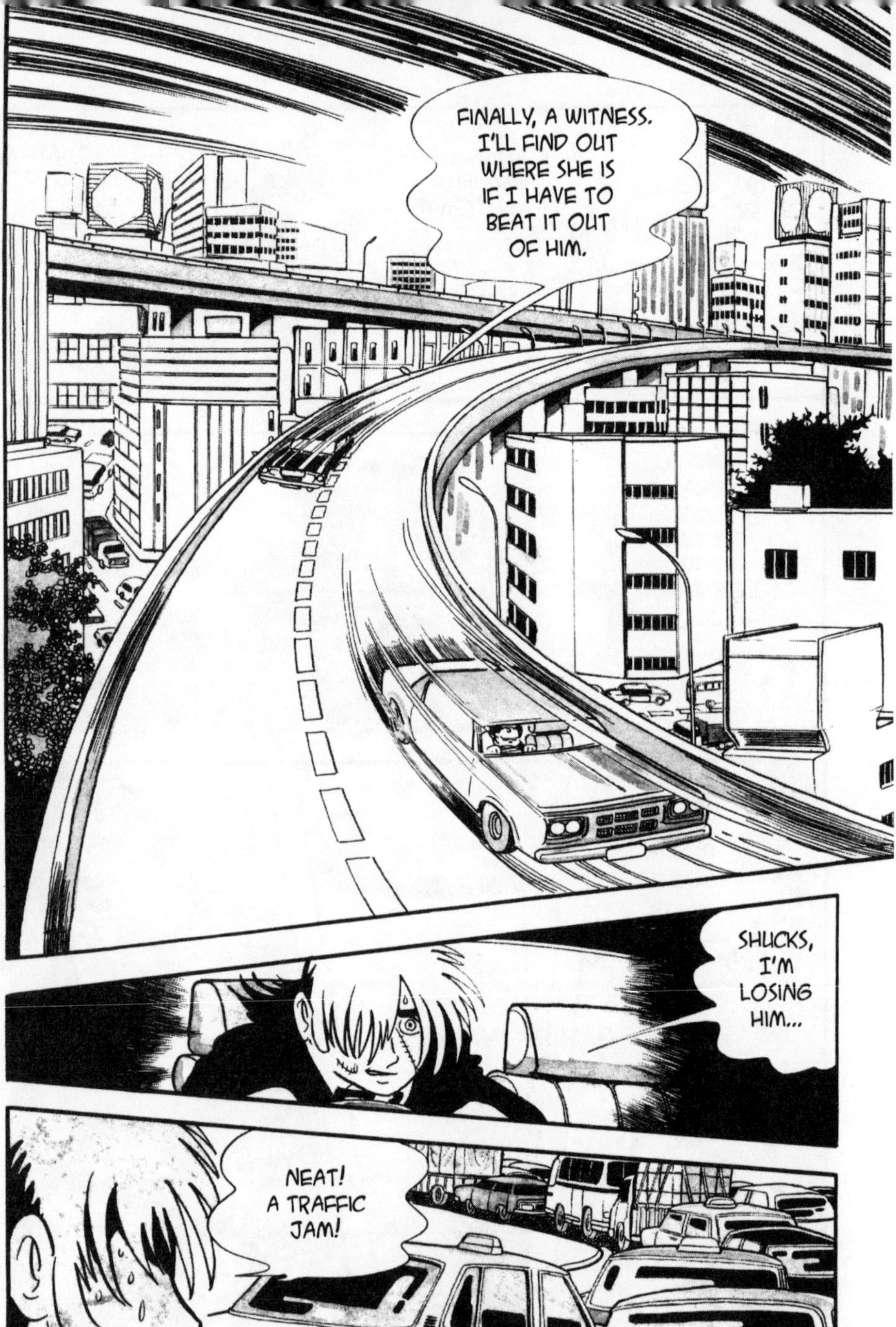
FINALLY, A WITNESS. I'LL FIND OUT WHERE SHE IS IF I HAVE TO BEAT IT OUT OF HIM.
SHUCKS, I'M LOSING HIM...
NEAT! A TRAFFIC JAM!

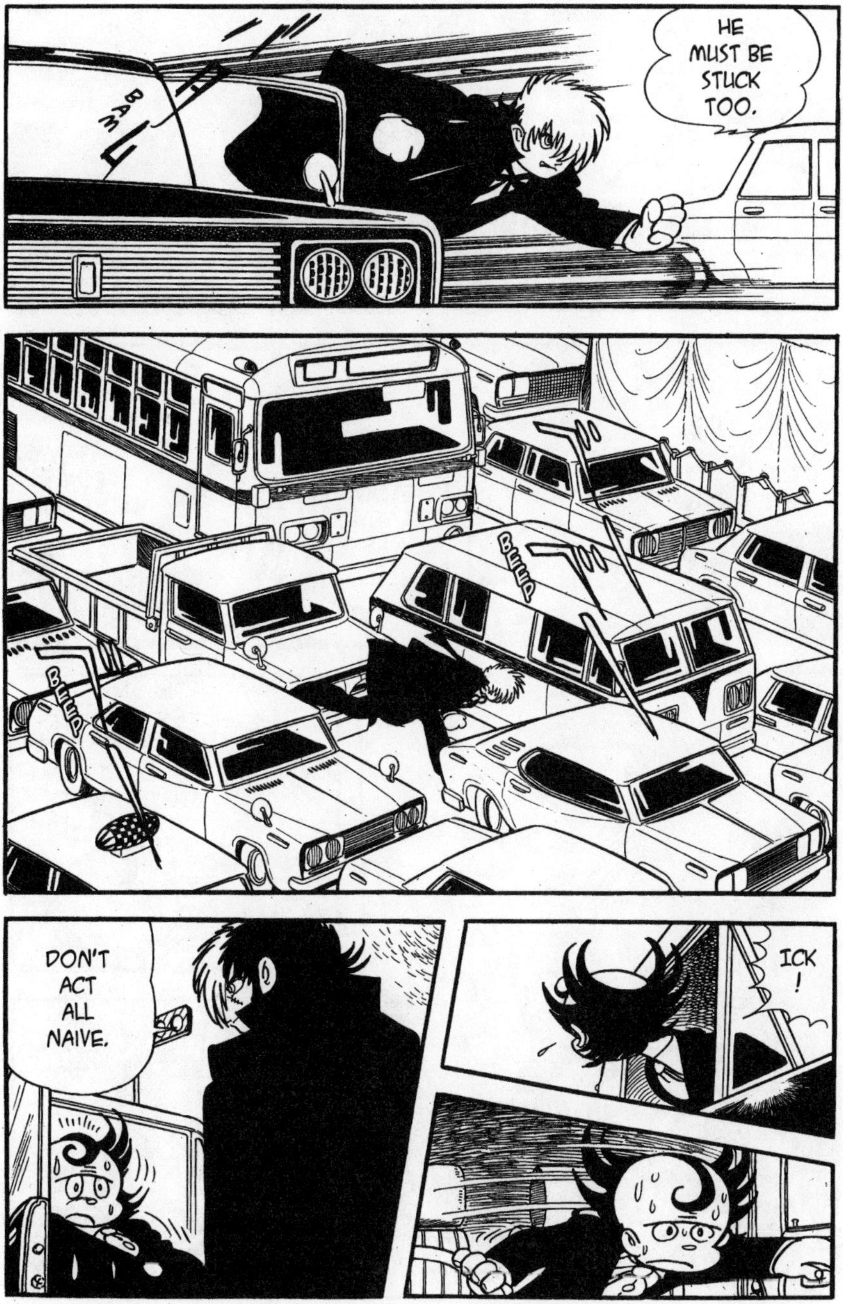
HE MUST BE STUCK TOO.
BAM
BEEP
BEEP
ICK!
DON'T ACT ALL NAIVE.

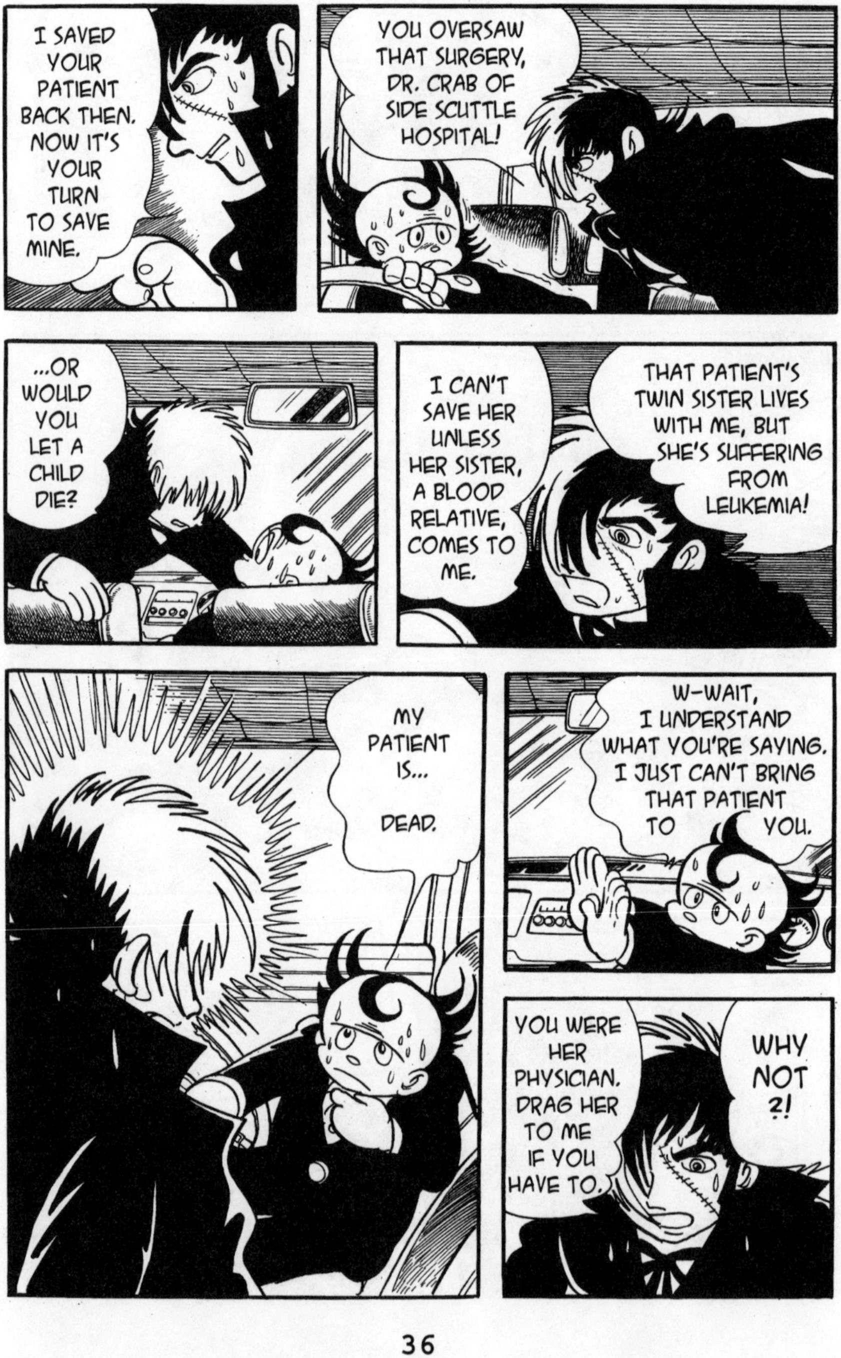
YOU OVERSAW THAT SURGERY, DR. CRAB OF SIDE SCUTTLE HOSPITAL!
I SAVED YOUR PATIENT BACK THEN. NOW IT'S YOUR TURN TO SAVE MINE.
THAT PATIENT'S TWIN SISTER LIVES WITH ME, BUT SHE'S SUFFERING FROM LEUKEMIA!
I CAN'T SAVE HER UNLESS HER SISTER, A BLOOD RELATIVE, COMES TO ME.
...OR WOULD YOU LET A CHILD DIE?
W-WAIT, I UNDERSTAND WHAT YOU'RE SAYING. I JUST CAN'T BRING THAT PATIENT TO YOU.
WHY NOT ?!
YOU WERE HER PHYSICIAN. DRAG HER TO ME IF YOU HAVE TO.
MY PATIENT IS... DEAD.

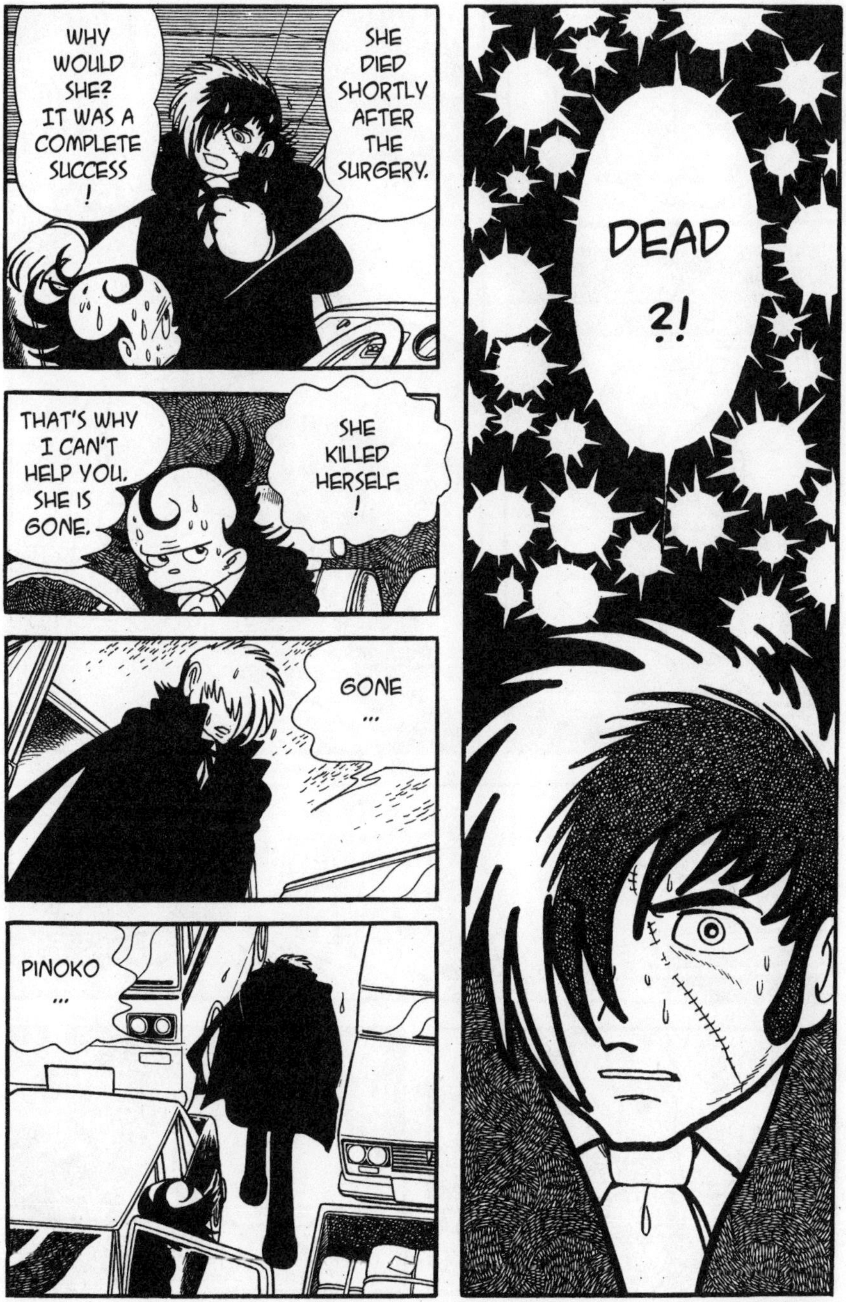
DEAD ?!
SHE DIED SHORTLY AFTER THE SURGERY.
WHY WOULD SHE? IT WAS A COMPLETE SUCCESS !
SHE KILLED HERSELF !
THAT'S WHY I CAN'T HELP YOU. SHE IS GONE.
GONE ...
PINOKO ...

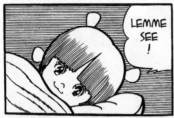

LEMME SEE!
WOW, THOSE ARE PINOKO'S NEW ARMS AND LEGS? SHEKSHY!
AND THE FACE?
YUKKO. IT'S ALL EMPTY.
THIS IS A SYNTHETIC-FIBER SKULL. I'LL PLACE YOUR BRAIN, NOSE, MOUTH AND ALL INTO THIS.

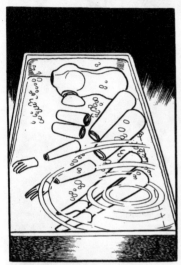

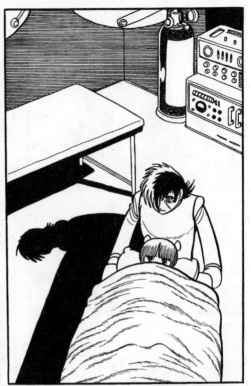

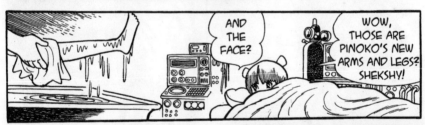

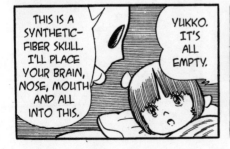

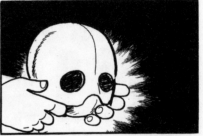

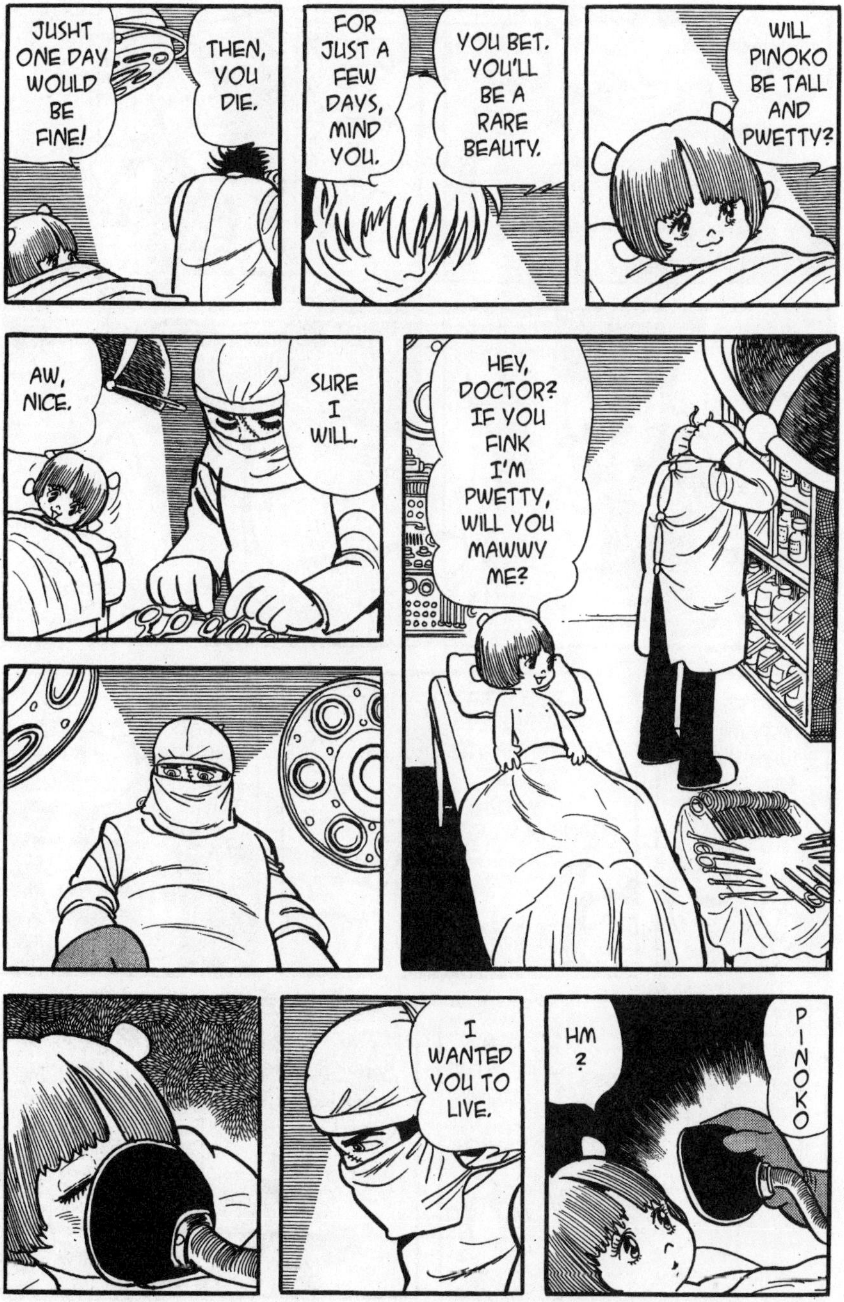
WILL PINOKO BE TALL AND PWETTY?
YOU BET. YOU'LL BE A RARE BEAUTY.
FOR JUST A FEW DAYS, MIND YOU.
THEN, YOU DIE.
JUSHT ONE DAY WOULD BE FINE!
HEY, DOCTOR? IF YOU FINK I'M PWETTY, WILL YOU MAWWY ME?
SURE I WILL.
AW, NICE.
PINOKO
HM?
I WANTED YOU TO LIVE.

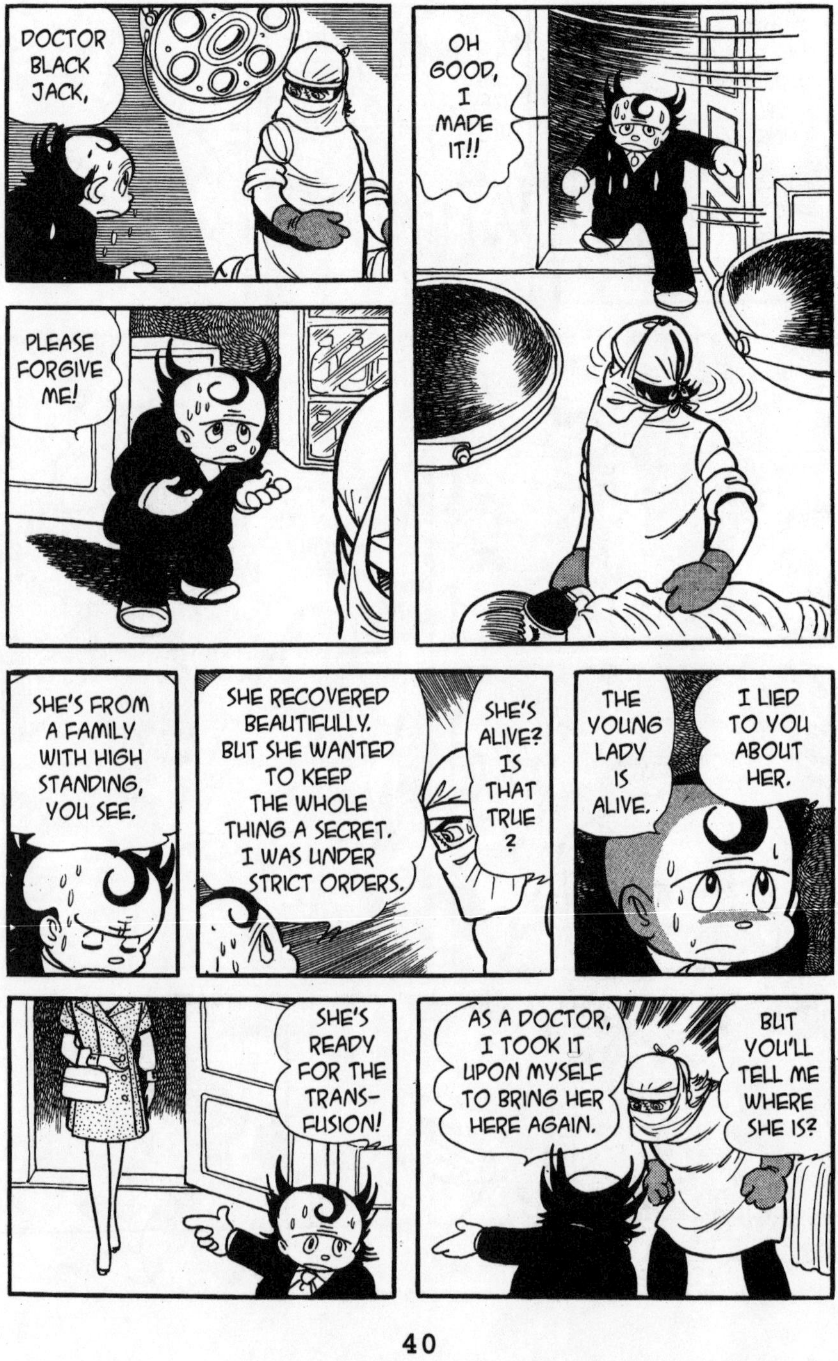
OH GOOD, I MADE IT!!
DOCTOR BLACK JACK,
PLEASE FORGIVE ME!
I LIED TO YOU ABOUT HER.
THE YOUNG LADY IS ALIVE.
SHE'S ALIVE? IS THAT TRUE?
SHE RECOVERED BEAUTIFULLY. BUT SHE WANTED TO KEEP THE WHOLE THING A SECRET. I WAS UNDER STRICT ORDERS.
SHE'S FROM A FAMILY WITH HIGH STANDING, YOU SEE.
BUT YOU'LL TELL ME WHERE SHE IS?
AS A DOCTOR, I TOOK IT UPON MYSELF TO BRING HER HERE AGAIN.
SHE'S READY FOR THE TRANS-FUSION!

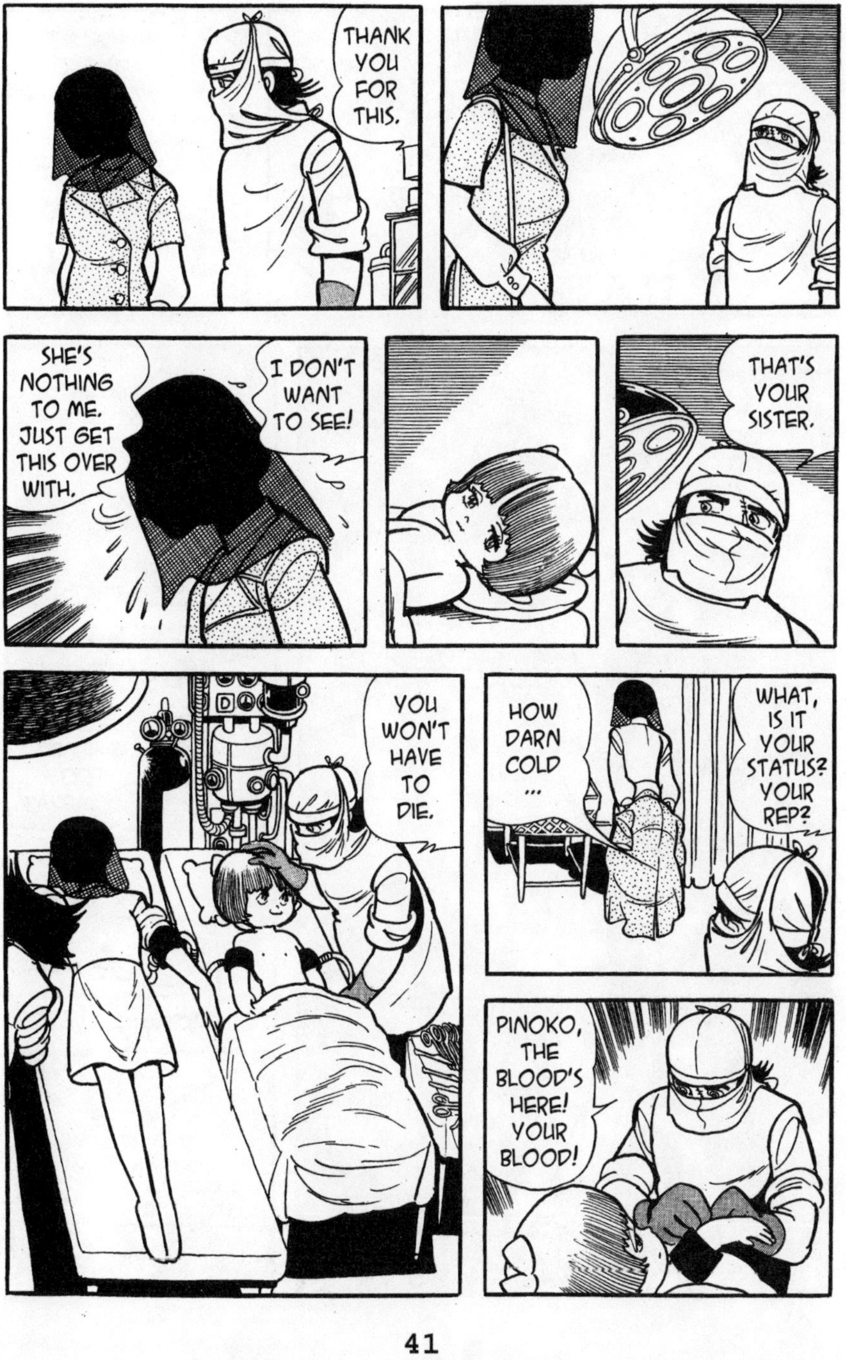
THANK YOU FOR THIS.
THAT'S YOUR SISTER.
I DON'T WANT TO SEE!
SHE'S NOTHING TO ME. JUST GET THIS OVER WITH.
WHAT, IS IT YOUR STATUS? YOUR REP?
HOW DARN COLD ...
PINOKO, THE BLOOD'S HERE! YOUR BLOOD!
YOU WON'T HAVE TO DIE.

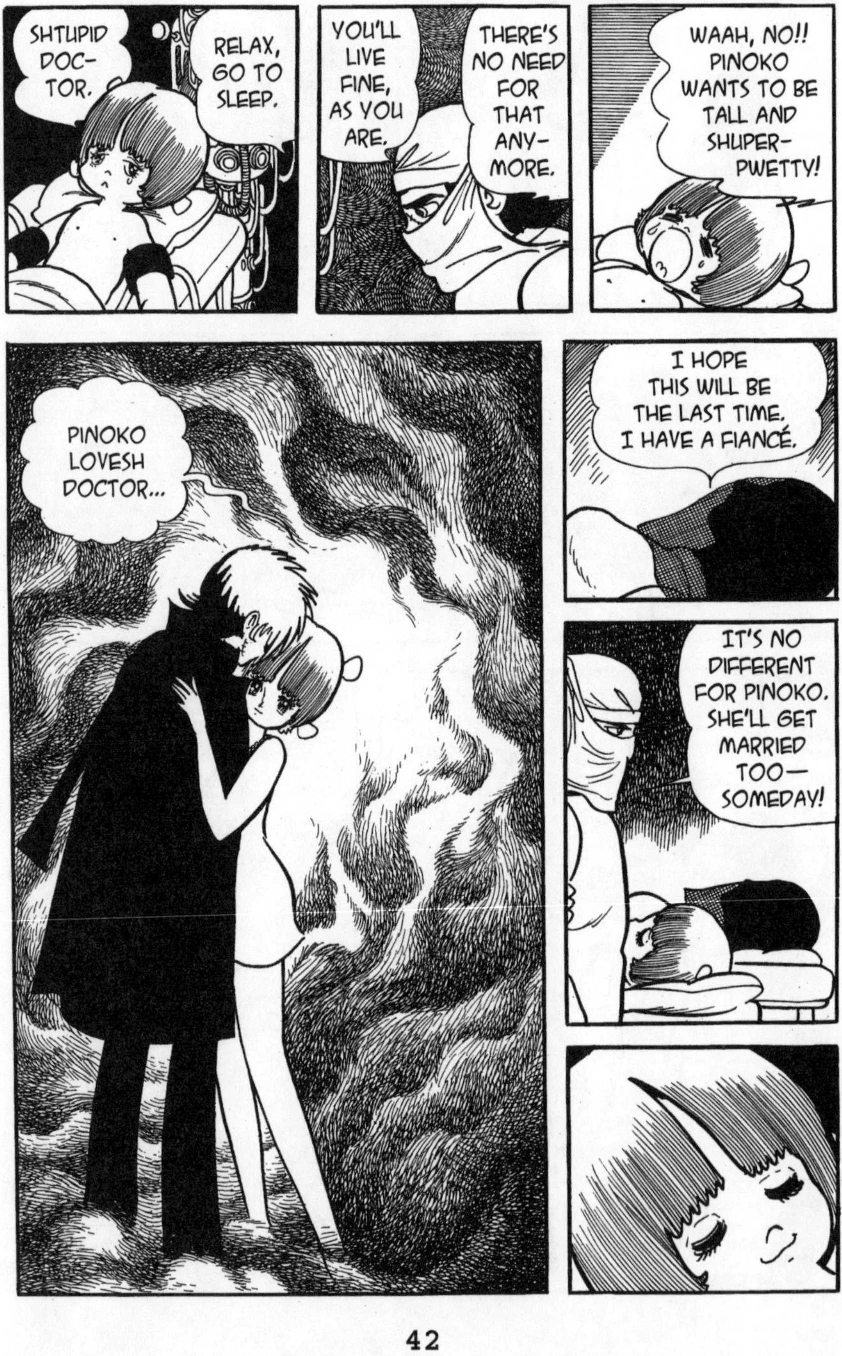
WAAH, NO!! PINOKO WANTS TO BE TALL AND SHUPER-PWETTY!
THERE'S NO NEED FOR THAT ANYMORE.
YOU'LL LIVE FINE, AS YOU ARE.
RELAX, GO TO SLEEP.
SHTUPID DOCTOR.
I HOPE THIS WILL BE THE LAST TIME. I HAVE A FIANCÉ.
IT'S NO DIFFERENT FOR PINOKO. SHE'LL GET MARRIED TOO— SOMEDAY!
PINOKO LOVESH DOCTOR...

EYEWITNESS

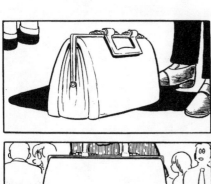

A HIKARI EXPRESS WILL BE ARRIVING IN TWO MINUTES...

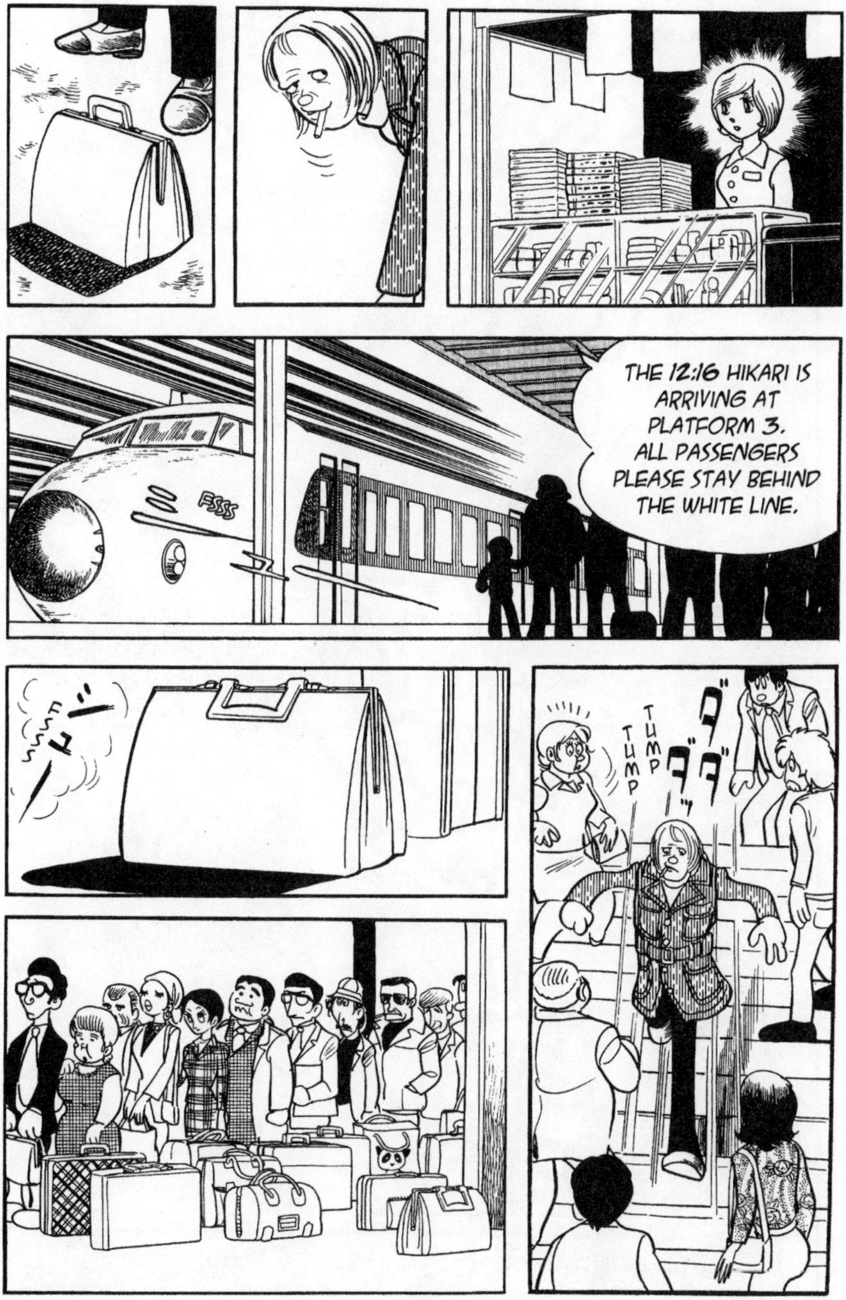
THE 12:16 HIKARI IS ARRIVING AT PLATFORM 3. ALL PASSENGERS PLEASE STAY BEHIND THE WHITE LINE.
FSSS
TUMP TUMP
FSSS

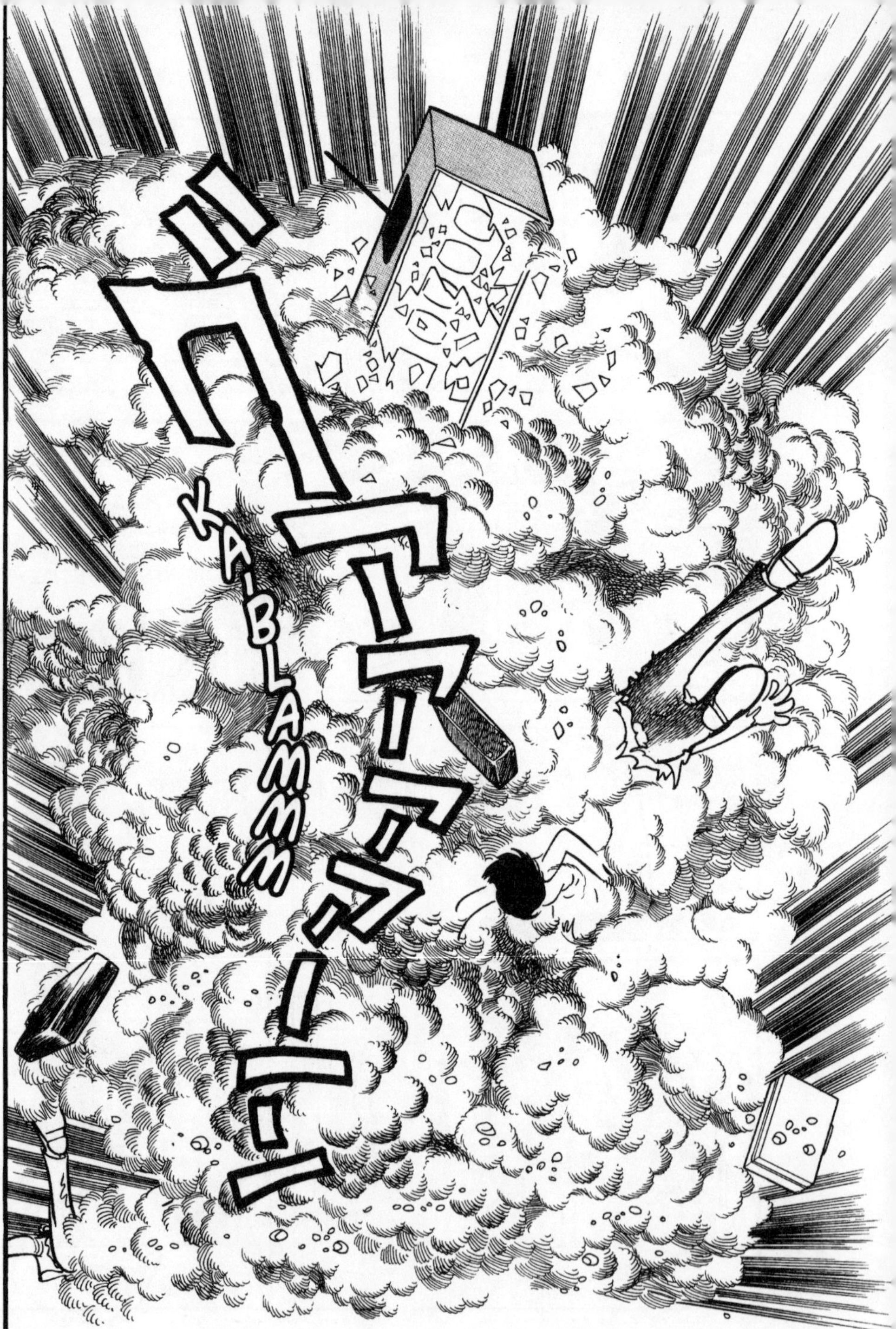
KA-BLAMMM

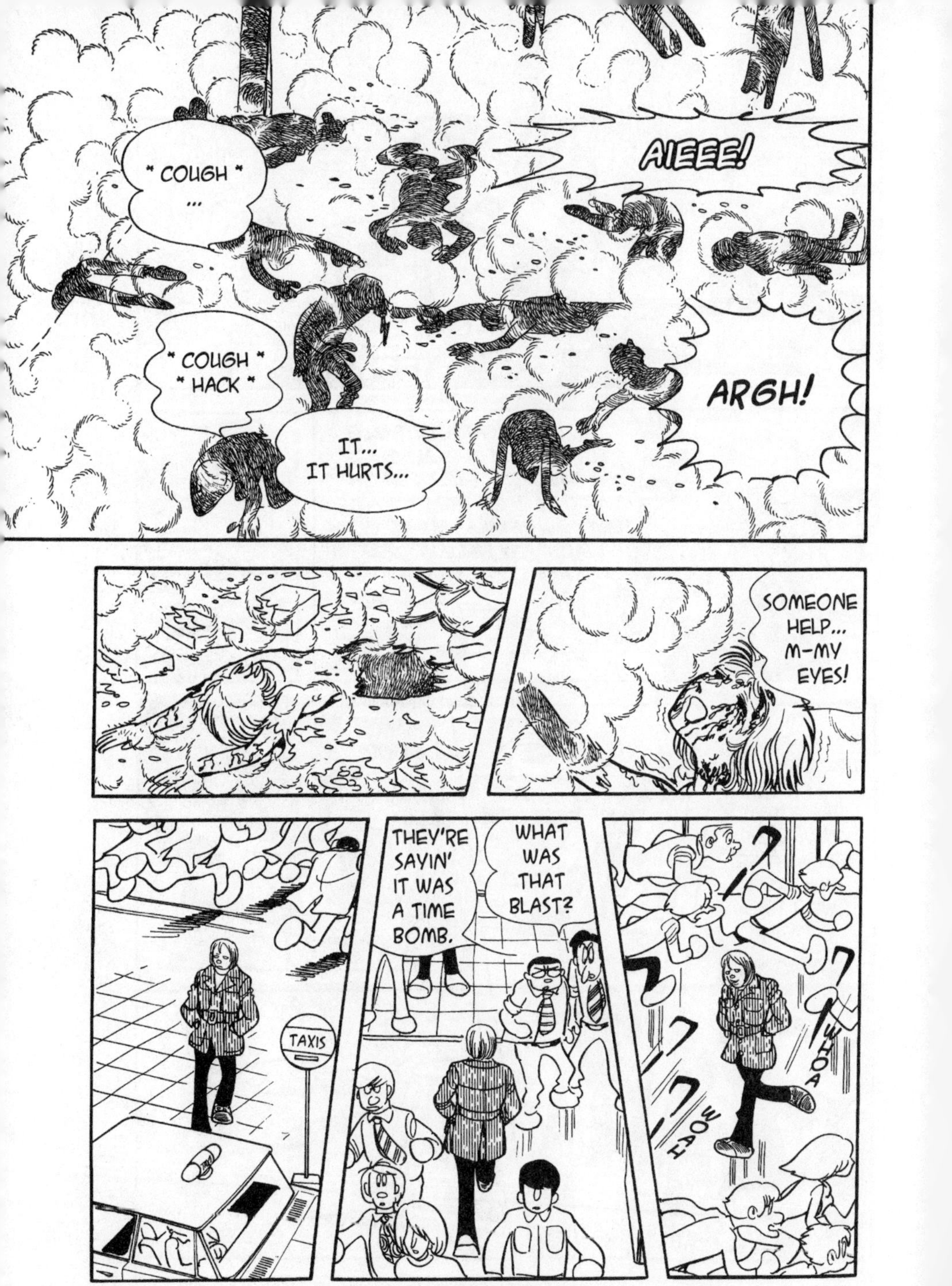
AIEEE!
"COUGH" ...
ARGH!
"COUGH" "HACK"
IT... IT HURTS...
SOMEONE HELP... M-MY EYES!
WHOA
WHOA
WHAT WAS THAT BLAST?
THEY'RE SAYIN' IT WAS A TIME BOMB.
TAXIS

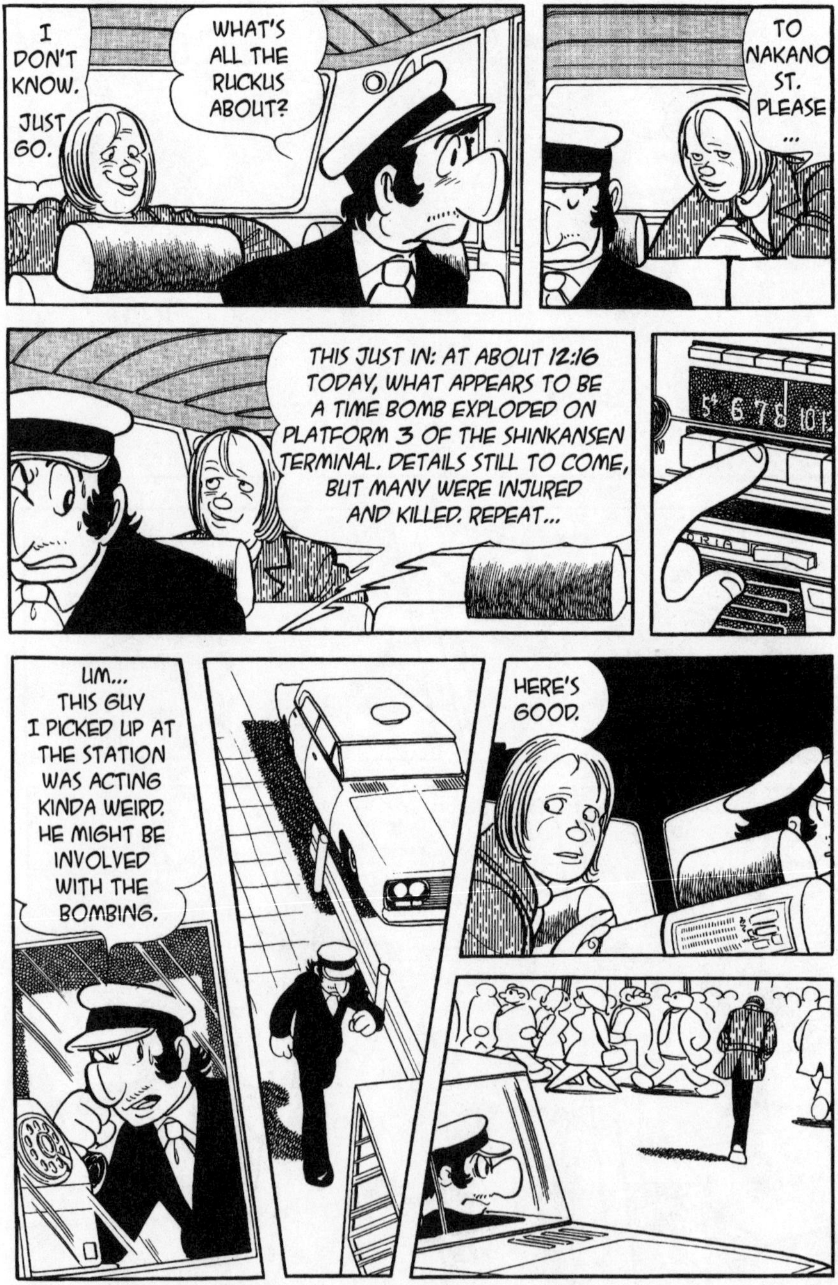
TO NAKANO ST. PLEASE ...
WHAT'S ALL THE RUCKUS ABOUT?
I DON'T KNOW. JUST GO.
THIS JUST IN: AT ABOUT 12:16 TODAY, WHAT APPEARS TO BE A TIME BOMB EXPLODED ON PLATFORM 3 OF THE SHINKANSEN TERMINAL. DETAILS STILL TO COME, BUT MANY WERE INJURED AND KILLED. REPEAT...
HERE'S GOOD.
UM... THIS GUY I PICKED UP AT THE STATION WAS ACTING KINDA WEIRD. HE MIGHT BE INVOLVED WITH THE BOMBING.

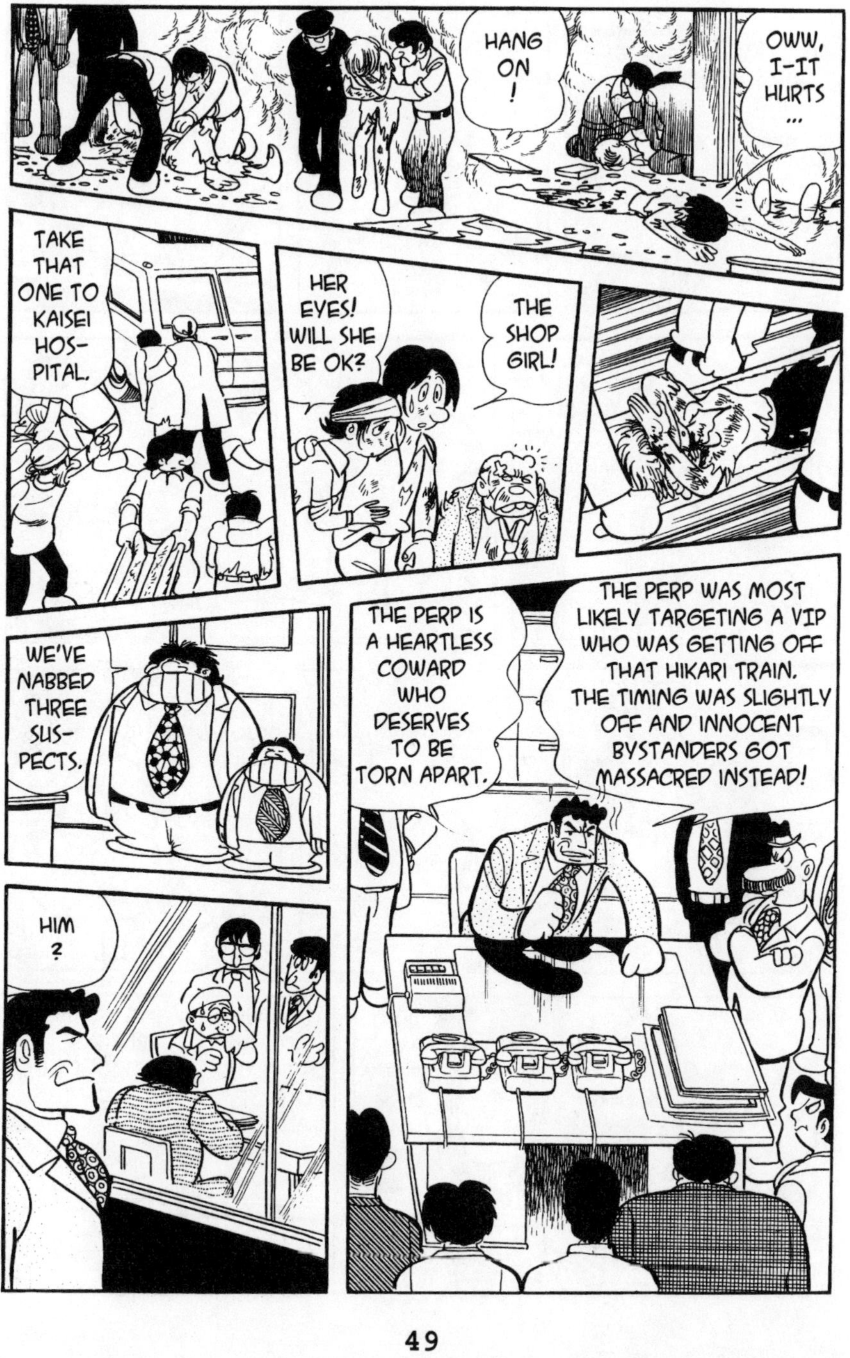
OWW, I-IT HURTS ...
HANG ON !
THE SHOP GIRL!
HER EYES! WILL SHE BE OK?
TAKE THAT ONE TO KAISEI HOS-PITAL.
THE PERP WAS MOST LIKELY TARGETING A VIP WHO WAS GETTING OFF THAT HIKARI TRAIN. THE TIMING WAS SLIGHTLY OFF AND INNOCENT BYSTANDERS GOT MASSACRED INSTEAD!
THE PERP IS A HEARTLESS COWARD WHO DESERVES TO BE TORN APART.
WE'VE NABBED THREE SUS-PECTS.
HIM ?

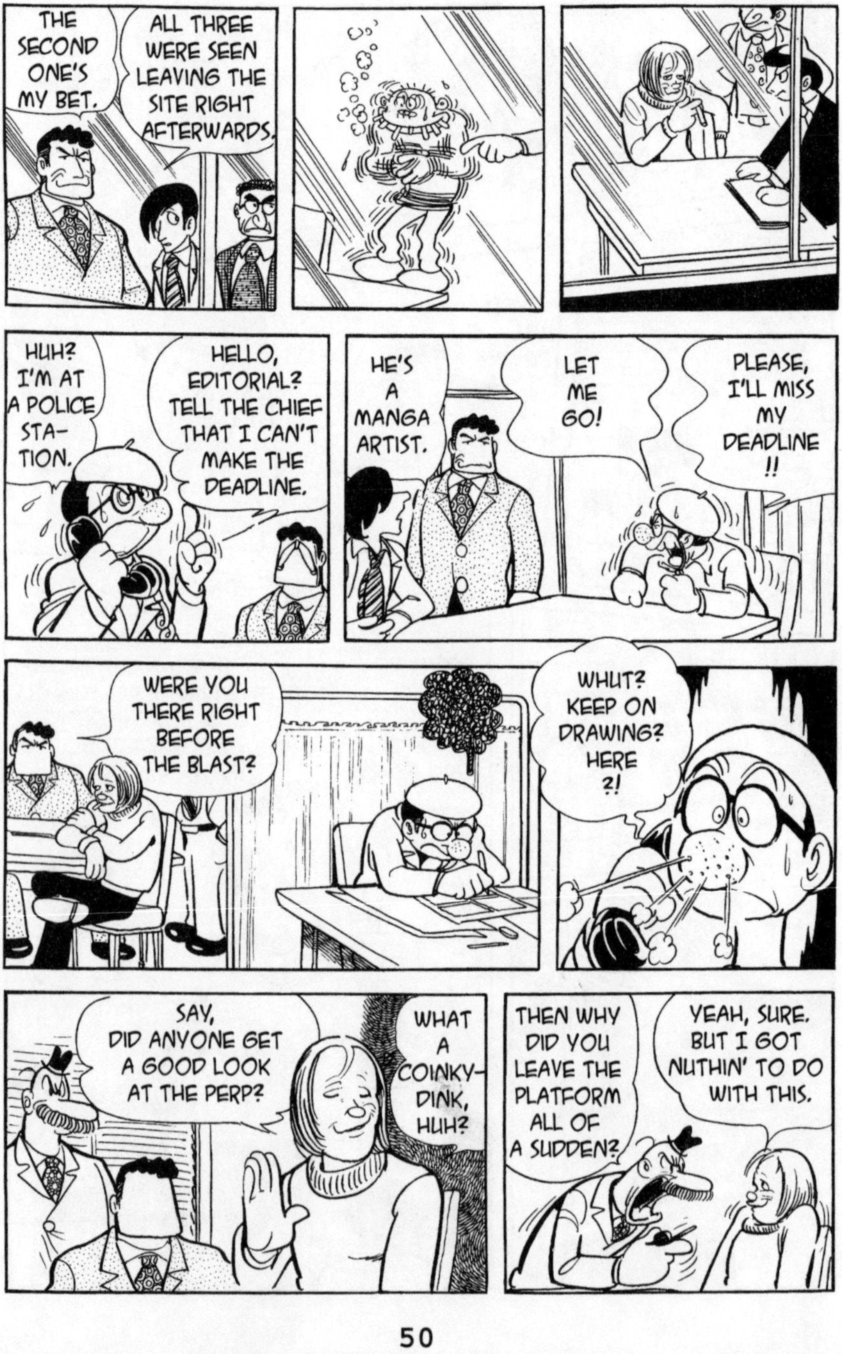
ALL THREE WERE SEEN LEAVING THE SITE RIGHT AFTERWARDS.
THE SECOND ONE'S MY BET.
PLEASE, I'LL MISS MY DEADLINE !!
LET ME GO!
HE'S A MANGA ARTIST.
HELLO, EDITORIAL? TELL THE CHIEF THAT I CAN'T MAKE THE DEADLINE.
HUH? I'M AT A POLICE STATION.
WHUT? KEEP ON DRAWING? HERE ?!
WERE YOU THERE RIGHT BEFORE THE BLAST?
YEAH, SURE. BUT I GOT NUTHIN' TO DO WITH THIS.
THEN WHY DID YOU LEAVE THE PLATFORM ALL OF A SUDDEN?
WHAT A COINKY-DINK, HUH?
SAY, DID ANYONE GET A GOOD LOOK AT THE PERP?

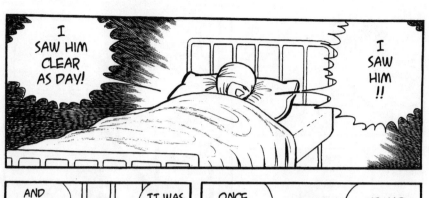

I SAW HIM !!
I SAW HIM CLEAR AS DAY!
HE HAD A BAG WITH HIM.
ONCE THE HIKARI CAME IN, HE LEFT IT AND RAN.
IT WAS THAT BAG THAT BLEW UP.
AND THAT'S THE LAST THING I SAW ...
WHAT DID HE LOOK LIKE? TELL US WHAT YOU REMEMBER.
WELL, UHM... HE WAS WEARING A COAT AND BLACK PANTS. AND HIS FACE...
HE WAS PALE. HE LOOKED MEAN.
WHAT ELSE ?
I CAN'T DESCRIBE HIM WITH WORDS!
I COULD POINT HIM OUT TO YOU
IF I COULD SEE HIM !

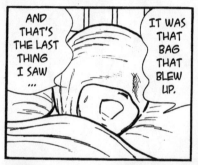

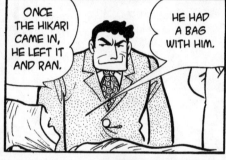

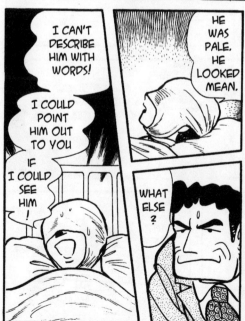

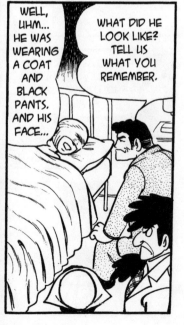

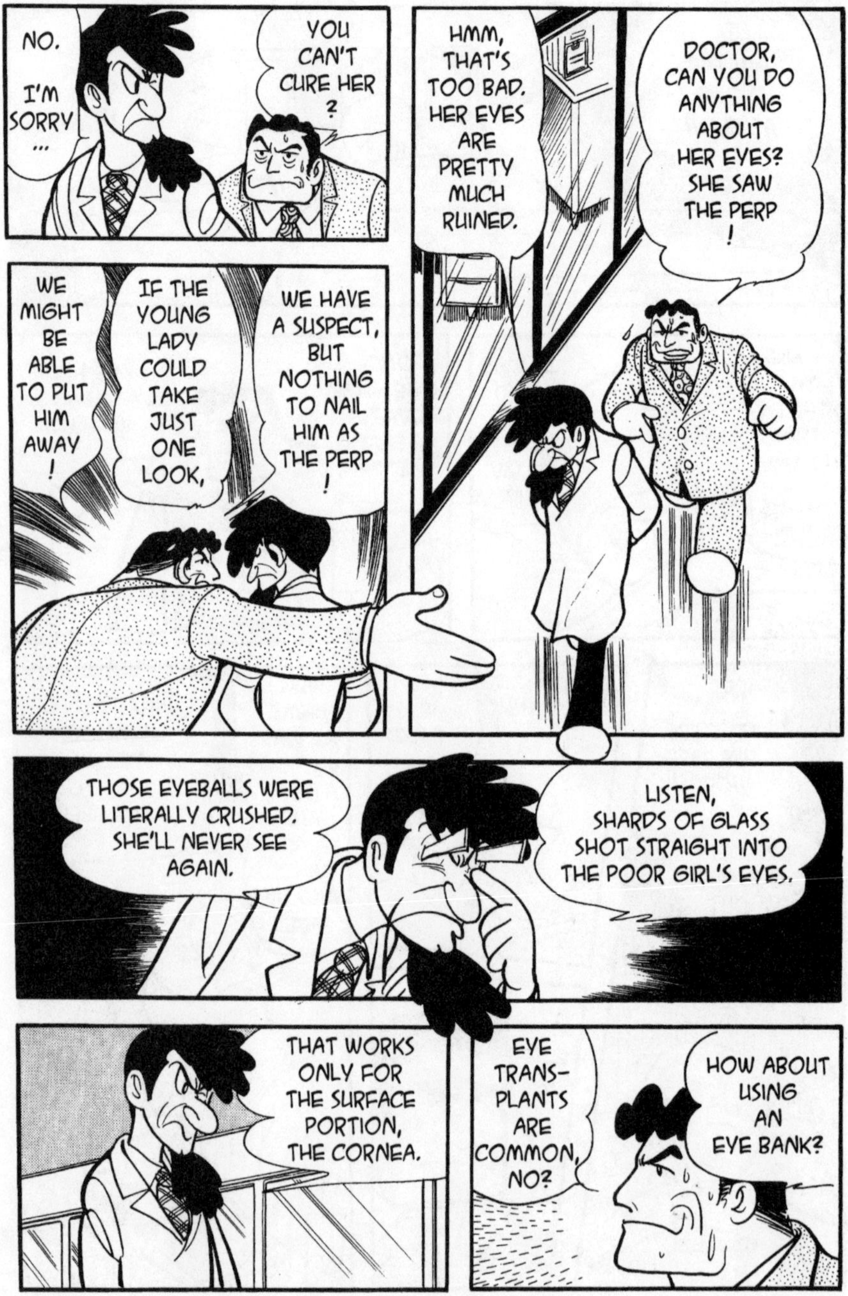
DOCTOR, CAN YOU DO ANYTHING ABOUT HER EYES? SHE SAW THE PERP!
HMM, THAT'S TOO BAD. HER EYES ARE PRETTY MUCH RUINED.
YOU CAN'T CURE HER?
NO. I'M SORRY...
WE HAVE A SUSPECT, BUT NOTHING TO NAIL HIM AS THE PERP!
IF THE YOUNG LADY COULD TAKE JUST ONE LOOK,
WE MIGHT BE ABLE TO PUT HIM AWAY!
LISTEN, SHARDS OF GLASS SHOT STRAIGHT INTO THE POOR GIRL'S EYES.
THOSE EYEBALLS WERE LITERALLY CRUSHED. SHE'LL NEVER SEE AGAIN.
HOW ABOUT USING AN EYE BANK?
EYE TRANS-PLANTS ARE COMMON, NO?
THAT WORKS ONLY FOR THE SURFACE PORTION, THE CORNEA.

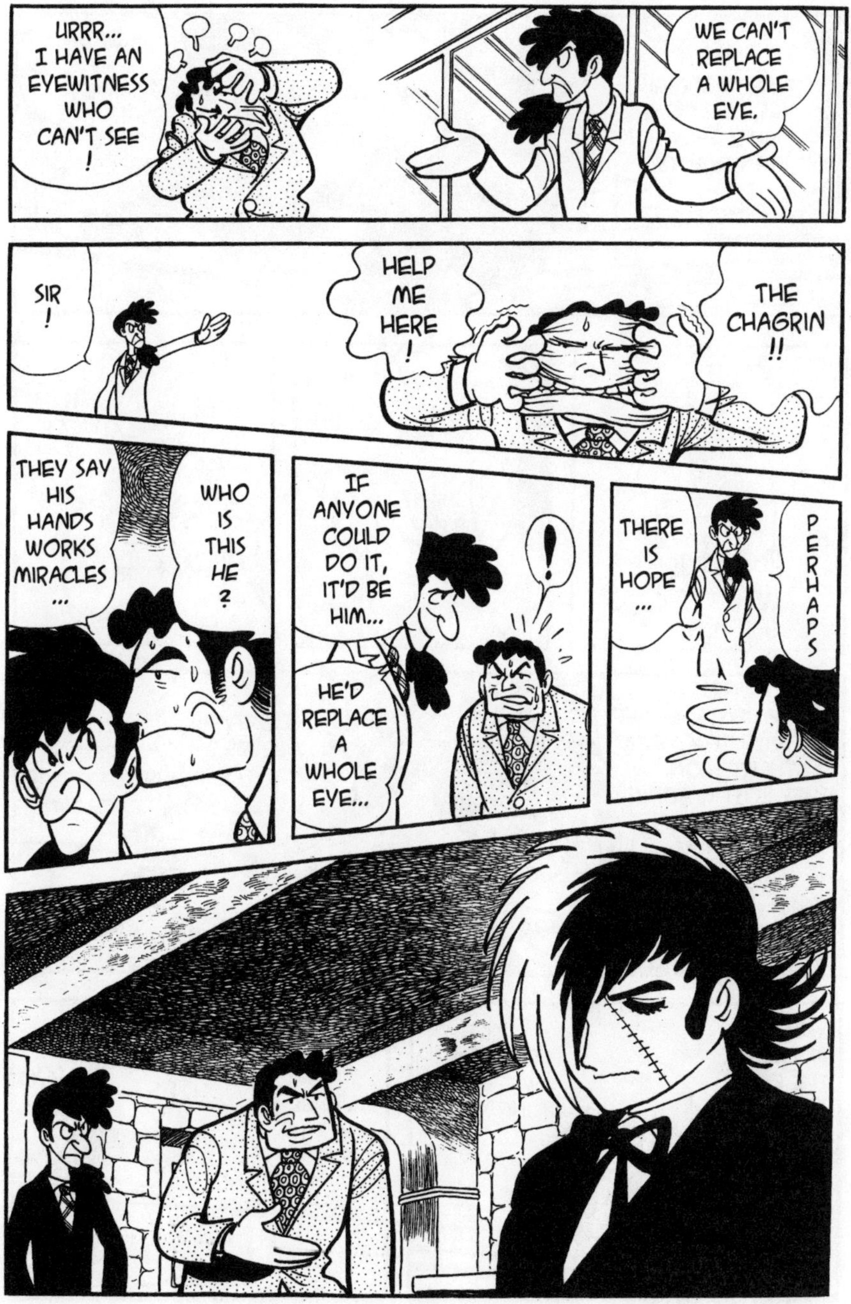
WE CAN'T REPLACE A WHOLE EYE.
URRR... I HAVE AN EYEWITNESS WHO CAN'T SEE!
THE CHAGRIN!!
HELP ME HERE!
SIR!
PERHAPS
THERE IS HOPE...
!
IF ANYONE COULD DO IT, IT'D BE HIM...
HE'D REPLACE A WHOLE EYE...
WHO IS THIS HE?
THEY SAY HIS HANDS WORKS MIRACLES...

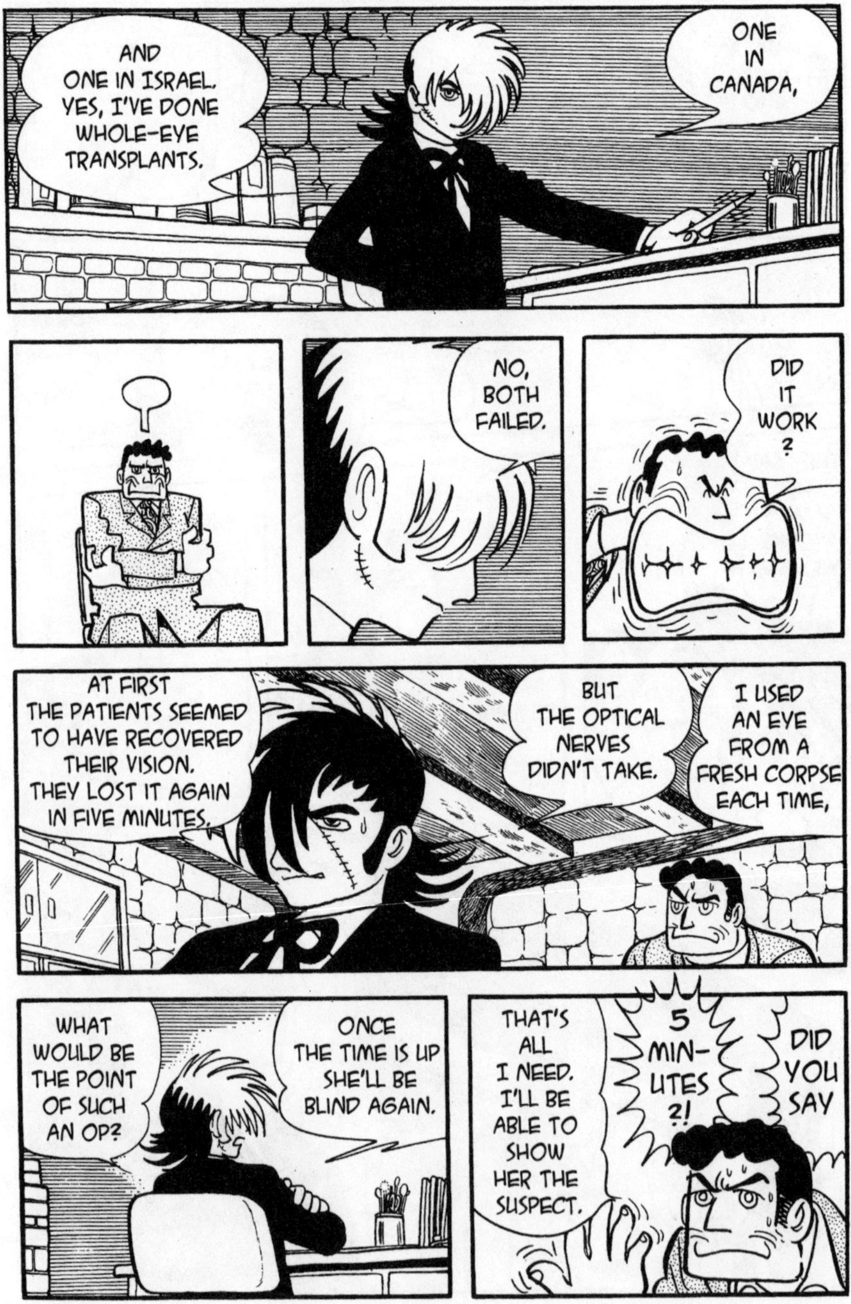
ONE IN CANADA,
AND ONE IN ISRAEL. YES, I'VE DONE WHOLE-EYE TRANSPLANTS.
DID IT WORK ?
NO, BOTH FAILED.
I USED AN EYE FROM A FRESH CORPSE EACH TIME,
BUT THE OPTICAL NERVES DIDN'T TAKE.
AT FIRST THE PATIENTS SEEMED TO HAVE RECOVERED THEIR VISION. THEY LOST IT AGAIN IN FIVE MINUTES.
DID YOU SAY
5 MIN-UTES ?!
THAT'S ALL I NEED. I'LL BE ABLE TO SHOW HER THE SUSPECT.
ONCE THE TIME IS UP SHE'LL BE BLIND AGAIN.
WHAT WOULD BE THE POINT OF SUCH AN OP?

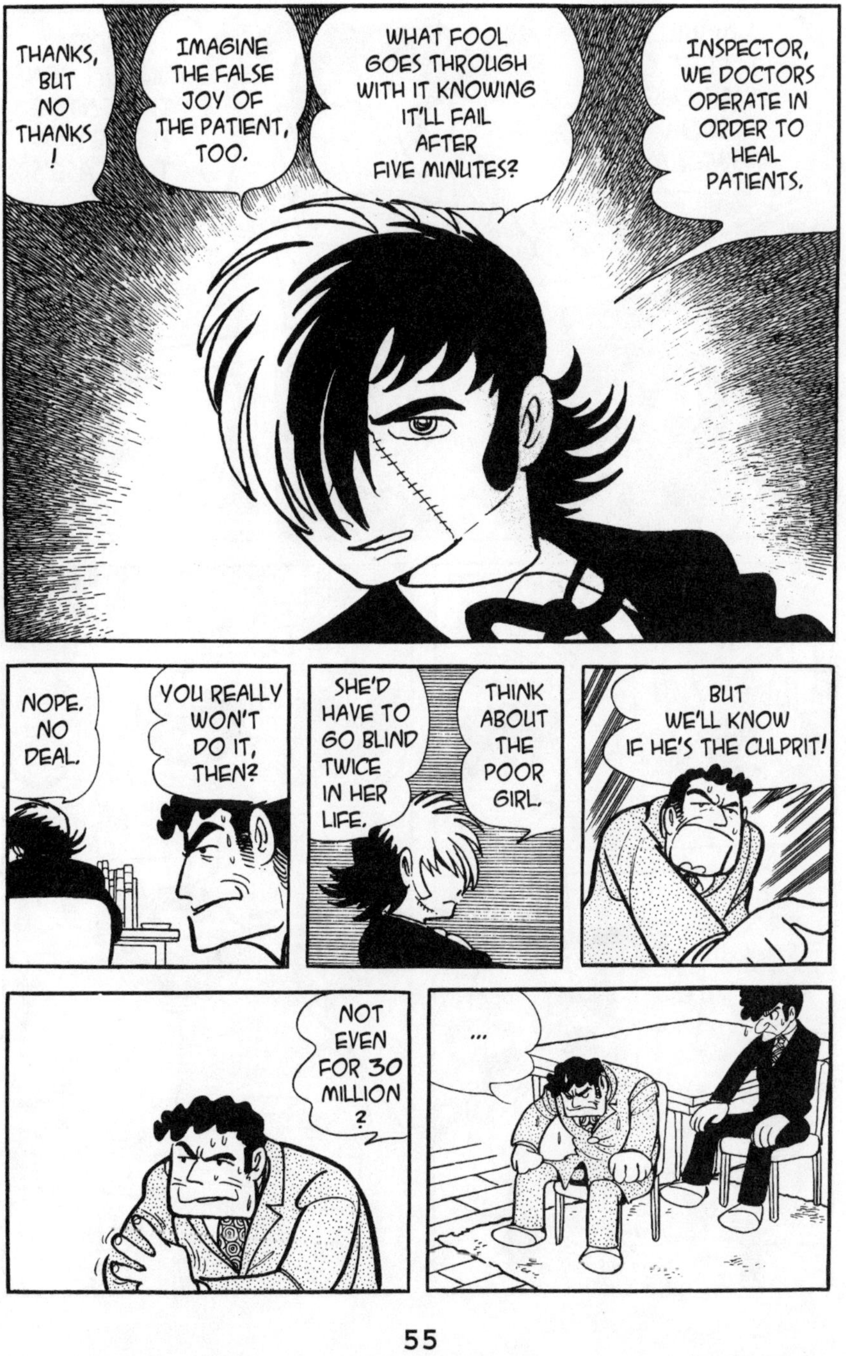
INSPECTOR, WE DOCTORS OPERATE IN ORDER TO HEAL PATIENTS.
WHAT FOOL GOES THROUGH WITH IT KNOWING IT'LL FAIL AFTER FIVE MINUTES?
IMAGINE THE FALSE JOY OF THE PATIENT, TOO.
THANKS, BUT NO THANKS!
BUT WE'LL KNOW IF HE'S THE CULPRIT!
THINK ABOUT THE POOR GIRL.
SHE'D HAVE TO GO BLIND TWICE IN HER LIFE.
YOU REALLY WON'T DO IT, THEN?
NOPE. NO DEAL.
...
NOT EVEN FOR 30 MILLION?

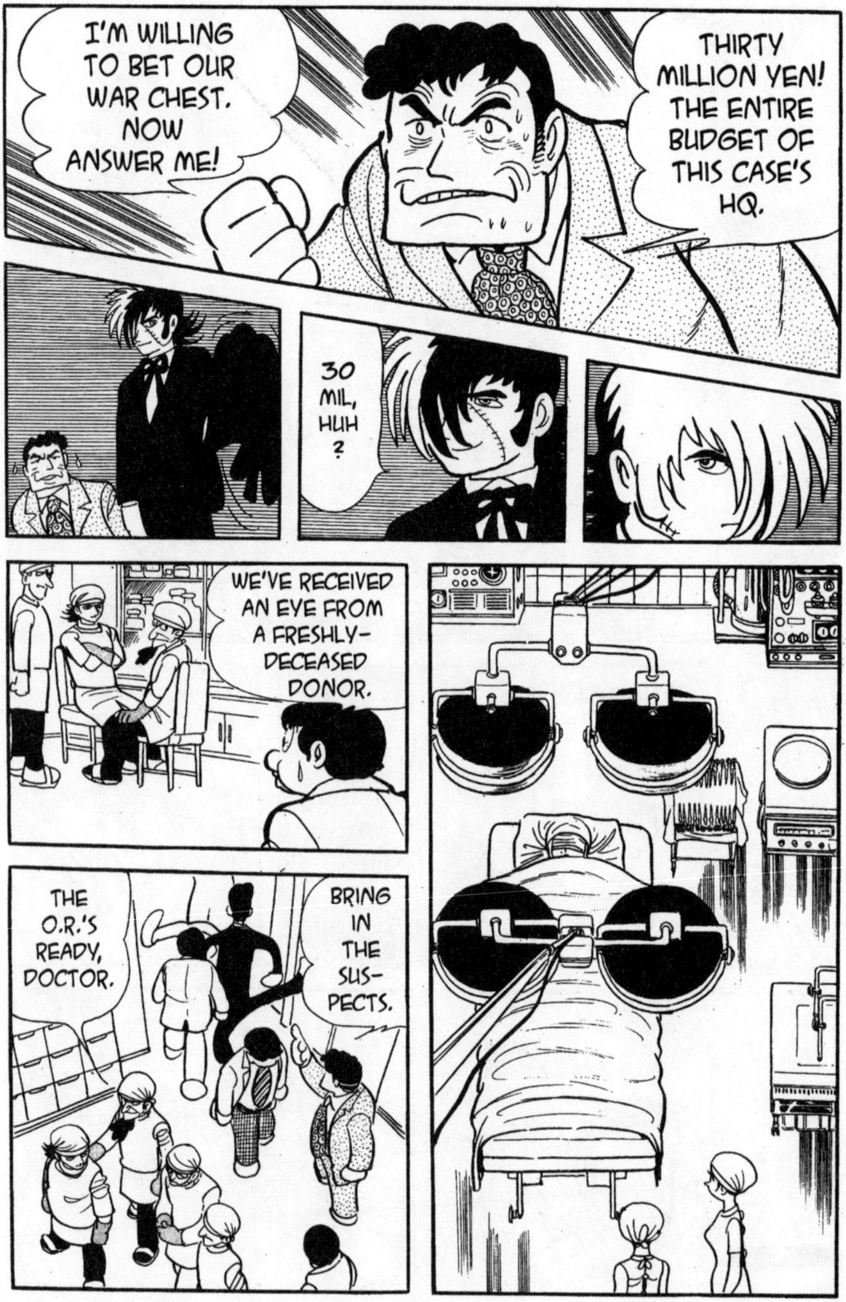
THIRTY MILLION YEN! THE ENTIRE BUDGET OF THIS CASE'S HQ.
I'M WILLING TO BET OUR WAR CHEST. NOW ANSWER ME!
30 MIL, HUH?
WE'VE RECEIVED AN EYE FROM A FRESHLY-DECEASED DONOR.
BRING IN THE SUS-PECTS.
THE O.R.'S READY, DOCTOR.

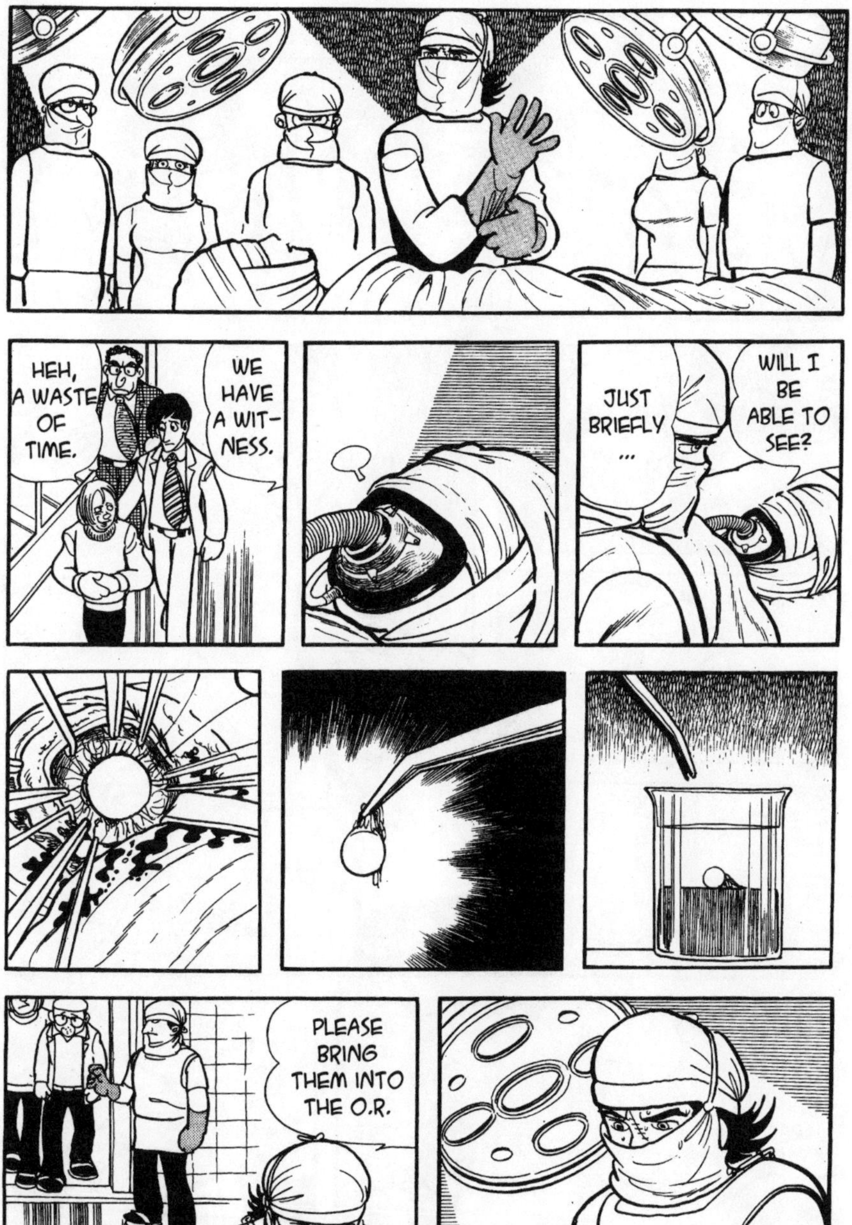
WILL I BE ABLE TO SEE?
JUST BRIEFLY ...
WE HAVE A WIT-NESS.
HEH, A WASTE OF TIME.
PLEASE BRING THEM INTO THE O.R.

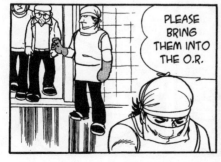

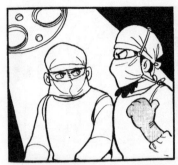

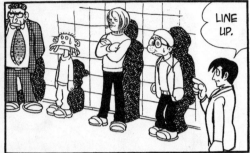

LINE UP.
I-IT'S HIM, IN THE MIDDLE! THAT'S THE ONE!
M... ME? CUT THIS OUT!
SHE'S TOTALLY LYING!
HE LEFT HIS BAG THEN RAN!

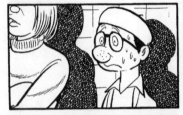

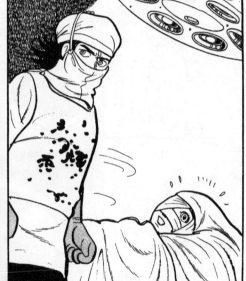

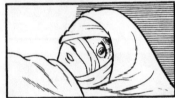

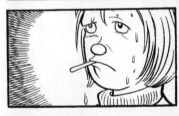

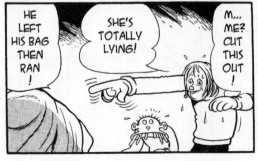

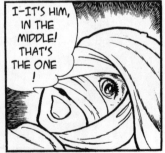

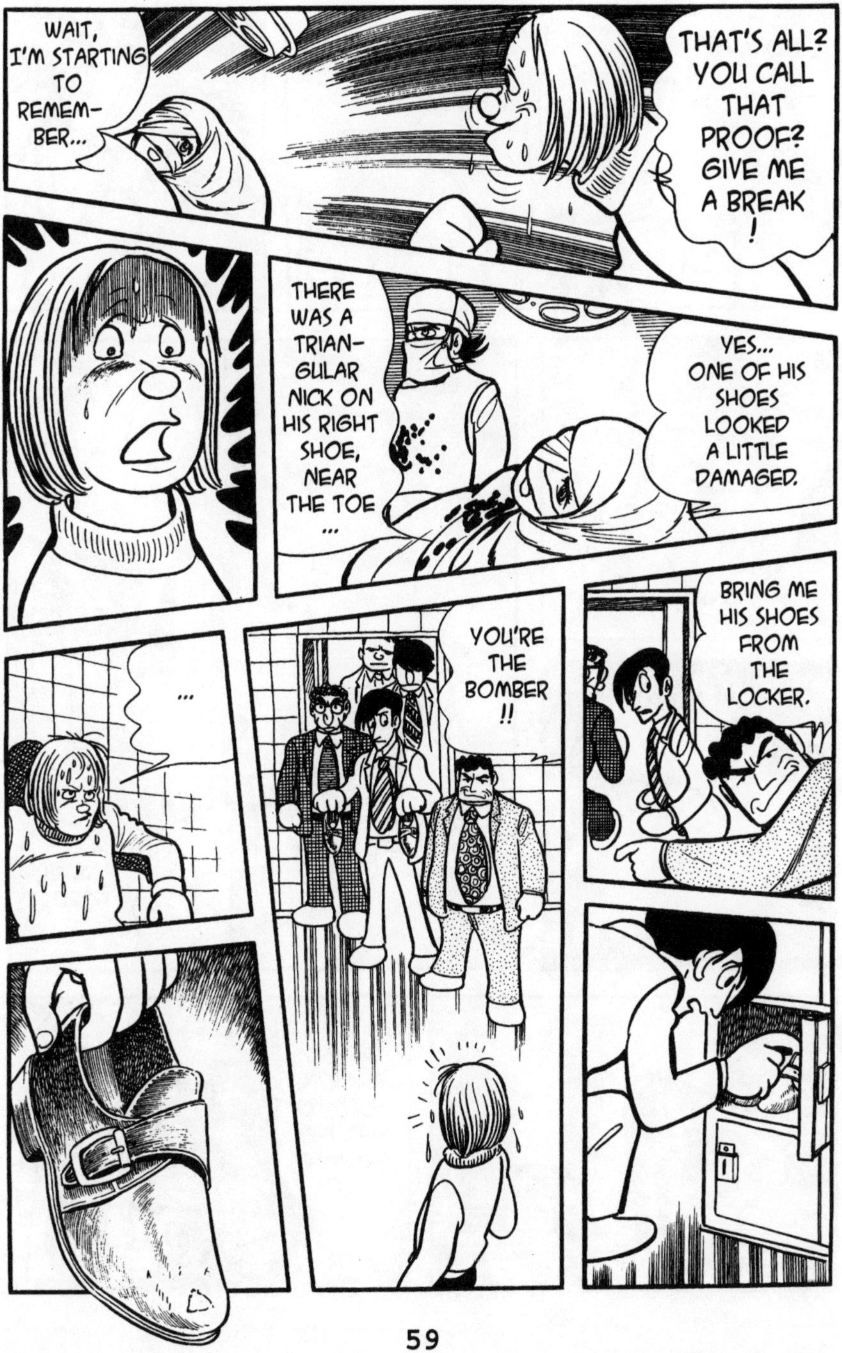
THAT'S ALL? YOU CALL THAT PROOF? GIVE ME A BREAK!
WAIT, I'M STARTING TO REMEMBER...
YES... ONE OF HIS SHOES LOOKED A LITTLE DAMAGED.
THERE WAS A TRIANGULAR NICK ON HIS RIGHT SHOE, NEAR THE TOE...
BRING ME HIS SHOES FROM THE LOCKER.
YOU'RE THE BOMBER!!
...

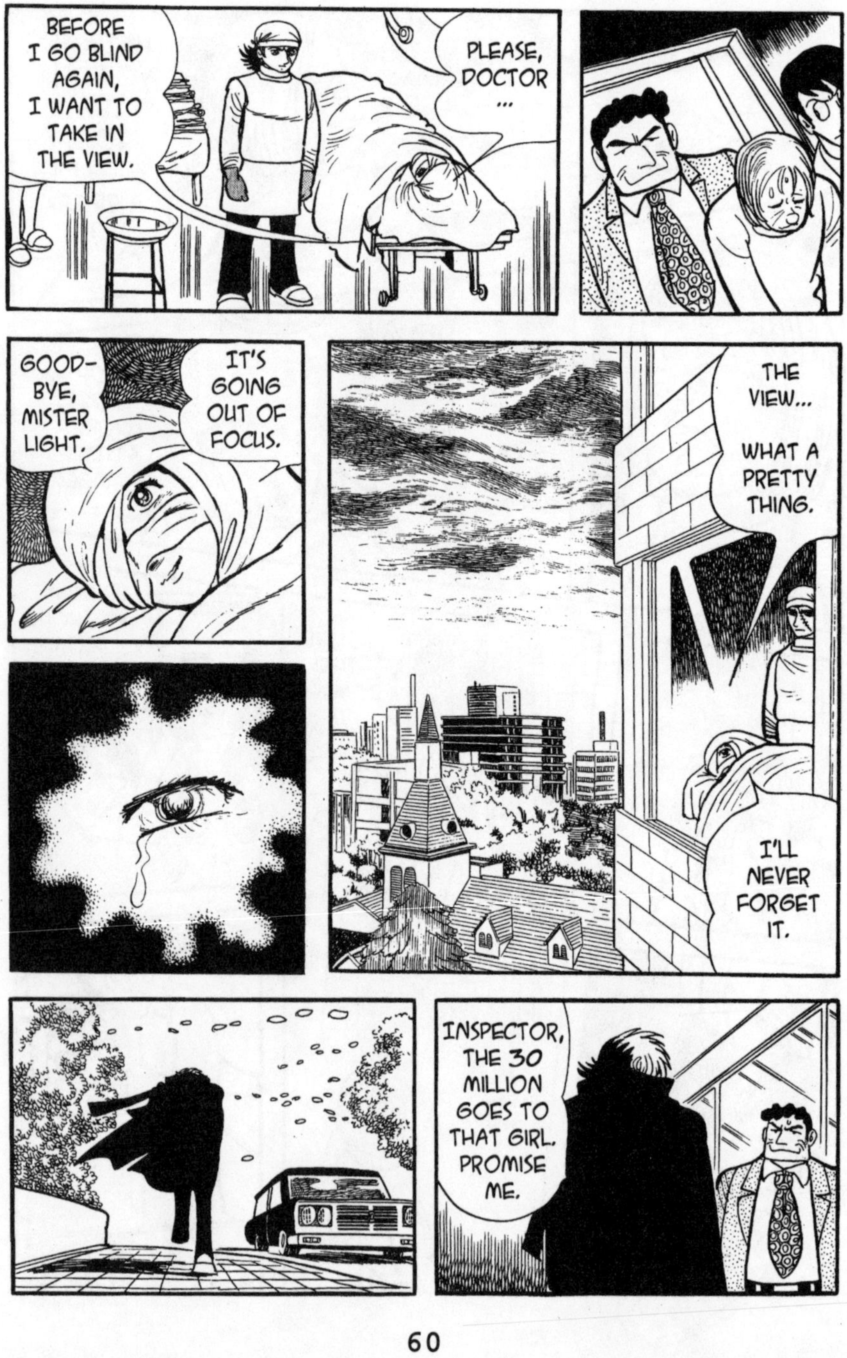
PLEASE, DOCTOR ...
BEFORE I GO BLIND AGAIN, I WANT TO TAKE IN THE VIEW.
THE VIEW... WHAT A PRETTY THING.
I'LL NEVER FORGET IT.
IT'S GOING OUT OF FOCUS.
GOOD-BYE, MISTER LIGHT.
INSPECTOR, THE 30 MILLION GOES TO THAT GIRL. PROMISE ME.

AS HE WILLS

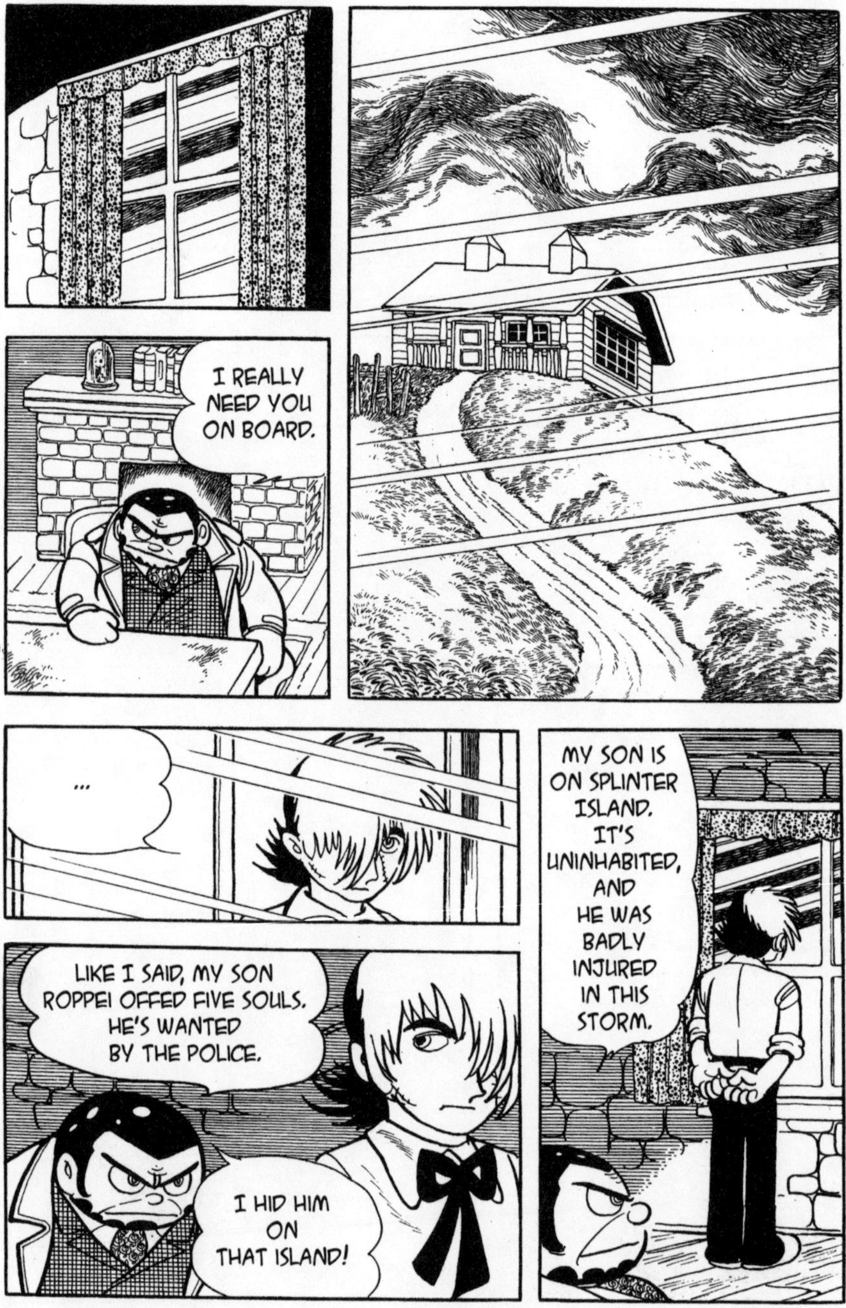
I REALLY NEED YOU ON BOARD.
MY SON IS ON SPLINTER ISLAND. IT'S UNINHABITED, AND HE WAS BADLY INJURED IN THIS STORM.
...
LIKE I SAID, MY SON ROPPEI OFFED FIVE SOULS. HE'S WANTED BY THE POLICE.
I HID HIM ON THAT ISLAND!

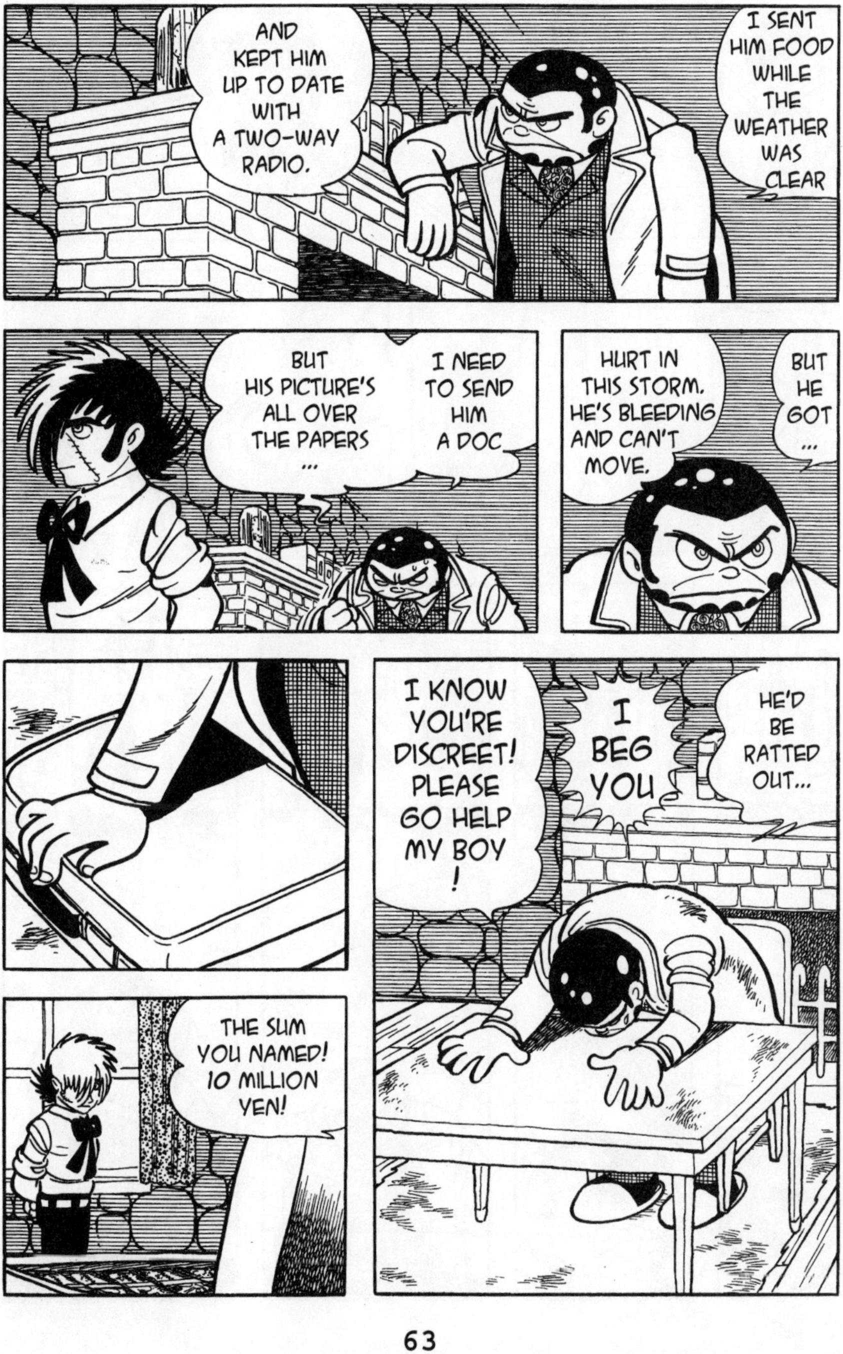
I SENT HIM FOOD WHILE THE WEATHER WAS CLEAR
AND KEPT HIM UP TO DATE WITH A TWO-WAY RADIO.
BUT HE GOT ...
HURT IN THIS STORM. HE'S BLEEDING AND CAN'T MOVE.
I NEED TO SEND HIM A DOC
BUT HIS PICTURE'S ALL OVER THE PAPERS ...
HE'D BE RATTED OUT...
I BEG YOU
I KNOW YOU'RE DISCREET! PLEASE GO HELP MY BOY !
THE SUM YOU NAMED! 10 MILLION YEN!

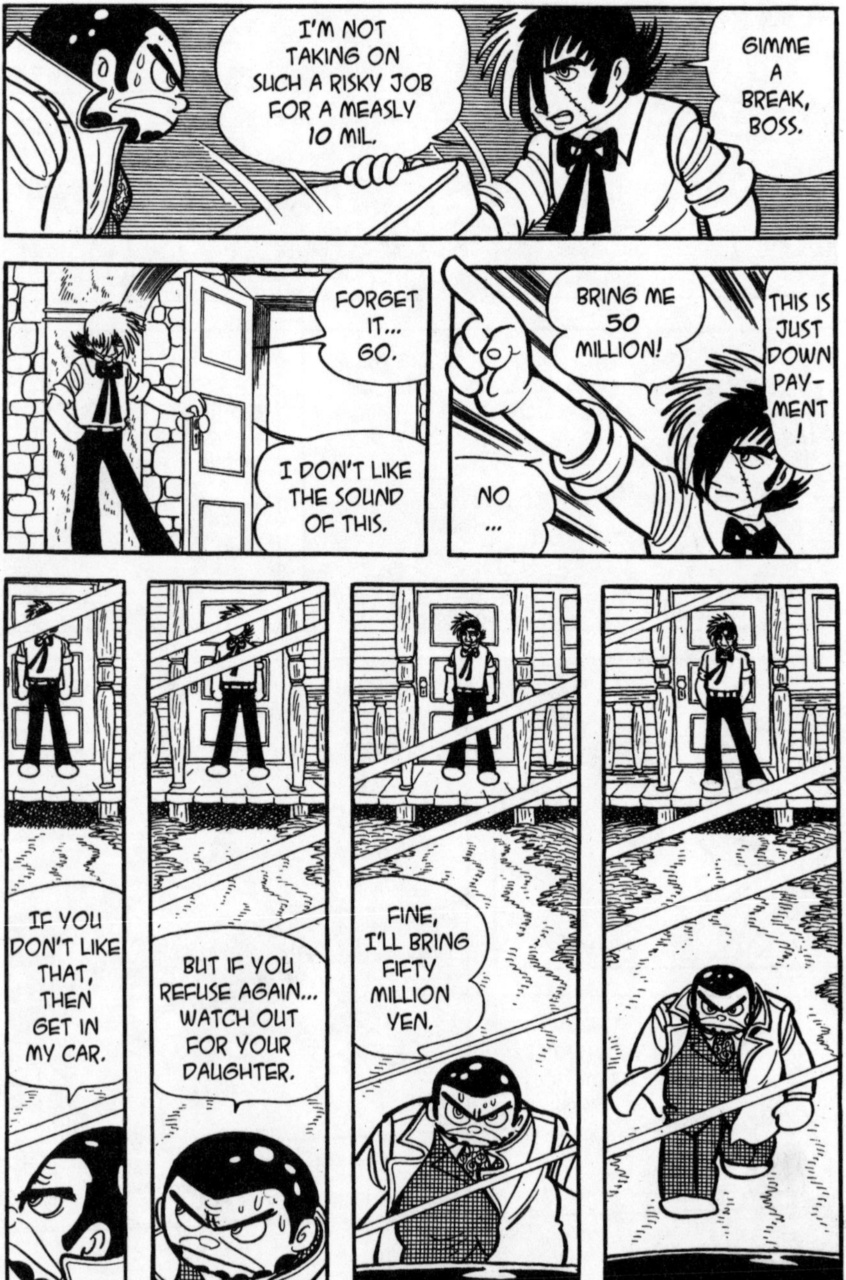
GIMME A BREAK, BOSS.
I'M NOT TAKING ON SUCH A RISKY JOB FOR A MEASLY 10 MIL.
THIS IS JUST DOWN PAY-MENT!
BRING ME 50 MILLION!
NO ...
FORGET IT... GO.
I DON'T LIKE THE SOUND OF THIS.
FINE, I'LL BRING FIFTY MILLION YEN.
BUT IF YOU REFUSE AGAIN... WATCH OUT FOR YOUR DAUGHTER.
IF YOU DON'T LIKE THAT, THEN GET IN MY CAR.

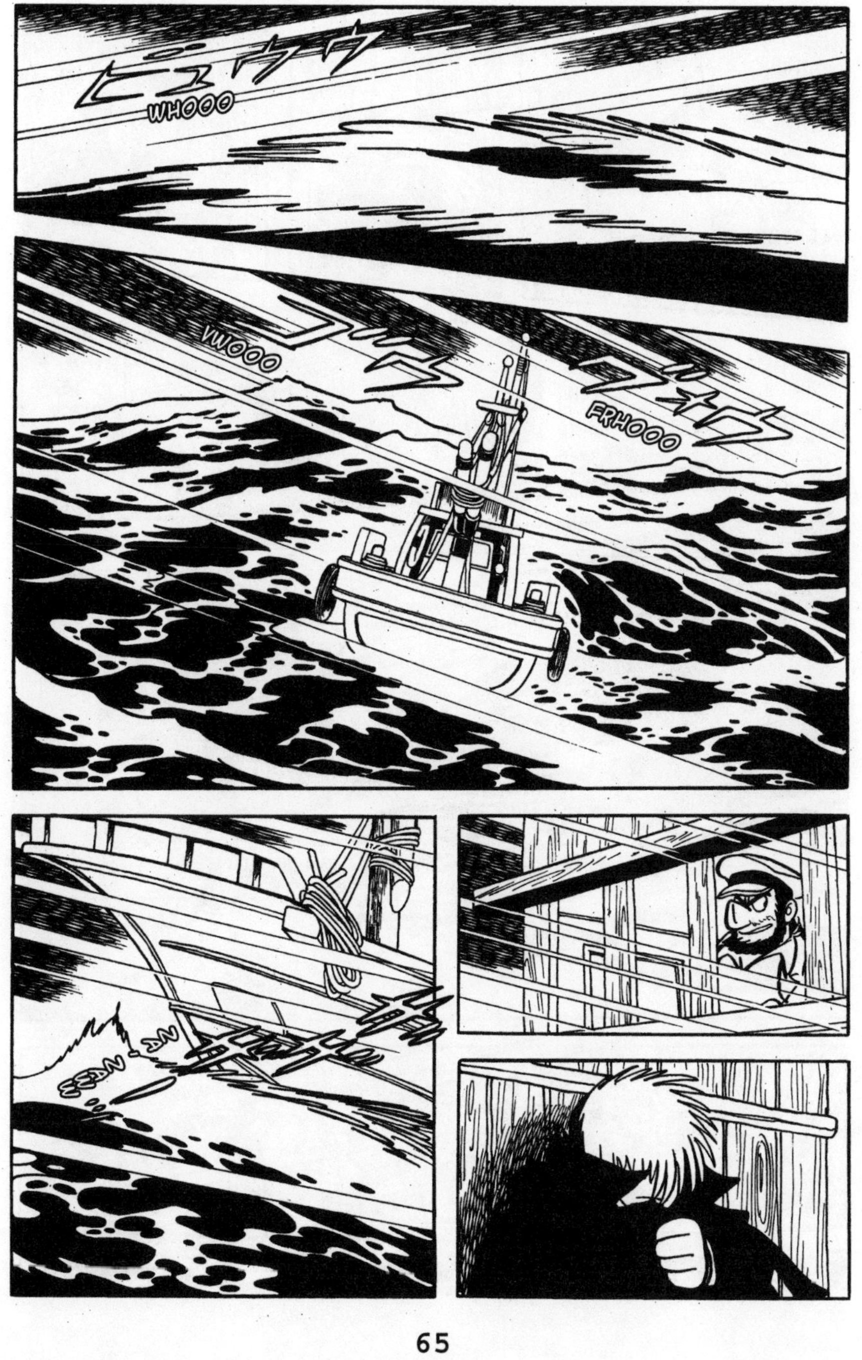

WHOOO
FRHOOO
VWOOO
ZA-ZAAN

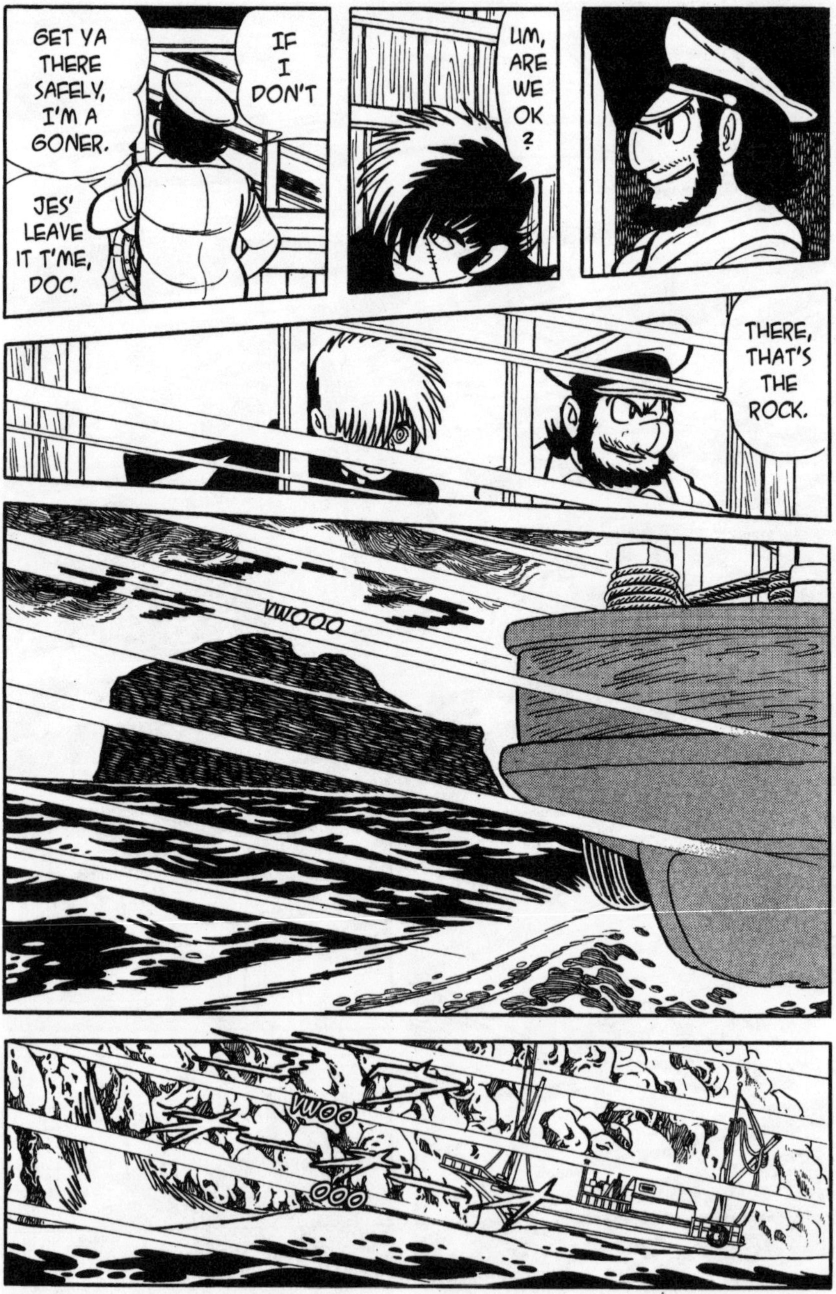
UM, ARE WE OK?
IF I DON'T
GET YA THERE SAFELY, I'M A GONER.
JES' LEAVE IT T'ME, DOC.
THERE, THAT'S THE ROCK.
VWOOO
VWOO

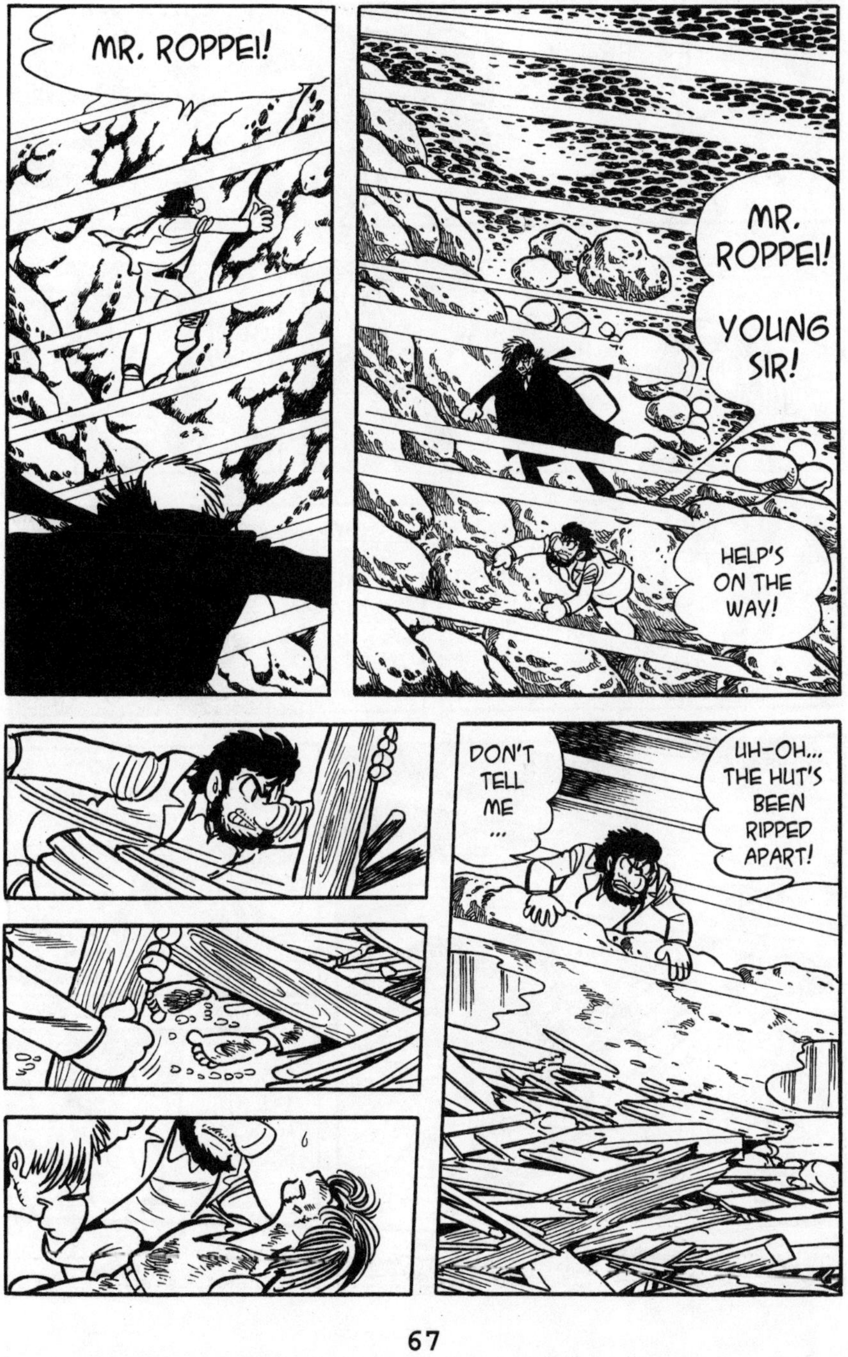
MR. ROPPEI! YOUNG SIR!
HELP'S ON THE WAY!
MR. ROPPEI!
UH-OH... THE HUT'S BEEN RIPPED APART!
DON'T TELL ME ...

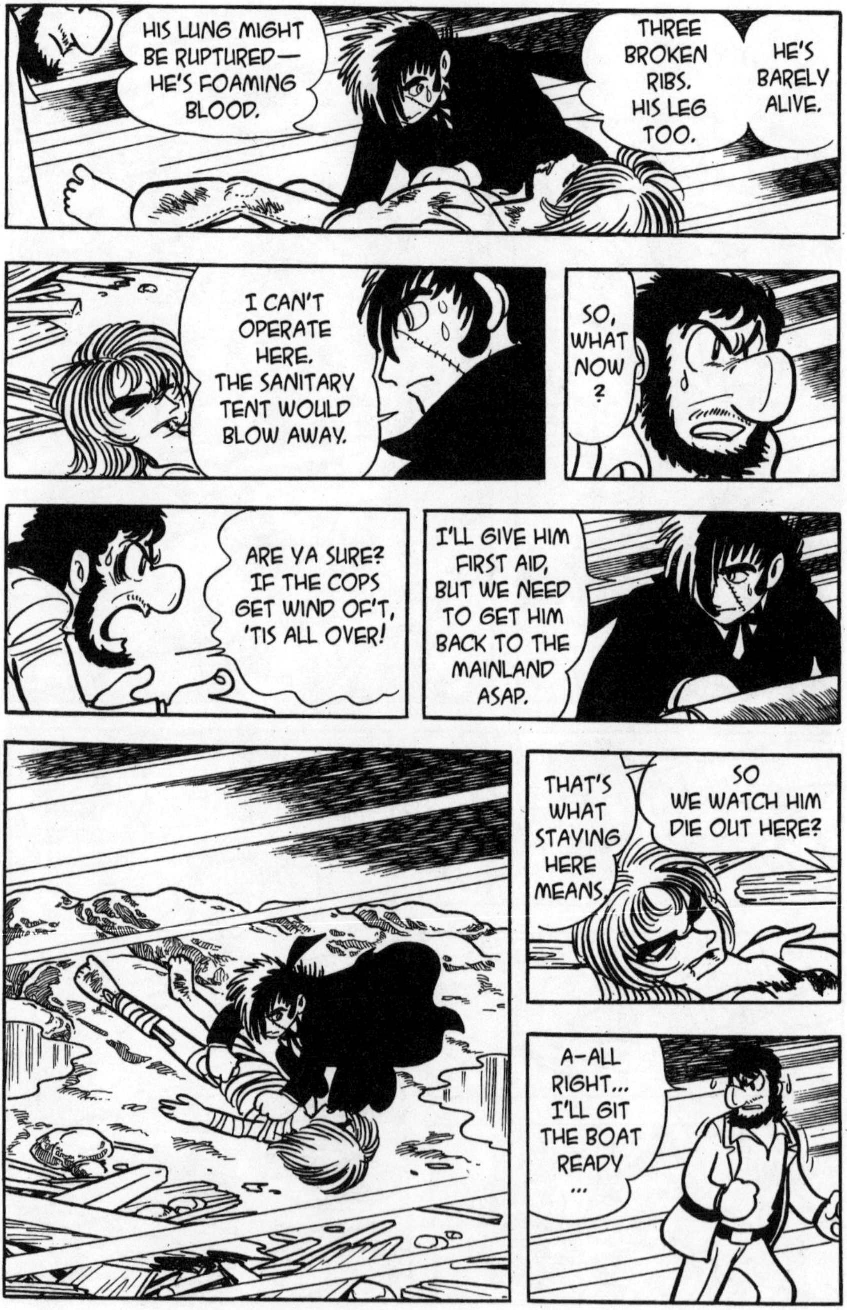
HE'S BARELY ALIVE.
THREE BROKEN RIBS. HIS LEG TOO.
HIS LUNG MIGHT BE RUPTURED— HE'S FOAMING BLOOD.
SO, WHAT NOW ?
I CAN'T OPERATE HERE. THE SANITARY TENT WOULD BLOW AWAY.
I'LL GIVE HIM FIRST AID, BUT WE NEED TO GET HIM BACK TO THE MAINLAND ASAP.
ARE YA SURE? IF THE COPS GET WIND OF'T, 'TIS ALL OVER!
SO WE WATCH HIM DIE OUT HERE?
THAT'S WHAT STAYING HERE MEANS.
A-ALL RIGHT... I'LL GIT THE BOAT READY ...

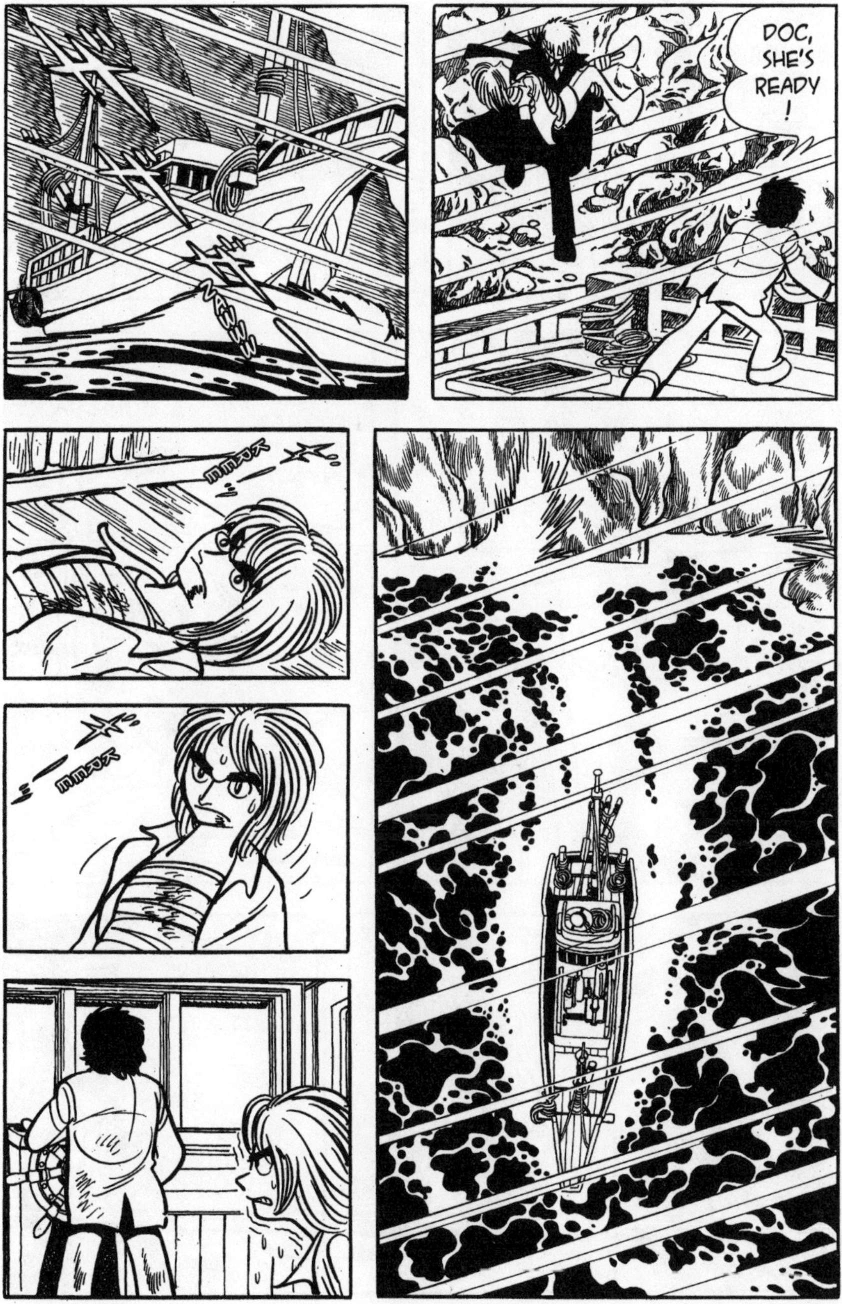
DOC, SHE'S READY !

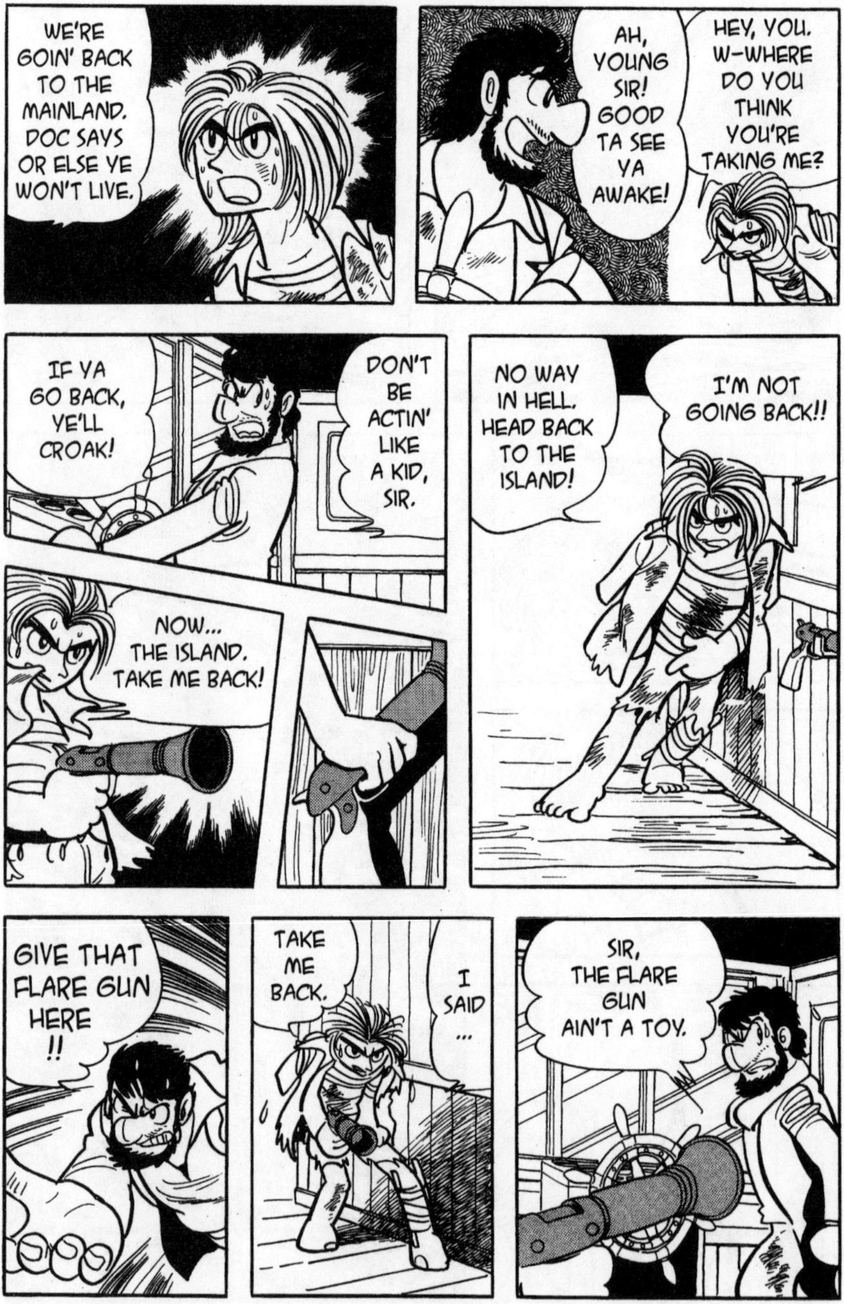
HEY, YOU. W-WHERE DO YOU THINK YOU'RE TAKING ME?
AH, YOUNG SIR! GOOD TA SEE YA AWAKE!
WE'RE GOIN' BACK TO THE MAINLAND. DOC SAYS OR ELSE YE WON'T LIVE.
I'M NOT GOING BACK!!
NO WAY IN HELL. HEAD BACK TO THE ISLAND!
DON'T BE ACTIN' LIKE A KID, SIR.
IF YA GO BACK, YE'LL CROAK!
NOW... THE ISLAND. TAKE ME BACK!
SIR, THE FLARE GUN AIN'T A TOY.
I SAID ...
TAKE ME BACK.
GIVE THAT FLARE GUN HERE !!

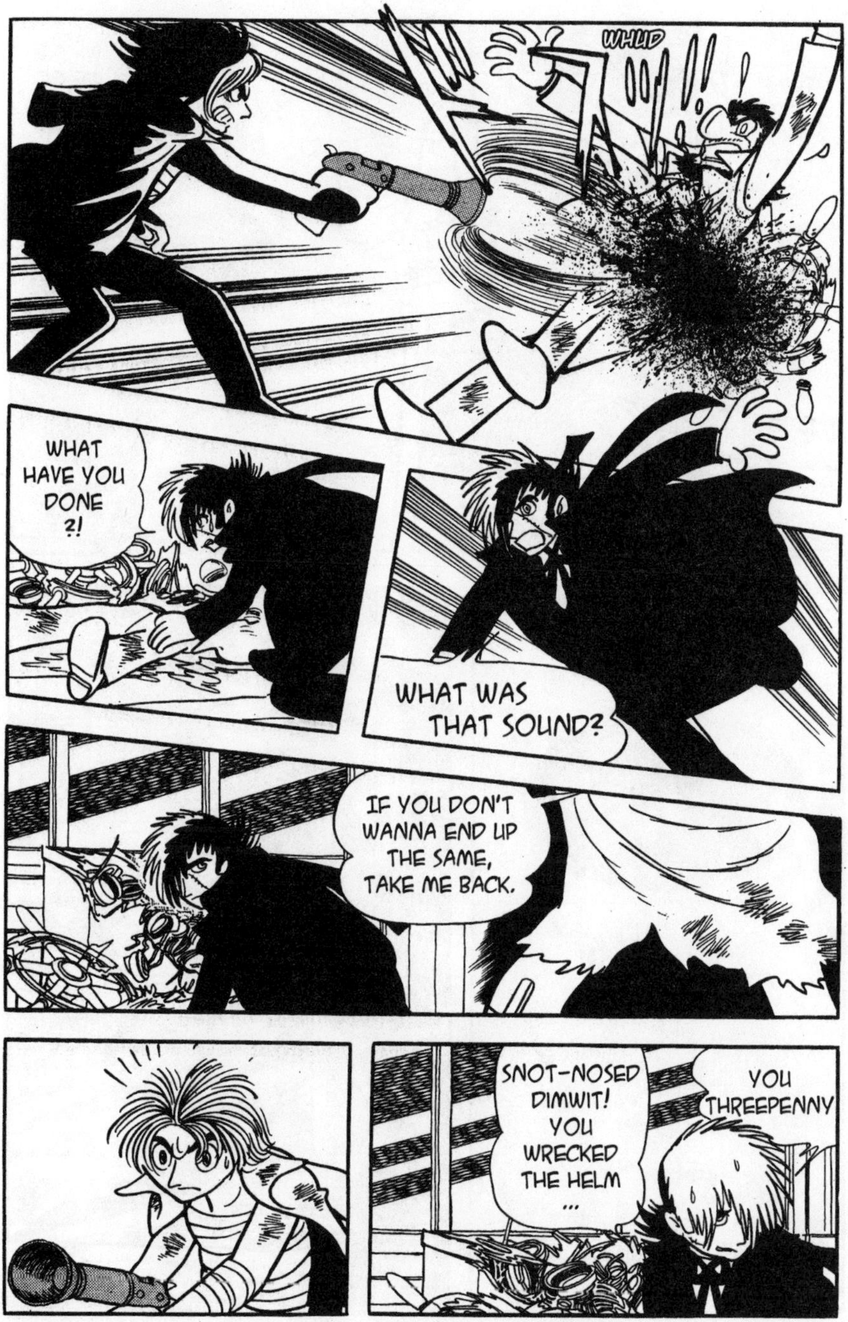
WHUD
WHAT WAS THAT SOUND?
WHAT HAVE YOU DONE ?!
IF YOU DON'T WANNA END UP THE SAME, TAKE ME BACK.
YOU THREEPENNY
SNOT-NOSED DIMWIT! YOU WRECKED THE HELM ...

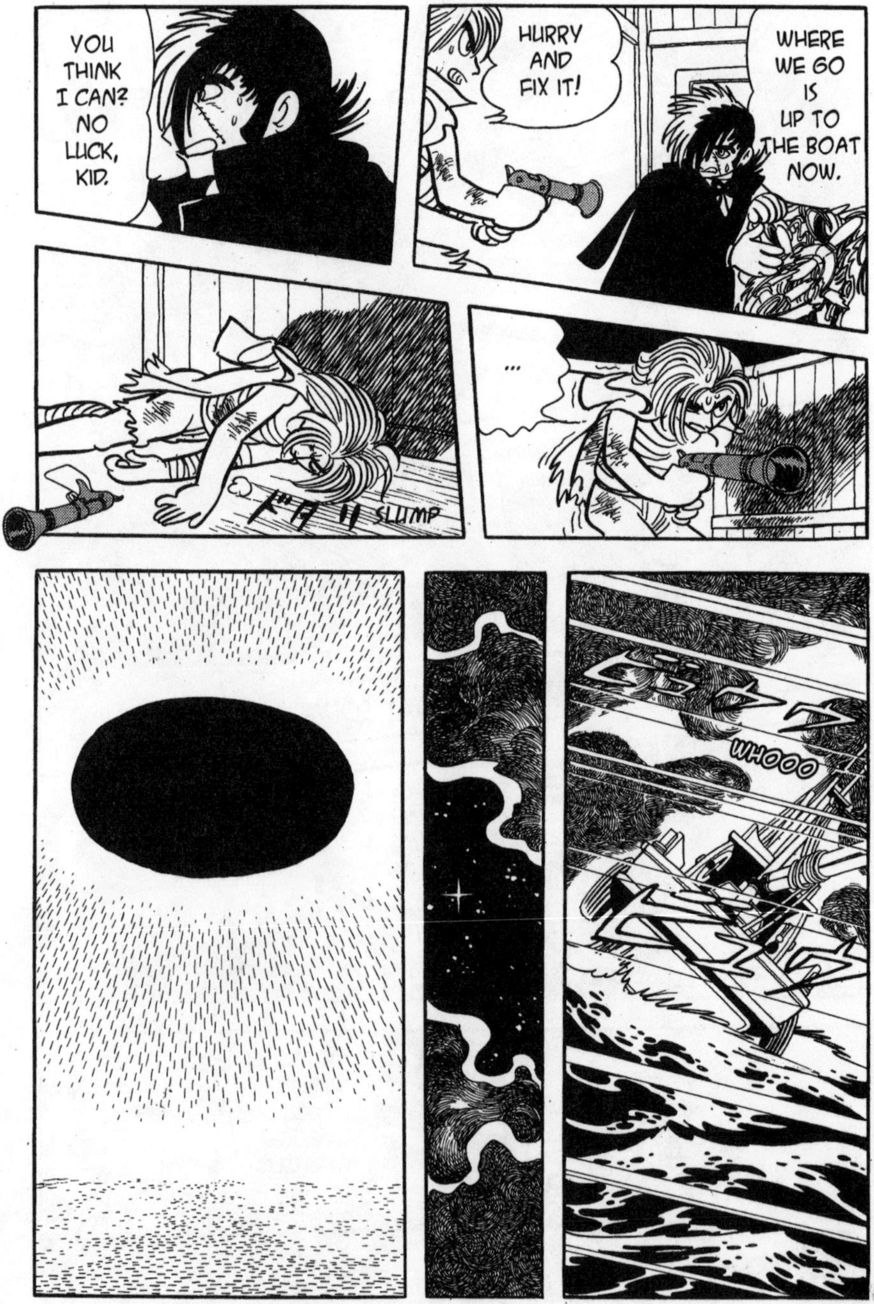
WHERE WE GO IS UP TO THE BOAT NOW.
HURRY AND FIX IT!
YOU THINK I CAN? NO LUCK, KID.
...
SLUMP
WHOOO

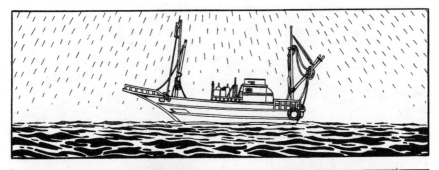

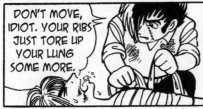

KOFF
KOFF KOFF
DON'T MOVE, IDIOT. YOUR RIBS JUST TORE UP YOUR LUNG SOME MORE.
WHERE ARE WE?
DON'T ASK ME. YOU SHOT THE COMPASS ALONG WITH THE HELM!
WERE IT NOT FOR MY DEAL WITH YOUR DAD I'D TOSS YOU OVER-BOARD.
ACK!! WATER! WE'RE TAKING ON WATER!
WE'RE SINKING !!

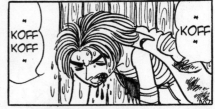

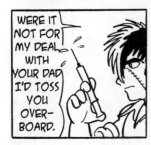

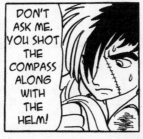

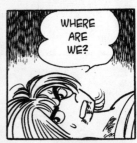

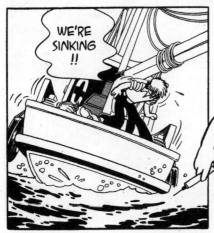

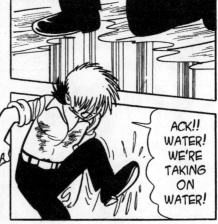

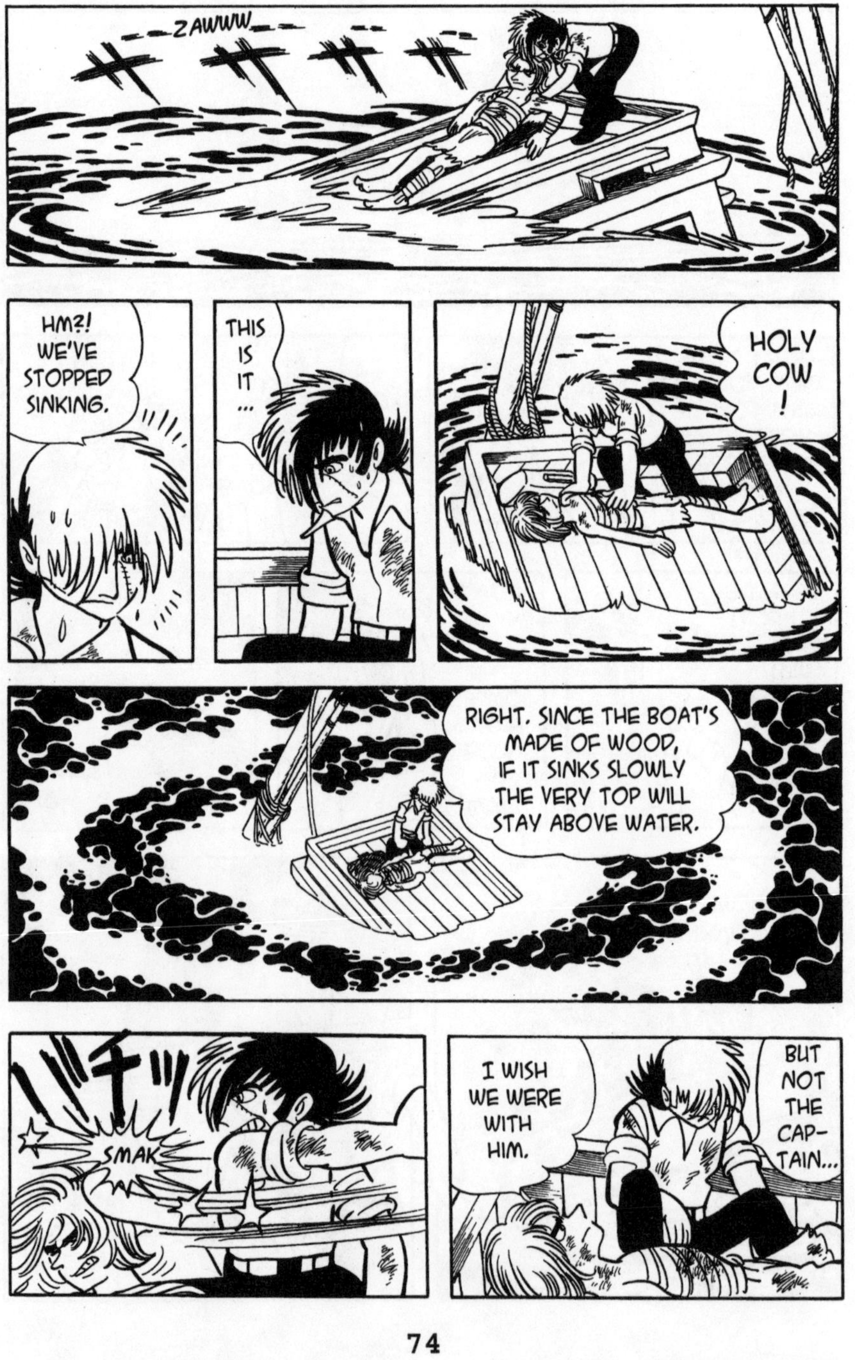
ZAWWW
HOLY COW !
THIS IS IT ...
HM?! WE'VE STOPPED SINKING.
RIGHT. SINCE THE BOAT'S MADE OF WOOD, IF IT SINKS SLOWLY THE VERY TOP WILL STAY ABOVE WATER.
BUT NOT THE CAP-TAIN...
I WISH WE WERE WITH HIM.
SMAK

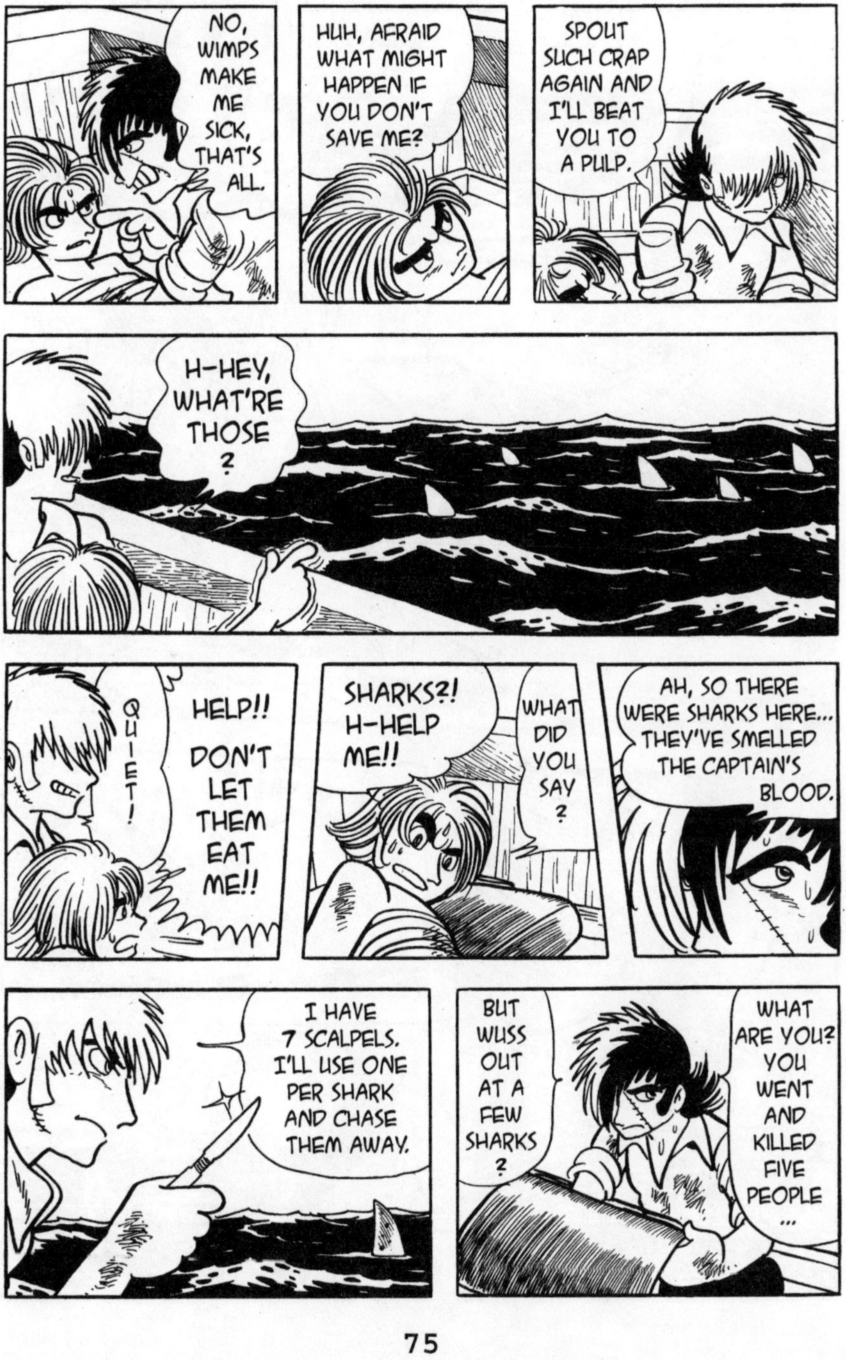
SPOUT SUCH CRAP AGAIN AND I'LL BEAT YOU TO A PULP.
HUH, AFRAID WHAT MIGHT HAPPEN IF YOU DON'T SAVE ME?
NO, WIMPS MAKE ME SICK, THAT'S ALL.
H-HEY, WHAT'RE THOSE?
AH, SO THERE WERE SHARKS HERE... THEY'VE SMELLED THE CAPTAIN'S BLOOD.
WHAT DID YOU SAY?
SHARKS?! H-HELP ME!!
HELP!! DON'T LET THEM EAT ME!!
QUIET!
WHAT ARE YOU? YOU WENT AND KILLED FIVE PEOPLE...
BUT WUSS OUT AT A FEW SHARKS?
I HAVE 7 SCALPELS. I'LL USE ONE PER SHARK AND CHASE THEM AWAY.

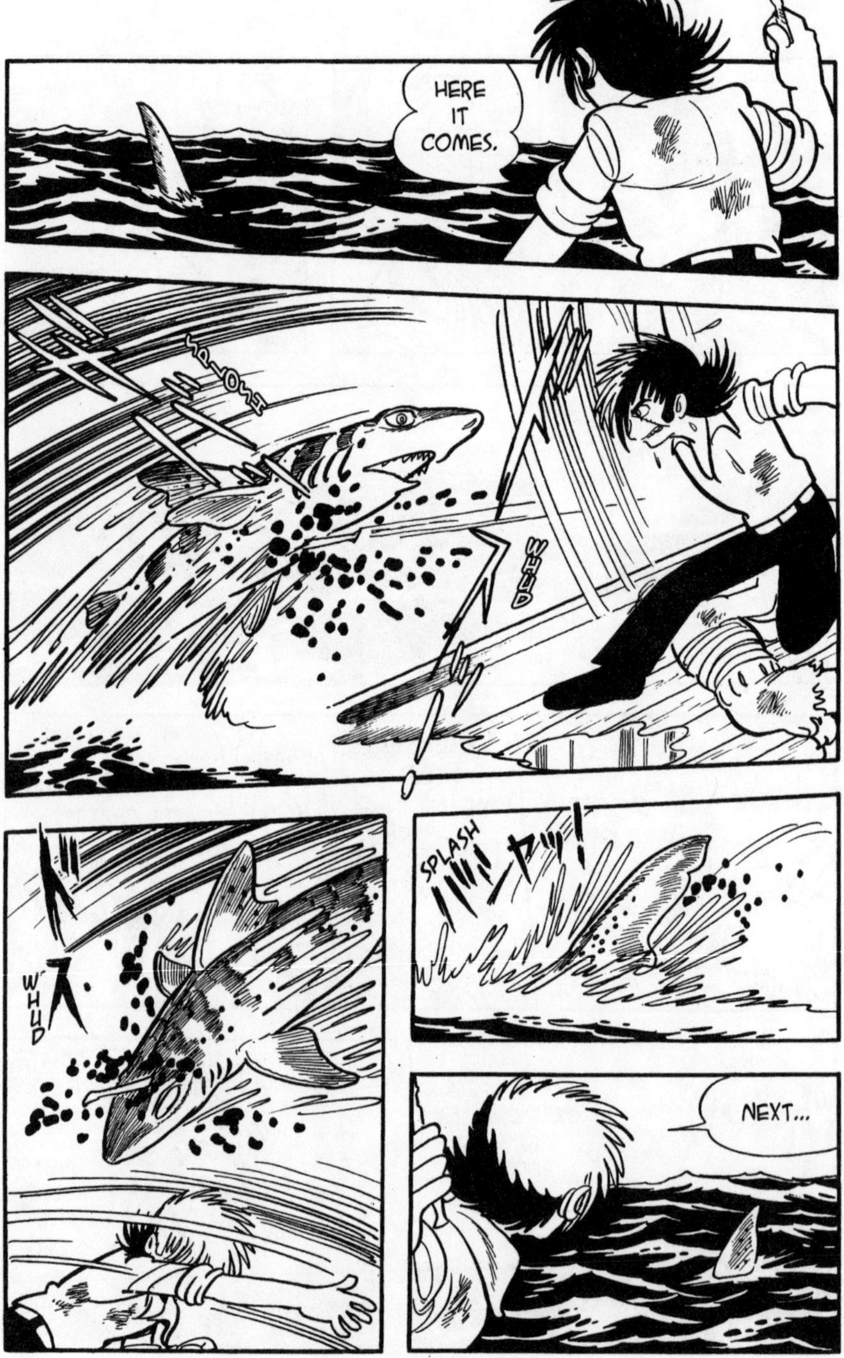
HERE IT COMES.
WHUD
SPLASH
WHUD
NEXT...

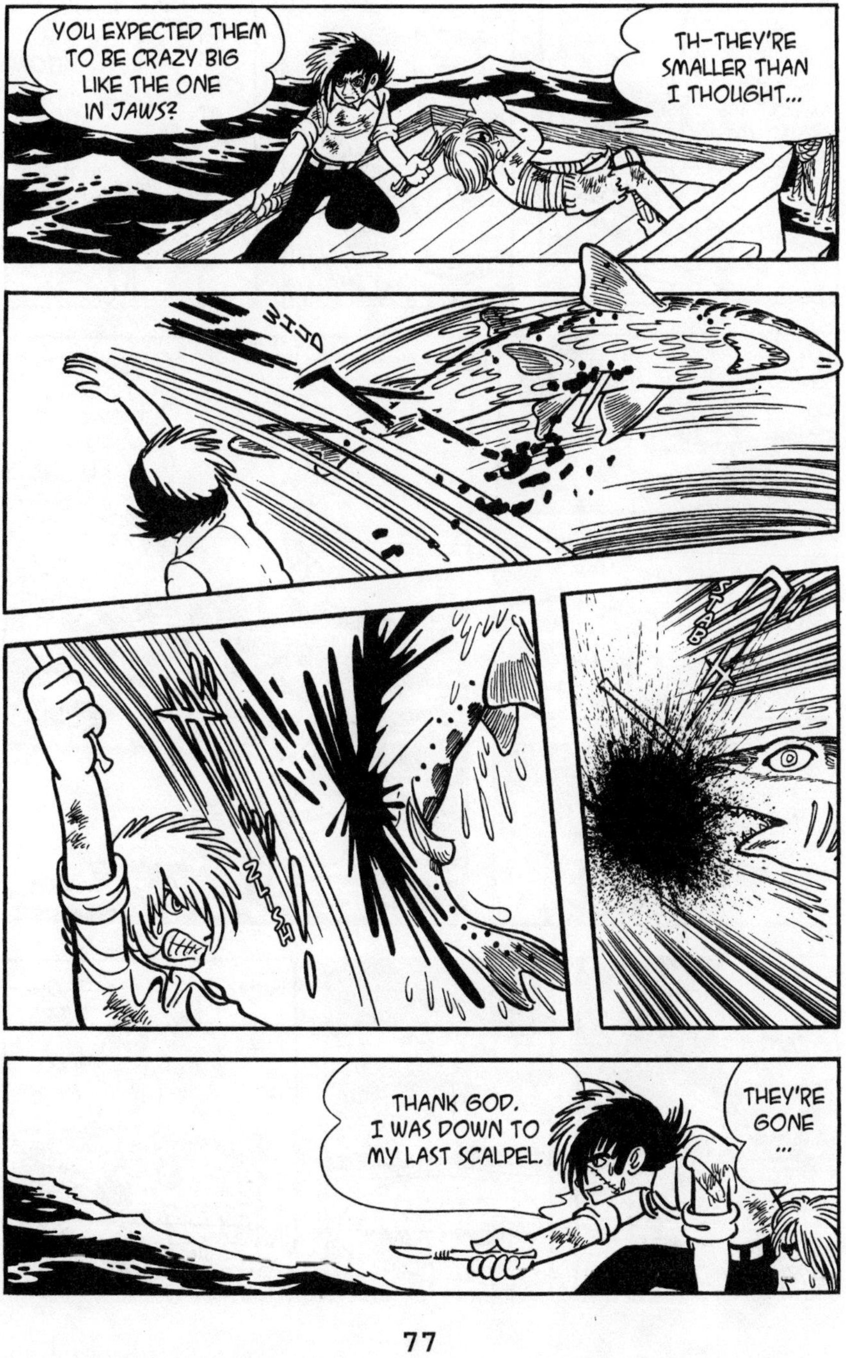
TH-THEY'RE SMALLER THAN I THOUGHT...
YOU EXPECTED THEM TO BE CRAZY BIG LIKE THE ONE IN JAWS?
STAB
THEY'RE GONE ...
THANK GOD. I WAS DOWN TO MY LAST SCALPEL.

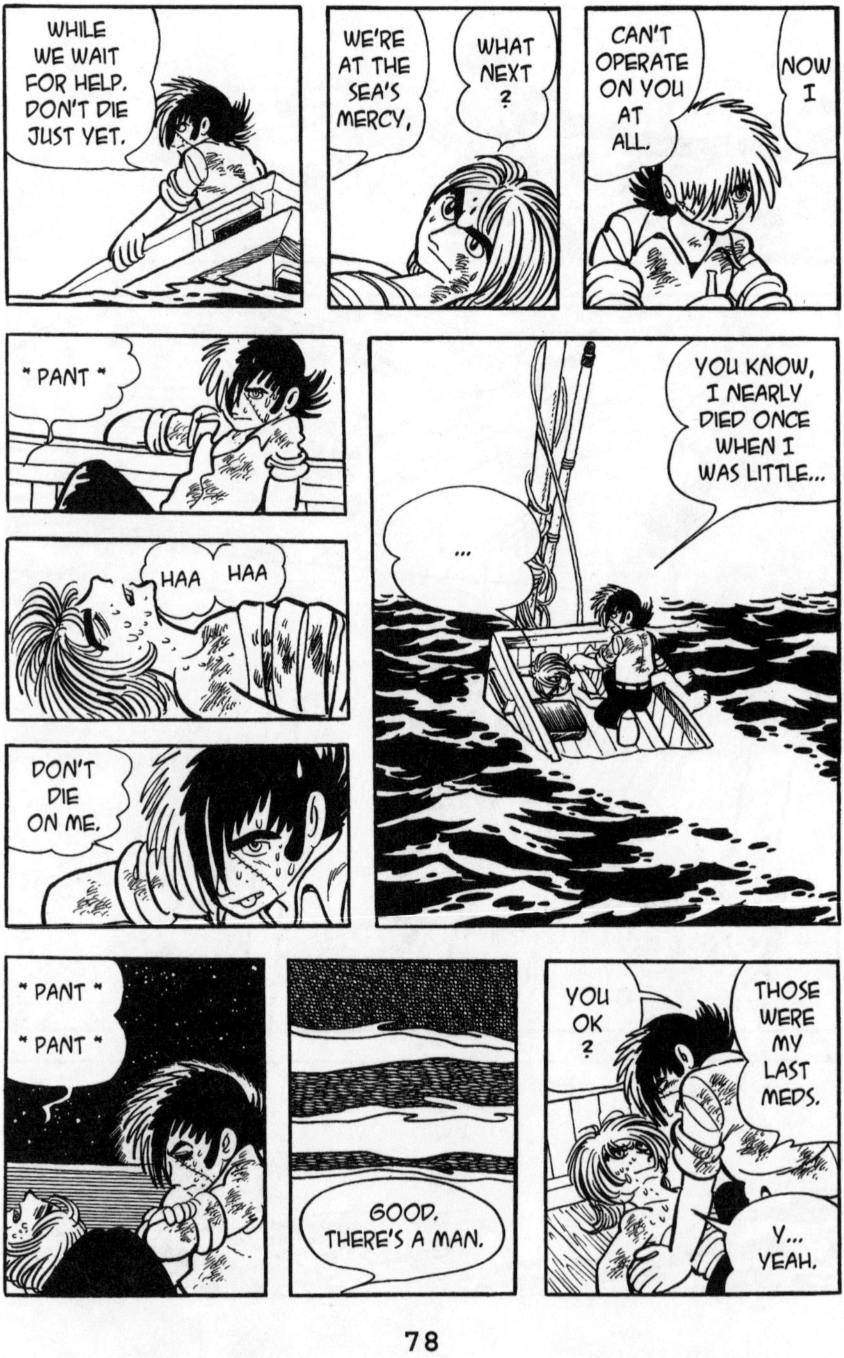
NOW I
CAN'T OPERATE ON YOU AT ALL.
WHAT NEXT?
WE'RE AT THE SEA'S MERCY,
WHILE WE WAIT FOR HELP. DON'T DIE JUST YET.
YOU KNOW, I NEARLY DIED ONCE WHEN I WAS LITTLE...
...
* PANT *
HAA HAA
DON'T DIE ON ME.
THOSE WERE MY LAST MEDS.
YOU OK?
Y... YEAH.
GOOD. THERE'S A MAN.
* PANT *
* PANT *

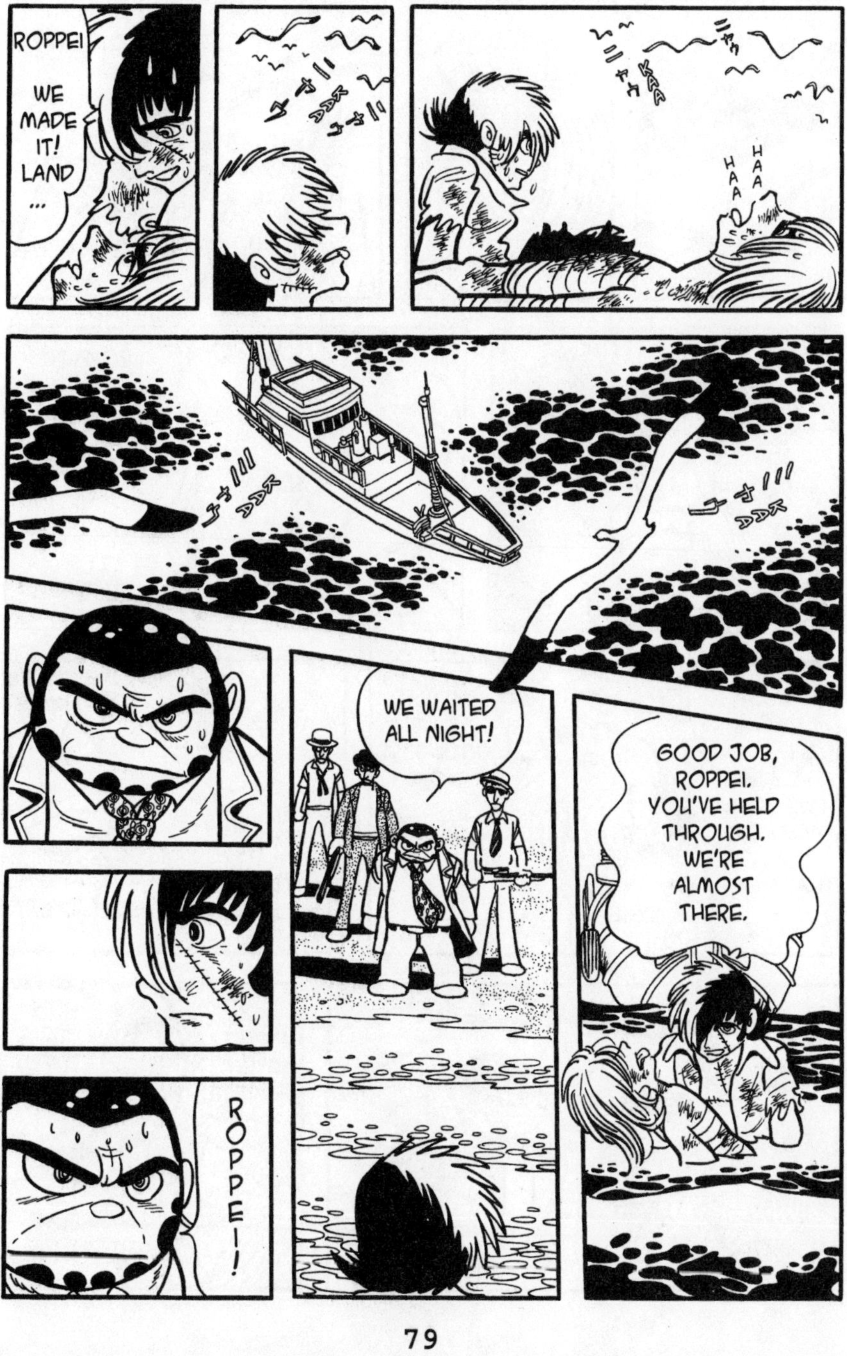
KAA
HAA
HAA
KAA
ROPPEI
WE MADE IT! LAND ...
KAA
KAA
GOOD JOB, ROPPEI. YOU'VE HELD THROUGH. WE'RE ALMOST THERE.
WE WAITED ALL NIGHT!
ROPPEI!

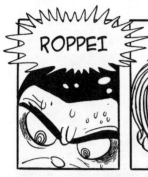

ROPPEI!!
ROPPEI
ROPPEI ...
ROPPEI, A-ARE YOU DEAD?
IT'S DADDY!
YOU POOR THING!
YOU LET HIM DIE?
HE WAS ALIVE UNTIL JUST NOW.
HE WAS BRAVE. SEEING YOU, HE MUST HAVE RELAXED AND LOST SOME OF THAT FIGHT.
YOU DIDN'T EVEN OPERATE!
YOU JUST LET HIM DIE.
SAY YOUR PRAYERS!

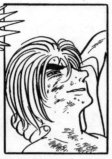

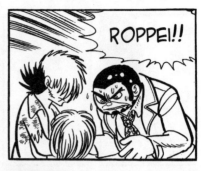

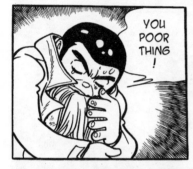

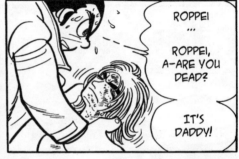

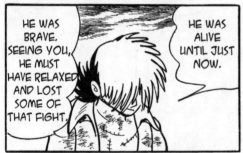

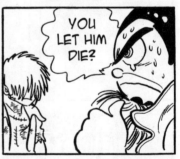

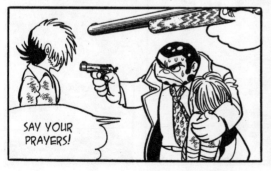

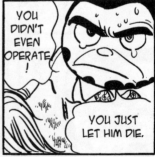

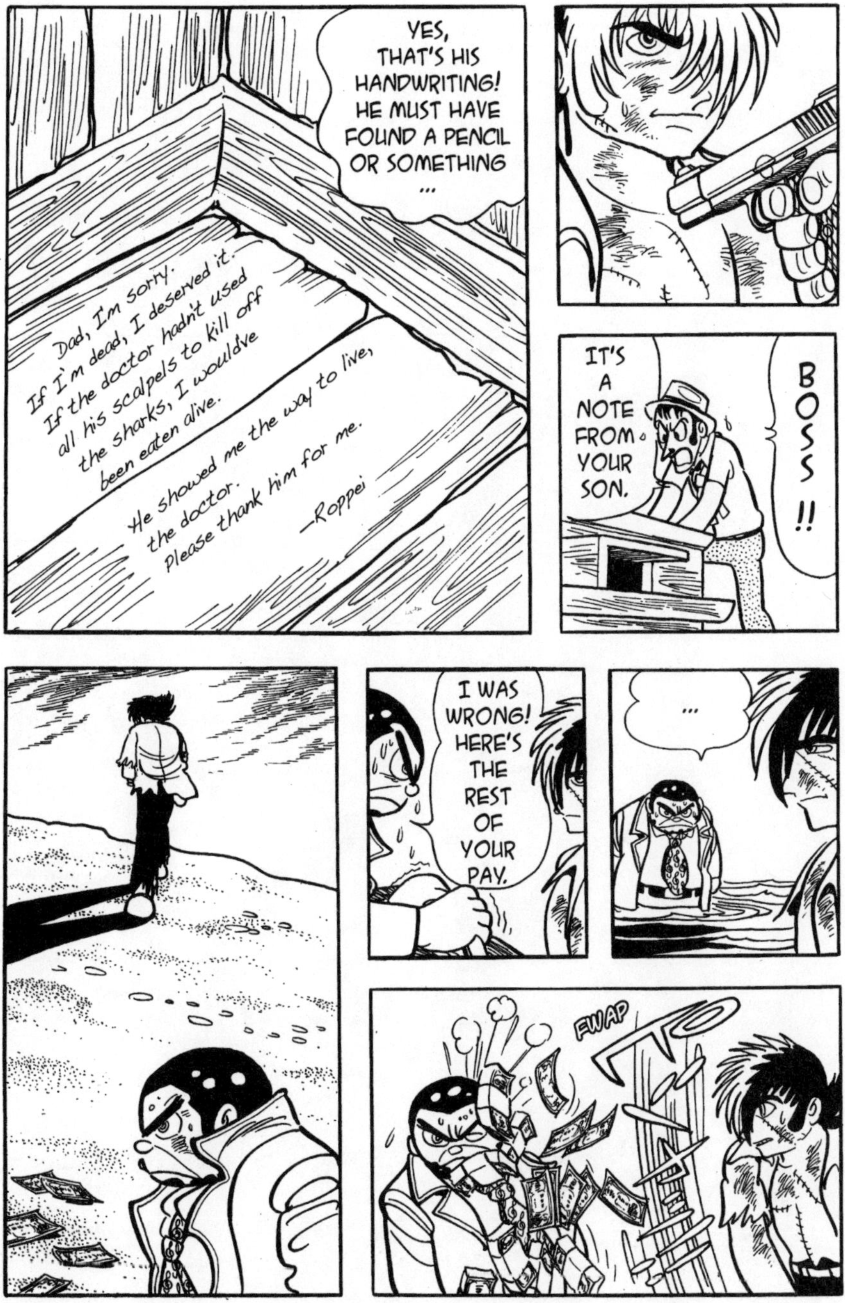
BOSS!!
IT'S A NOTE FROM YOUR SON.
YES, THAT'S HIS HANDWRITING! HE MUST HAVE FOUND A PENCIL OR SOMETHING ...
Dad, I'm sorry. If I'm dead, I deserved it. If the doctor hadn't used all his scalpels to kill off the sharks, I would've been eaten alive.
He showed me the way to live, the doctor. Please thank him for me.
—Roppei
...
I WAS WRONG! HERE'S THE REST OF YOUR PAY.
FWAP

THE PROMISE

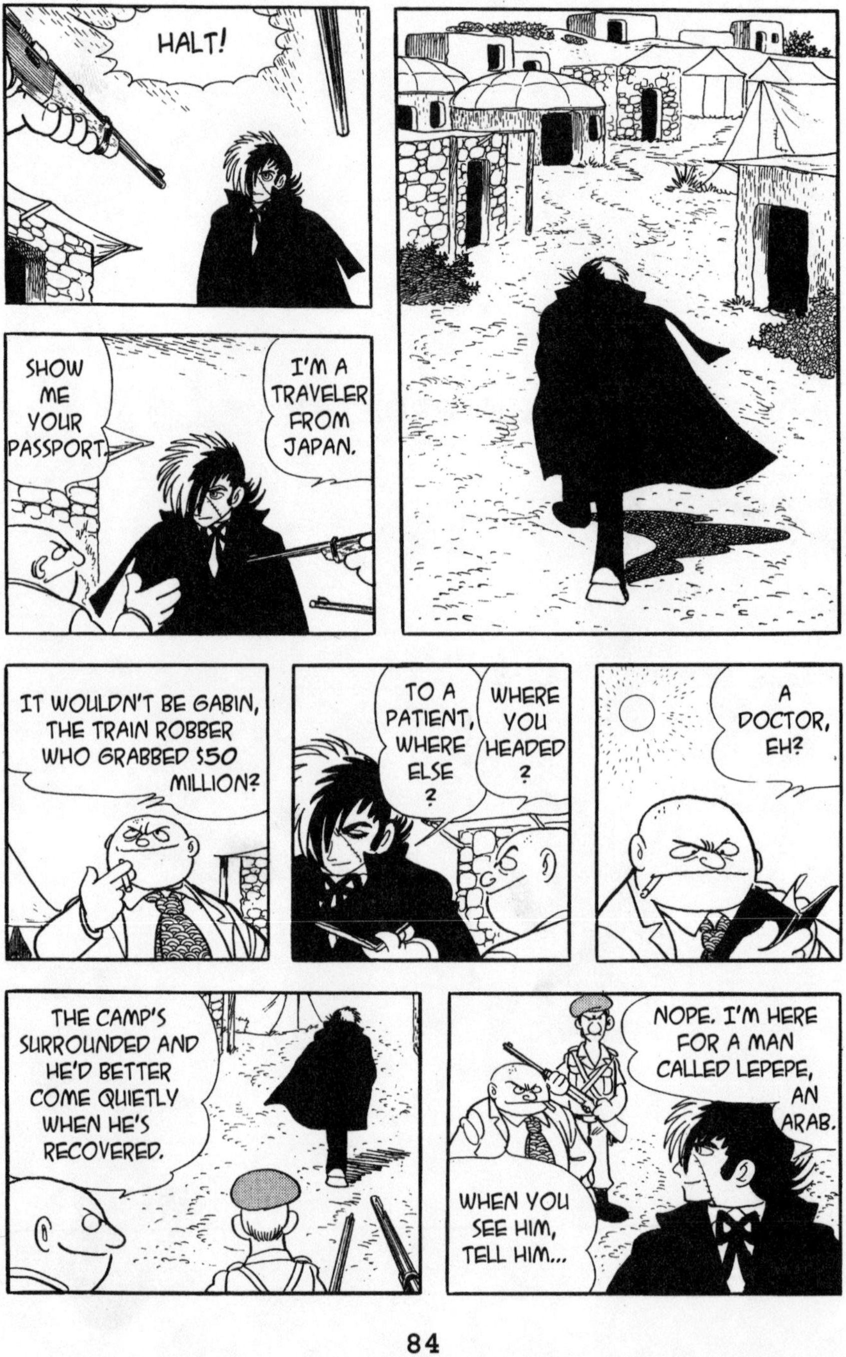
HALT!
I'M A TRAVELER FROM JAPAN.
SHOW ME YOUR PASSPORT.
A DOCTOR, EH?
WHERE YOU HEADED?
TO A PATIENT, WHERE ELSE?
IT WOULDN'T BE GABIN, THE TRAIN ROBBER WHO GRABBED $50 MILLION?
NOPE. I'M HERE FOR A MAN CALLED LEPEPE, AN ARAB.
WHEN YOU SEE HIM, TELL HIM...
THE CAMP'S SURROUNDED AND HE'D BETTER COME QUIETLY WHEN HE'S RECOVERED.

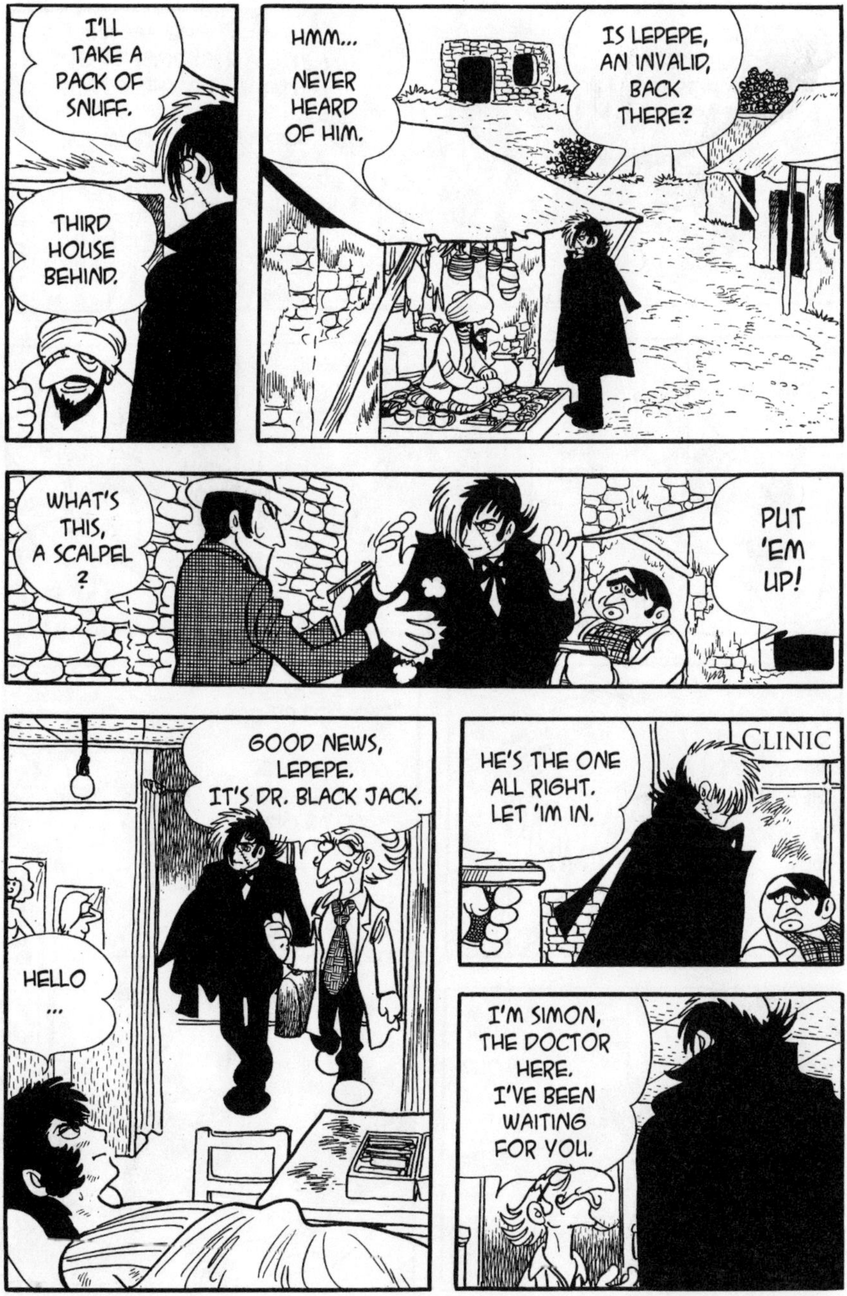
IS LEPEPE, AN INVALID, BACK THERE?
HMM... NEVER HEARD OF HIM.
I'LL TAKE A PACK OF SNUFF.
THIRD HOUSE BEHIND.
PUT 'EM UP!
WHAT'S THIS, A SCALPEL?
CLINIC
HE'S THE ONE ALL RIGHT. LET 'IM IN.
I'M SIMON, THE DOCTOR HERE. I'VE BEEN WAITING FOR YOU.
GOOD NEWS, LEPEPE. IT'S DR. BLACK JACK.
HELLO ...

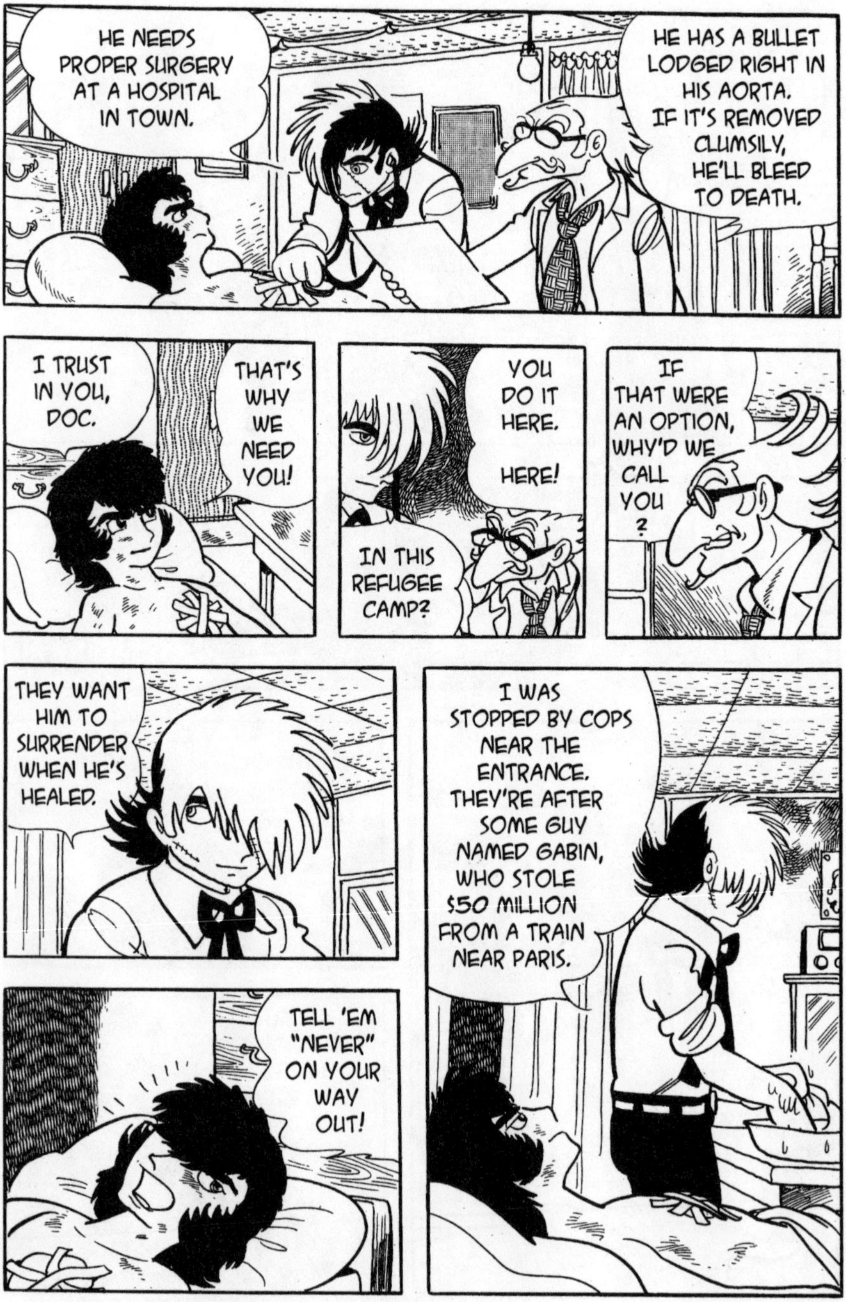
HE HAS A BULLET LODGED RIGHT IN HIS AORTA. IF IT'S REMOVED CLUMSILY, HE'LL BLEED TO DEATH.
HE NEEDS PROPER SURGERY AT A HOSPITAL IN TOWN.
IF THAT WERE AN OPTION, WHY'D WE CALL YOU?
YOU DO IT HERE. HERE!
IN THIS REFUGEE CAMP?
THAT'S WHY WE NEED YOU!
I TRUST IN YOU, DOC.
I WAS STOPPED BY COPS NEAR THE ENTRANCE. THEY'RE AFTER SOME GUY NAMED GABIN, WHO STOLE $50 MILLION FROM A TRAIN NEAR PARIS.
THEY WANT HIM TO SURRENDER WHEN HE'S HEALED.
TELL 'EM "NEVER" ON YOUR WAY OUT!

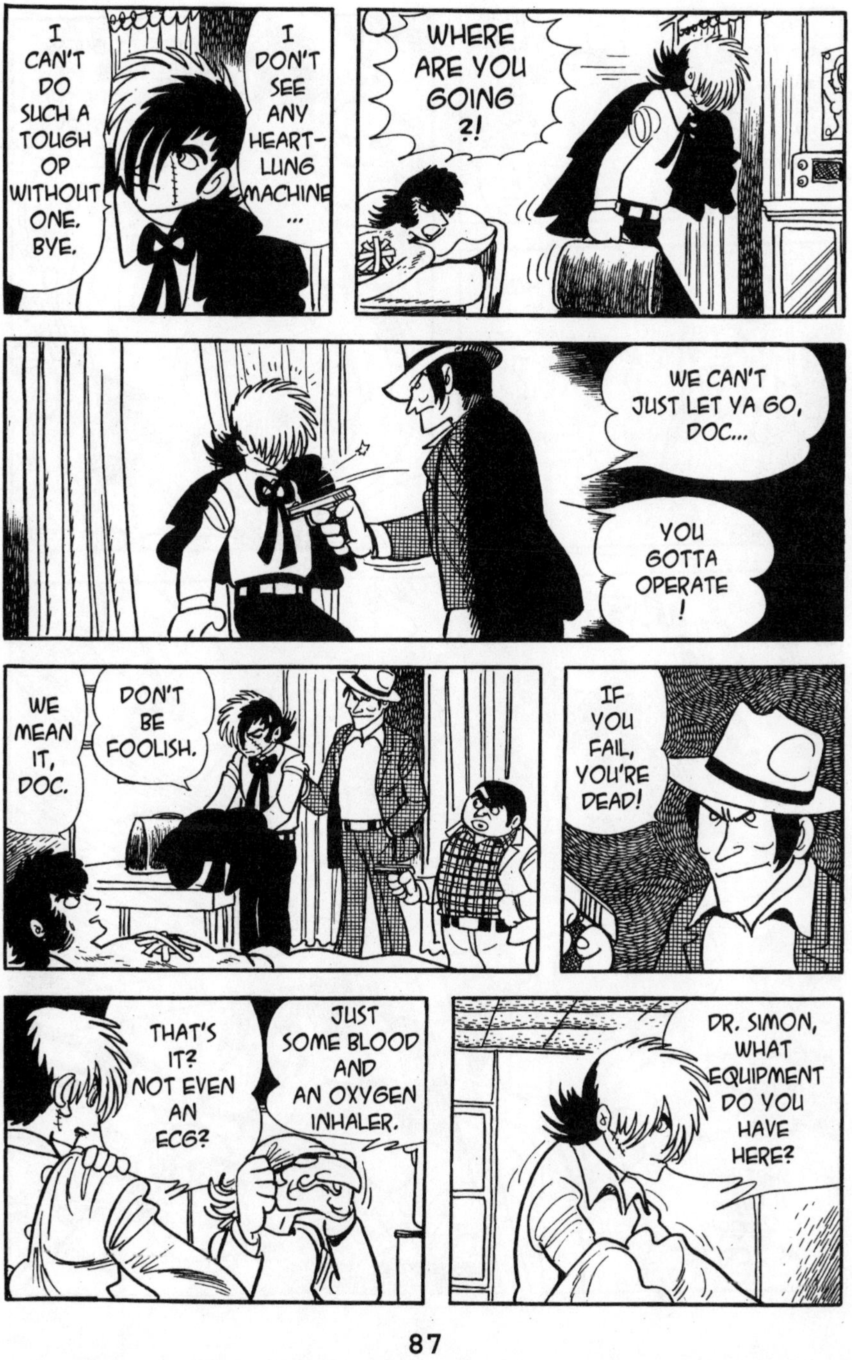
WHERE ARE YOU GOING ?!
I DON'T SEE ANY HEART-LUNG MACHINE ...
I CAN'T DO SUCH A TOUGH OP WITHOUT ONE. BYE.
WE CAN'T JUST LET YA GO, DOC...
YOU GOTTA OPERATE !
IF YOU FAIL, YOU'RE DEAD!
DON'T BE FOOLISH.
WE MEAN IT, DOC.
DR. SIMON, WHAT EQUIPMENT DO YOU HAVE HERE?
JUST SOME BLOOD AND AN OXYGEN INHALER.
THAT'S IT? NOT EVEN AN ECG?

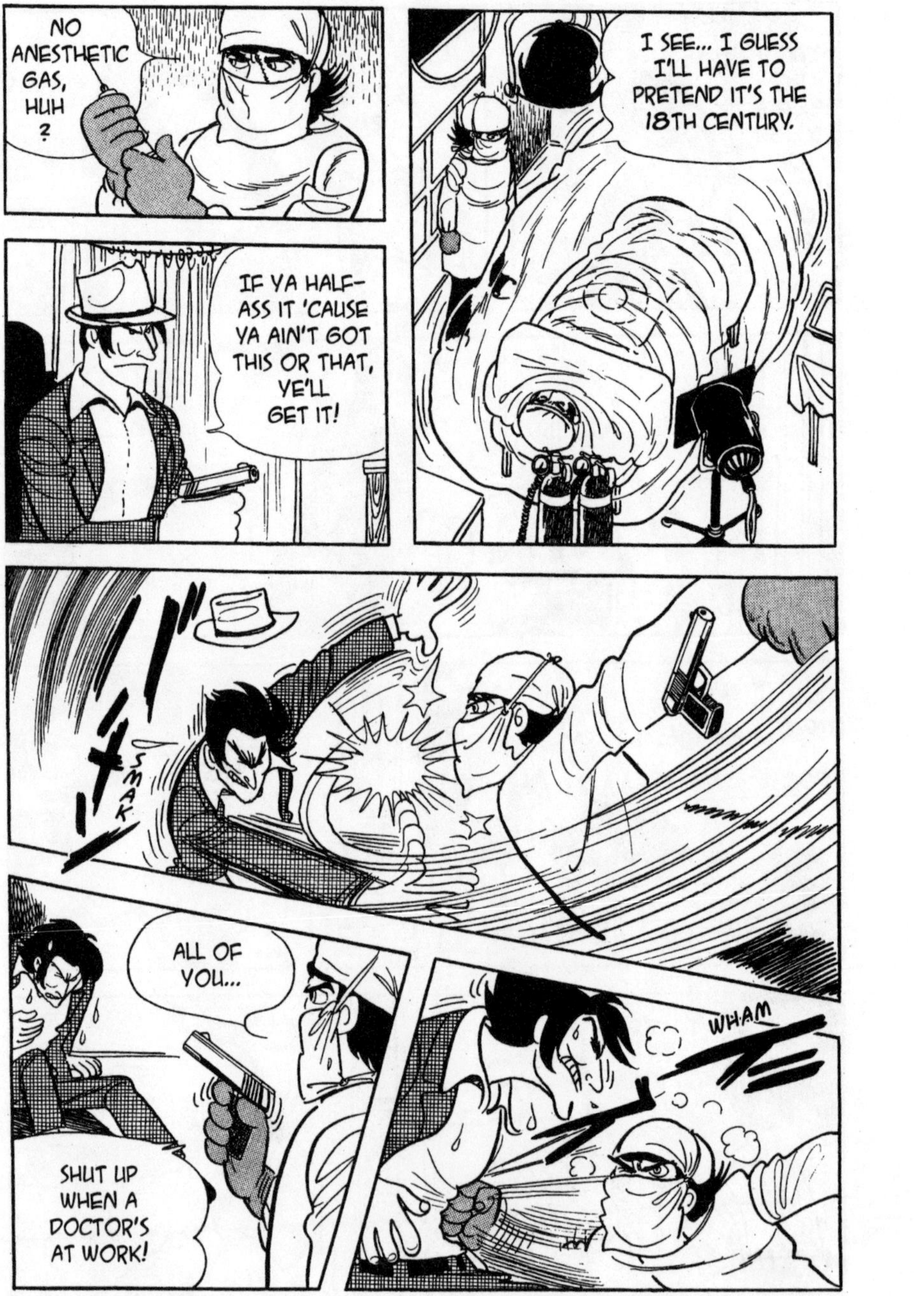
I SEE... I GUESS I'LL HAVE TO PRETEND IT'S THE 18TH CENTURY.
NO ANESTHETIC GAS, HUH ?
IF YA HALF-ASS IT 'CAUSE YA AIN'T GOT THIS OR THAT, YE'LL GET IT!
SMAK
WHAM
ALL OF YOU...
SHUT UP WHEN A DOCTOR'S AT WORK!

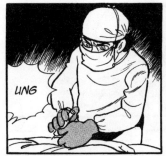

UNG

TRUST THE DOC. JUST GET OUT OF THIS ROOM...

NO!

HERE YOU ARE.

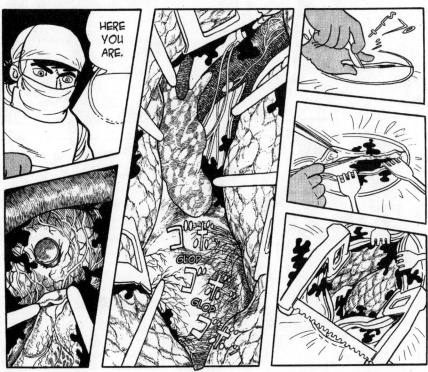

GLOP

GLOP

W... WAIT !!
DON'T TOUCH IT!
SHUSH. HOW DO I TAKE IT OUT WITHOUT TOUCHING IT?
ONE FALSE MOVE AND HE'LL DIE OF MASSIVE BLOOD LOSS.
DON'T WORRY. I AM A SURGEON AFTER ALL.
TRUE, IT'S STUCK SMACK DAB IN THE AORTA ...
THIS WON'T BE EASY.
DAMMIT, IF I HAD A HEART-LUNG MACHINE, I'D DIVERT THE BLOOD AND PLUCK IT RIGHT OUT...
WHAT'LL YOU DO?
THERE'S ONLY ONE WAY. WE'LL HAVE TO DO THIS IN TWO STAGES.
FIRST, I'LL ADD ANOTHER WALL TO THE AORTA.

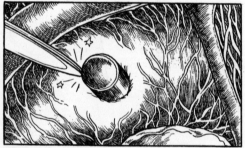

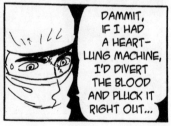

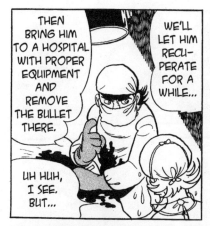

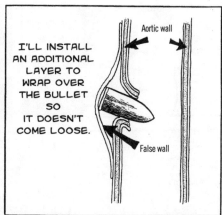

I'LL INSTALL AN ADDITIONAL LAYER TO WRAP OVER THE BULLET SO IT DOESN'T COME LOOSE.
Aortic wall
False wall
WE'LL LET HIM RECU-PERATE FOR A WHILE...
THEN BRING HIM TO A HOSPITAL WITH PROPER EQUIPMENT AND REMOVE THE BULLET THERE.
UH HUH, I SEE. BUT...
THERE'S REALLY NO OTHER WAY.
I'LL TAKE A VESSEL SECTION FROM HIS THIGH.

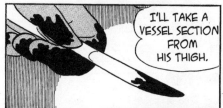

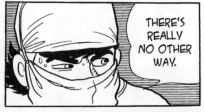

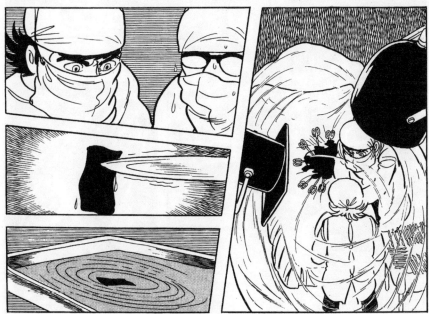

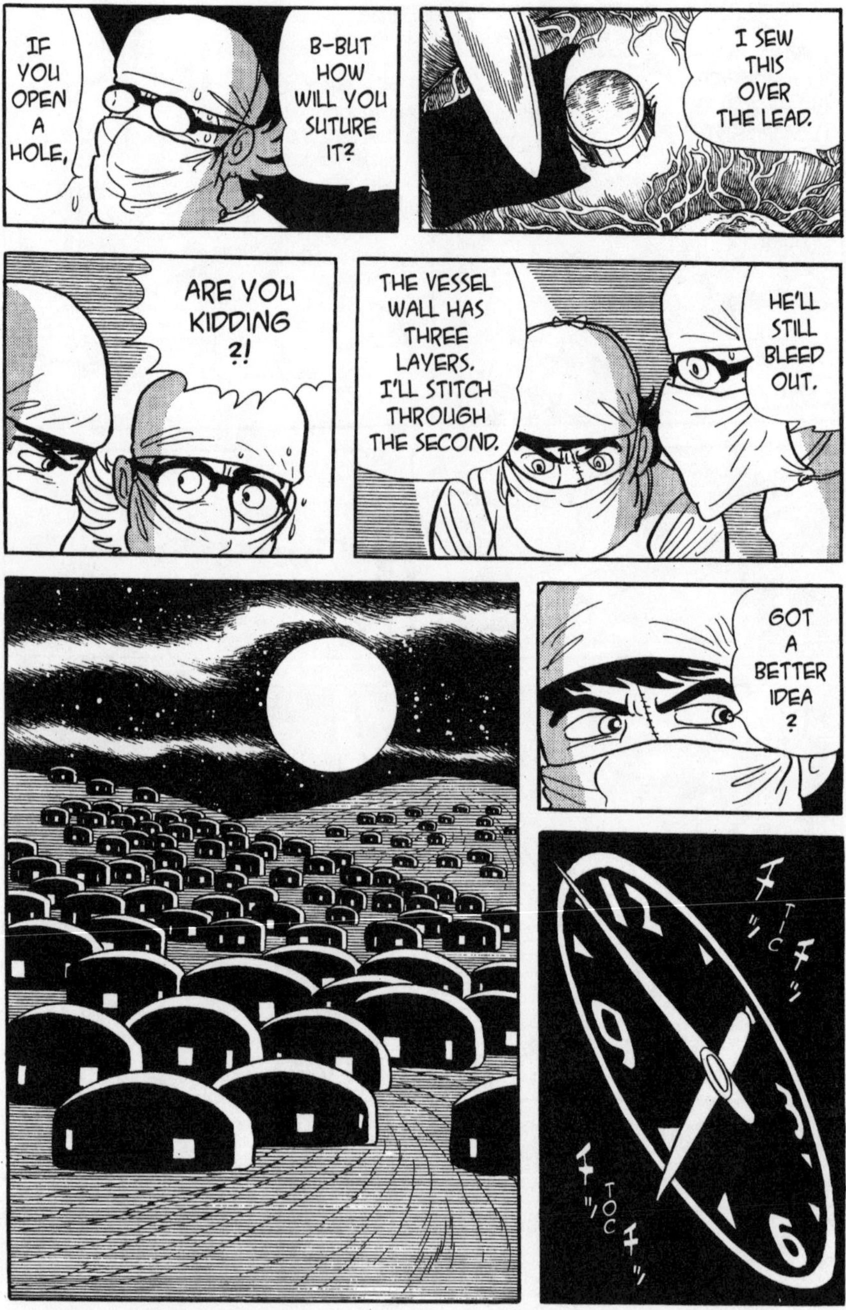
IF YOU OPEN A HOLE,
B-BUT HOW WILL YOU SUTURE IT?
I SEW THIS OVER THE LEAD.
ARE YOU KIDDING?!
THE VESSEL WALL HAS THREE LAYERS. I'LL STITCH THROUGH THE SECOND.
HE'LL STILL BLEED OUT.
GOT A BETTER IDEA?
チッ TIC チッ
チッ TOC チッ

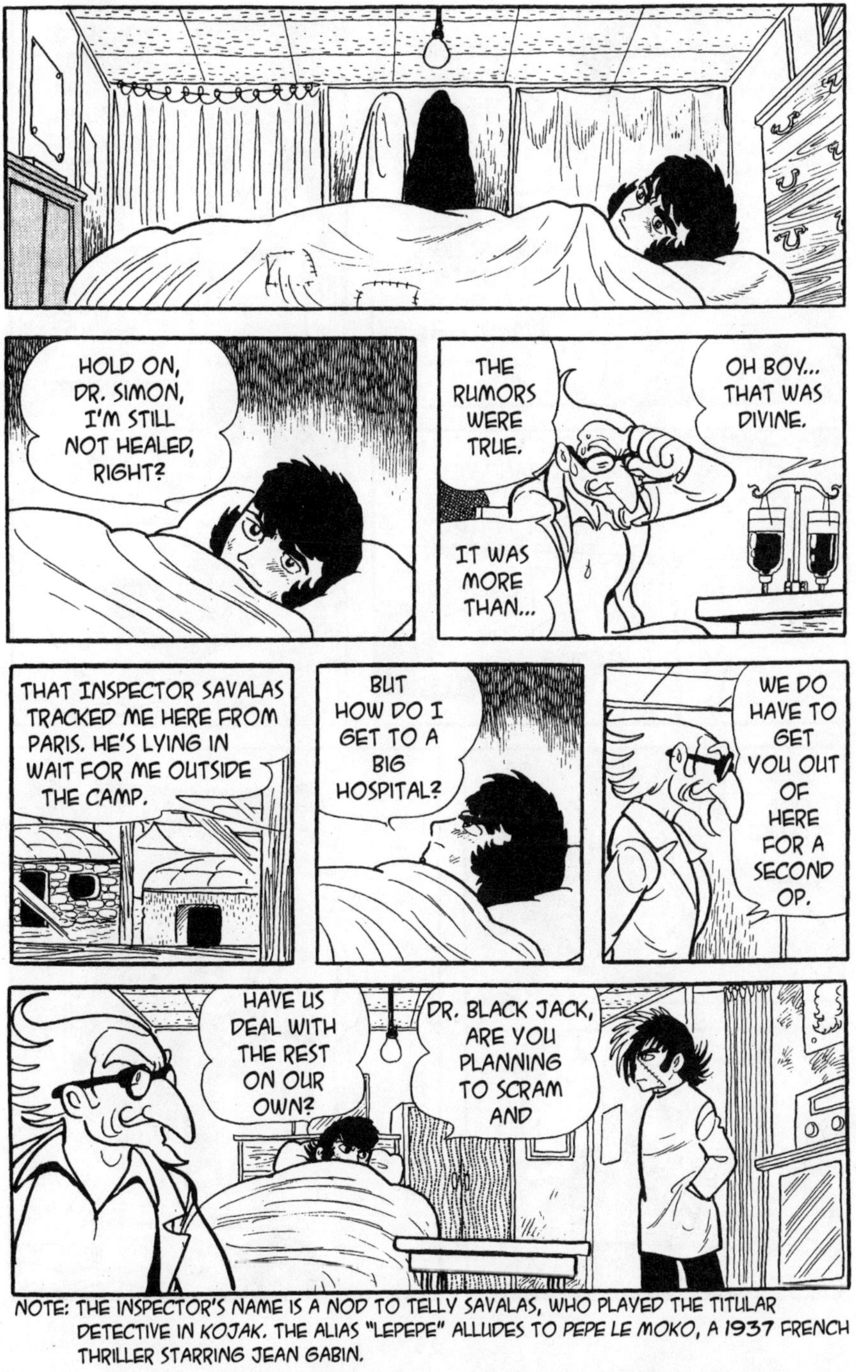
OH BOY... THAT WAS DIVINE.
THE RUMORS WERE TRUE.
IT WAS MORE THAN...
HOLD ON, DR. SIMON, I'M STILL NOT HEALED, RIGHT?
WE DO HAVE TO GET YOU OUT OF HERE FOR A SECOND OP.
BUT HOW DO I GET TO A BIG HOSPITAL?
THAT INSPECTOR SAVALAS TRACKED ME HERE FROM PARIS. HE'S LYING IN WAIT FOR ME OUTSIDE THE CAMP.
DR. BLACK JACK, ARE YOU PLANNING TO SCRAM AND
HAVE US DEAL WITH THE REST ON OUR OWN?

NOTE: THE INSPECTOR'S NAME IS A NOD TO TELLY SAVALAS, WHO PLAYED THE TITULAR DETECTIVE IN *KOJAK*. THE ALIAS "LEPEPE" ALLUDES TO *PEPE LE MOKO*, A 1937 FRENCH THRILLER STARRING JEAN GABIN.

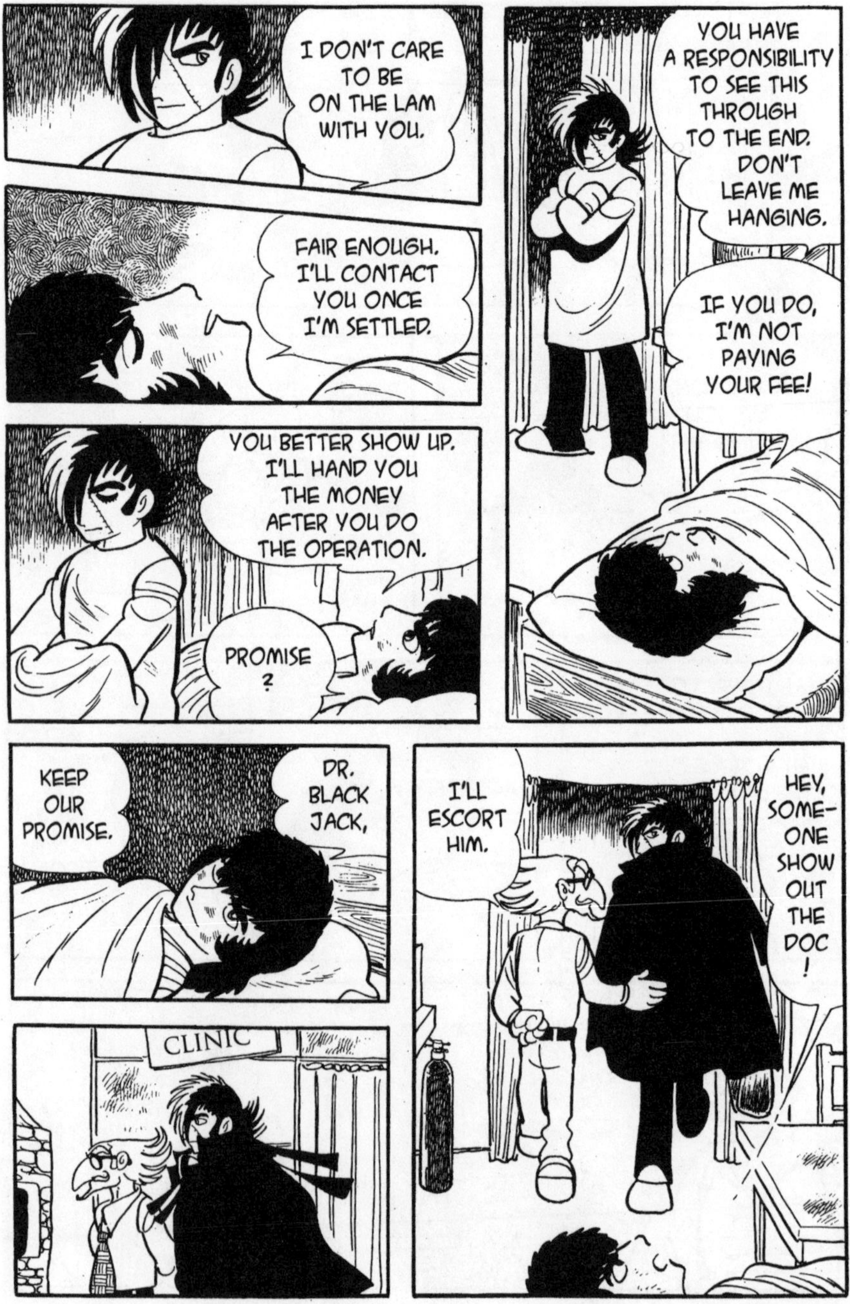
YOU HAVE A RESPONSIBILITY TO SEE THIS THROUGH TO THE END. DON'T LEAVE ME HANGING.
IF YOU DO, I'M NOT PAYING YOUR FEE!
I DON'T CARE TO BE ON THE LAM WITH YOU.
FAIR ENOUGH. I'LL CONTACT YOU ONCE I'M SETTLED.
YOU BETTER SHOW UP. I'LL HAND YOU THE MONEY AFTER YOU DO THE OPERATION.
PROMISE?
HEY, SOMEONE SHOW OUT THE DOC!
I'LL ESCORT HIM.
DR. BLACK JACK,
KEEP OUR PROMISE.
CLINIC

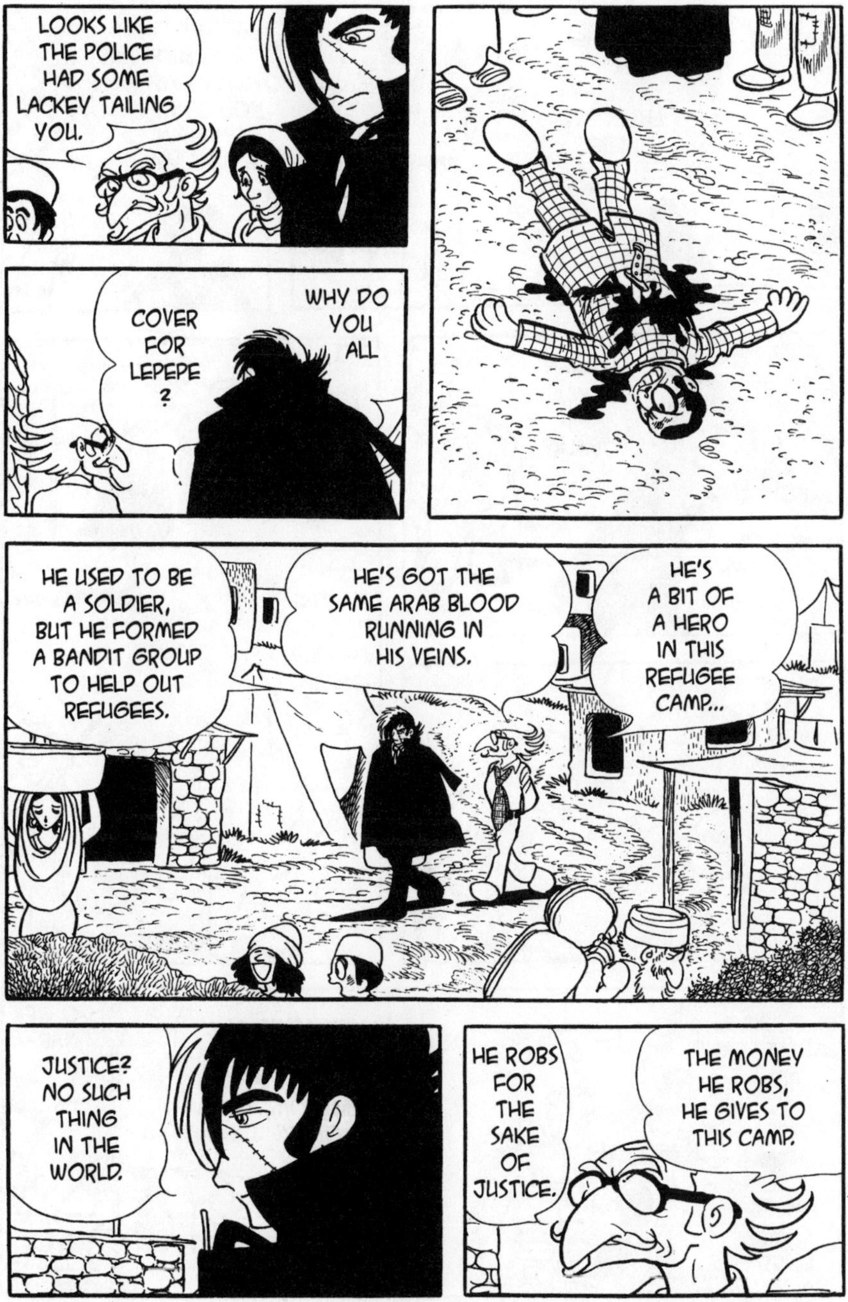
LOOKS LIKE THE POLICE HAD SOME LACKEY TAILING YOU.
WHY DO YOU ALL COVER FOR LEPEPE?
HE'S A BIT OF A HERO IN THIS REFUGEE CAMP...
HE'S GOT THE SAME ARAB BLOOD RUNNING IN HIS VEINS.
HE USED TO BE A SOLDIER, BUT HE FORMED A BANDIT GROUP TO HELP OUT REFUGEES.
THE MONEY HE ROBS, HE GIVES TO THIS CAMP.
HE ROBS FOR THE SAKE OF JUSTICE.
JUSTICE? NO SUCH THING IN THE WORLD.

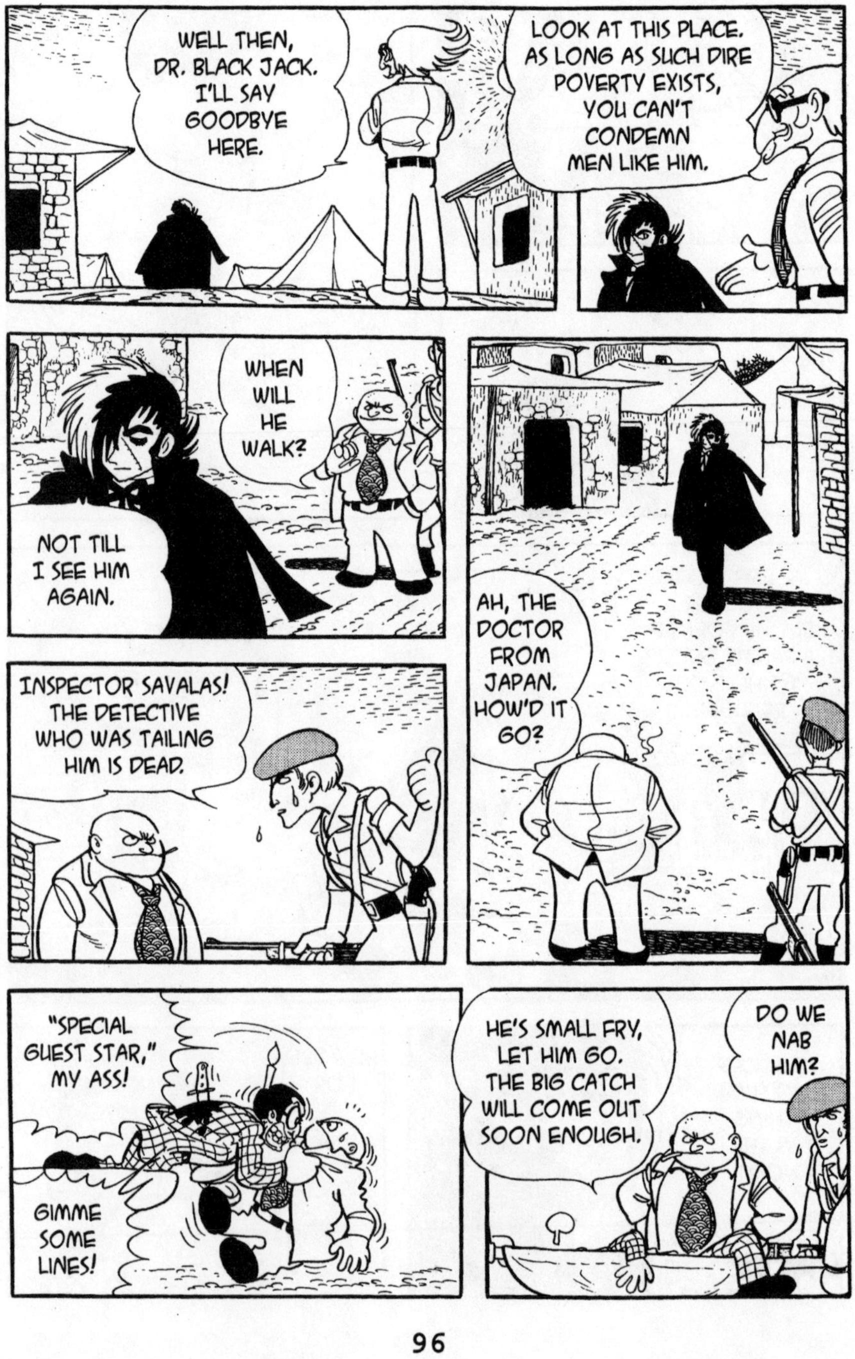
LOOK AT THIS PLACE. AS LONG AS SUCH DIRE POVERTY EXISTS, YOU CAN'T CONDEMN MEN LIKE HIM.
WELL THEN, DR. BLACK JACK. I'LL SAY GOODBYE HERE.
AH, THE DOCTOR FROM JAPAN. HOW'D IT GO?
WHEN WILL HE WALK?
NOT TILL I SEE HIM AGAIN.
INSPECTOR SAVALAS! THE DETECTIVE WHO WAS TAILING HIM IS DEAD.
DO WE NAB HIM?
HE'S SMALL FRY, LET HIM GO. THE BIG CATCH WILL COME OUT SOON ENOUGH.
"SPECIAL GUEST STAR," MY ASS!
GIMME SOME LINES!

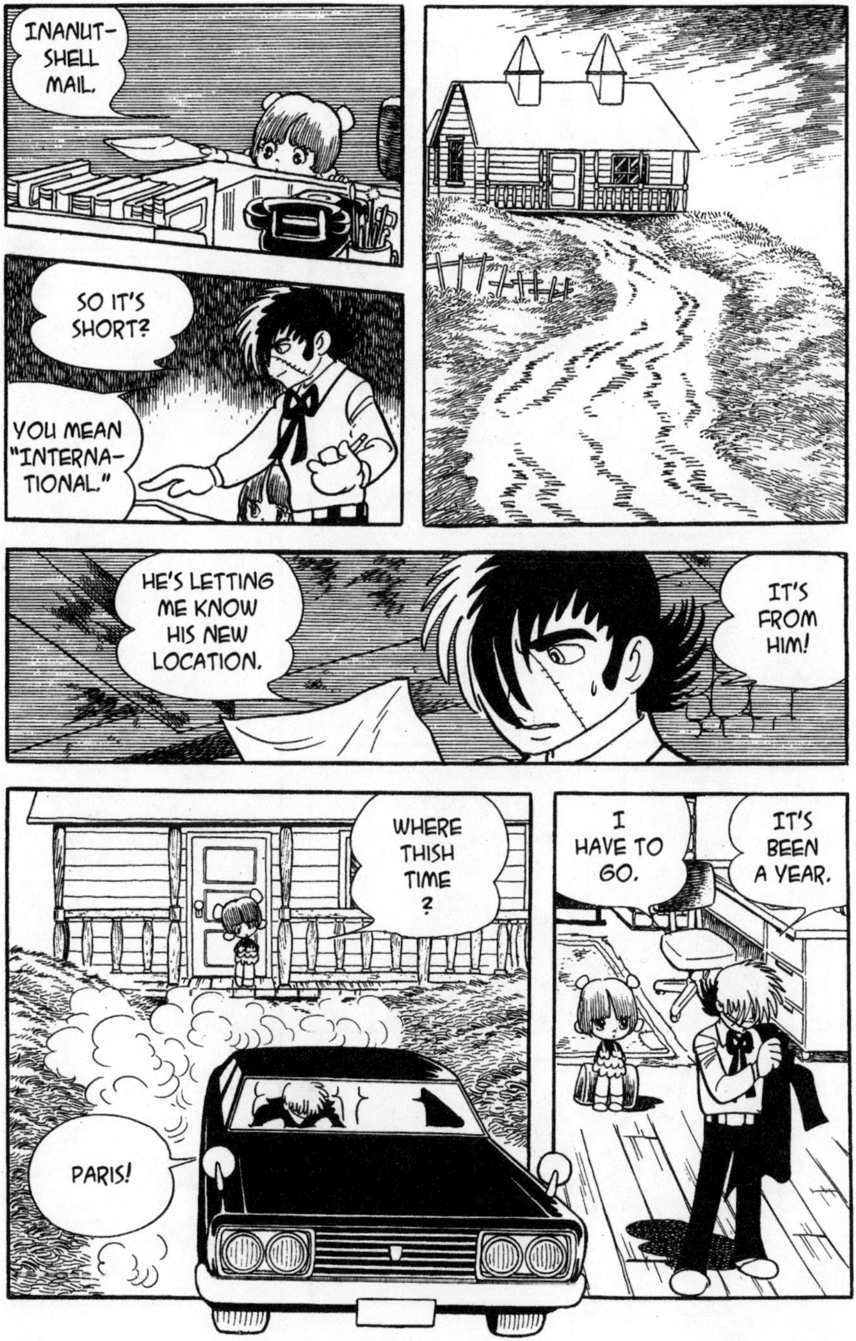
INANUT-SHELL MAIL.
SO IT'S SHORT?
YOU MEAN "INTERNA-TIONAL."
IT'S FROM HIM!
HE'S LETTING ME KNOW HIS NEW LOCATION.
IT'S BEEN A YEAR.
I HAVE TO GO.
WHERE THISH TIME ?
PARIS!

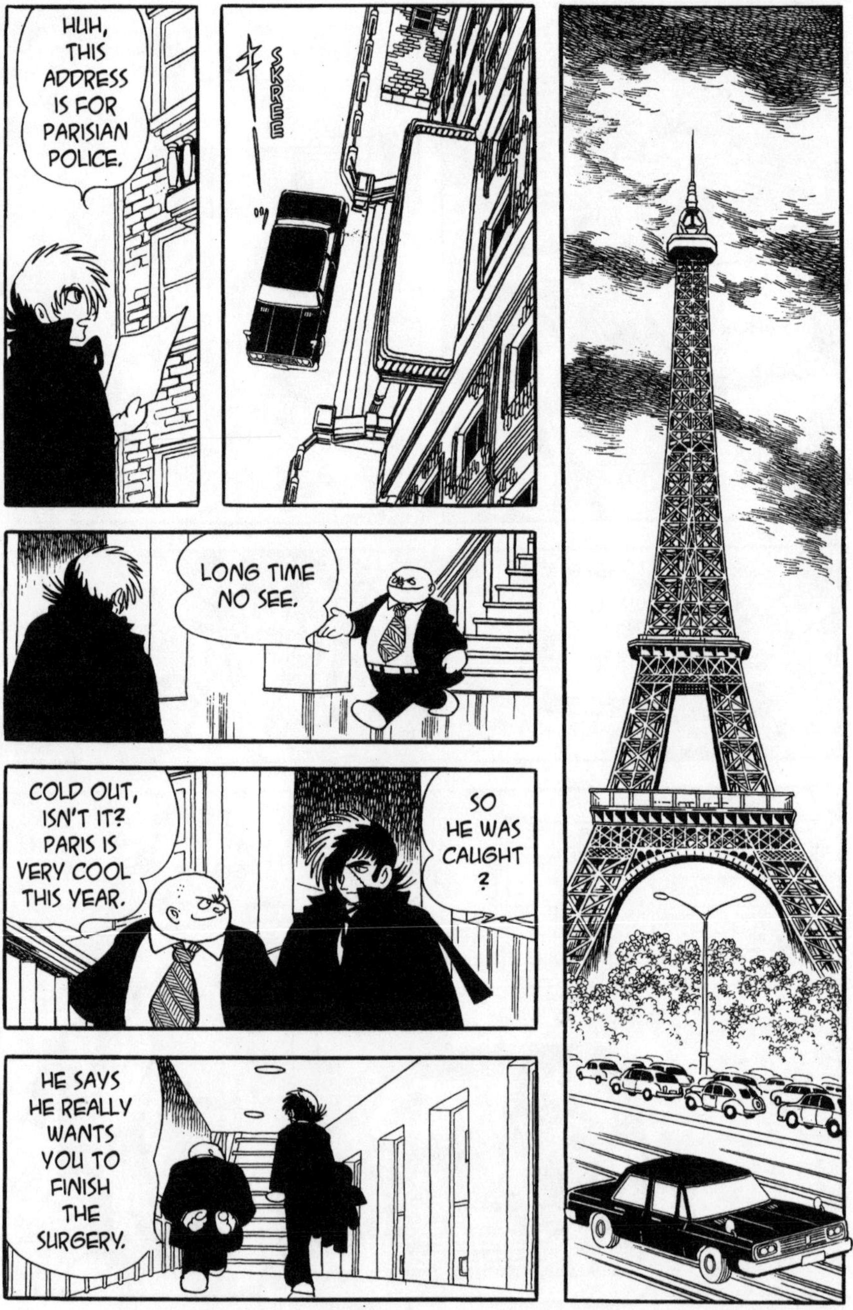
SKREE
HUH, THIS ADDRESS IS FOR PARISIAN POLICE.
LONG TIME NO SEE.
SO HE WAS CAUGHT?
COLD OUT, ISN'T IT? PARIS IS VERY COOL THIS YEAR.
HE SAYS HE REALLY WANTS YOU TO FINISH THE SURGERY.

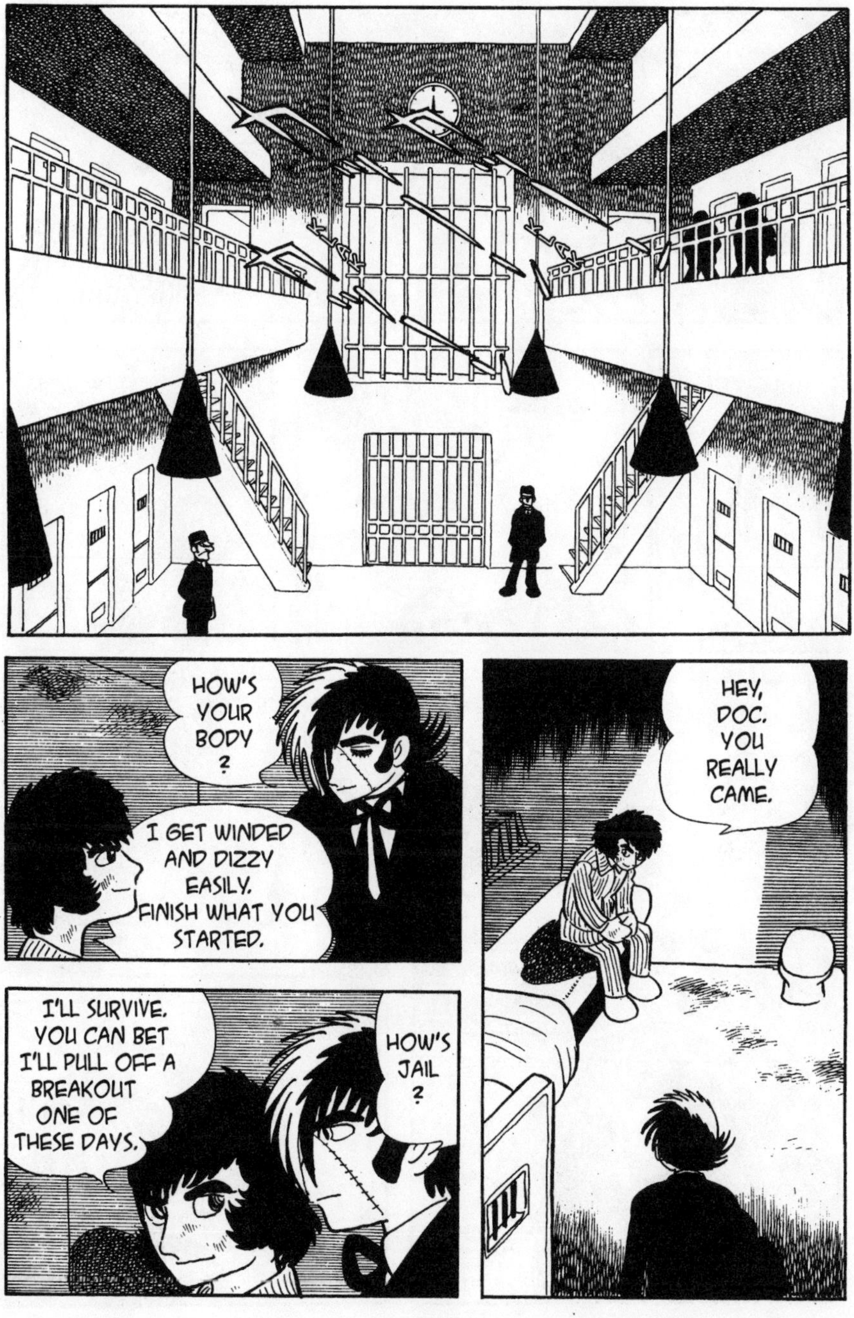
HEY, DOC. YOU REALLY CAME.
HOW'S YOUR BODY?
I GET WINDED AND DIZZY EASILY. FINISH WHAT YOU STARTED.
HOW'S JAIL?
I'LL SURVIVE. YOU CAN BET I'LL PULL OFF A BREAKOUT ONE OF THESE DAYS.

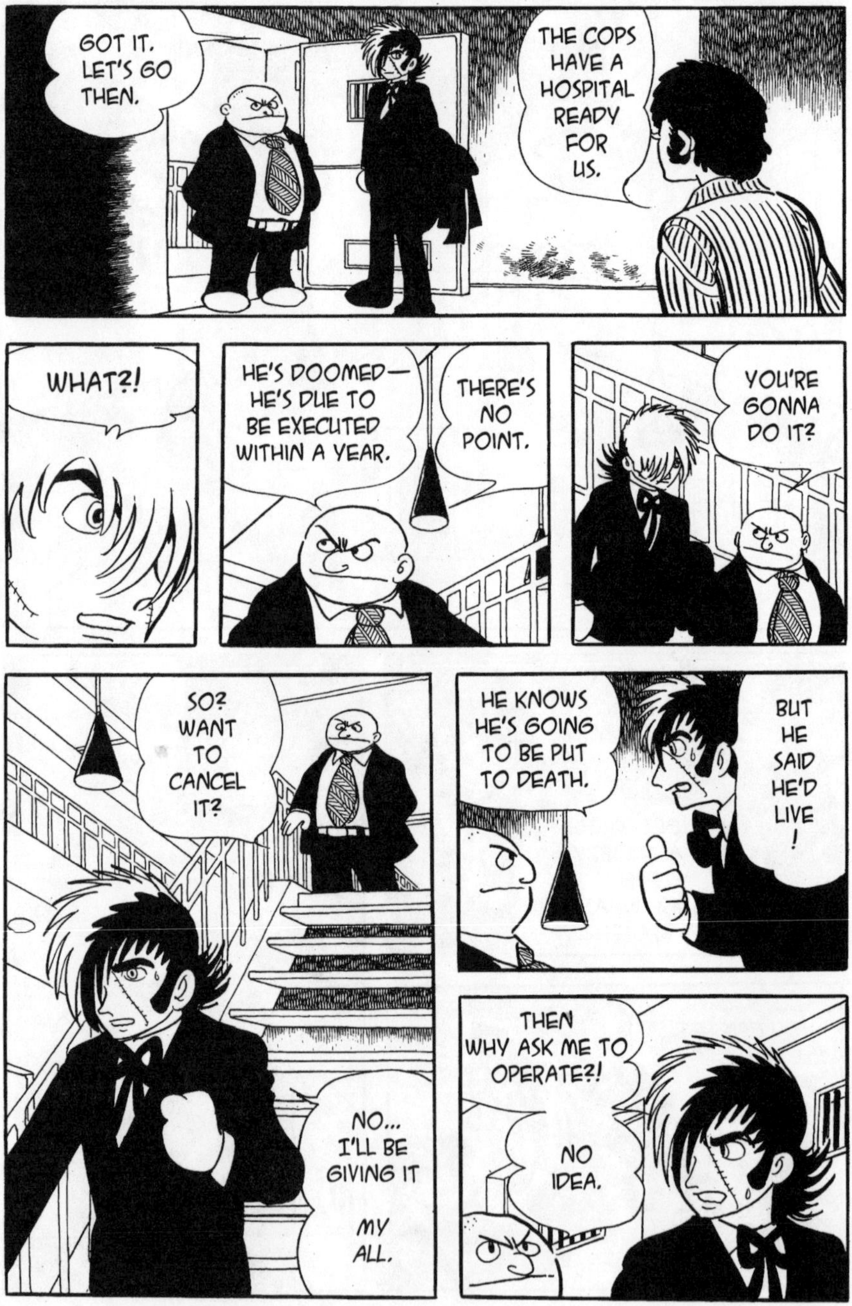
THE COPS HAVE A HOSPITAL READY FOR US.
GOT IT. LET'S GO THEN.
YOU'RE GONNA DO IT?
THERE'S NO POINT.
HE'S DOOMED— HE'S DUE TO BE EXECUTED WITHIN A YEAR.
WHAT?!
BUT HE SAID HE'D LIVE!
HE KNOWS HE'S GOING TO BE PUT TO DEATH.
THEN WHY ASK ME TO OPERATE?!
NO IDEA.
SO? WANT TO CANCEL IT?
NO... I'LL BE GIVING IT MY ALL.

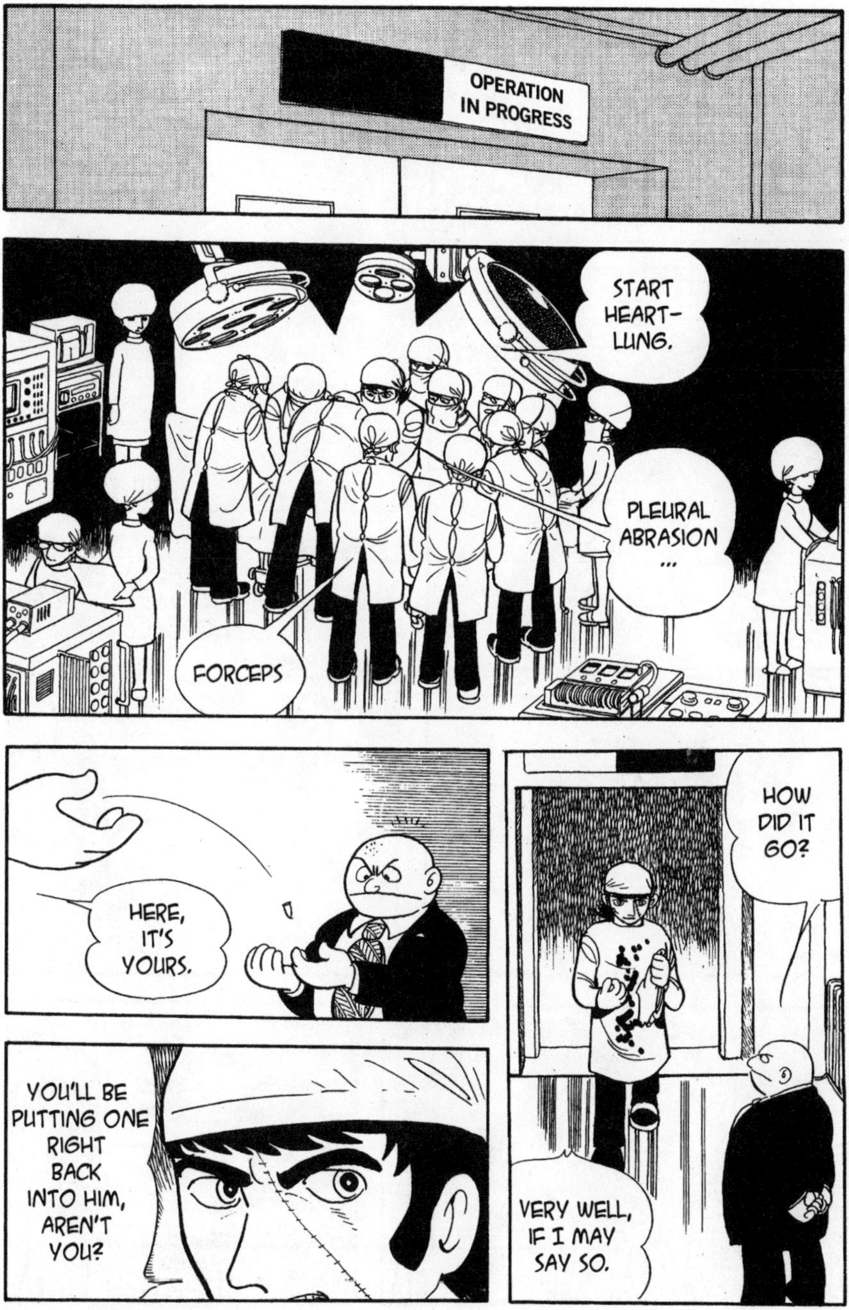
OPERATION IN PROGRESS
START HEART-LUNG.
PLEURAL ABRASION ...
FORCEPS
HOW DID IT GO?
VERY WELL, IF I MAY SAY SO.
HERE, IT'S YOURS.
YOU'LL BE PUTTING ONE RIGHT BACK INTO HIM, AREN'T YOU?

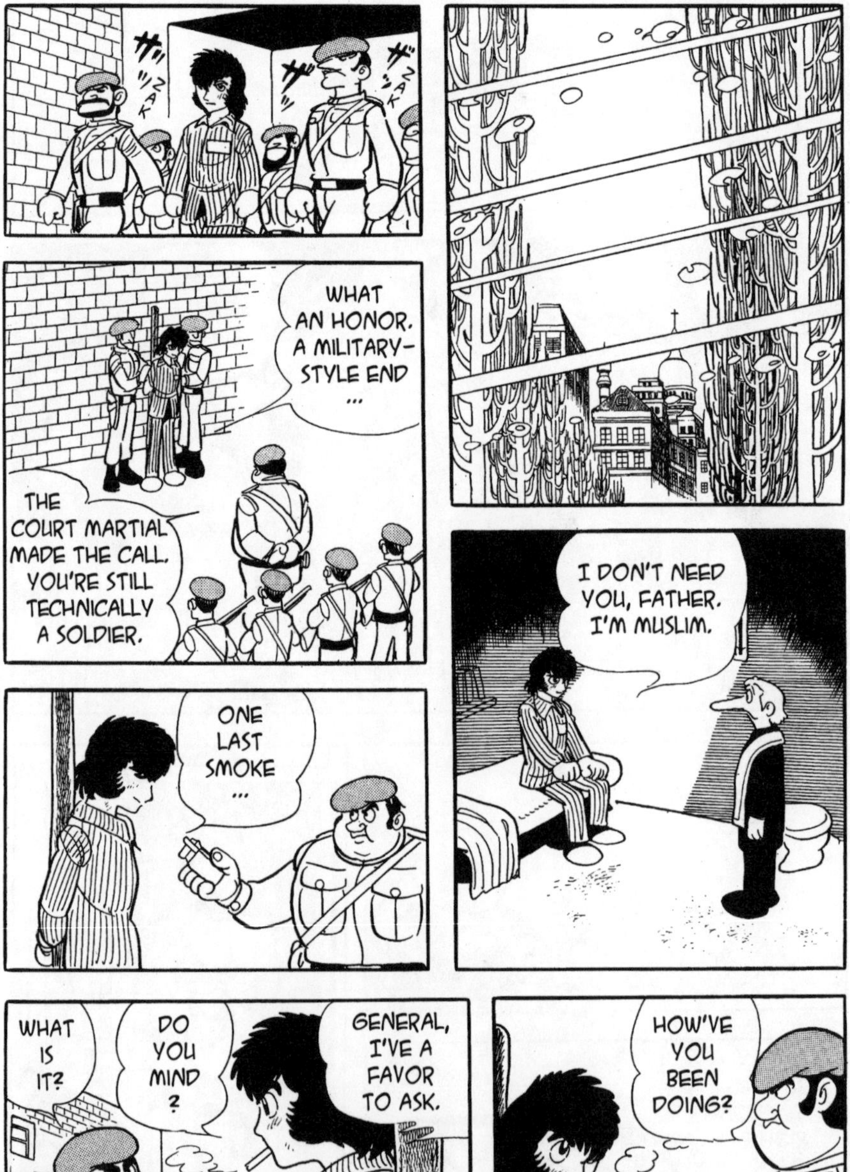
I DON'T NEED YOU, FATHER. I'M MUSLIM.
ZAK
ZAK
WHAT AN HONOR. A MILITARY-STYLE END ...
THE COURT MARTIAL MADE THE CALL. YOU'RE STILL TECHNICALLY A SOLDIER.
ONE LAST SMOKE ...
HOW'VE YOU BEEN DOING?
VERY WELL, THANKS.
GENERAL, I'VE A FAVOR TO ASK.
DO YOU MIND?
WHAT IS IT?

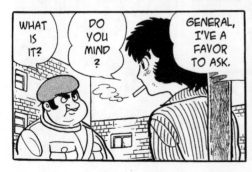

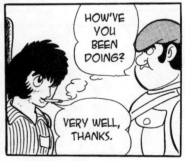

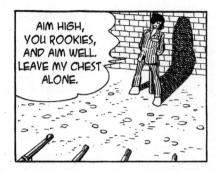

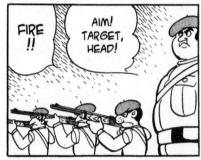

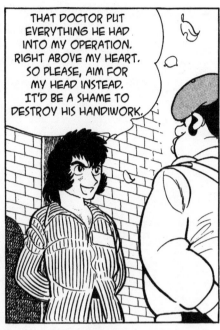

THAT DOCTOR PUT EVERYTHING HE HAD INTO MY OPERATION. RIGHT ABOVE MY HEART. SO PLEASE, AIM FOR MY HEAD INSTEAD. IT'D BE A SHAME TO DESTROY HIS HANDIWORK.
AIM HIGH, YOU ROOKIES, AND AIM WELL. LEAVE MY CHEST ALONE.
AIM! TARGET, HEAD!
FIRE !!
BANG
BANG BANG
IS DR. BLACK JACK HERE? I HAVE HIS REMUNERATION.
HE DEPARTED A GOOD WHILE AGO... HE LEFT A MESSAGE.
HE WON'T ACCEPT PAYMENT FOR A PATIENT HE COULDN'T SAVE.

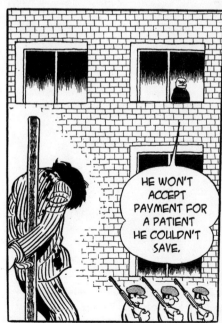

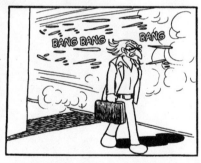

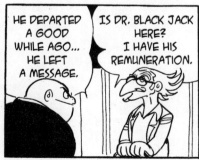

THREE-LEGGED RACE

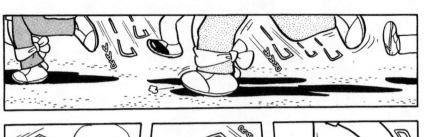

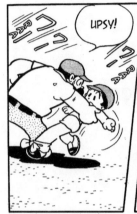

UPSY!
HEAVE-HO!
HA HA HA
HE'S FACING BACKWARDS.
I KNOW, BLOCKHEAD!
JUST GOT A LITTLE LOOSE, IS ALL.

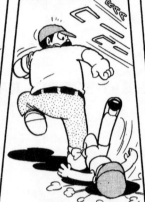

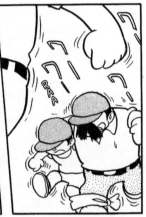

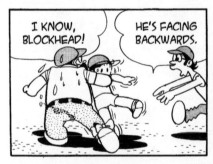

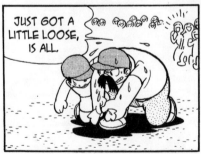

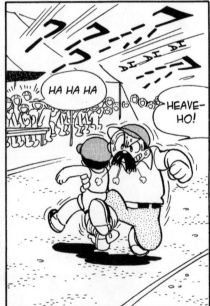

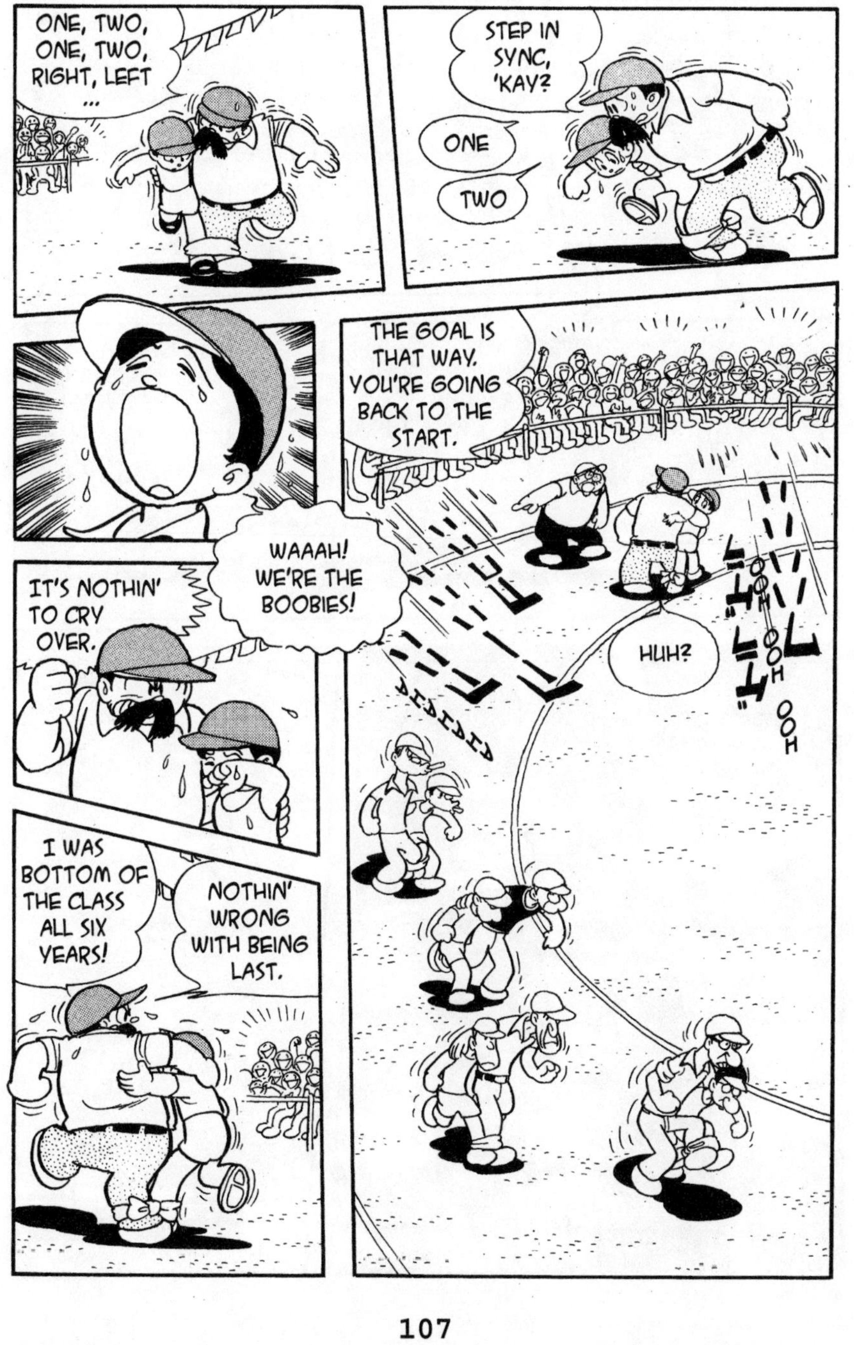
STEP IN SYNC, 'KAY?
ONE
TWO
ONE, TWO, ONE, TWO, RIGHT, LEFT ...
THE GOAL IS THAT WAY. YOU'RE GOING BACK TO THE START.
HUH?
OOH
OOH
OOH
WAAAH! WE'RE THE BOOBIES!
IT'S NOTHIN' TO CRY OVER.
NOTHIN' WRONG WITH BEING LAST.
I WAS BOTTOM OF THE CLASS ALL SIX YEARS!

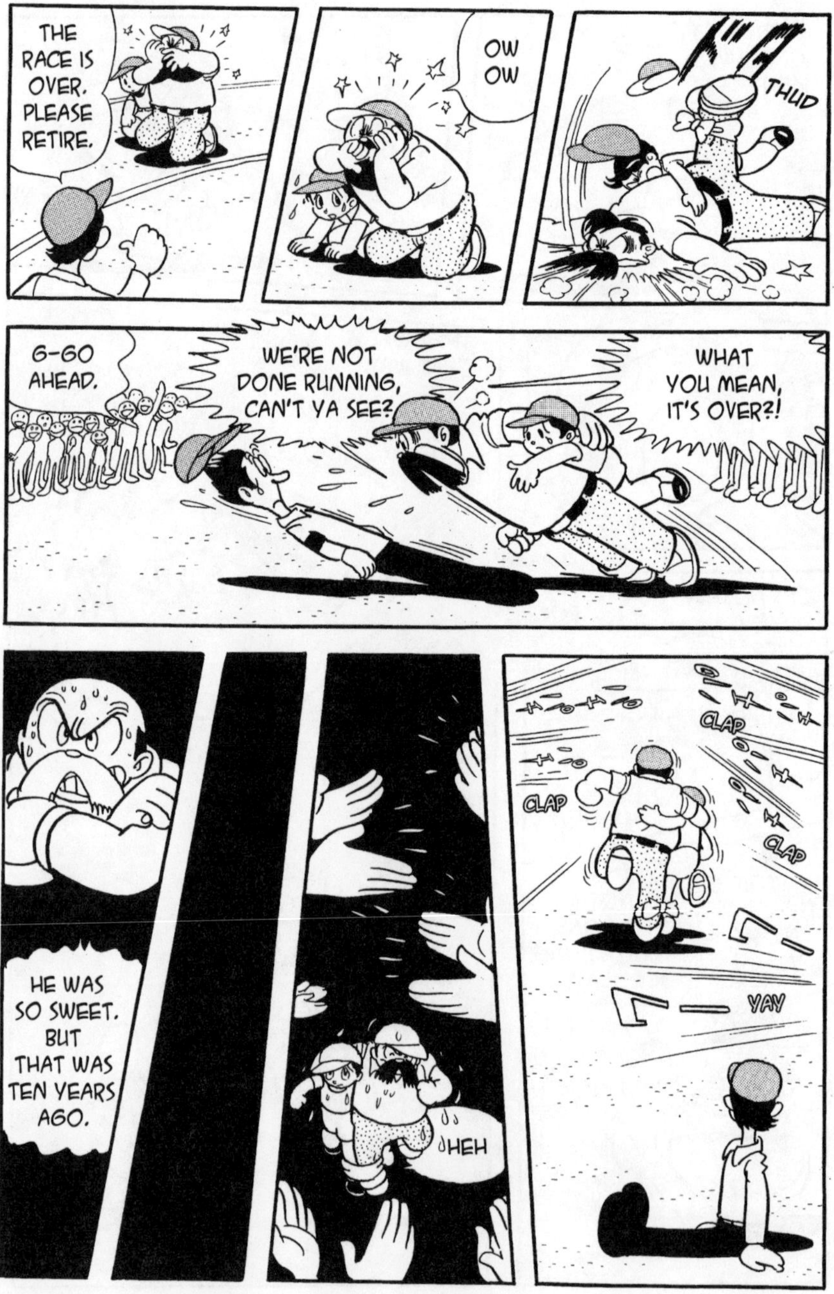
THUD
OW OW
THE RACE IS OVER. PLEASE RETIRE.
WHAT YOU MEAN, IT'S OVER?!
WE'RE NOT DONE RUNNING, CAN'T YA SEE?
G-GO AHEAD.
CLAP
CLAP
CLAP
YAY
HEH
HE WAS SO SWEET. BUT THAT WAS TEN YEARS AGO.

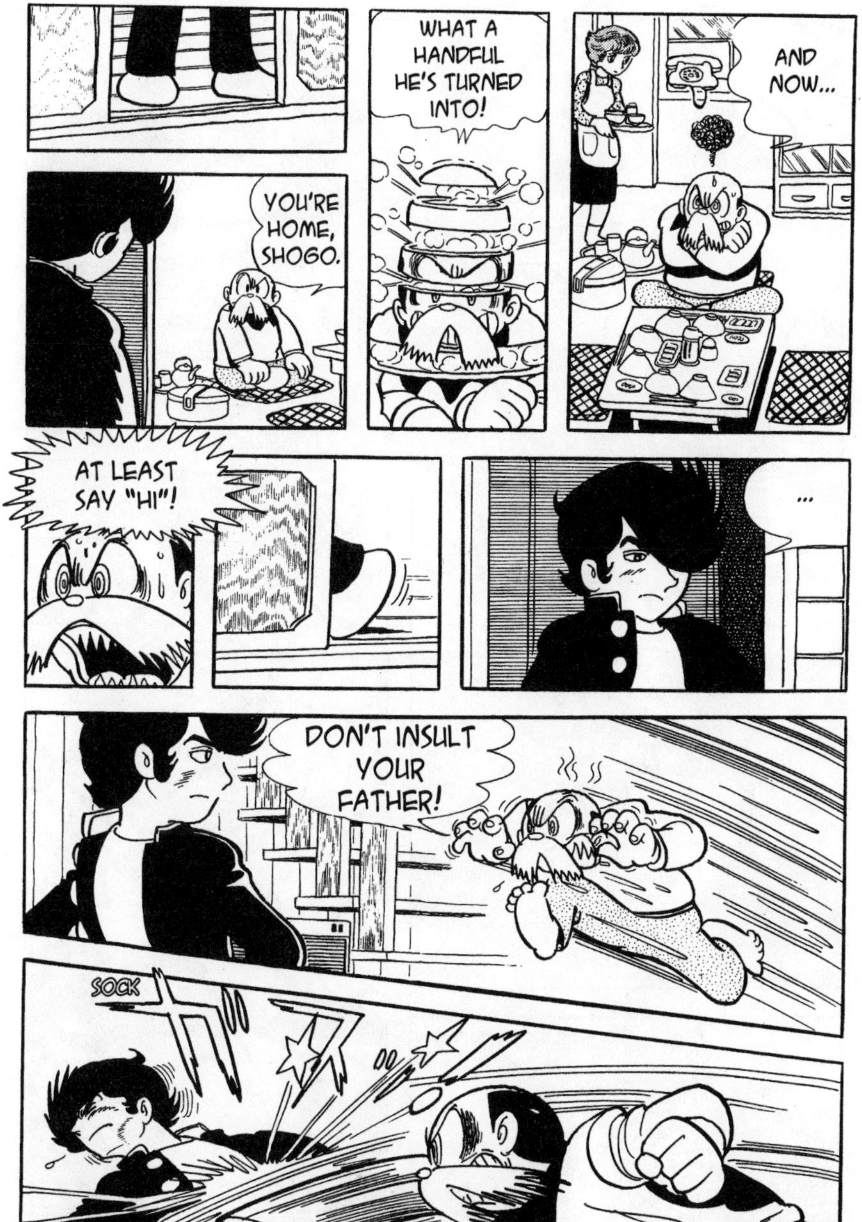
AND NOW...
WHAT A HANDFUL HE'S TURNED INTO!
YOU'RE HOME, SHOGO.
...
AT LEAST SAY "HI"!
DON'T INSULT YOUR FATHER!
SOCK

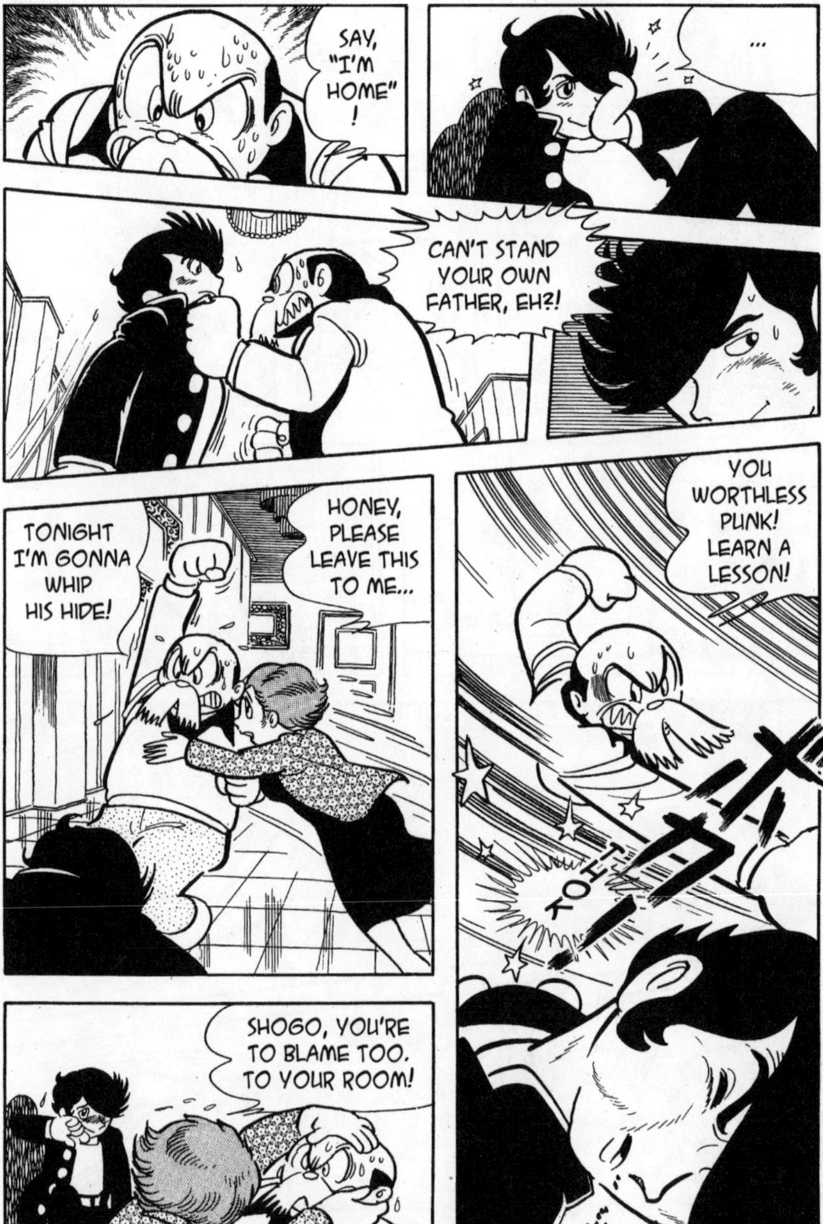
...
SAY, "I'M HOME"!
CAN'T STAND YOUR OWN FATHER, EH?!
YOU WORTHLESS PUNK! LEARN A LESSON!
THOK
HONEY, PLEASE LEAVE THIS TO ME...
TONIGHT I'M GONNA WHIP HIS HIDE!
SHOGO, YOU'RE TO BLAME TOO. TO YOUR ROOM!

I DON'T LIKE HIS FRIENDS. THEY'RE A BUNCH OF THUGS.

IT'S JUST A PHASE HE'S GOING THROUGH.

WHERE DID THAT GOOD-NATURED, GENTLE BOY GO?

WE DID THREE-LEGGED RACES ON SPORTS DAY.

WHY DOES HE HATE ME SO MUCH?

I DIDN'T RAISE HIM LIKE THAT.

enemy of the people, of the poor,

Black Jack, enemy of the people, robber and tormentor OF THE poor, HAND over THE 100 million yen you've stolen or we'll blow up YOUR house

—Japan Lunatic RED Faction

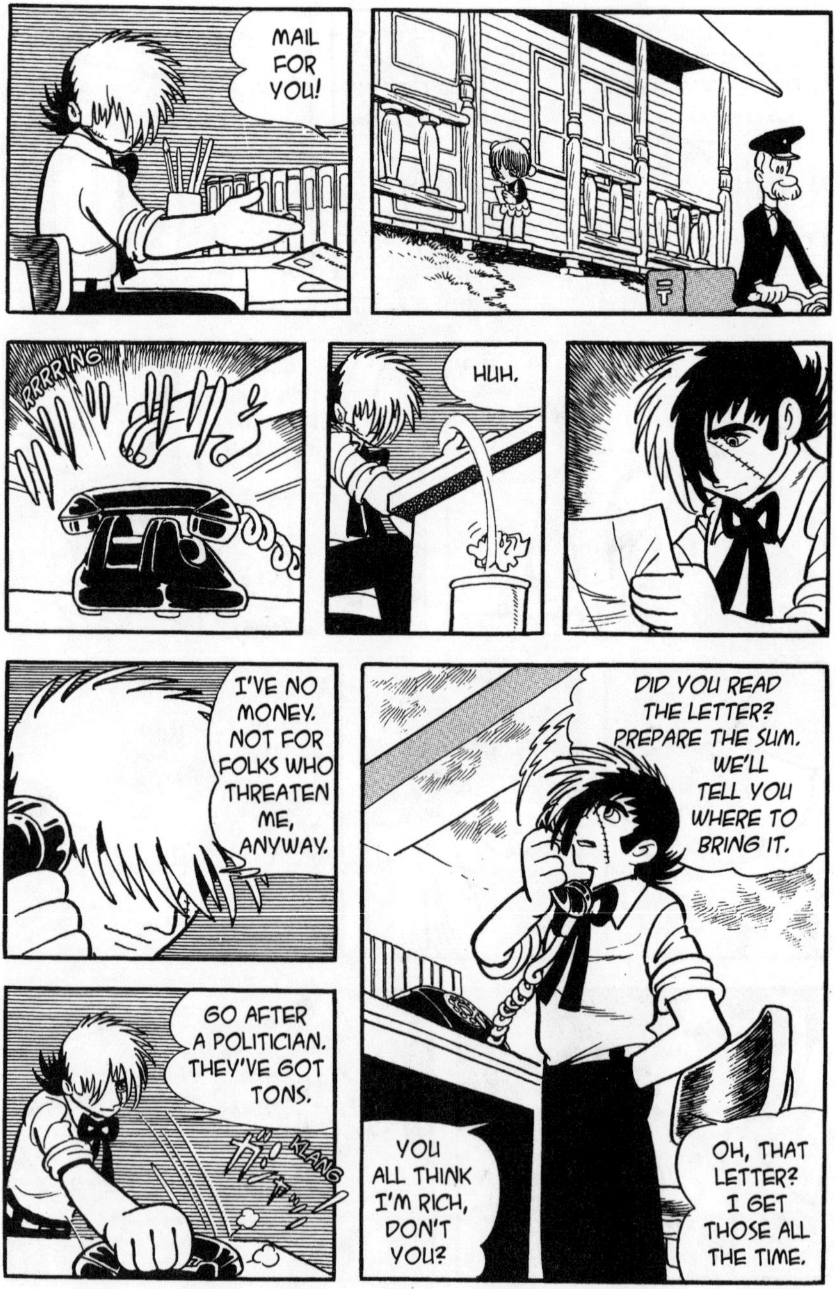
MAIL FOR YOU!
HUH.
RRRRING
DID YOU READ THE LETTER? PREPARE THE SUM. WE'LL TELL YOU WHERE TO BRING IT.
OH, THAT LETTER? I GET THOSE ALL THE TIME.
YOU ALL THINK I'M RICH, DON'T YOU?
I'VE NO MONEY. NOT FOR FOLKS WHO THREATEN ME, ANYWAY.
GO AFTER A POLITICIAN. THEY'VE GOT TONS.
KLANG

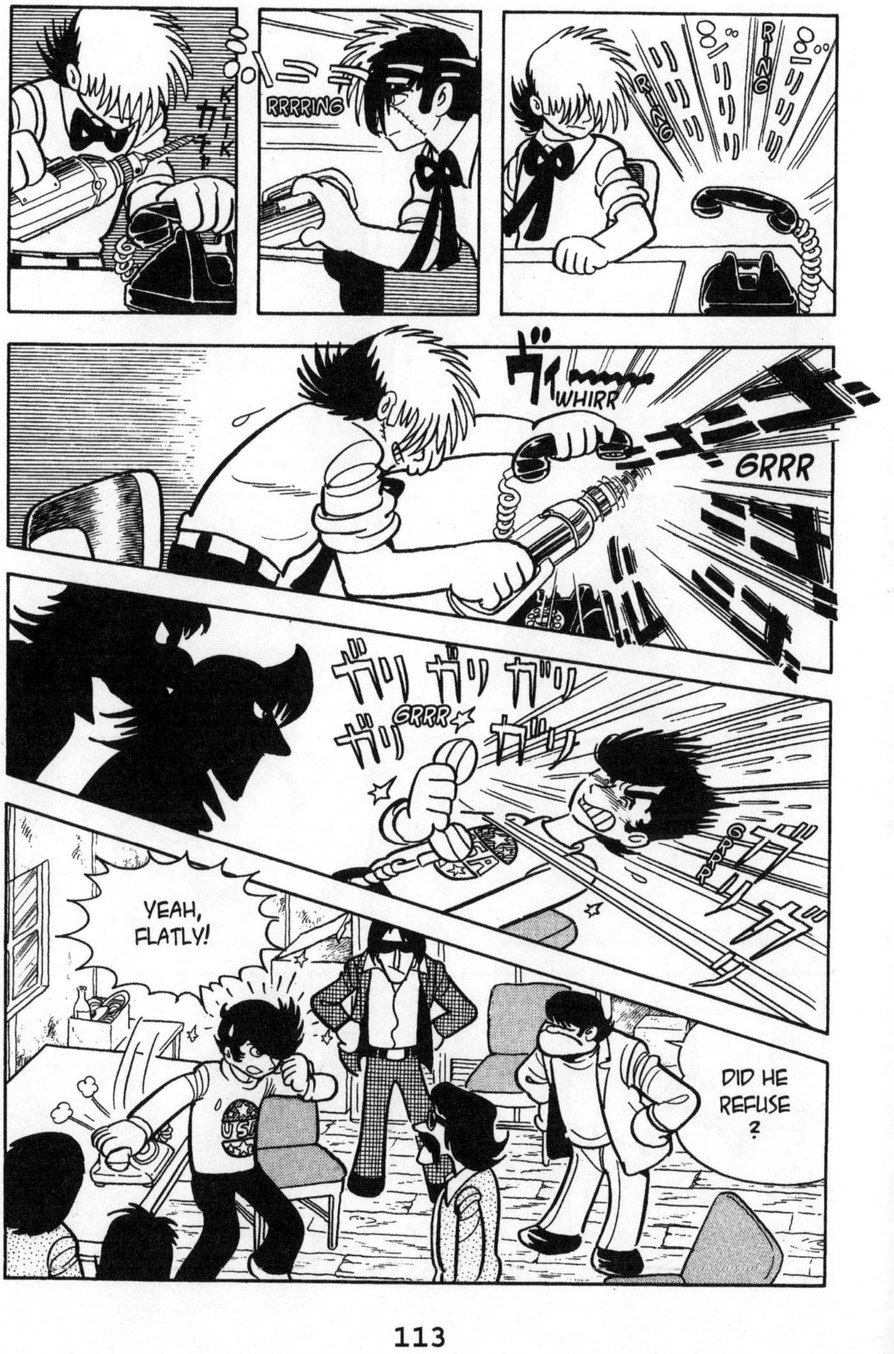
RING
RING
RRRRING
KLIK
WHIRR
GRRR
GRRR
GRRR
DID HE REFUSE?
YEAH, FLATLY!

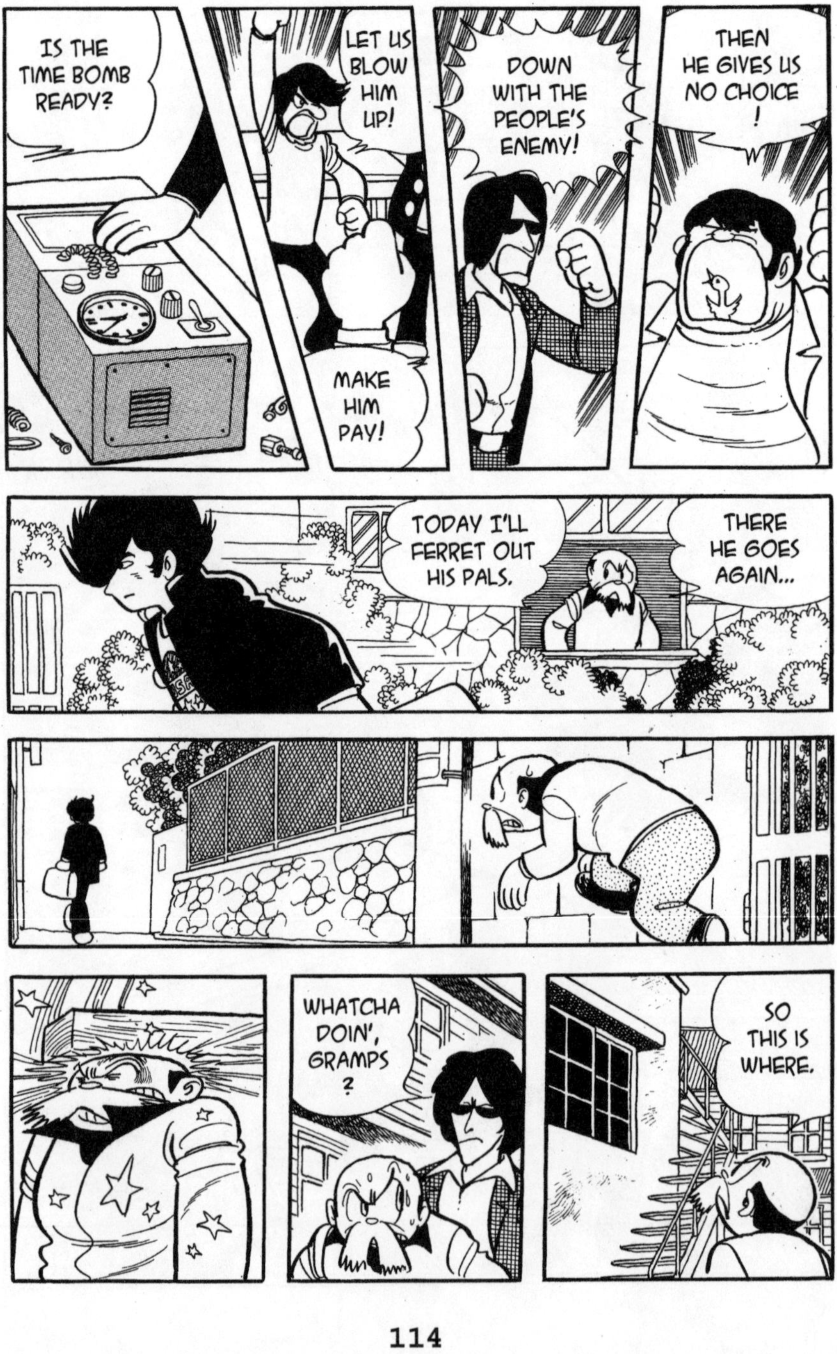
THEN HE GIVES US NO CHOICE !
DOWN WITH THE PEOPLE'S ENEMY!
LET US BLOW HIM UP!
MAKE HIM PAY!
IS THE TIME BOMB READY?
THERE HE GOES AGAIN...
TODAY I'LL FERRET OUT HIS PALS.
SO THIS IS WHERE.
WHATCHA DOIN', GRAMPS ?

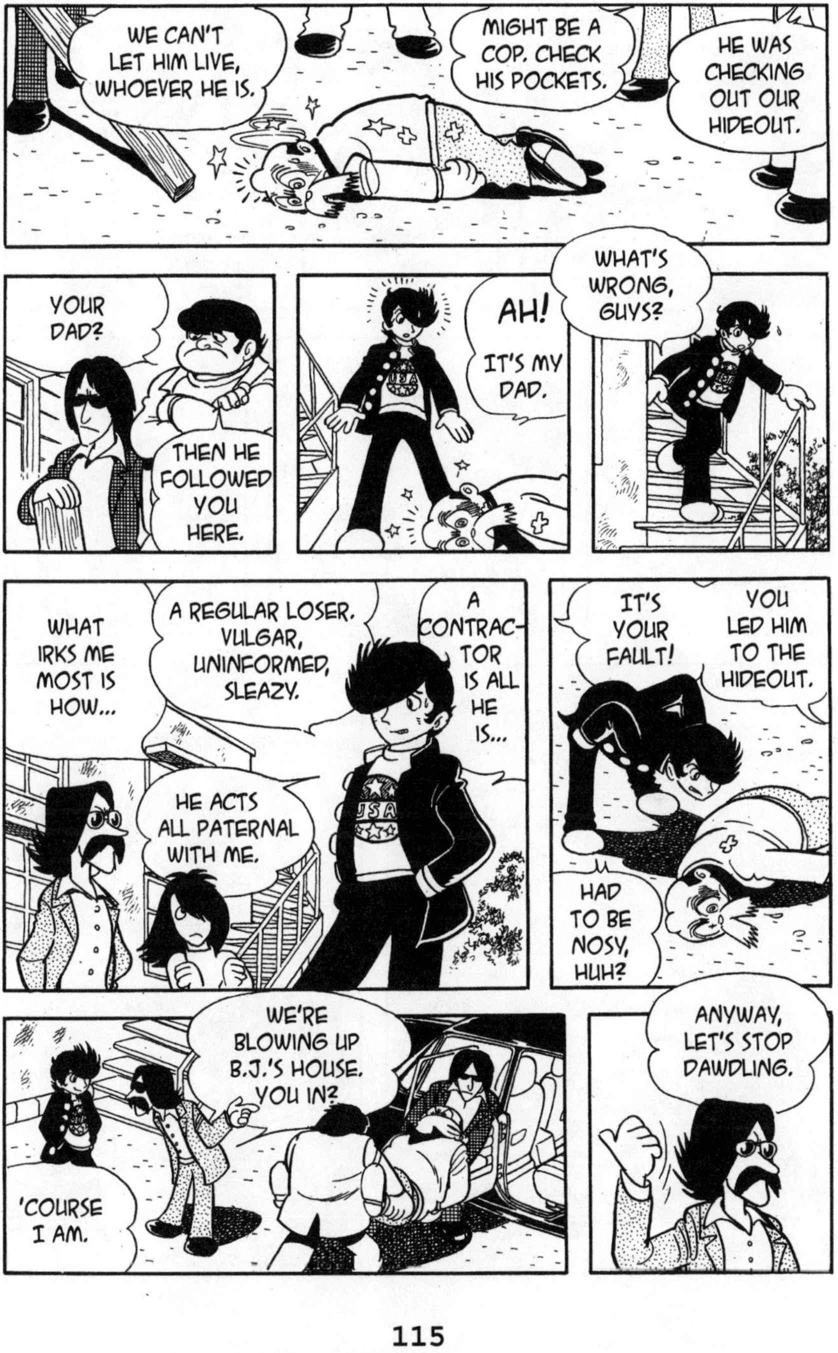
HE WAS CHECKING OUT OUR HIDEOUT.
MIGHT BE A COP. CHECK HIS POCKETS.
WE CAN'T LET HIM LIVE, WHOEVER HE IS.
WHAT'S WRONG, GUYS?
AH!
IT'S MY DAD.
YOUR DAD?
THEN HE FOLLOWED YOU HERE.
YOU LED HIM TO THE HIDEOUT.
IT'S YOUR FAULT!
HAD TO BE NOSY, HUH?
A CONTRAC-TOR IS ALL HE IS...
A REGULAR LOSER. VULGAR, UNINFORMED, SLEAZY.
WHAT IRKS ME MOST IS HOW...
HE ACTS ALL PATERNAL WITH ME.
ANYWAY, LET'S STOP DAWDLING.
WE'RE BLOWING UP B.J.'S HOUSE. YOU IN?
'COURSE I AM.

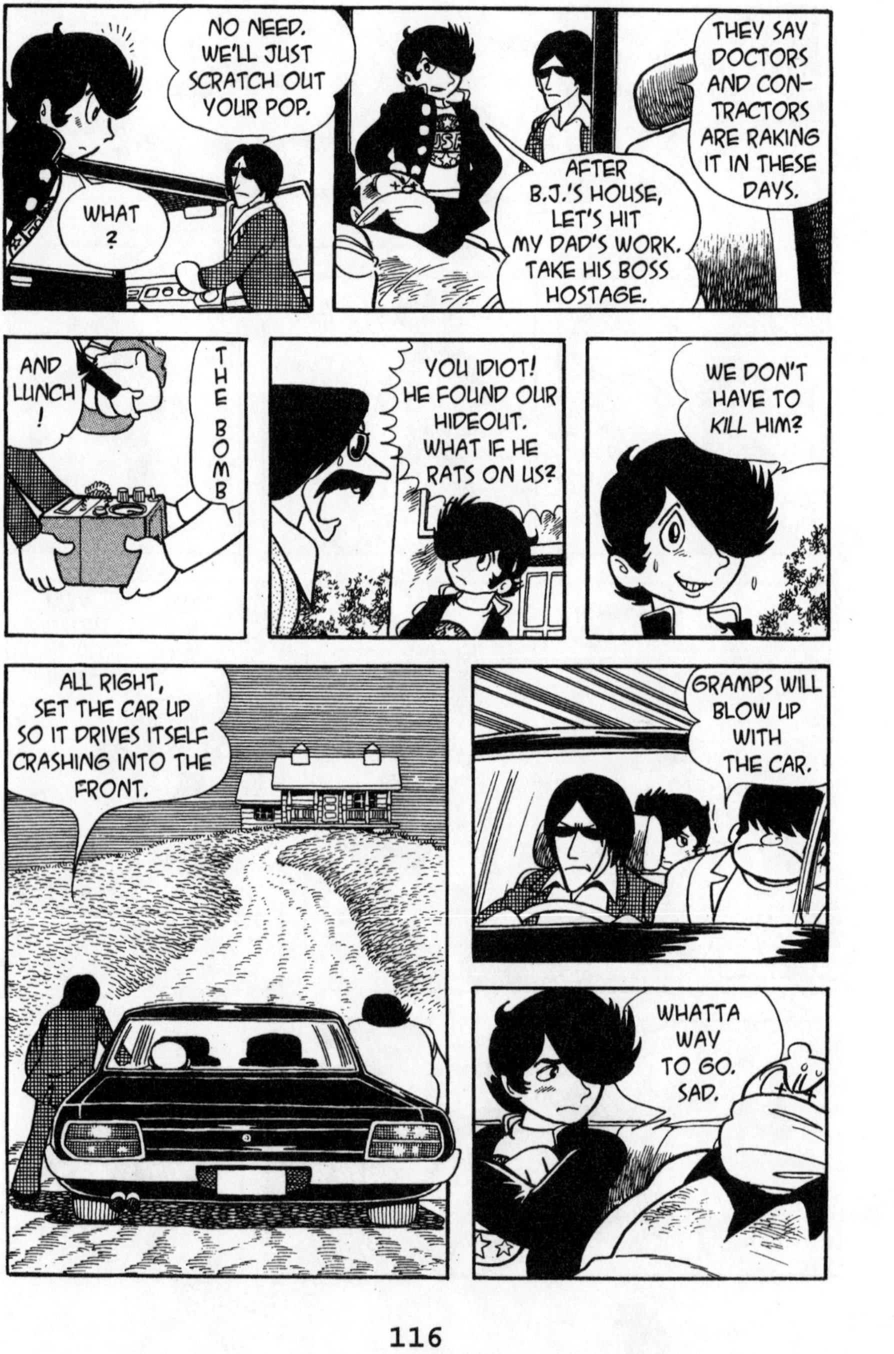
NO NEED. WE'LL JUST SCRATCH OUT YOUR POP.
WHAT?
AFTER B.J.'S HOUSE, LET'S HIT MY DAD'S WORK. TAKE HIS BOSS HOSTAGE.
THEY SAY DOCTORS AND CONTRACTORS ARE RAKING IT IN THESE DAYS.
THE BOMB
AND LUNCH!
YOU IDIOT! HE FOUND OUR HIDEOUT. WHAT IF HE RATS ON US?
WE DON'T HAVE TO KILL HIM?
ALL RIGHT, SET THE CAR UP SO IT DRIVES ITSELF CRASHING INTO THE FRONT.
GRAMPS WILL BLOW UP WITH THE CAR.
WHATTA WAY TO GO. SAD.

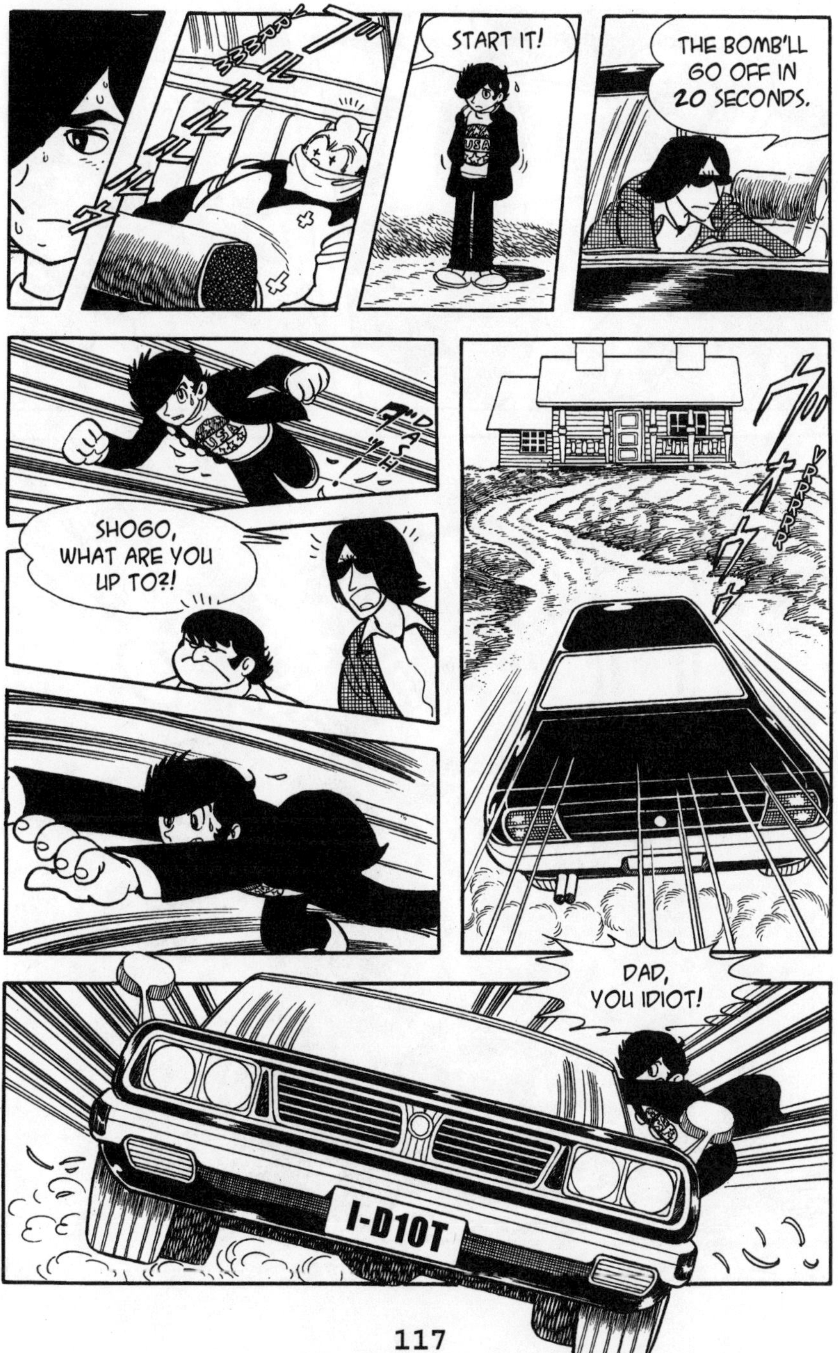
THE BOMB'LL GO OFF IN 20 SECONDS.
START IT!
BBBRRV
VRRRRR
DASH
SHOGO, WHAT ARE YOU UP TO?!
DAD, YOU IDIOT!
I-D10T

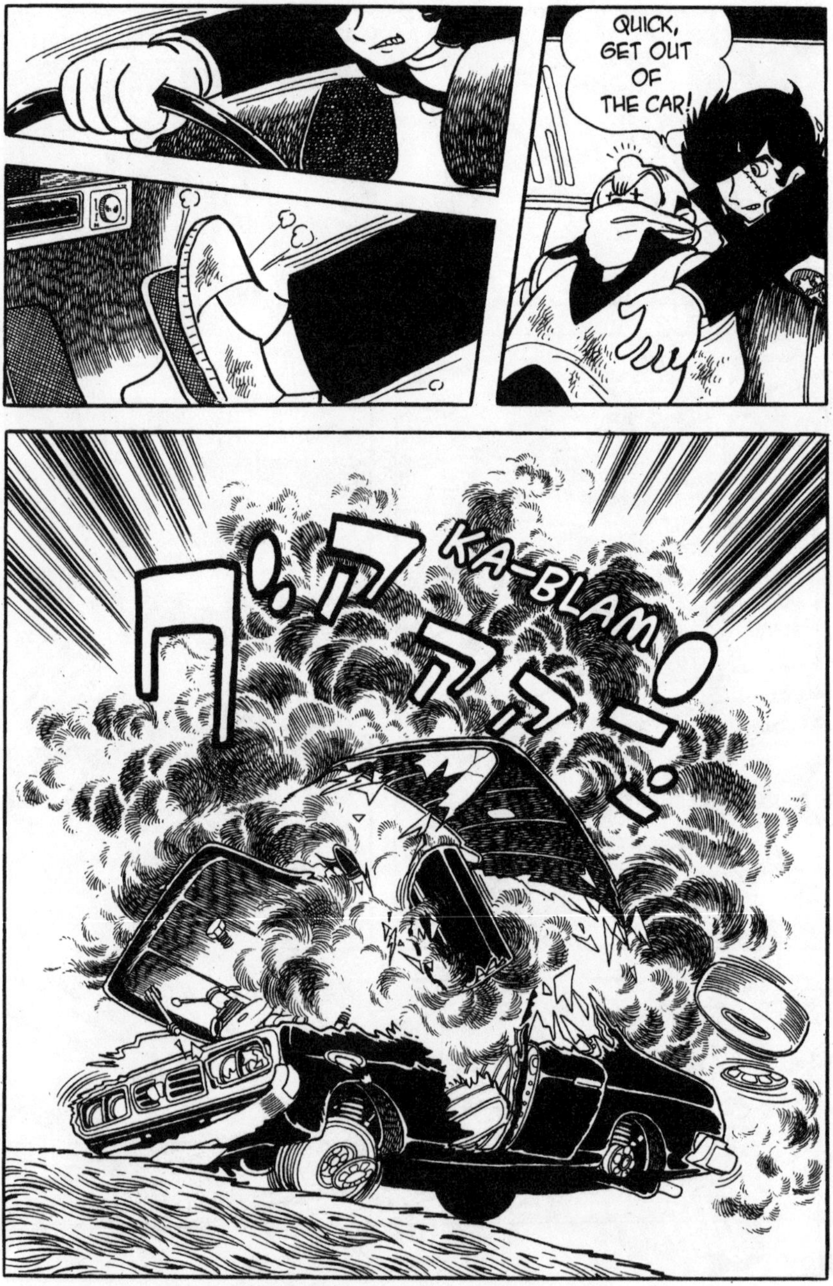
QUICK, GET OUT OF THE CAR!
KA-BLAM

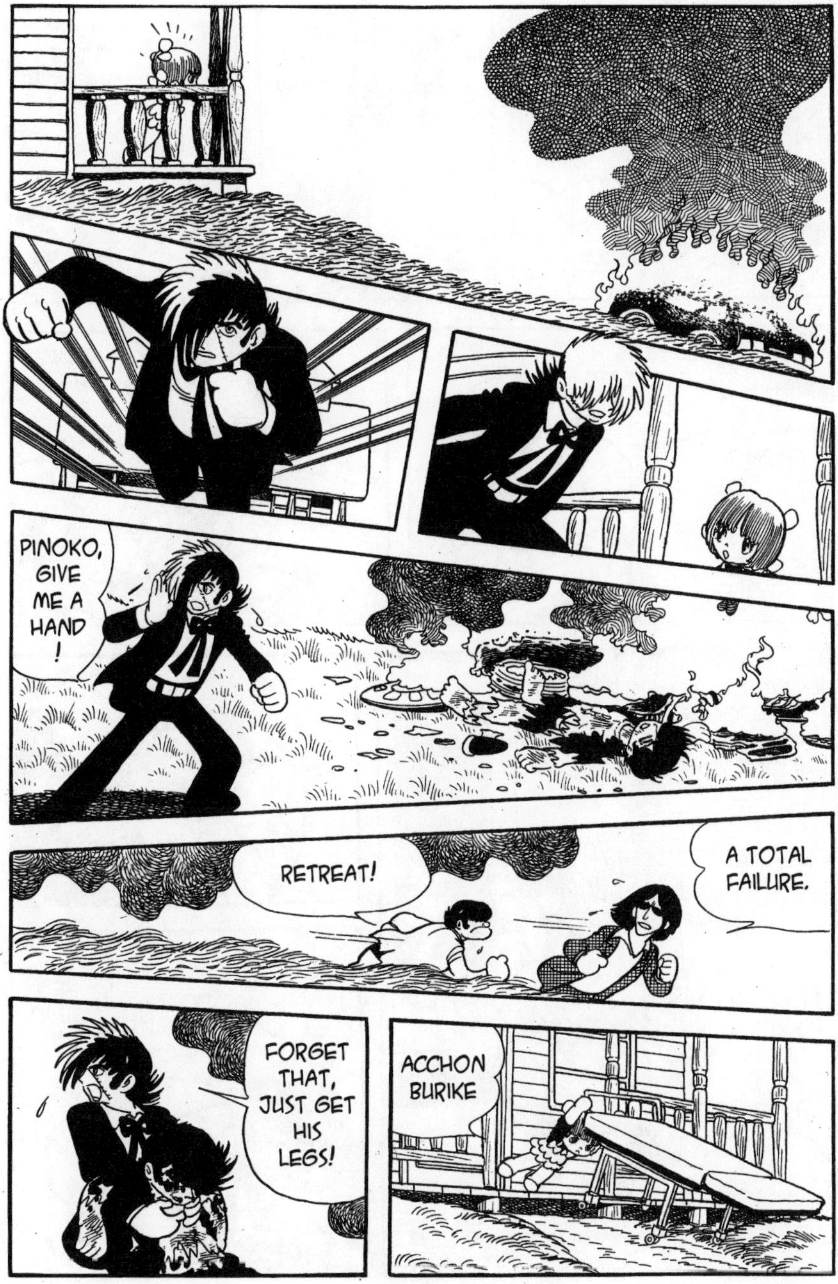
PINOKO, GIVE ME A HAND!
A TOTAL FAILURE.
RETREAT!
ACCHON BURIKE
FORGET THAT, JUST GET HIS LEGS!

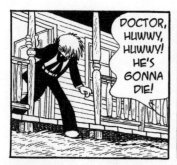

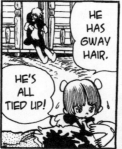

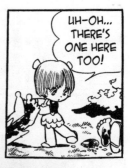

UH-OH... THERE'S ONE HERE TOO!
HE HAS GWAY HAIR.
HE'S ALL TIED UP!
DOCTOR, HUWWY, HUWWY! HE'S GONNA DIE!
WOW, THIS IS BAD.
UNH...
UHH...
IT'S TOO LATE FOR HIM.
SHO... SHOGO.
UNGH
ガクリ
SLUMP
HE'S DEAD !!
DAMMIT... IF WE'D NOTICED ONLY A MINUTE SOONER!
A CEREBRAL EMBOLISM. A BLOCKAGE IN HIS BRAIN'S BLOOD VESSEL ...
IT KILLED HIS BRAIN TISSUE.
YOU'RE TAKING HIM IN?

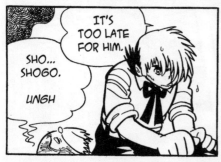

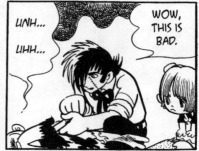

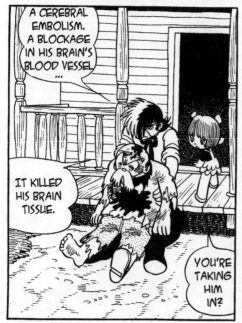

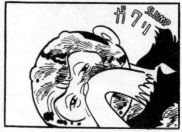

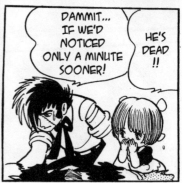

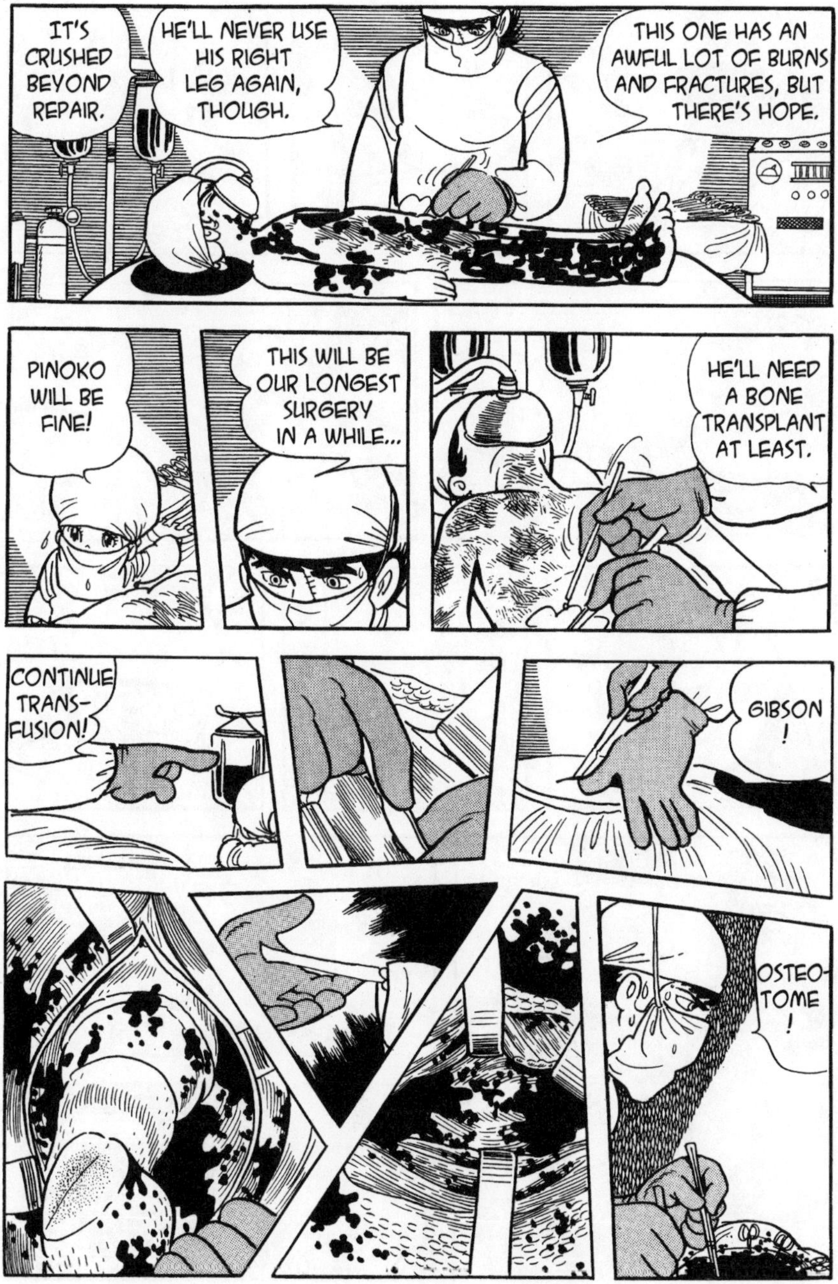
THIS ONE HAS AN AWFUL LOT OF BURNS AND FRACTURES, BUT THERE'S HOPE.
HE'LL NEVER USE HIS RIGHT LEG AGAIN, THOUGH.
IT'S CRUSHED BEYOND REPAIR.
HE'LL NEED A BONE TRANSPLANT AT LEAST.
THIS WILL BE OUR LONGEST SURGERY IN A WHILE...
PINOKO WILL BE FINE!
GIBSON!
CONTINUE TRANS-FUSION!
OSTEO-TOME!

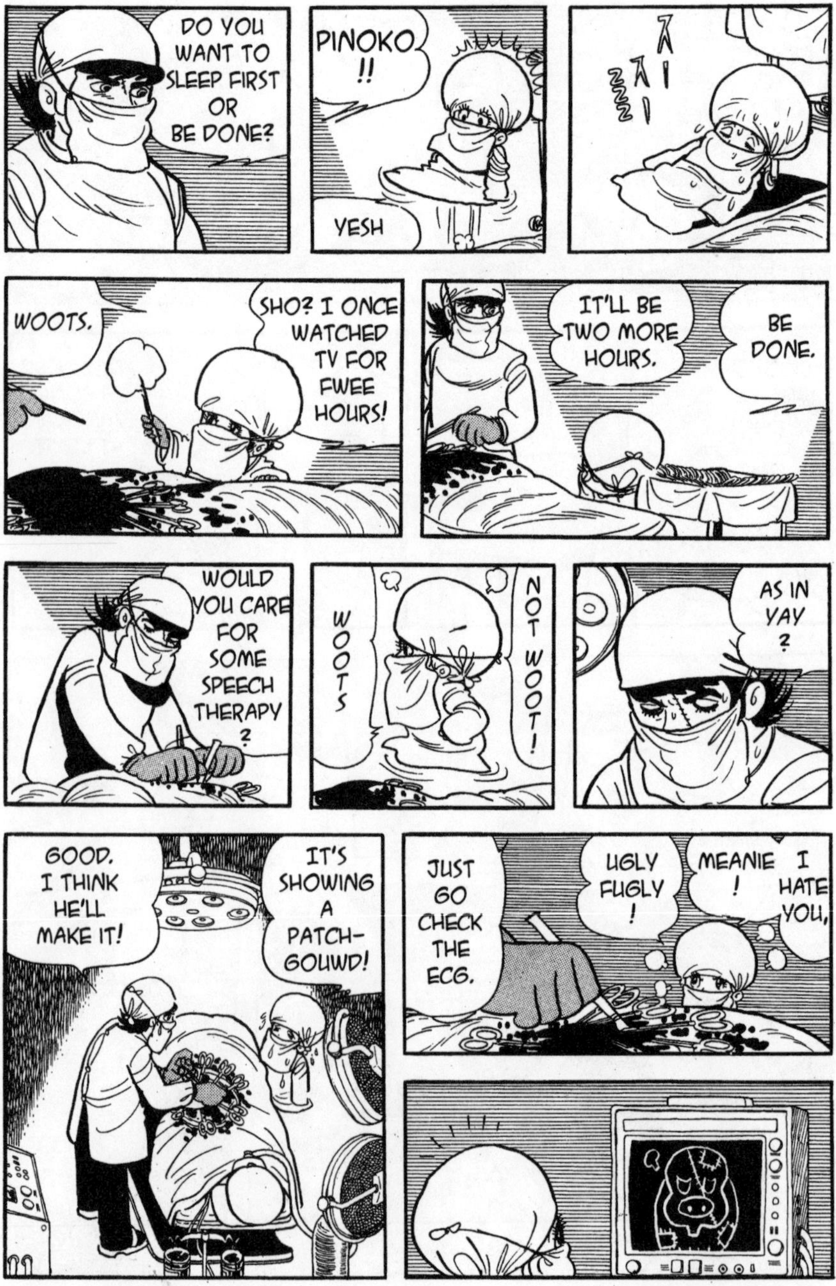
スー
スー
ZZZ
PINOKO !!
YESH
DO YOU WANT TO SLEEP FIRST OR BE DONE?
BE DONE.
IT'LL BE TWO MORE HOURS.
SHO? I ONCE WATCHED TV FOR FWEE HOURS!
WOOTS.
AS IN YAY ?
NOT WOOT!
WOOTS
WOULD YOU CARE FOR SOME SPEECH THERAPY ?
I HATE YOU,
MEANIE !
UGLY FUGLY !
JUST GO CHECK THE ECG.
IT'S SHOWING A PATCH-GOUWD!
GOOD. I THINK HE'LL MAKE IT!

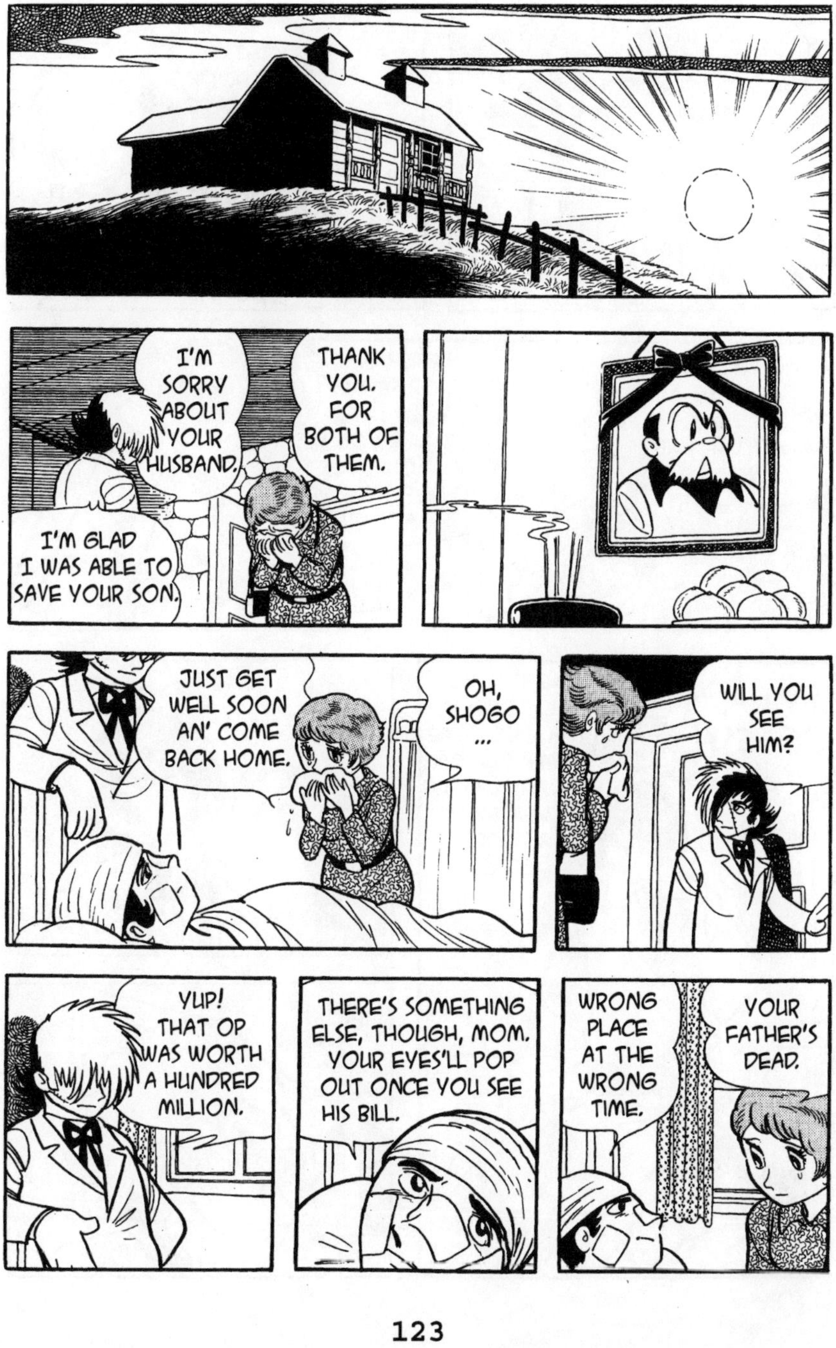
THANK YOU. FOR BOTH OF THEM.
I'M SORRY ABOUT YOUR HUSBAND.
I'M GLAD I WAS ABLE TO SAVE YOUR SON.
WILL YOU SEE HIM?
OH, SHOGO ...
JUST GET WELL SOON AN' COME BACK HOME.
YOUR FATHER'S DEAD.
WRONG PLACE AT THE WRONG TIME.
THERE'S SOMETHING ELSE, THOUGH, MOM. YOUR EYES'LL POP OUT ONCE YOU SEE HIS BILL.
YUP! THAT OP WAS WORTH A HUNDRED MILLION.

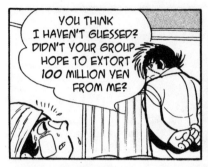

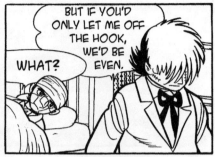

BUT IF YOU'D ONLY LET ME OFF THE HOOK, WE'D BE EVEN.
WHAT?
YOU THINK I HAVEN'T GUESSED? DIDN'T YOUR GROUP HOPE TO EXTORT 100 MILLION YEN FROM ME?
IN EXCHANGE FOR SAVING YOUR LIFE, I'D LIKE YOU TO TELL YOUR PALS TO STOP PLAYING AT BLACKMAIL.
NOT A CHANCE. AS LONG AS YOU'RE RAKING IT IN, WE'LL HOUND YOU.
WITH THAT LEG?
HUH ??
NEARLY ALL THE BONES IN THAT LEG CAME FROM YOUR DAD. I TRANSPLANTED THEM FROM HIS CORPSE.
MY DAD'S BONES?!

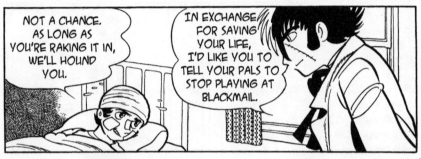

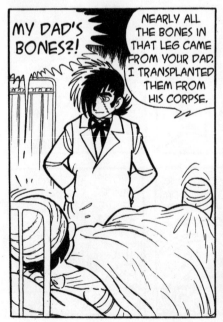

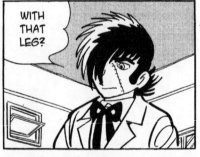

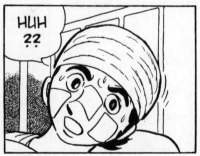

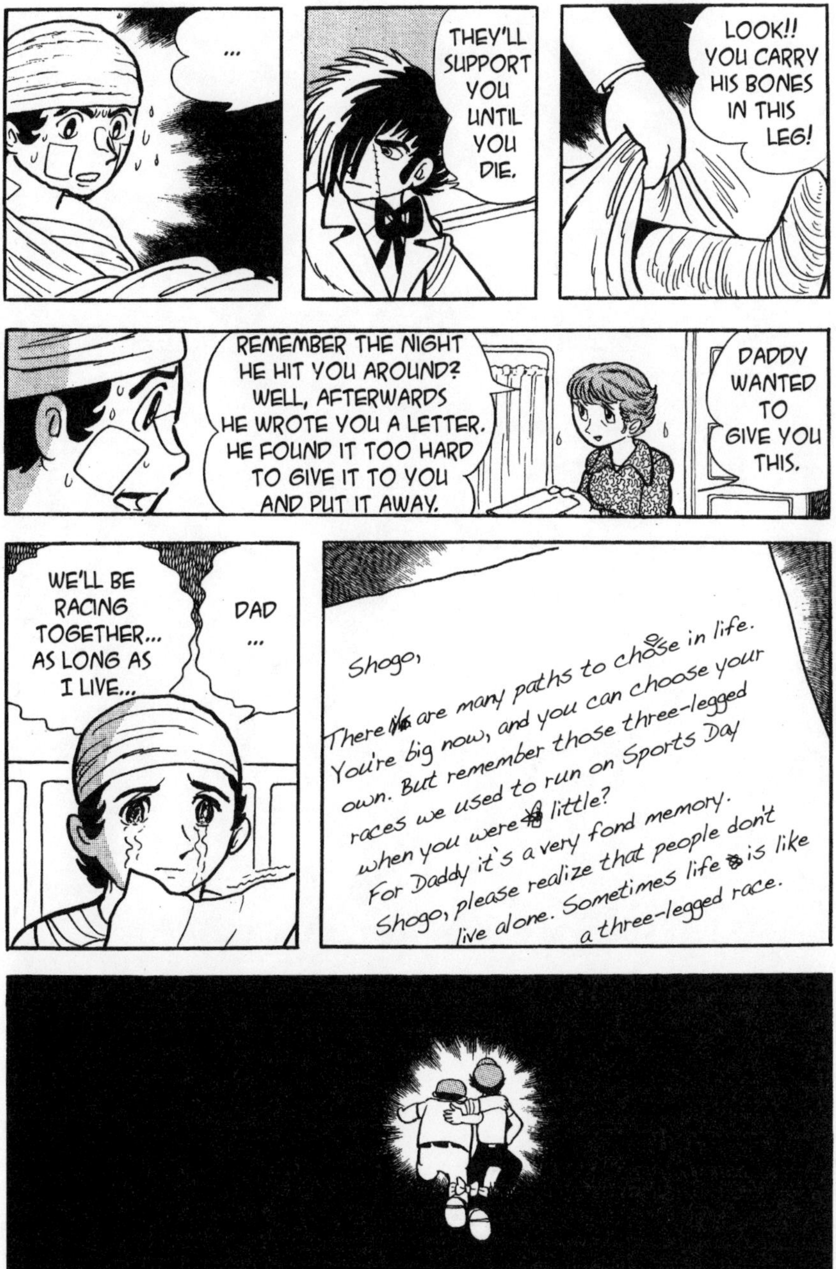
LOOK!! YOU CARRY HIS BONES IN THIS LEG!
THEY'LL SUPPORT YOU UNTIL YOU DIE.
...
DADDY WANTED TO GIVE YOU THIS.
REMEMBER THE NIGHT HE HIT YOU AROUND? WELL, AFTERWARDS HE WROTE YOU A LETTER. HE FOUND IT TOO HARD TO GIVE IT TO YOU AND PUT IT AWAY.
Shogo,
There are many paths to choose in life. You're big now, and you can choose your own. But remember those three-legged races we used to run on Sports Day when you were little?
For Daddy it's a very fond memory.
Shogo, please realize that people don't live alone. Sometimes life is like a three-legged race.
DAD ...
WE'LL BE RACING TOGETHER... AS LONG AS I LIVE...

A QUESTION OF PRIORITIES

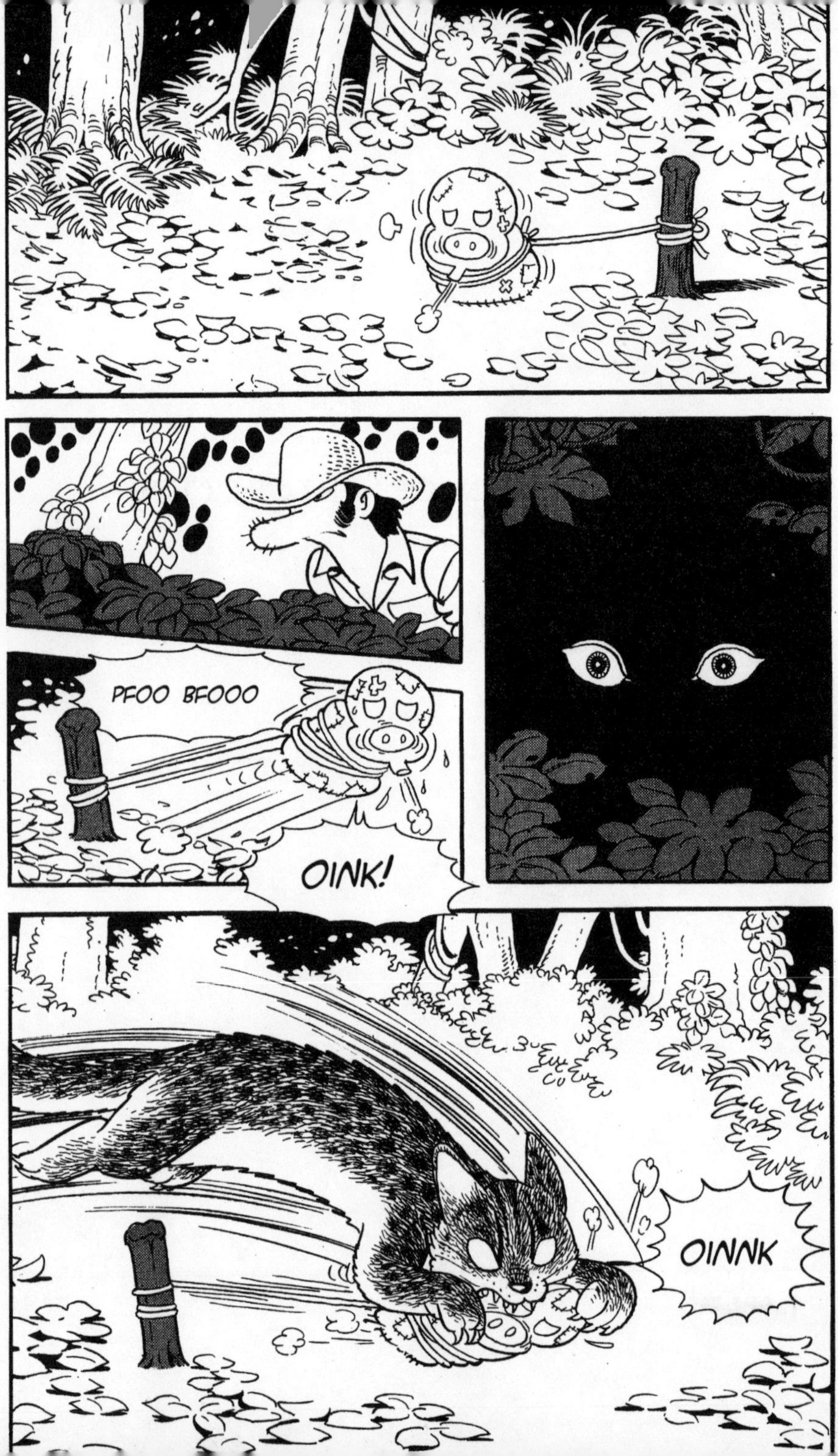
PFOO BFOOO
OINK!
OINNK

HRF
HRF
HRF
LURCH
THWAP
MMRAOW RAWRRR
IT WAS WORT CAMPING OUT FOR TWO WEEKS,
MISTER IRIOMOTE CAT!
RAOWR
NICE AND EASY ...

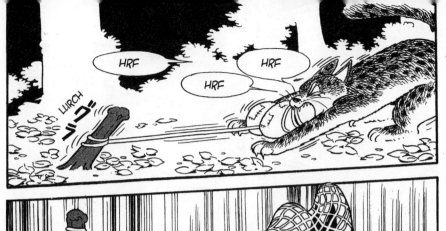

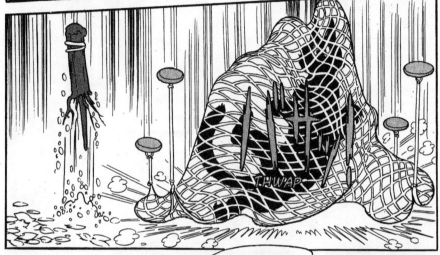

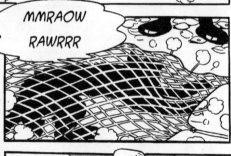

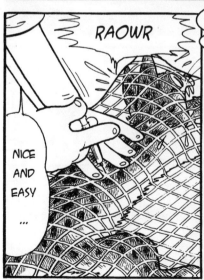

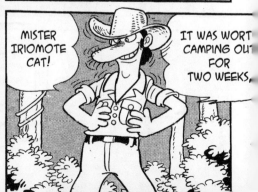

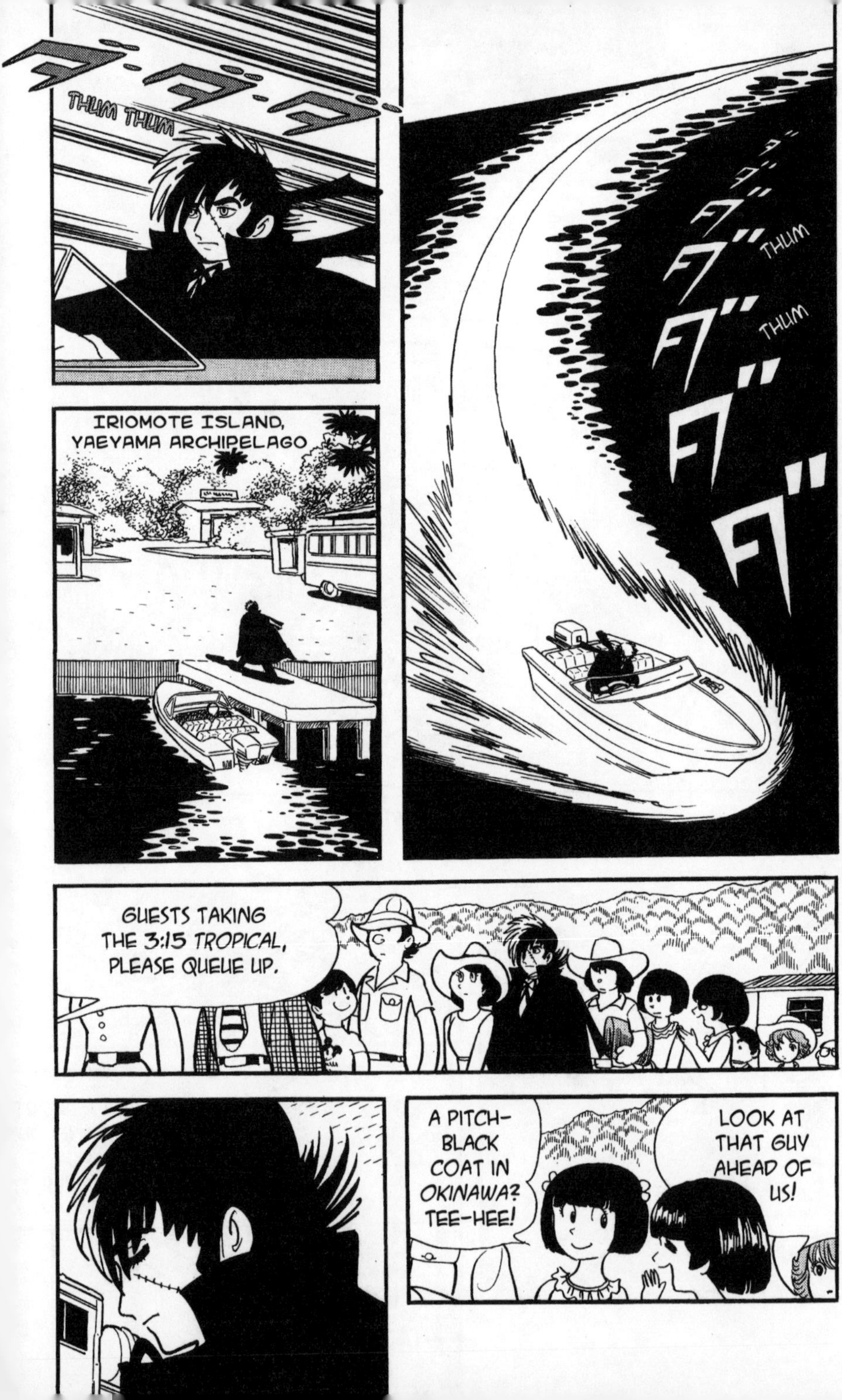
THUM
THUM
THUM THUM
IRIOMOTE ISLAND, YAEYAMA ARCHIPELAGO
GUESTS TAKING THE 3:15 TROPICAL, PLEASE QUEUE UP.
LOOK AT THAT GUY AHEAD OF US!
A PITCH-BLACK COAT IN OKINAWA? TEE-HEE!

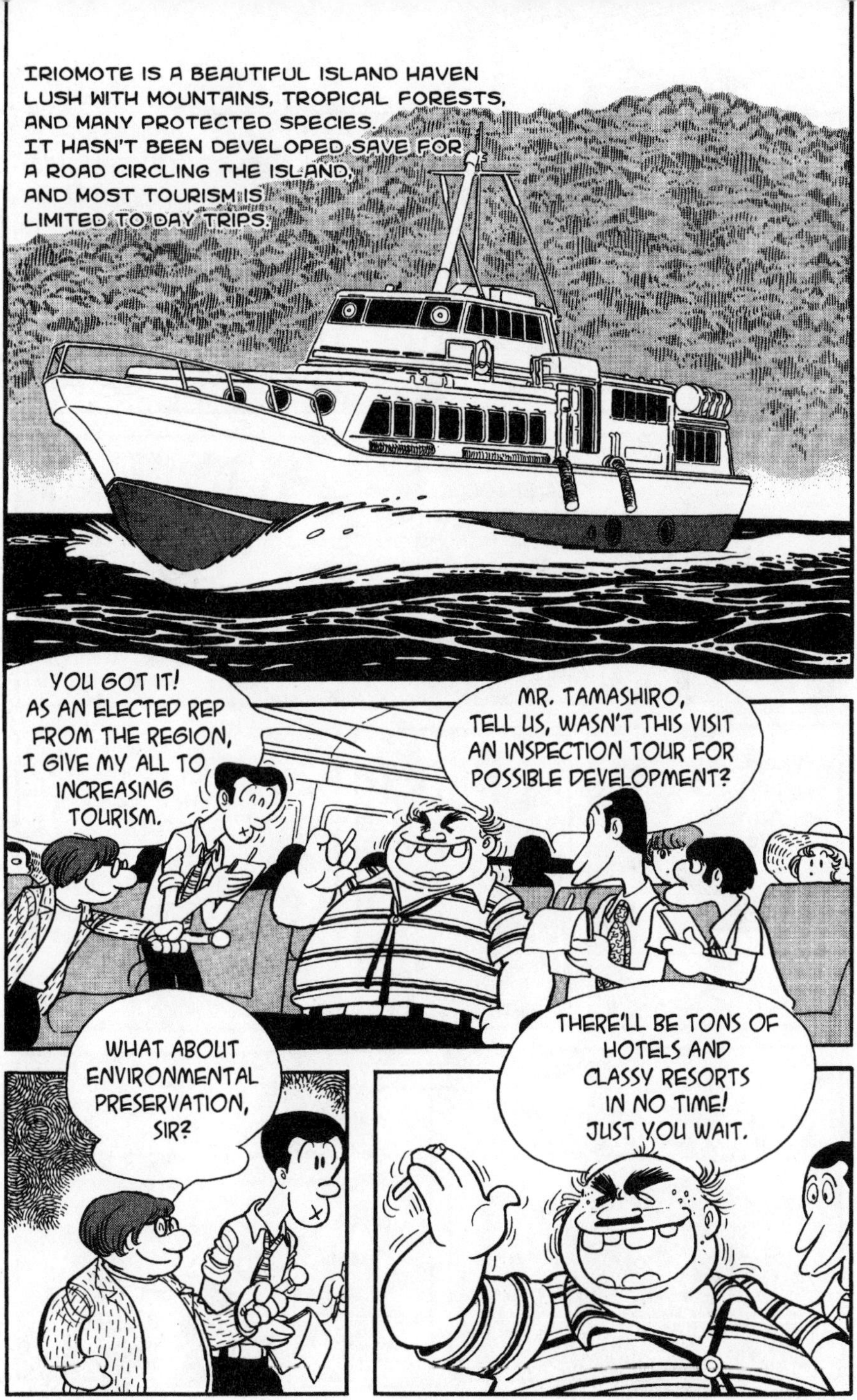
IRIOMOTE IS A BEAUTIFUL ISLAND HAVEN LUSH WITH MOUNTAINS, TROPICAL FORESTS, AND MANY PROTECTED SPECIES. IT HASN'T BEEN DEVELOPED SAVE FOR A ROAD CIRCLING THE ISLAND, AND MOST TOURISM IS LIMITED TO DAY TRIPS.
MR. TAMASHIRO, TELL US, WASN'T THIS VISIT AN INSPECTION TOUR FOR POSSIBLE DEVELOPMENT?
YOU GOT IT! AS AN ELECTED REP FROM THE REGION, I GIVE MY ALL TO INCREASING TOURISM.
THERE'LL BE TONS OF HOTELS AND CLASSY RESORTS IN NO TIME! JUST YOU WAIT.
WHAT ABOUT ENVIRONMENTAL PRESERVATION, SIR?

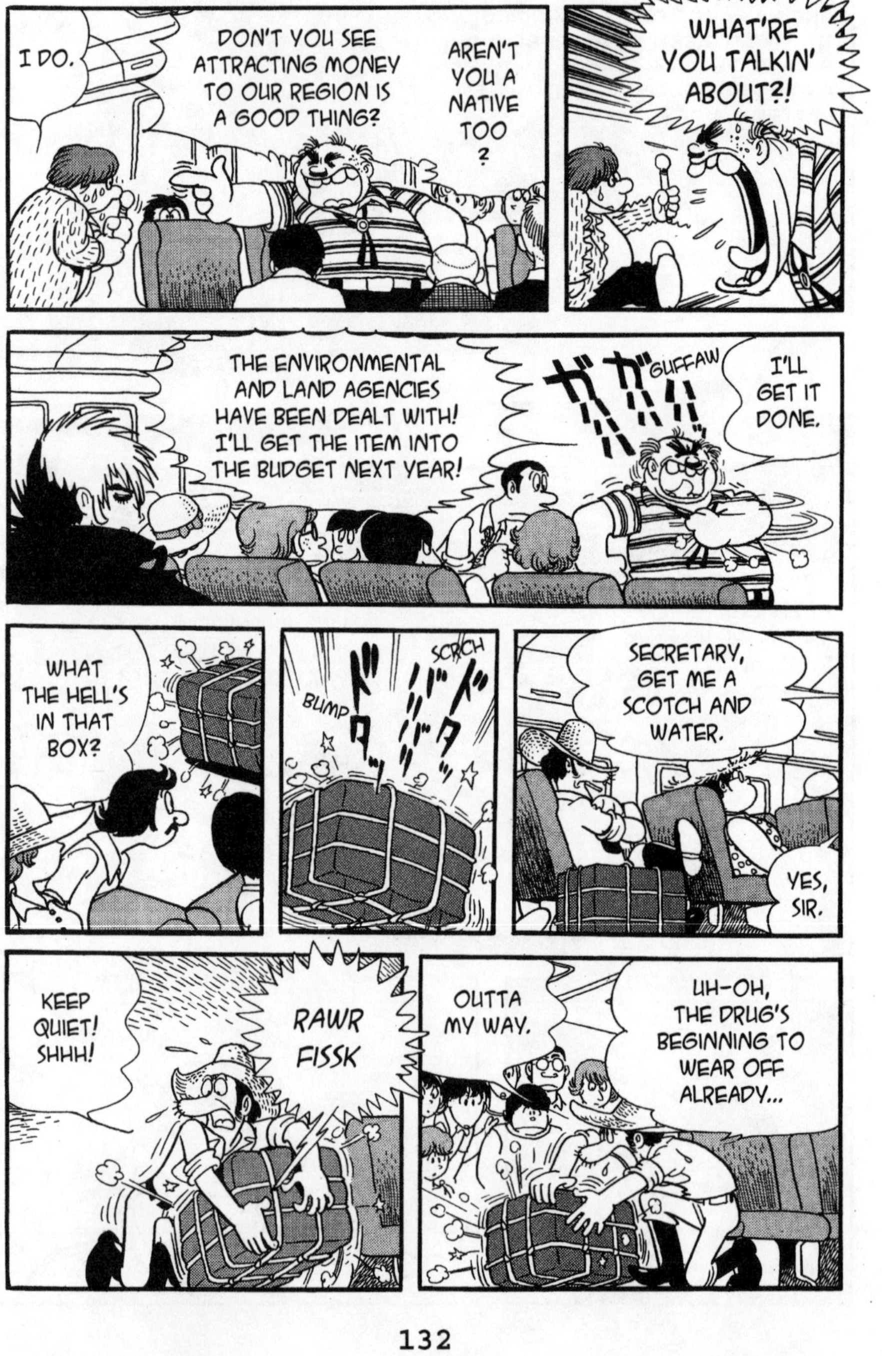
WHAT'RE YOU TALKIN' ABOUT?!
AREN'T YOU A NATIVE TOO ?
DON'T YOU SEE ATTRACTING MONEY TO OUR REGION IS A GOOD THING?
I DO.
I'LL GET IT DONE.
GUFFAW
THE ENVIRONMENTAL AND LAND AGENCIES HAVE BEEN DEALT WITH! I'LL GET THE ITEM INTO THE BUDGET NEXT YEAR!
SECRETARY, GET ME A SCOTCH AND WATER.
YES, SIR.
SCRCH
BUMP
WHAT THE HELL'S IN THAT BOX?
UH-OH, THE DRUG'S BEGINNING TO WEAR OFF ALREADY...
OUTTA MY WAY.
RAWR FISSK
KEEP QUIET! SHHH!

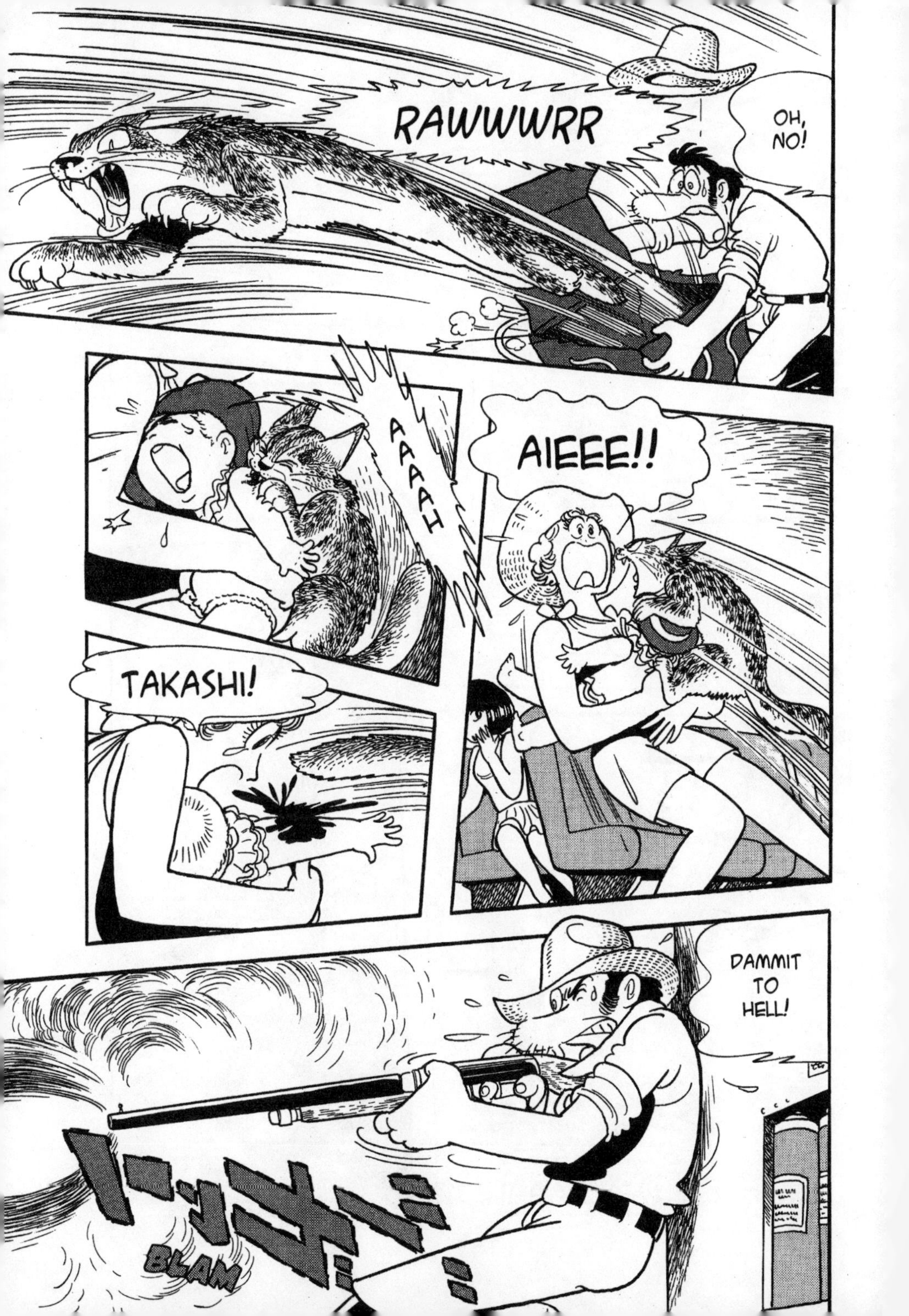
OH, NO!
RAWWWRR
AIEEE!!
AAAAAH
TAKASHI!
DAMMIT TO HELL!
BLAM

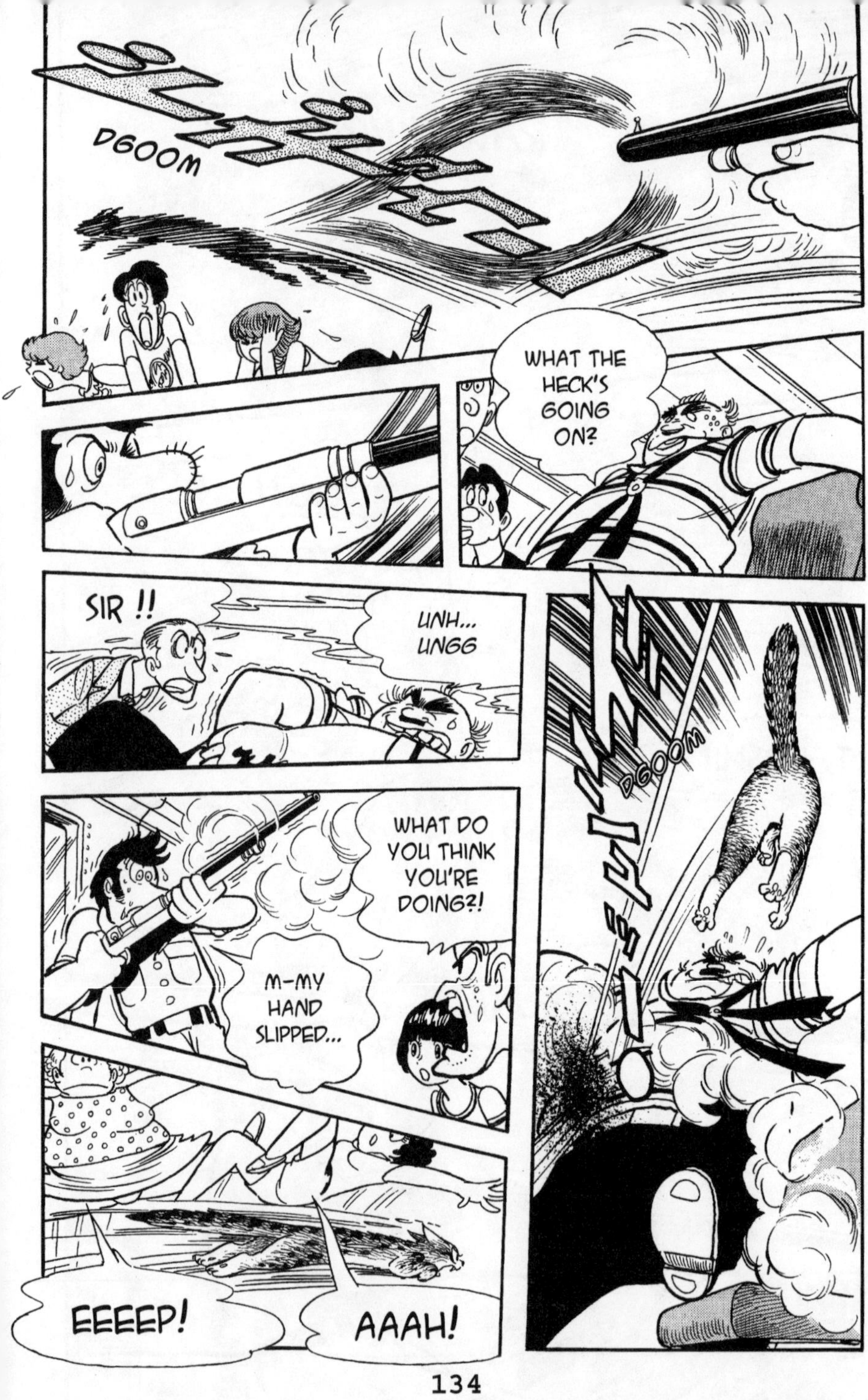
DGOOM
WHAT THE HECK'S GOING ON?
DGOOM
UNH... UNGG
SIR !!
WHAT DO YOU THINK YOU'RE DOING?!
M-MY HAND SLIPPED...
AAAH!
EEEEP!

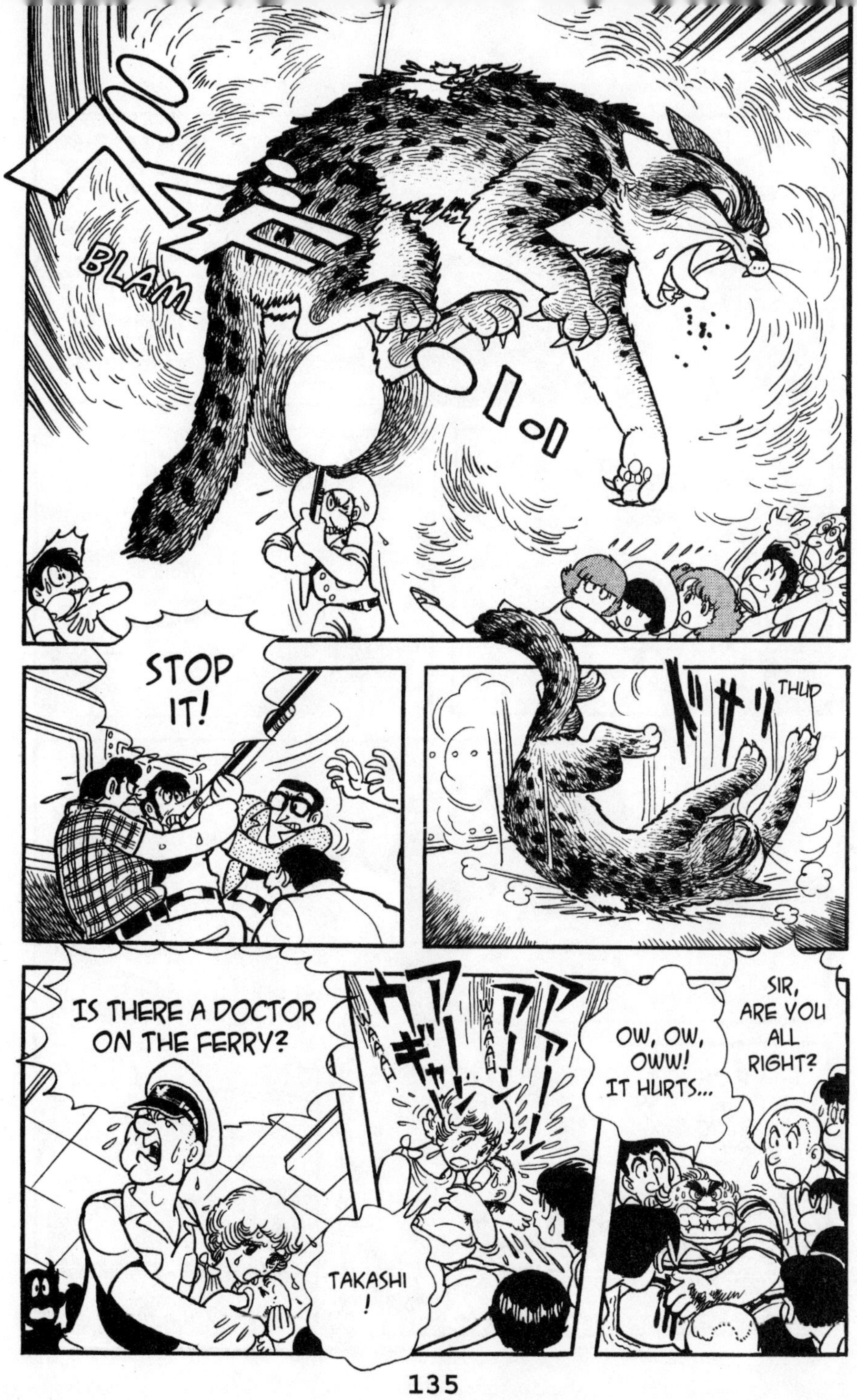
BLAM
THUD
STOP IT!
SIR, ARE YOU ALL RIGHT?
OW, OW, OWW! IT HURTS...
WAAAH
WAAAAH
IS THERE A DOCTOR ON THE FERRY?
TAKASHI!

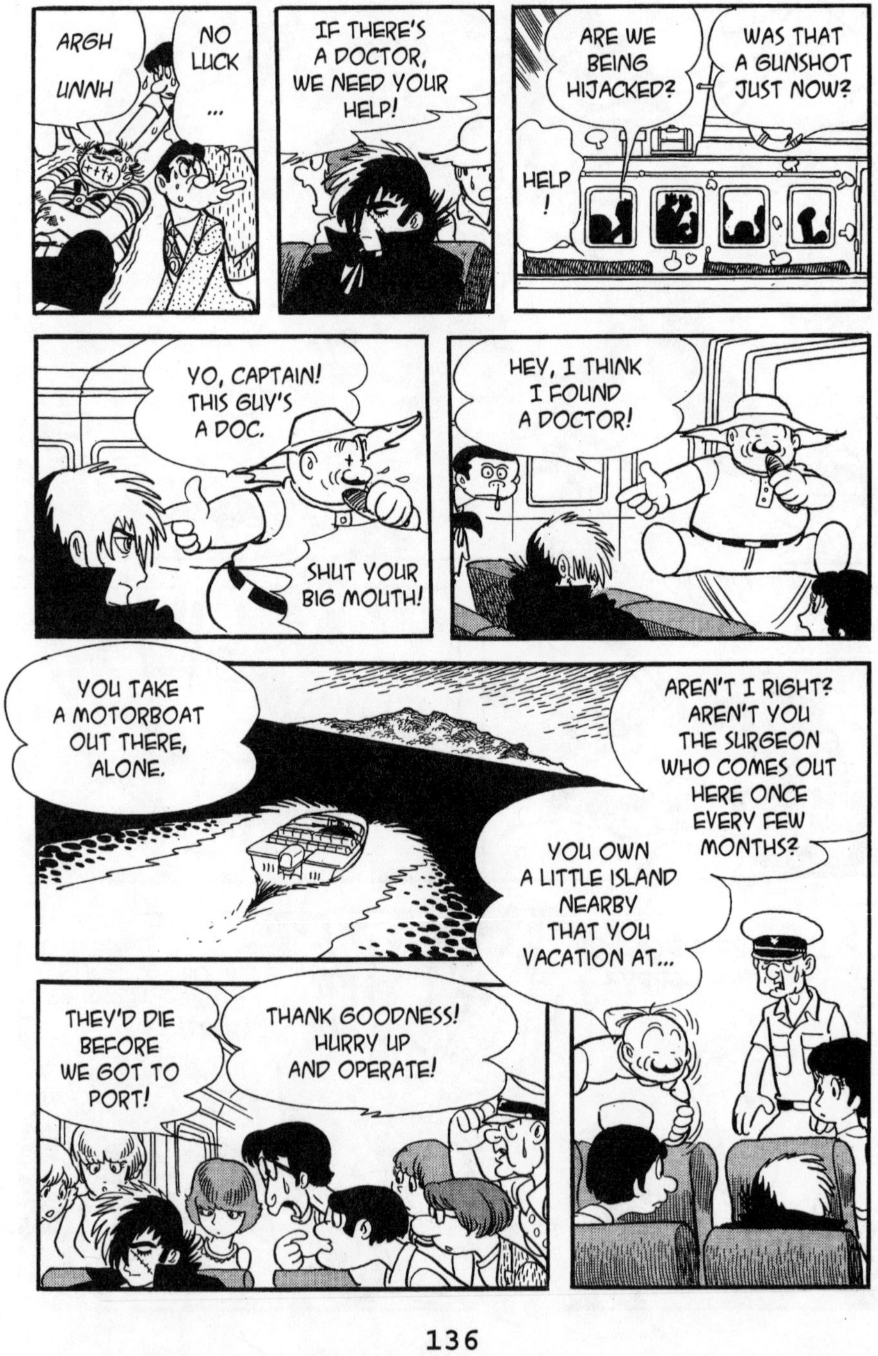
WAS THAT A GUNSHOT JUST NOW?
ARE WE BEING HIJACKED?
HELP!
IF THERE'S A DOCTOR, WE NEED YOUR HELP!
NO LUCK ...
ARGH UNNH
HEY, I THINK I FOUND A DOCTOR!
YO, CAPTAIN! THIS GUY'S A DOC.
SHUT YOUR BIG MOUTH!
AREN'T I RIGHT? AREN'T YOU THE SURGEON WHO COMES OUT HERE ONCE EVERY FEW MONTHS?
YOU OWN A LITTLE ISLAND NEARBY THAT YOU VACATION AT...
YOU TAKE A MOTORBOAT OUT THERE, ALONE.
THANK GOODNESS! HURRY UP AND OPERATE!
THEY'D DIE BEFORE WE GOT TO PORT!

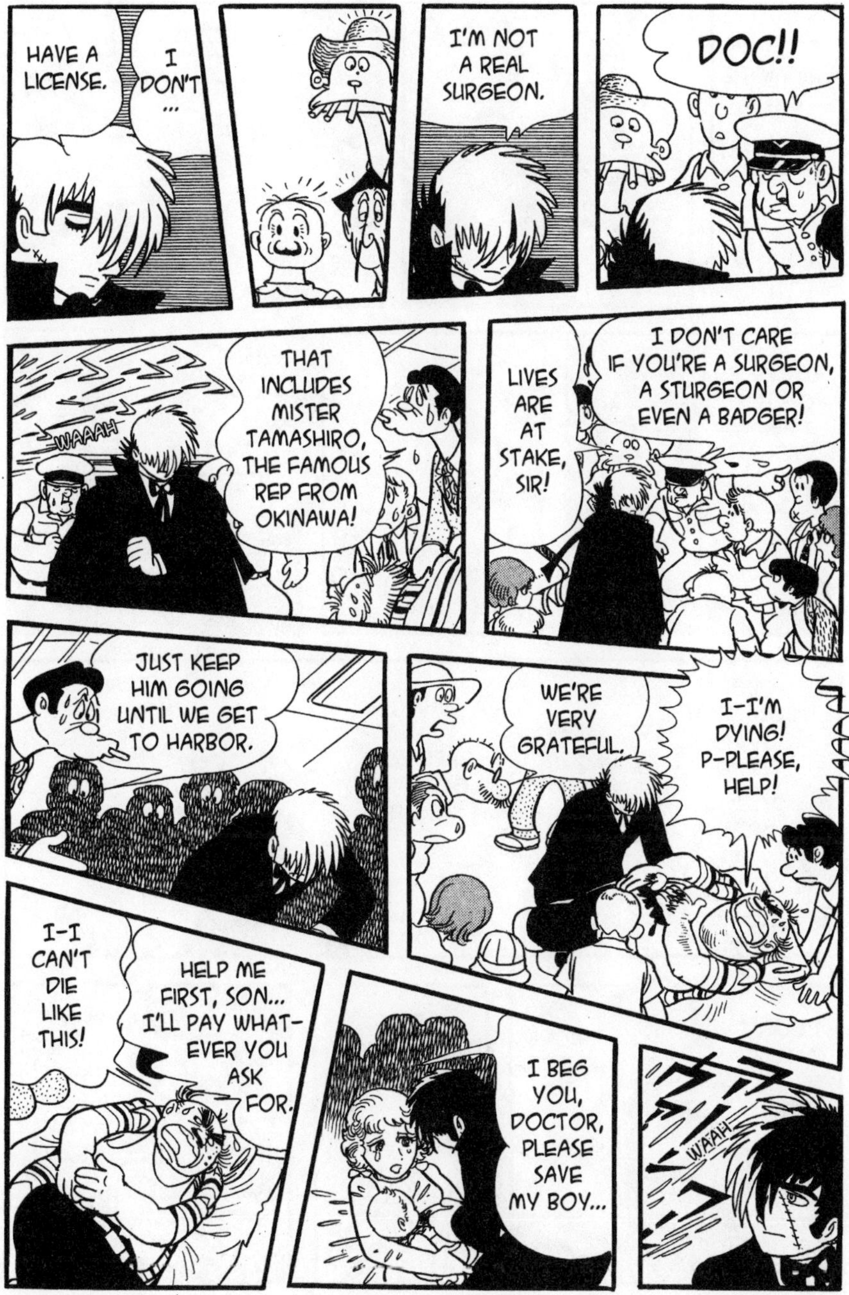
DOC!!
I'M NOT A REAL SURGEON.
I DON'T ...
HAVE A LICENSE.
I DON'T CARE IF YOU'RE A SURGEON, A STURGEON OR EVEN A BADGER!
LIVES ARE AT STAKE, SIR!
THAT INCLUDES MISTER TAMASHIRO, THE FAMOUS REP FROM OKINAWA!
WAAAH
I-I'M DYING! P-PLEASE, HELP!
WE'RE VERY GRATEFUL.
JUST KEEP HIM GOING UNTIL WE GET TO HARBOR.
WAAAH
I BEG YOU, DOCTOR, PLEASE SAVE MY BOY...
HELP ME FIRST, SON... I'LL PAY WHATEVER YOU ASK FOR.
I-I CAN'T DIE LIKE THIS!

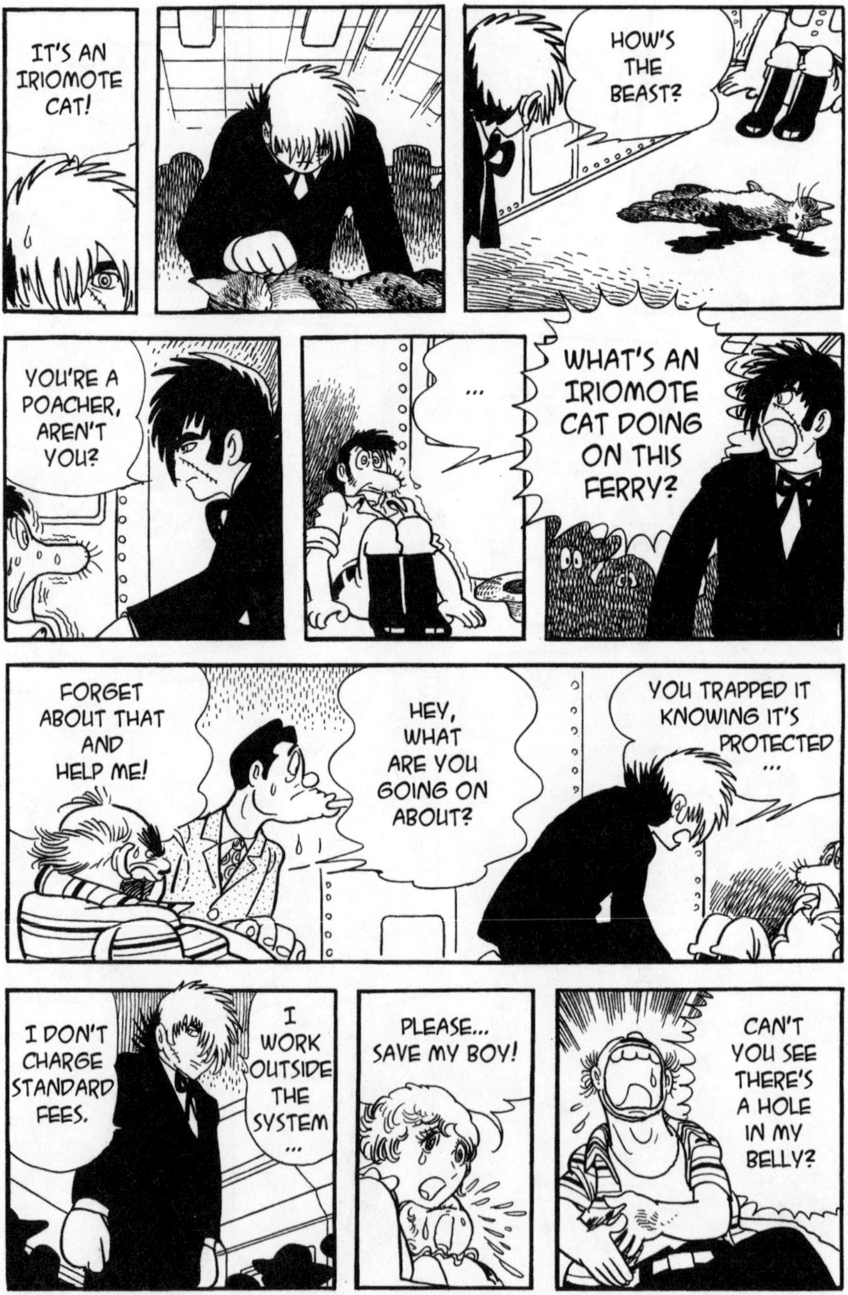
HOW'S THE BEAST?
IT'S AN IRIOMOTE CAT!
WHAT'S AN IRIOMOTE CAT DOING ON THIS FERRY?
...
YOU'RE A POACHER, AREN'T YOU?
YOU TRAPPED IT KNOWING IT'S PROTECTED ...
HEY, WHAT ARE YOU GOING ON ABOUT?
FORGET ABOUT THAT AND HELP ME!
CAN'T YOU SEE THERE'S A HOLE IN MY BELLY?
PLEASE... SAVE MY BOY!
I WORK OUTSIDE THE SYSTEM ...
I DON'T CHARGE STANDARD FEES.

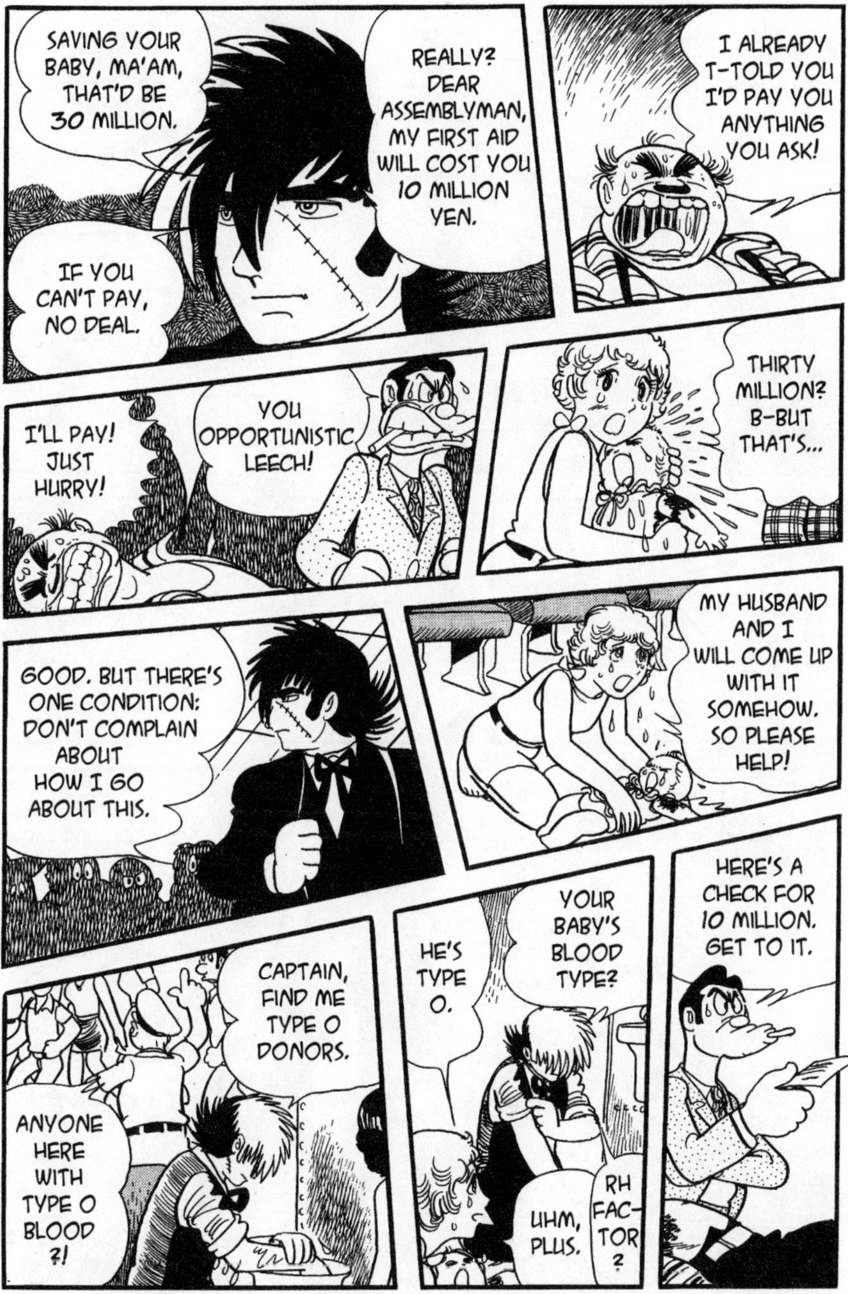
I ALREADY T-TOLD YOU I'D PAY YOU ANYTHING YOU ASK!
REALLY? DEAR ASSEMBLYMAN, MY FIRST AID WILL COST YOU 10 MILLION YEN.
SAVING YOUR BABY, MA'AM, THAT'D BE 30 MILLION.
IF YOU CAN'T PAY, NO DEAL.
THIRTY MILLION? B-BUT THAT'S...
YOU OPPORTUNISTIC LEECH!
I'LL PAY! JUST HURRY!
MY HUSBAND AND I WILL COME UP WITH IT SOMEHOW. SO PLEASE HELP!
GOOD. BUT THERE'S ONE CONDITION: DON'T COMPLAIN ABOUT HOW I GO ABOUT THIS.
HERE'S A CHECK FOR 10 MILLION. GET TO IT.
YOUR BABY'S BLOOD TYPE?
HE'S TYPE O.
RH FACTOR?
UHM, PLUS.
CAPTAIN, FIND ME TYPE O DONORS.
ANYONE HERE WITH TYPE O BLOOD ?!

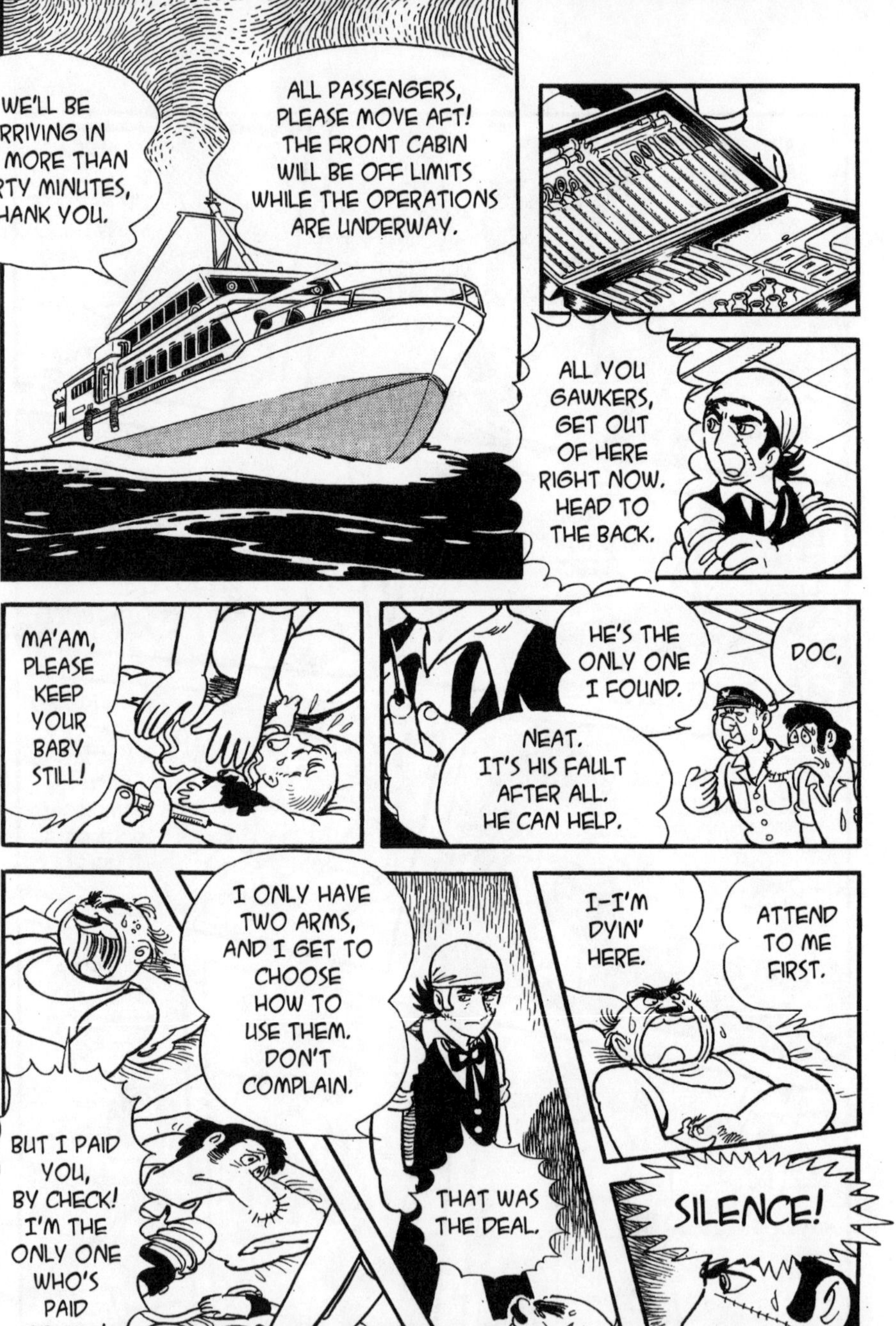
ALL YOU GAWKERS, GET OUT OF HERE RIGHT NOW. HEAD TO THE BACK.
ALL PASSENGERS, PLEASE MOVE AFT! THE FRONT CABIN WILL BE OFF LIMITS WHILE THE OPERATIONS ARE UNDERWAY.
WE'LL BE ARRIVING IN NO MORE THAN THIRTY MINUTES, THANK YOU.
DOC,
HE'S THE ONLY ONE I FOUND.
NEAT. IT'S HIS FAULT AFTER ALL. HE CAN HELP.
MA'AM, PLEASE KEEP YOUR BABY STILL!
ATTEND TO ME FIRST.
I-I'M DYIN' HERE.
I ONLY HAVE TWO ARMS, AND I GET TO CHOOSE HOW TO USE THEM. DON'T COMPLAIN.
BUT I PAID YOU, BY CHECK! I'M THE ONLY ONE WHO'S PAID SO FAR!
THAT WAS THE DEAL.
SILENCE!

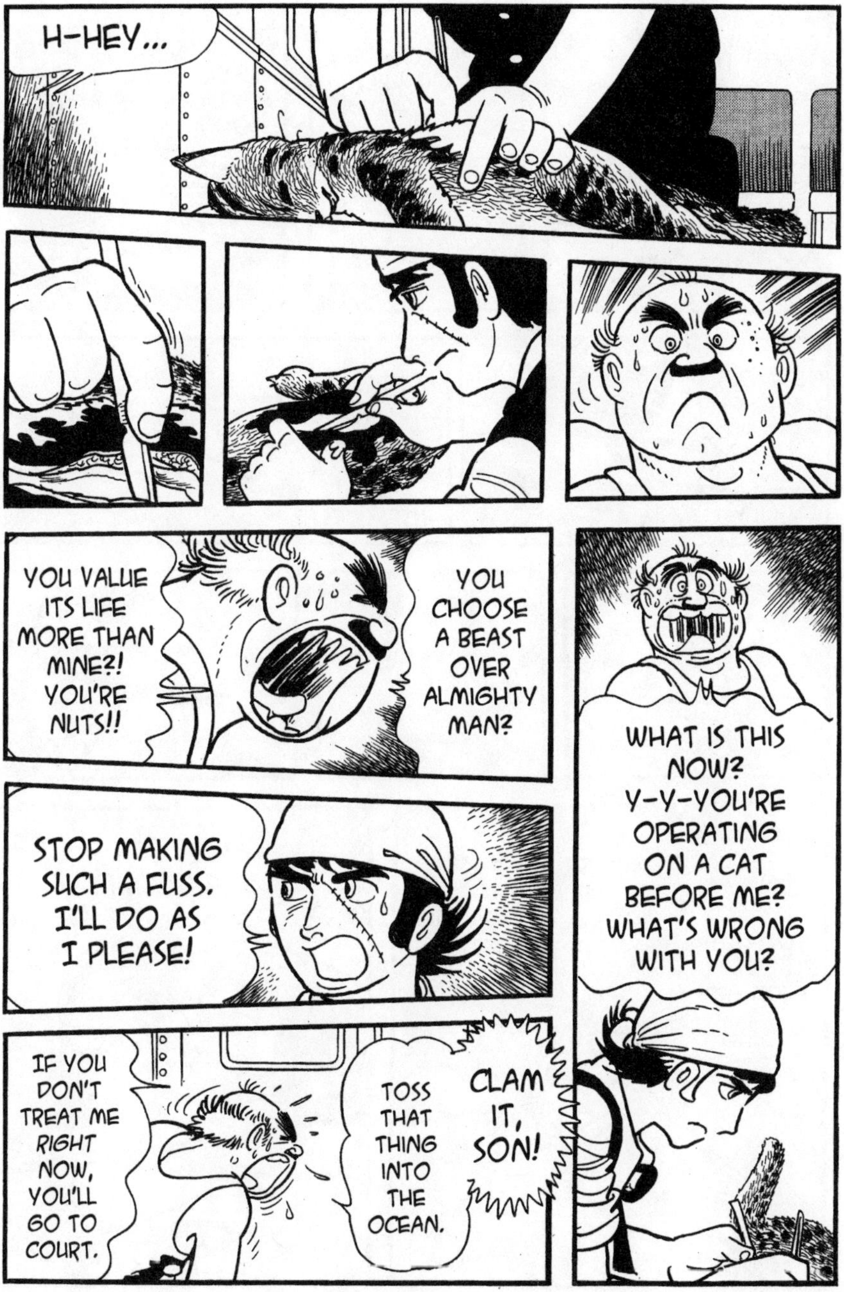
H-HEY...
WHAT IS THIS NOW? Y-Y-YOU'RE OPERATING ON A CAT BEFORE ME? WHAT'S WRONG WITH YOU?
YOU CHOOSE A BEAST OVER ALMIGHTY MAN?
YOU VALUE ITS LIFE MORE THAN MINE?! YOU'RE NUTS!!
STOP MAKING SUCH A FUSS. I'LL DO AS I PLEASE!
CLAM IT, SON!
TOSS THAT THING INTO THE OCEAN.
IF YOU DON'T TREAT ME RIGHT NOW, YOU'LL GO TO COURT.

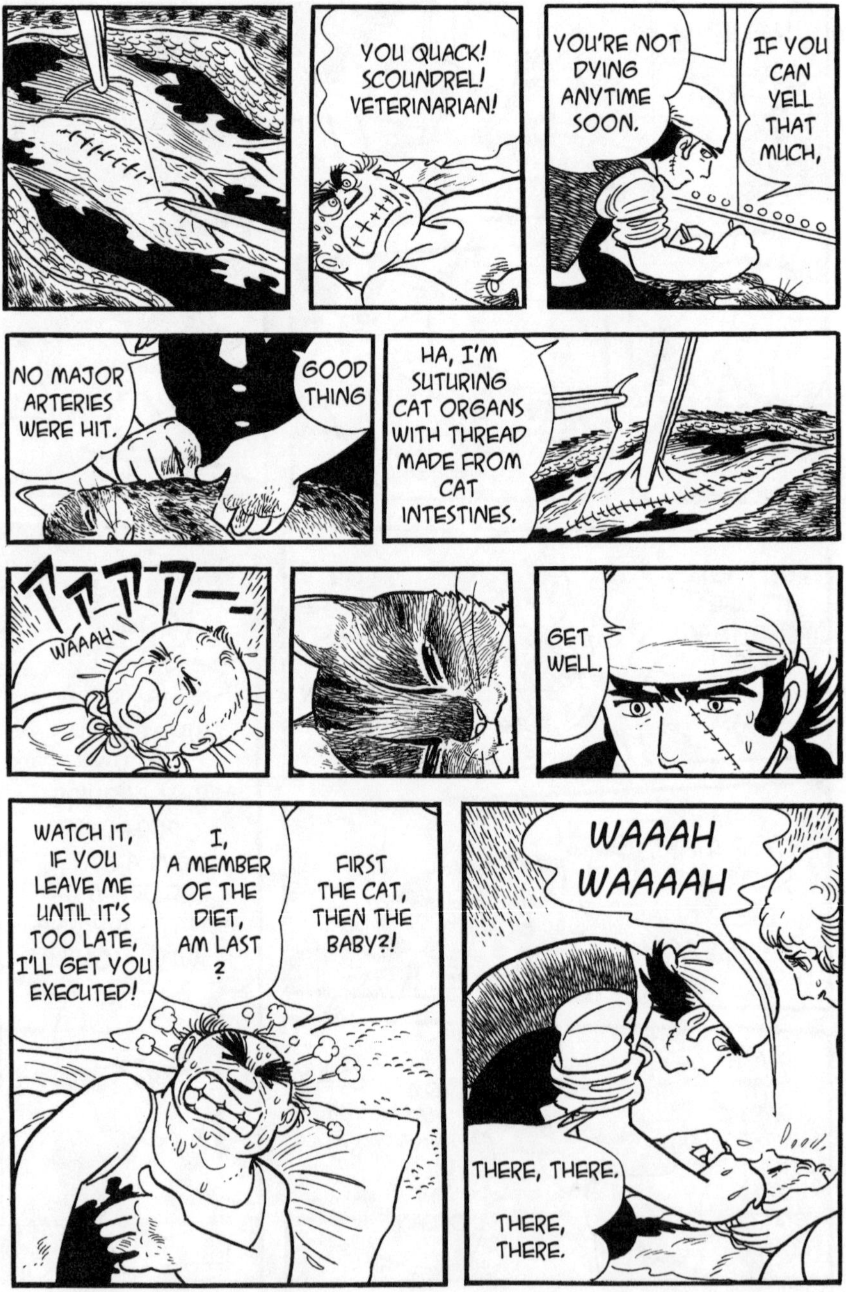
IF YOU CAN YELL THAT MUCH,
YOU'RE NOT DYING ANYTIME SOON.
YOU QUACK! SCOUNDREL! VETERINARIAN!
HA, I'M SUTURING CAT ORGANS WITH THREAD MADE FROM CAT INTESTINES.
GOOD THING
NO MAJOR ARTERIES WERE HIT.
GET WELL.
WAAAH
WAAAH WAAAAH
THERE, THERE.
THERE, THERE.
FIRST THE CAT, THEN THE BABY?!
I, A MEMBER OF THE DIET, AM LAST?
WATCH IT, IF YOU LEAVE ME UNTIL IT'S TOO LATE, I'LL GET YOU EXECUTED!

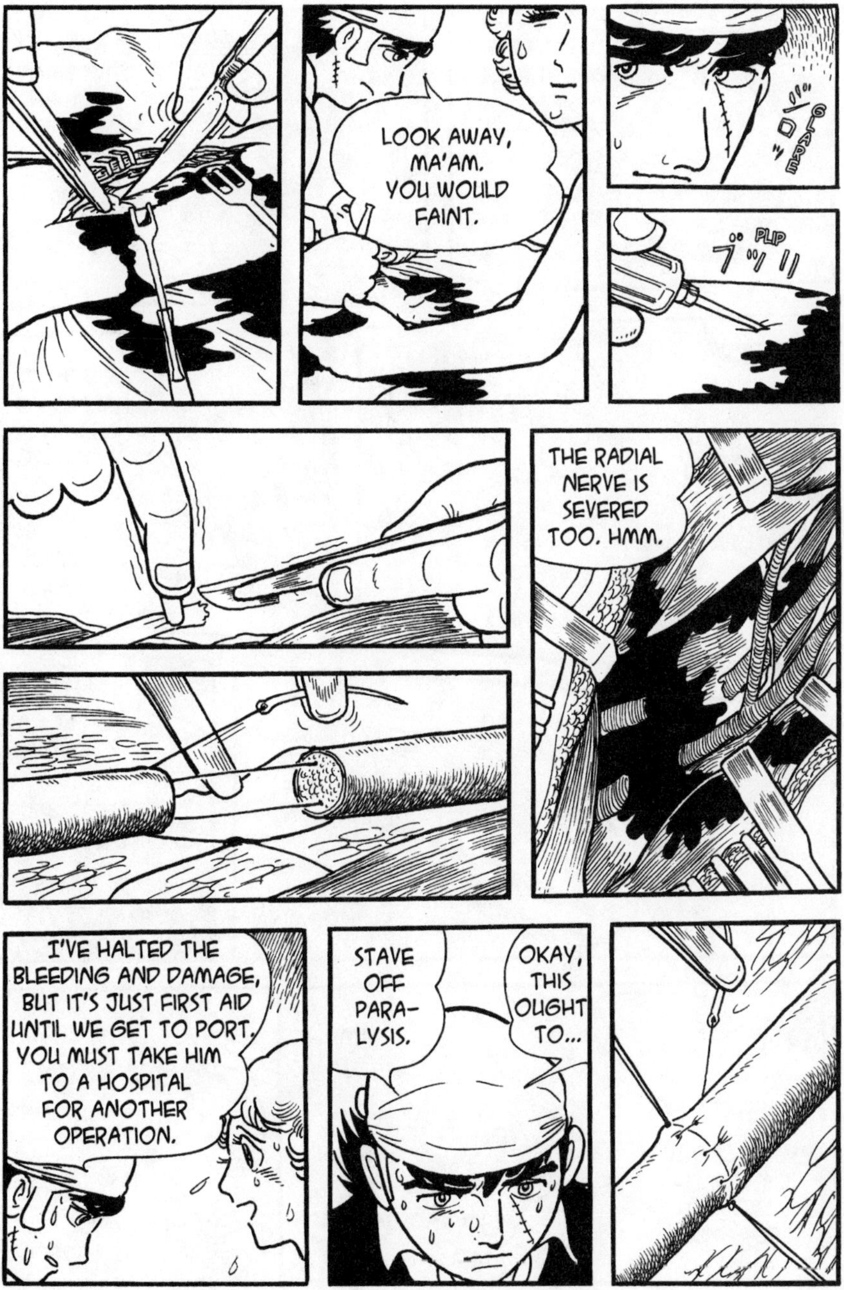
GLARE
PLIP
LOOK AWAY, MA'AM. YOU WOULD FAINT.
THE RADIAL NERVE IS SEVERED TOO. HMM.
OKAY, THIS OUGHT TO...
STAVE OFF PARA-LYSIS.
I'VE HALTED THE BLEEDING AND DAMAGE, BUT IT'S JUST FIRST AID UNTIL WE GET TO PORT. YOU MUST TAKE HIM TO A HOSPITAL FOR ANOTHER OPERATION.

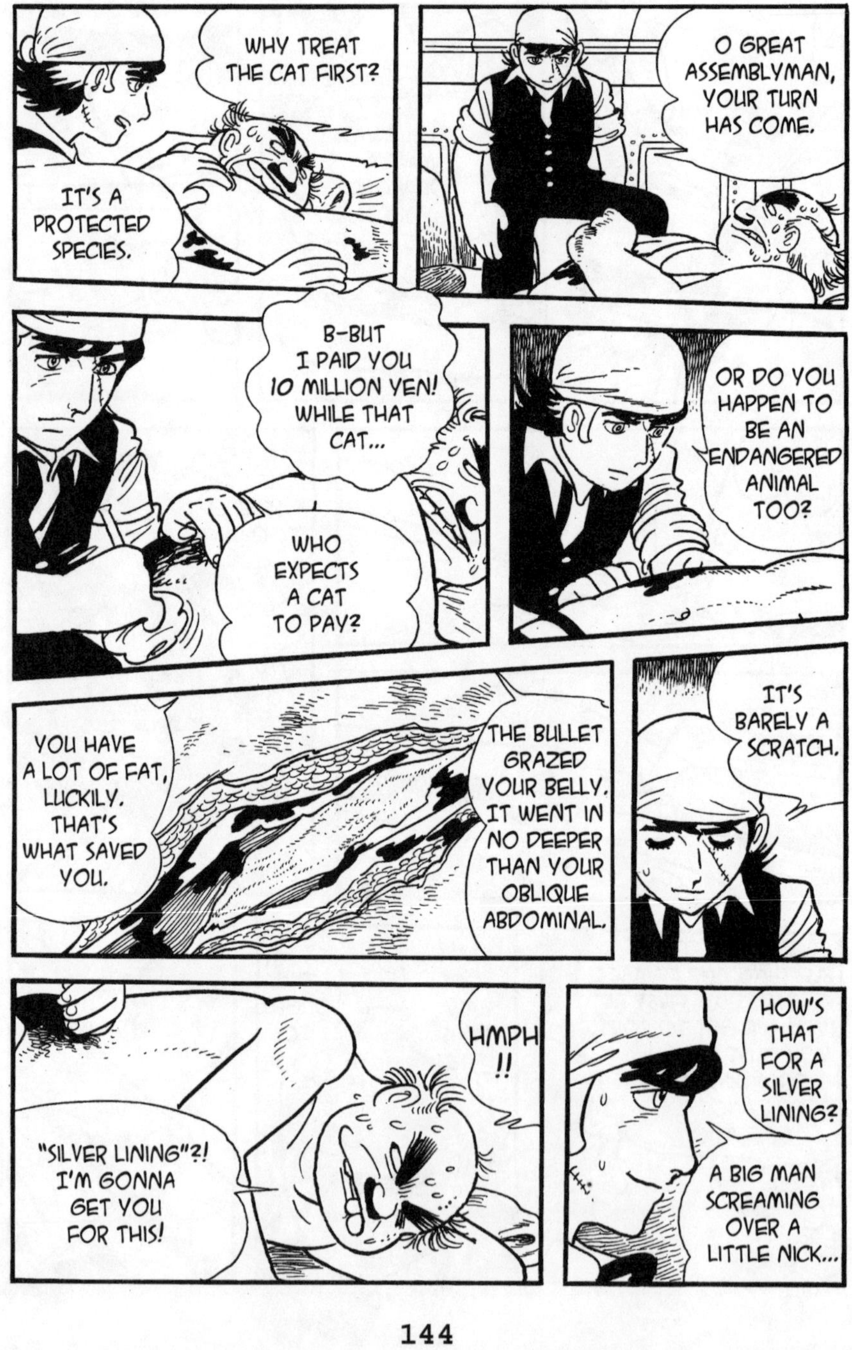
O GREAT ASSEMBLYMAN, YOUR TURN HAS COME.
WHY TREAT THE CAT FIRST?
IT'S A PROTECTED SPECIES.
OR DO YOU HAPPEN TO BE AN ENDANGERED ANIMAL TOO?
B-BUT I PAID YOU 10 MILLION YEN! WHILE THAT CAT...
WHO EXPECTS A CAT TO PAY?
IT'S BARELY A SCRATCH.
THE BULLET GRAZED YOUR BELLY. IT WENT IN NO DEEPER THAN YOUR OBLIQUE ABDOMINAL.
YOU HAVE A LOT OF FAT, LUCKILY. THAT'S WHAT SAVED YOU.
HOW'S THAT FOR A SILVER LINING?
A BIG MAN SCREAMING OVER A LITTLE NICK...
HMPH !!
"SILVER LINING"?! I'M GONNA GET YOU FOR THIS!

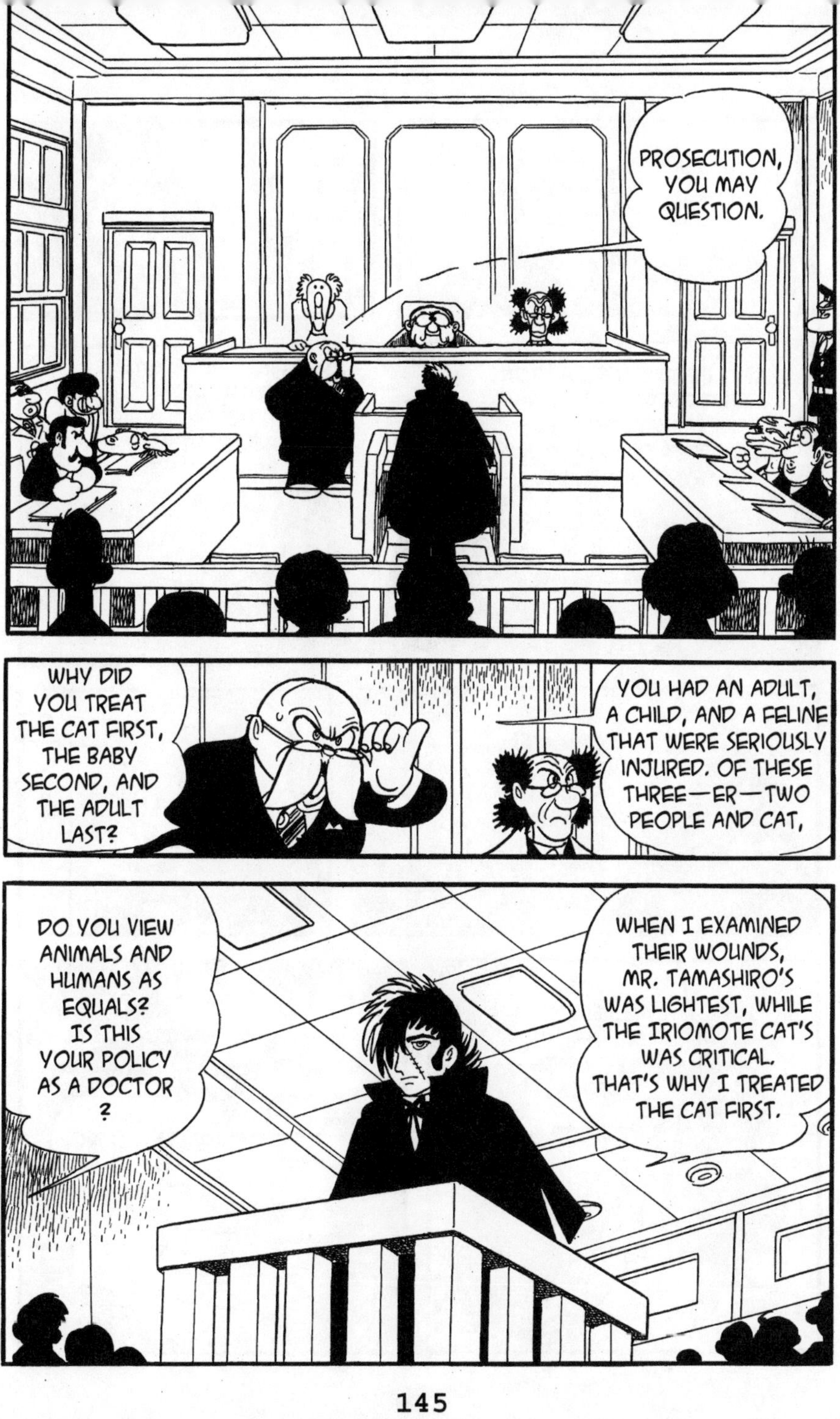
PROSECUTION, YOU MAY QUESTION.
YOU HAD AN ADULT, A CHILD, AND A FELINE THAT WERE SERIOUSLY INJURED. OF THESE THREE—ER—TWO PEOPLE AND CAT,
WHY DID YOU TREAT THE CAT FIRST, THE BABY SECOND, AND THE ADULT LAST?
WHEN I EXAMINED THEIR WOUNDS, MR. TAMASHIRO'S WAS LIGHTEST, WHILE THE IRIOMOTE CAT'S WAS CRITICAL. THAT'S WHY I TREATED THE CAT FIRST.
DO YOU VIEW ANIMALS AND HUMANS AS EQUALS? IS THIS YOUR POLICY AS A DOCTOR?

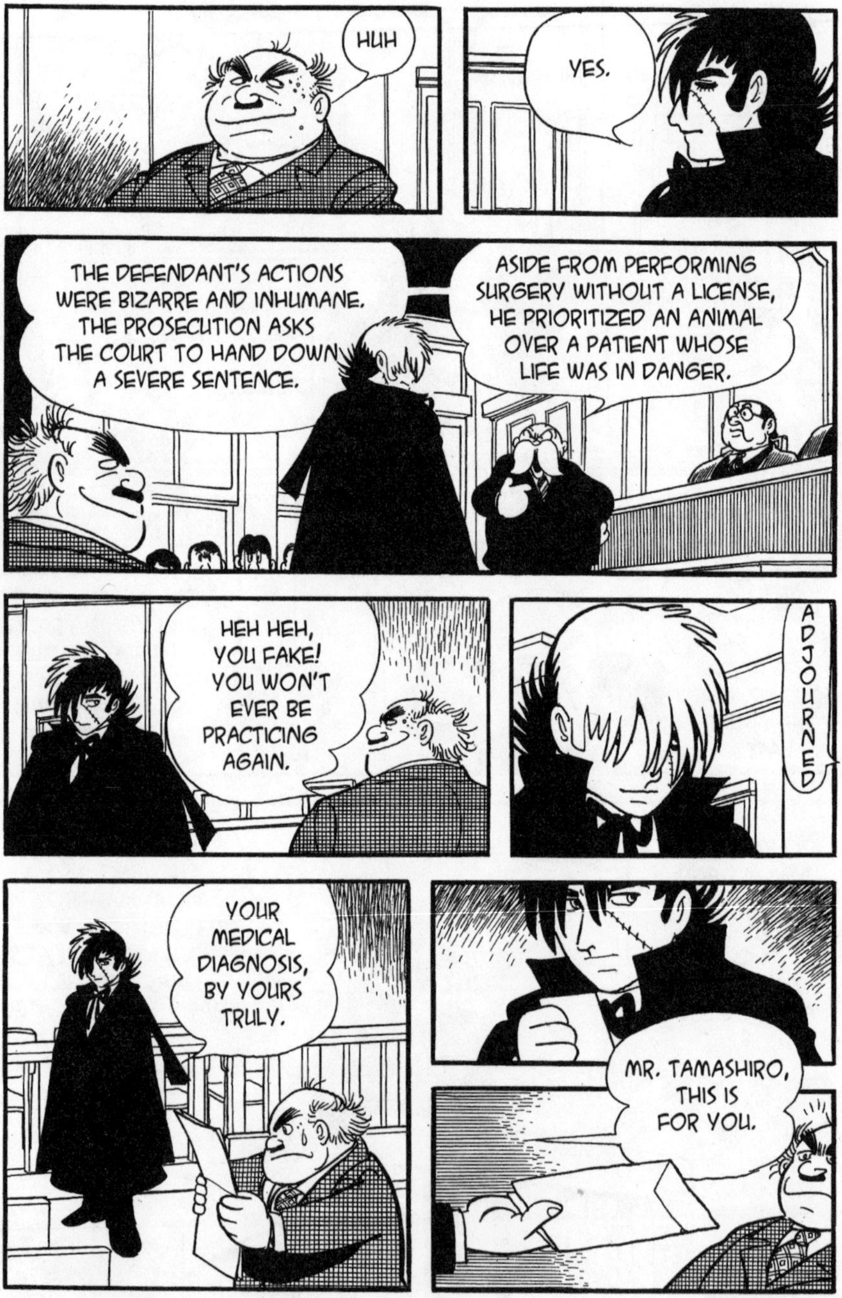
YES.
HUH
ASIDE FROM PERFORMING SURGERY WITHOUT A LICENSE, HE PRIORITIZED AN ANIMAL OVER A PATIENT WHOSE LIFE WAS IN DANGER.
THE DEFENDANT'S ACTIONS WERE BIZARRE AND INHUMANE. THE PROSECUTION ASKS THE COURT TO HAND DOWN A SEVERE SENTENCE.
ADJOURNED
HEH HEH, YOU FAKE! YOU WON'T EVER BE PRACTICING AGAIN.
MR. TAMASHIRO, THIS IS FOR YOU.
YOUR MEDICAL DIAGNOSIS, BY YOURS TRULY.

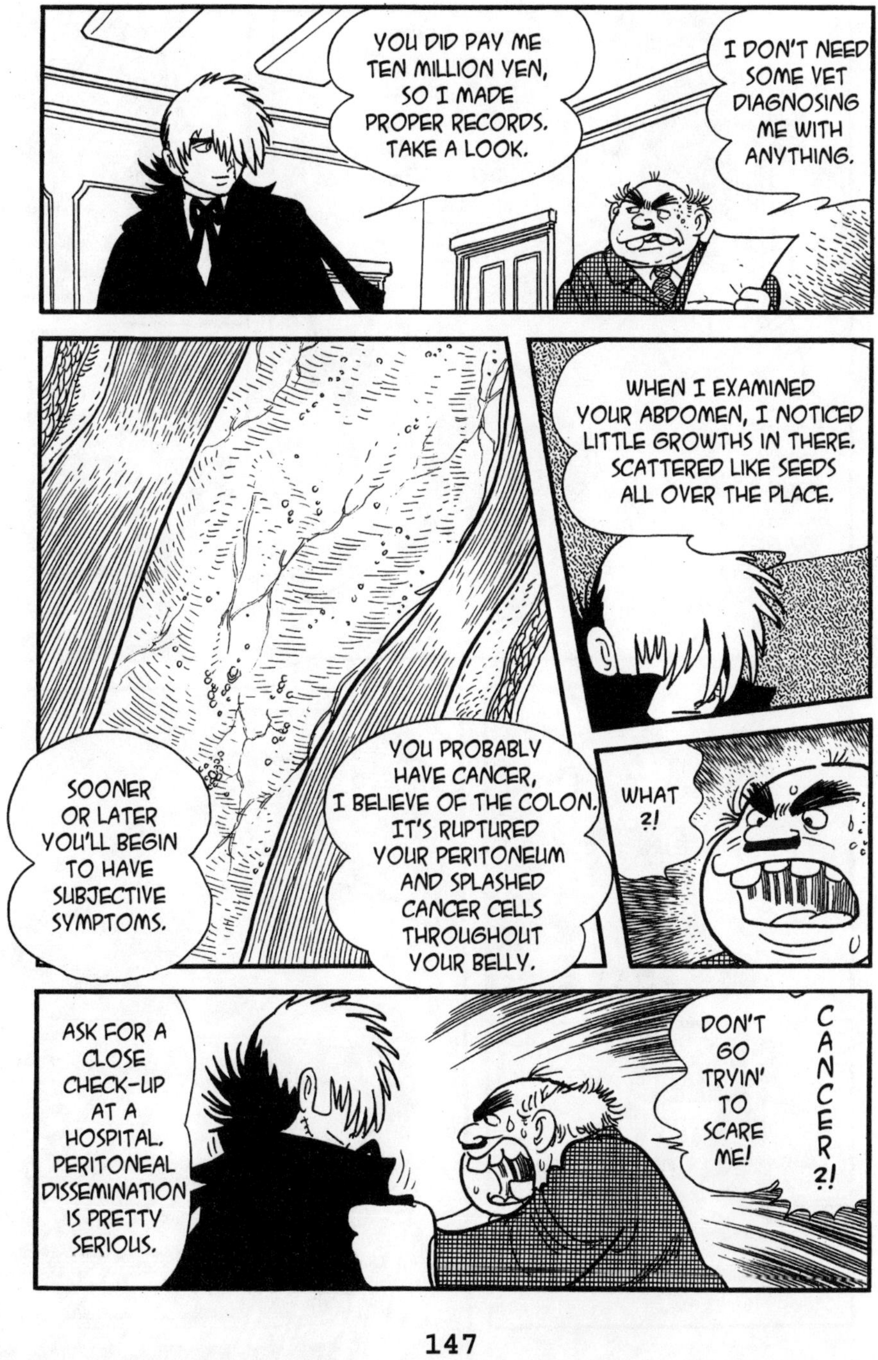
I DON'T NEED SOME VET DIAGNOSING ME WITH ANYTHING.
YOU DID PAY ME TEN MILLION YEN, SO I MADE PROPER RECORDS. TAKE A LOOK.
WHEN I EXAMINED YOUR ABDOMEN, I NOTICED LITTLE GROWTHS IN THERE. SCATTERED LIKE SEEDS ALL OVER THE PLACE.
WHAT?!
YOU PROBABLY HAVE CANCER, I BELIEVE OF THE COLON. IT'S RUPTURED YOUR PERITONEUM AND SPLASHED CANCER CELLS THROUGHOUT YOUR BELLY.
SOONER OR LATER YOU'LL BEGIN TO HAVE SUBJECTIVE SYMPTOMS.
CANCER?!
DON'T GO TRYIN' TO SCARE ME!
ASK FOR A CLOSE CHECK-UP AT A HOSPITAL. PERITONEAL DISSEMINATION IS PRETTY SERIOUS.

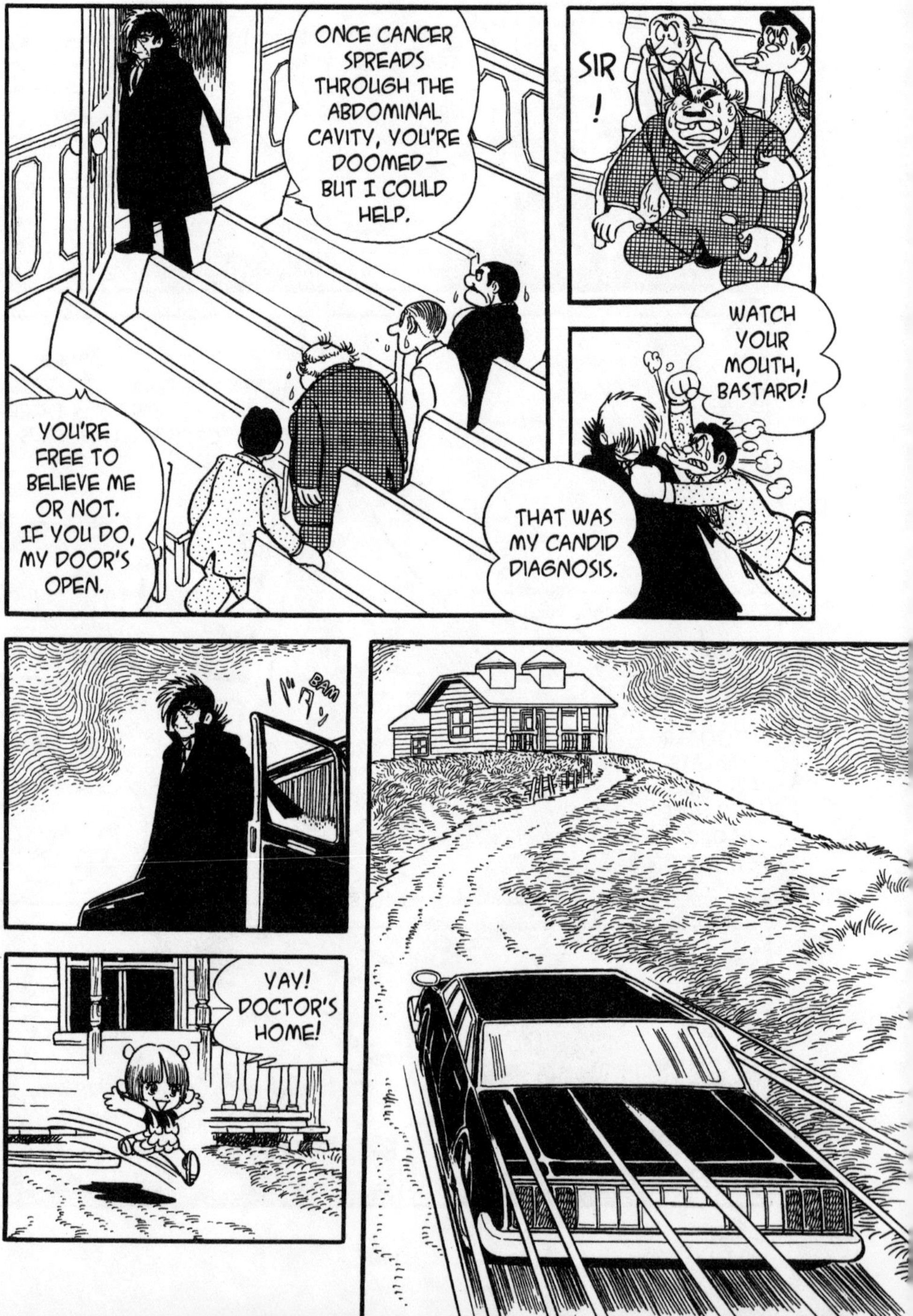
SIR!
WATCH YOUR MOUTH, BASTARD!
THAT WAS MY CANDID DIAGNOSIS.
ONCE CANCER SPREADS THROUGH THE ABDOMINAL CAVITY, YOU'RE DOOMED— BUT I COULD HELP.
YOU'RE FREE TO BELIEVE ME OR NOT. IF YOU DO, MY DOOR'S OPEN.
バタン
BAM
YAY! DOCTOR'S HOME!

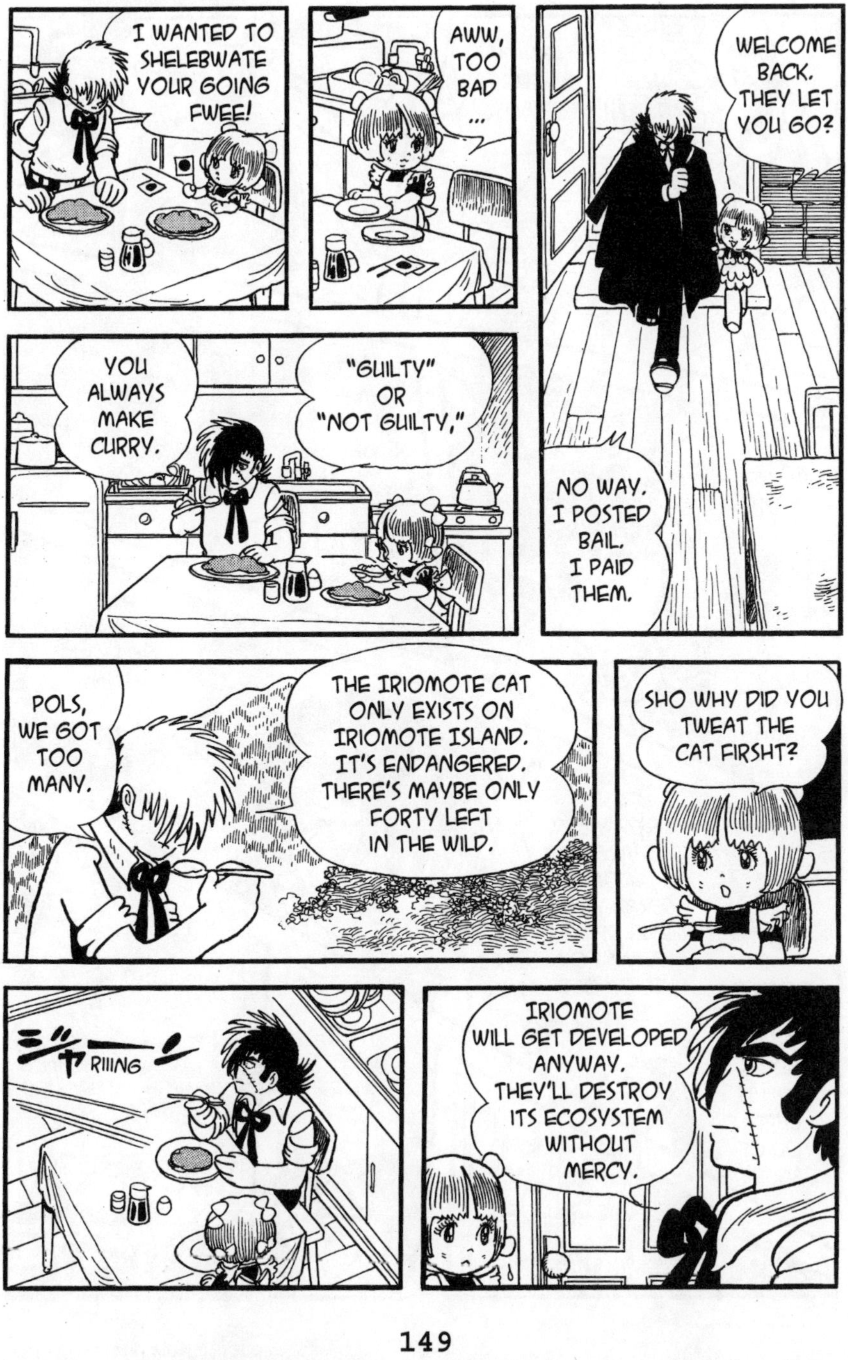
WELCOME BACK. THEY LET YOU GO?
NO WAY. I POSTED BAIL. I PAID THEM.
AWW, TOO BAD ...
I WANTED TO SHELEBWATE YOUR GOING FWEE!
"GUILTY" OR "NOT GUILTY,"
YOU ALWAYS MAKE CURRY.
SHO WHY DID YOU TWEAT THE CAT FIRSHT?
THE IRIOMOTE CAT ONLY EXISTS ON IRIOMOTE ISLAND. IT'S ENDANGERED. THERE'S MAYBE ONLY FORTY LEFT IN THE WILD.
POLS, WE GOT TOO MANY.
IRIOMOTE WILL GET DEVELOPED ANYWAY. THEY'LL DESTROY ITS ECOSYSTEM WITHOUT MERCY.
ジャーン
RIIING

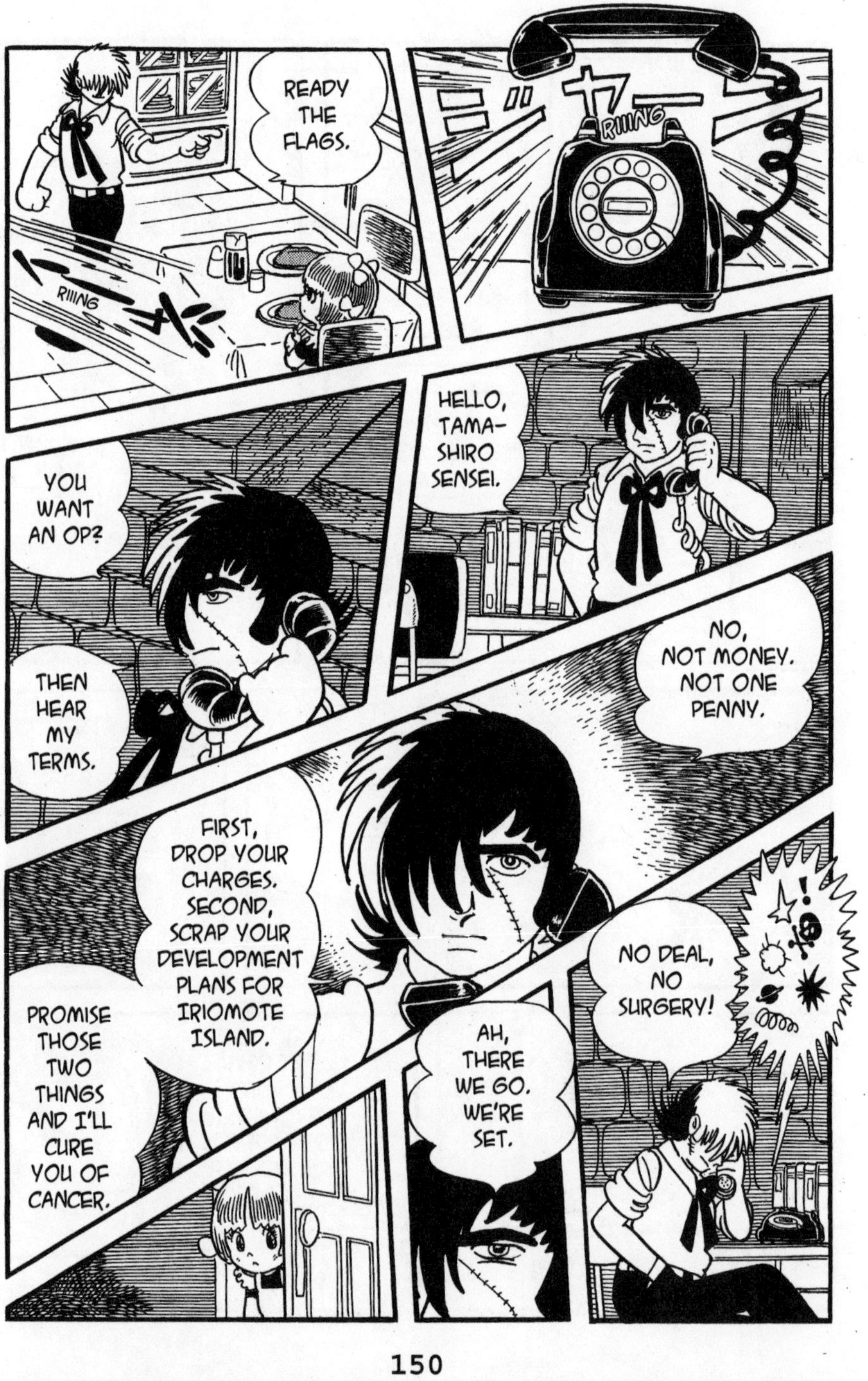
RIIING
READY THE FLAGS.
RIIING
HELLO, TAMA-SHIRO SENSEI.
YOU WANT AN OP?
THEN HEAR MY TERMS.
NO, NOT MONEY. NOT ONE PENNY.
FIRST, DROP YOUR CHARGES. SECOND, SCRAP YOUR DEVELOPMENT PLANS FOR IRIOMOTE ISLAND.
PROMISE THOSE TWO THINGS AND I'LL CURE YOU OF CANCER.
NO DEAL, NO SURGERY!
AH, THERE WE GO. WE'RE SET.

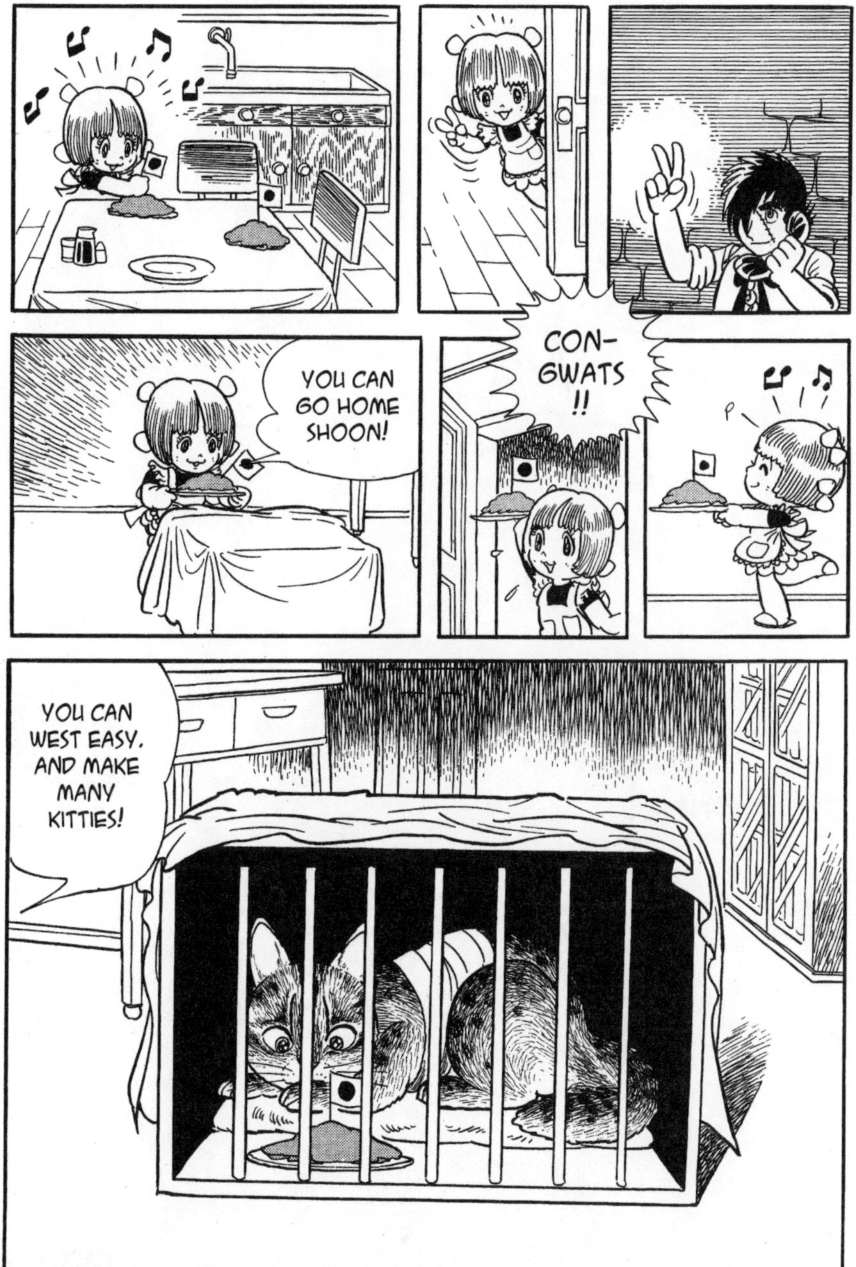
CON-GWATS !!
YOU CAN GO HOME SHOON!
YOU CAN WEST EASY. AND MAKE MANY KITTIES!

YOU DID IT!!

DROP THE BAG. THERE'S MONEY IN IT, YEAH?

SPLIIT

WHAT? IT'S OUR EMPLOYEES' PAY...

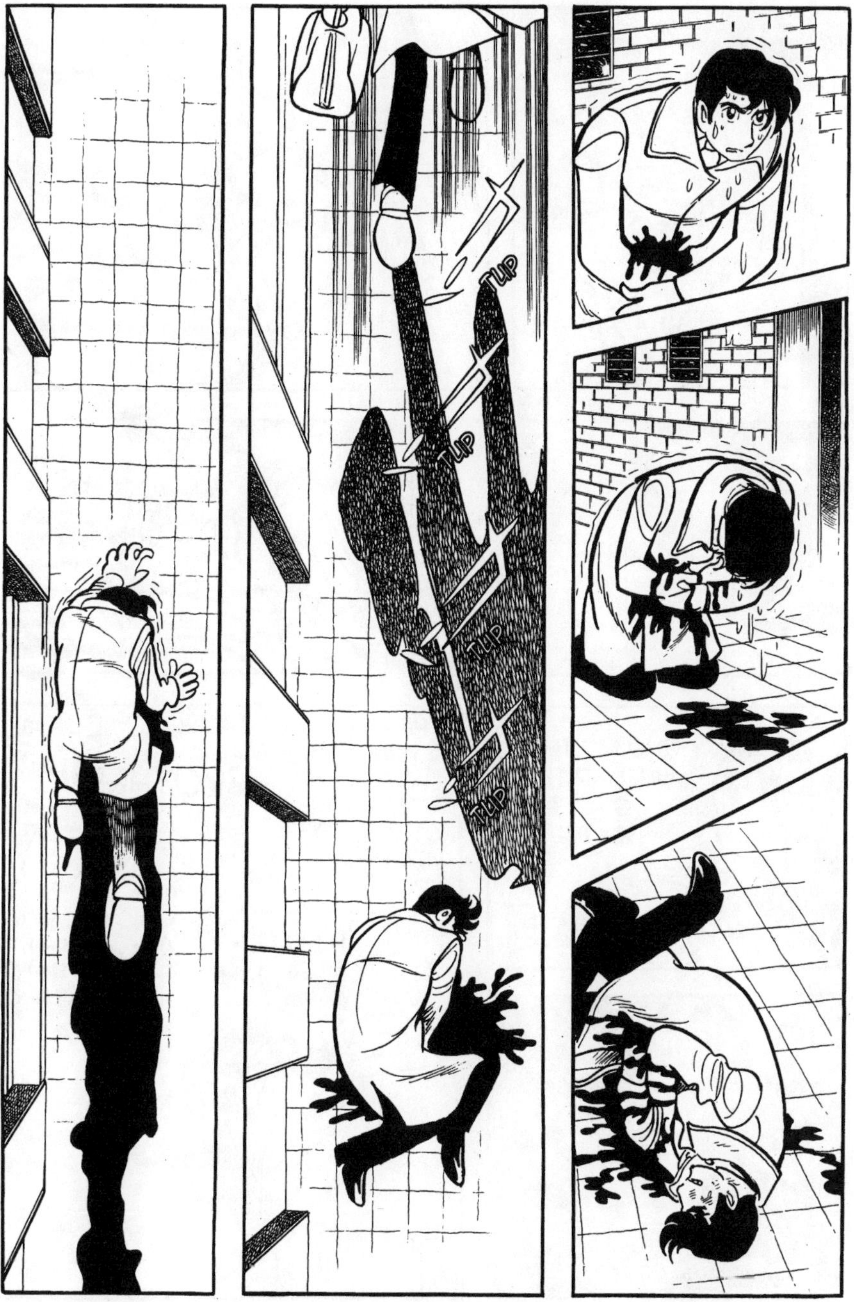
TUP
TUP
TUP
TUP

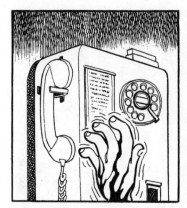

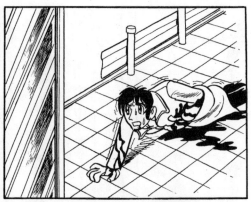

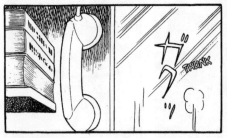

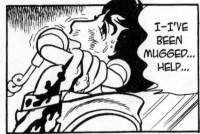

I-I'VE BEEN MUGGED... HELP...
THUNK
HE'S BEYOND HELP. THERE'S NOTHING WE CAN DO.
BROTHER!!
WHO DID THIS? WHO DID THIS TO HIM? TELL ME!
"SOB"
"SOB"

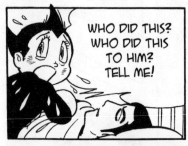

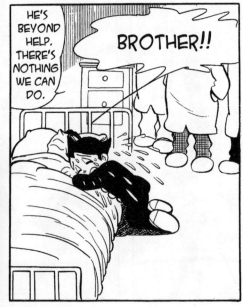

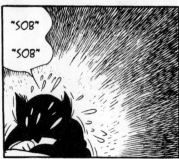

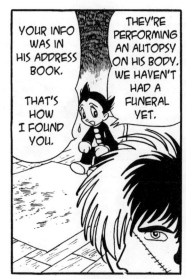

THEY'RE PERFORMING AN AUTOPSY ON HIS BODY. WE HAVEN'T HAD A FUNERAL YET.
YOUR INFO WAS IN HIS ADDRESS BOOK.
THAT'S HOW I FOUND YOU.
HOW CAN I HELP YOU?
DOCTOR, I WANT TO AVENGE MY BROTHER!
AVENGE? HOW DO YOU MEAN?
I'LL FIND THE PERP. HE ATTACKED MY BROTHER AS HE CAME OUT OF THE BANK.
I'LL GO TO THAT BANK WITH A BAG EVERY DAY UNTIL HE COMES TO ATTACK ME.

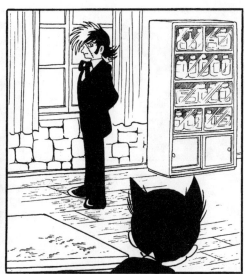

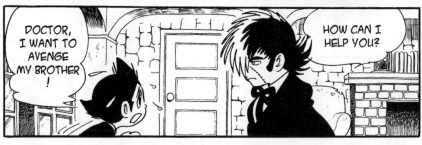

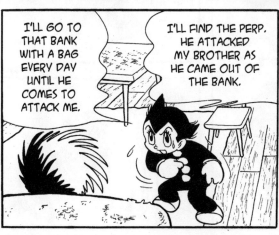

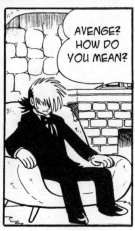

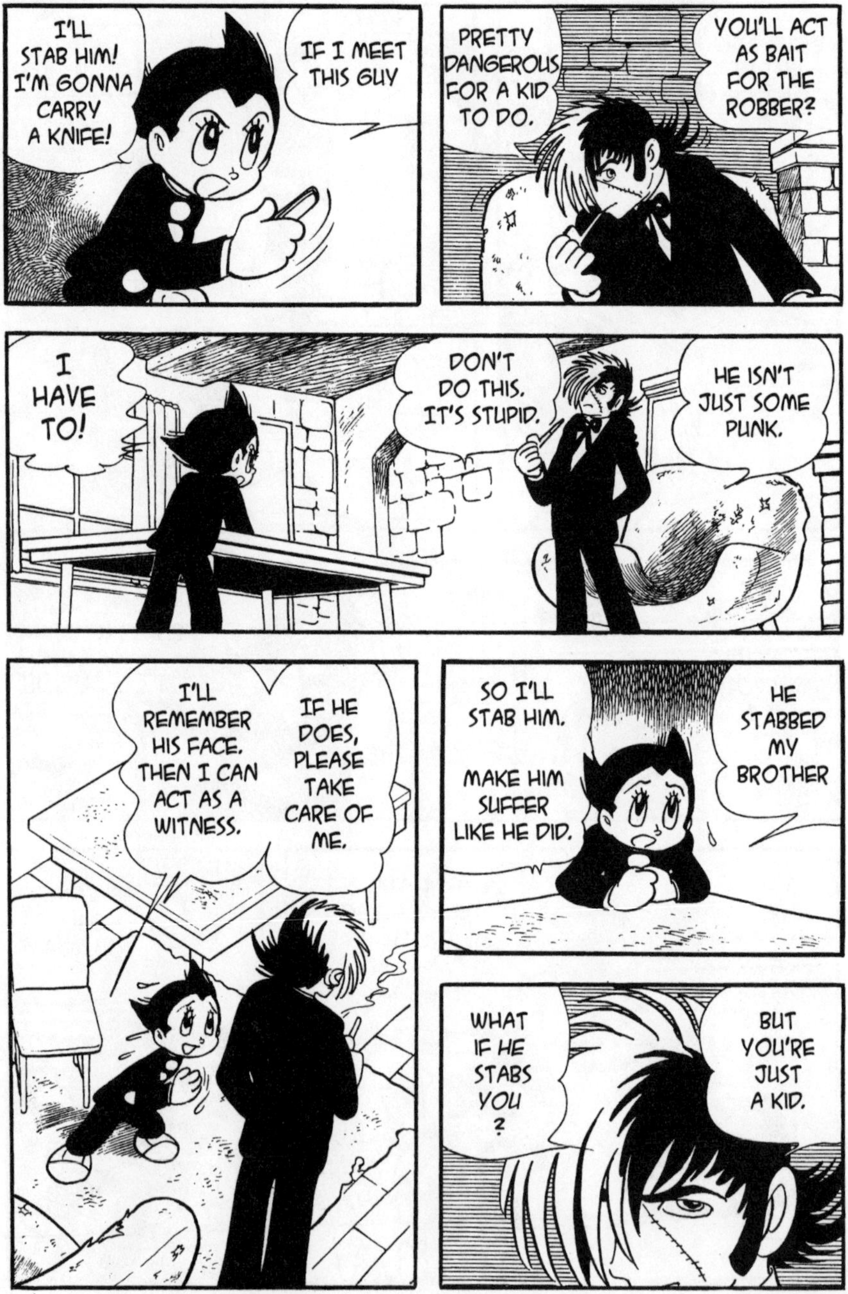
YOU'LL ACT AS BAIT FOR THE ROBBER?
PRETTY DANGEROUS FOR A KID TO DO.
IF I MEET THIS GUY
I'LL STAB HIM! I'M GONNA CARRY A KNIFE!
HE ISN'T JUST SOME PUNK.
DON'T DO THIS. IT'S STUPID.
I HAVE TO!
HE STABBED MY BROTHER
SO I'LL STAB HIM.
MAKE HIM SUFFER LIKE HE DID.
BUT YOU'RE JUST A KID.
WHAT IF HE STABS YOU ?
IF HE DOES, PLEASE TAKE CARE OF ME.
I'LL REMEMBER HIS FACE. THEN I CAN ACT AS A WITNESS.

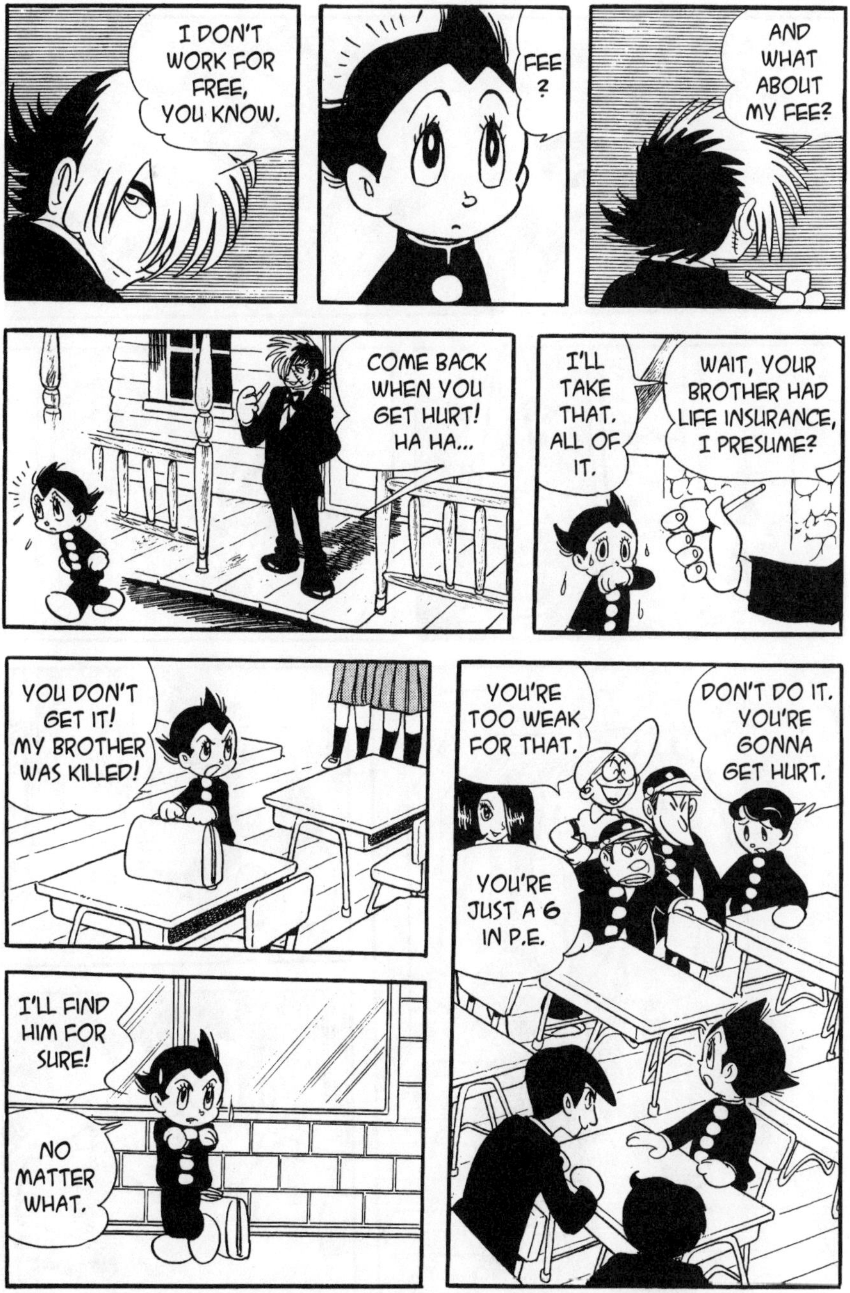
AND WHAT ABOUT MY FEE?
FEE ?
I DON'T WORK FOR FREE, YOU KNOW.
WAIT, YOUR BROTHER HAD LIFE INSURANCE, I PRESUME?
I'LL TAKE THAT. ALL OF IT.
COME BACK WHEN YOU GET HURT! HA HA...
DON'T DO IT. YOU'RE GONNA GET HURT.
YOU'RE TOO WEAK FOR THAT.
YOU'RE JUST A 6 IN P.E.
YOU DON'T GET IT! MY BROTHER WAS KILLED!
I'LL FIND HIM FOR SURE!
NO MATTER WHAT.

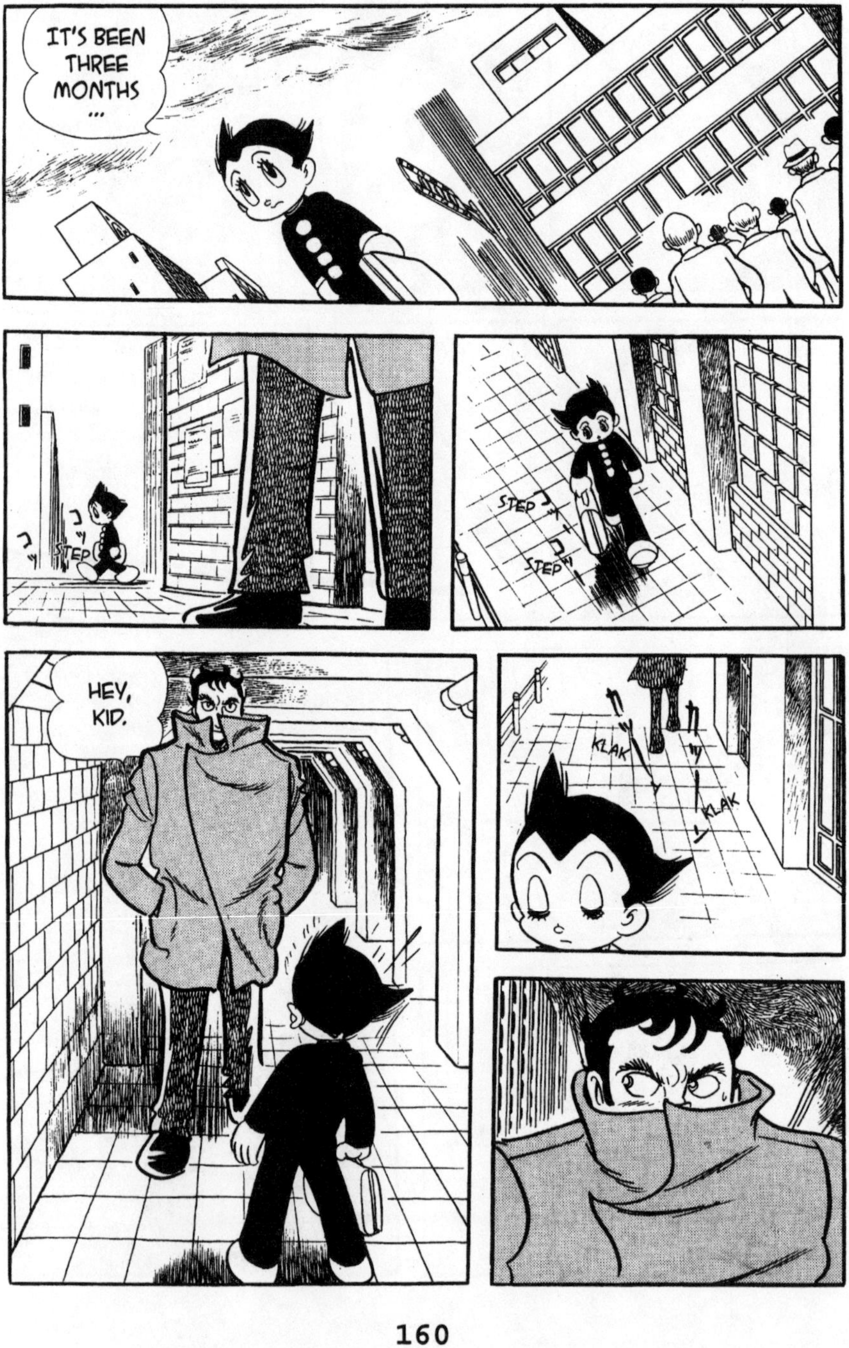

IT'S BEEN THREE MONTHS ...
STEP コッ
STEP コッ
コッ
STEP
コッ
カッ
KLAK
カッ
KLAK
HEY, KID.

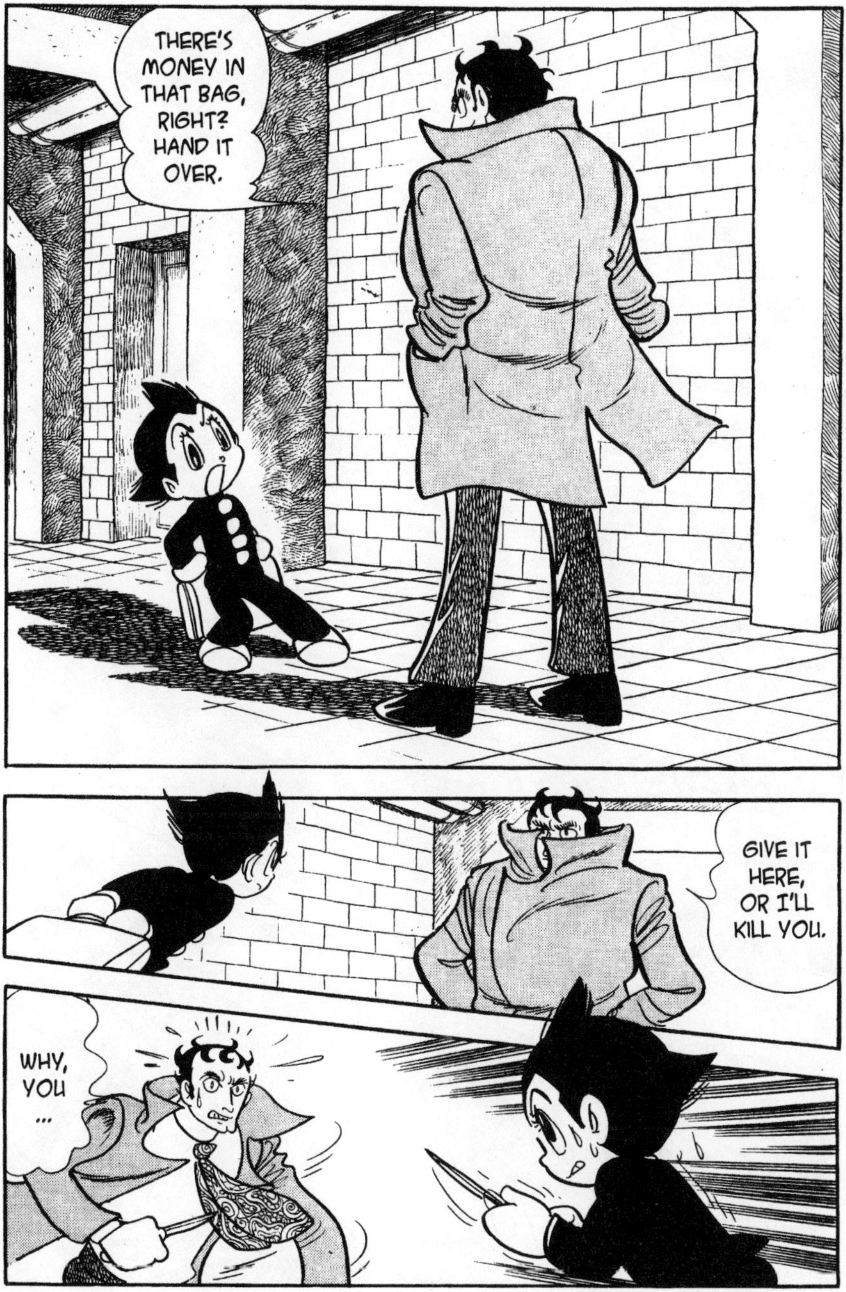
THERE'S MONEY IN THAT BAG, RIGHT? HAND IT OVER.
GIVE IT HERE, OR I'LL KILL YOU.
WHY, YOU ...

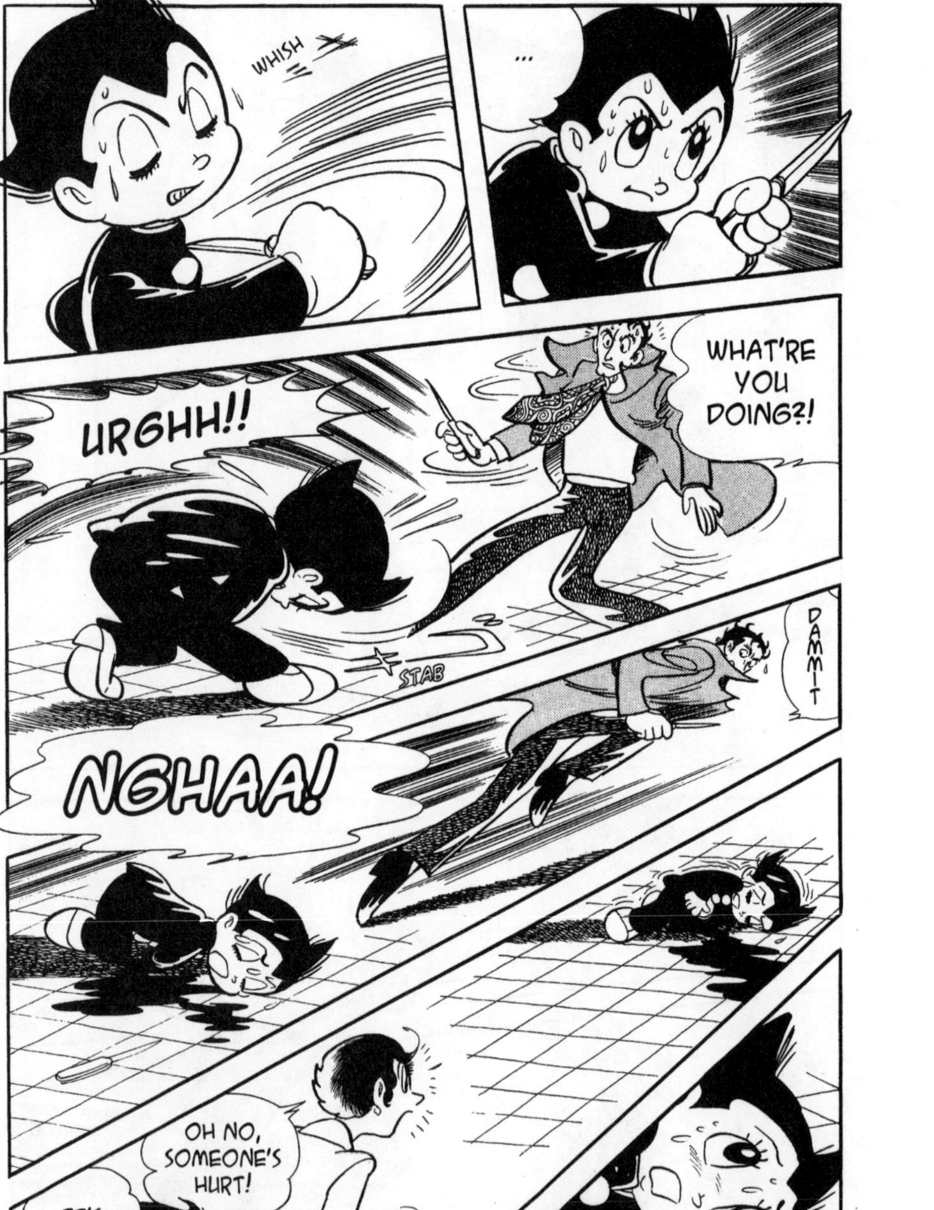
...
WHISH
WHAT'RE YOU DOING?!
URGHH!!
STAB
DAMMIT
NGHAA!
OH NO, SOMEONE'S HURT!
IT'S A CHILD!

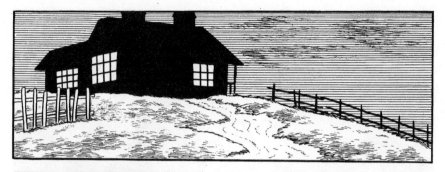

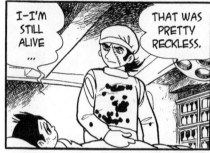

THAT WAS PRETTY RECKLESS.
I-I'M STILL ALIVE ...
WHY DID YOU STAB YOUR-SELF?
WHAT ?!
HE STABBED ME.
I CAN TELL BY LOOKING AT THE WOUND. YOU DID IT.
SUBCON-SCIOUSLY YOU MADE A SMALL, SAFE WOUND.
SO? WHY'D YOU DO IT ?
YOU WON'T TELL ANYONE? PROMISE ME!
AS SOON AS I SAW HIM, I THOUGHT "HE'D KILL ME!"
SO I DID IT FIRST. BUT I'LL SAY HE STABBED ME!

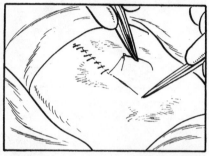

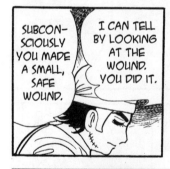

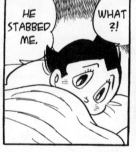

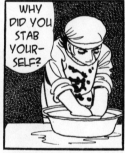

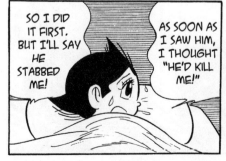

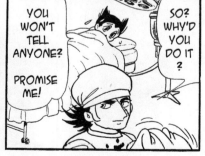

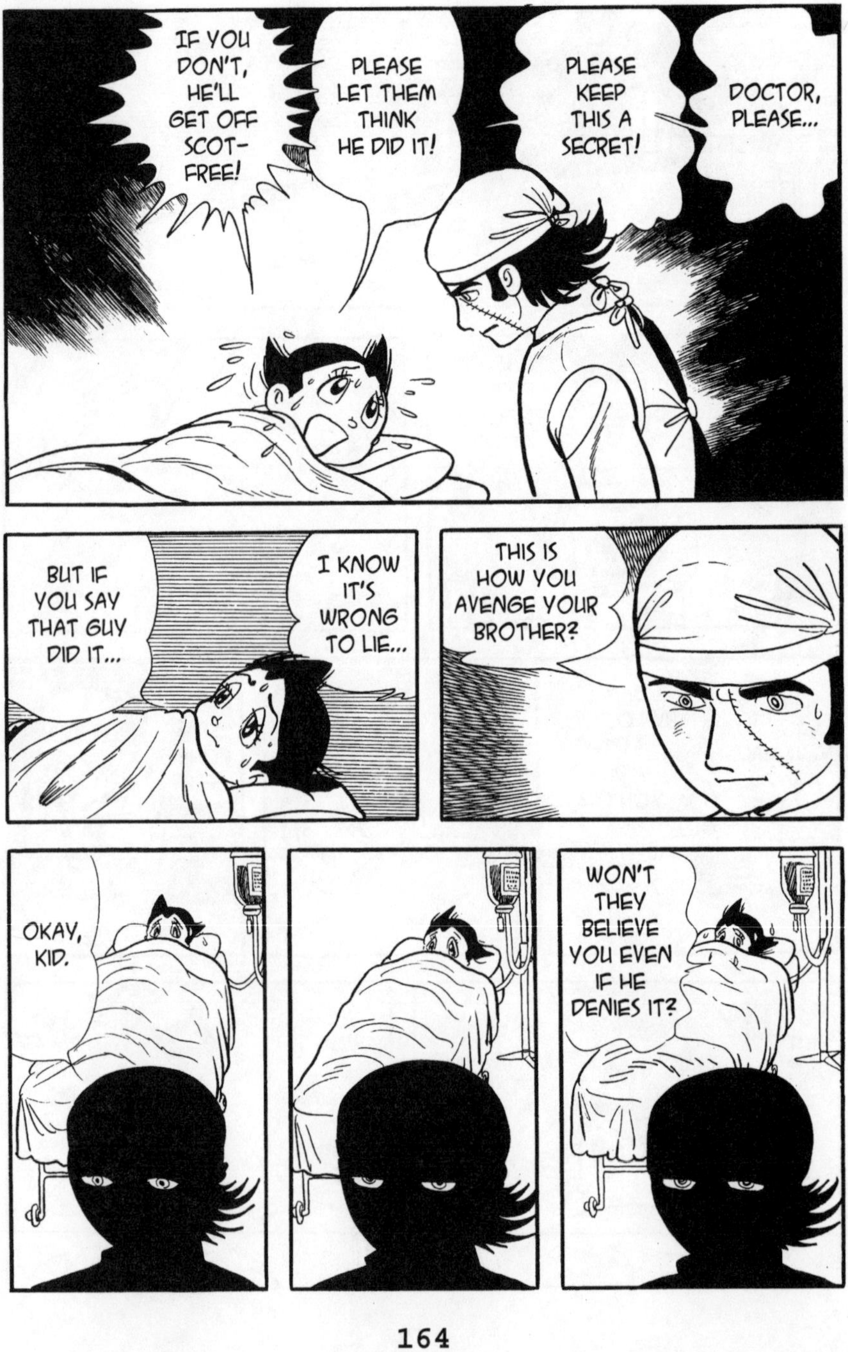
DOCTOR, PLEASE...
PLEASE KEEP THIS A SECRET!
PLEASE LET THEM THINK HE DID IT!
IF YOU DON'T, HE'LL GET OFF SCOT-FREE!
THIS IS HOW YOU AVENGE YOUR BROTHER?
I KNOW IT'S WRONG TO LIE...
BUT IF YOU SAY THAT GUY DID IT...
WON'T THEY BELIEVE YOU EVEN IF HE DENIES IT?
OKAY, KID.

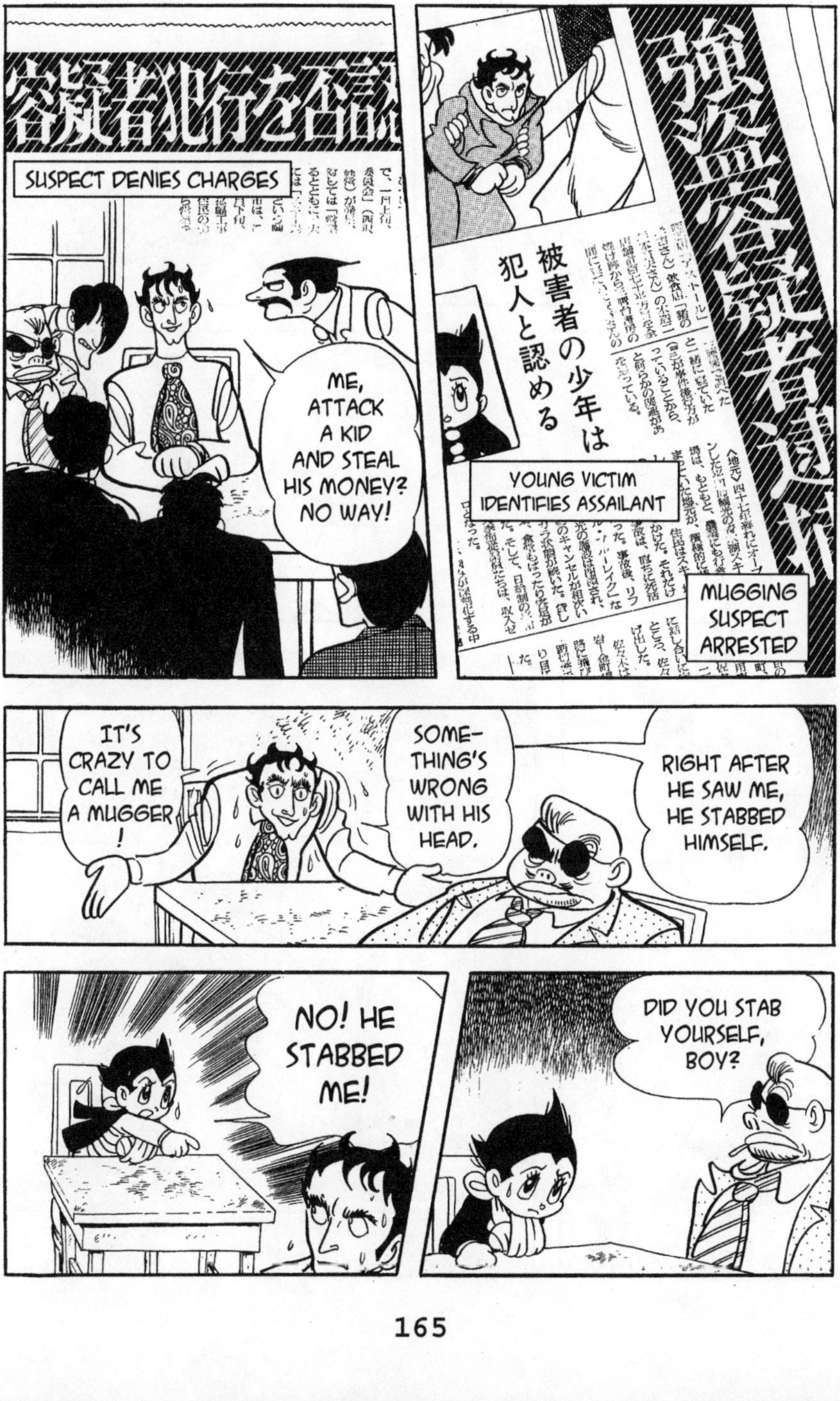
強盗容疑者逮
被害者の少年は犯人と認める
YOUNG VICTIM IDENTIFIES ASSAILANT
MUGGING SUSPECT ARRESTED
容疑者犯行を否認
SUSPECT DENIES CHARGES
ME, ATTACK A KID AND STEAL HIS MONEY? NO WAY!
RIGHT AFTER HE SAW ME, HE STABBED HIMSELF.
SOME-THING'S WRONG WITH HIS HEAD.
IT'S CRAZY TO CALL ME A MUGGER!
DID YOU STAB YOURSELF, BOY?
NO! HE STABBED ME!

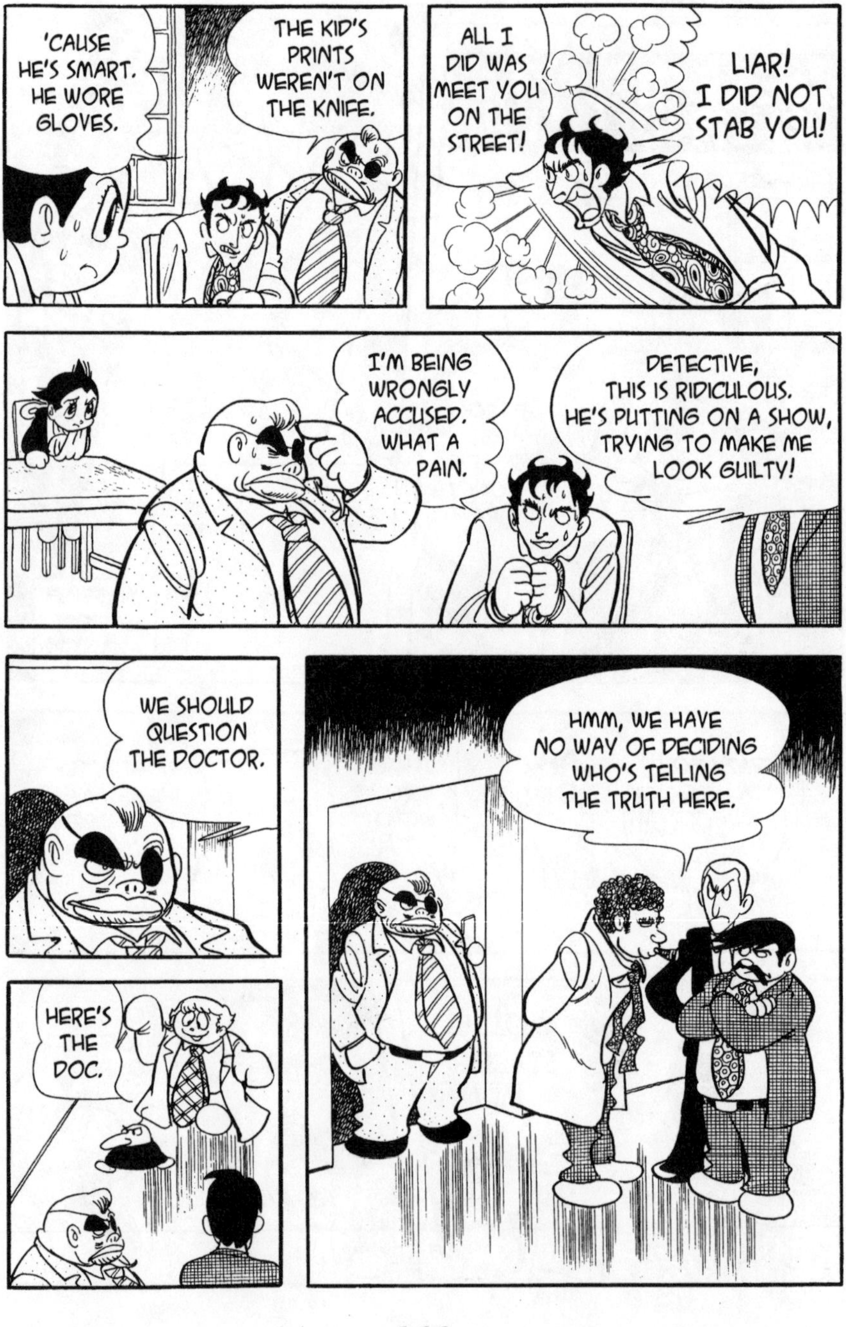
LIAR! I DID NOT STAB YOU!
ALL I DID WAS MEET YOU ON THE STREET!
THE KID'S PRINTS WEREN'T ON THE KNIFE.
'CAUSE HE'S SMART. HE WORE GLOVES.
DETECTIVE, THIS IS RIDICULOUS. HE'S PUTTING ON A SHOW, TRYING TO MAKE ME LOOK GUILTY!
I'M BEING WRONGLY ACCUSED. WHAT A PAIN.
HMM, WE HAVE NO WAY OF DECIDING WHO'S TELLING THE TRUTH HERE.
WE SHOULD QUESTION THE DOCTOR.
HERE'S THE DOC.

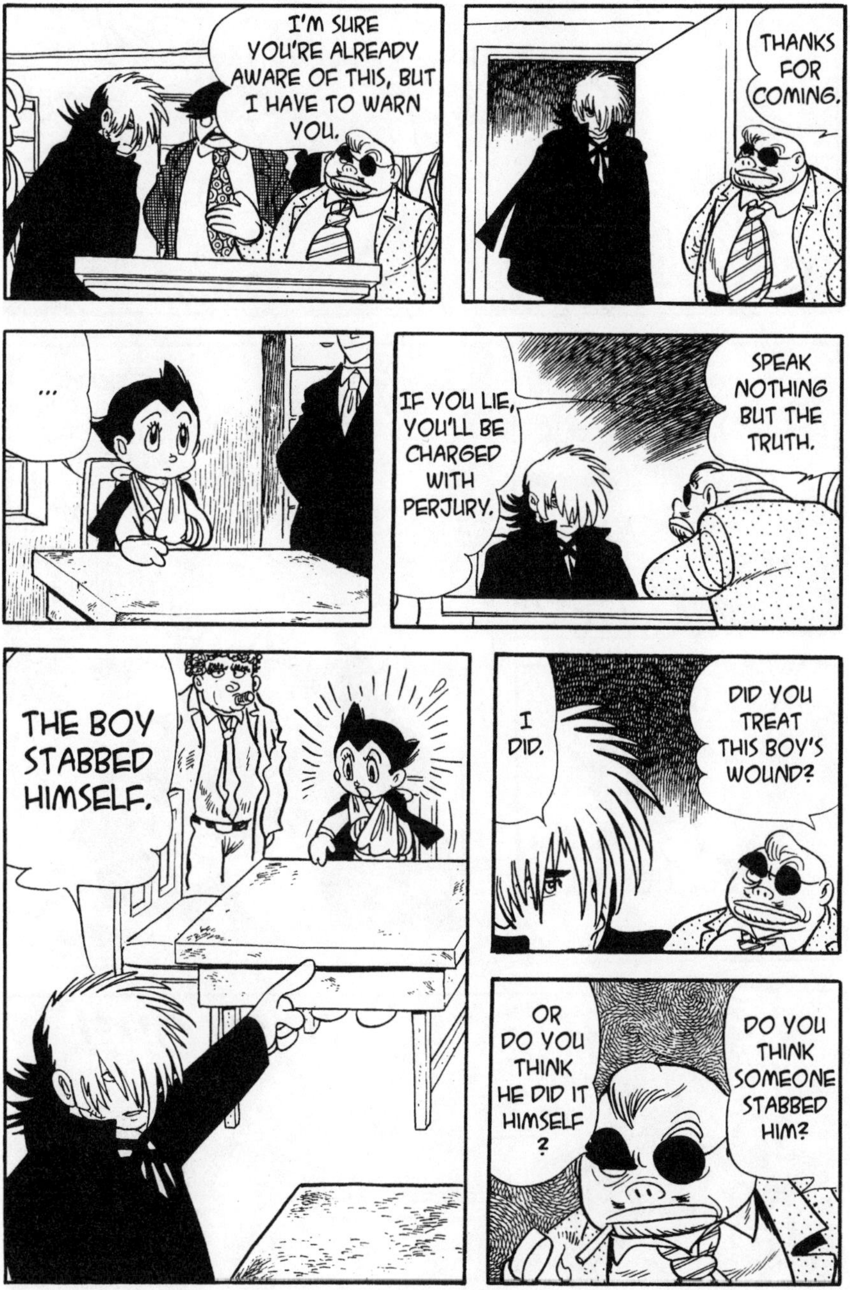
THANKS FOR COMING.
I'M SURE YOU'RE ALREADY AWARE OF THIS, BUT I HAVE TO WARN YOU.
SPEAK NOTHING BUT THE TRUTH.
IF YOU LIE, YOU'LL BE CHARGED WITH PERJURY.
...
DID YOU TREAT THIS BOY'S WOUND?
I DID.
DO YOU THINK SOMEONE STABBED HIM?
OR DO YOU THINK HE DID IT HIMSELF?
THE BOY STABBED HIMSELF.

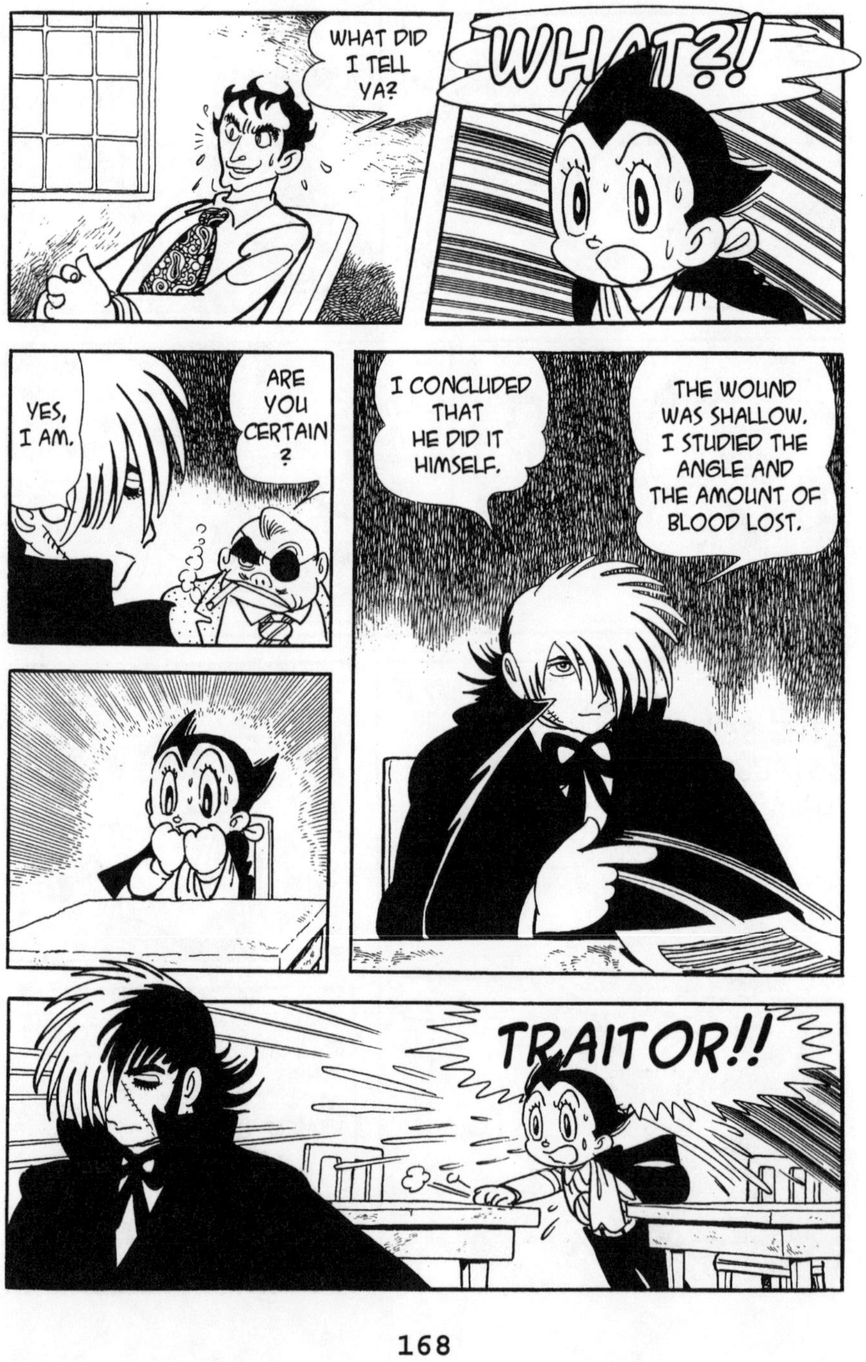

WHAT?!
WHAT DID I TELL YA?
THE WOUND WAS SHALLOW. I STUDIED THE ANGLE AND THE AMOUNT OF BLOOD LOST.
I CONCLUDED THAT HE DID IT HIMSELF.
ARE YOU CERTAIN?
YES, I AM.
TRAITOR!!

THANK YOU FOR YOUR TESTIMONY.
NO, NO, NO!
HE DID IT!
LET ME GO. ISN'T THIS CASE CLOSED?
YEAH, YOU'RE FREE TO LEAVE.
WHAT A LITTLE DEVIL.
SOMEONE HAS GOT TO PUT A MUZZLE ON THAT KID.
GASP
YOU...!!

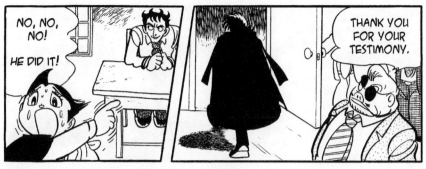

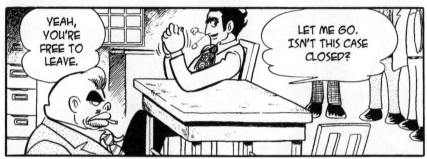

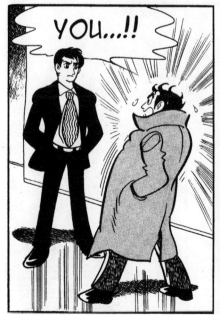

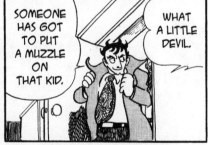

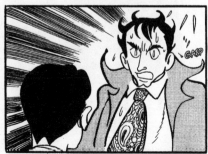

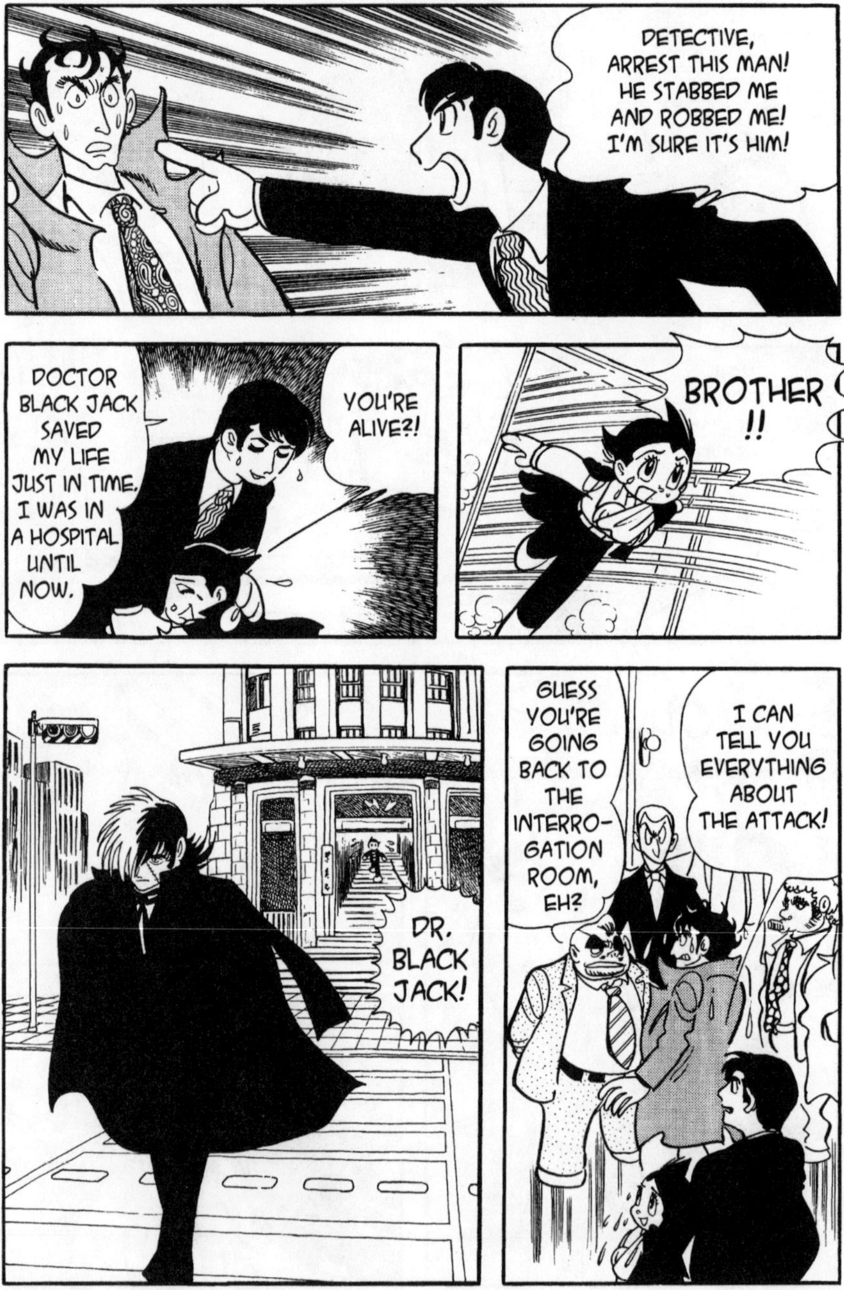
DETECTIVE, ARREST THIS MAN! HE STABBED ME AND ROBBED ME! I'M SURE IT'S HIM!
BROTHER !!
YOU'RE ALIVE?!
DOCTOR BLACK JACK SAVED MY LIFE JUST IN TIME. I WAS IN A HOSPITAL UNTIL NOW.
I CAN TELL YOU EVERYTHING ABOUT THE ATTACK!
GUESS YOU'RE GOING BACK TO THE INTERRO-GATION ROOM, EH?
DR. BLACK JACK!

GUNSHOT WOUND

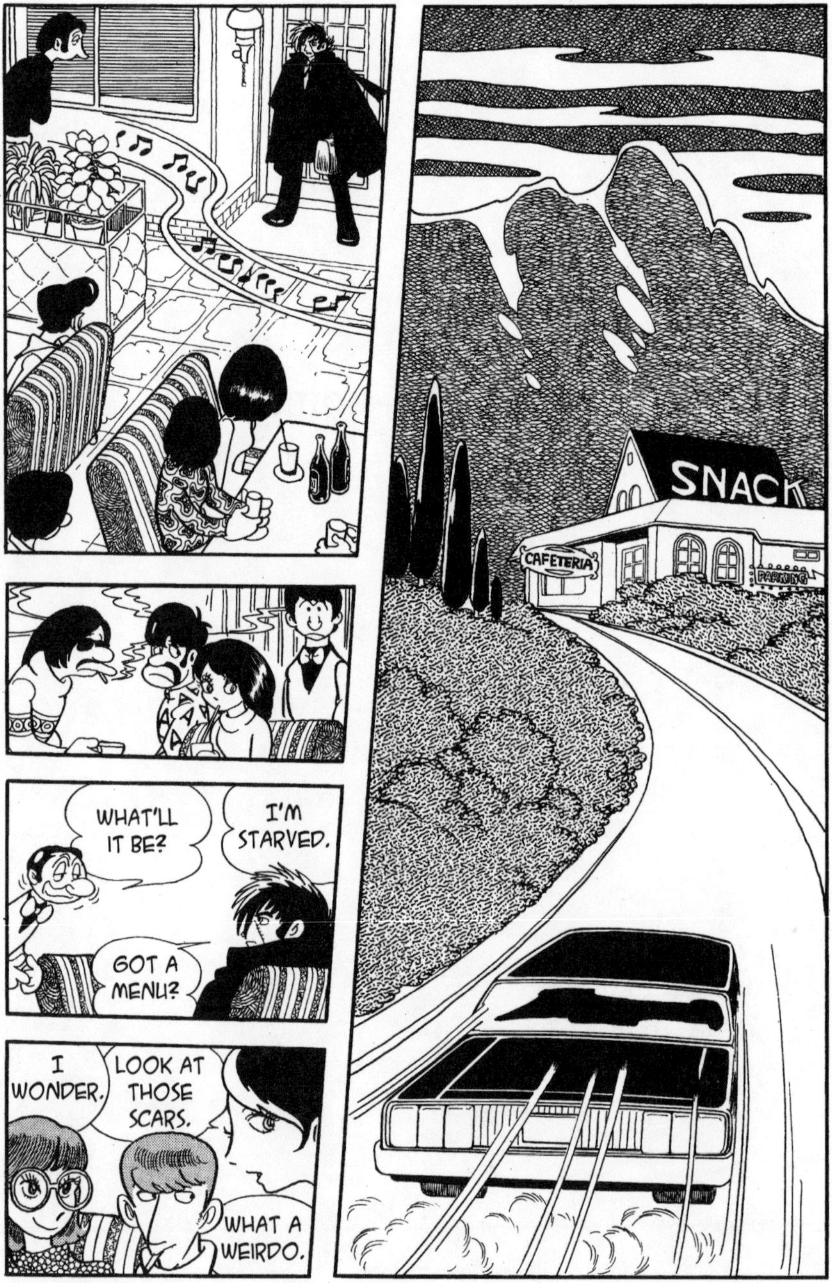
SNACK
CAFETERIA
PARKING
I'M STARVED.
WHAT'LL IT BE?
GOT A MENU?
LOOK AT THOSE SCARS.
I WONDER.
WHAT A WEIRDO.

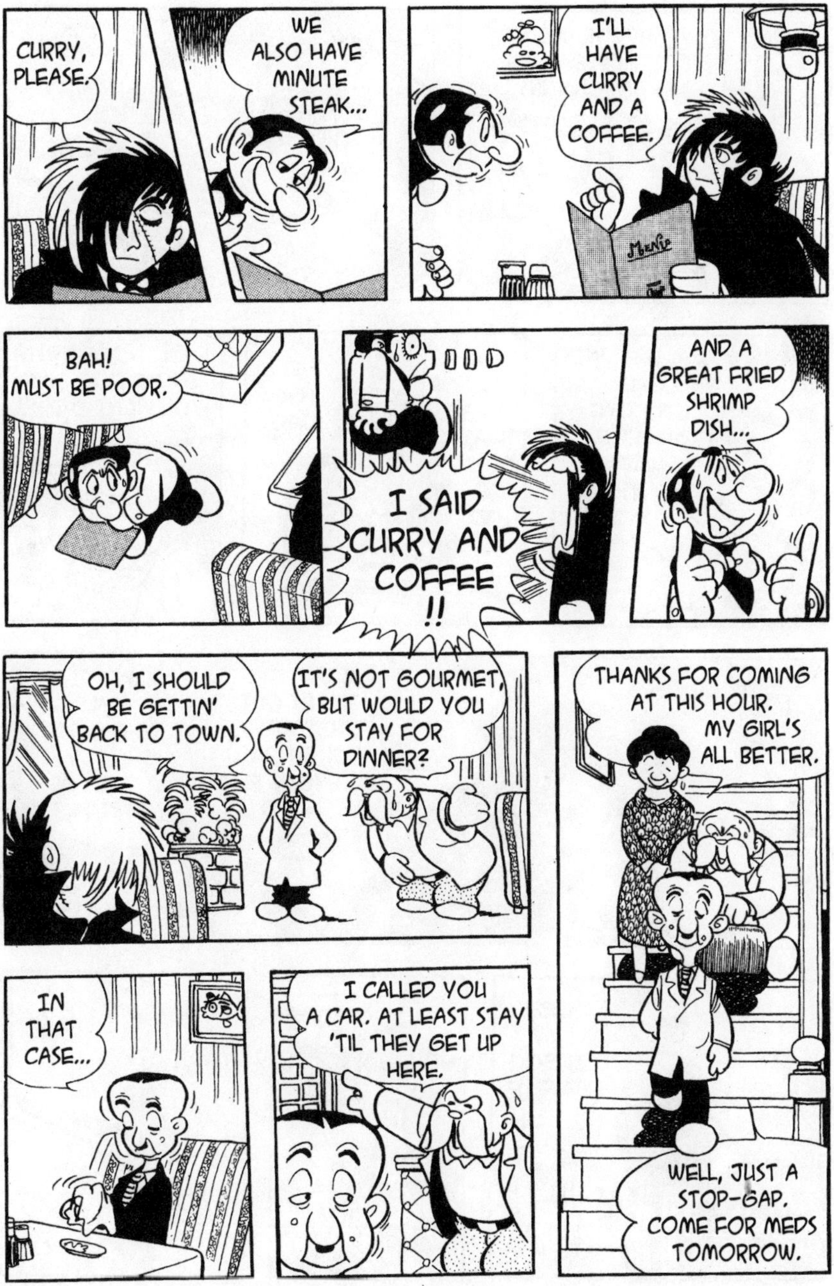
I'LL HAVE CURRY AND A COFFEE.
WE ALSO HAVE MINUTE STEAK...
CURRY, PLEASE.
AND A GREAT FRIED SHRIMP DISH...
I SAID CURRY AND COFFEE !!
BAH! MUST BE POOR.
THANKS FOR COMING AT THIS HOUR. MY GIRL'S ALL BETTER.
WELL, JUST A STOP-GAP. COME FOR MEDS TOMORROW.
IT'S NOT GOURMET, BUT WOULD YOU STAY FOR DINNER?
OH, I SHOULD BE GETTIN' BACK TO TOWN.
I CALLED YOU A CAR. AT LEAST STAY 'TIL THEY GET UP HERE.
IN THAT CASE...

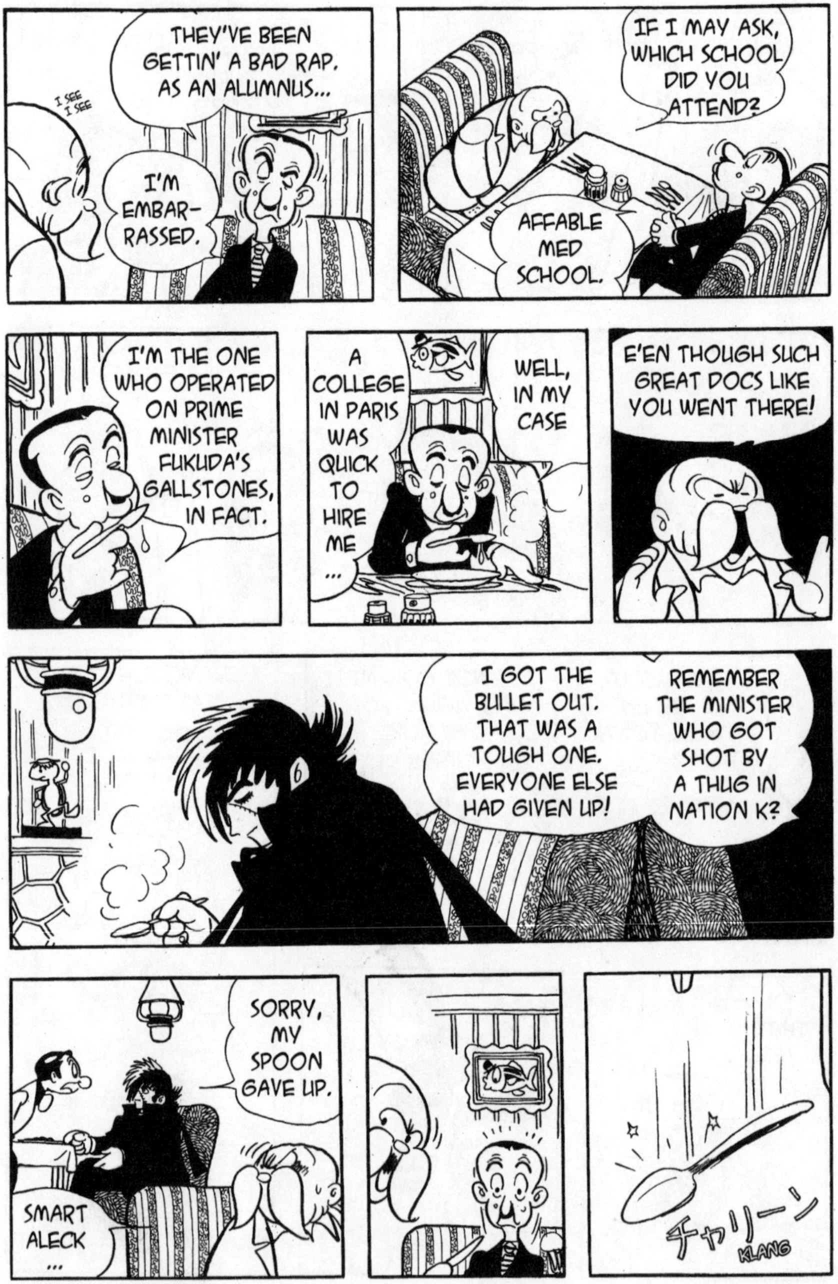
IF I MAY ASK, WHICH SCHOOL DID YOU ATTEND?
AFFABLE MED SCHOOL.
THEY'VE BEEN GETTIN' A BAD RAP. AS AN ALUMNUS...
I SEE I SEE
I'M EMBARRASSED.
E'EN THOUGH SUCH GREAT DOCS LIKE YOU WENT THERE!
WELL, IN MY CASE
A COLLEGE IN PARIS WAS QUICK TO HIRE ME ...
I'M THE ONE WHO OPERATED ON PRIME MINISTER FUKUDA'S GALLSTONES, IN FACT.
REMEMBER THE MINISTER WHO GOT SHOT BY A THUG IN NATION K?
I GOT THE BULLET OUT. THAT WAS A TOUGH ONE. EVERYONE ELSE HAD GIVEN UP!
チャリーン
KLANG
SORRY, MY SPOON GAVE UP.
SMART ALECK ...

THAT'S HIM.
THERE'S A GUY OUTSIDE, SAYS HE'S GOT BUSINESS WITH YA.
GET MOVIN'.
I'M EATING. HE CAN WAIT.
SORRY, BUT YA CAN'T DILLY-DALLY!
AIEEE!
SHEDDAP!
I GOT NO BUSINESS WITH YOU OTHERS. STAY PUT AND YOU'LL BE SAFE.
I'M JUST AFTER THIS GUY.

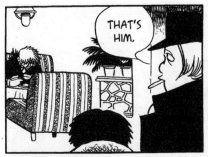

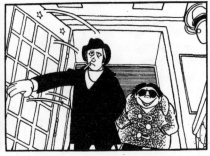

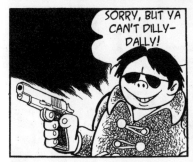

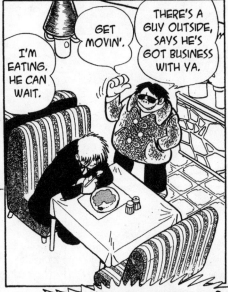

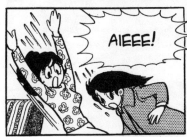

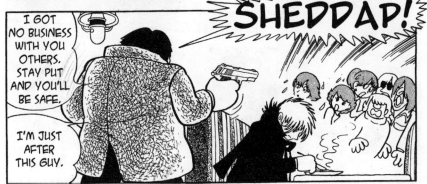

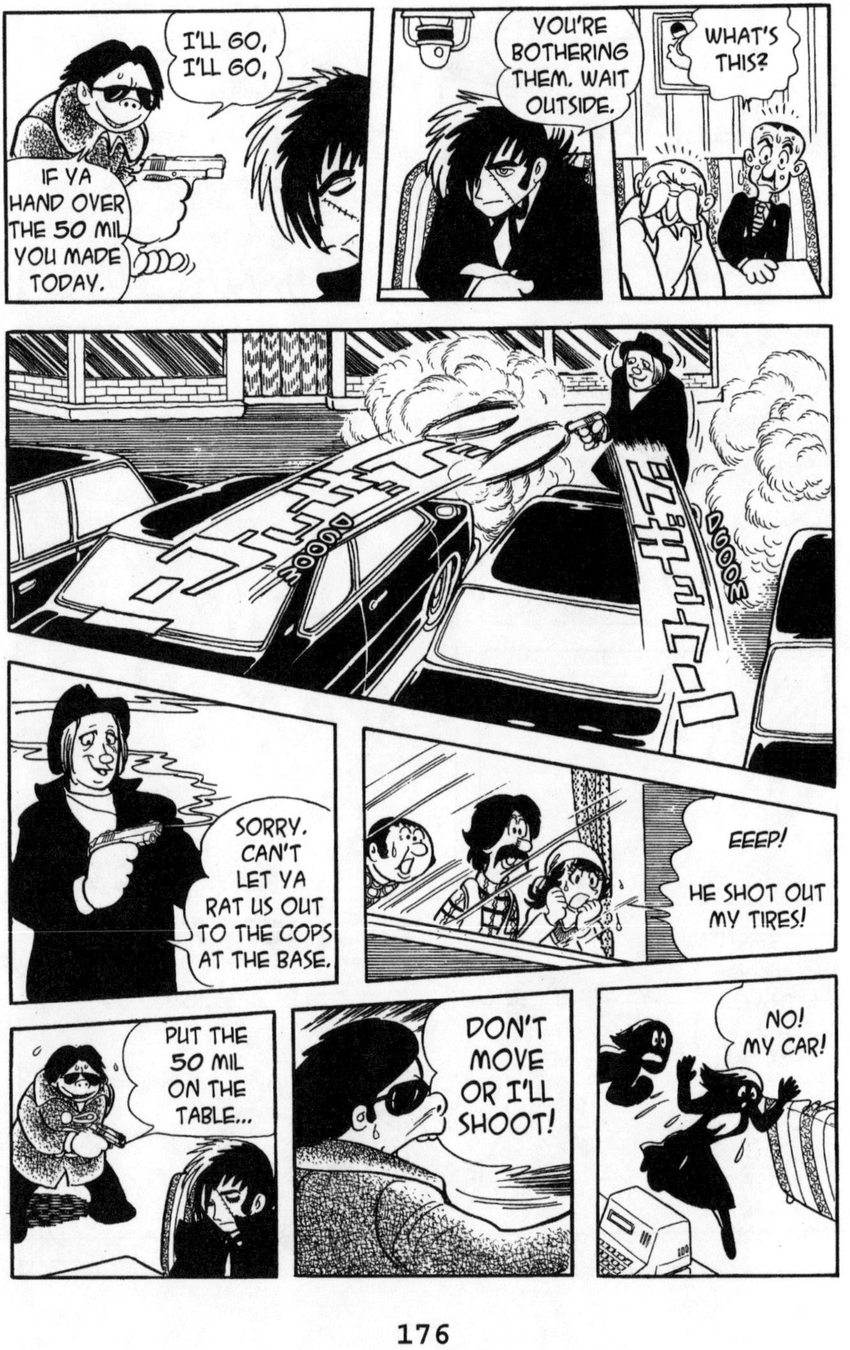
WHAT'S THIS?
YOU'RE BOTHERING THEM. WAIT OUTSIDE.
I'LL GO, I'LL GO,
IF YA HAND OVER THE 50 MIL YOU MADE TODAY.
DOOOM
DOOOM
EEEP!
HE SHOT OUT MY TIRES!
SORRY. CAN'T LET YA RAT US OUT TO THE COPS AT THE BASE.
NO! MY CAR!
DON'T MOVE OR I'LL SHOOT!
PUT THE 50 MIL ON THE TABLE...

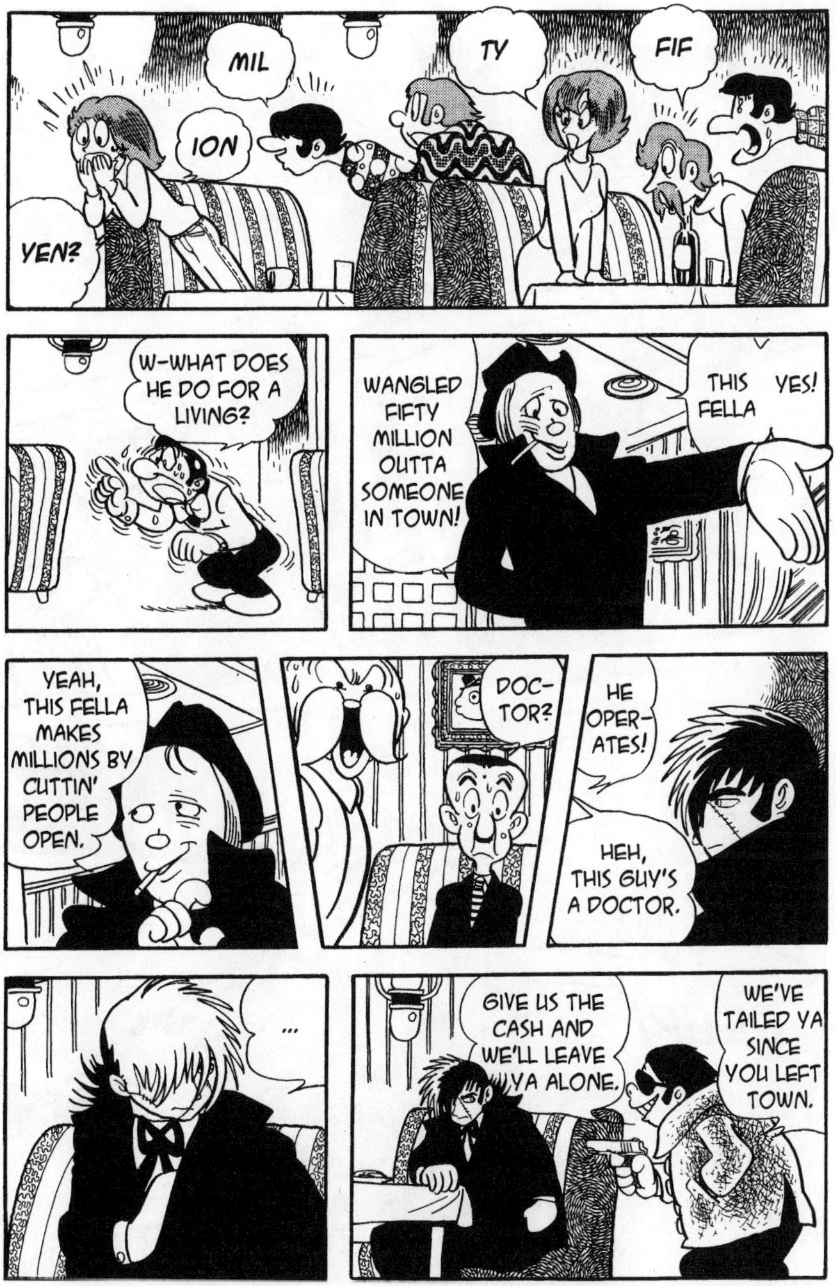
FIF
TY
MIL
ION
YEN?
YES!
THIS FELLA
WANGLED FIFTY MILLION OUTTA SOMEONE IN TOWN!
W-WHAT DOES HE DO FOR A LIVING?
HE OPERATES!
HEH, THIS GUY'S A DOCTOR.
DOCTOR?
YEAH, THIS FELLA MAKES MILLIONS BY CUTTIN' PEOPLE OPEN.
WE'VE TAILED YA SINCE YOU LEFT TOWN.
GIVE US THE CASH AND WE'LL LEAVE YA ALONE.
...

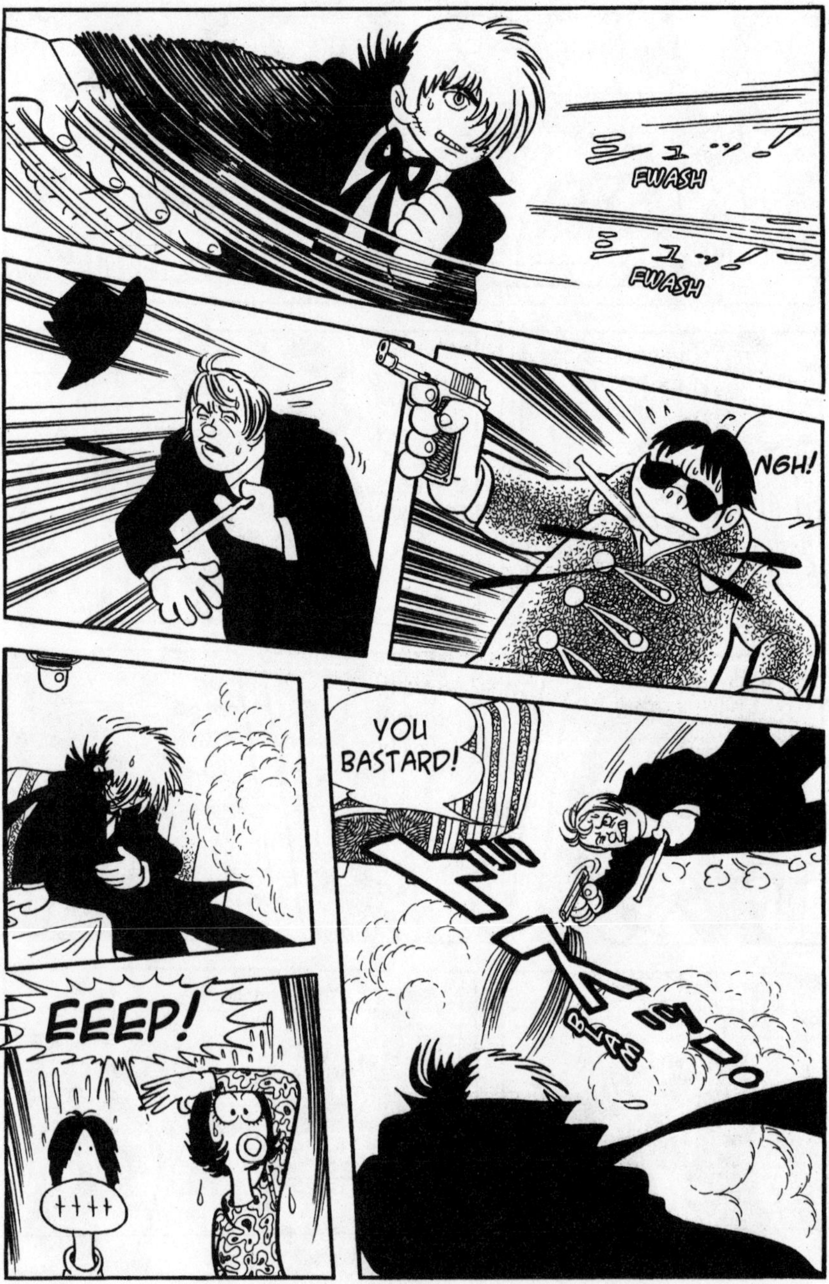
FWASH
FWASH
NGH!
YOU BASTARD!
BLAM
EEEP!

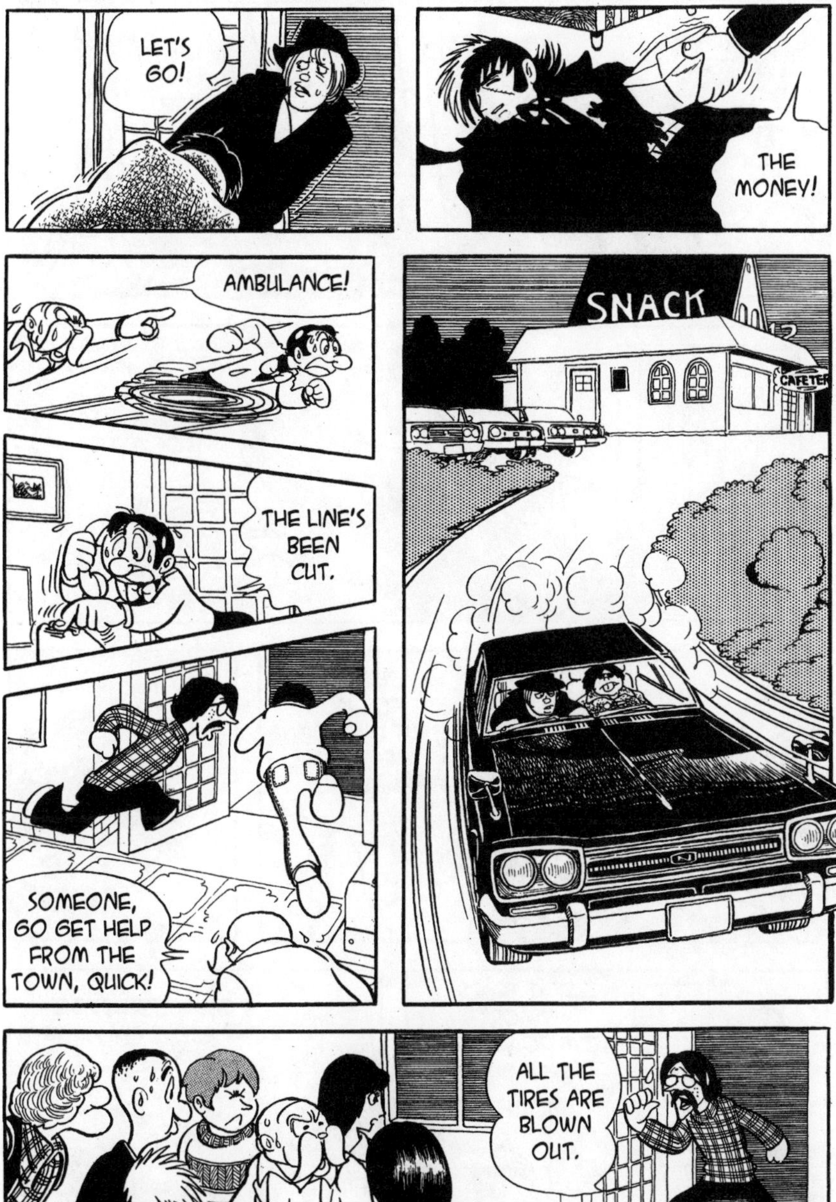
THE MONEY!
LET'S GO!
SNACK
AMBULANCE!
THE LINE'S BEEN CUT.
SOMEONE, GO GET HELP FROM THE TOWN, QUICK!
ALL THE TIRES ARE BLOWN OUT.

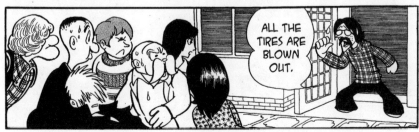

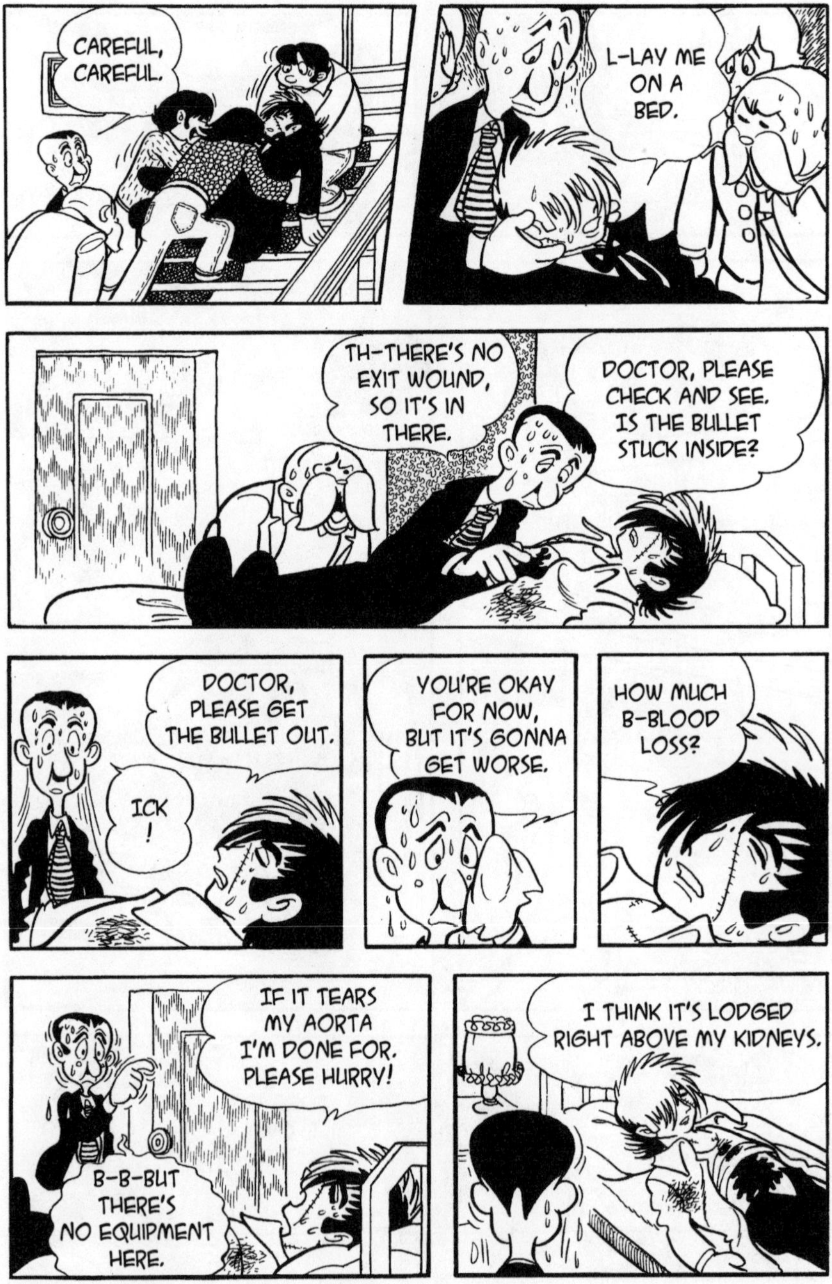
L-LAY ME ON A BED.
CAREFUL, CAREFUL.
DOCTOR, PLEASE CHECK AND SEE. IS THE BULLET STUCK INSIDE?
TH-THERE'S NO EXIT WOUND, SO IT'S IN THERE.
HOW MUCH B-BLOOD LOSS?
YOU'RE OKAY FOR NOW, BUT IT'S GONNA GET WORSE.
DOCTOR, PLEASE GET THE BULLET OUT.
ICK!
I THINK IT'S LODGED RIGHT ABOVE MY KIDNEYS.
IF IT TEARS MY AORTA I'M DONE FOR. PLEASE HURRY!
B-B-BUT THERE'S NO EQUIPMENT HERE.

GETTING A BULLET OUT CAN BE QUITE EASY.
BUT I NEED AN EK-EK-EK- X-RAY AND A STERILE ROOM.
I'LL GO TALK THIS OVER.
THE SHOCK IS MAKING ME FEEL ILL. PLEASE FIND SOMEONE ELSE.
BUT WE'RE STRANDED UP HERE!
DOCTOR, PLEASE. BESIDES, YOU'RE EXCELLENT!
NO EQUIPMENT. MY HANDS ARE TIED HERE.
BUT YOU REMOVED THAT FISHBONE FROM MY GIRL'S THROAT...
THIS ISN'T THE SAME!
NO CHOICE ...
STAY DOWN HERE, ALL OF YOU.
DOCTOR, PLEASE OPERATE!
W-WAIT A SEC...

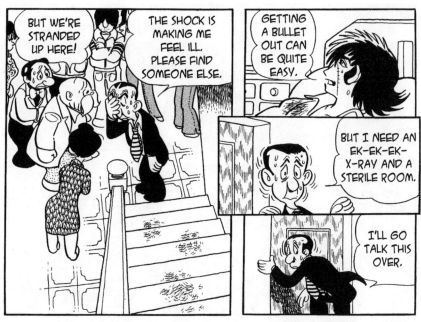

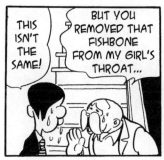

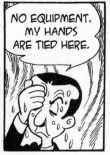

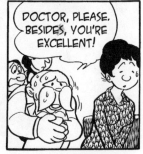

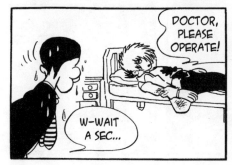

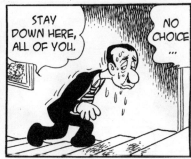

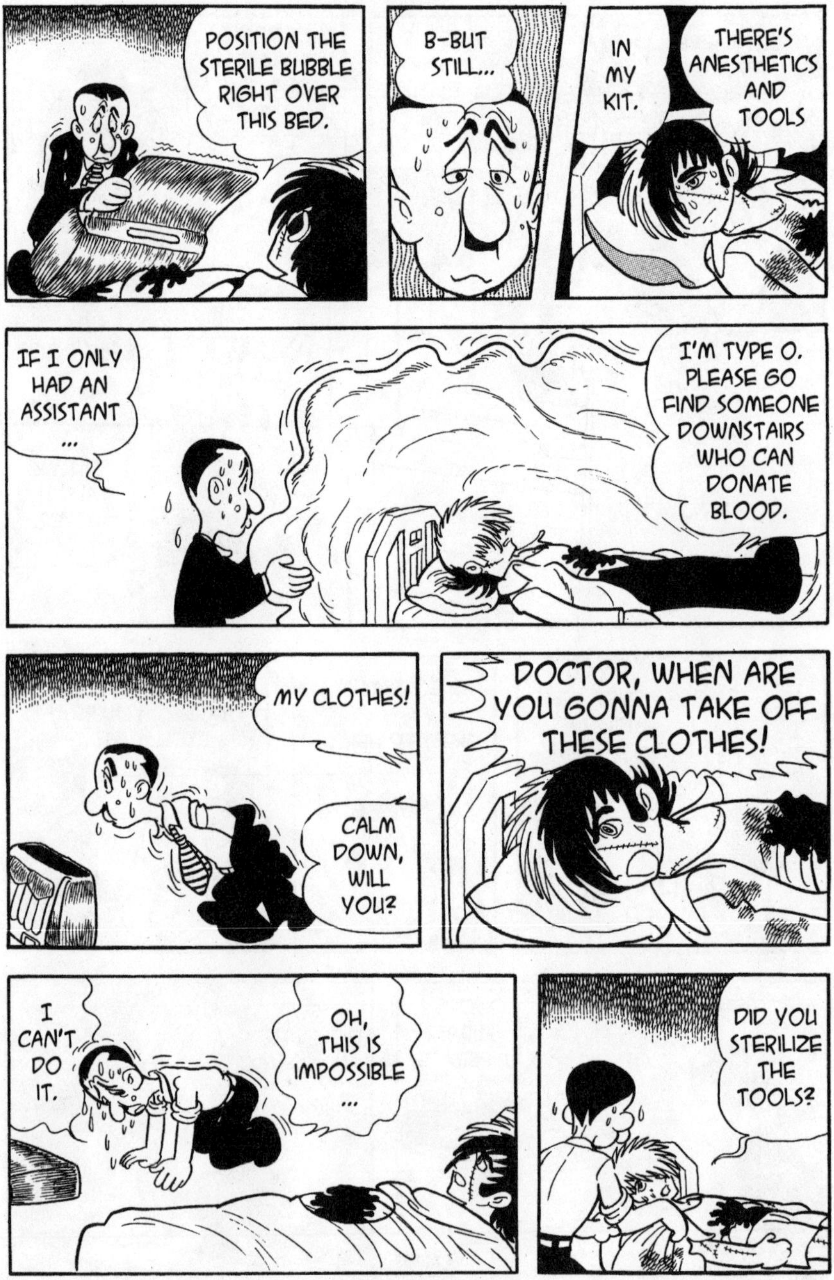
THERE'S ANESTHETICS AND TOOLS
IN MY KIT.
B-BUT STILL...
POSITION THE STERILE BUBBLE RIGHT OVER THIS BED.
I'M TYPE O. PLEASE GO FIND SOMEONE DOWNSTAIRS WHO CAN DONATE BLOOD.
IF I ONLY HAD AN ASSISTANT ...
DOCTOR, WHEN ARE YOU GONNA TAKE OFF THESE CLOTHES!
MY CLOTHES!
CALM DOWN, WILL YOU?
DID YOU STERILIZE THE TOOLS?
OH, THIS IS IMPOSSIBLE ...
I CAN'T DO IT.

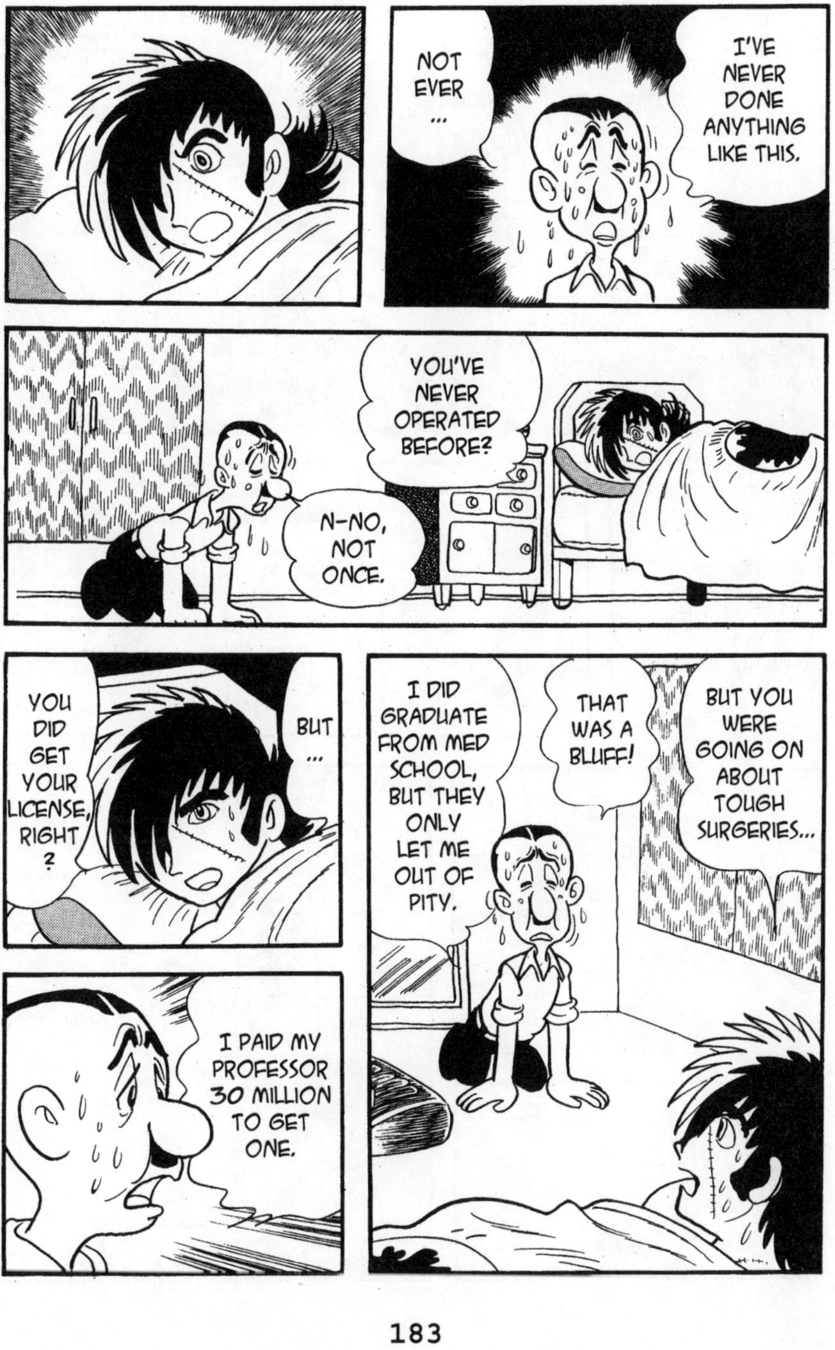
I'VE NEVER DONE ANYTHING LIKE THIS.
NOT EVER ...
YOU'VE NEVER OPERATED BEFORE?
N-NO, NOT ONCE.
BUT YOU WERE GOING ON ABOUT TOUGH SURGERIES...
THAT WAS A BLUFF!
I DID GRADUATE FROM MED SCHOOL, BUT THEY ONLY LET ME OUT OF PITY.
BUT ...
YOU DID GET YOUR LICENSE, RIGHT?
I PAID MY PROFESSOR 30 MILLION TO GET ONE.

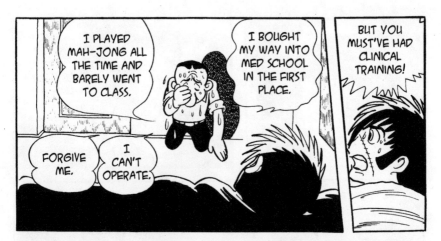

BUT YOU MUST'VE HAD CLINICAL TRAINING!
I BOUGHT MY WAY INTO MED SCHOOL IN THE FIRST PLACE.
I PLAYED MAH-JONG ALL THE TIME AND BARELY WENT TO CLASS.
I CAN'T OPERATE.
FORGIVE ME.
SOME DOCTOR.
IS THIS FRAUD MY ONLY CHOICE?
I'VE OPERATED ON MYSELF BEFORE.
BUT RIGHT NOW I CAN'T USE MY ARMS VERY WELL.
ICK!
I NEED YOU
TO BE MY HANDS!
DON'T SCRAM. GET READY.

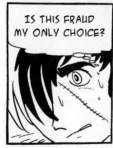

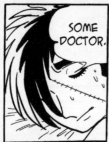

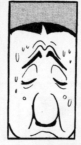

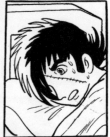

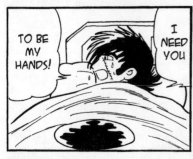

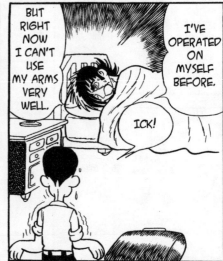

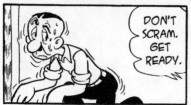

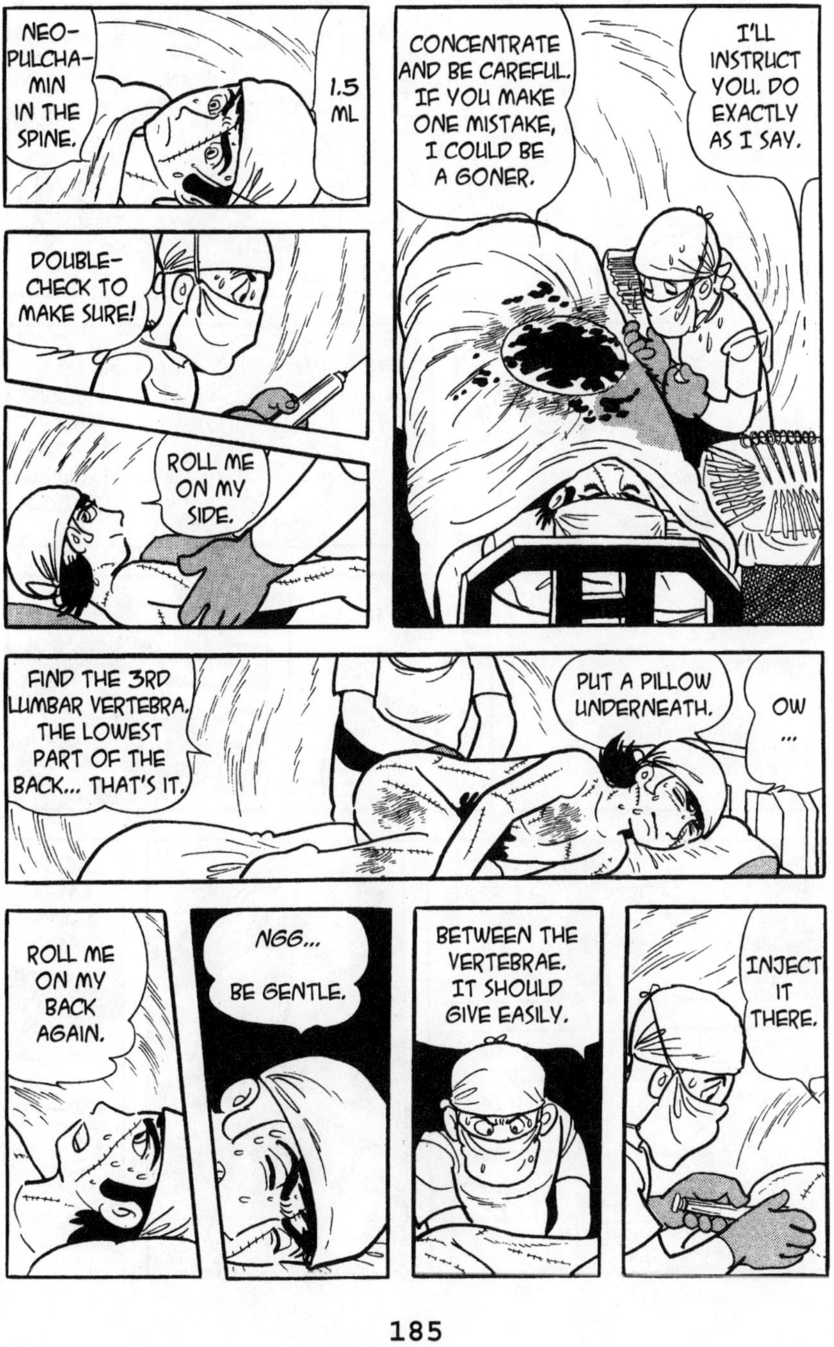
I'LL INSTRUCT YOU. DO EXACTLY AS I SAY.
CONCENTRATE AND BE CAREFUL. IF YOU MAKE ONE MISTAKE, I COULD BE A GONER.
1.5 ML
NEO-PULCHAMIN IN THE SPINE.
DOUBLE-CHECK TO MAKE SURE!
ROLL ME ON MY SIDE.
OW ...
PUT A PILLOW UNDERNEATH.
FIND THE 3RD LUMBAR VERTEBRA. THE LOWEST PART OF THE BACK... THAT'S IT.
INJECT IT THERE.
BETWEEN THE VERTEBRAE. IT SHOULD GIVE EASILY.
NGG...
BE GENTLE.
ROLL ME ON MY BACK AGAIN.

GET A SCALPEL.

I CAN'T FEEL ANYTHING.

OK, IT'S KICKING IN.

IDIOT! JUST USE GAUZE TO MOP IT UP!

B-BUT THERE'S A POOL OF BLOOD...!

CUT THE WOUND ALONG THE ABDOMINAL MUSCLE.

HURRY!

THERE'S A GAPING HOLE IN THE MUSCLE.

HOLD OPEN USING CLAMPS.

THE BLOOD'S FROM THERE.

OF COURSE THERE IS... NOW GET TO THE MESENTERY.

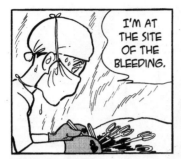

I'M AT THE SITE OF THE BLEEDING.
UGH
I GIVE UP!
YOU CAN'T GIVE UP NOW, YOU MORON!
BUT I CAN'T DO IT...
YOU CAN DO SIMPLE PROCEDURES, RIGHT?
I CAN STITCH UP A NASTY GASH...
THEN THINK OF THIS AS JUST A NASTY GASH, NOT MAJOR SURGERY.
IT'S ALL THE SAME.
EXAMINE THE MESENTERY.
DO YOU SEE ANY CUT VEIN?
AH, THIS ONE!

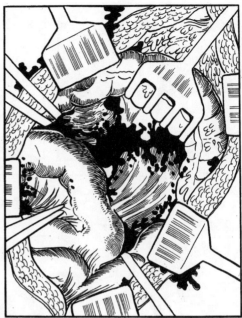

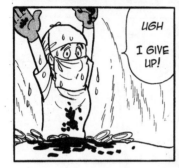

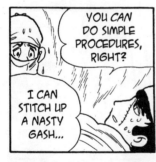

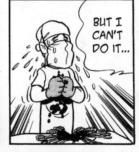

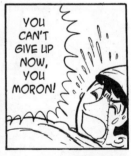

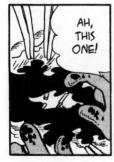

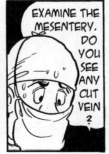

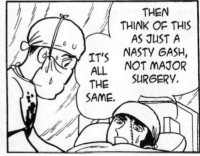

USE ANASTO-MOSING FORCEPS.
パチリ
PAK
ギクリ
GULP
THE BUL-LET!
I FOUND IT!
DR. BLACK JACK?
DOCTOR!
HE'S NOT BREATHING!
DOCTOR!
I WONDER IF HE HAS AN OXYGEN INHALER...
YES! NOW COME BACK!
カチリ
KLIK

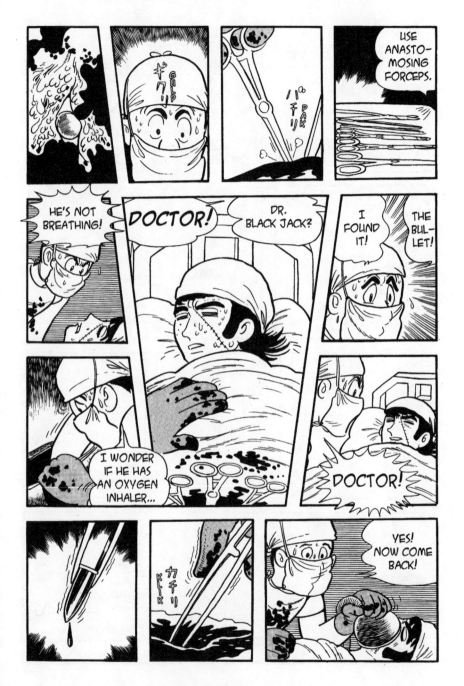

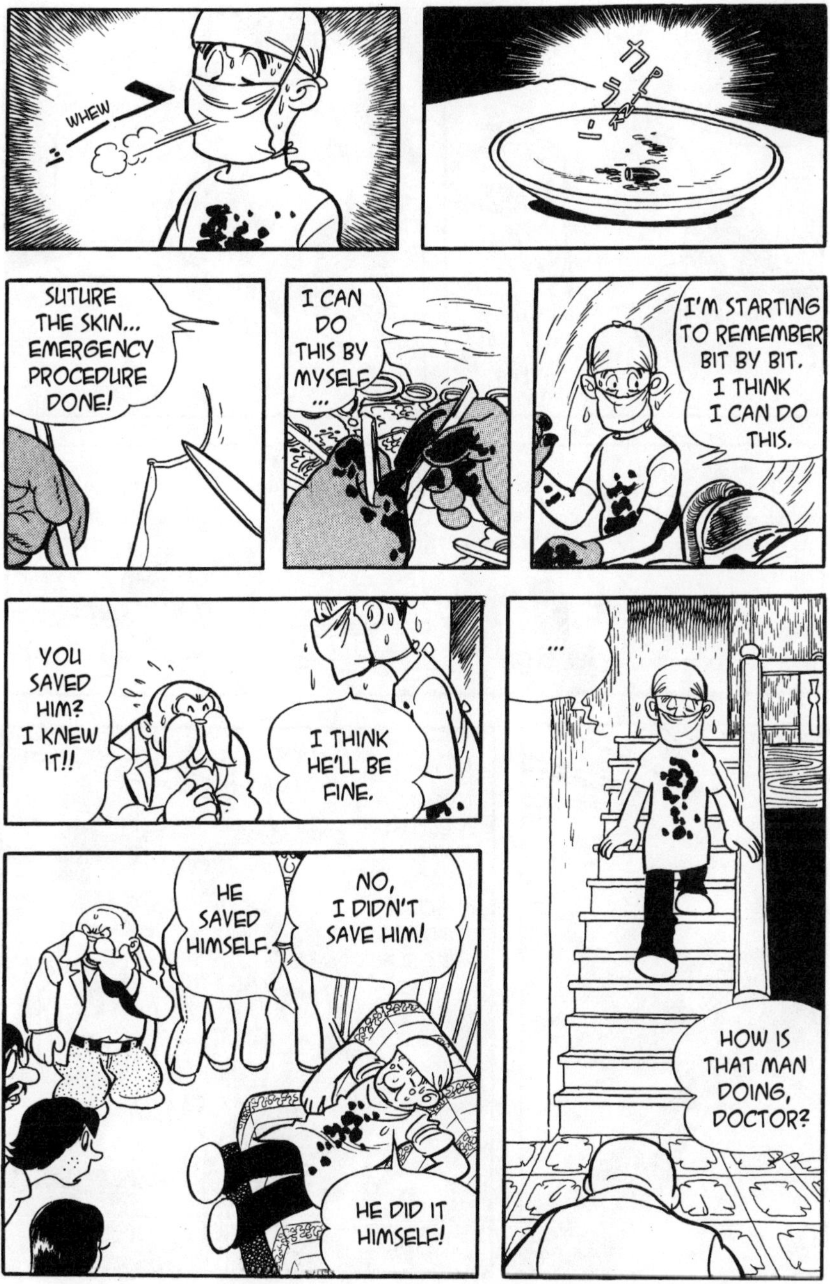
WHEW
I'M STARTING TO REMEMBER BIT BY BIT. I THINK I CAN DO THIS.
I CAN DO THIS BY MYSELF...
SUTURE THE SKIN... EMERGENCY PROCEDURE DONE!
...
HOW IS THAT MAN DOING, DOCTOR?
I THINK HE'LL BE FINE.
YOU SAVED HIM? I KNEW IT!!
NO, I DIDN'T SAVE HIM!
HE SAVED HIMSELF.
HE DID IT HIMSELF!

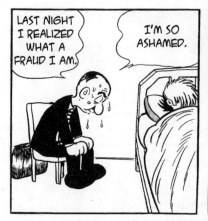

I'M SO ASHAMED.
LAST NIGHT I REALIZED WHAT A FRAUD I AM.
I SAID MEAN THINGS ...
NO, NO, NOT AT ALL.
I'M GOING BACK TO MED SCHOOL TO START OVER.
NOW YOU CAN BRAG TO EVERYONE FOR REAL!
YOU TOOK A BULLET NOT OUT OF SOME MINISTER, BUT *BLACK JACK*!
yes

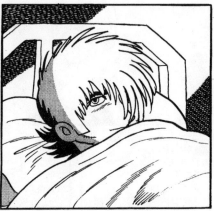

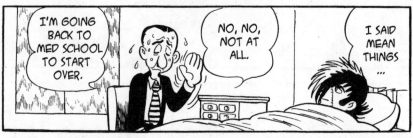

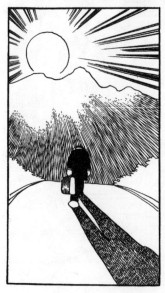

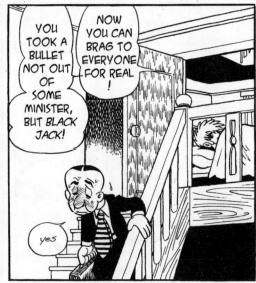

MISTRESS SHIRAHA

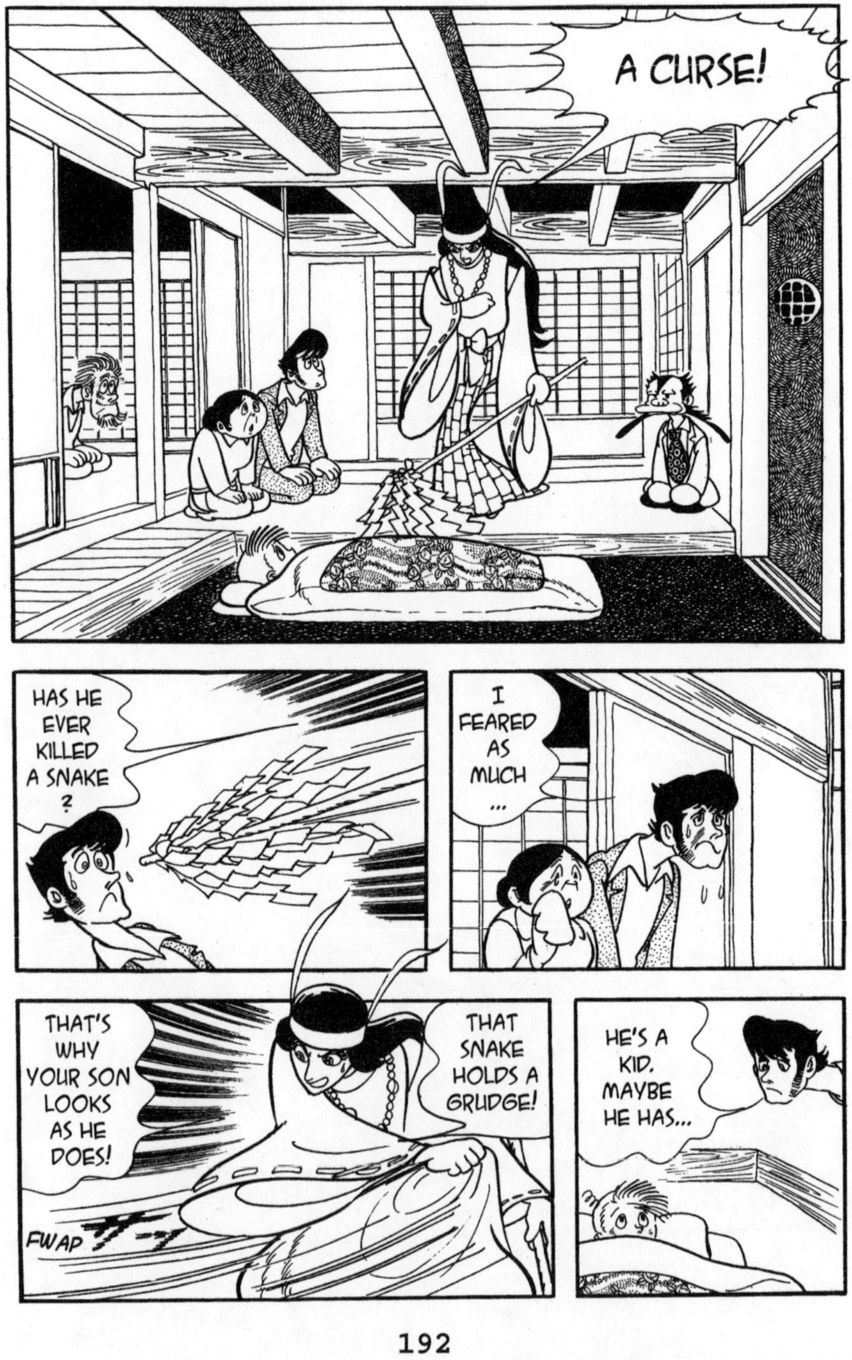
A CURSE!
I FEARED AS MUCH ...
HAS HE EVER KILLED A SNAKE ?
HE'S A KID. MAYBE HE HAS...
THAT SNAKE HOLDS A GRUDGE!
THAT'S WHY YOUR SON LOOKS AS HE DOES!
FWAP

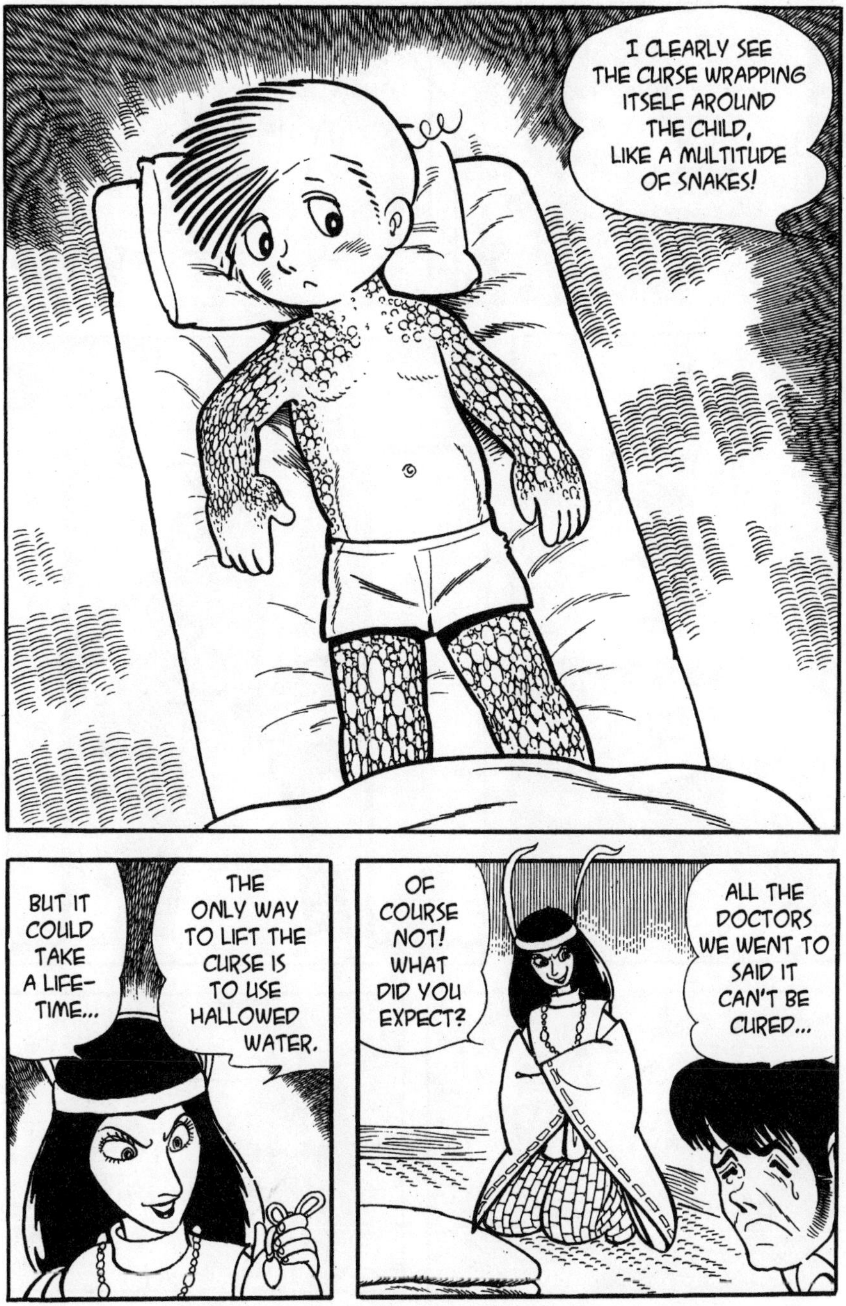
I CLEARLY SEE THE CURSE WRAPPING ITSELF AROUND THE CHILD, LIKE A MULTITUDE OF SNAKES!
ALL THE DOCTORS WE WENT TO SAID IT CAN'T BE CURED...
OF COURSE NOT! WHAT DID YOU EXPECT?
THE ONLY WAY TO LIFT THE CURSE IS TO USE HALLOWED WATER.
BUT IT COULD TAKE A LIFE-TIME...

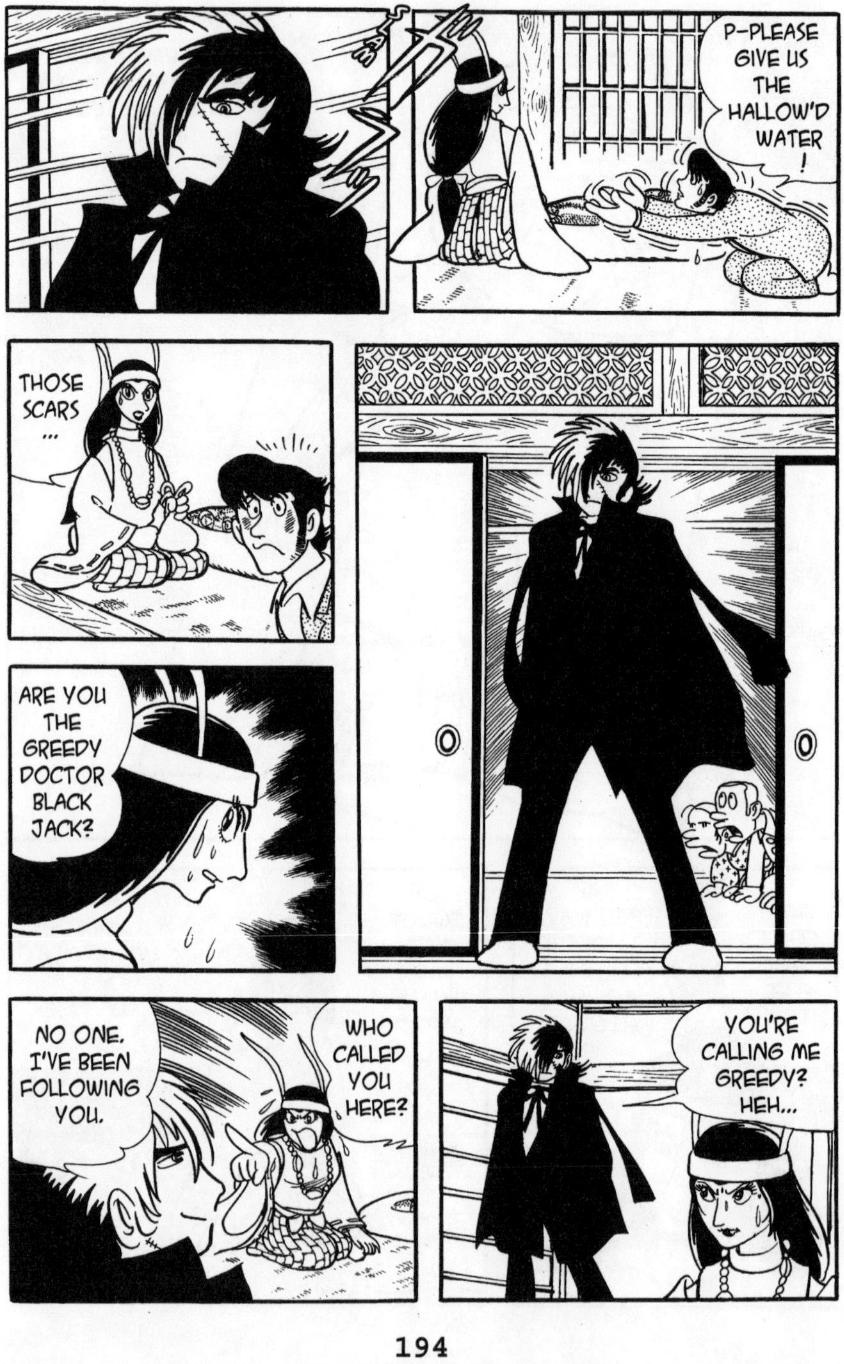
P-PLEASE GIVE US THE HALLOW'D WATER !
THOSE SCARS ...
ARE YOU THE GREEDY DOCTOR BLACK JACK?
YOU'RE CALLING ME GREEDY? HEH...
WHO CALLED YOU HERE?
NO ONE. I'VE BEEN FOLLOWING YOU.

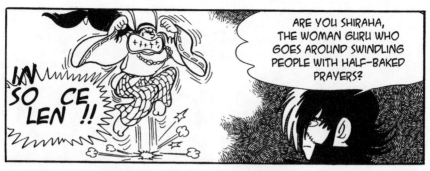

ARE YOU SHIRAHA, THE WOMAN GURU WHO GOES AROUND SWINDLING PEOPLE WITH HALF-BAKED PRAYERS?
IN SO CE LEN !!
HOW DARE YOU ?!
WHAT COULD A DOCTOR POSSIBLY KNOW ABOUT PRAYERS?
THERE ARE MANY ILLS THAT DOCTORS CAN'T CURE.
THEY ARE CAUSED BY INTERFERING SPIRITS.
ONLY PRAYERS CAN BANISH THEM!
OH HO ...
WANT TO MAKE A BET?
IF I CAN'T CURE THIS BOY'S ILLNESS
I'LL PROSTRATE MYSELF BEFORE YOU AND SWEAR OFF PRACTICING MEDICINE.

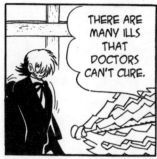

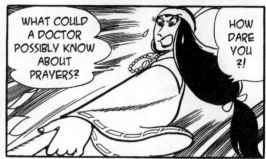

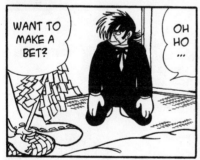

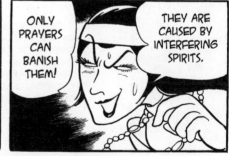

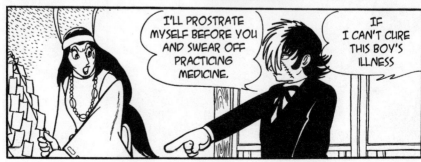

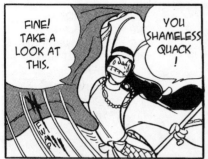

BUT, IF I DO CURE HIM, YOU HAVE TO GIVE ME ALL THE MONEY YOU'VE MADE.
LIKE THE BET ?
YOU SHAMELESS QUACK !
FINE! TAKE A LOOK AT THIS.
FWAP
THIS IS ICHTHYOSIS ... ...
ICHTHYOSIS— A DISORDER WHERE THE SKIN TURNS THICK AND HARD, CRACKS, AND AS A RESULT RESEMBLES FISH SCALES. THE CAUSE IS UNKNOWN, AND THERE IS NO CURE.
YOU THINK YOU CAN CURE HIM?

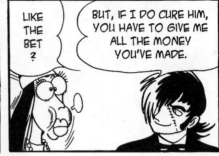

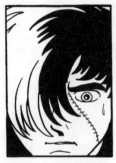

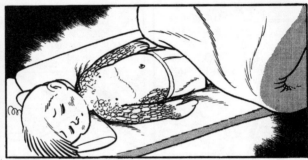

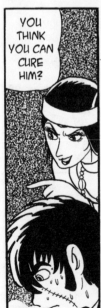

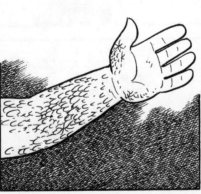

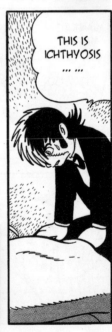

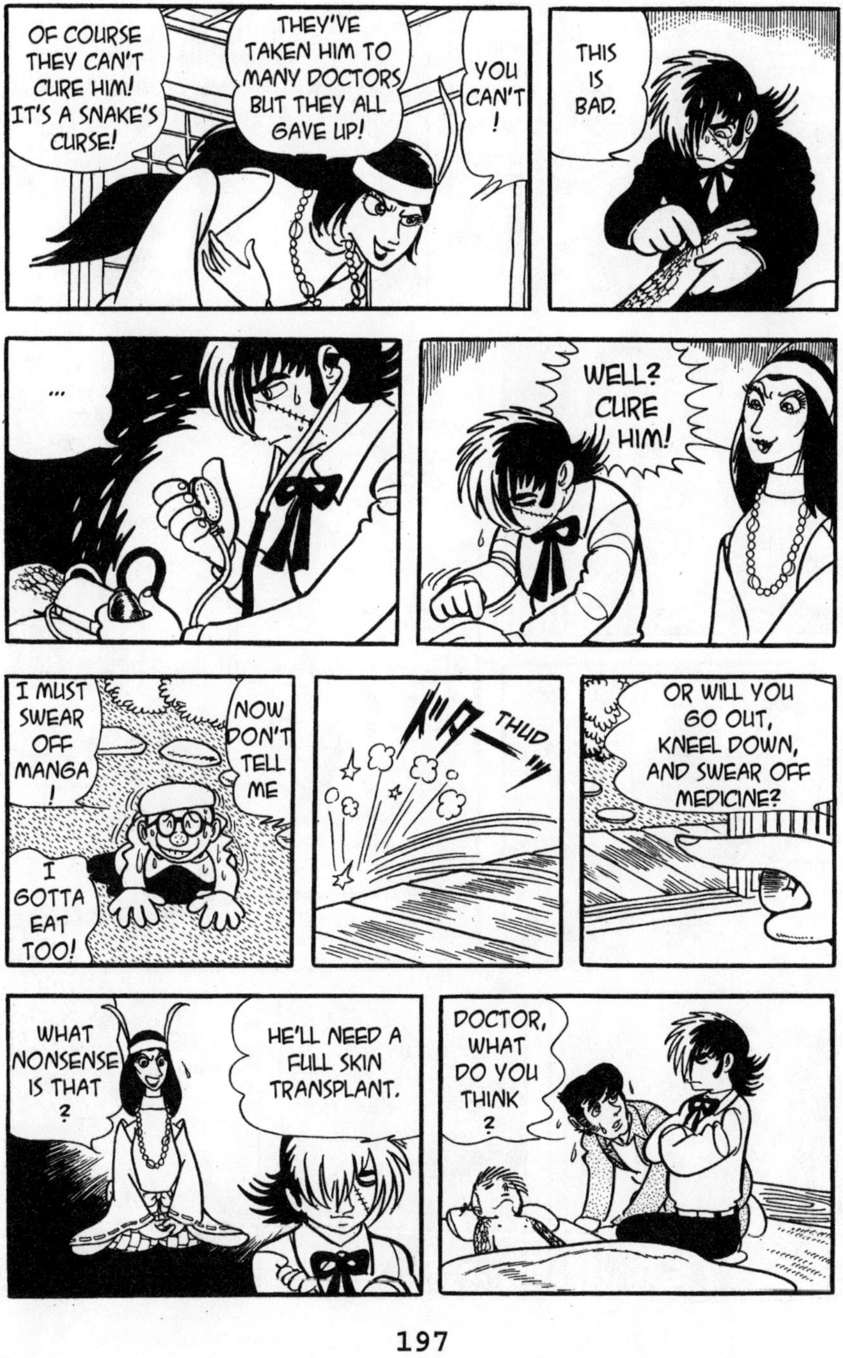
THIS IS BAD.
YOU CAN'T!
THEY'VE TAKEN HIM TO MANY DOCTORS BUT THEY ALL GAVE UP!
OF COURSE THEY CAN'T CURE HIM! IT'S A SNAKE'S CURSE!
WELL? CURE HIM!
...
OR WILL YOU GO OUT, KNEEL DOWN, AND SWEAR OFF MEDICINE?
THUD
NOW DON'T TELL ME
I MUST SWEAR OFF MANGA!
I GOTTA EAT TOO!
DOCTOR, WHAT DO YOU THINK?
HE'LL NEED A FULL SKIN TRANSPLANT.
WHAT NONSENSE IS THAT?

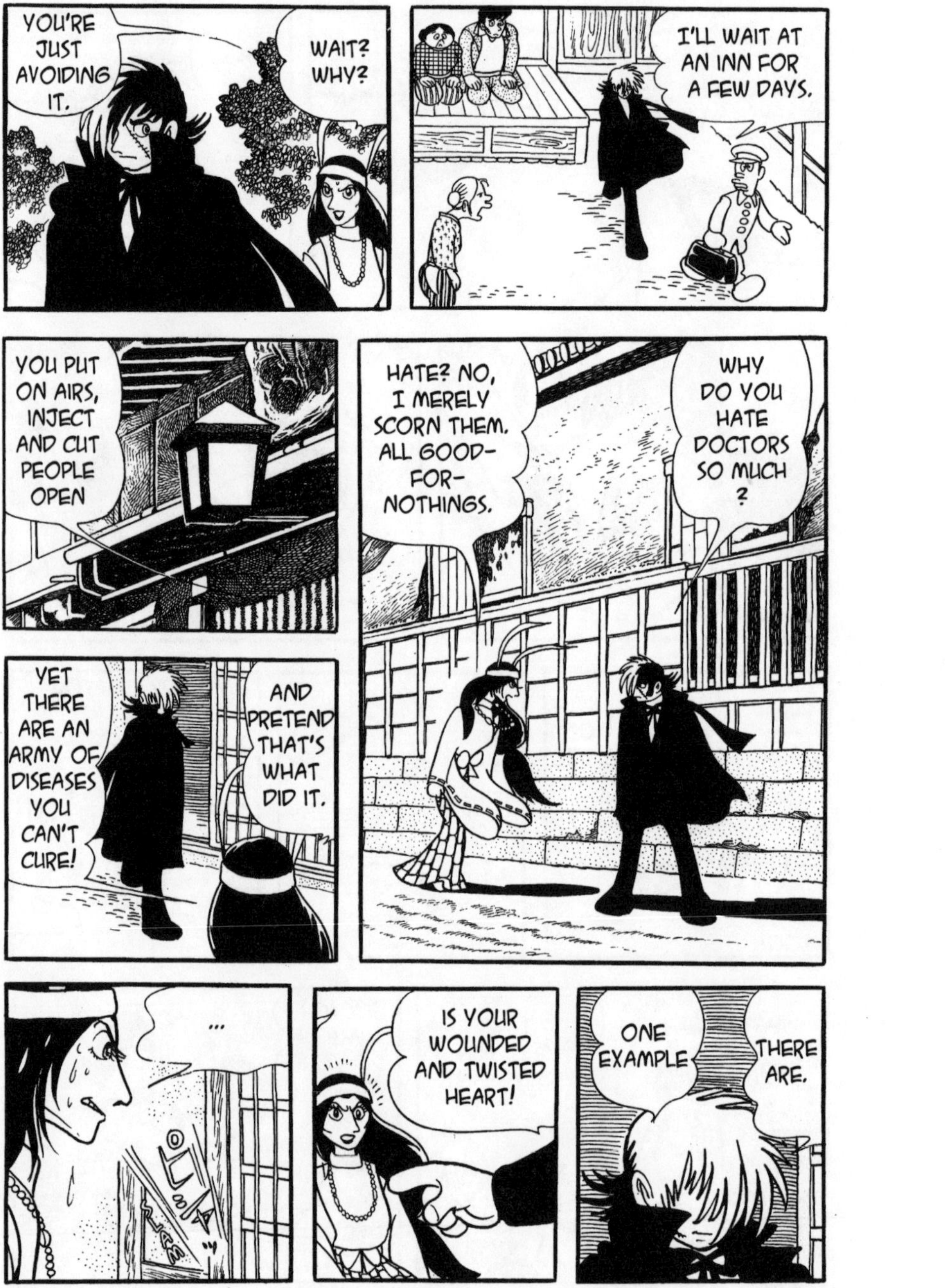
I'LL WAIT AT AN INN FOR A FEW DAYS.
WAIT? WHY?
YOU'RE JUST AVOIDING IT.
WHY DO YOU HATE DOCTORS SO MUCH ?
HATE? NO, I MERELY SCORN THEM. ALL GOOD-FOR-NOTHINGS.
YOU PUT ON AIRS, INJECT AND CUT PEOPLE OPEN
AND PRETEND THAT'S WHAT DID IT.
YET THERE ARE AN ARMY OF DISEASES YOU CAN'T CURE!
THERE ARE.
ONE EXAMPLE
IS YOUR WOUNDED AND TWISTED HEART!
...

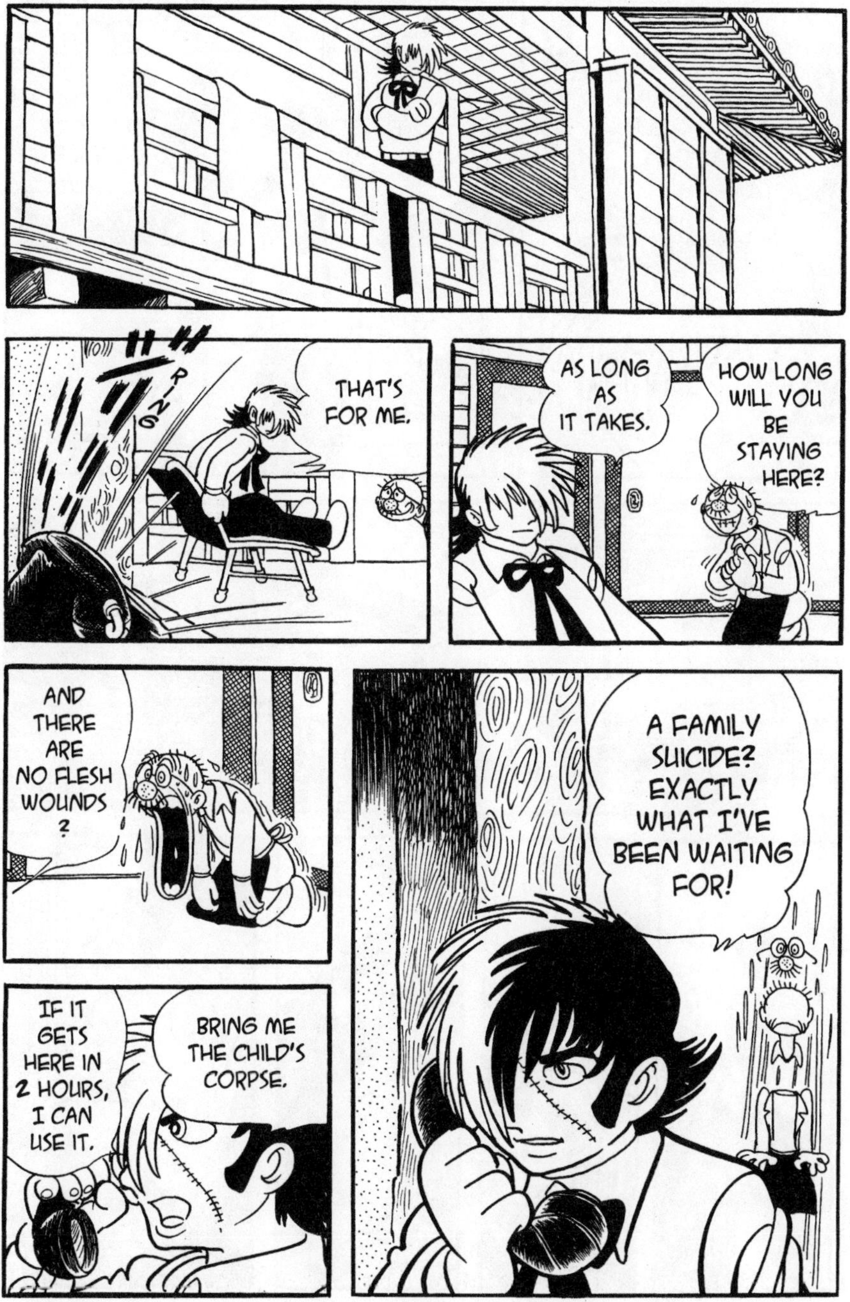
HOW LONG WILL YOU BE STAYING HERE?
AS LONG AS IT TAKES.
THAT'S FOR ME.
RING
A FAMILY SUICIDE? EXACTLY WHAT I'VE BEEN WAITING FOR!
AND THERE ARE NO FLESH WOUNDS?
BRING ME THE CHILD'S CORPSE.
IF IT GETS HERE IN 2 HOURS, I CAN USE IT.

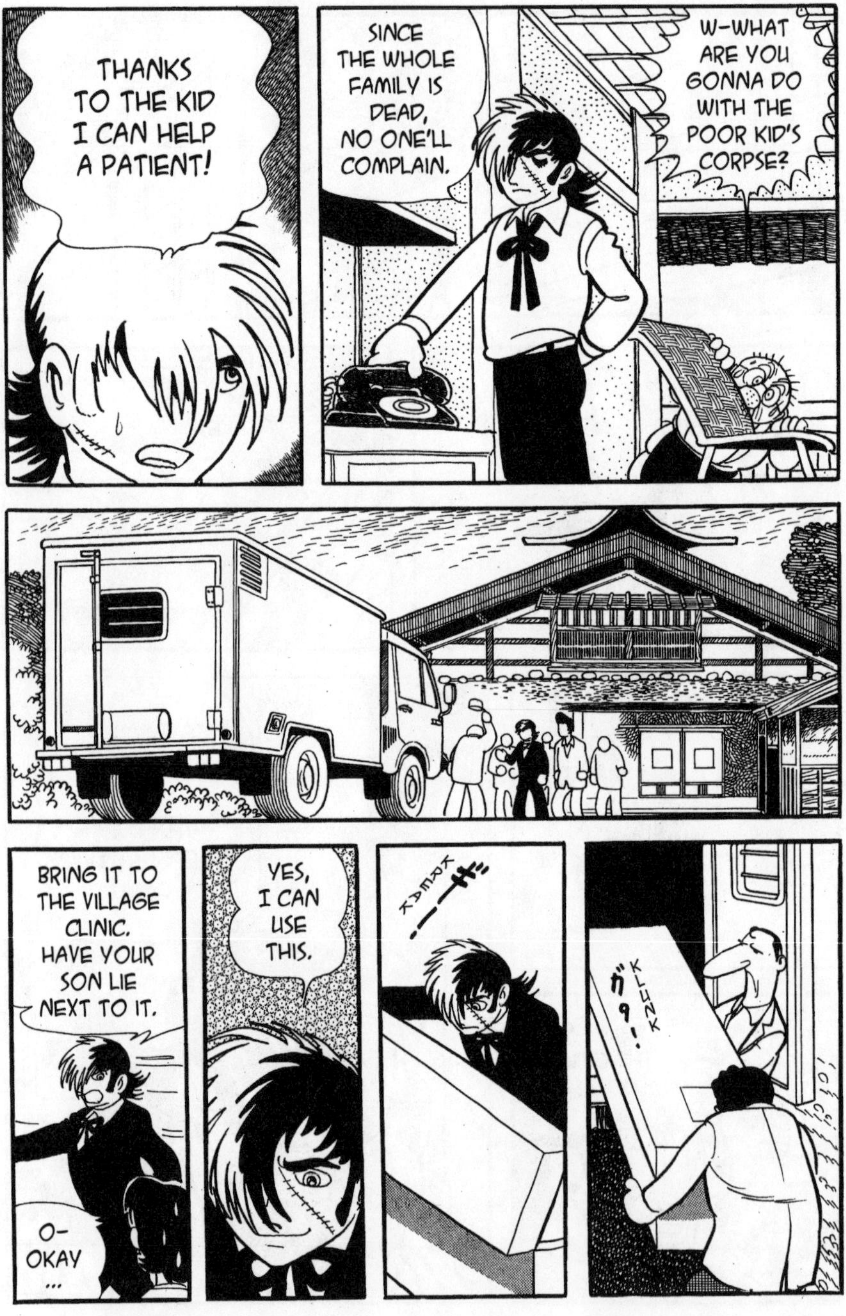
W-WHAT ARE YOU GONNA DO WITH THE POOR KID'S CORPSE?
SINCE THE WHOLE FAMILY IS DEAD, NO ONE'LL COMPLAIN.
THANKS TO THE KID I CAN HELP A PATIENT!
ガタ!
KLUNK
ギーー!
KREAK
YES, I CAN USE THIS.
BRING IT TO THE VILLAGE CLINIC. HAVE YOUR SON LIE NEXT TO IT.
O-OKAY ...

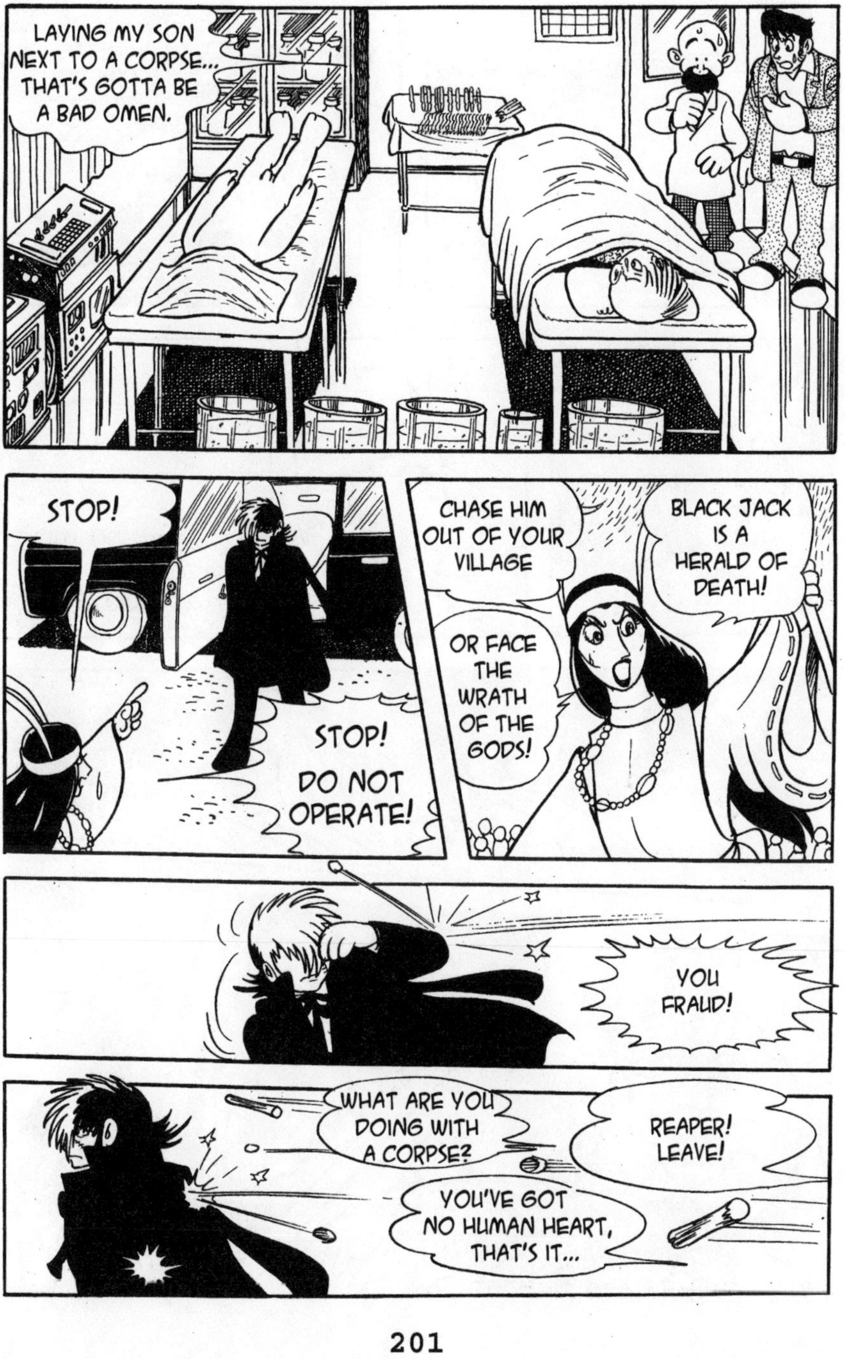
LAYING MY SON NEXT TO A CORPSE... THAT'S GOTTA BE A BAD OMEN.
BLACK JACK IS A HERALD OF DEATH!
CHASE HIM OUT OF YOUR VILLAGE
OR FACE THE WRATH OF THE GODS!
STOP!
STOP!
DO NOT OPERATE!
YOU FRAUD!
REAPER! LEAVE!
WHAT ARE YOU DOING WITH A CORPSE?
YOU'VE GOT NO HUMAN HEART, THAT'S IT...

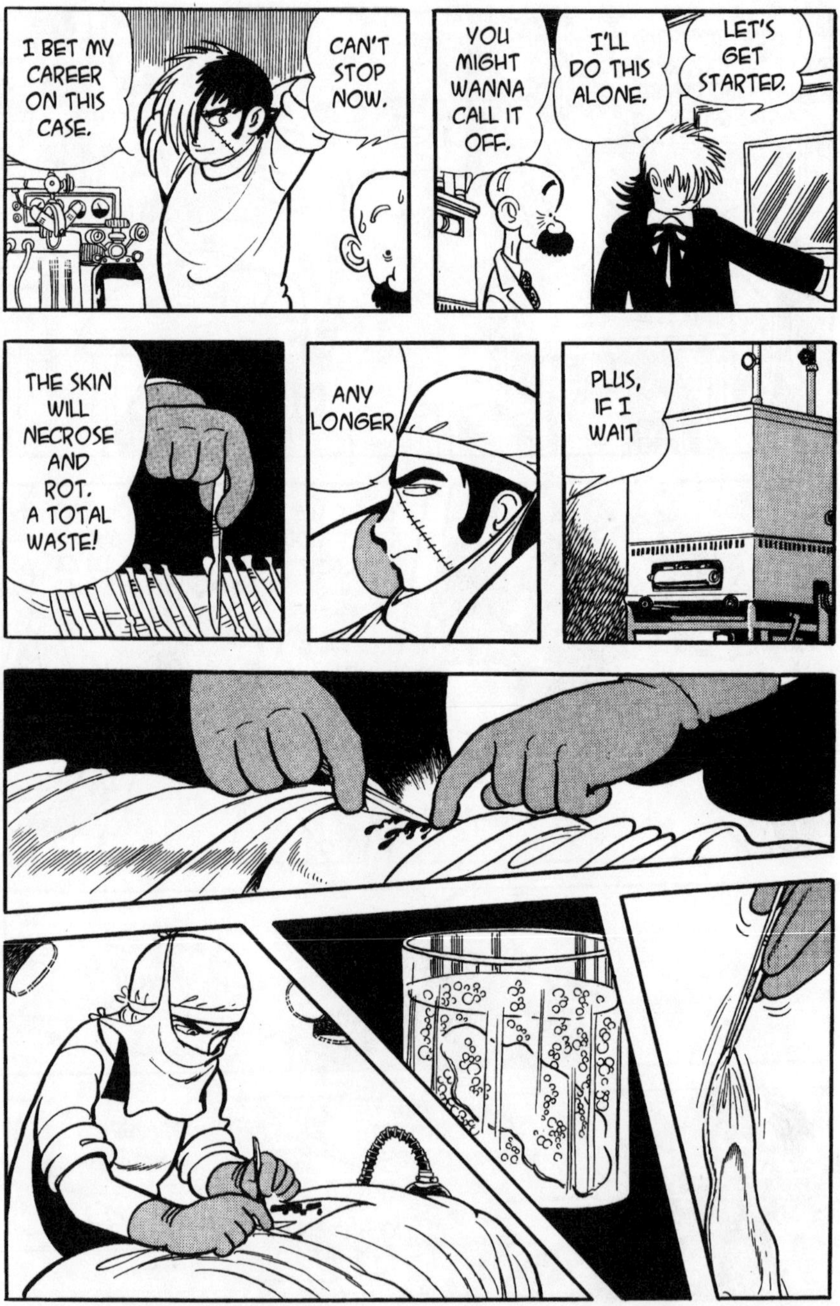
LET'S GET STARTED.
I'LL DO THIS ALONE.
YOU MIGHT WANNA CALL IT OFF.
CAN'T STOP NOW.
I BET MY CAREER ON THIS CASE.
PLUS, IF I WAIT
ANY LONGER
THE SKIN WILL NECROSE AND ROT. A TOTAL WASTE!

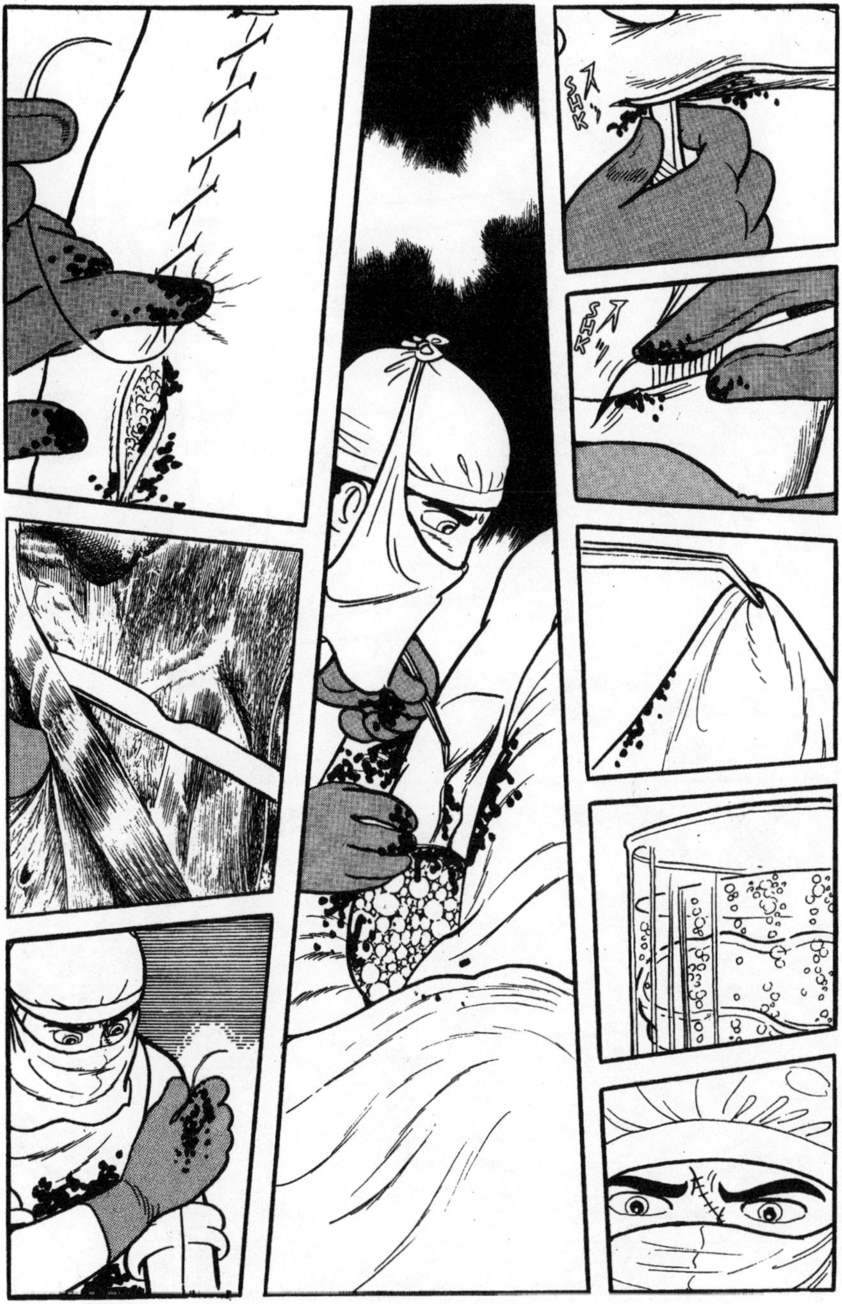
SHK
SHK

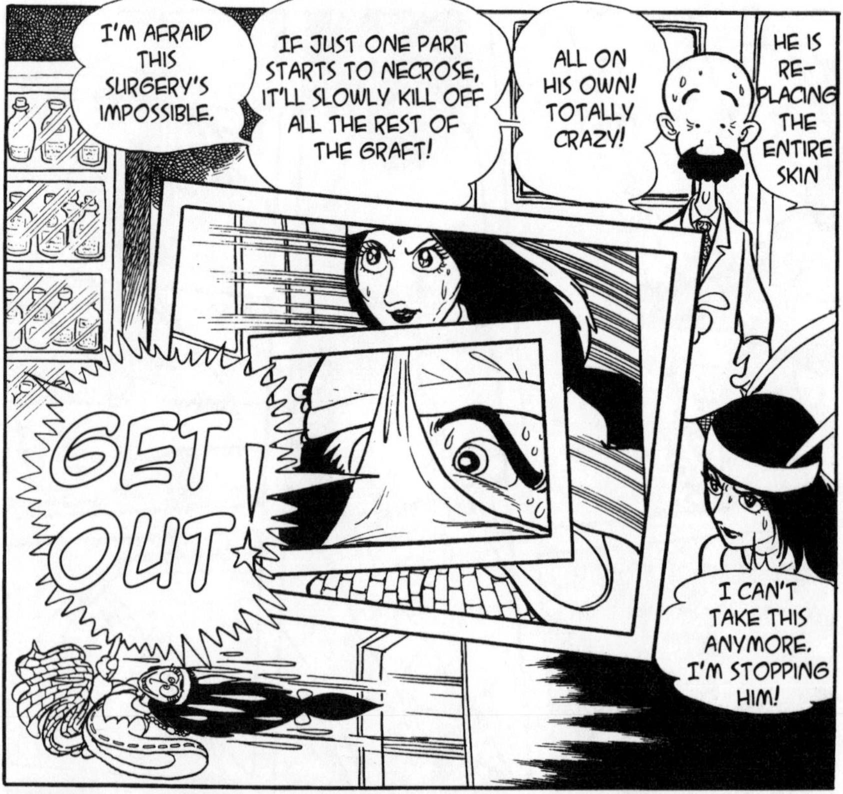
HE IS RE-PLACING THE ENTIRE SKIN
ALL ON HIS OWN! TOTALLY CRAZY!
IF JUST ONE PART STARTS TO NECROSE, IT'LL SLOWLY KILL OFF ALL THE REST OF THE GRAFT!
I'M AFRAID THIS SURGERY'S IMPOSSIBLE.
I CAN'T TAKE THIS ANYMORE. I'M STOPPING HIM!
GET OUT!

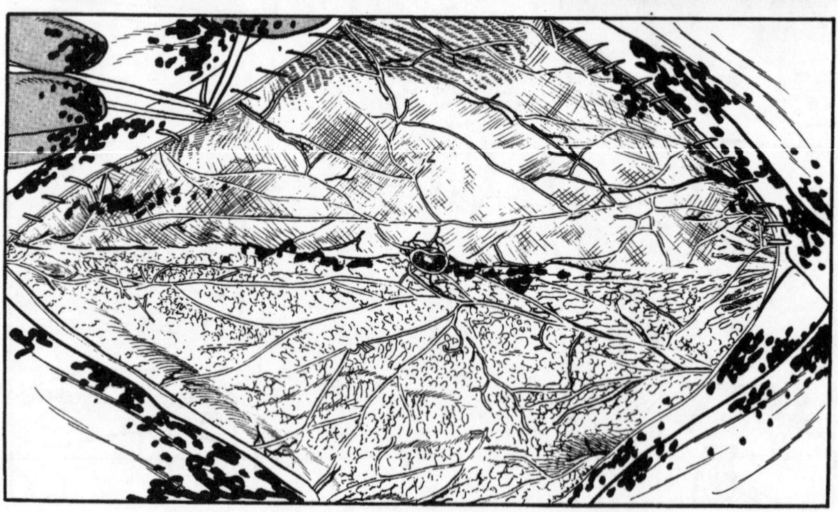

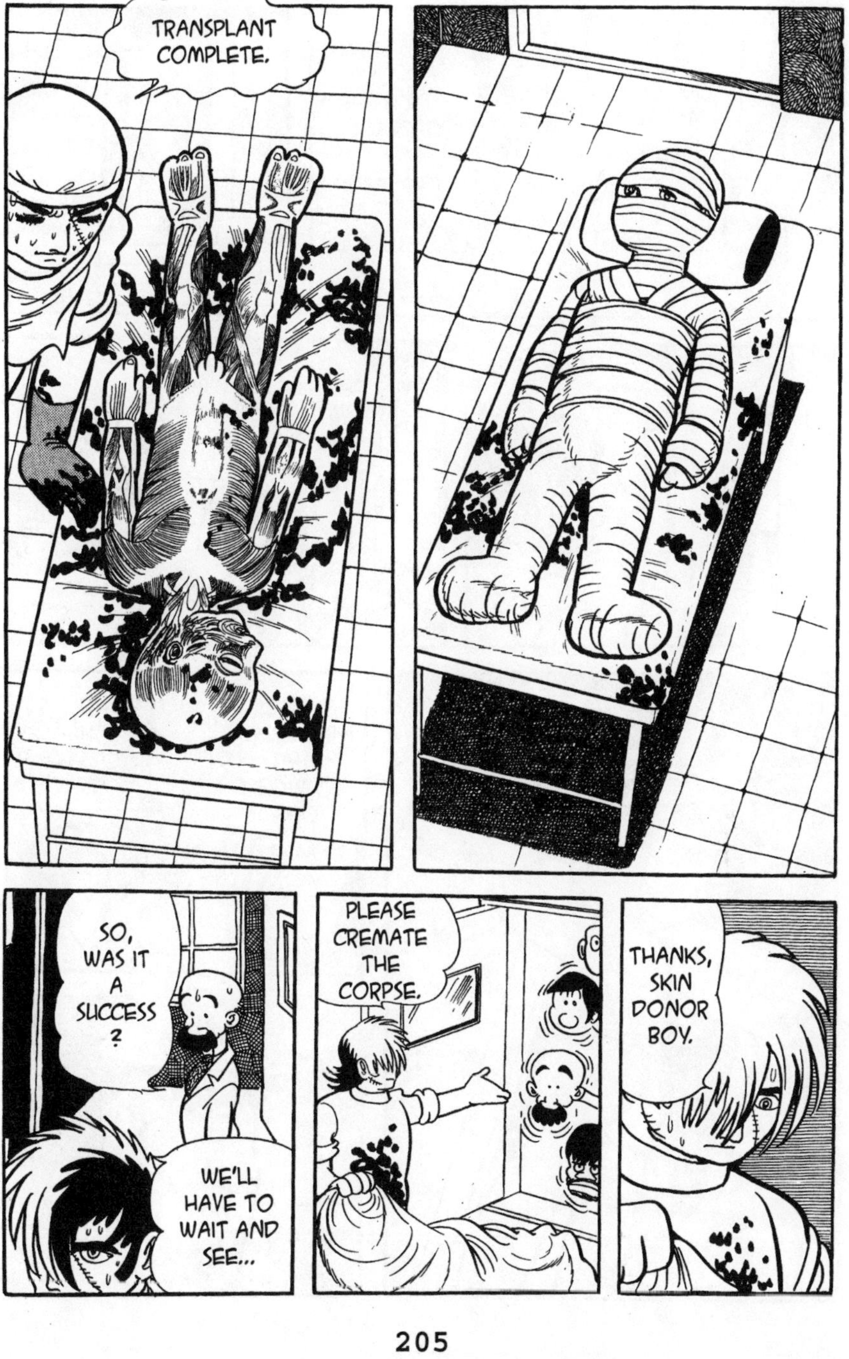
TRANSPLANT COMPLETE.
THANKS, SKIN DONOR BOY.
PLEASE CREMATE THE CORPSE.
SO, WAS IT A SUCCESS?
WE'LL HAVE TO WAIT AND SEE...

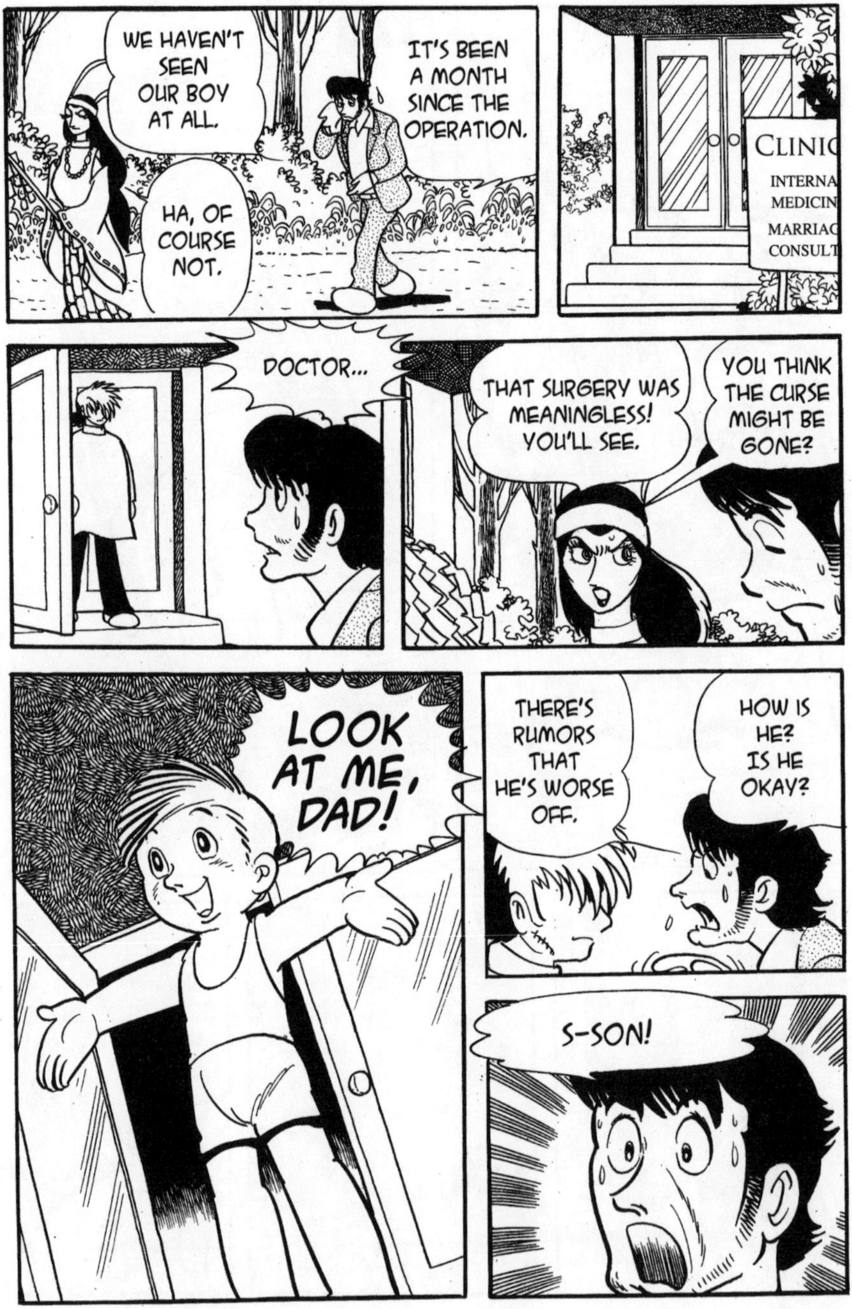
CLINIC
INTERNA
MEDICIN
MARRIAG
CONSULT
IT'S BEEN A MONTH SINCE THE OPERATION.
WE HAVEN'T SEEN OUR BOY AT ALL.
HA, OF COURSE NOT.
YOU THINK THE CURSE MIGHT BE GONE?
THAT SURGERY WAS MEANINGLESS! YOU'LL SEE.
DOCTOR...
HOW IS HE? IS HE OKAY?
THERE'S RUMORS THAT HE'S WORSE OFF.
S-SON!
LOOK AT ME, DAD!

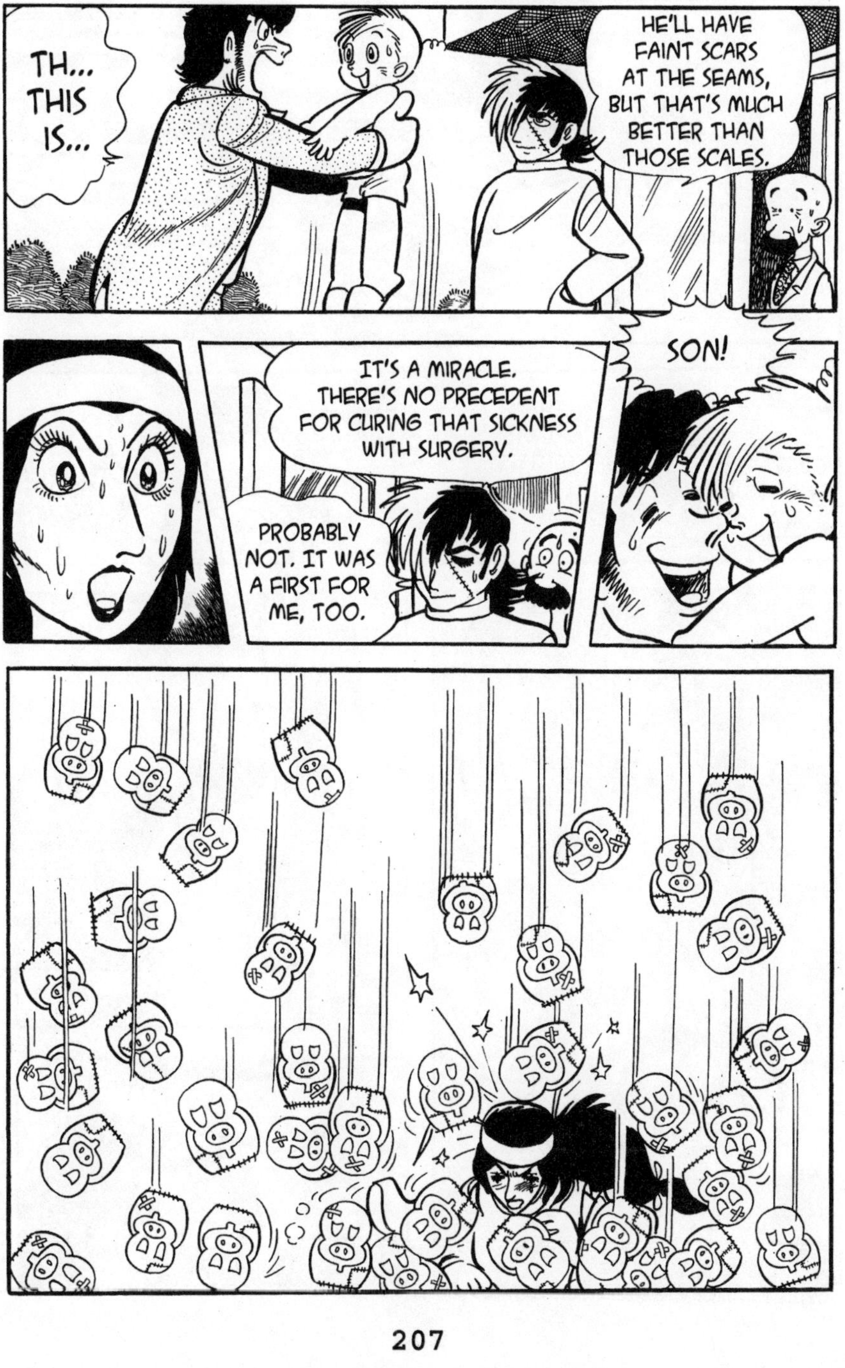
HE'LL HAVE FAINT SCARS AT THE SEAMS, BUT THAT'S MUCH BETTER THAN THOSE SCALES.
TH... THIS IS...
SON!
IT'S A MIRACLE. THERE'S NO PRECEDENT FOR CURING THAT SICKNESS WITH SURGERY.
PROBABLY NOT. IT WAS A FIRST FOR ME, TOO.

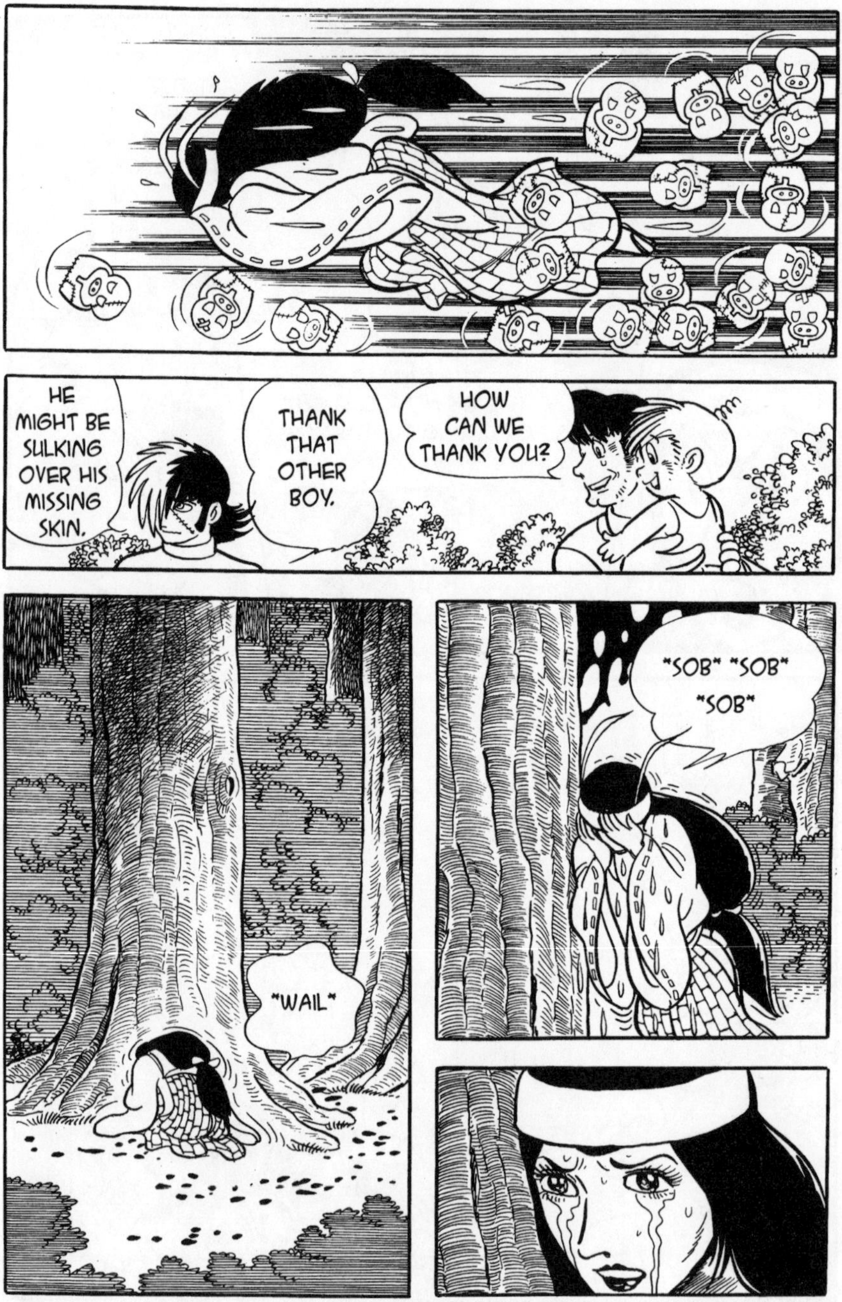
HOW CAN WE THANK YOU?
THANK THAT OTHER BOY.
HE MIGHT BE SULKING OVER HIS MISSING SKIN.
"SOB" "SOB" "SOB"
"WAIL"

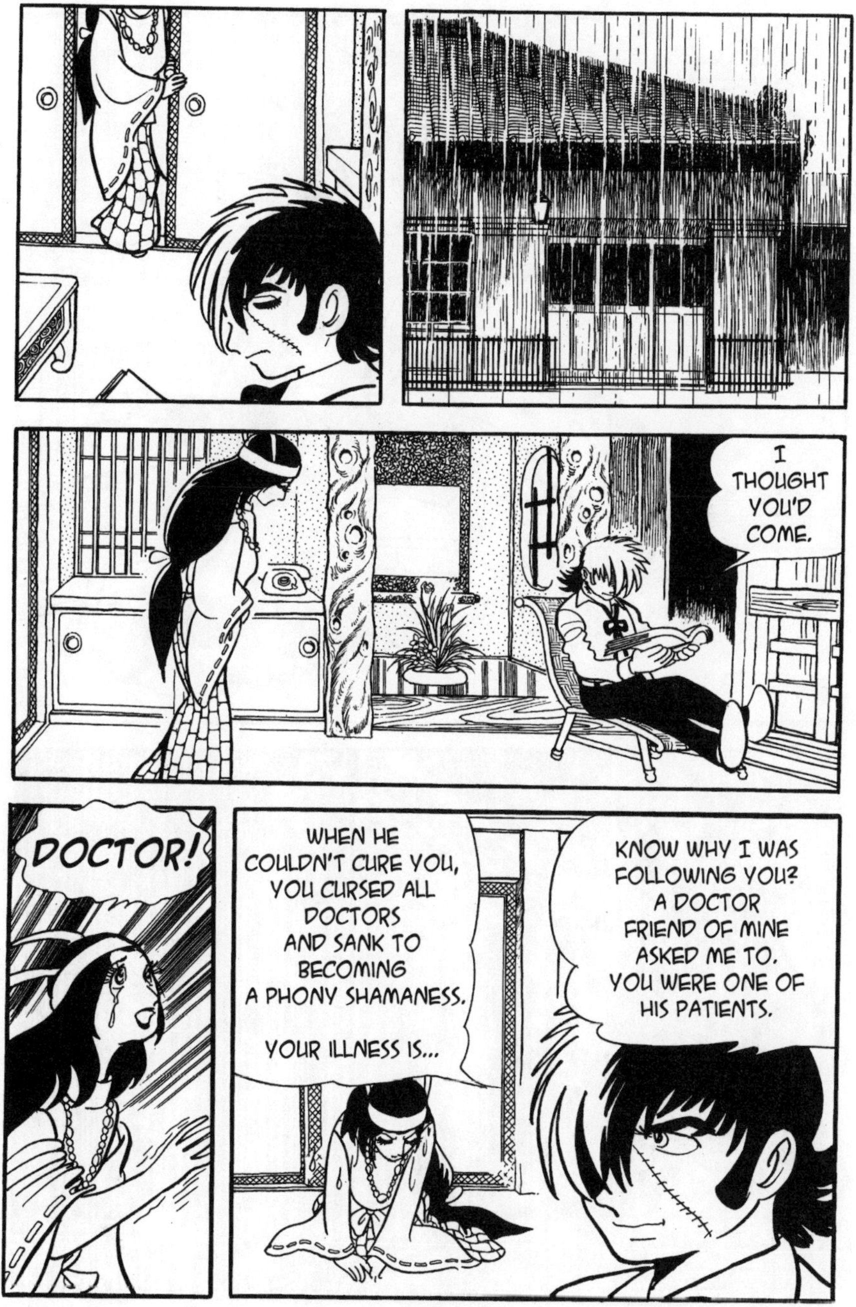
I THOUGHT YOU'D COME.
KNOW WHY I WAS FOLLOWING YOU? A DOCTOR FRIEND OF MINE ASKED ME TO. YOU WERE ONE OF HIS PATIENTS.
WHEN HE COULDN'T CURE YOU, YOU CURSED ALL DOCTORS AND SANK TO BECOMING A PHONY SHAMANESS.
YOUR ILLNESS IS...
DOCTOR!

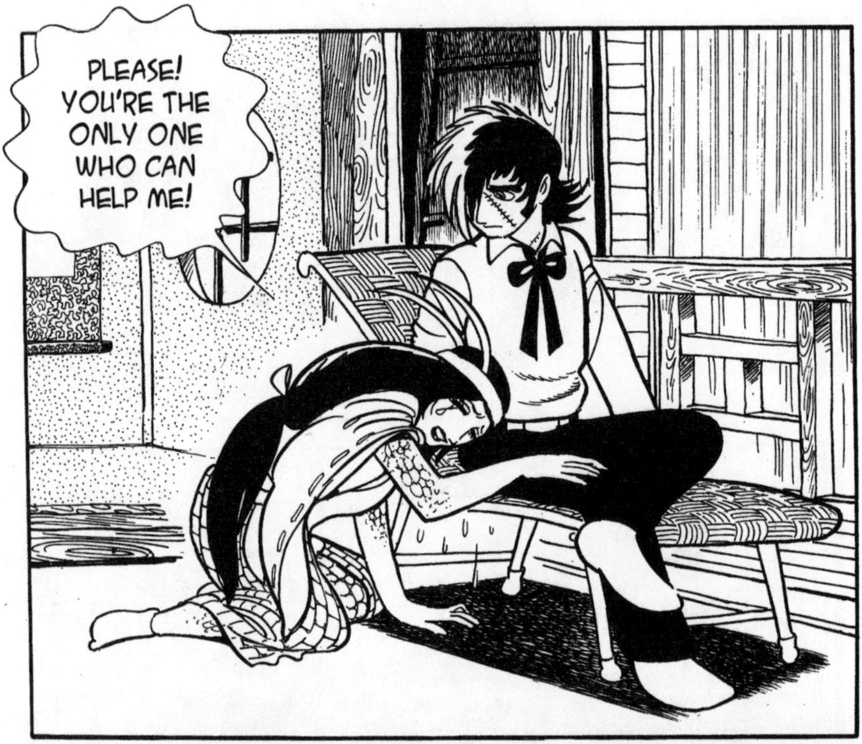
PLEASE! YOU'RE THE ONLY ONE WHO CAN HELP ME!

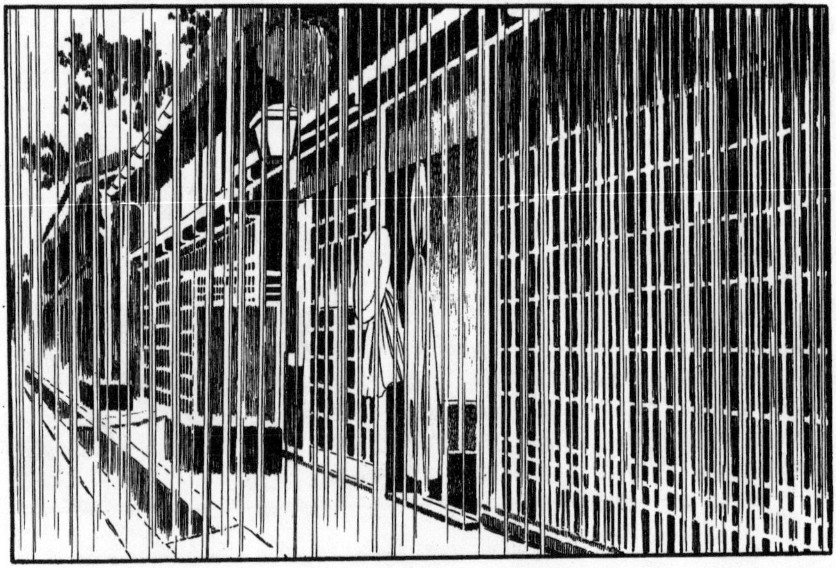

GIFT TO THE FUTURE

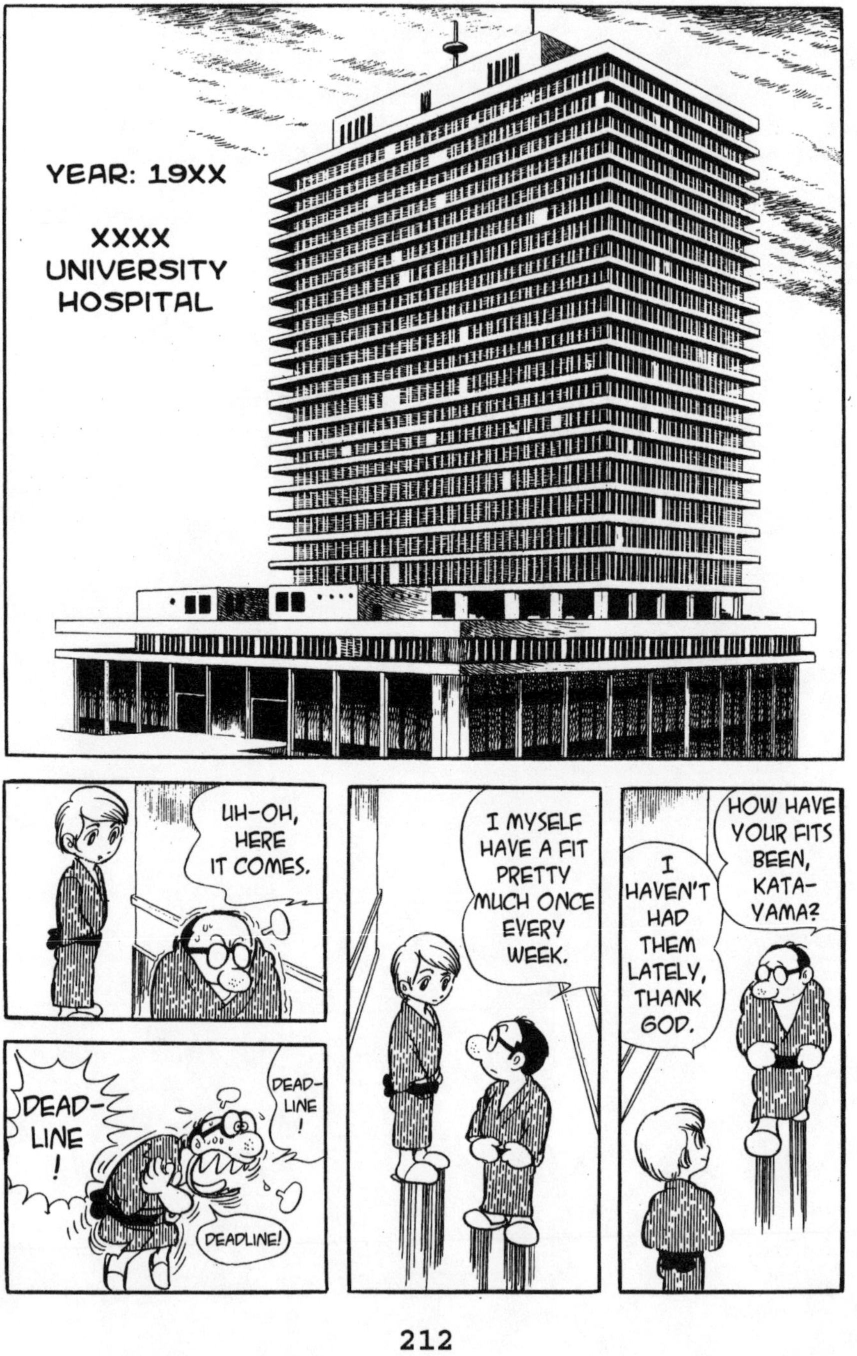
YEAR: 19XX
XXXX UNIVERSITY HOSPITAL
HOW HAVE YOUR FITS BEEN, KATA-YAMA?
I HAVEN'T HAD THEM LATELY, THANK GOD.
I MYSELF HAVE A FIT PRETTY MUCH ONCE EVERY WEEK.
UH-OH, HERE IT COMES.
DEAD-LINE!
DEAD-LINE!
DEADLINE!

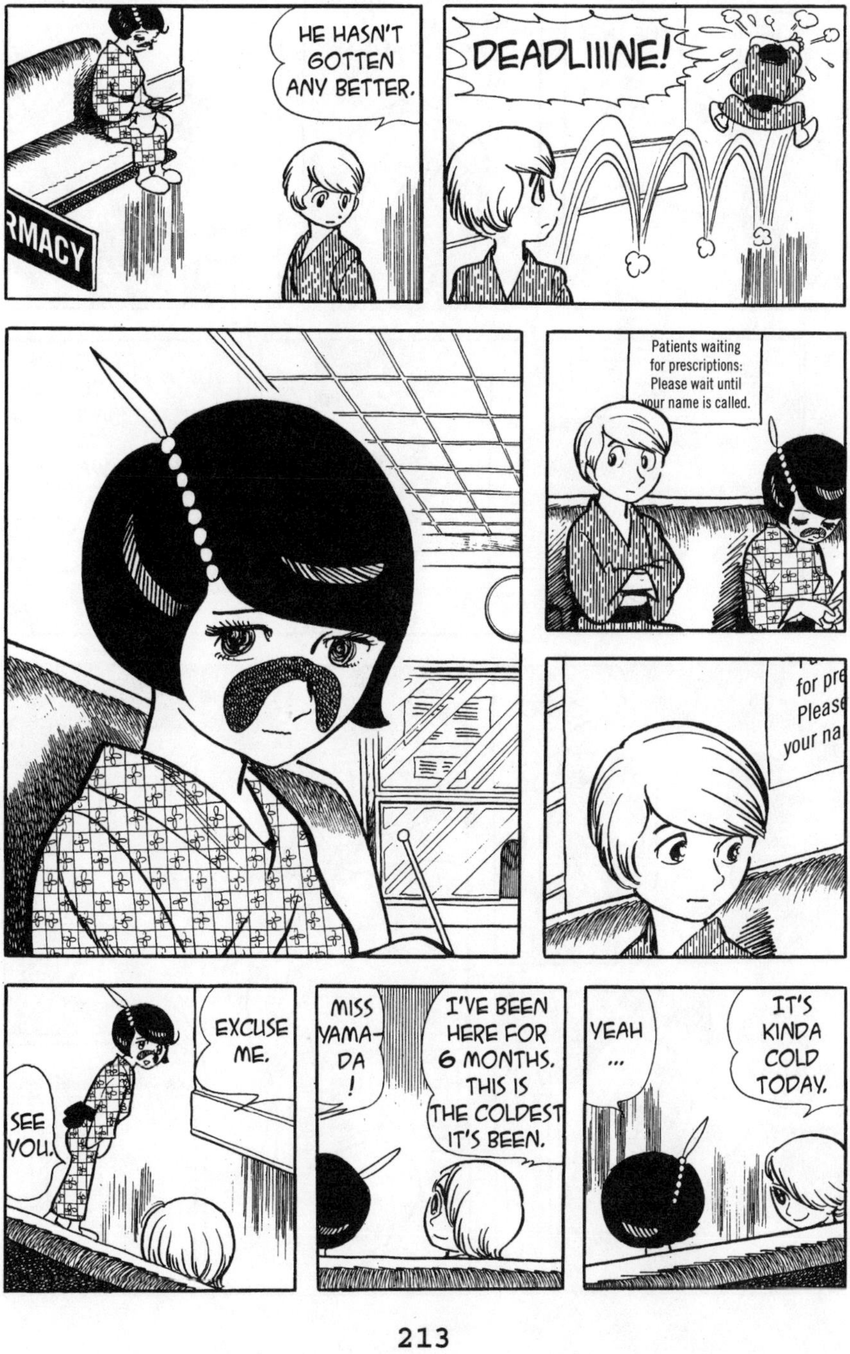
DEADLIIINE!
HE HASN'T GOTTEN ANY BETTER.
RMACY
Patients waiting for prescriptions: Please wait until your name is called.
IT'S KINDA COLD TODAY.
YEAH ...
I'VE BEEN HERE FOR 6 MONTHS. THIS IS THE COLDEST IT'S BEEN.
MISS YAMA-DA!
EXCUSE ME.
SEE YOU.

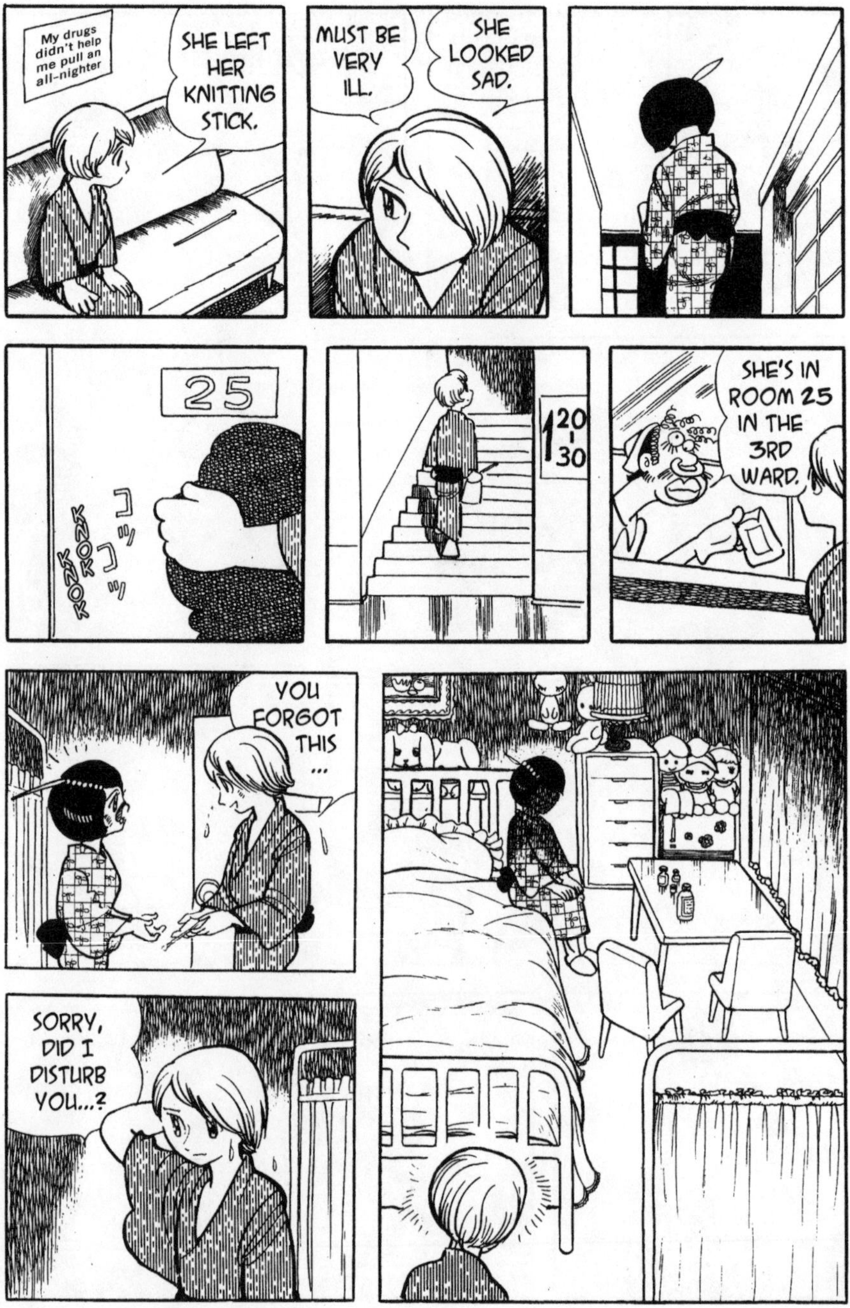
SHE LOOKED SAD.
MUST BE VERY ILL.
My drugs didn't help me pull an all-nighter
SHE LEFT HER KNITTING STICK.
SHE'S IN ROOM 25 IN THE 3RD WARD.
1 20 - 30
25
コツ コツ
KNOK KNOK
YOU FORGOT THIS ...
SORRY, DID I DISTURB YOU...?

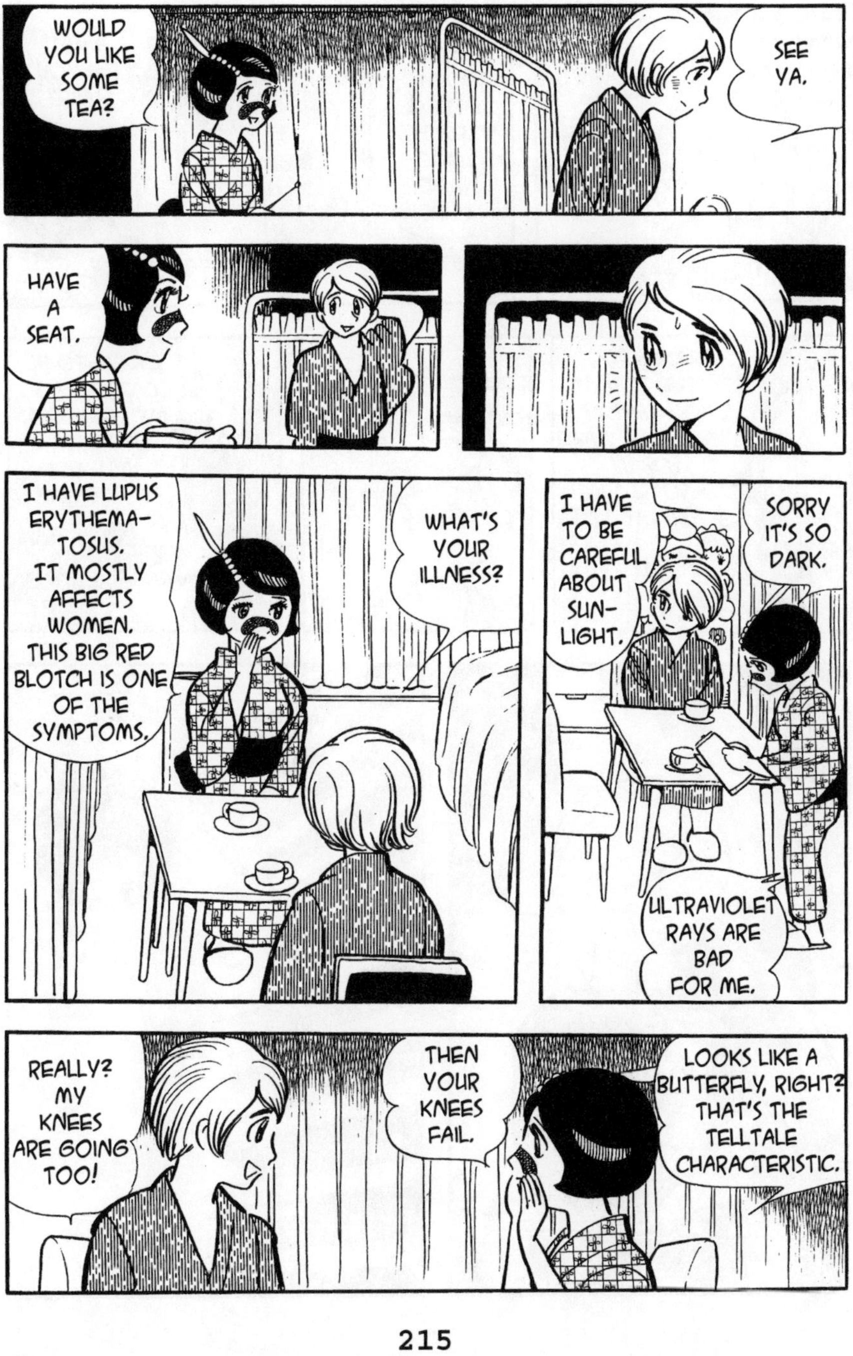

SEE YA.
WOULD YOU LIKE SOME TEA?
HAVE A SEAT.
SORRY IT'S SO DARK.
I HAVE TO BE CAREFUL ABOUT SUN-LIGHT.
ULTRAVIOLET RAYS ARE BAD FOR ME.
WHAT'S YOUR ILLNESS?
I HAVE LUPUS ERYTHEMA-TOSUS. IT MOSTLY AFFECTS WOMEN. THIS BIG RED BLOTCH IS ONE OF THE SYMPTOMS.
LOOKS LIKE A BUTTERFLY, RIGHT? THAT'S THE TELLTALE CHARACTERISTIC.
THEN YOUR KNEES FAIL.
REALLY? MY KNEES ARE GOING TOO!

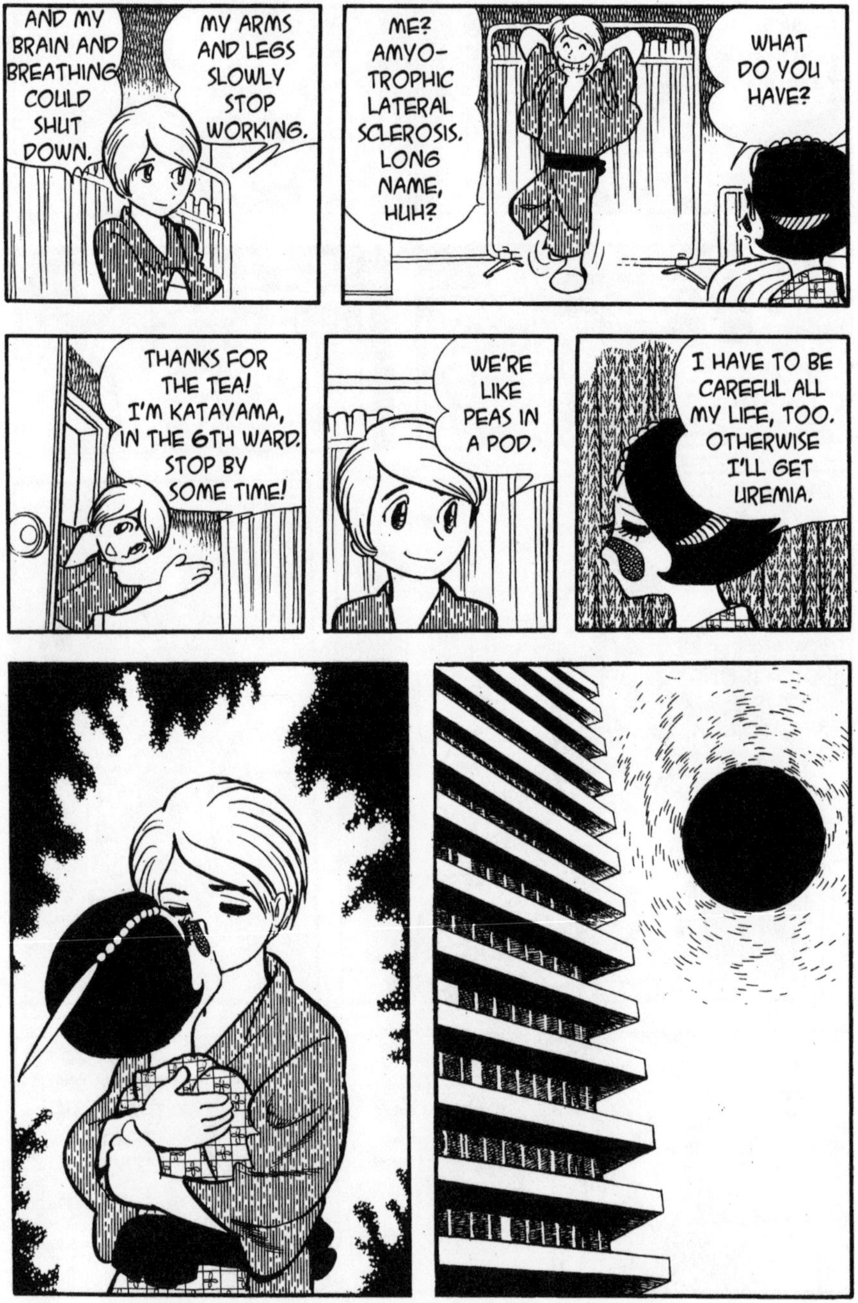

WHAT DO YOU HAVE?
ME? AMYO-TROPHIC LATERAL SCLEROSIS. LONG NAME, HUH?
MY ARMS AND LEGS SLOWLY STOP WORKING.
AND MY BRAIN AND BREATHING COULD SHUT DOWN.
I HAVE TO BE CAREFUL ALL MY LIFE, TOO. OTHERWISE I'LL GET UREMIA.
WE'RE LIKE PEAS IN A POD.
THANKS FOR THE TEA! I'M KATAYAMA, IN THE 6TH WARD. STOP BY SOME TIME!

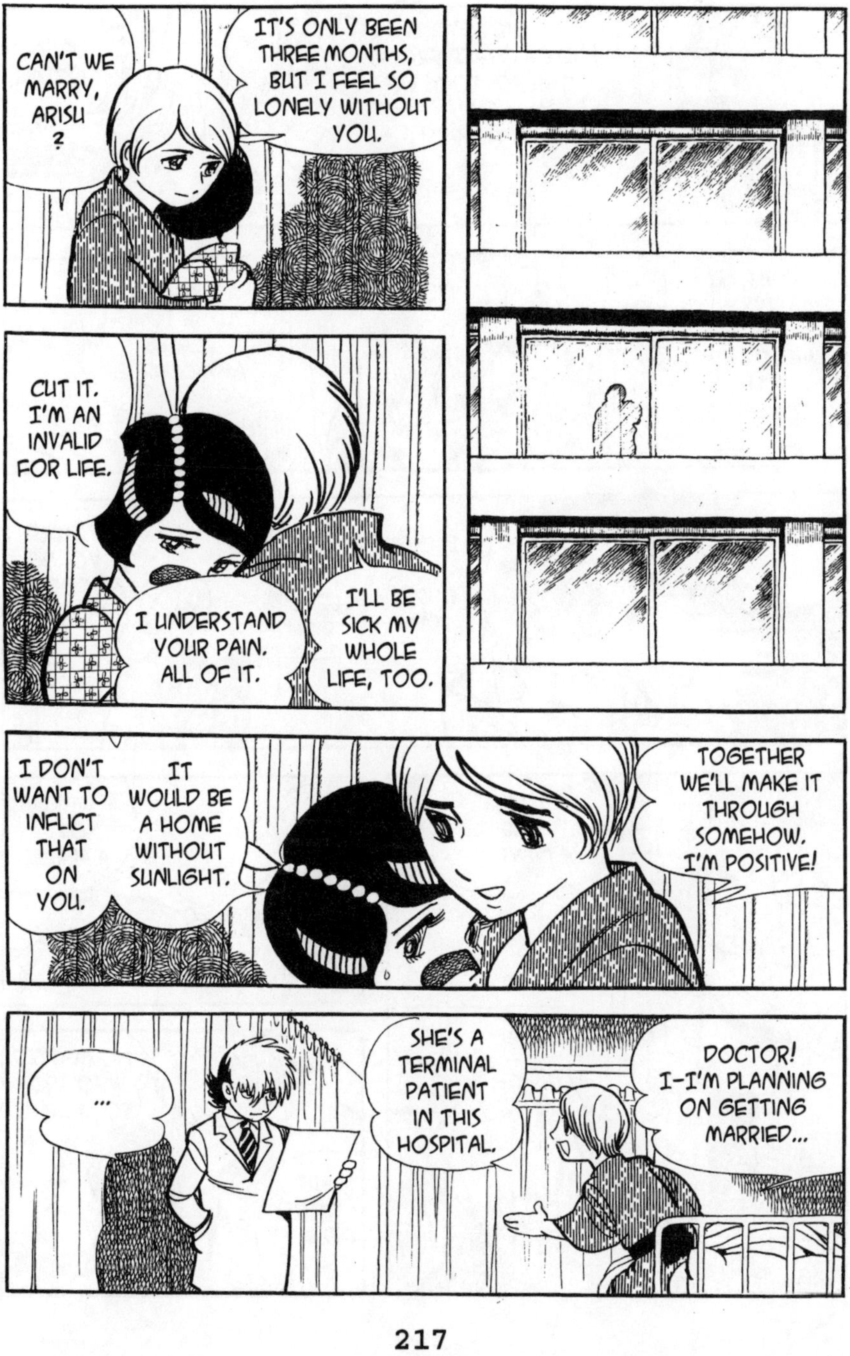
IT'S ONLY BEEN THREE MONTHS, BUT I FEEL SO LONELY WITHOUT YOU.
CAN'T WE MARRY, ARISU?
CUT IT. I'M AN INVALID FOR LIFE.
I UNDERSTAND YOUR PAIN. ALL OF IT.
I'LL BE SICK MY WHOLE LIFE, TOO.
TOGETHER WE'LL MAKE IT THROUGH SOMEHOW. I'M POSITIVE!
IT WOULD BE A HOME WITHOUT SUNLIGHT.
I DON'T WANT TO INFLICT THAT ON YOU.
DOCTOR! I-I'M PLANNING ON GETTING MARRIED...
SHE'S A TERMINAL PATIENT IN THIS HOSPITAL.
...

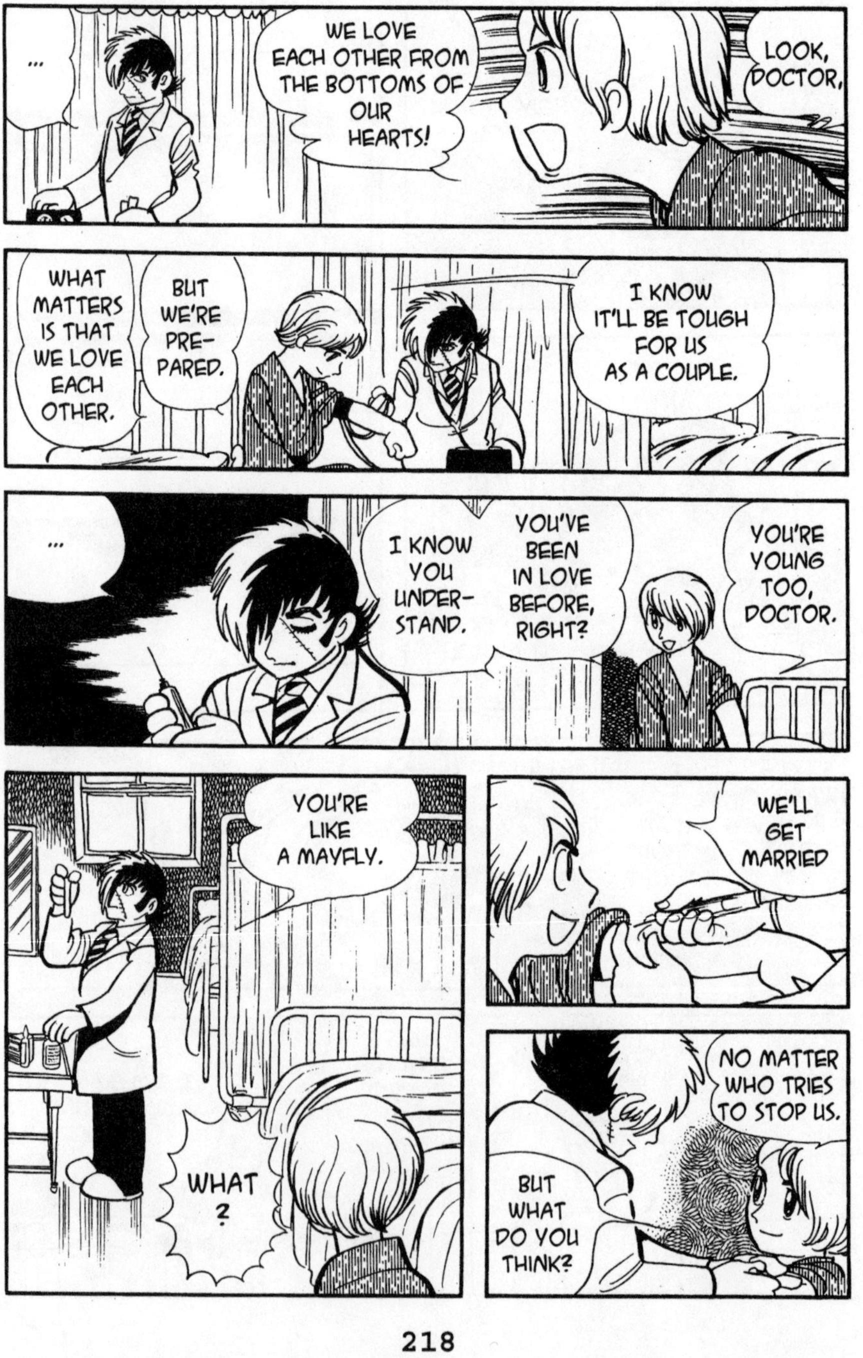
LOOK, DOCTOR,
WE LOVE EACH OTHER FROM THE BOTTOMS OF OUR HEARTS!
...
I KNOW IT'LL BE TOUGH FOR US AS A COUPLE.
BUT WE'RE PRE-PARED.
WHAT MATTERS IS THAT WE LOVE EACH OTHER.
YOU'RE YOUNG TOO, DOCTOR.
YOU'VE BEEN IN LOVE BEFORE, RIGHT?
I KNOW YOU UNDER-STAND.
...
WE'LL GET MARRIED
NO MATTER WHO TRIES TO STOP US.
BUT WHAT DO YOU THINK?
YOU'RE LIKE A MAYFLY.
WHAT?

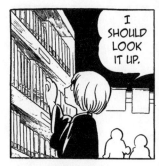

MAYFLY ?
WHAT A THING TO SAY ...
HE THINKS I'M FLITTY?
I SHOULD LOOK IT UP.
ONCE MATURE, MAYFLIES CAN NEITHER EAT NOR DRINK. LIVING FOR JUST A WEEK OR TWO, THEY MERELY SEEK A MATE, AFTER WHICH DEATH AWAITS.
IT HURTS...
MY KNEES HURT!
PLEASE GIVE ME MY INJECTION. I CAN'T STAND IT!
YOU'RE STILL PLANNING A WEDDING EVEN WITH SO MUCH PAIN?
YES ...
THEY'RE SEPARATE ISSUES.
SILLY. YOU'LL NEED TREATMENT YOUR WHOLE LIFE.
YOU CAN'T LEAD A MARRIED LIFE!
BUT I WILL.

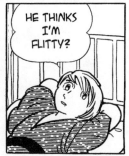

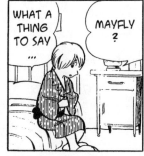

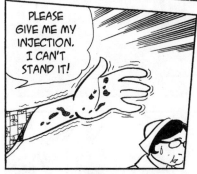

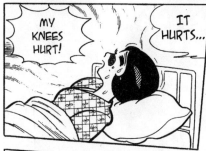

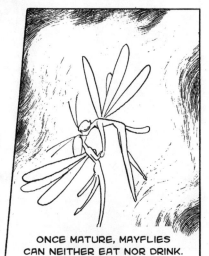

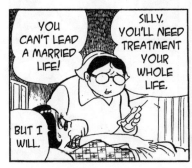

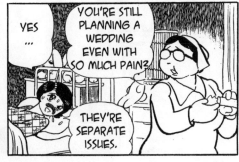

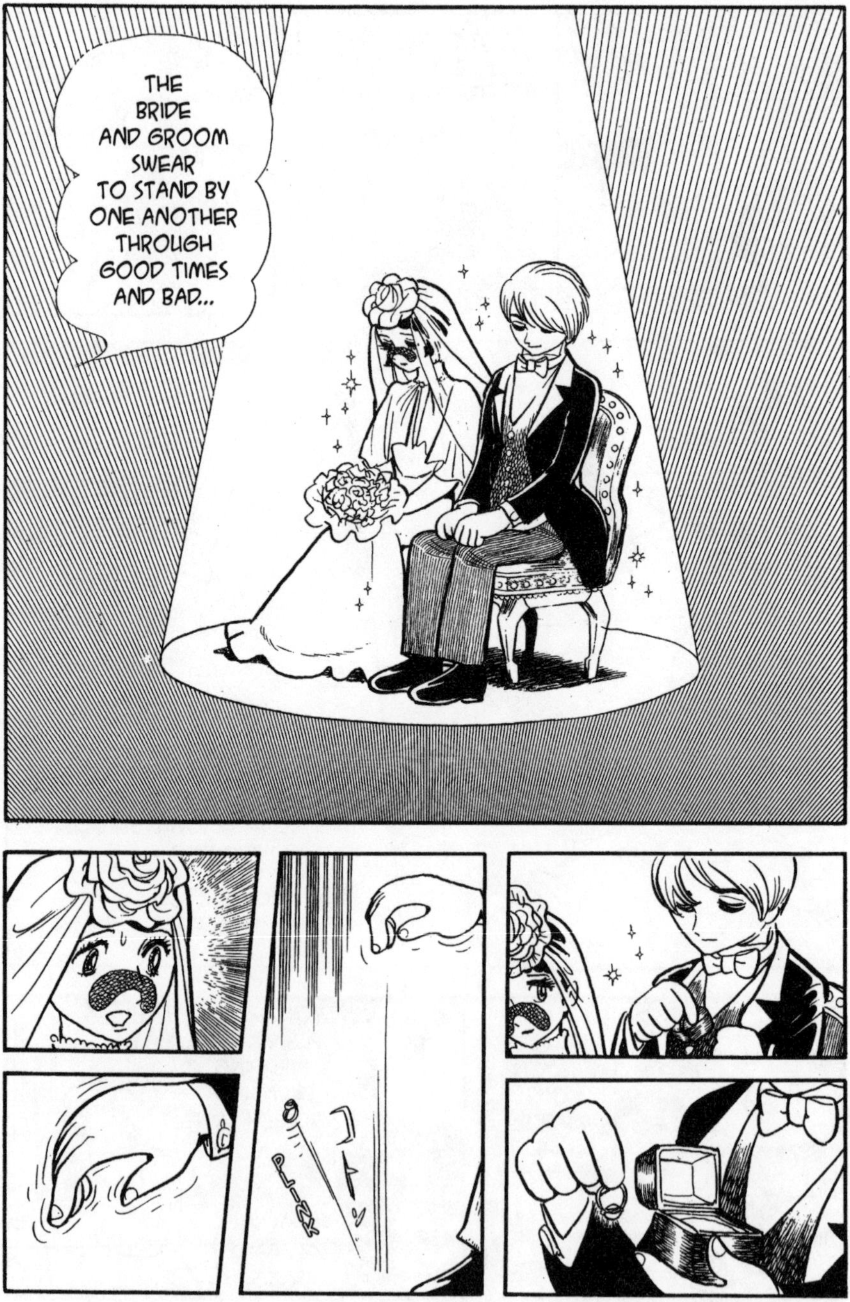
THE BRIDE AND GROOM SWEAR TO STAND BY ONE ANOTHER THROUGH GOOD TIMES AND BAD...
PLINK

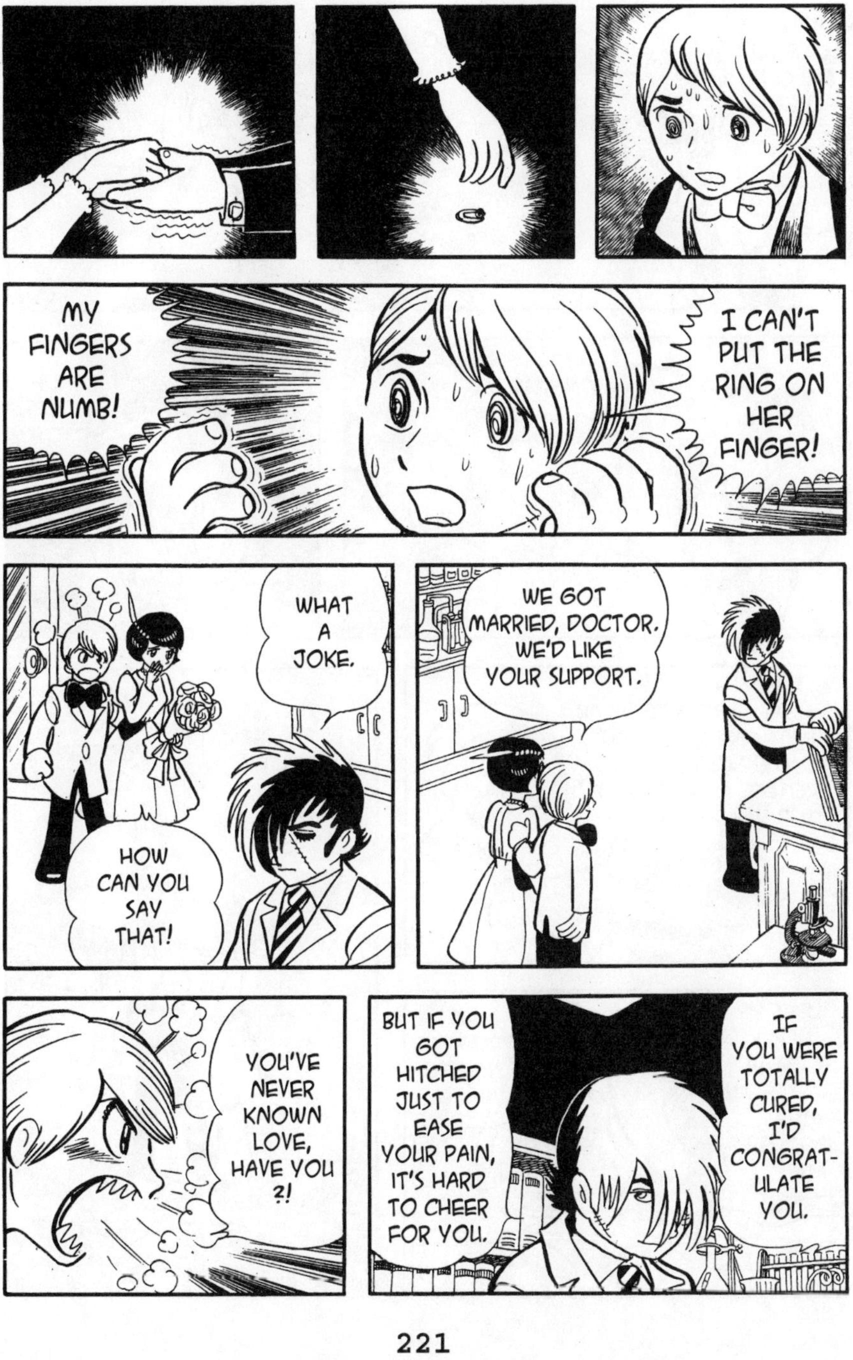
I CAN'T PUT THE RING ON HER FINGER!
MY FINGERS ARE NUMB!
WE GOT MARRIED, DOCTOR. WE'D LIKE YOUR SUPPORT.
WHAT A JOKE.
HOW CAN YOU SAY THAT!
IF YOU WERE TOTALLY CURED, I'D CONGRAT-ULATE YOU.
BUT IF YOU GOT HITCHED JUST TO EASE YOUR PAIN, IT'S HARD TO CHEER FOR YOU.
YOU'VE NEVER KNOWN LOVE, HAVE YOU ?!

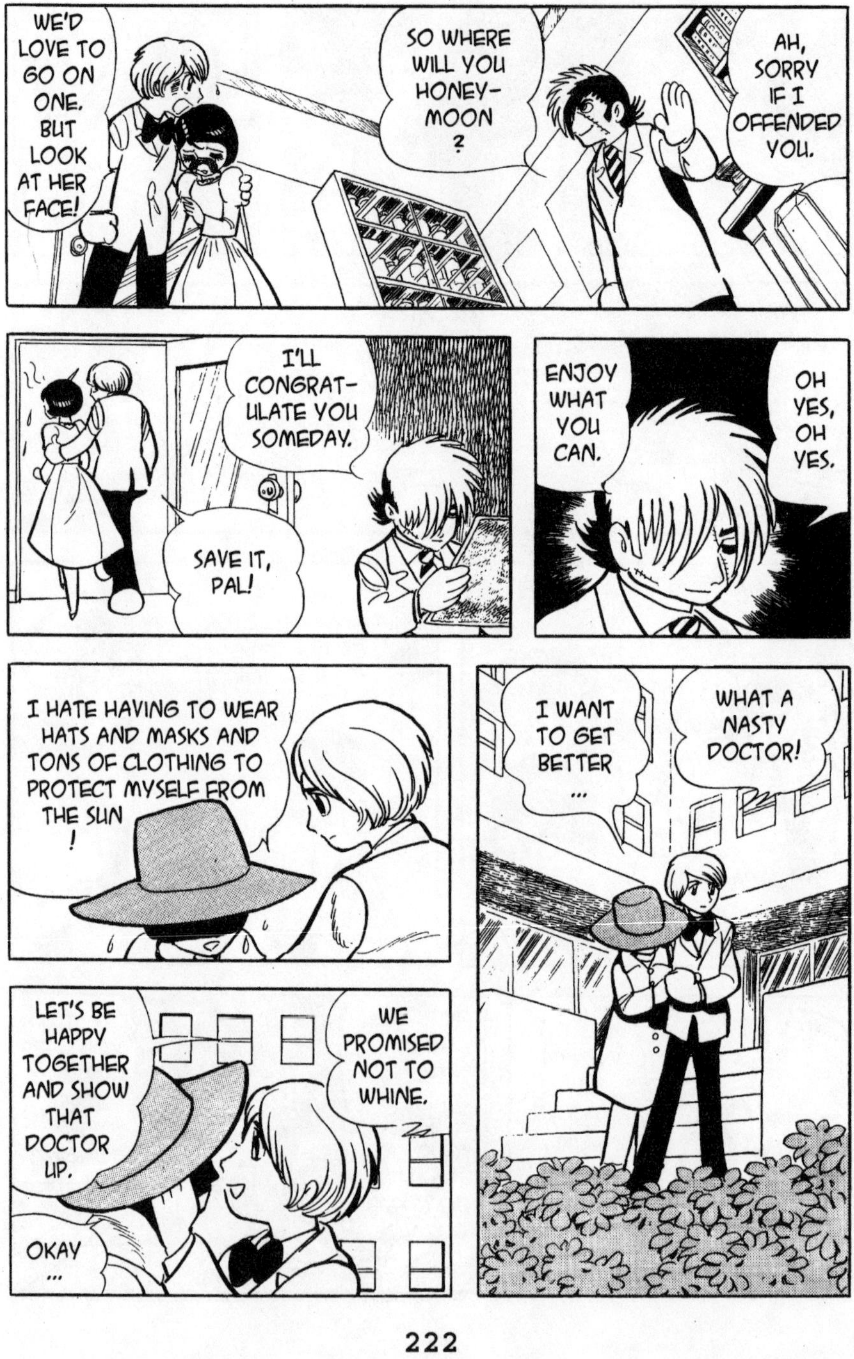
AH, SORRY IF I OFFENDED YOU.
SO WHERE WILL YOU HONEY-MOON?
WE'D LOVE TO GO ON ONE. BUT LOOK AT HER FACE!
OH YES, OH YES.
ENJOY WHAT YOU CAN.
I'LL CONGRAT-ULATE YOU SOMEDAY.
SAVE IT, PAL!
WHAT A NASTY DOCTOR!
I WANT TO GET BETTER ...
I HATE HAVING TO WEAR HATS AND MASKS AND TONS OF CLOTHING TO PROTECT MYSELF FROM THE SUN!
WE PROMISED NOT TO WHINE.
LET'S BE HAPPY TOGETHER AND SHOW THAT DOCTOR UP.
OKAY ...

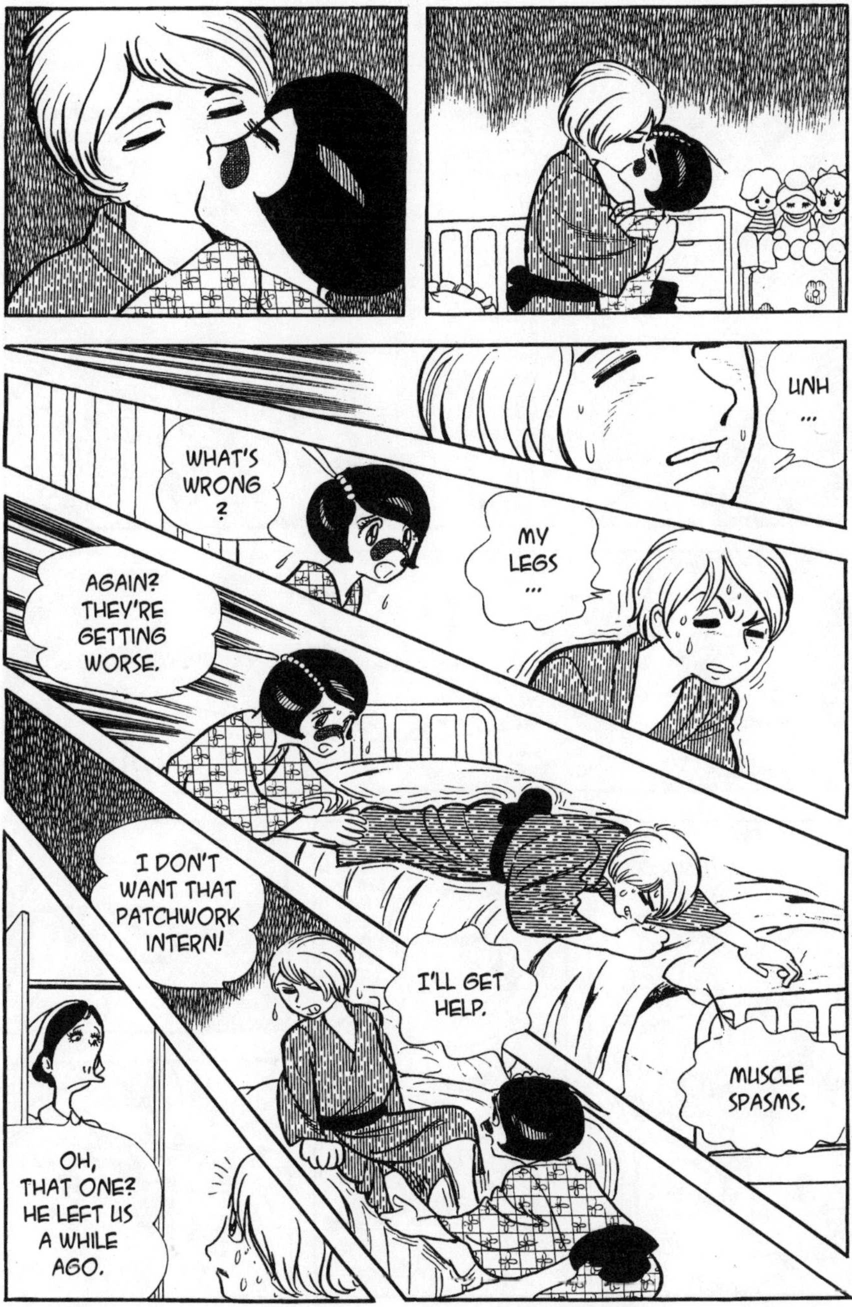
UNH ...
WHAT'S WRONG?
MY LEGS ...
AGAIN? THEY'RE GETTING WORSE.
MUSCLE SPASMS.
I'LL GET HELP.
I DON'T WANT THAT PATCHWORK INTERN!
OH, THAT ONE? HE LEFT US A WHILE AGO.

10 YEARS LATER— THE ACADEMY OF SCIENCES, MOSCOW...

SURGERY COMPLETE.

MEMBRANE ARACHNOID SUTURING

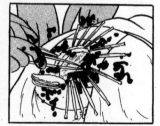

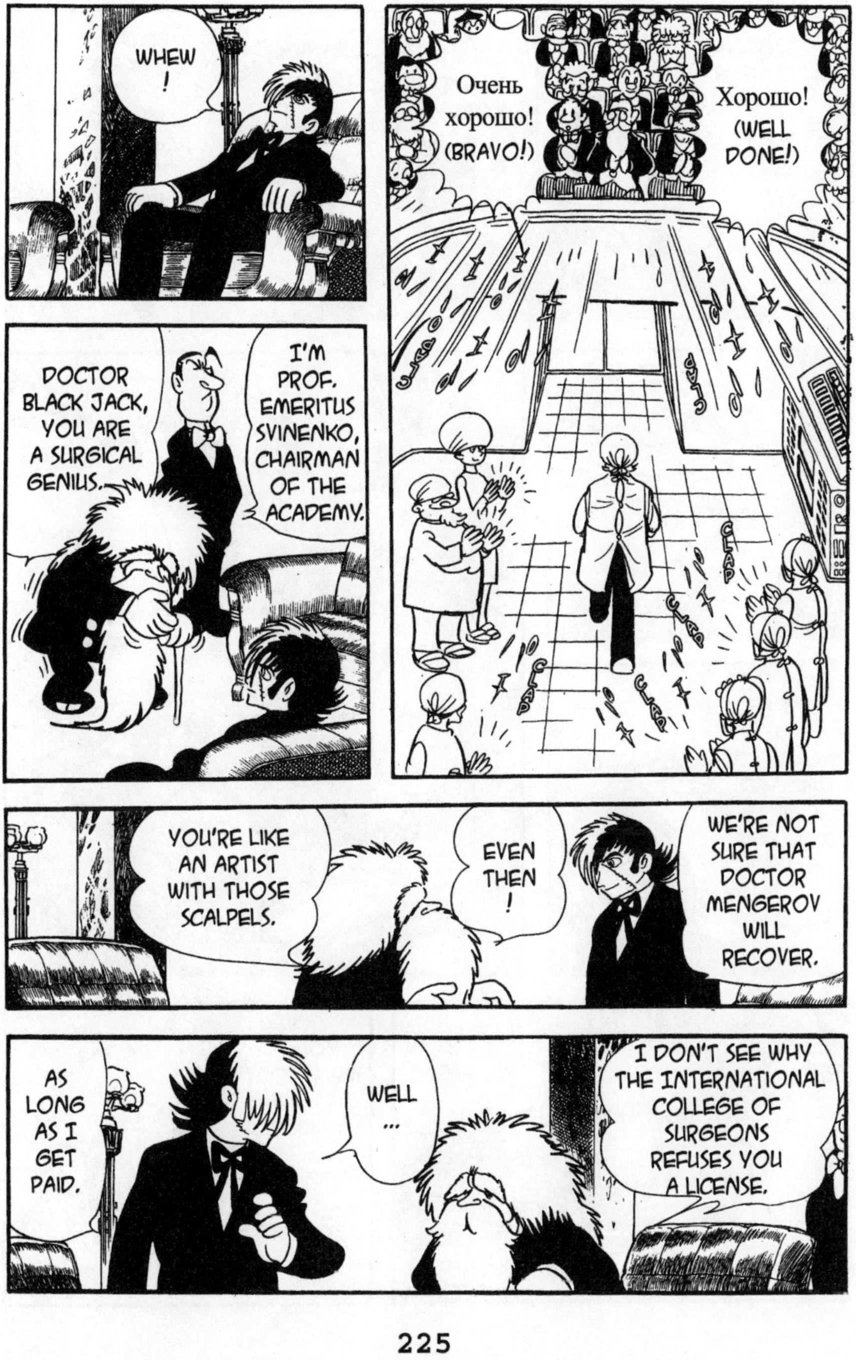
Хорошо! (WELL DONE!)
Очень хорошо! (BRAVO!)
CLAP
CLAP
CLAP
CLAP
CLAP
CLAP
WHEW!
I'M PROF. EMERITUS SVINENKO, CHAIRMAN OF THE ACADEMY.
DOCTOR BLACK JACK, YOU ARE A SURGICAL GENIUS...
WE'RE NOT SURE THAT DOCTOR MENGEROV WILL RECOVER.
EVEN THEN!
YOU'RE LIKE AN ARTIST WITH THOSE SCALPELS.
I DON'T SEE WHY THE INTERNATIONAL COLLEGE OF SURGEONS REFUSES YOU A LICENSE.
WELL...
AS LONG AS I GET PAID.

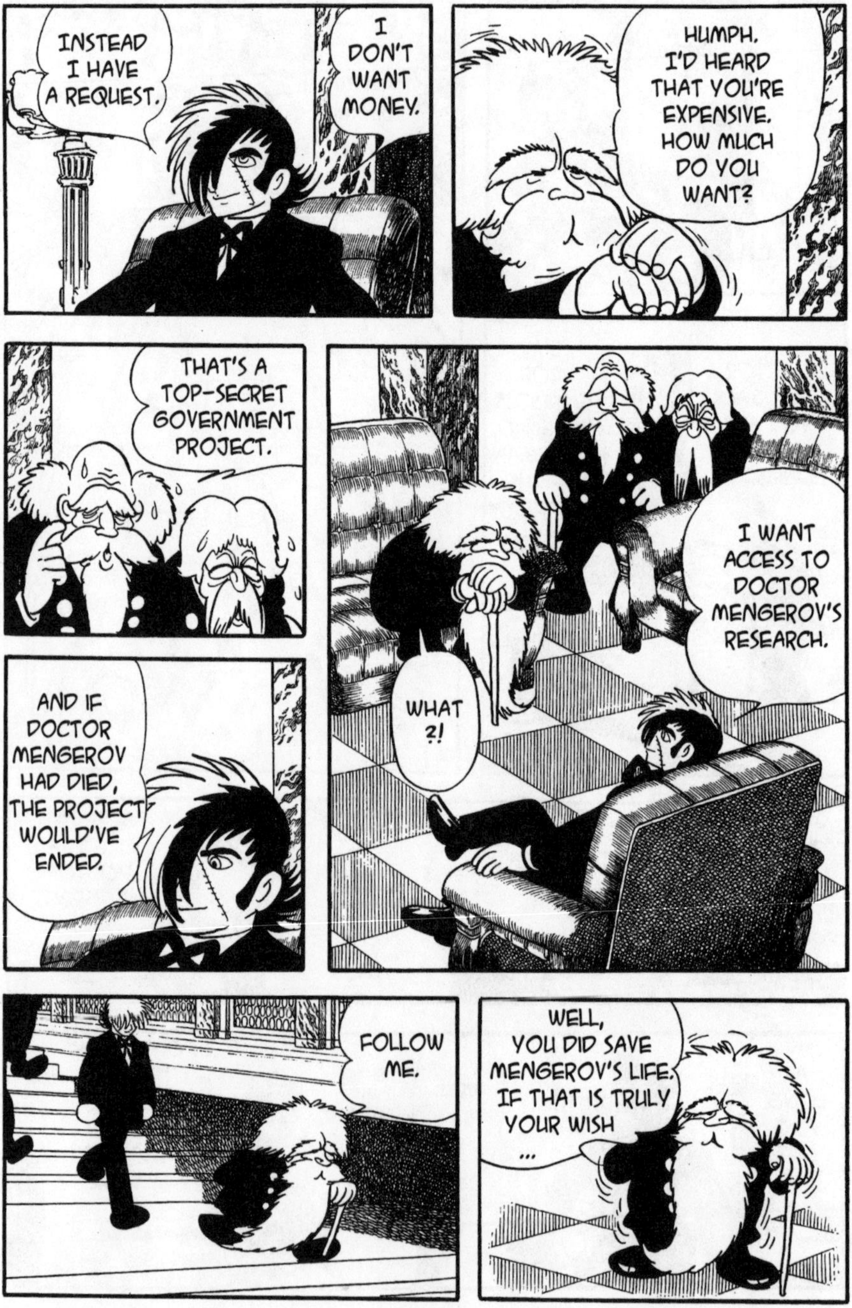
HUMPH. I'D HEARD THAT YOU'RE EXPENSIVE. HOW MUCH DO YOU WANT?
I DON'T WANT MONEY.
INSTEAD I HAVE A REQUEST.
I WANT ACCESS TO DOCTOR MENGEROV'S RESEARCH.
WHAT ?!
THAT'S A TOP-SECRET GOVERNMENT PROJECT.
AND IF DOCTOR MENGEROV HAD DIED, THE PROJECT WOULD'VE ENDED.
WELL, YOU DID SAVE MENGEROV'S LIFE. IF THAT IS TRULY YOUR WISH ...
FOLLOW ME.

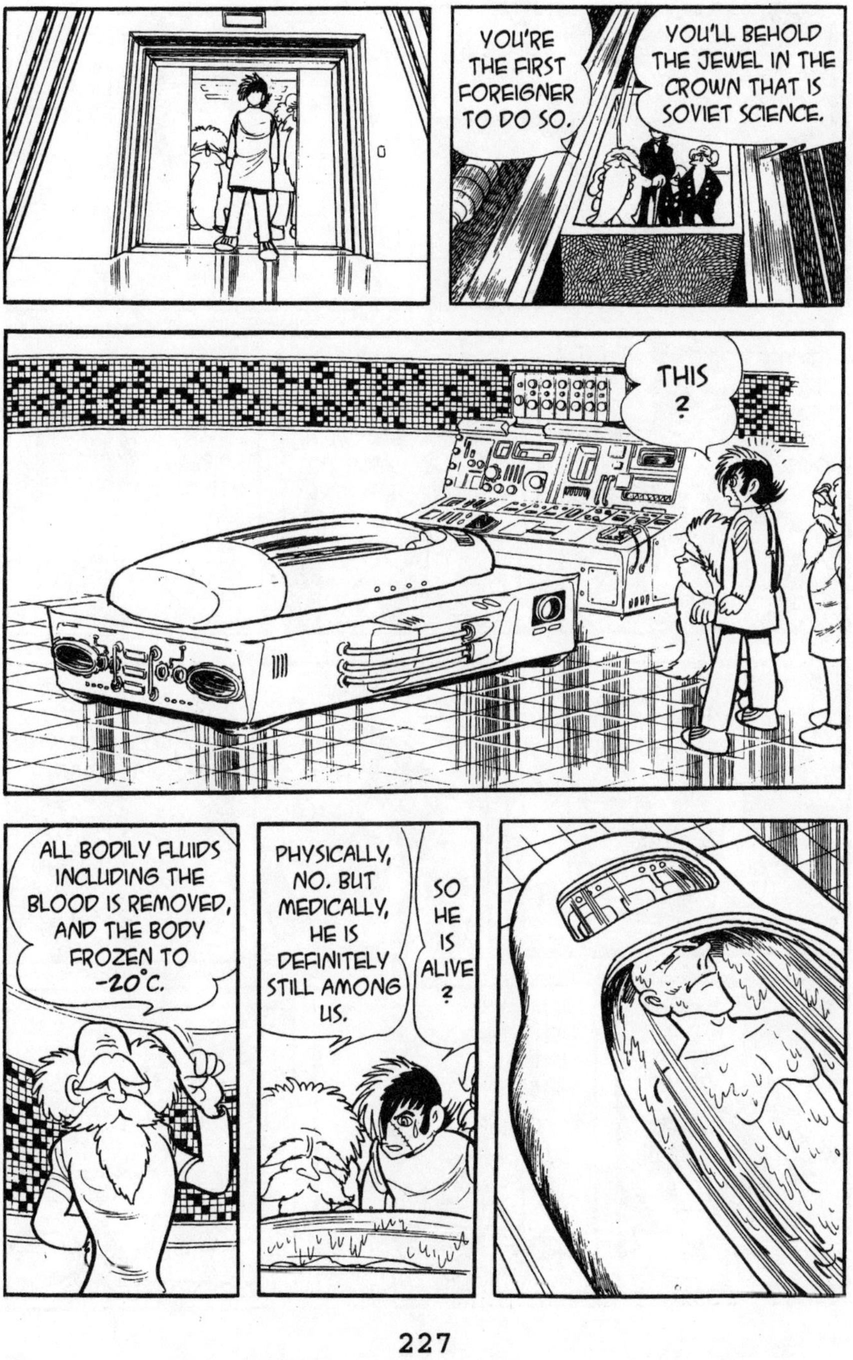
YOU'LL BEHOLD THE JEWEL IN THE CROWN THAT IS SOVIET SCIENCE.
YOU'RE THE FIRST FOREIGNER TO DO SO.
THIS ?
SO HE IS ALIVE ?
PHYSICALLY, NO. BUT MEDICALLY, HE IS DEFINITELY STILL AMONG US.
ALL BODILY FLUIDS INCLUDING THE BLOOD IS REMOVED, AND THE BODY FROZEN TO -20°C.

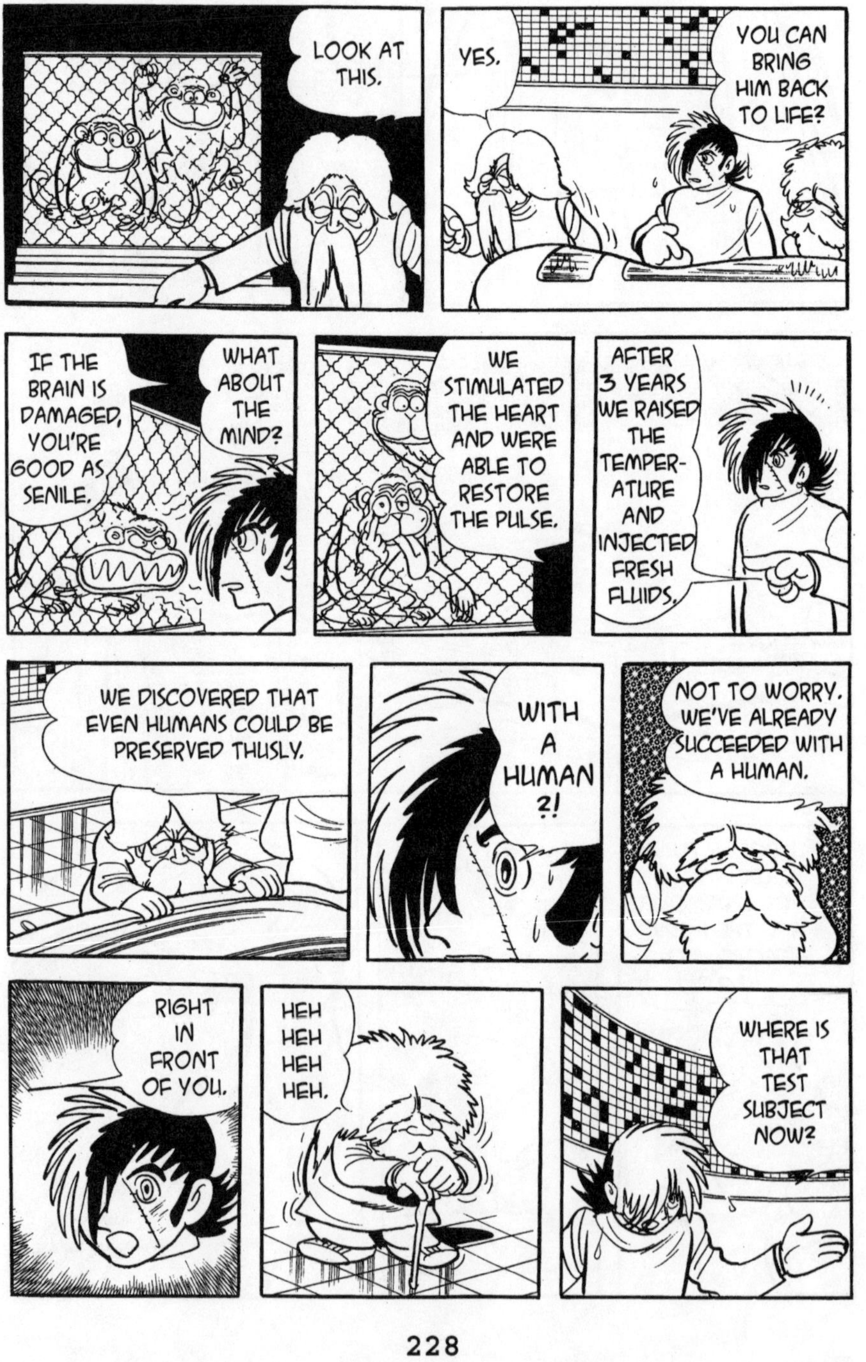
YOU CAN BRING HIM BACK TO LIFE?
YES.
LOOK AT THIS.
AFTER 3 YEARS WE RAISED THE TEMPER-ATURE AND INJECTED FRESH FLUIDS.
WE STIMULATED THE HEART AND WERE ABLE TO RESTORE THE PULSE.
WHAT ABOUT THE MIND?
IF THE BRAIN IS DAMAGED, YOU'RE GOOD AS SENILE.
NOT TO WORRY. WE'VE ALREADY SUCCEEDED WITH A HUMAN.
WITH A HUMAN ?!
WE DISCOVERED THAT EVEN HUMANS COULD BE PRESERVED THUSLY.
WHERE IS THAT TEST SUBJECT NOW?
HEH HEH HEH HEH.
RIGHT IN FRONT OF YOU.

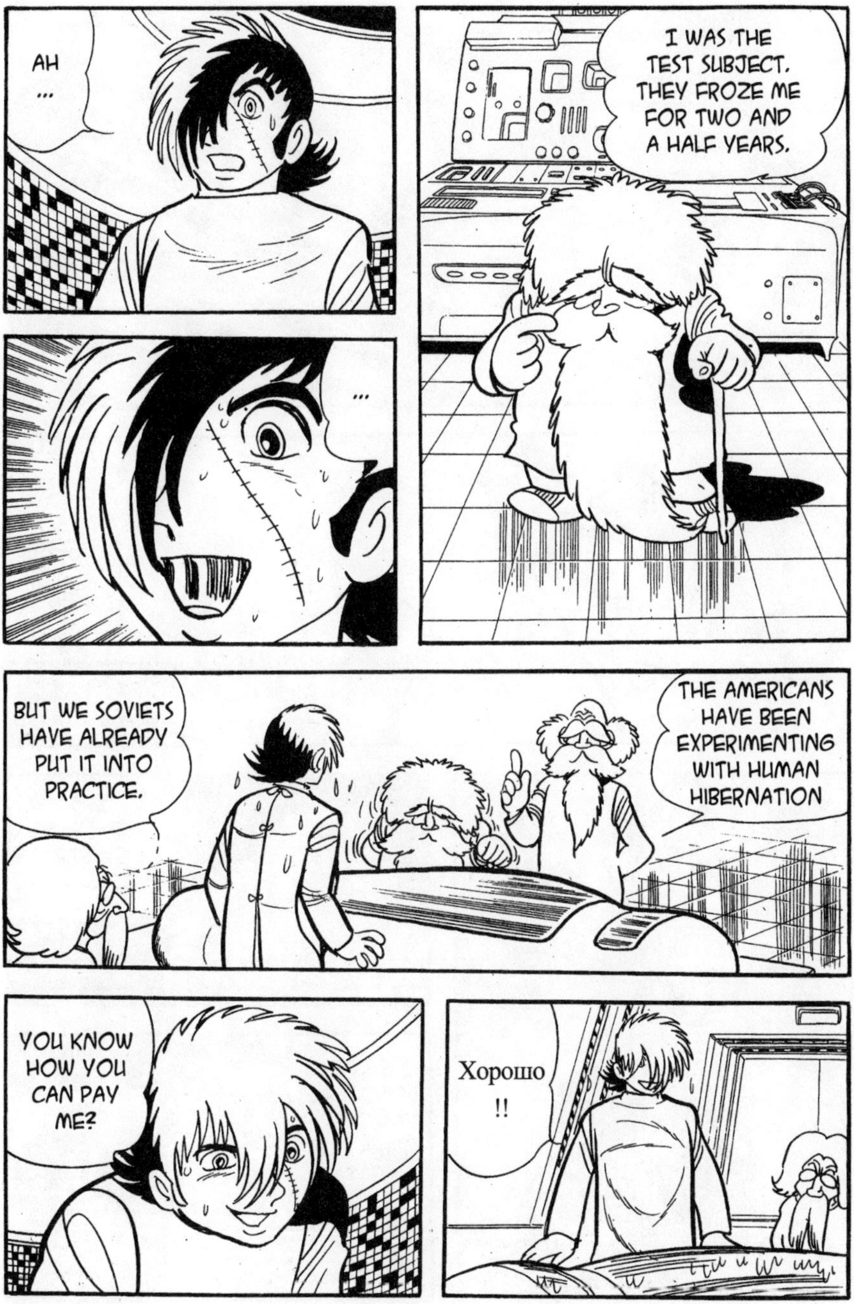
I WAS THE TEST SUBJECT. THEY FROZE ME FOR TWO AND A HALF YEARS.
AH ...
...
THE AMERICANS HAVE BEEN EXPERIMENTING WITH HUMAN HIBERNATION
BUT WE SOVIETS HAVE ALREADY PUT IT INTO PRACTICE.
Хорошо !!
YOU KNOW HOW YOU CAN PAY ME?

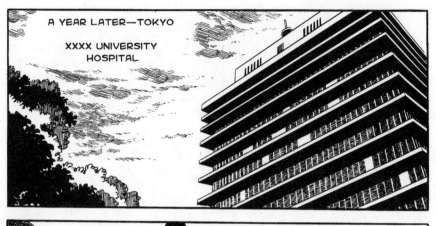

A YEAR LATER—TOKYO
XXXX UNIVERSITY HOSPITAL
IT'S END-STAGE BULBAR PALSY.
HE CAN'T USE HIS TONGUE, NEITHER SPEAK NOR EAT.
WE HAVE HIM ON A RESPIRATOR FOR NOW,
BUT IF HIS LUNGS TOTALLY GIVE OUT, THE END WILL NOT BE FAR AWAY ...
DARLING!

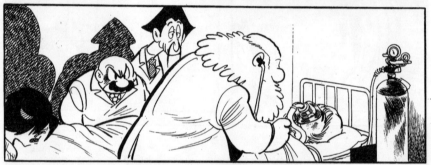

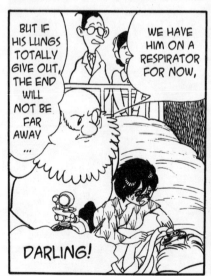

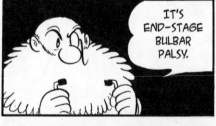

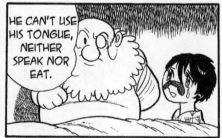

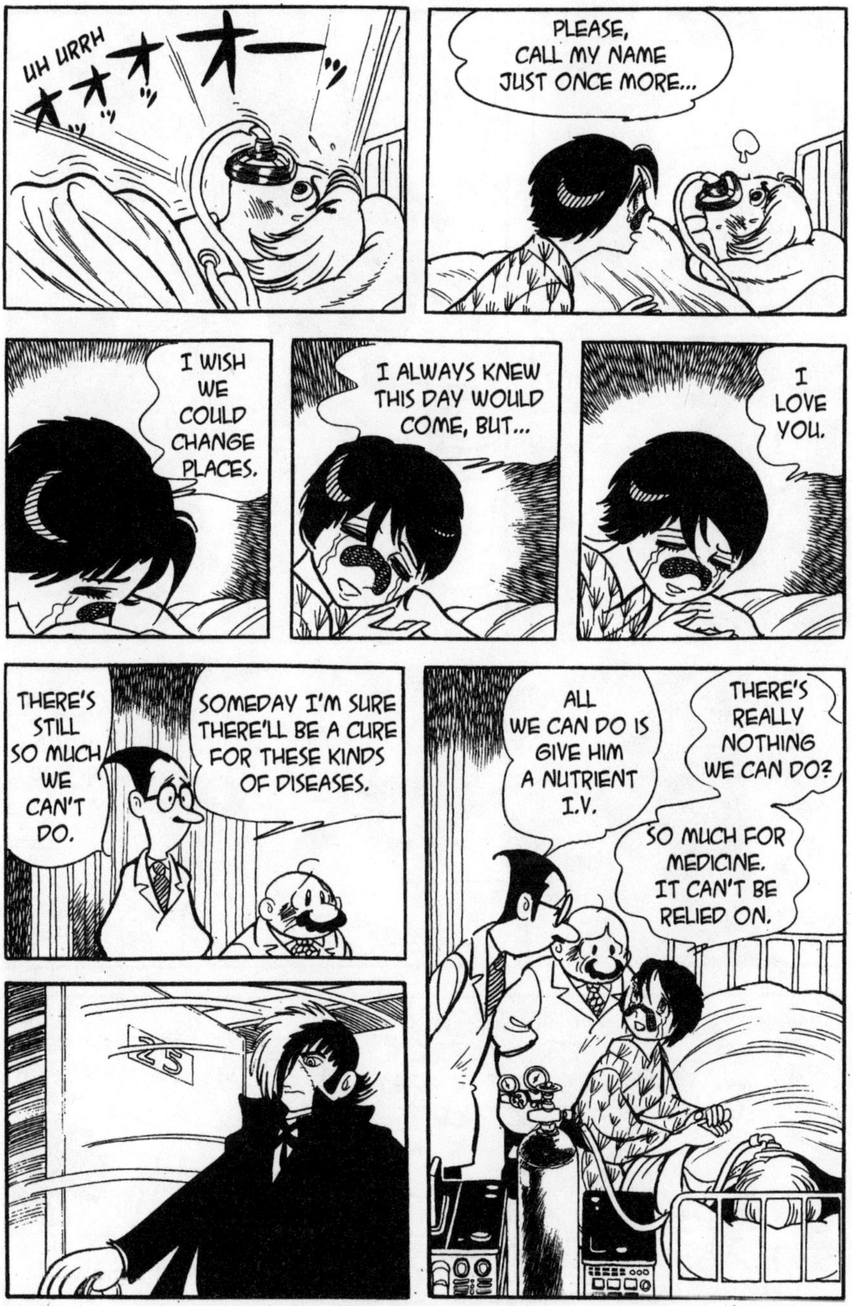
PLEASE, CALL MY NAME JUST ONCE MORE...
UH URRH
I LOVE YOU.
I ALWAYS KNEW THIS DAY WOULD COME, BUT...
I WISH WE COULD CHANGE PLACES.
THERE'S REALLY NOTHING WE CAN DO?
ALL WE CAN DO IS GIVE HIM A NUTRIENT I.V.
SO MUCH FOR MEDICINE. IT CAN'T BE RELIED ON.
SOMEDAY I'M SURE THERE'LL BE A CURE FOR THESE KINDS OF DISEASES.
THERE'S STILL SO MUCH WE CAN'T DO.
25

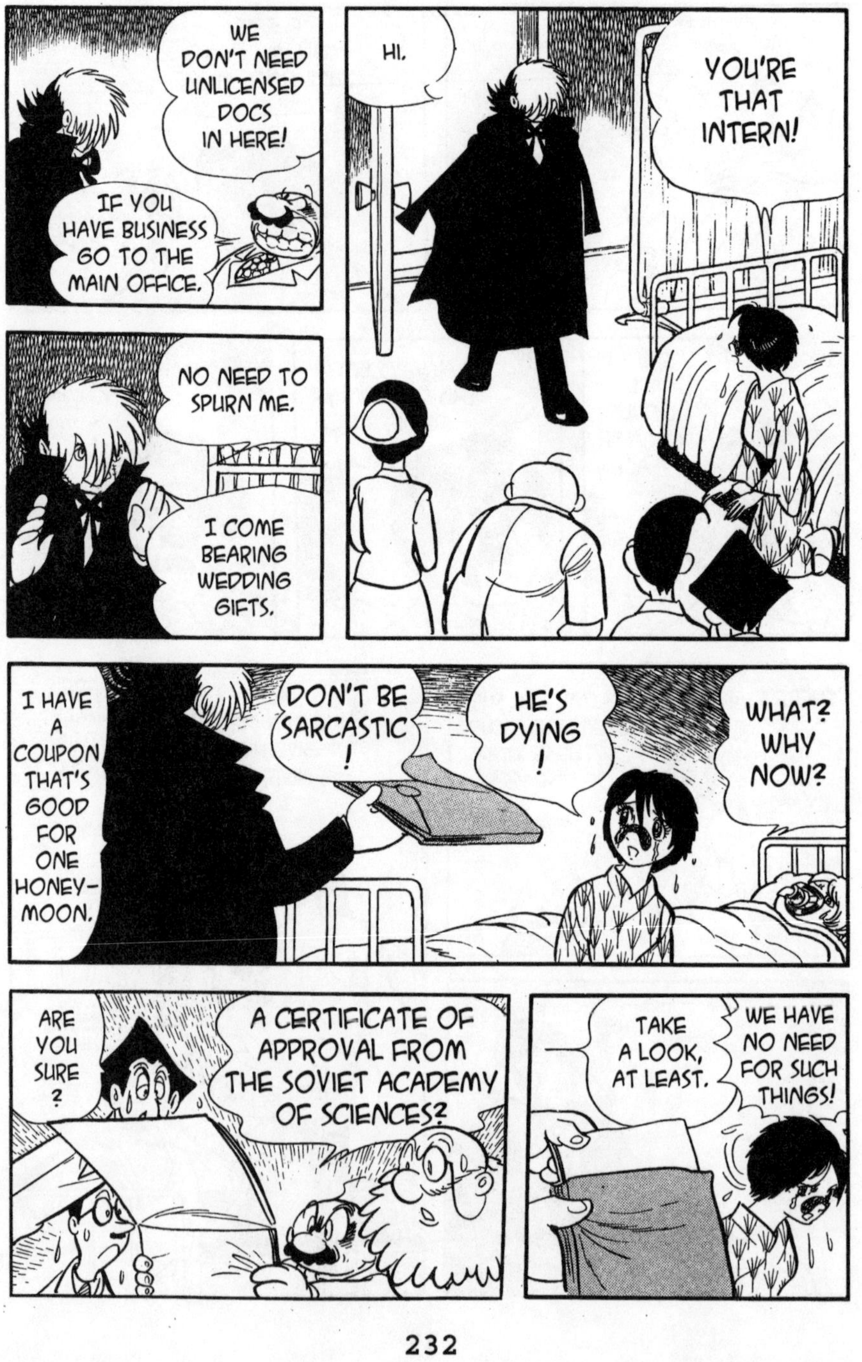
WE DON'T NEED UNLICENSED DOCS IN HERE!
IF YOU HAVE BUSINESS GO TO THE MAIN OFFICE.
HI.
YOU'RE THAT INTERN!
NO NEED TO SPURN ME.
I COME BEARING WEDDING GIFTS.
I HAVE A COUPON THAT'S GOOD FOR ONE HONEY-MOON.
DON'T BE SARCASTIC!
HE'S DYING!
WHAT? WHY NOW?
ARE YOU SURE?
A CERTIFICATE OF APPROVAL FROM THE SOVIET ACADEMY OF SCIENCES?
TAKE A LOOK, AT LEAST.
WE HAVE NO NEED FOR SUCH THINGS!

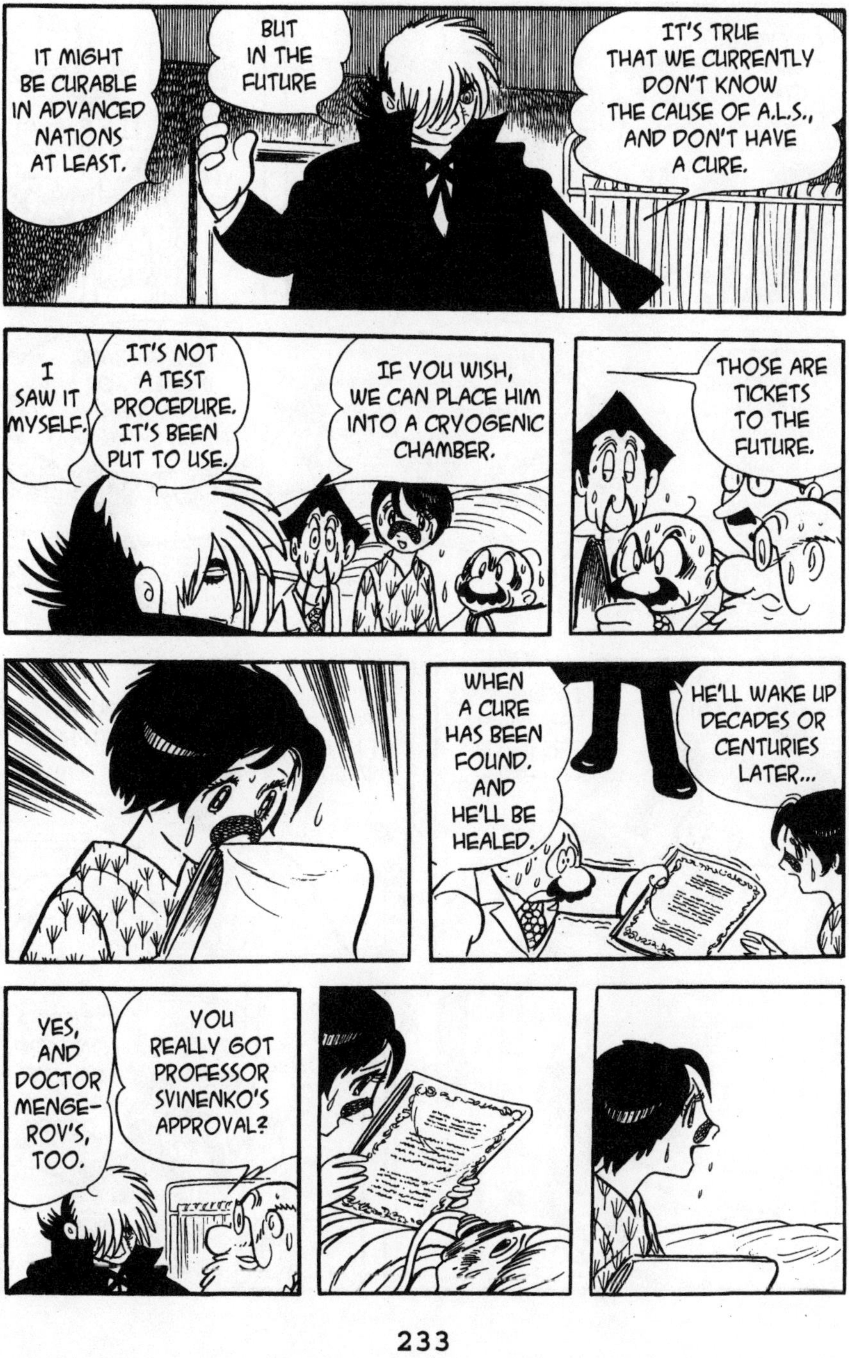
IT'S TRUE THAT WE CURRENTLY DON'T KNOW THE CAUSE OF A.L.S., AND DON'T HAVE A CURE.
BUT IN THE FUTURE
IT MIGHT BE CURABLE IN ADVANCED NATIONS AT LEAST.
THOSE ARE TICKETS TO THE FUTURE.
IF YOU WISH, WE CAN PLACE HIM INTO A CRYOGENIC CHAMBER.
IT'S NOT A TEST PROCEDURE. IT'S BEEN PUT TO USE.
I SAW IT MYSELF.
HE'LL WAKE UP DECADES OR CENTURIES LATER...
WHEN A CURE HAS BEEN FOUND. AND HE'LL BE HEALED.
YOU REALLY GOT PROFESSOR SVINENKO'S APPROVAL?
YES, AND DOCTOR MENGE-ROV'S, TOO.

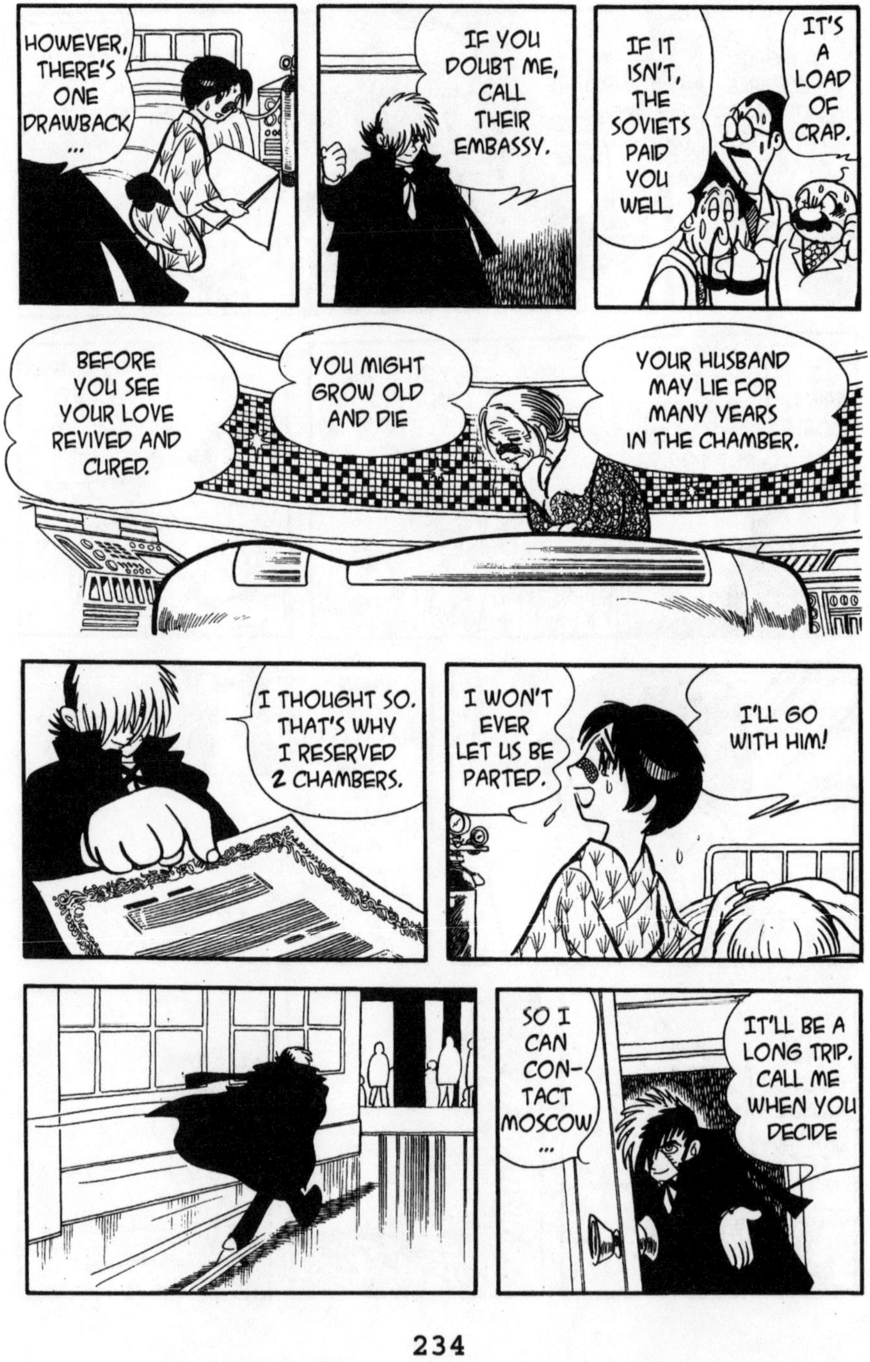
IT'S A LOAD OF CRAP.
IF IT ISN'T, THE SOVIETS PAID YOU WELL.
IF YOU DOUBT ME, CALL THEIR EMBASSY.
HOWEVER, THERE'S ONE DRAWBACK ...
YOUR HUSBAND MAY LIE FOR MANY YEARS IN THE CHAMBER.
YOU MIGHT GROW OLD AND DIE
BEFORE YOU SEE YOUR LOVE REVIVED AND CURED.
I'LL GO WITH HIM!
I WON'T EVER LET US BE PARTED.
I THOUGHT SO. THAT'S WHY I RESERVED 2 CHAMBERS.
IT'LL BE A LONG TRIP. CALL ME WHEN YOU DECIDE
SO I CAN CON-TACT MOSCOW ...

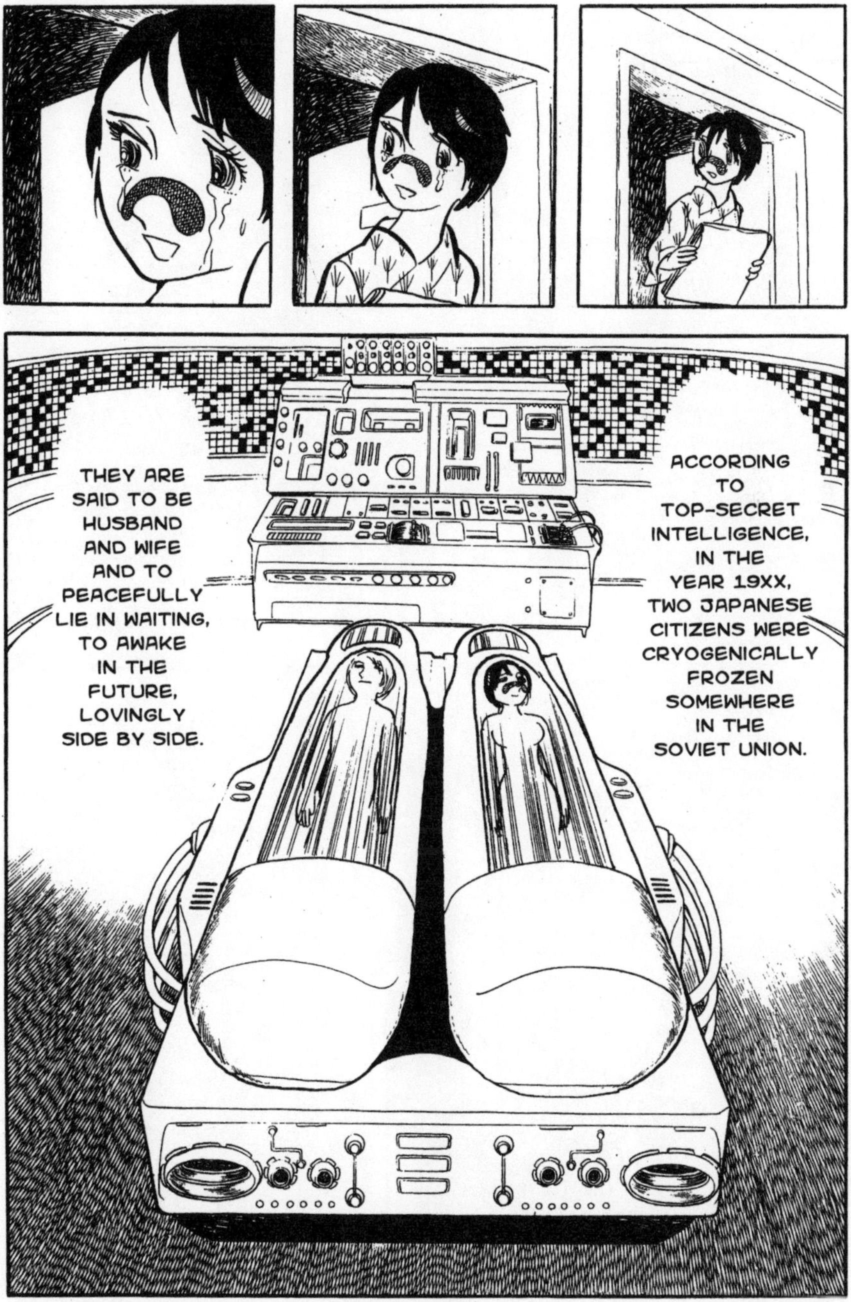
ACCORDING TO TOP-SECRET INTELLIGENCE, IN THE YEAR 19XX, TWO JAPANESE CITIZENS WERE CRYOGENICALLY FROZEN SOMEWHERE IN THE SOVIET UNION.
THEY ARE SAID TO BE HUSBAND AND WIFE AND TO PEACEFULLY LIE IN WAITING, TO AWAKE IN THE FUTURE, LOVINGLY SIDE BY SIDE.

SUN DOLLS

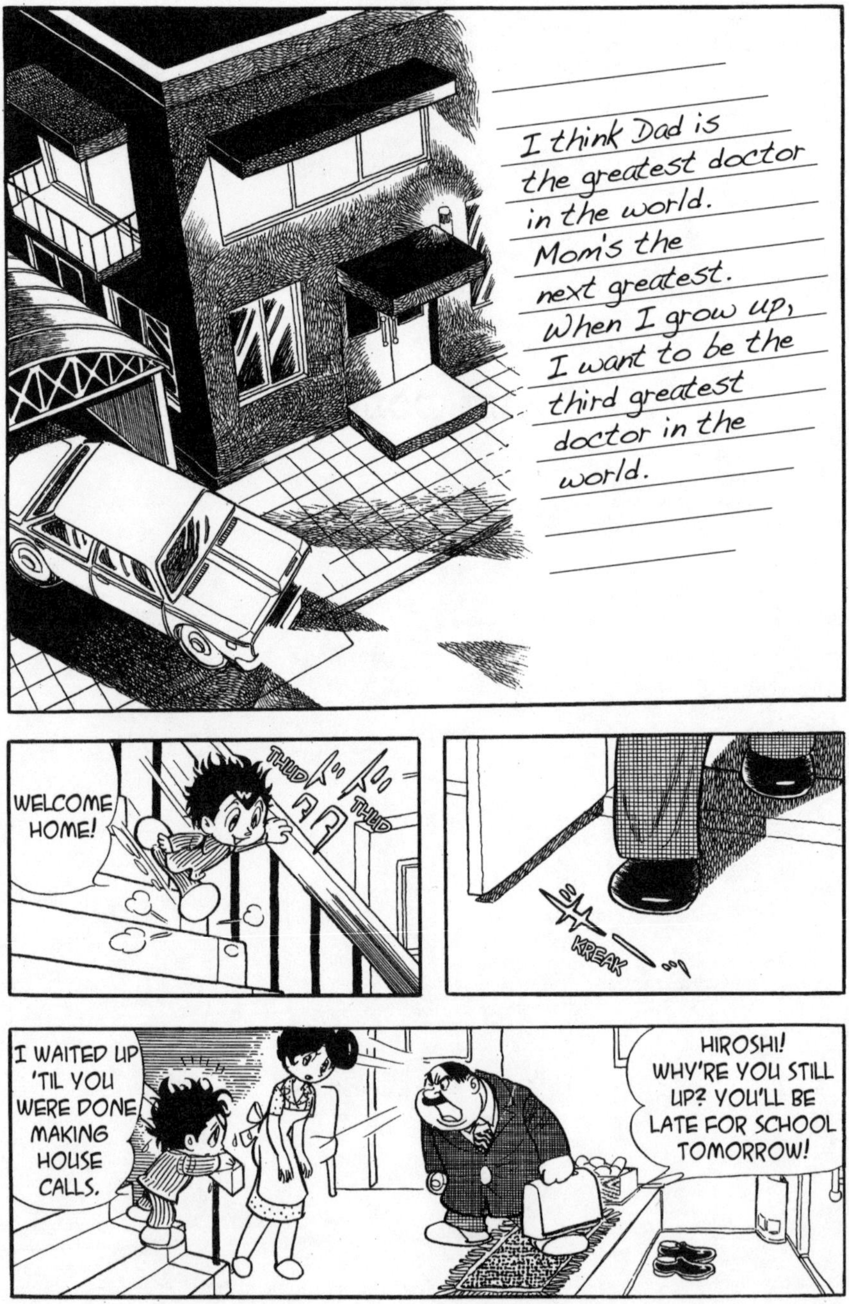
I think Dad is the greatest doctor in the world. Mom's the next greatest. When I grow up, I want to be the third greatest doctor in the world.
KREAK
THUD
THUD
WELCOME HOME!
HIROSHI! WHY'RE YOU STILL UP? YOU'LL BE LATE FOR SCHOOL TOMORROW!
I WAITED UP 'TIL YOU WERE DONE MAKING HOUSE CALLS.

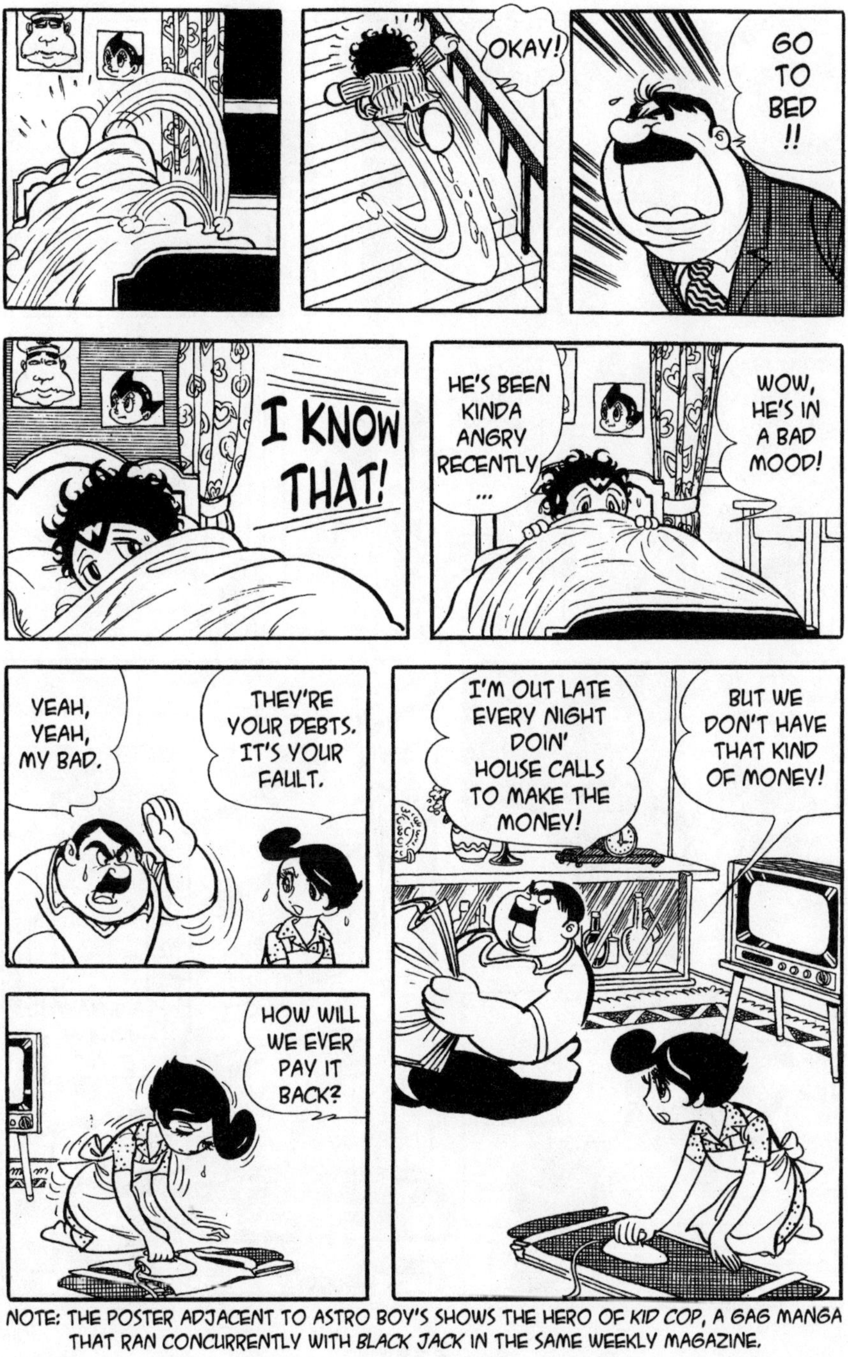
GO TO BED !!
OKAY!
WOW, HE'S IN A BAD MOOD!
HE'S BEEN KINDA ANGRY RECENTLY ...
I KNOW THAT!
BUT WE DON'T HAVE THAT KIND OF MONEY!
I'M OUT LATE EVERY NIGHT DOIN' HOUSE CALLS TO MAKE THE MONEY!
THEY'RE YOUR DEBTS. IT'S YOUR FAULT.
YEAH, YEAH, MY BAD.
HOW WILL WE EVER PAY IT BACK?

NOTE: THE POSTER ADJACENT TO ASTRO BOY'S SHOWS THE HERO OF *KID COP*, A GAG MANGA THAT RAN CONCURRENTLY WITH *BLACK JACK* IN THE SAME WEEKLY MAGAZINE.

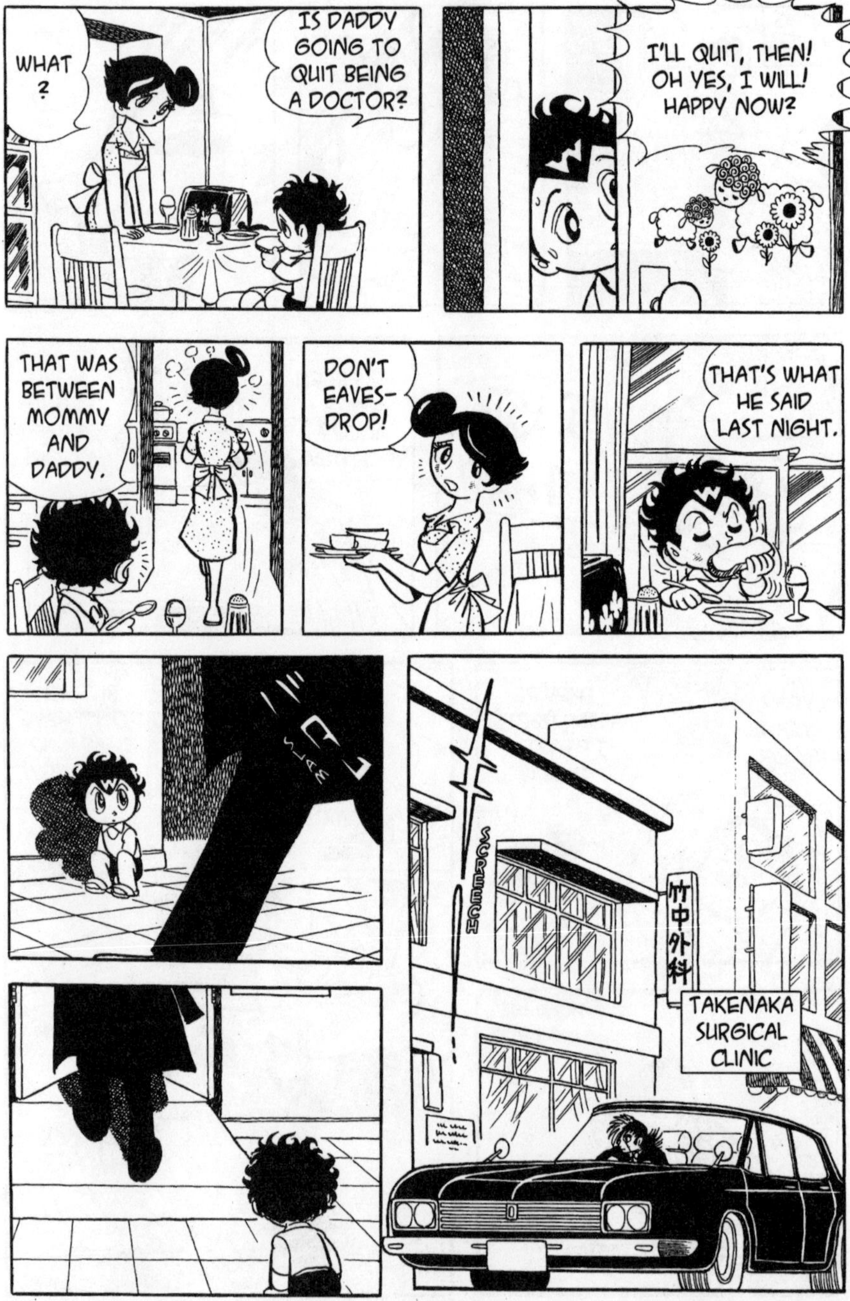
I'LL QUIT, THEN! OH YES, I WILL! HAPPY NOW?
IS DADDY GOING TO QUIT BEING A DOCTOR?
WHAT ?
THAT'S WHAT HE SAID LAST NIGHT.
DON'T EAVES-DROP!
THAT WAS BETWEEN MOMMY AND DADDY.
SCREECH
竹中外科
TAKENAKA SURGICAL CLINIC
SLAM

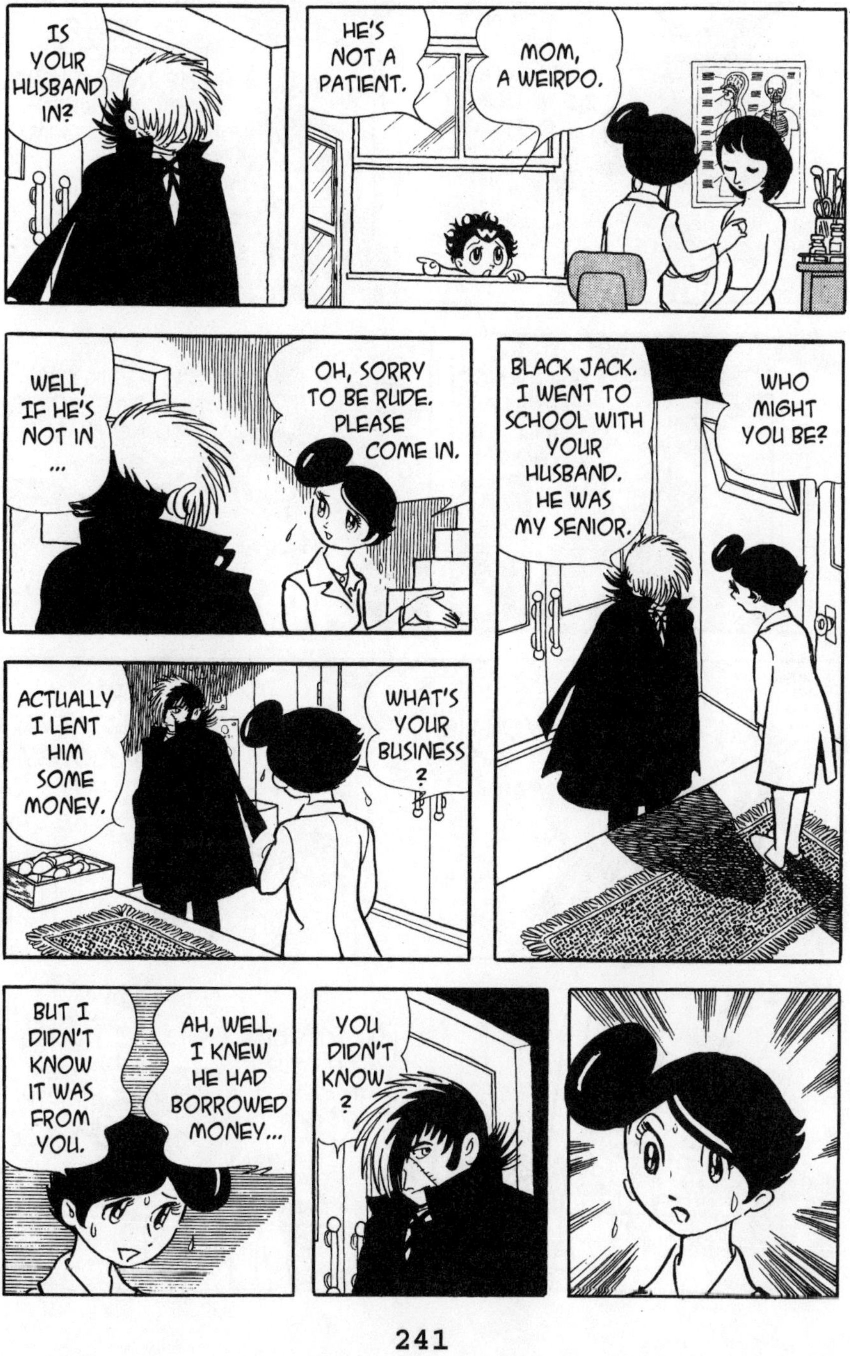
MOM, A WEIRDO.
HE'S NOT A PATIENT.
IS YOUR HUSBAND IN?
WHO MIGHT YOU BE?
BLACK JACK. I WENT TO SCHOOL WITH YOUR HUSBAND. HE WAS MY SENIOR.
OH, SORRY TO BE RUDE. PLEASE COME IN.
WELL, IF HE'S NOT IN ...
WHAT'S YOUR BUSINESS?
ACTUALLY I LENT HIM SOME MONEY.
YOU DIDN'T KNOW?
AH, WELL, I KNEW HE HAD BORROWED MONEY...
BUT I DIDN'T KNOW IT WAS FROM YOU.

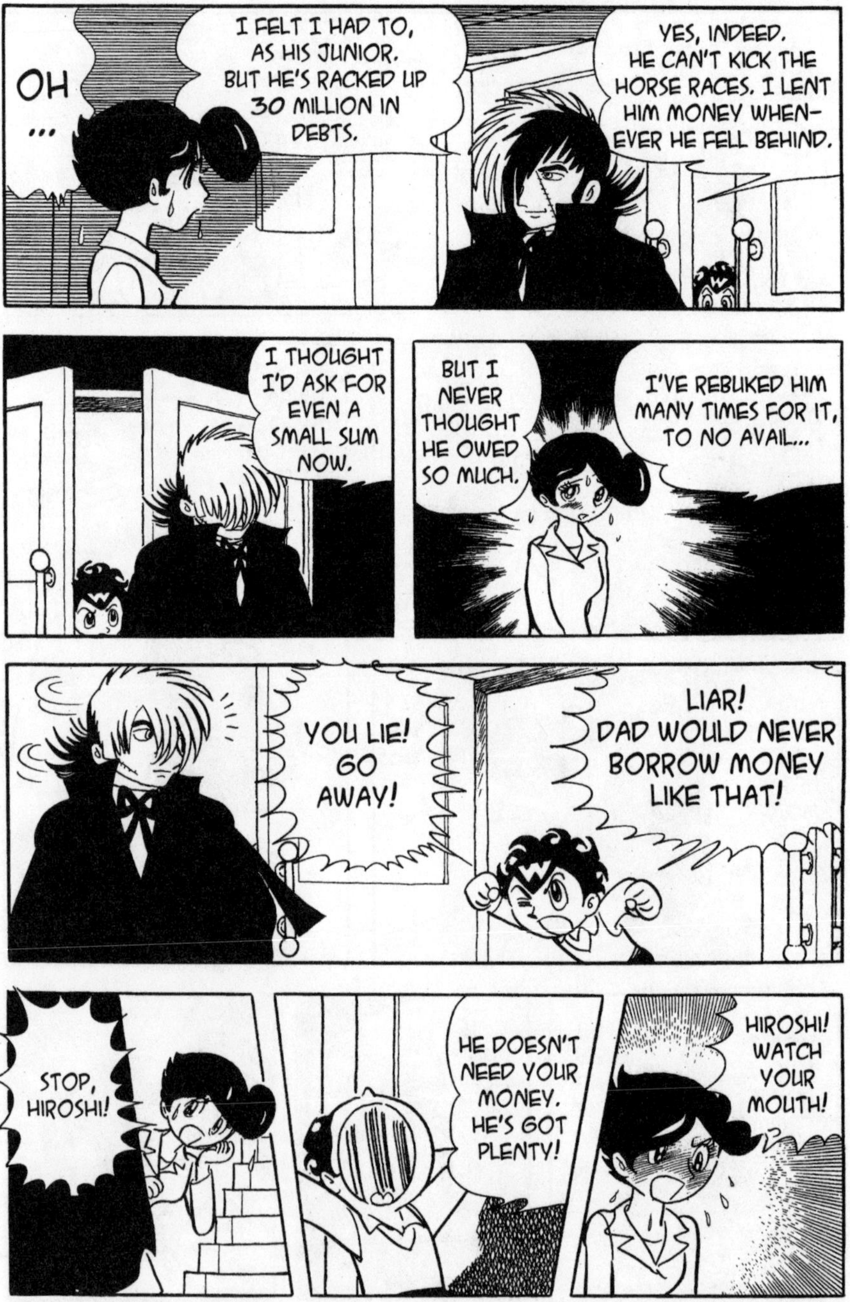

YES, INDEED. HE CAN'T KICK THE HORSE RACES. I LENT HIM MONEY WHEN-EVER HE FELL BEHIND.
I FELT I HAD TO, AS HIS JUNIOR. BUT HE'S RACKED UP 30 MILLION IN DEBTS.
OH ...
I'VE REBUKED HIM MANY TIMES FOR IT, TO NO AVAIL...
BUT I NEVER THOUGHT HE OWED SO MUCH.
I THOUGHT I'D ASK FOR EVEN A SMALL SUM NOW.
LIAR! DAD WOULD NEVER BORROW MONEY LIKE THAT!
YOU LIE! GO AWAY!
HIROSHI! WATCH YOUR MOUTH!
HE DOESN'T NEED YOUR MONEY. HE'S GOT PLENTY!
STOP, HIROSHI!

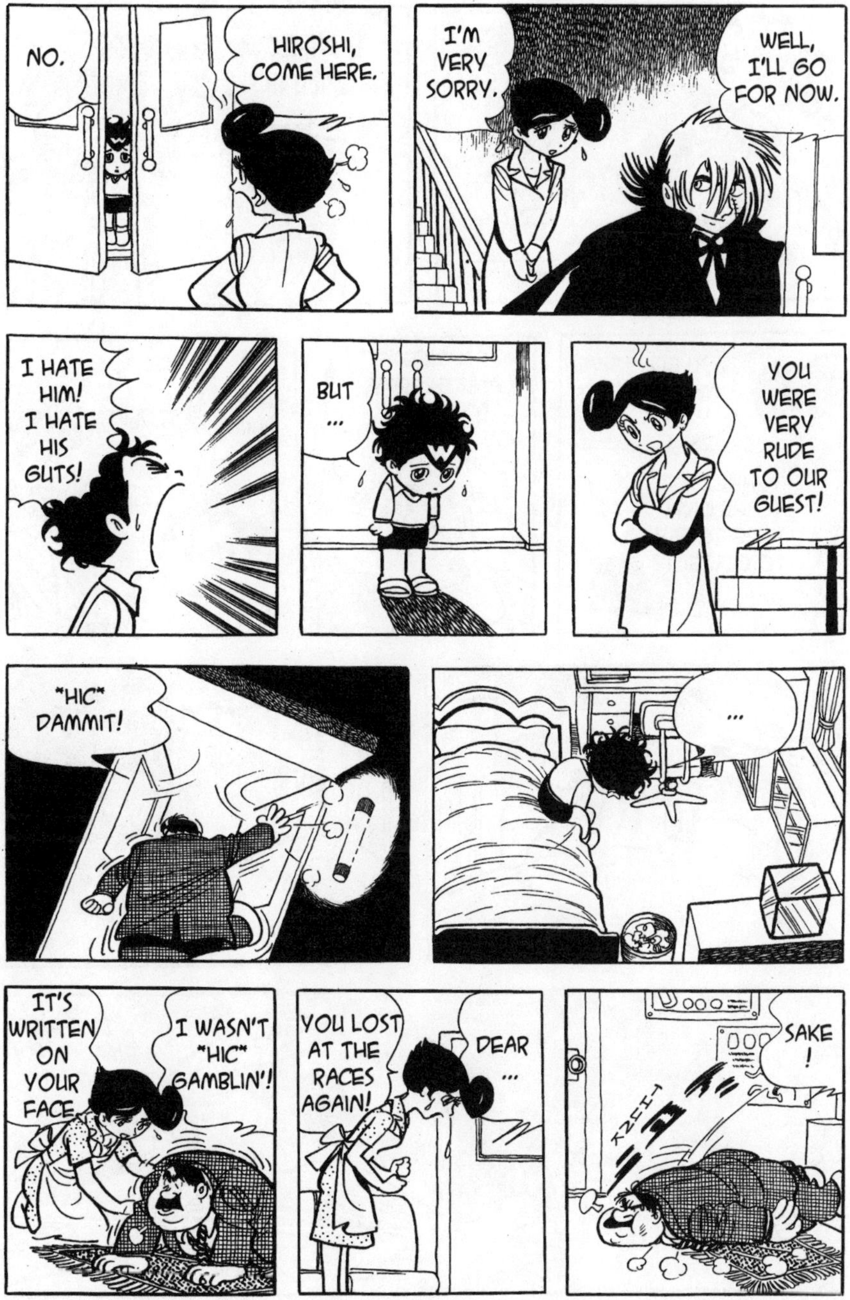
WELL, I'LL GO FOR NOW.
I'M VERY SORRY.
HIROSHI, COME HERE.
NO.
YOU WERE VERY RUDE TO OUR GUEST!
BUT ...
I HATE HIM! I HATE HIS GUTS!
...
"HIC" DAMMIT!
SAKE !
DEAR ...
YOU LOST AT THE RACES AGAIN!
I WASN'T "HIC" GAMBLIN'!
IT'S WRITTEN ON YOUR FACE

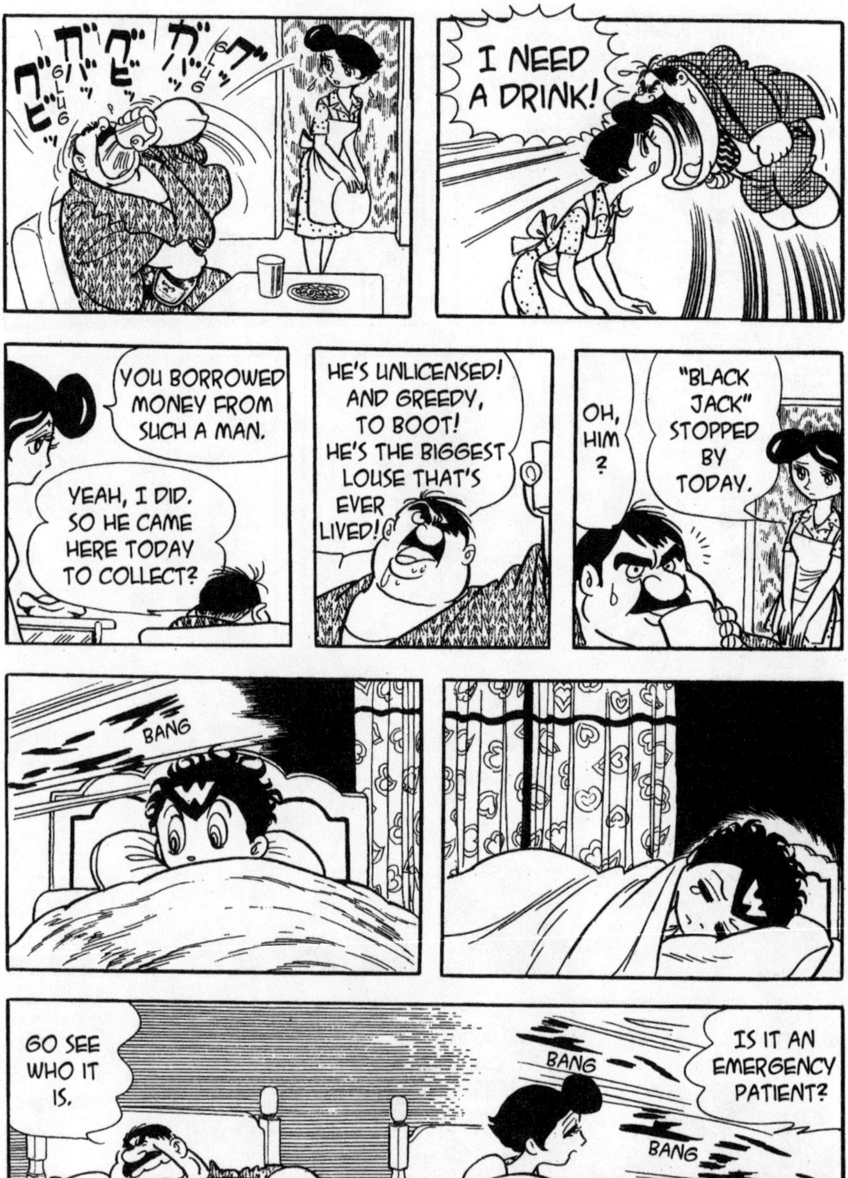
I NEED A DRINK!
GLUG
GLUG
"BLACK JACK" STOPPED BY TODAY.
OH, HIM?
HE'S UNLICENSED! AND GREEDY, TO BOOT! HE'S THE BIGGEST LOUSE THAT'S EVER LIVED!
YOU BORROWED MONEY FROM SUCH A MAN.
YEAH, I DID. SO HE CAME HERE TODAY TO COLLECT?
BANG
IS IT AN EMERGENCY PATIENT?
BANG
BANG
BANG
GO SEE WHO IT IS.

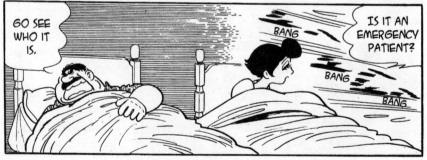

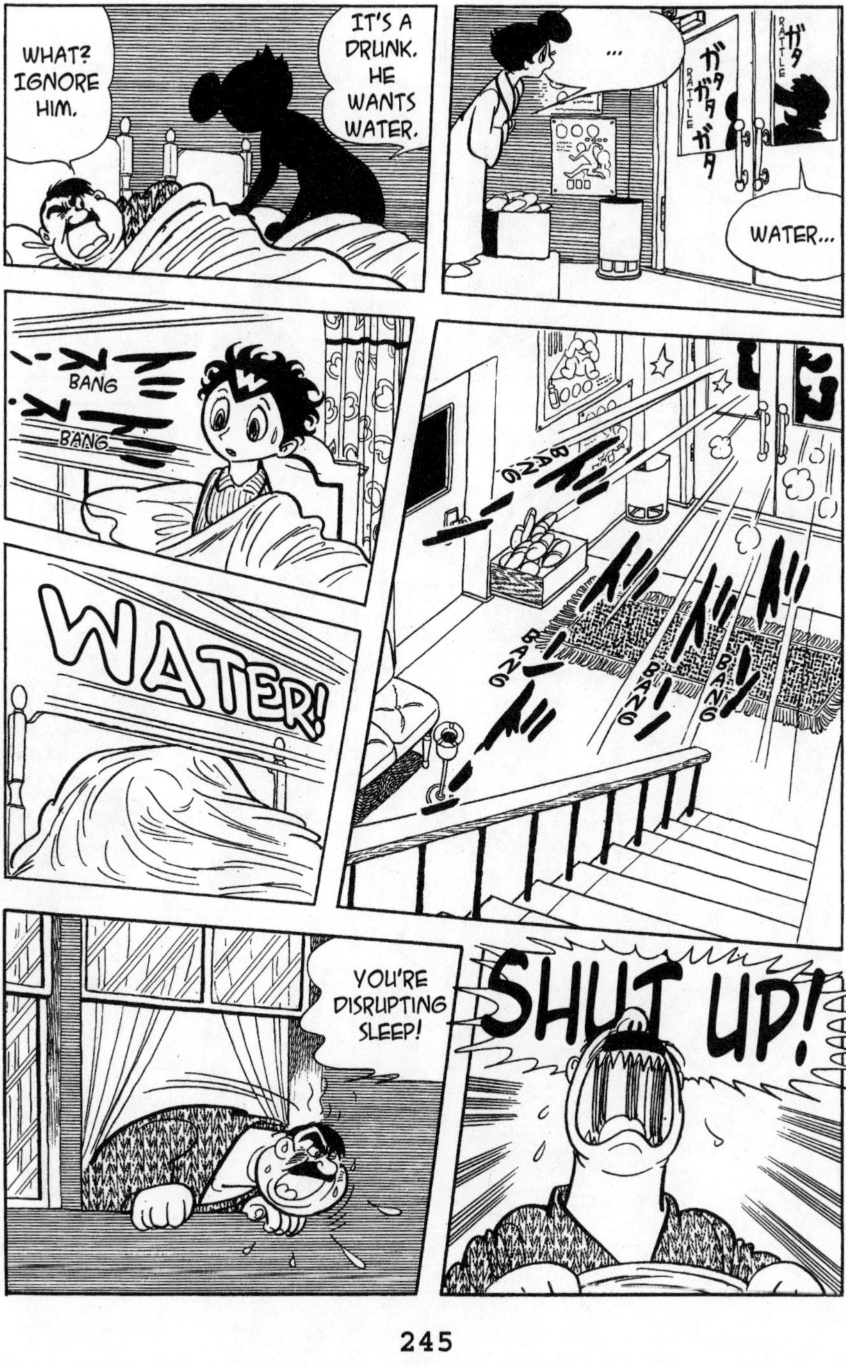
...
ガタ
RATTLE
ガタガタガタ
RATTLE
WATER...
IT'S A DRUNK. HE WANTS WATER.
WHAT? IGNORE HIM.
BANG
BANG
BANG
BANG
BANG
BANG
BANG
WATER!
SHUT UP!
YOU'RE DISRUPTING SLEEP!

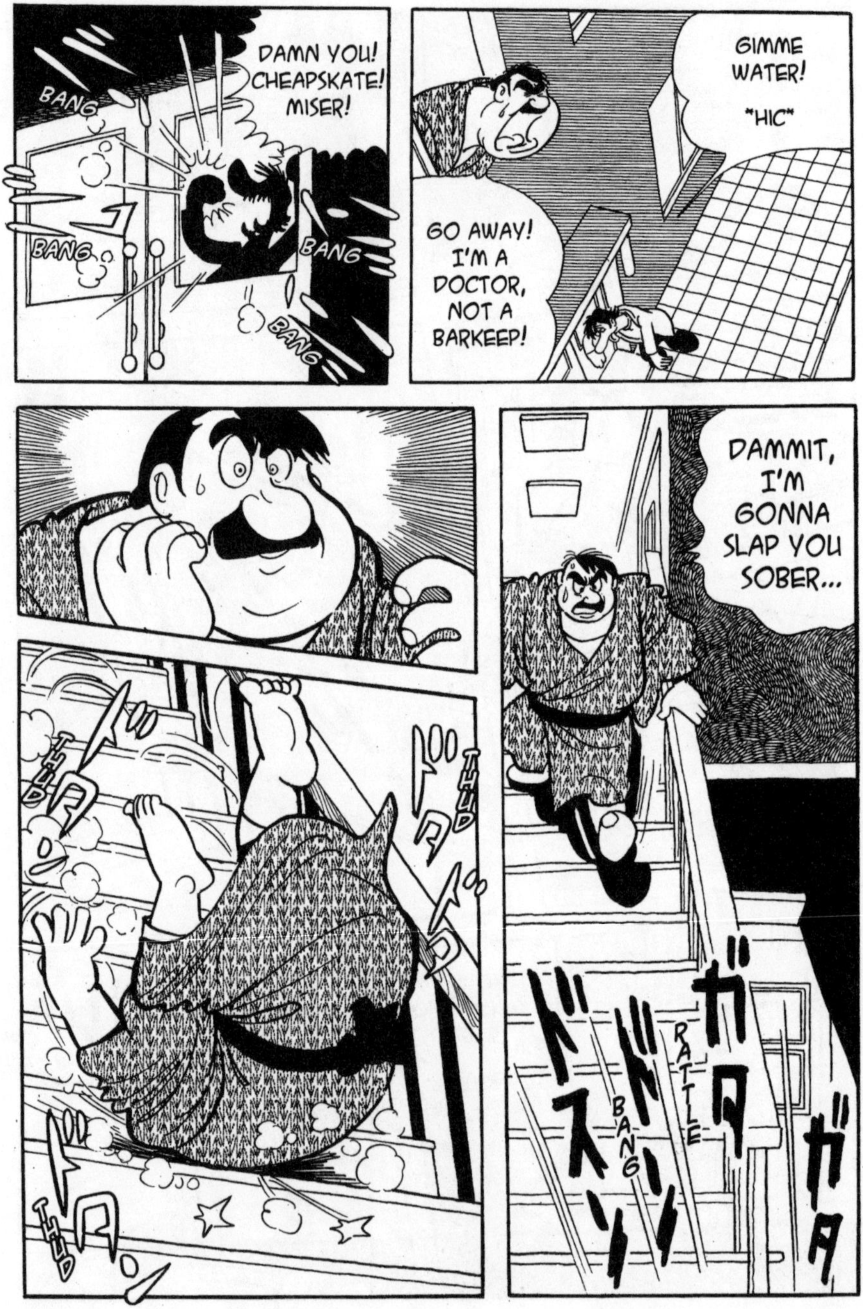
GIMME WATER!
HIC
GO AWAY! I'M A DOCTOR, NOT A BARKEEP!
DAMN YOU! CHEAPSKATE! MISER!
BANG
BANG
BANG
BANG
DAMMIT, I'M GONNA SLAP YOU SOBER...
RATTLE
BANG
THUD
THUD

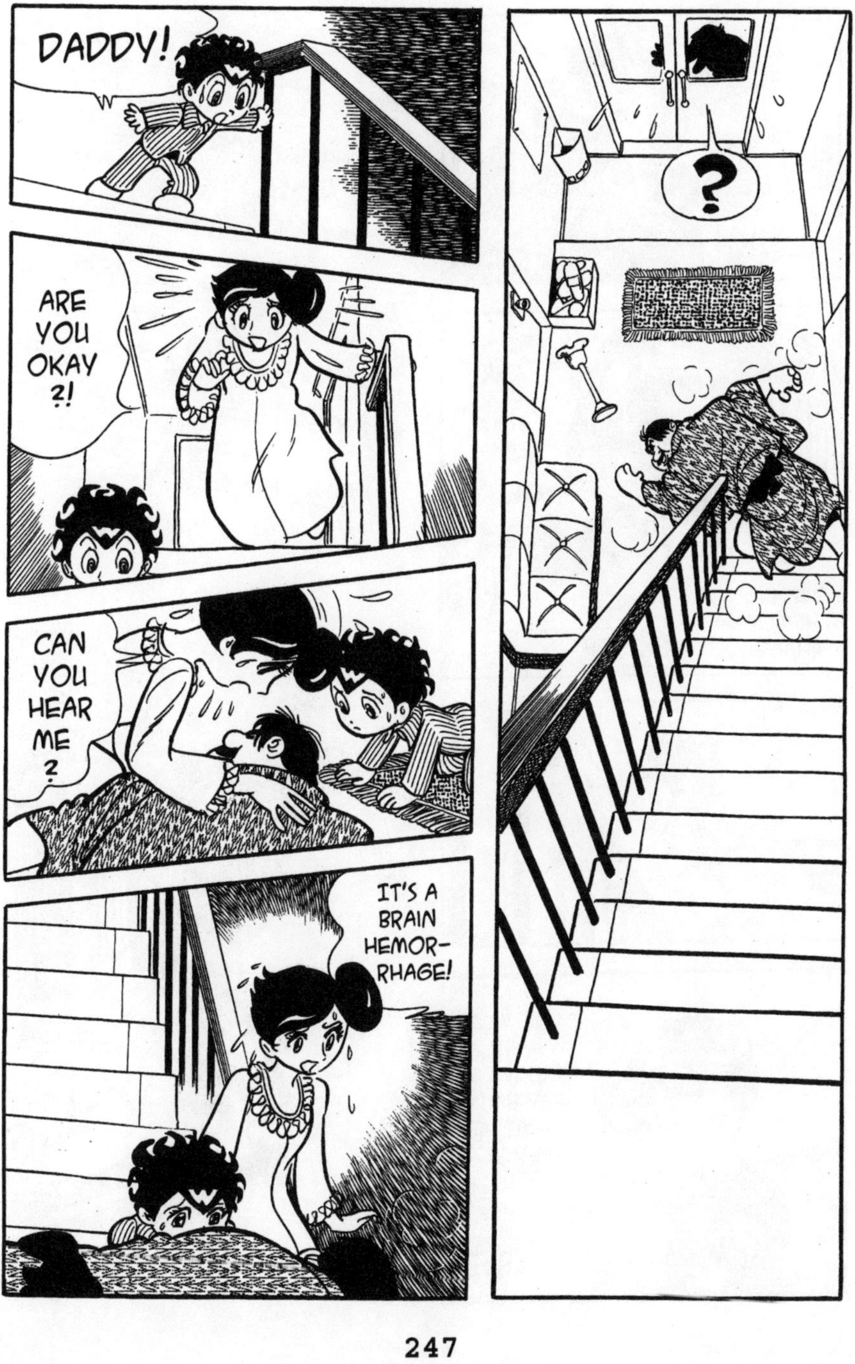
?
DADDY!
ARE YOU OKAY ?!
CAN YOU HEAR ME ?
IT'S A BRAIN HEMOR-RHAGE!

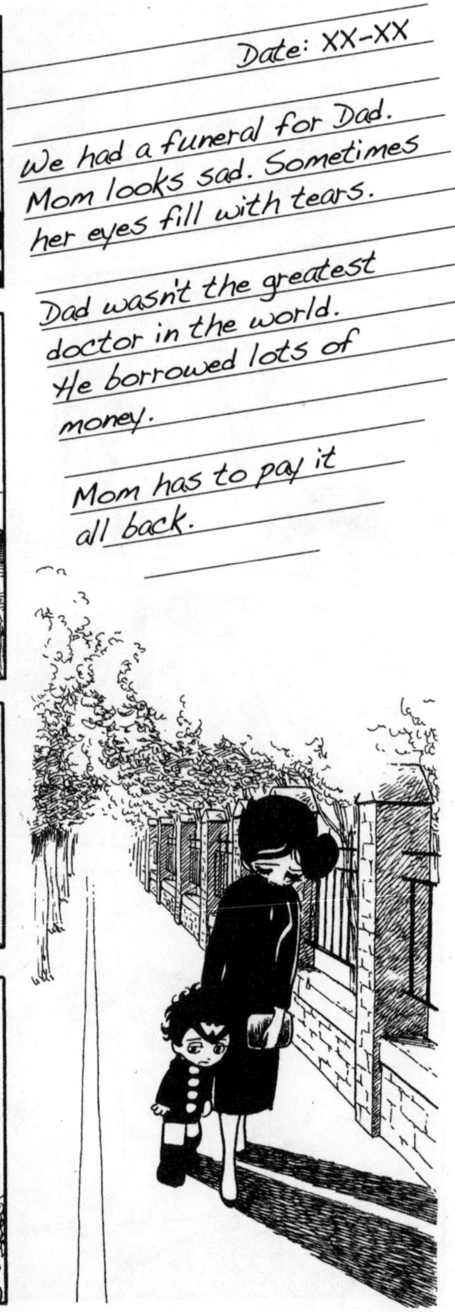
Date: XX-XX
We had a funeral for Dad. Mom looks sad. Sometimes her eyes fill with tears.
Dad wasn't the greatest doctor in the world. He borrowed lots of money.
Mom has to pay it all back.

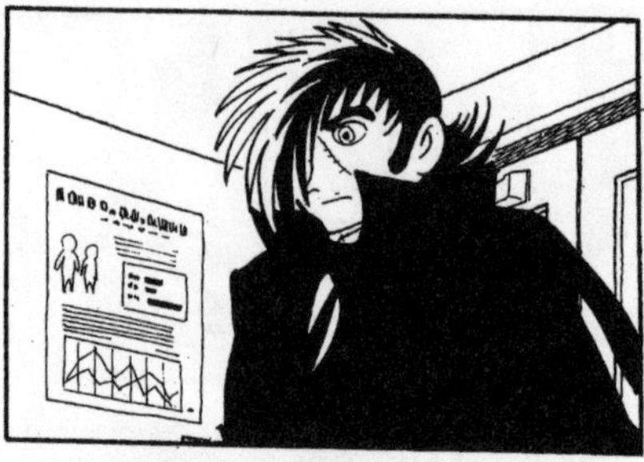

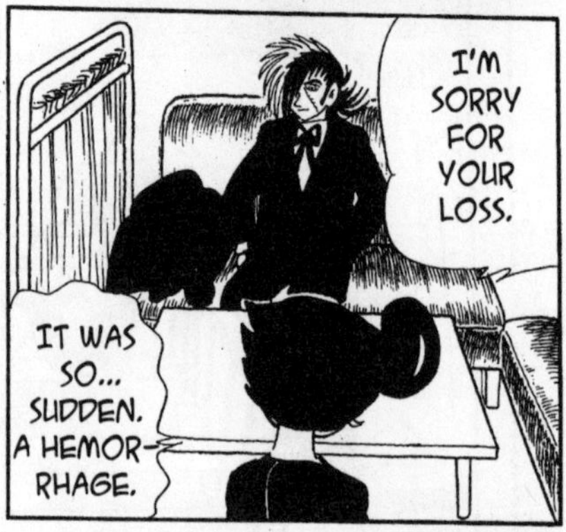
I'M SORRY FOR YOUR LOSS.
IT WAS SO... SUDDEN. A HEMOR-RHAGE.

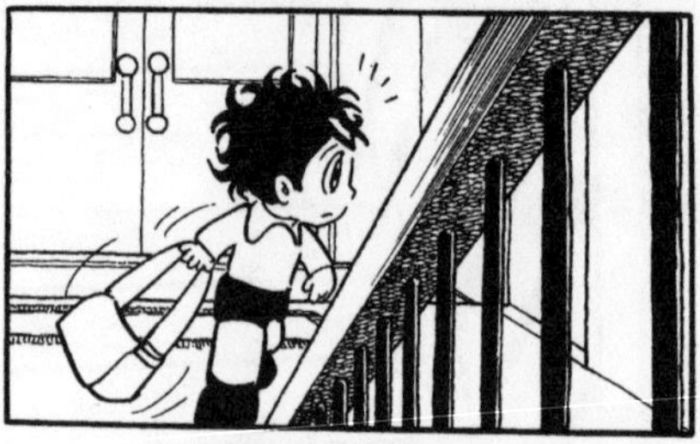

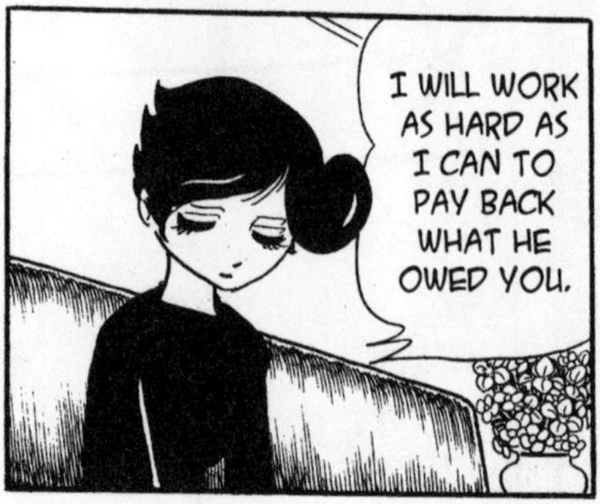
I WILL WORK AS HARD AS I CAN TO PAY BACK WHAT HE OWED YOU.

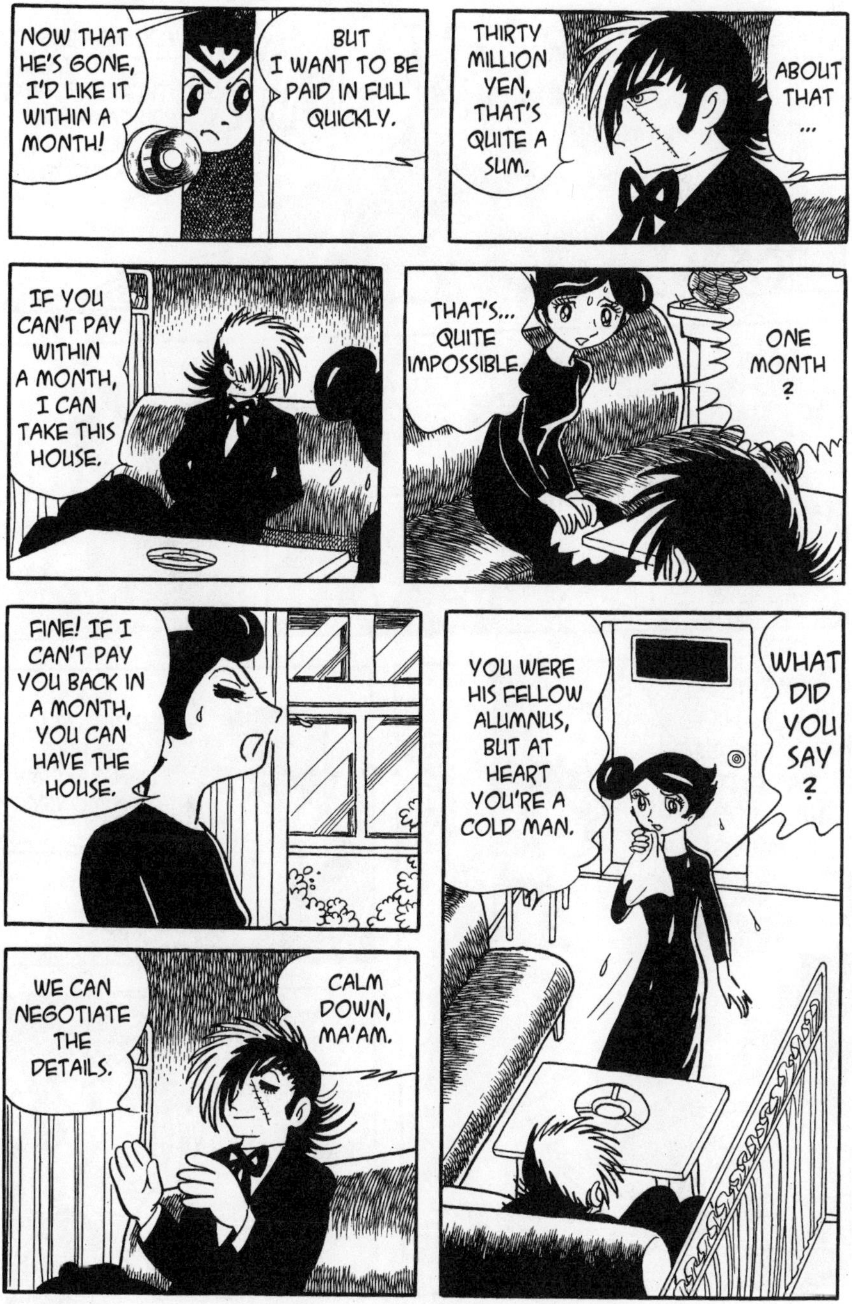
ABOUT THAT ...
THIRTY MILLION YEN, THAT'S QUITE A SUM.
BUT I WANT TO BE PAID IN FULL QUICKLY.
NOW THAT HE'S GONE, I'D LIKE IT WITHIN A MONTH!
ONE MONTH?
THAT'S... QUITE IMPOSSIBLE.
IF YOU CAN'T PAY WITHIN A MONTH, I CAN TAKE THIS HOUSE.
WHAT DID YOU SAY?
YOU WERE HIS FELLOW ALUMNUS, BUT AT HEART YOU'RE A COLD MAN.
FINE! IF I CAN'T PAY YOU BACK IN A MONTH, YOU CAN HAVE THE HOUSE.
CALM DOWN, MA'AM.
WE CAN NEGOTIATE THE DETAILS.

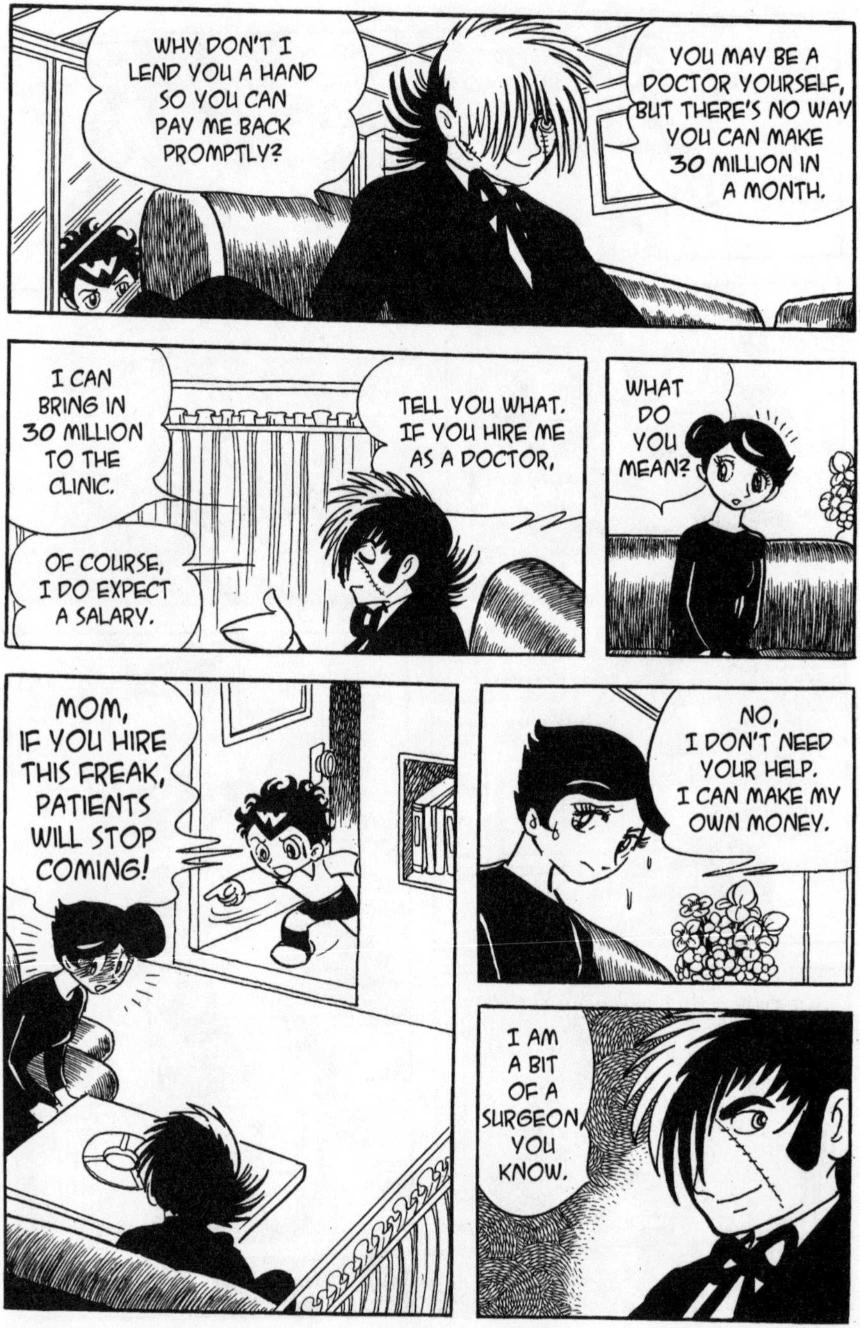
YOU MAY BE A DOCTOR YOURSELF, BUT THERE'S NO WAY YOU CAN MAKE 30 MILLION IN A MONTH.
WHY DON'T I LEND YOU A HAND SO YOU CAN PAY ME BACK PROMPTLY?
WHAT DO YOU MEAN?
TELL YOU WHAT. IF YOU HIRE ME AS A DOCTOR,
I CAN BRING IN 30 MILLION TO THE CLINIC.
OF COURSE, I DO EXPECT A SALARY.
NO, I DON'T NEED YOUR HELP. I CAN MAKE MY OWN MONEY.
I AM A BIT OF A SURGEON, YOU KNOW.
MOM, IF YOU HIRE THIS FREAK, PATIENTS WILL STOP COMING!

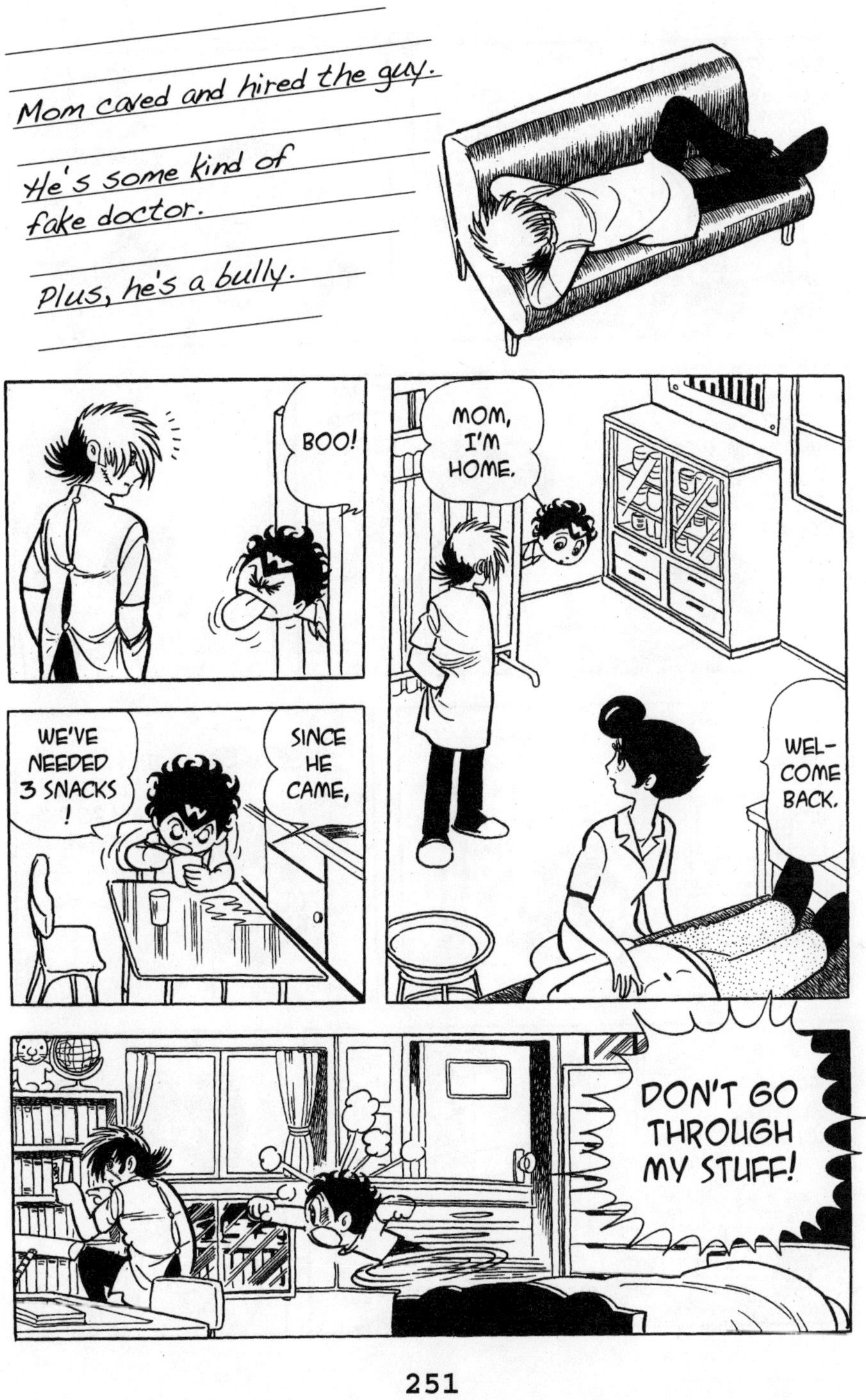

Mom caved and hired the guy.
He's some kind of fake doctor.
Plus, he's a bully.
MOM, I'M HOME.
WEL-COME BACK.
BOO!
SINCE HE CAME,
WE'VE NEEDED 3 SNACKS !
DON'T GO THROUGH MY STUFF!

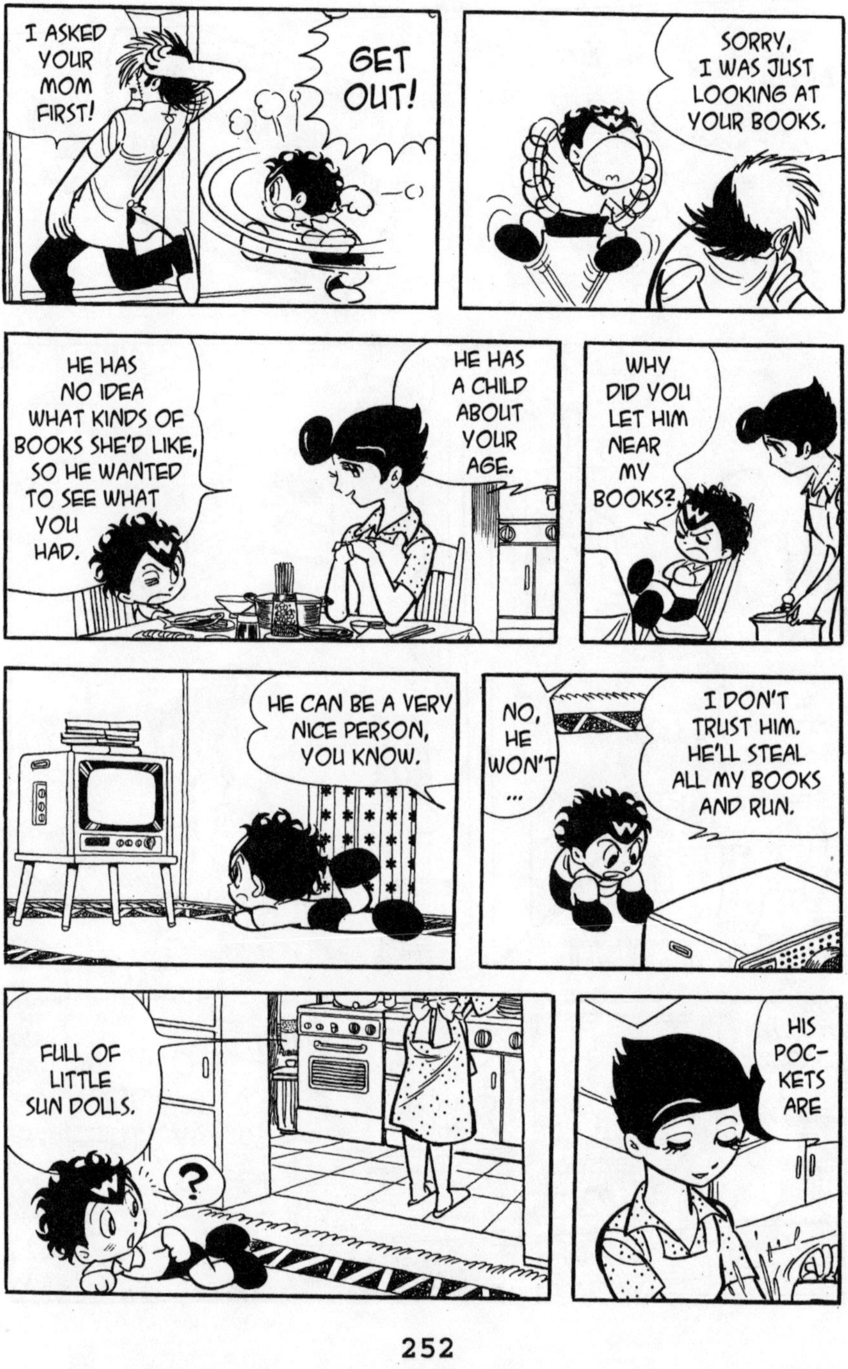
SORRY, I WAS JUST LOOKING AT YOUR BOOKS.
GET OUT!
I ASKED YOUR MOM FIRST!
WHY DID YOU LET HIM NEAR MY BOOKS?
HE HAS A CHILD ABOUT YOUR AGE.
HE HAS NO IDEA WHAT KINDS OF BOOKS SHE'D LIKE, SO HE WANTED TO SEE WHAT YOU HAD.
I DON'T TRUST HIM. HE'LL STEAL ALL MY BOOKS AND RUN.
NO, HE WON'T ...
HE CAN BE A VERY NICE PERSON, YOU KNOW.
HIS POC-KETS ARE
FULL OF LITTLE SUN DOLLS.
?

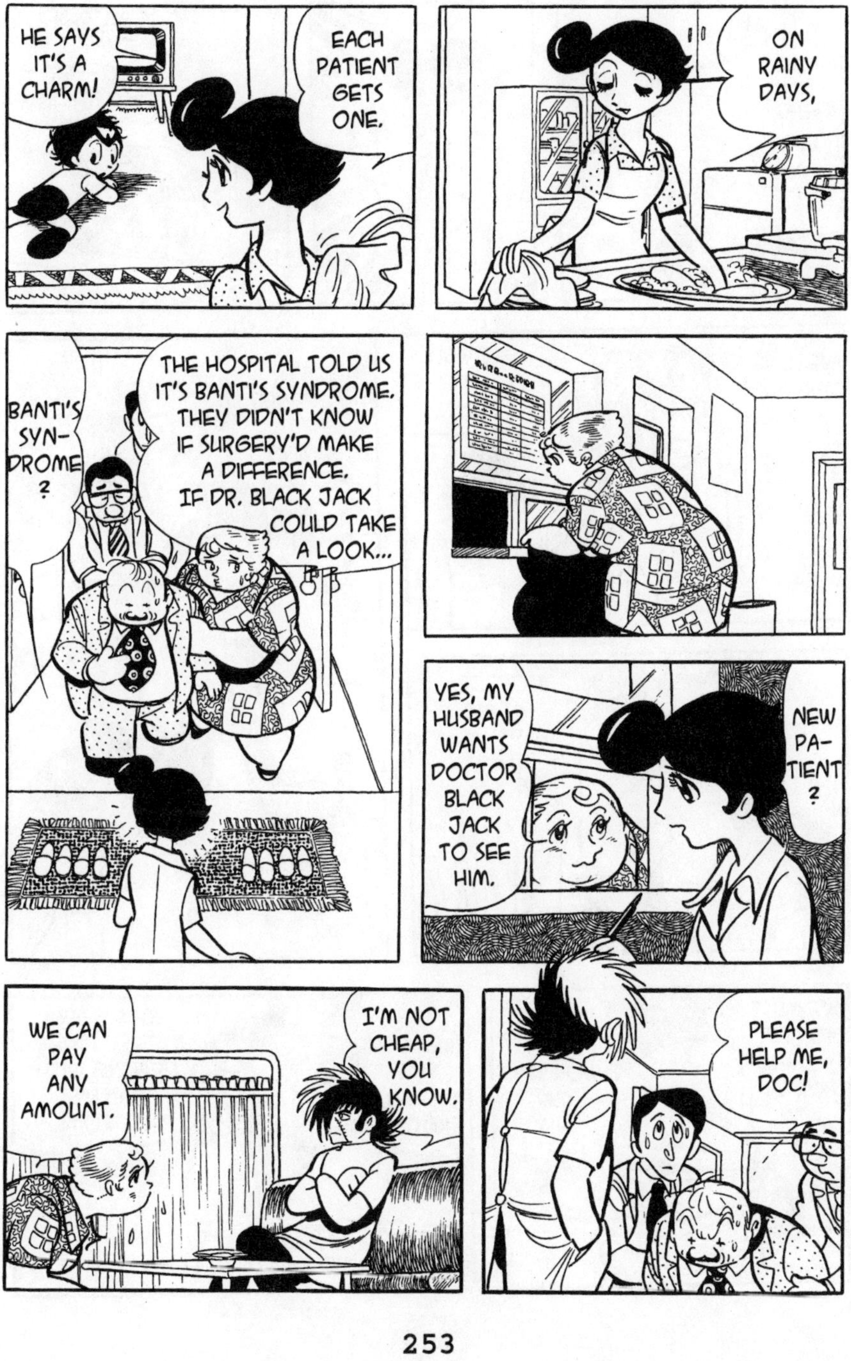
ON RAINY DAYS,
EACH PATIENT GETS ONE.
HE SAYS IT'S A CHARM!
NEW PATIENT?
YES, MY HUSBAND WANTS DOCTOR BLACK JACK TO SEE HIM.
THE HOSPITAL TOLD US IT'S BANTI'S SYNDROME. THEY DIDN'T KNOW IF SURGERY'D MAKE A DIFFERENCE. IF DR. BLACK JACK COULD TAKE A LOOK...
BANTI'S SYNDROME?
PLEASE HELP ME, DOC!
I'M NOT CHEAP, YOU KNOW.
WE CAN PAY ANY AMOUNT.

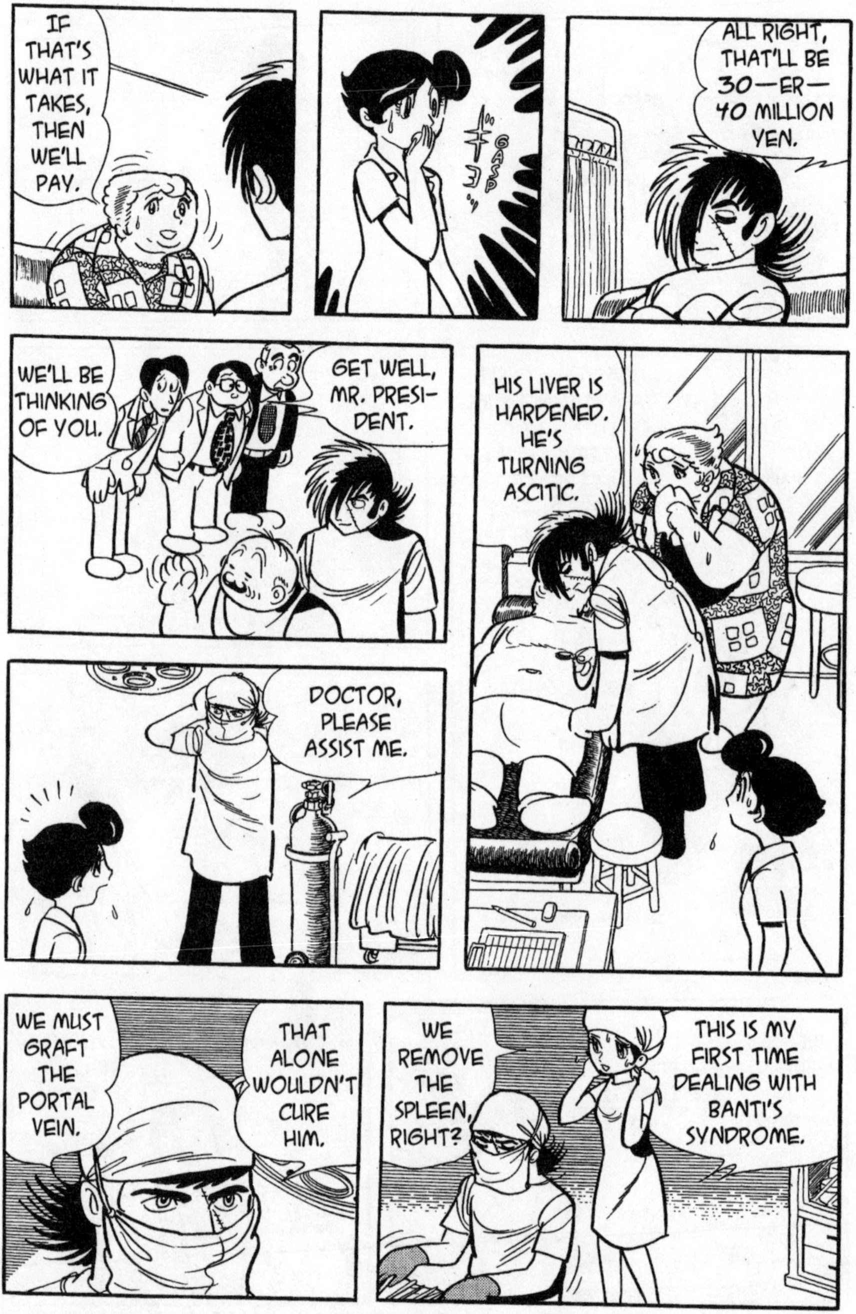
ALL RIGHT, THAT'LL BE 30—ER—40 MILLION YEN.
GASP
IF THAT'S WHAT IT TAKES, THEN WE'LL PAY.
HIS LIVER IS HARDENED. HE'S TURNING ASCITIC.
GET WELL, MR. PRESIDENT.
WE'LL BE THINKING OF YOU.
DOCTOR, PLEASE ASSIST ME.
THIS IS MY FIRST TIME DEALING WITH BANTI'S SYNDROME.
WE REMOVE THE SPLEEN, RIGHT?
THAT ALONE WOULDN'T CURE HIM.
WE MUST GRAFT THE PORTAL VEIN.

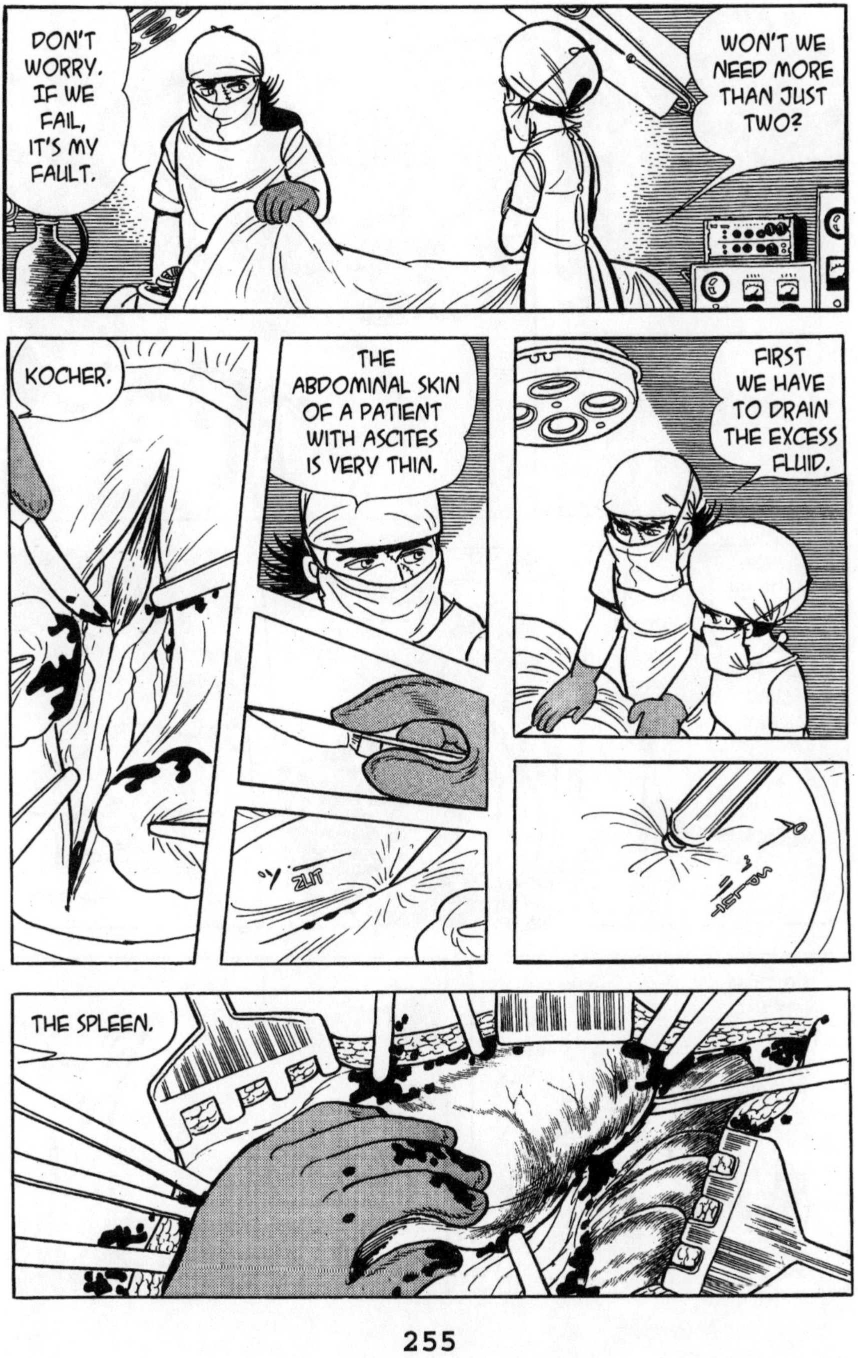
WON'T WE NEED MORE THAN JUST TWO?
DON'T WORRY. IF WE FAIL, IT'S MY FAULT.
FIRST WE HAVE TO DRAIN THE EXCESS FLUID.
THE ABDOMINAL SKIN OF A PATIENT WITH ASCITES IS VERY THIN.
KOCHER.
THE SPLEEN.

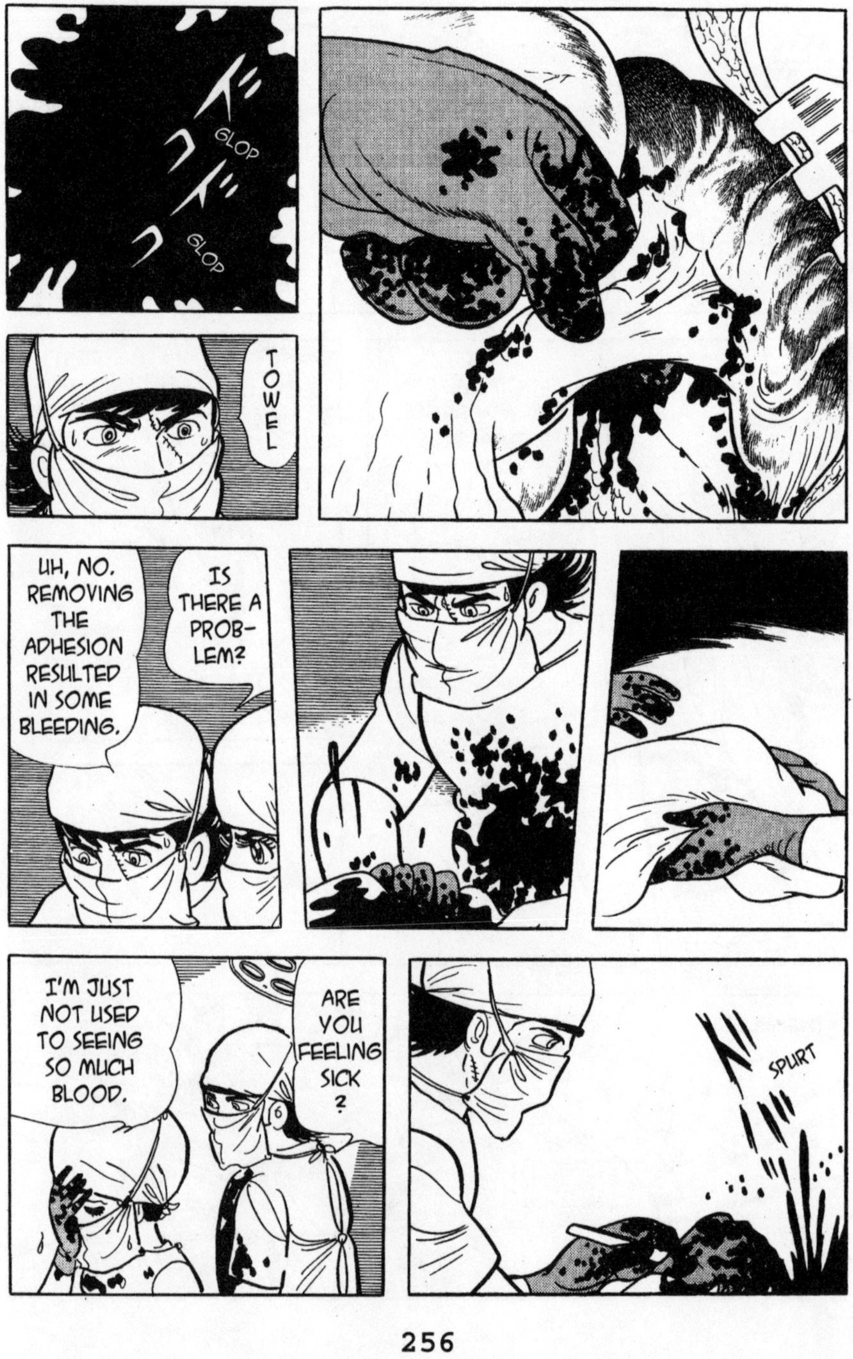
GLOP
GLOP
TOWEL
IS THERE A PROBLEM?
UH, NO. REMOVING THE ADHESION RESULTED IN SOME BLEEDING.
SPURT
ARE YOU FEELING SICK?
I'M JUST NOT USED TO SEEING SO MUCH BLOOD.

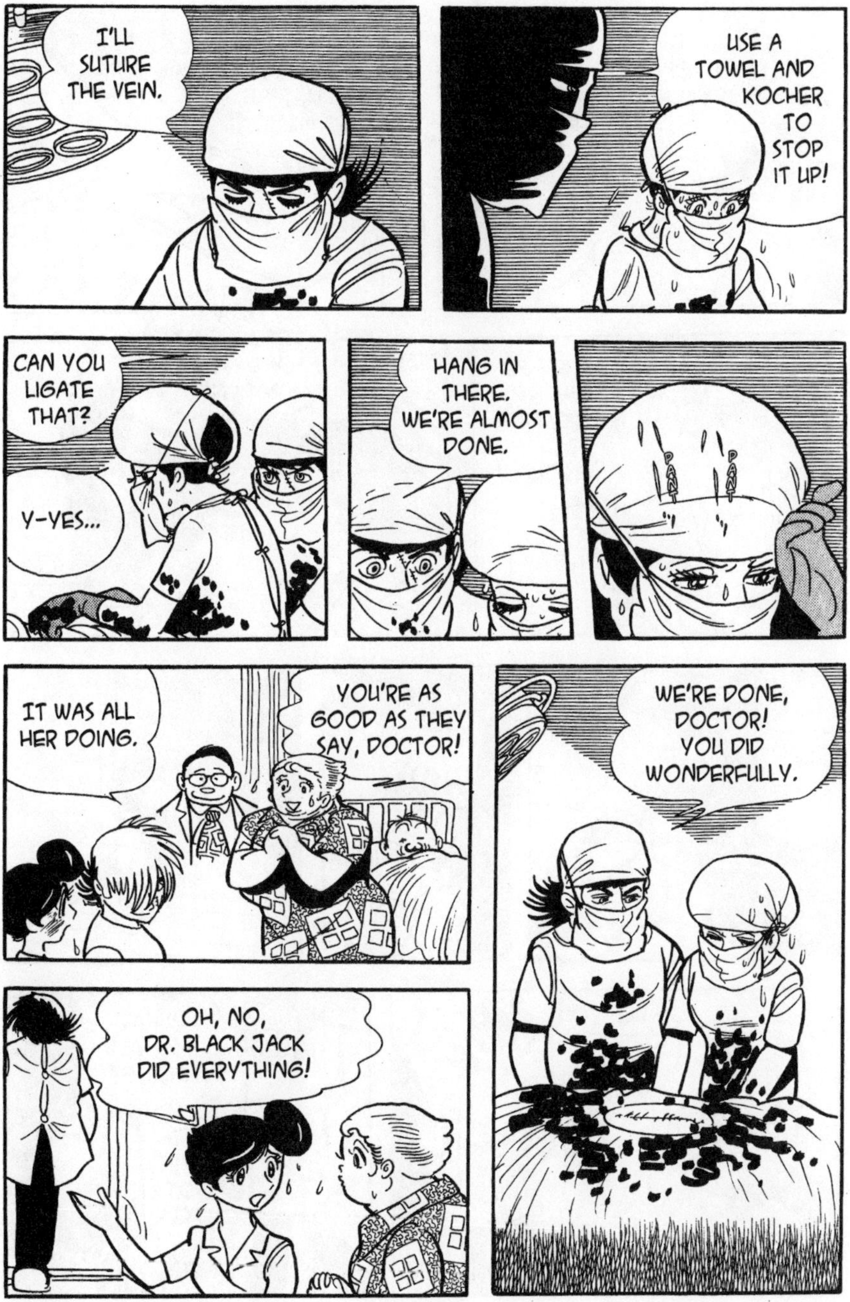
USE A TOWEL AND KOCHER TO STOP IT UP!
I'LL SUTURE THE VEIN.
PANT PANT
HANG IN THERE. WE'RE ALMOST DONE.
CAN YOU LIGATE THAT?
Y-YES...
WE'RE DONE, DOCTOR! YOU DID WONDERFULLY.
YOU'RE AS GOOD AS THEY SAY, DOCTOR!
IT WAS ALL HER DOING.
OH, NO, DR. BLACK JACK DID EVERYTHING!

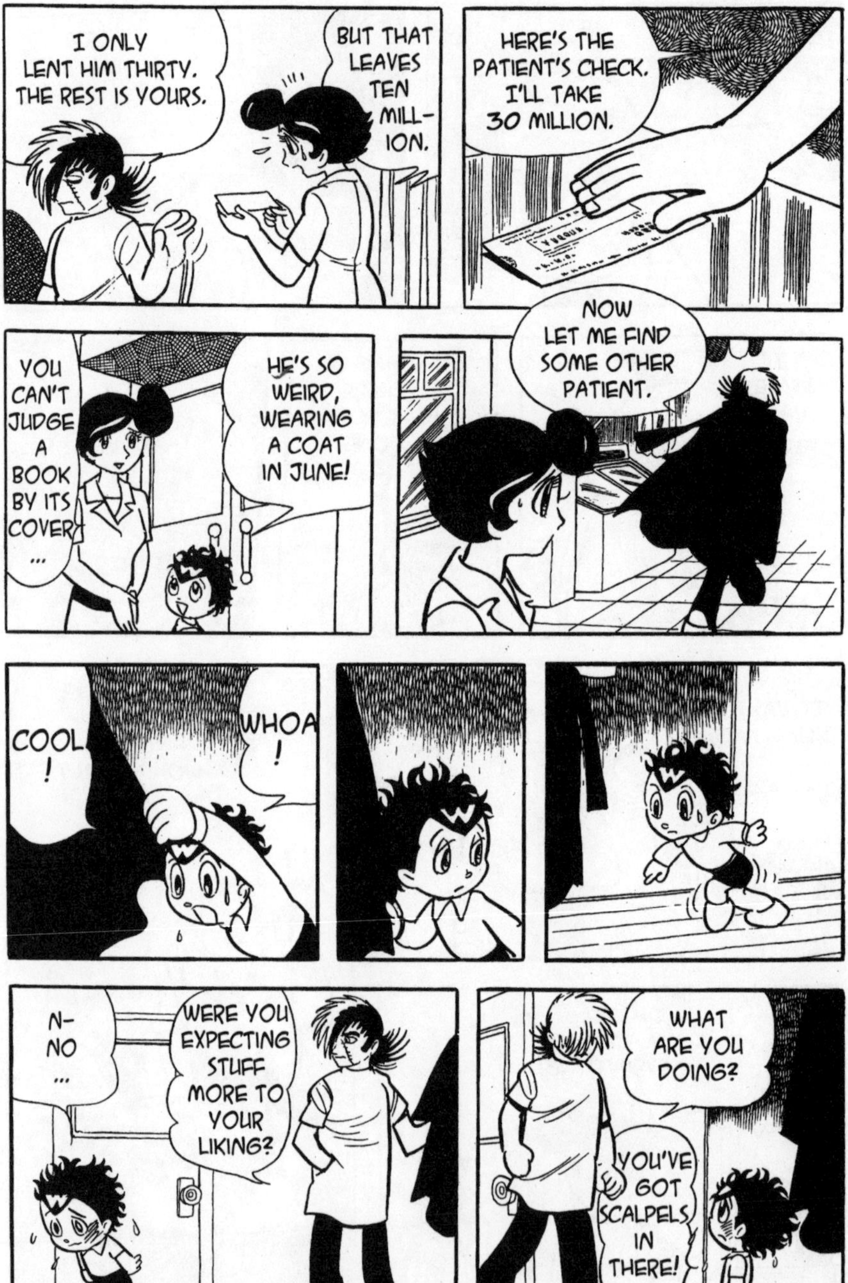
HERE'S THE PATIENT'S CHECK. I'LL TAKE 30 MILLION.
BUT THAT LEAVES TEN MILL-ION.
I ONLY LENT HIM THIRTY. THE REST IS YOURS.
NOW LET ME FIND SOME OTHER PATIENT.
HE'S SO WEIRD, WEARING A COAT IN JUNE!
YOU CAN'T JUDGE A BOOK BY ITS COVER ...
WHOA!
COOL!
WHAT ARE YOU DOING?
YOU'VE GOT SCALPELS IN THERE!
WERE YOU EXPECTING STUFF MORE TO YOUR LIKING?
N-NO ...

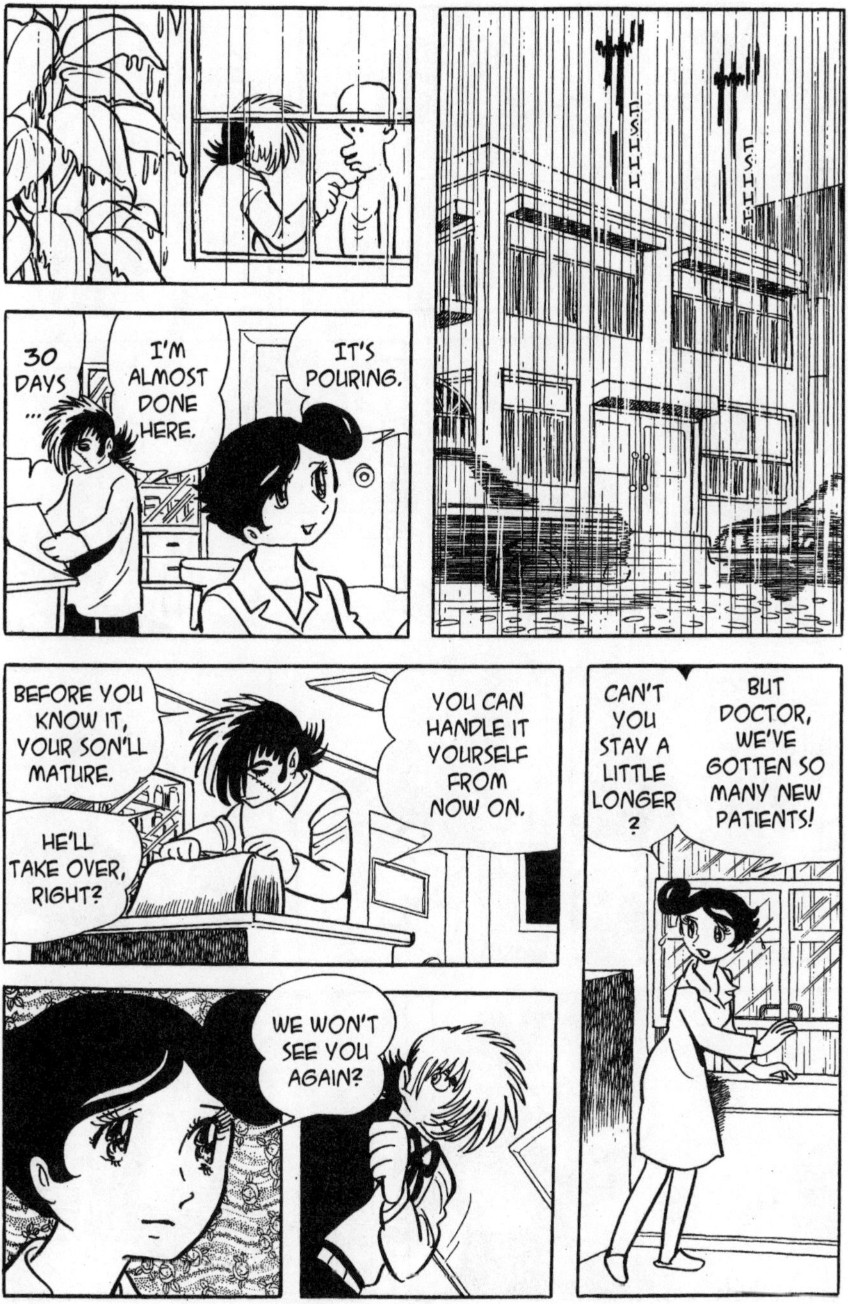
FSHHH
FSHHH
IT'S POURING.
I'M ALMOST DONE HERE.
30 DAYS ...
BUT DOCTOR, WE'VE GOTTEN SO MANY NEW PATIENTS!
CAN'T YOU STAY A LITTLE LONGER?
YOU CAN HANDLE IT YOURSELF FROM NOW ON.
BEFORE YOU KNOW IT, YOUR SON'LL MATURE.
HE'LL TAKE OVER, RIGHT?
WE WON'T SEE YOU AGAIN?

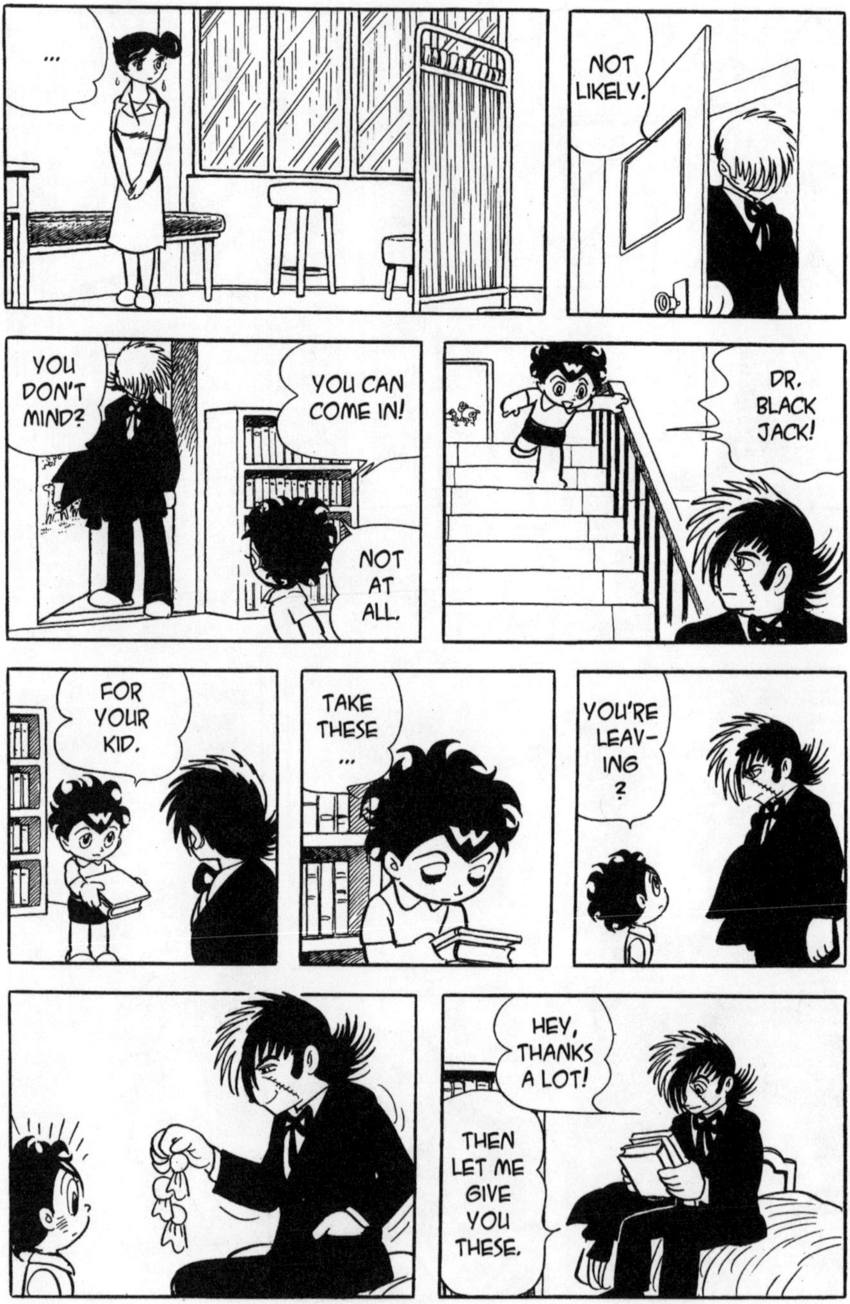
NOT LIKELY.
...
DR. BLACK JACK!
YOU CAN COME IN!
YOU DON'T MIND?
NOT AT ALL.
YOU'RE LEAV-ING?
TAKE THESE ...
FOR YOUR KID.
HEY, THANKS A LOT!
THEN LET ME GIVE YOU THESE.

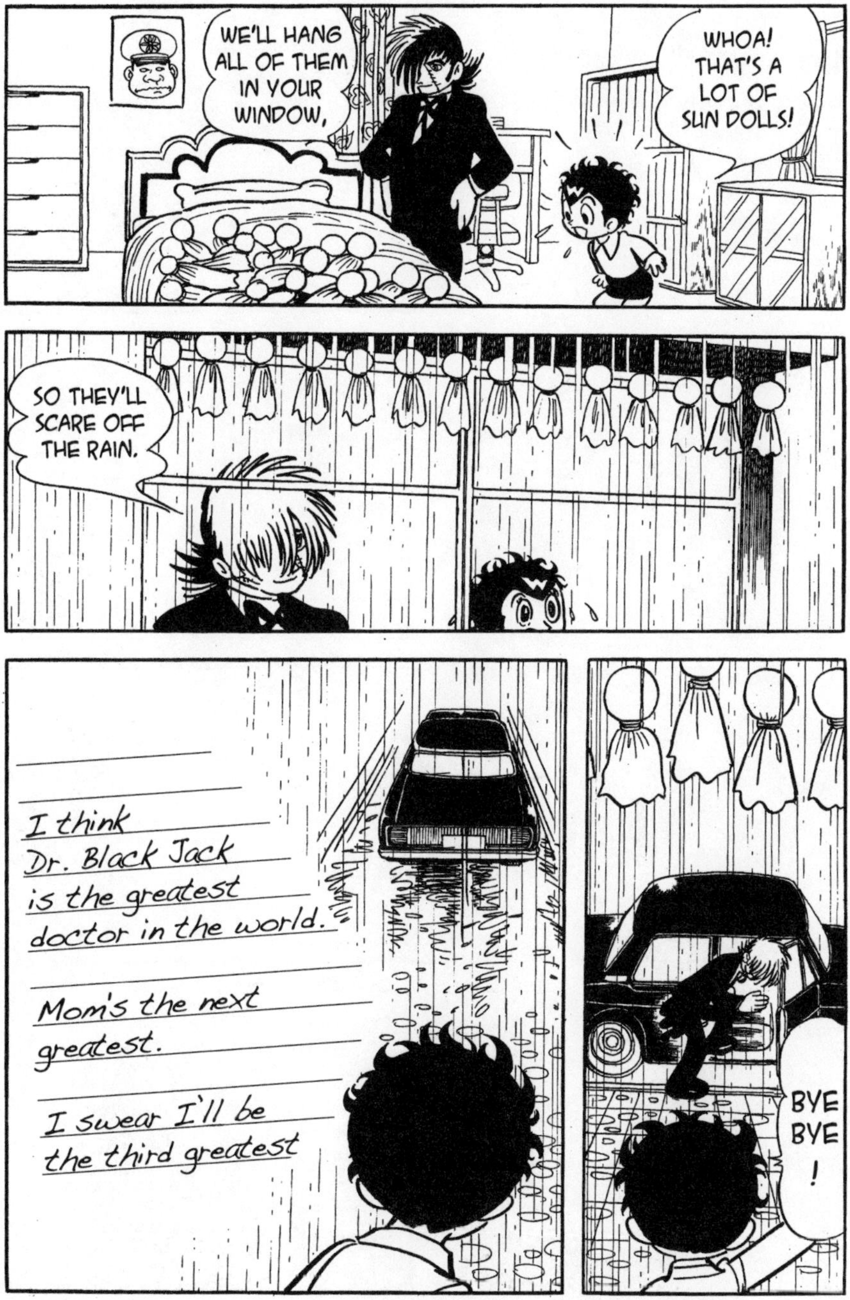
WHOA! THAT'S A LOT OF SUN DOLLS!
WE'LL HANG ALL OF THEM IN YOUR WINDOW,
SO THEY'LL SCARE OFF THE RAIN.
BYE BYE !
I think Dr. Black Jack is the greatest doctor in the world.
Mom's the next greatest.
I swear I'll be the third greatest

THIRD TIME'S THE CHARM

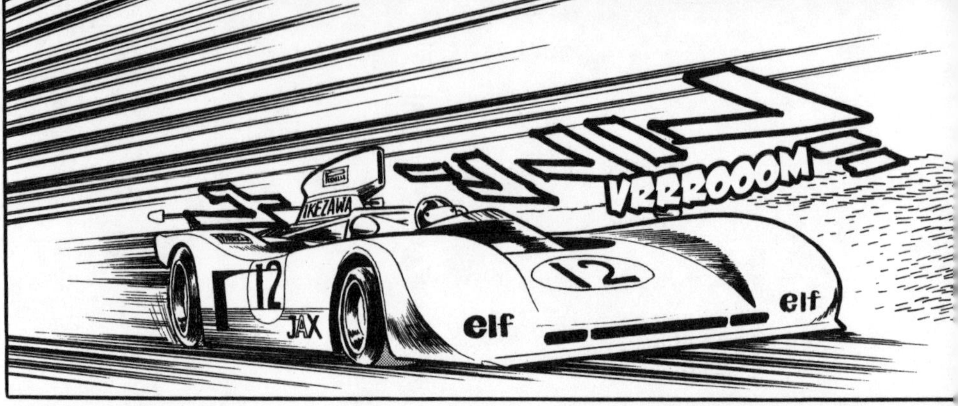

VRRROOOM
IKEZAWA
12
JAX
elf

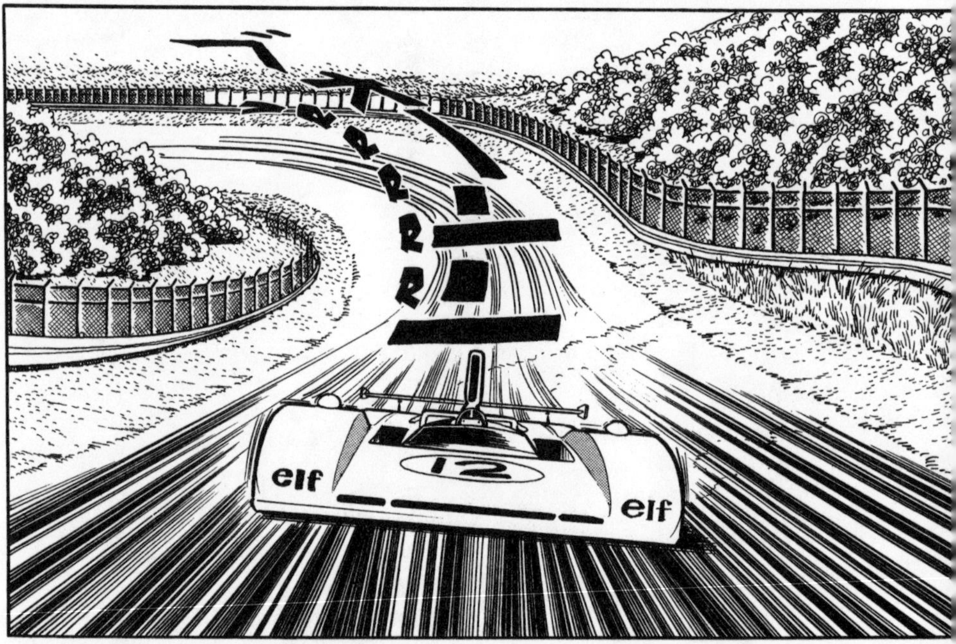

RRRRR
12
elf

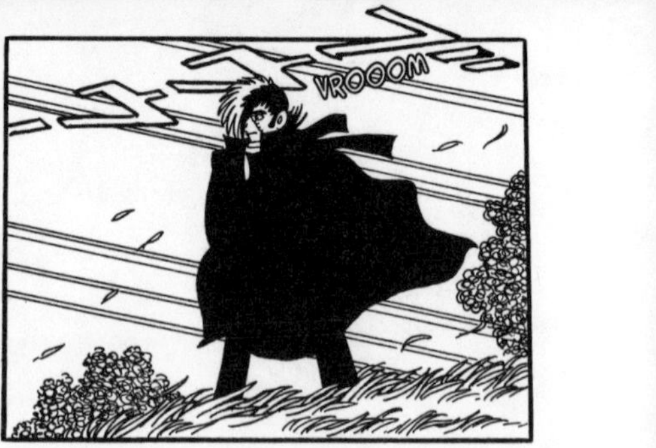

VROOOM

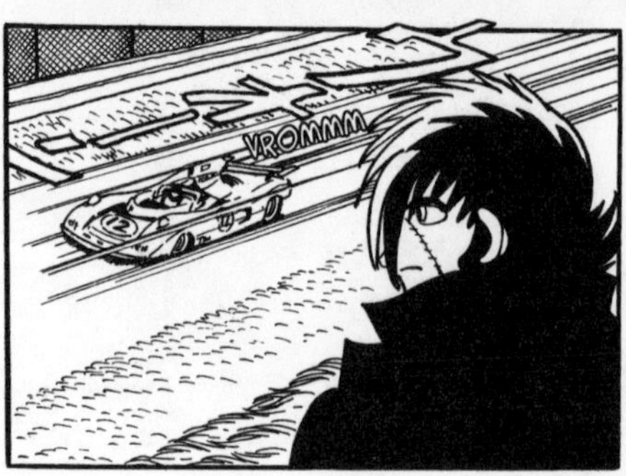

VROMMM

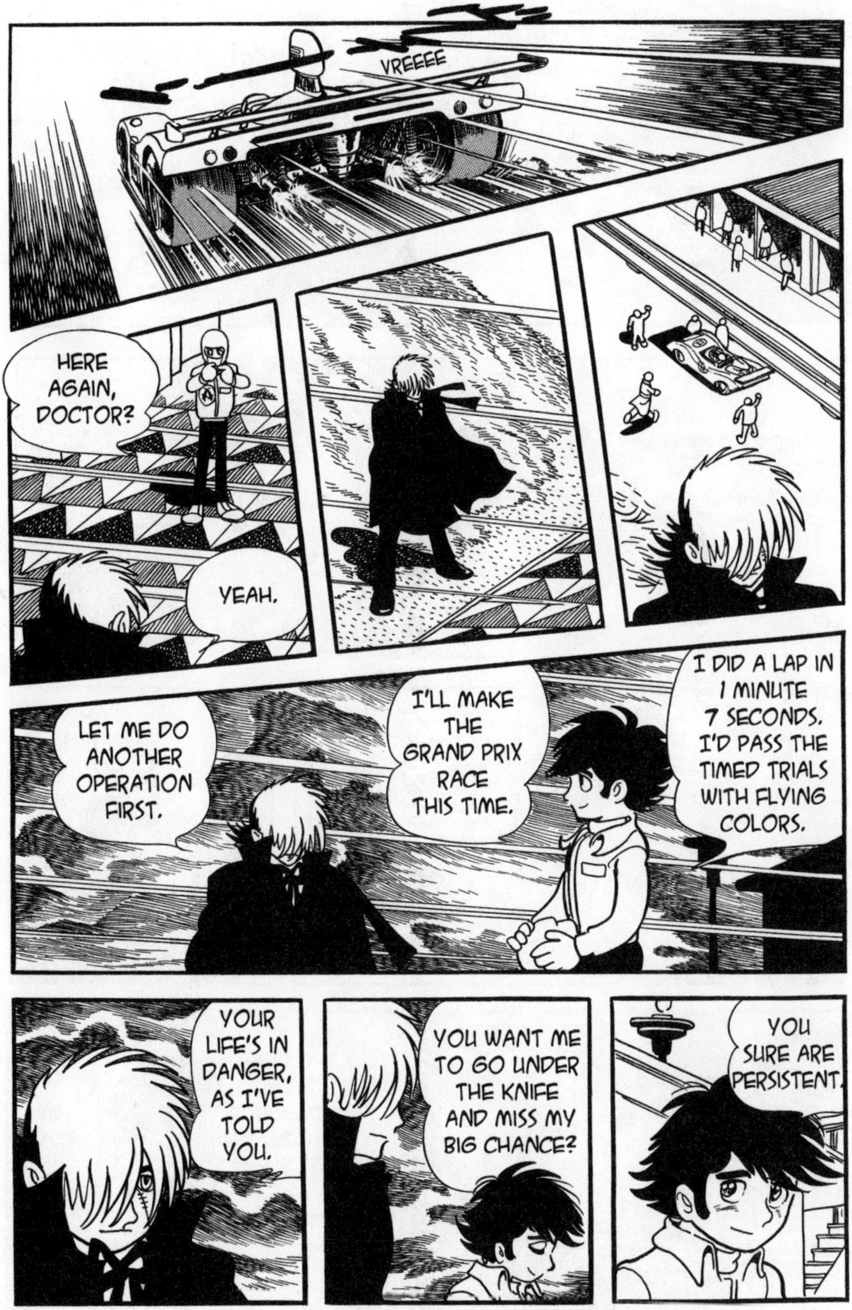
VREEEE
HERE AGAIN, DOCTOR?
YEAH.
I DID A LAP IN 1 MINUTE 7 SECONDS. I'D PASS THE TIMED TRIALS WITH FLYING COLORS.
I'LL MAKE THE GRAND PRIX RACE THIS TIME.
LET ME DO ANOTHER OPERATION FIRST.
YOU SURE ARE PERSISTENT.
YOU WANT ME TO GO UNDER THE KNIFE AND MISS MY BIG CHANCE?
YOUR LIFE'S IN DANGER, AS I'VE TOLD YOU.

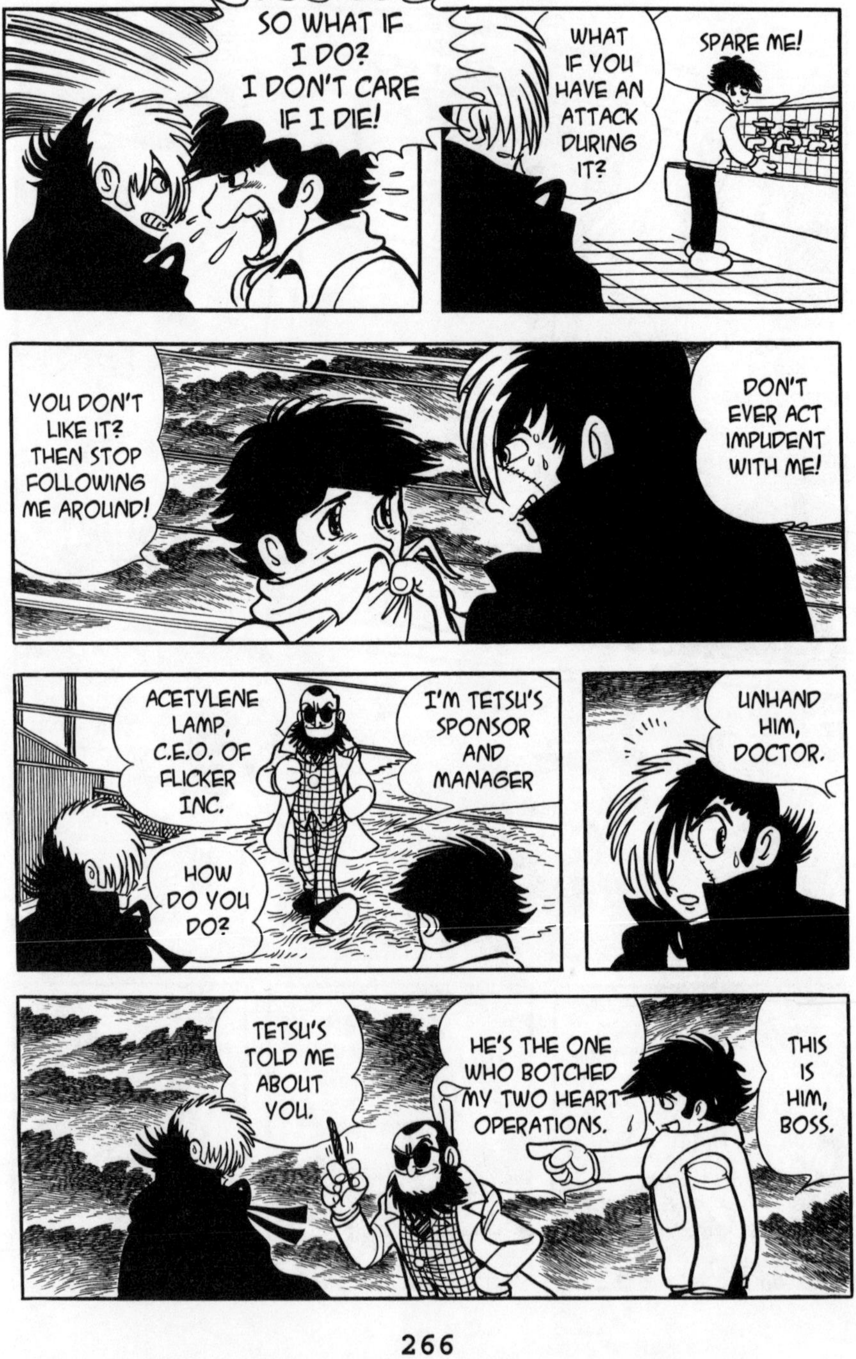
SPARE ME!
WHAT IF YOU HAVE AN ATTACK DURING IT?
SO WHAT IF I DO? I DON'T CARE IF I DIE!
DON'T EVER ACT IMPUDENT WITH ME!
YOU DON'T LIKE IT? THEN STOP FOLLOWING ME AROUND!
UNHAND HIM, DOCTOR.
I'M TETSU'S SPONSOR AND MANAGER
ACETYLENE LAMP, C.E.O. OF FLICKER INC.
HOW DO YOU DO?
THIS IS HIM, BOSS.
HE'S THE ONE WHO BOTCHED MY TWO HEART OPERATIONS.
TETSU'S TOLD ME ABOUT YOU.

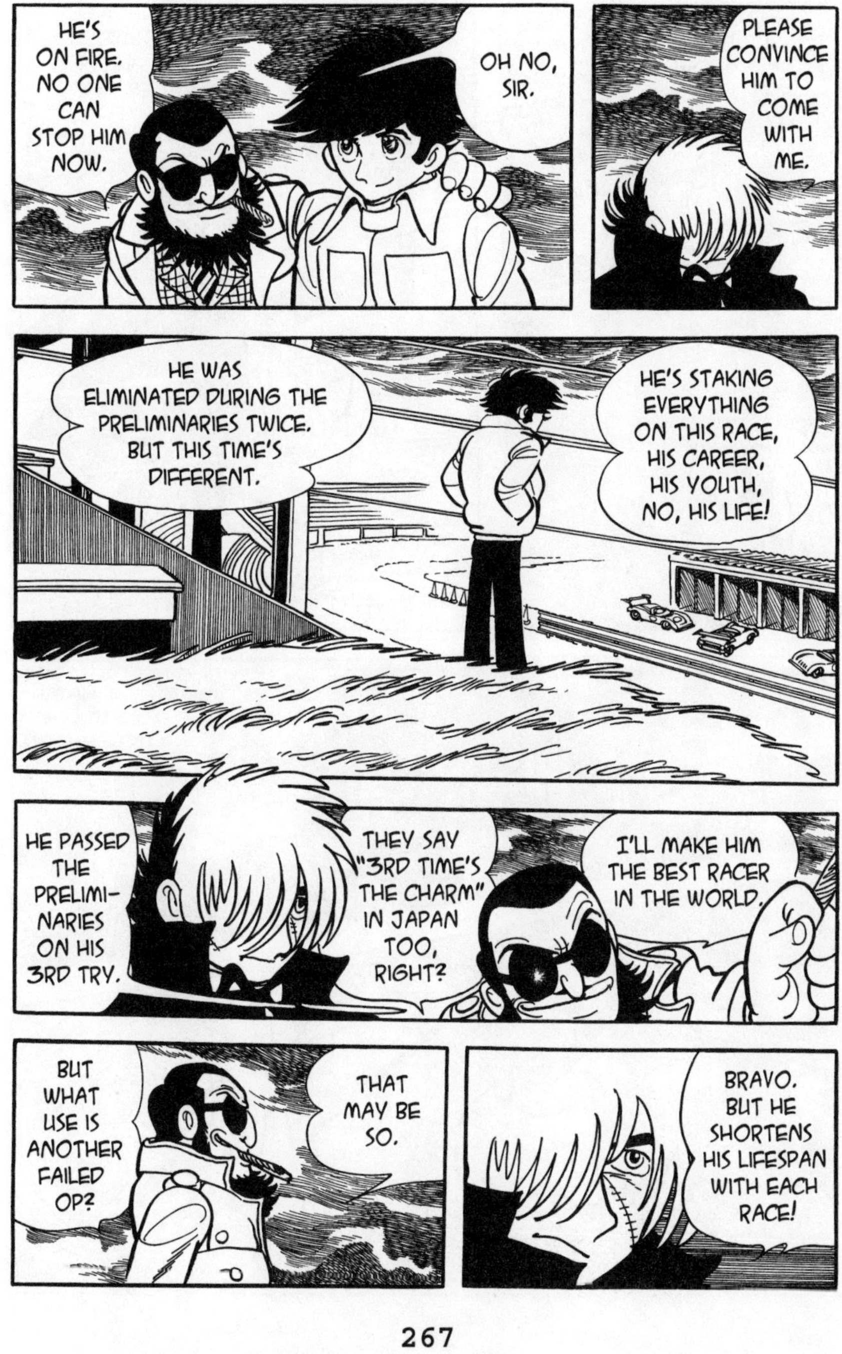
PLEASE CONVINCE HIM TO COME WITH ME.
OH NO, SIR.
HE'S ON FIRE. NO ONE CAN STOP HIM NOW.
HE'S STAKING EVERYTHING ON THIS RACE, HIS CAREER, HIS YOUTH, NO, HIS LIFE!
HE WAS ELIMINATED DURING THE PRELIMINARIES TWICE. BUT THIS TIME'S DIFFERENT.
I'LL MAKE HIM THE BEST RACER IN THE WORLD.
THEY SAY "3RD TIME'S THE CHARM" IN JAPAN TOO, RIGHT?
HE PASSED THE PRELIMI-NARIES ON HIS 3RD TRY.
BRAVO. BUT HE SHORTENS HIS LIFESPAN WITH EACH RACE!
THAT MAY BE SO.
BUT WHAT USE IS ANOTHER FAILED OP?

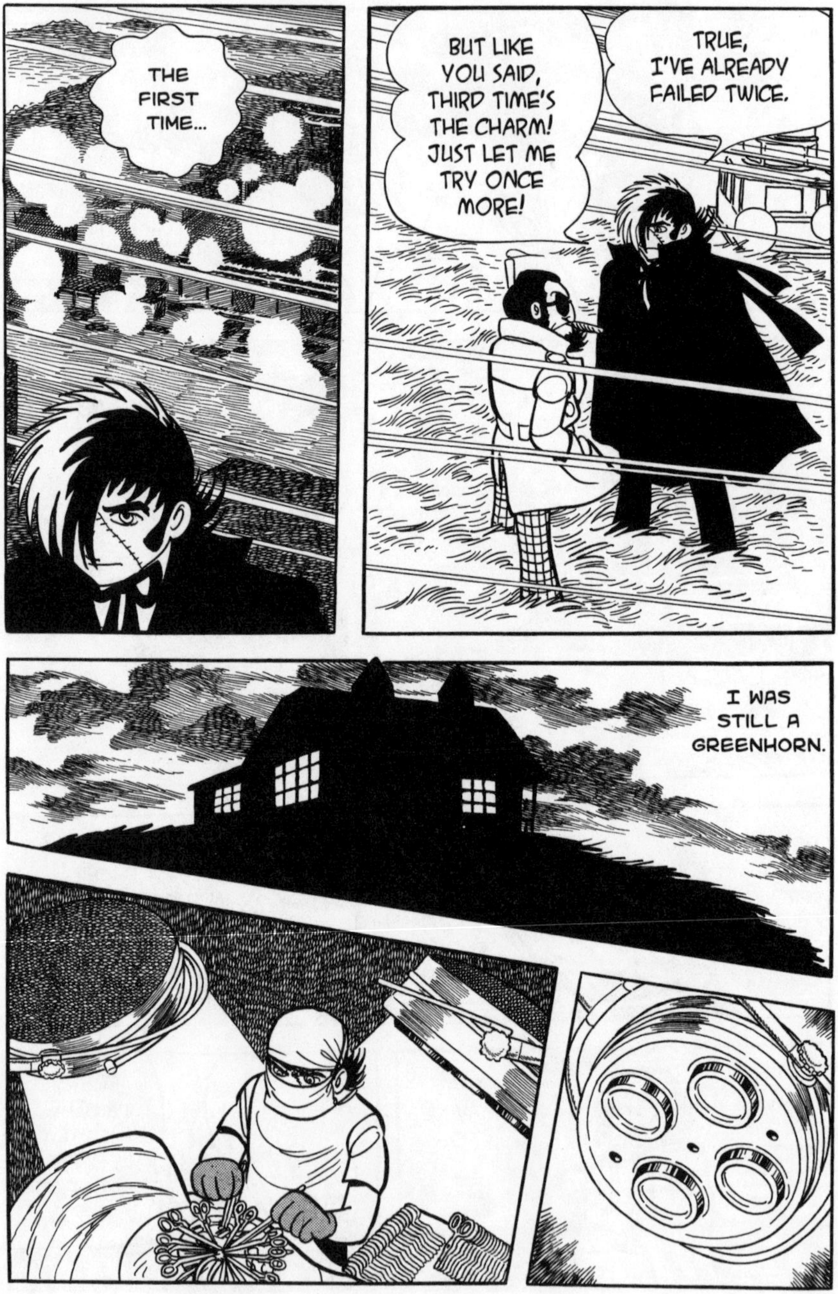
TRUE, I'VE ALREADY FAILED TWICE.
BUT LIKE YOU SAID, THIRD TIME'S THE CHARM! JUST LET ME TRY ONCE MORE!
THE FIRST TIME...
I WAS STILL A GREENHORN.

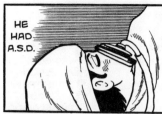

TETSU IKEZAWA WAS TWELVE YEARS OLD.
HE HAD A.S.D.
WHAT DO YOU KNOW ABOUT THE HEART? IT HAS TWO ATRIA AND TWO VENTRICLES, EACH PAIR DIVIDED INTO RIGHT AND LEFT SIDES BY A WALL. BUT SOME PEOPLE ARE BORN WITH A HOLE IN THE WALL, OR WITH NO WALL AT ALL. ATRIAL SEPTAL DEFECT (A.S.D.) IS ONE EXAMPLE.
Left Atrium
Inter-atrial Septum
Right Atrium
Left Ventricle
Right Ventricle
Inter-ventricular Septum

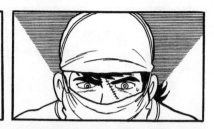

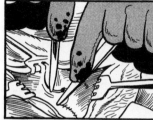

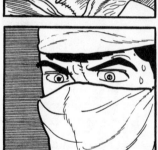

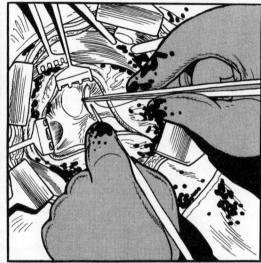

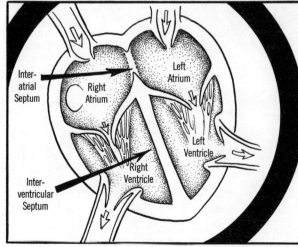

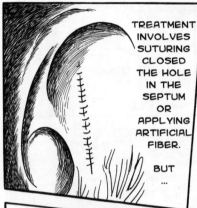

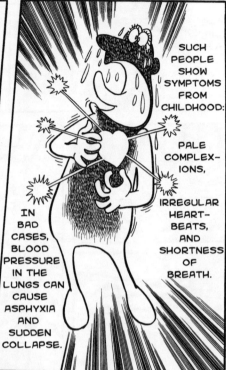

SUCH PEOPLE SHOW SYMPTOMS FROM CHILDHOOD:
PALE COMPLEX-IONS,
IRREGULAR HEART-BEATS, AND SHORTNESS OF BREATH.
IN BAD CASES, BLOOD PRESSURE IN THE LUNGS CAN CAUSE ASPHYXIA AND SUDDEN COLLAPSE.
TREATMENT INVOLVES SUTURING CLOSED THE HOLE IN THE SEPTUM OR APPLYING ARTIFICIAL FIBER.
BUT ...
I FAILED TO DO THAT WITH THE BOY.
DURING SURGERY HIS HEART STARTED TO CONVULSE ALL OF A SUDDEN.
I HAD TO ABORT THE OP RIGHT AWAY.
IT WAS THE FIRST TIME
I'D FACED DEFEAT AS A PRACTICING SURGEON!

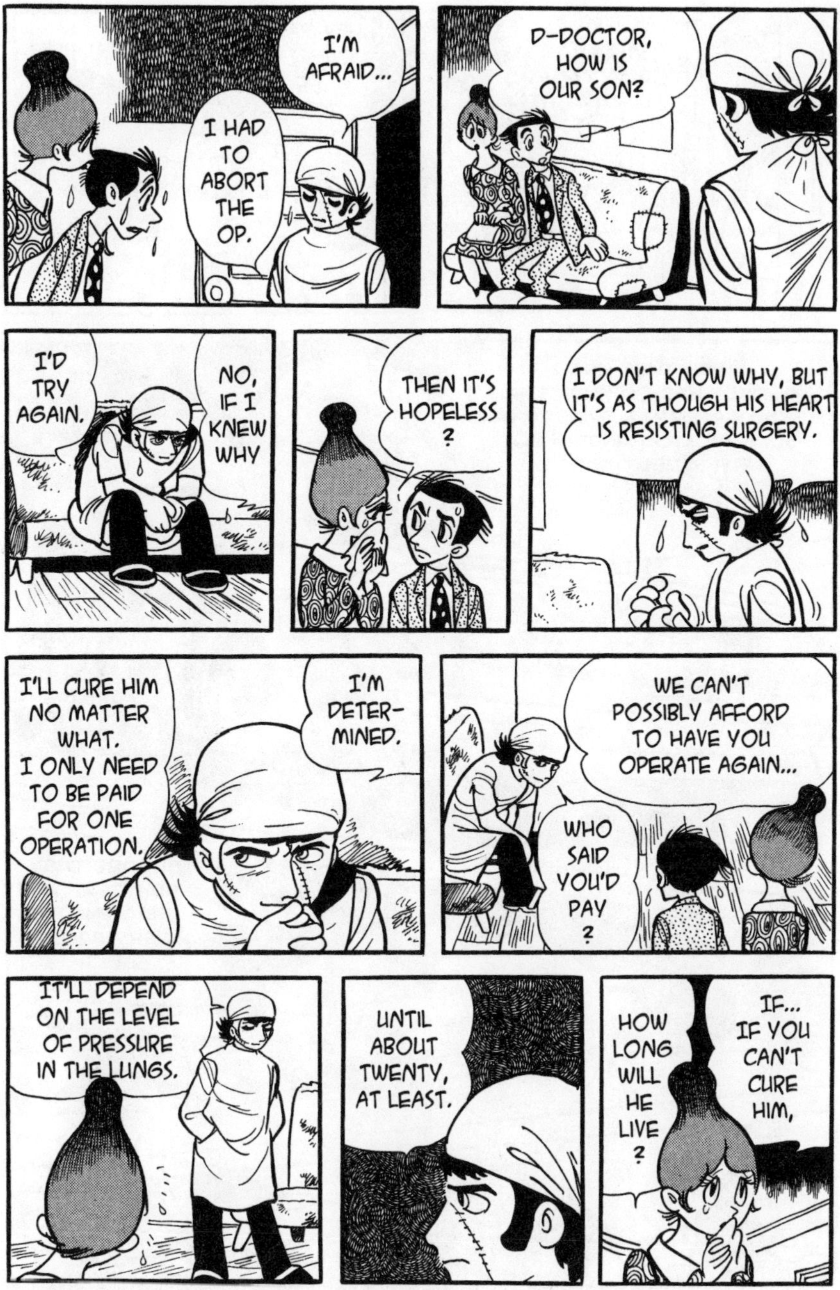
D-DOCTOR, HOW IS OUR SON?
I'M AFRAID...
I HAD TO ABORT THE OP.
I DON'T KNOW WHY, BUT IT'S AS THOUGH HIS HEART IS RESISTING SURGERY.
THEN IT'S HOPELESS?
NO, IF I KNEW WHY
I'D TRY AGAIN.
WE CAN'T POSSIBLY AFFORD TO HAVE YOU OPERATE AGAIN...
WHO SAID YOU'D PAY?
I'M DETER-MINED.
I'LL CURE HIM NO MATTER WHAT. I ONLY NEED TO BE PAID FOR ONE OPERATION.
IF... IF YOU CAN'T CURE HIM,
HOW LONG WILL HE LIVE?
UNTIL ABOUT TWENTY, AT LEAST.
IT'LL DEPEND ON THE LEVEL OF PRESSURE IN THE LUNGS.

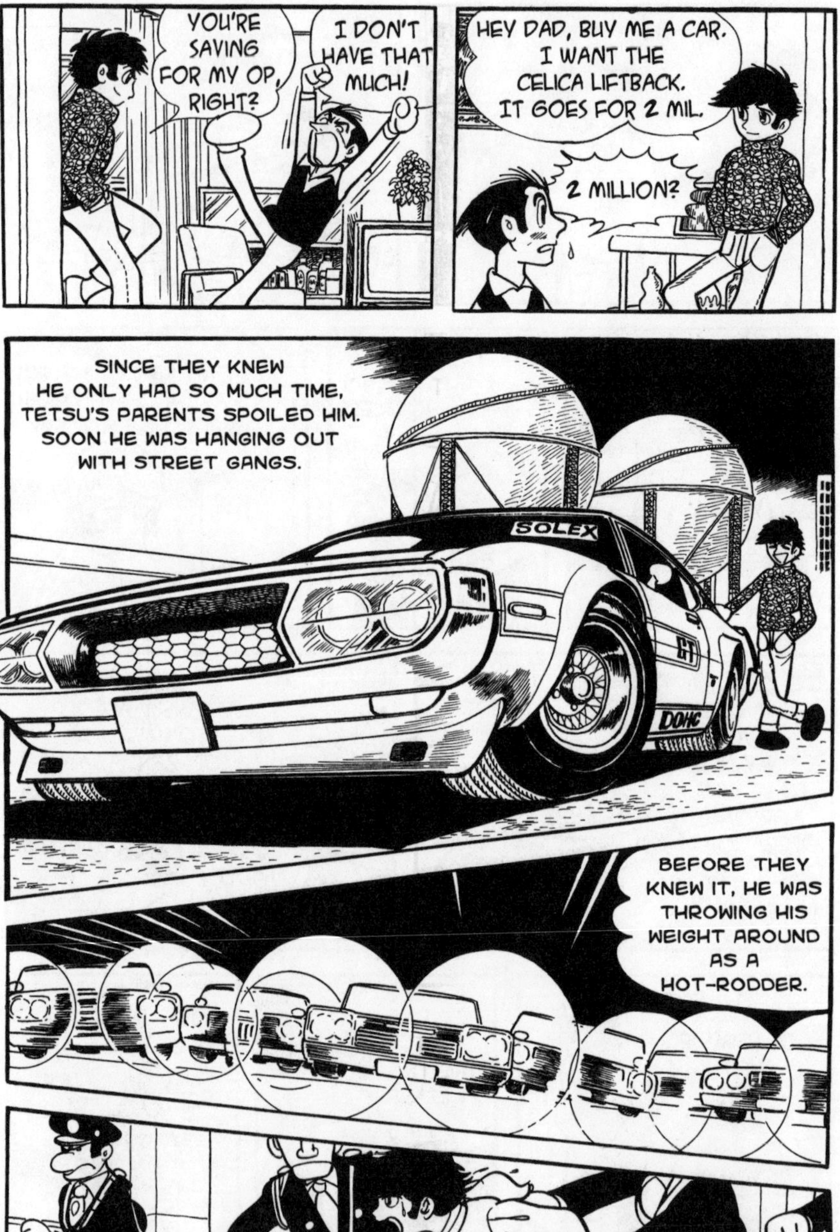
HEY DAD, BUY ME A CAR. I WANT THE CELICA LIFTBACK. IT GOES FOR 2 MIL.
2 MILLION?
I DON'T HAVE THAT MUCH!
YOU'RE SAVING FOR MY OP, RIGHT?
SINCE THEY KNEW HE ONLY HAD SO MUCH TIME, TETSU'S PARENTS SPOILED HIM. SOON HE WAS HANGING OUT WITH STREET GANGS.
SOLEX
GT
DOHC
BEFORE THEY KNEW IT, HE WAS THROWING HIS WEIGHT AROUND AS A HOT-RODDER.

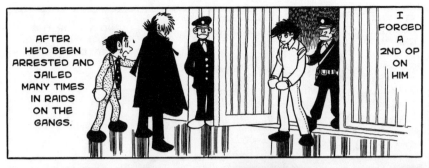

I FORCED A 2ND OP ON HIM
AFTER HE'D BEEN ARRESTED AND JAILED MANY TIMES IN RAIDS ON THE GANGS.
THIS WON'T BE
A REPEAT OF THE LAST TIME.
DURING HEART SURGERY, THE PATIENT IS HOOKED UP TO A HEART-LUNG MACHINE.
THE MACHINE ACTS IN PLACE OF THE REAL HEART AND LUNGS ...

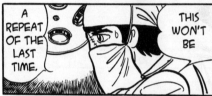

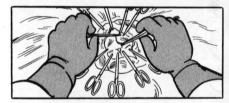

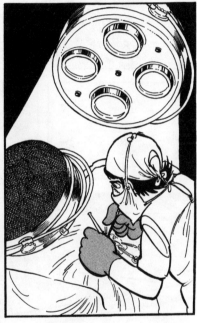

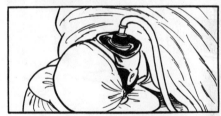

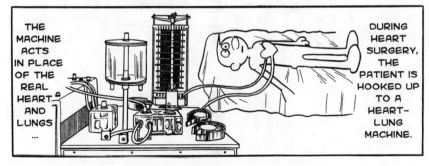

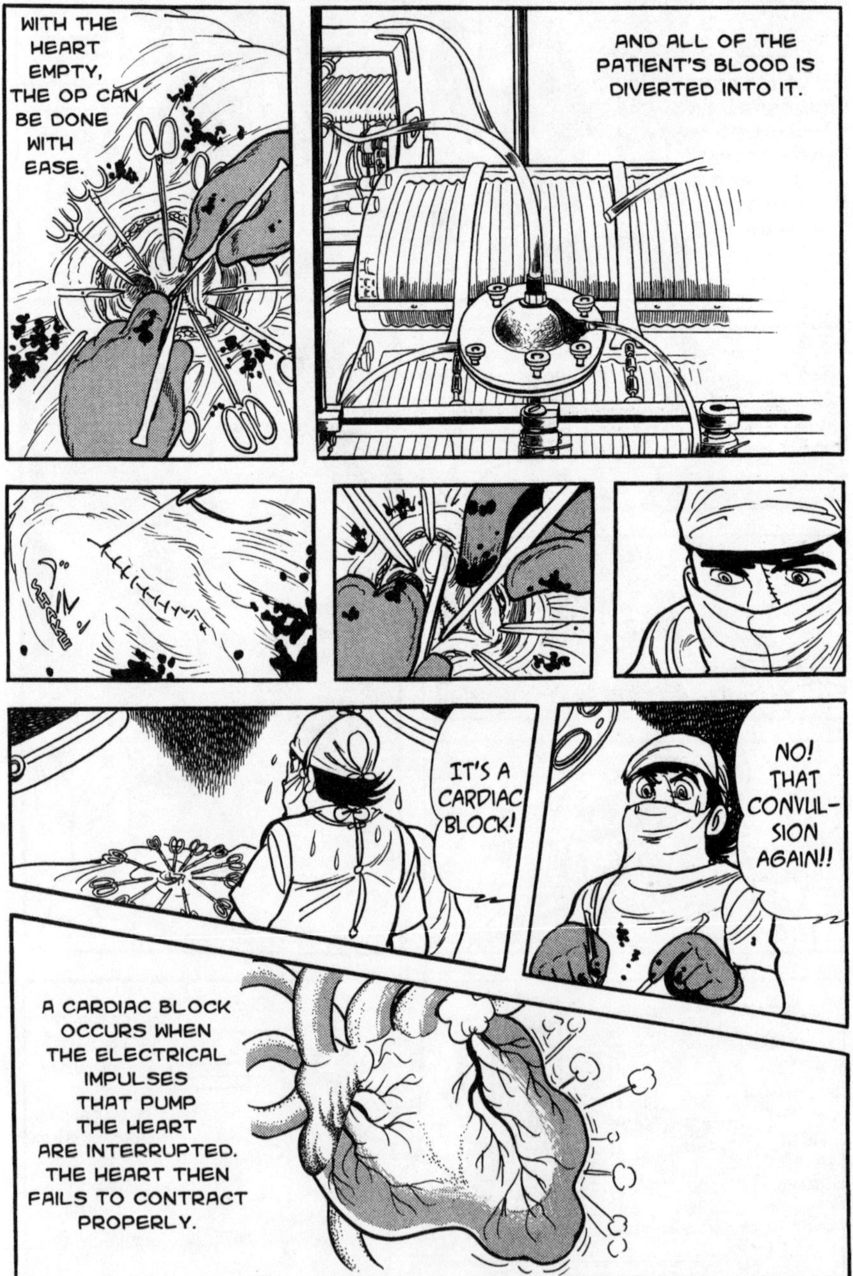
AND ALL OF THE PATIENT'S BLOOD IS DIVERTED INTO IT.
WITH THE HEART EMPTY, THE OP CAN BE DONE WITH EASE.
NO! THAT CONVUL-SION AGAIN!!
IT'S A CARDIAC BLOCK!
A CARDIAC BLOCK OCCURS WHEN THE ELECTRICAL IMPULSES THAT PUMP THE HEART ARE INTERRUPTED. THE HEART THEN FAILS TO CONTRACT PROPERLY.

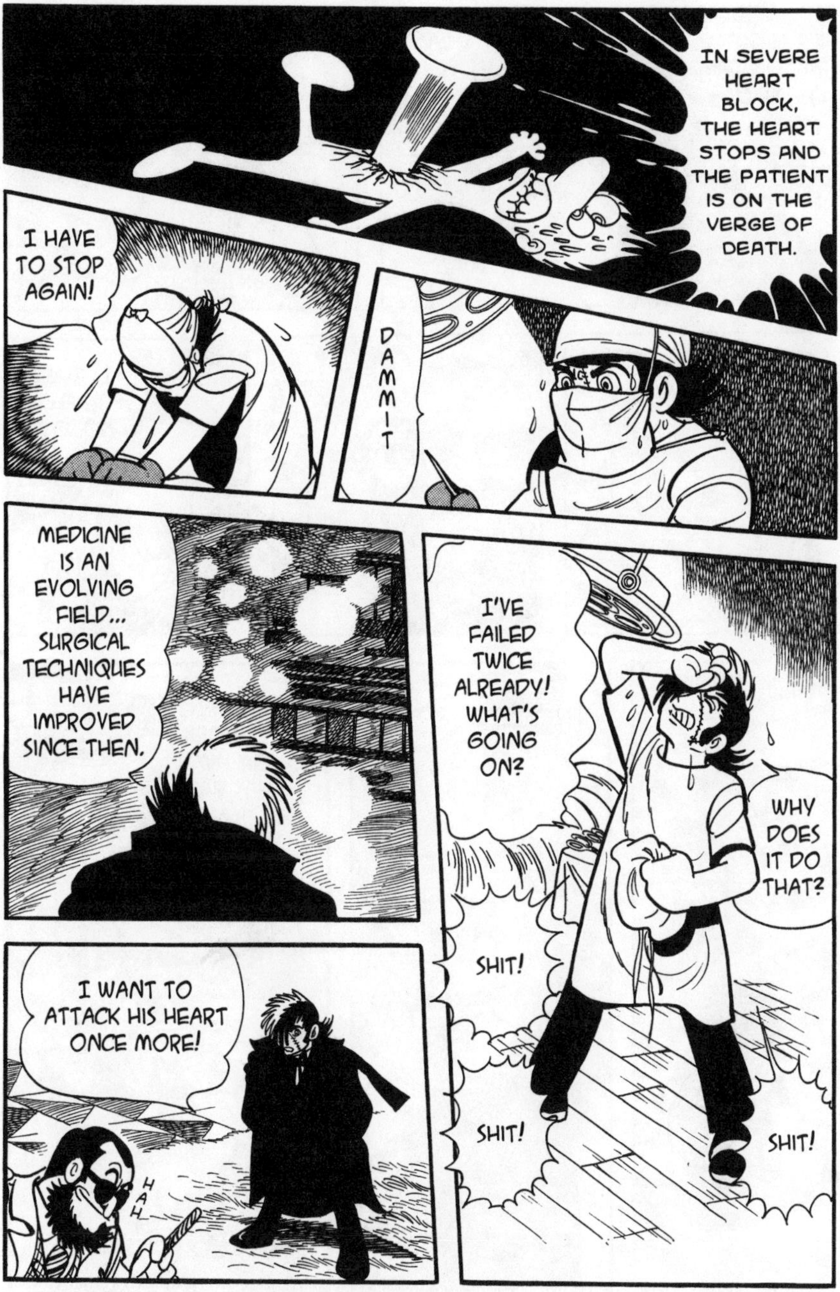
IN SEVERE HEART BLOCK, THE HEART STOPS AND THE PATIENT IS ON THE VERGE OF DEATH.
DAMMIT
I HAVE TO STOP AGAIN!
I'VE FAILED TWICE ALREADY! WHAT'S GOING ON?
WHY DOES IT DO THAT?
SHIT!
SHIT!
SHIT!
MEDICINE IS AN EVOLVING FIELD... SURGICAL TECHNIQUES HAVE IMPROVED SINCE THEN.
I WANT TO ATTACK HIS HEART ONCE MORE!
HAH

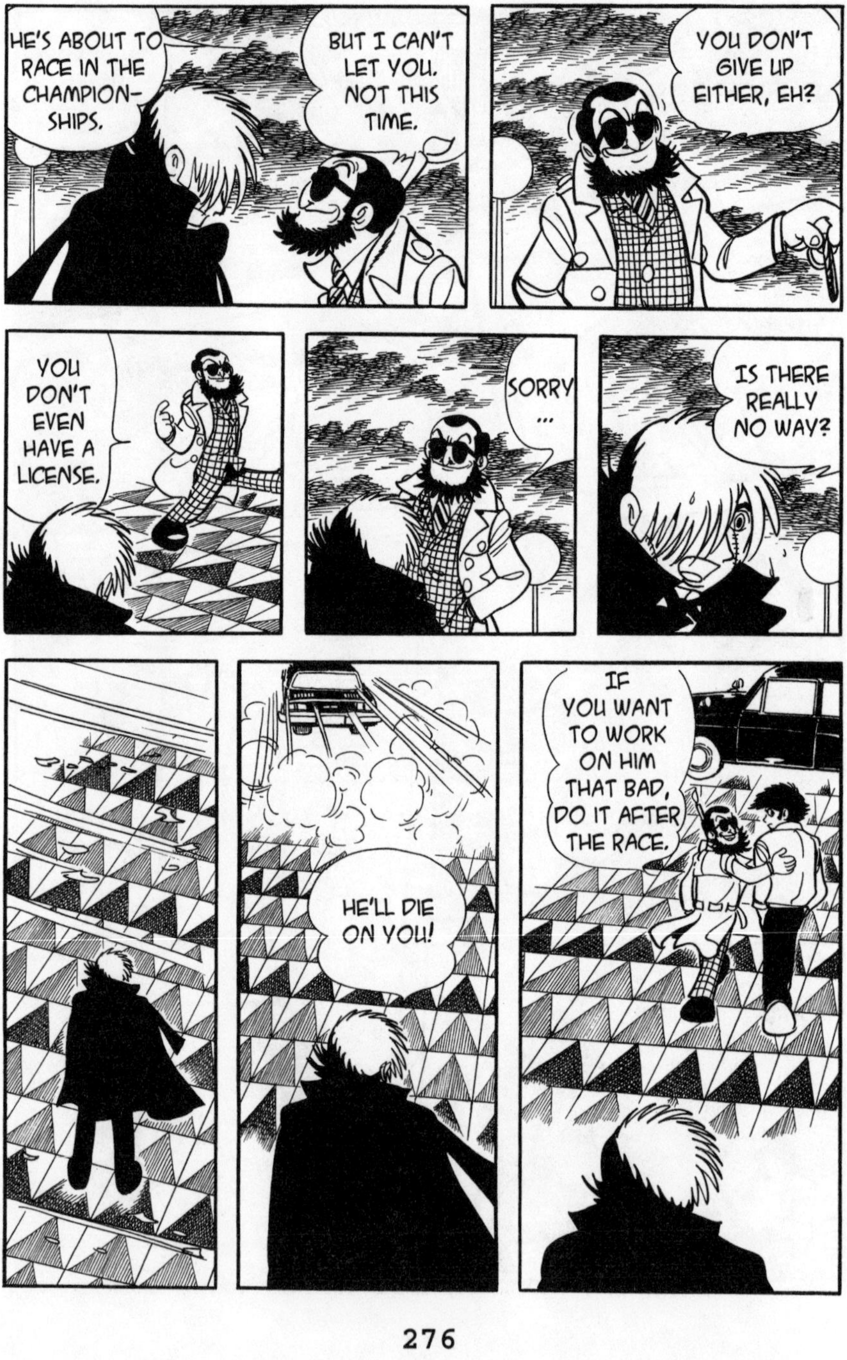
YOU DON'T GIVE UP EITHER, EH?
BUT I CAN'T LET YOU. NOT THIS TIME.
HE'S ABOUT TO RACE IN THE CHAMPION-SHIPS.
IS THERE REALLY NO WAY?
SORRY ...
YOU DON'T EVEN HAVE A LICENSE.
IF YOU WANT TO WORK ON HIM THAT BAD, DO IT AFTER THE RACE.
HE'LL DIE ON YOU!

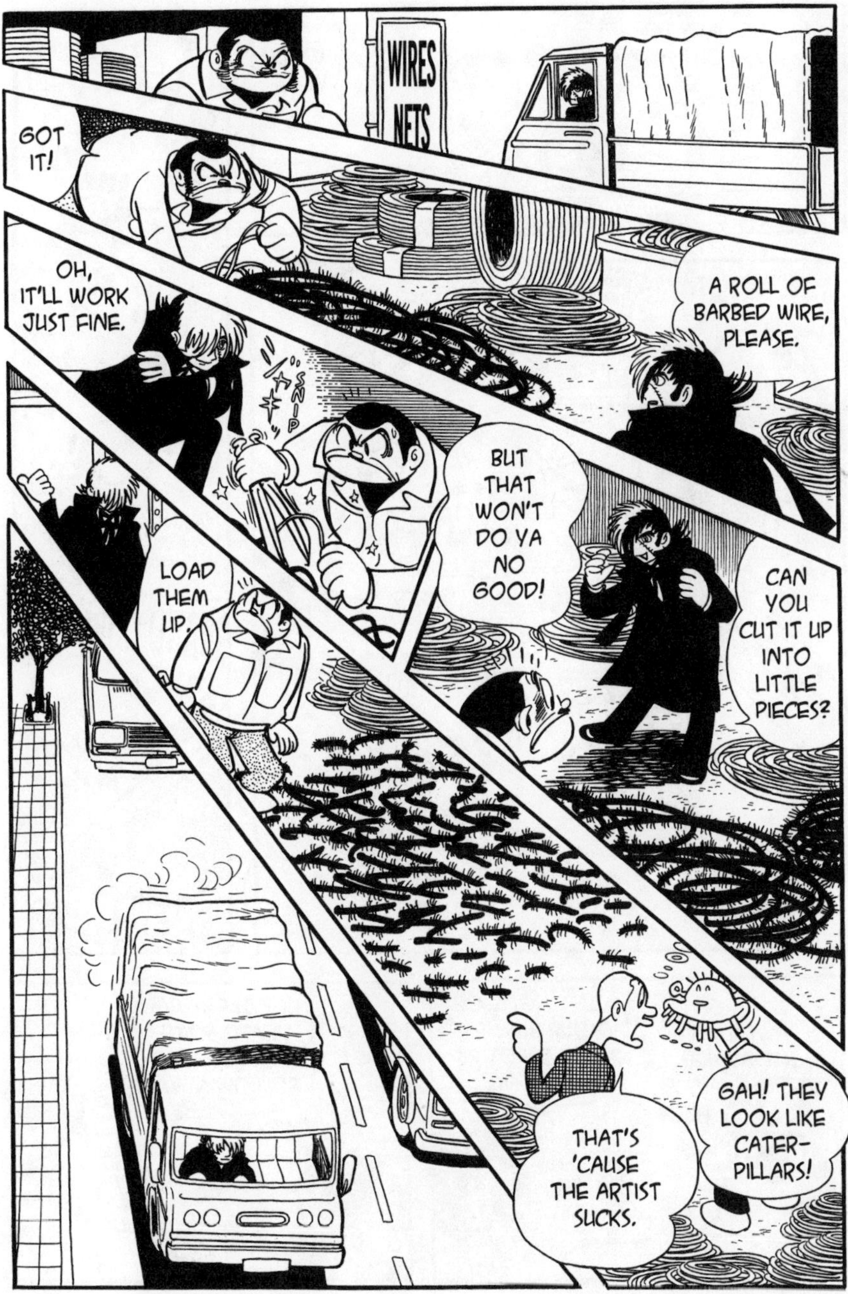
WIRES
NETS
GOT IT!
A ROLL OF BARBED WIRE, PLEASE.
CAN YOU CUT IT UP INTO LITTLE PIECES?
BUT THAT WON'T DO YA NO GOOD!
OH, IT'LL WORK JUST FINE.
SNIP
LOAD THEM UP.
GAH! THEY LOOK LIKE CATER-PILLARS!
THAT'S 'CAUSE THE ARTIST SUCKS.

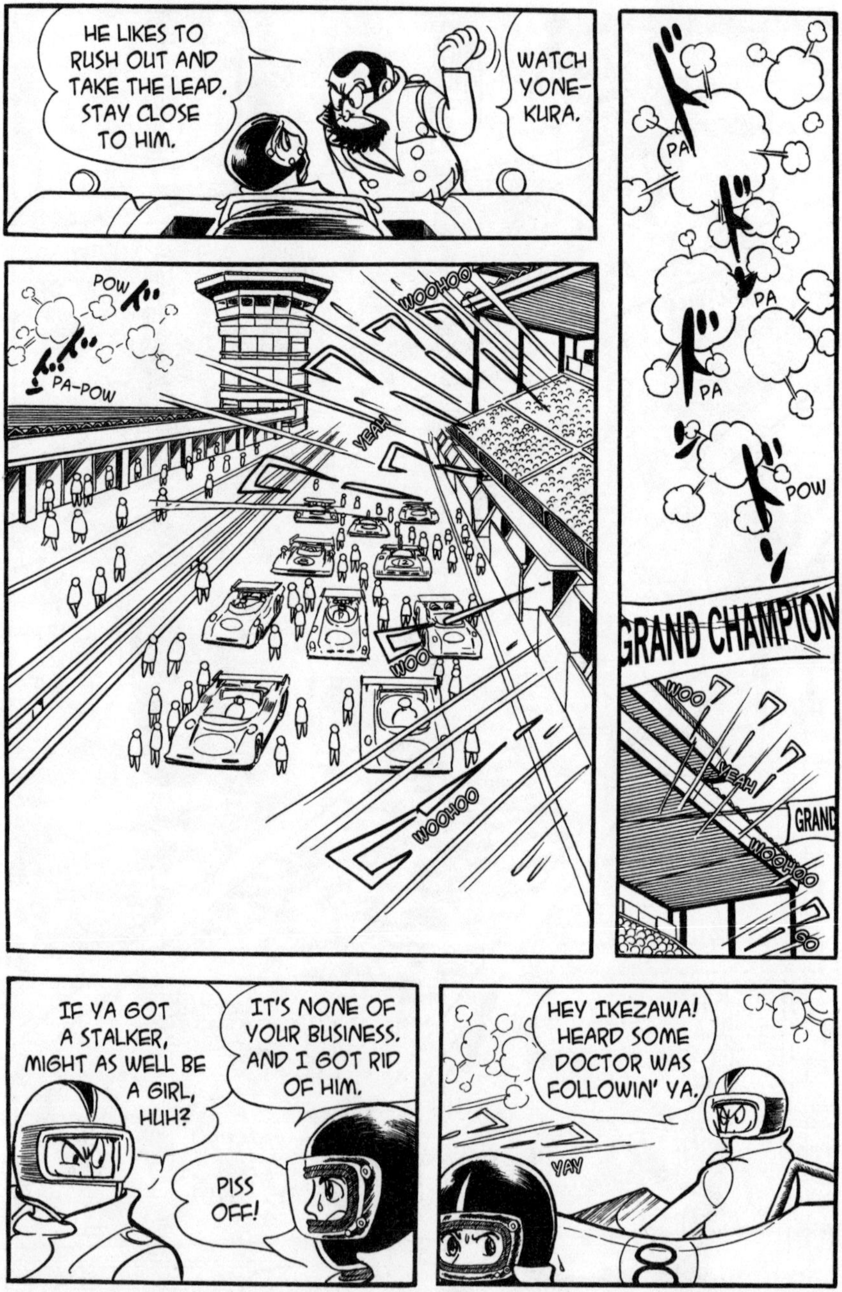
PA
PA
PA
POW
GRAND CHAMPION
WOO
YEAH
GRAND
WOOHOO
GO
WATCH YONE-KURA.
HE LIKES TO RUSH OUT AND TAKE THE LEAD. STAY CLOSE TO HIM.
POW
PA-POW
WOOHOO
YEAH
WOO
WOOHOO
HEY IKEZAWA! HEARD SOME DOCTOR WAS FOLLOWIN' YA.
YAY
IT'S NONE OF YOUR BUSINESS. AND I GOT RID OF HIM.
IF YA GOT A STALKER, MIGHT AS WELL BE A GIRL, HUH?
PISS OFF!

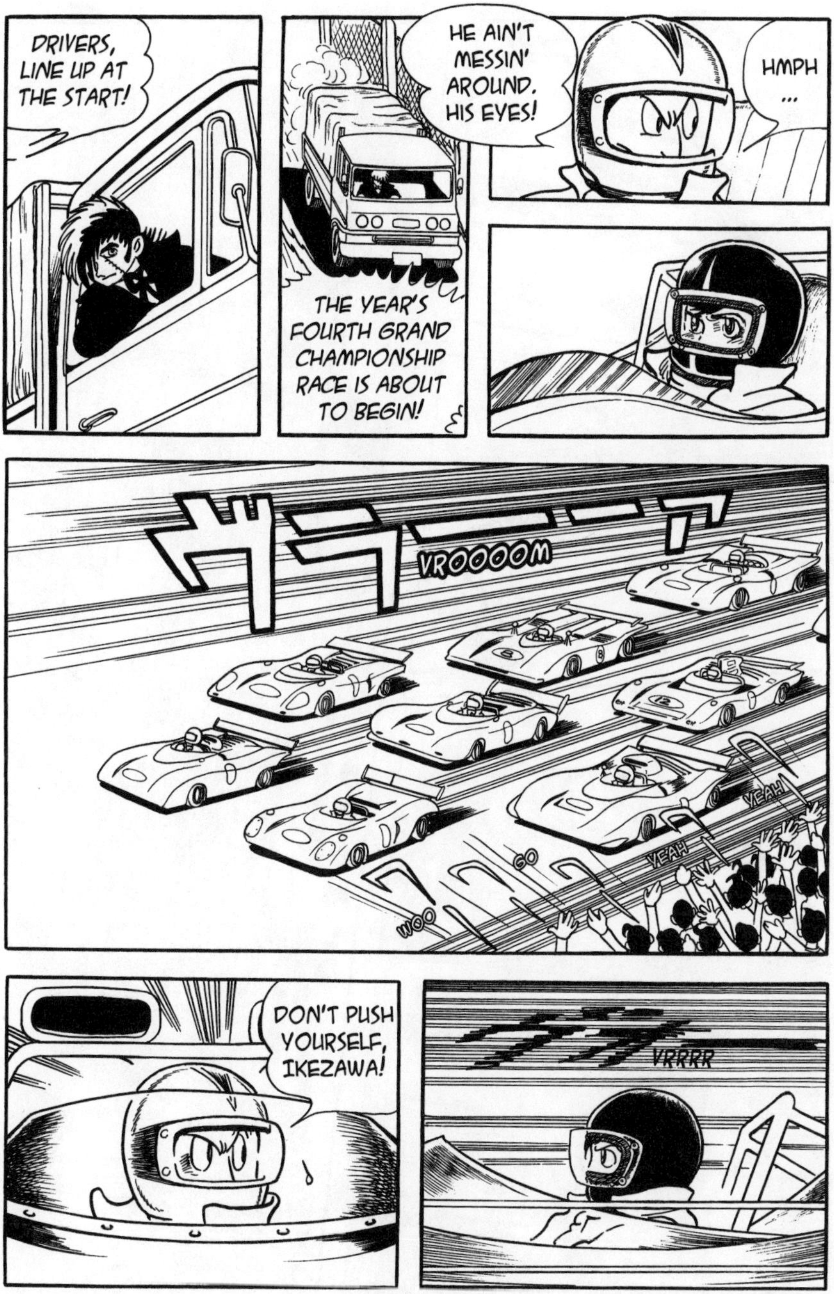
HMPH ...
HE AIN'T MESSIN' AROUND. HIS EYES!
THE YEAR'S FOURTH GRAND CHAMPIONSHIP RACE IS ABOUT TO BEGIN!
DRIVERS, LINE UP AT THE START!
VROOOOM
YEAH
YEAH
GO
WOO
VRRRR
DON'T PUSH YOURSELF, IKEZAWA!

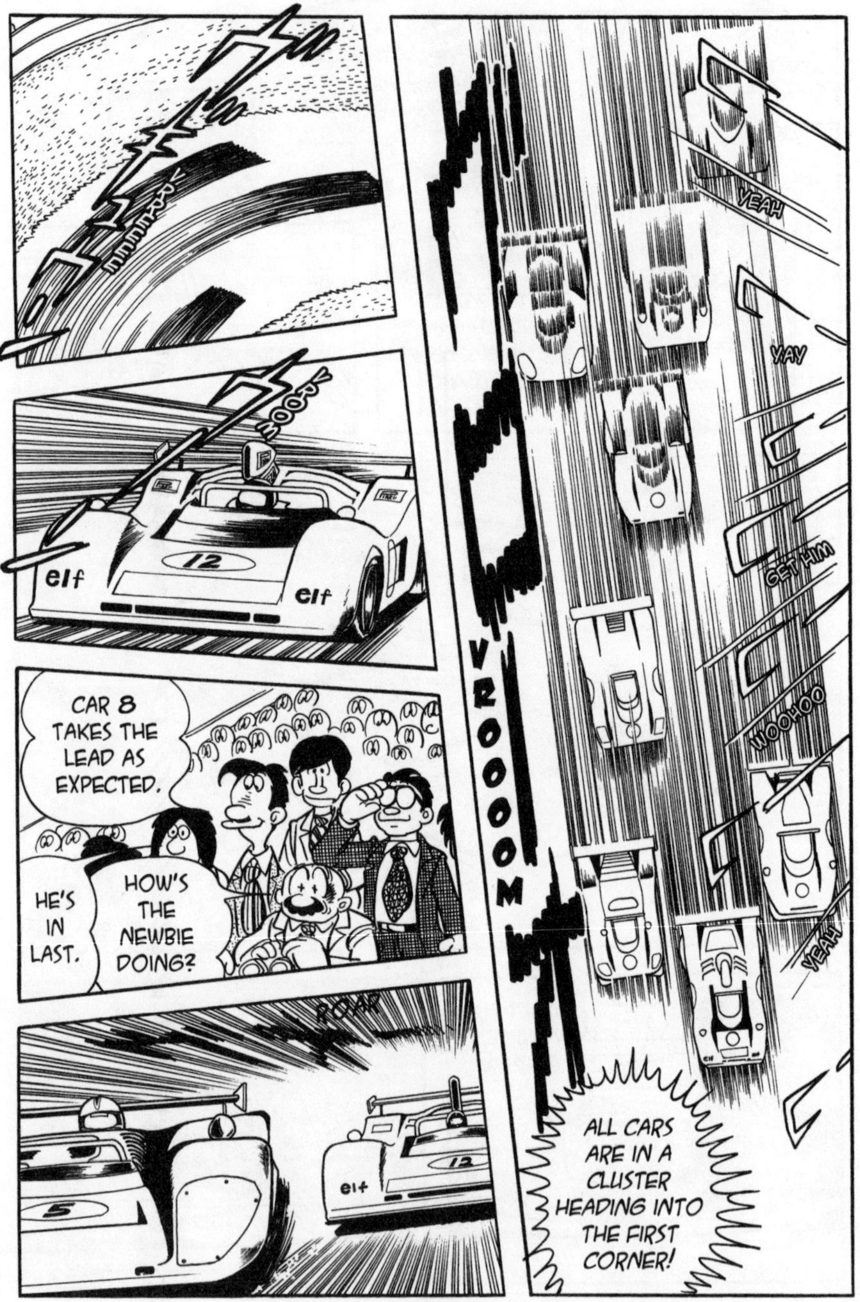
YEAH
YAY
GET HIM
WOOHOO
VROOOOOM
YEAH
ALL CARS ARE IN A CLUSTER HEADING INTO THE FIRST CORNER!
VROOM
CAR 8 TAKES THE LEAD AS EXPECTED.
HOW'S THE NEWBIE DOING?
HE'S IN LAST.
ROAR

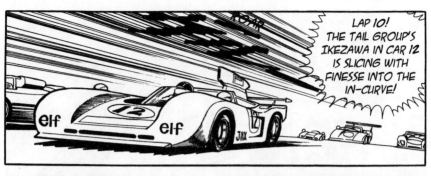

ROAR
LAP 10! THE TAIL GROUP'S IKEZAWA IN CAR 12 IS SLICING WITH FINESSE INTO THE IN-CURVE!
elf
elf
12
JAX
WOO
YEAH
YAY
WOO
KEEP IT COOL! YOU'VE GOT 35 MORE LAPS!
LAP 14! YONEKURA IN CAR 8 IS IN THE LEAD! HE IS RUSHING INTO THE TAIL GROUP ON LAP 13!
8
VRRR
8
GOING AROUND THE FIRST CORNER, THREE CARS IN THE TAIL GROUP COLLIDED! THEY'RE OUT!

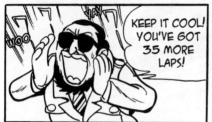

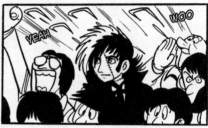

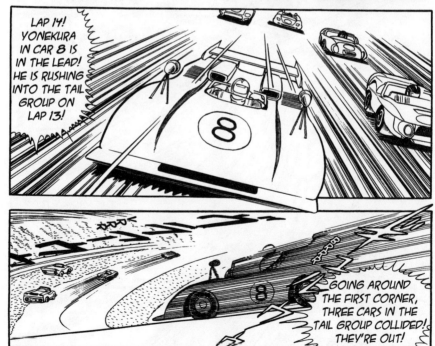

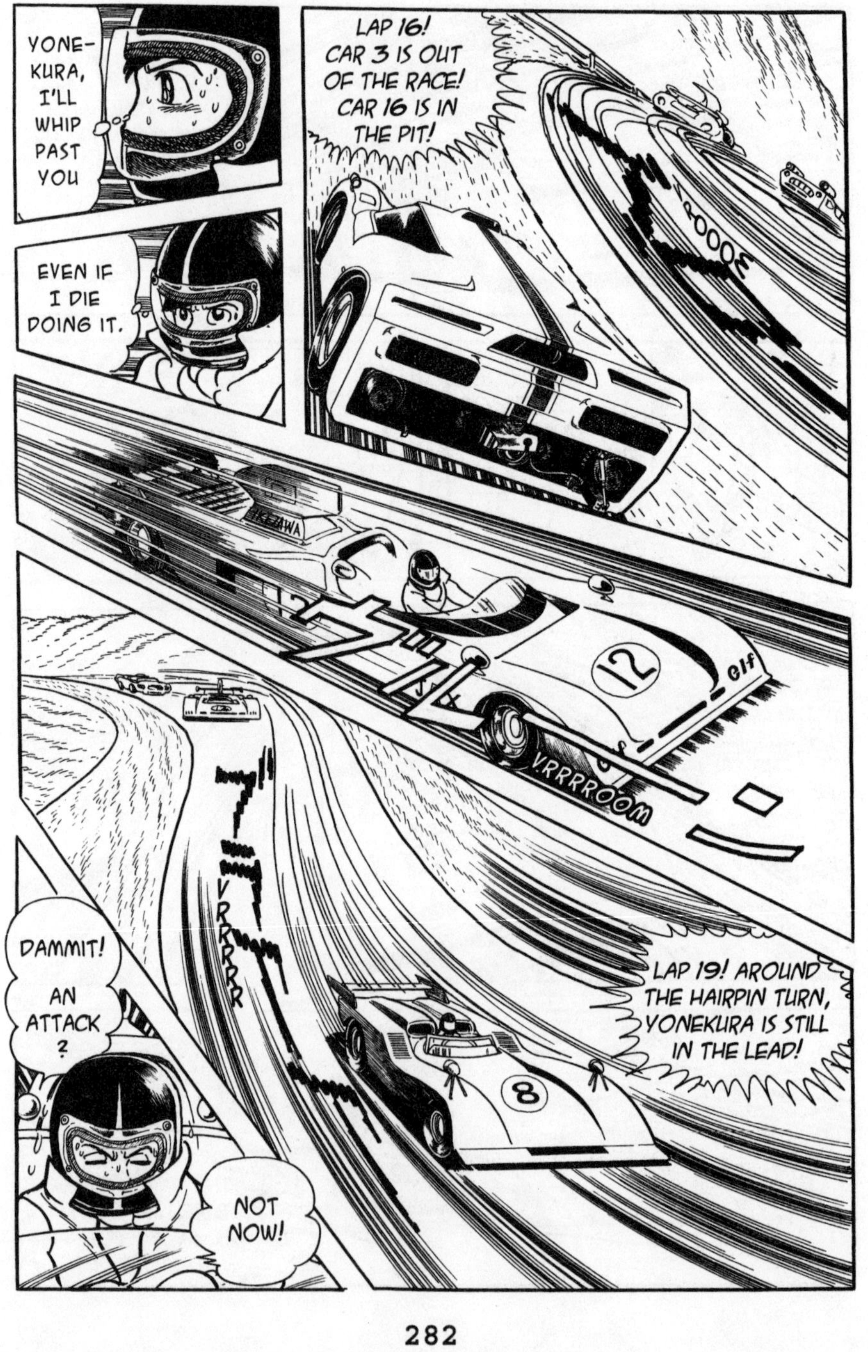
LAP 16! CAR 3 IS OUT OF THE RACE! CAR 16 IS IN THE PIT!
YONE-KURA, I'LL WHIP PAST YOU
EVEN IF I DIE DOING IT.
VRRRROOM
LAP 19! AROUND THE HAIRPIN TURN, YONEKURA IS STILL IN THE LEAD!
VRRRRRR
DAMMIT!
AN ATTACK?
NOT NOW!

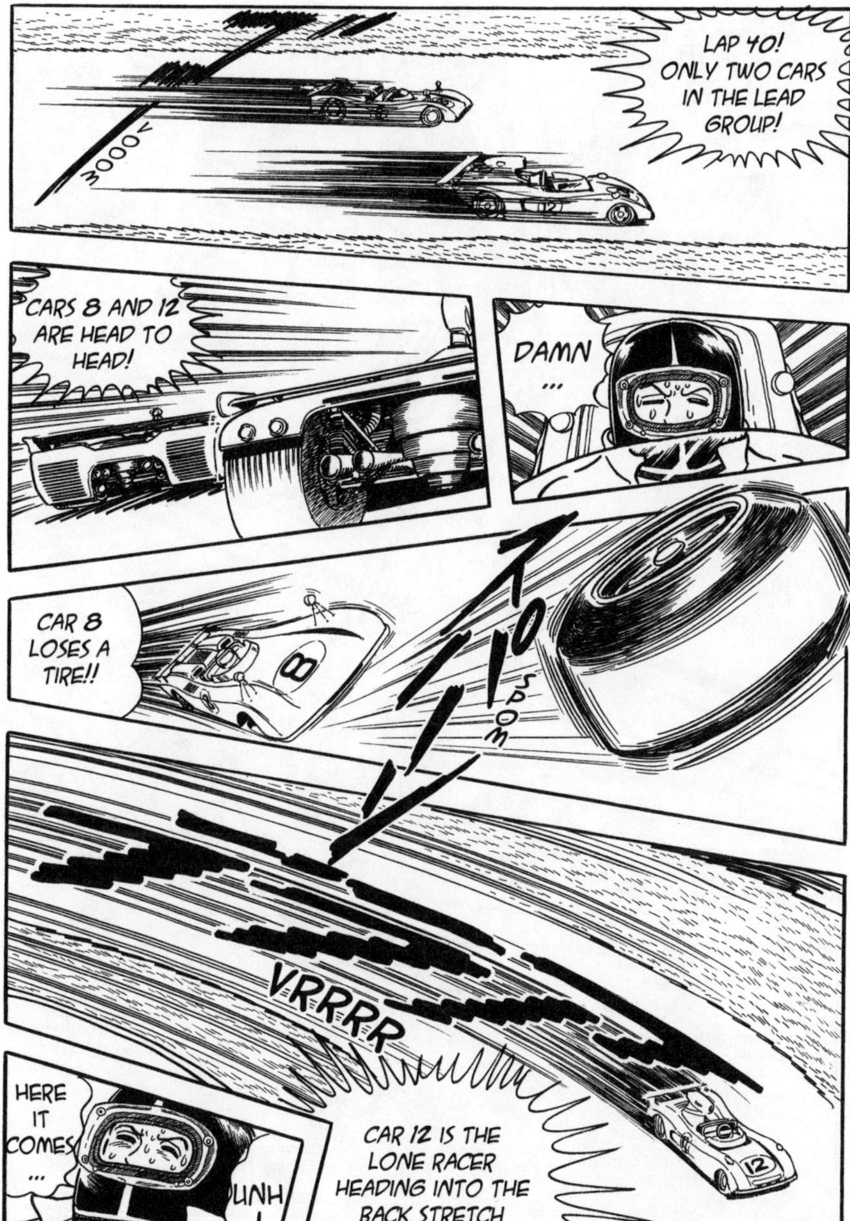
LAP 40! ONLY TWO CARS IN THE LEAD GROUP!
DAMN ...
CARS 8 AND 12 ARE HEAD TO HEAD!
CAR 8 LOSES A TIRE!!
SPOM
VRRRR
CAR 12 IS THE LONE RACER HEADING INTO THE BACK STRETCH OF LAP 40!
HERE IT COMES ...
UNH!

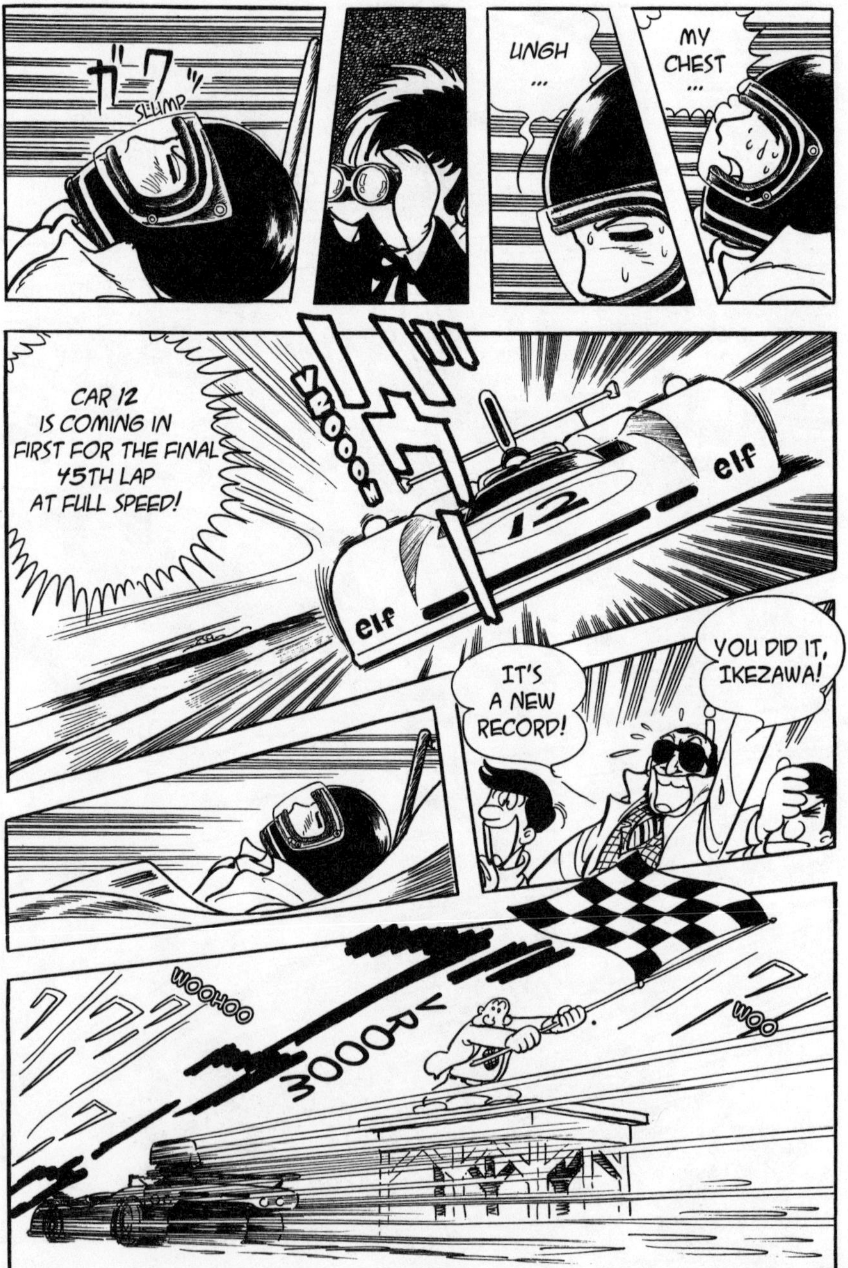
MY CHEST ...
UNGH ...
ガクッ
SLUMP
VROOOOM
CAR 12 IS COMING IN FIRST FOR THE FINAL 45TH LAP AT FULL SPEED!
YOU DID IT, IKEZAWA!
IT'S A NEW RECORD!
WOO
VROOOM
WOOHOO

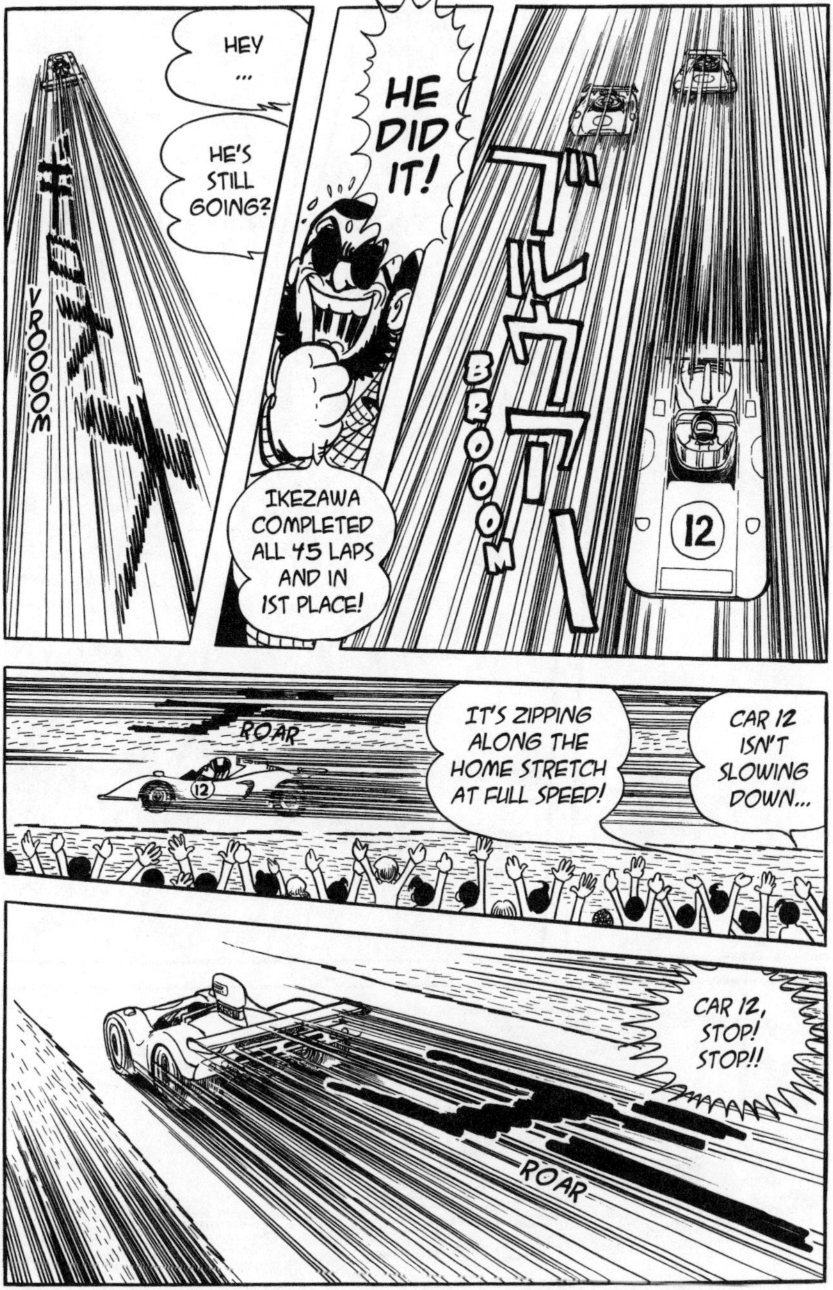
BROOOOM
HE DID IT!
IKEZAWA COMPLETED ALL 45 LAPS AND IN 1ST PLACE!
HEY ...
HE'S STILL GOING?
VROOOOM
CAR 12 ISN'T SLOWING DOWN...
IT'S ZIPPING ALONG THE HOME STRETCH AT FULL SPEED!
ROAR
CAR 12, STOP! STOP!!
ROAR

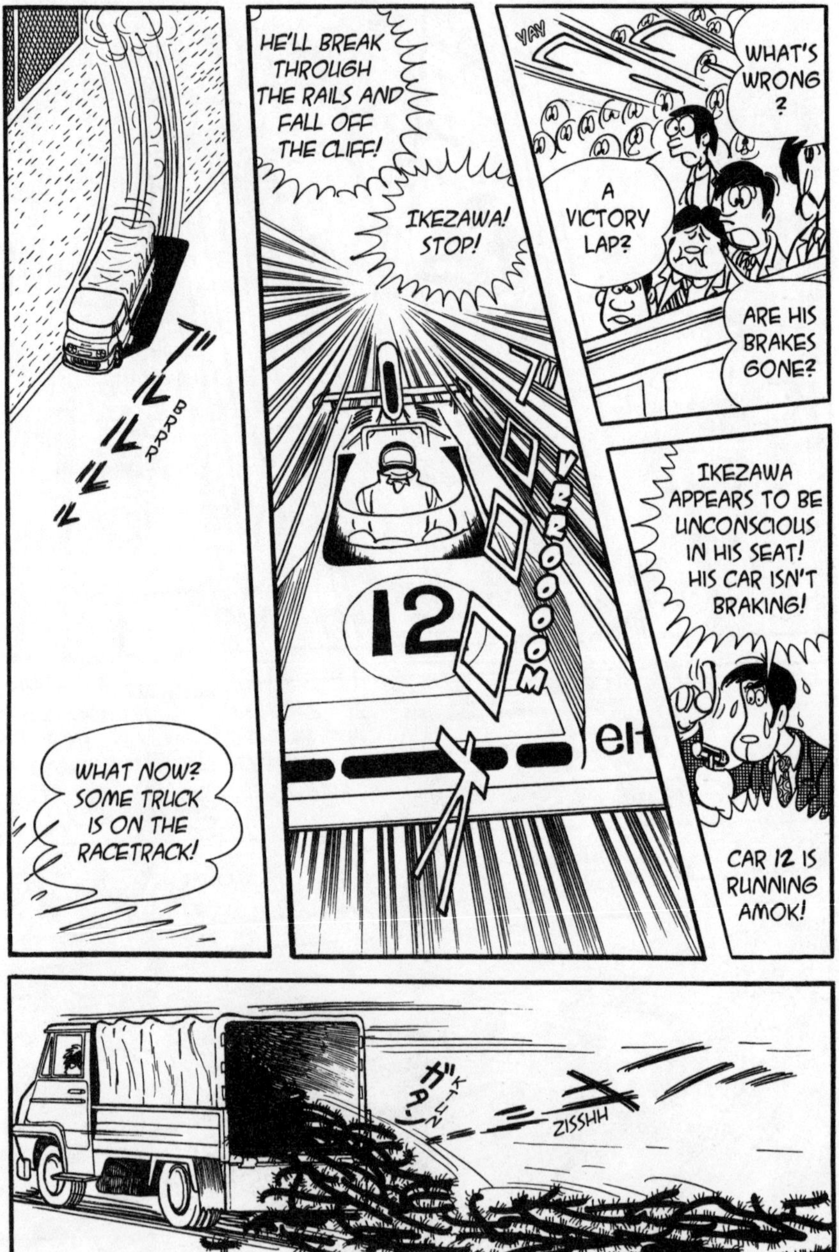
YAY
WHAT'S WRONG?
A VICTORY LAP?
ARE HIS BRAKES GONE?
IKEZAWA APPEARS TO BE UNCONSCIOUS IN HIS SEAT! HIS CAR ISN'T BRAKING!
CAR 12 IS RUNNING AMOK!
HE'LL BREAK THROUGH THE RAILS AND FALL OFF THE CLIFF!
IKEZAWA! STOP!
VRROOOOM
12
BRRRR
WHAT NOW? SOME TRUCK IS ON THE RACETRACK!
KTUN
ZISSHH

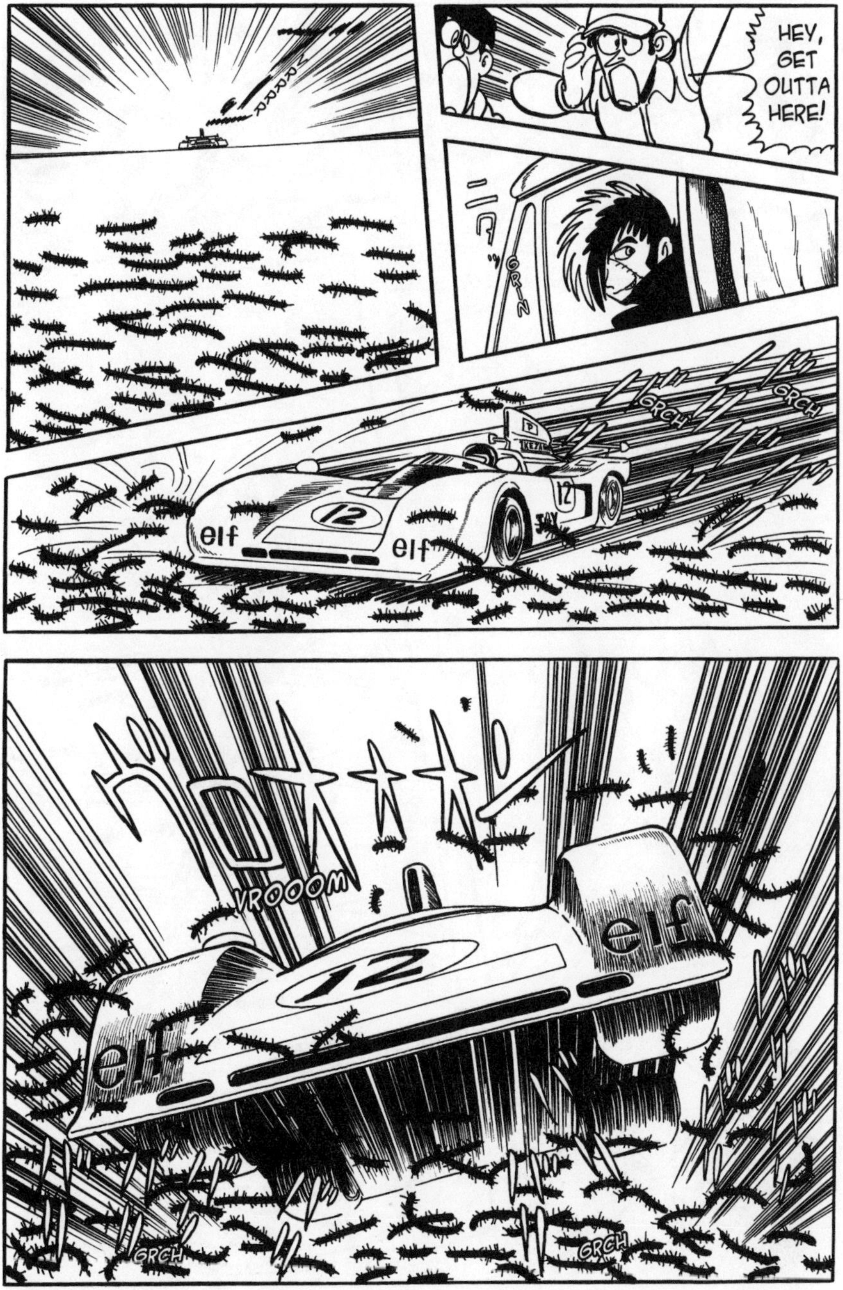
HEY, GET OUTTA HERE!
GRIN
GRCH
GRCH
VROOOM
GRCH
GRCH

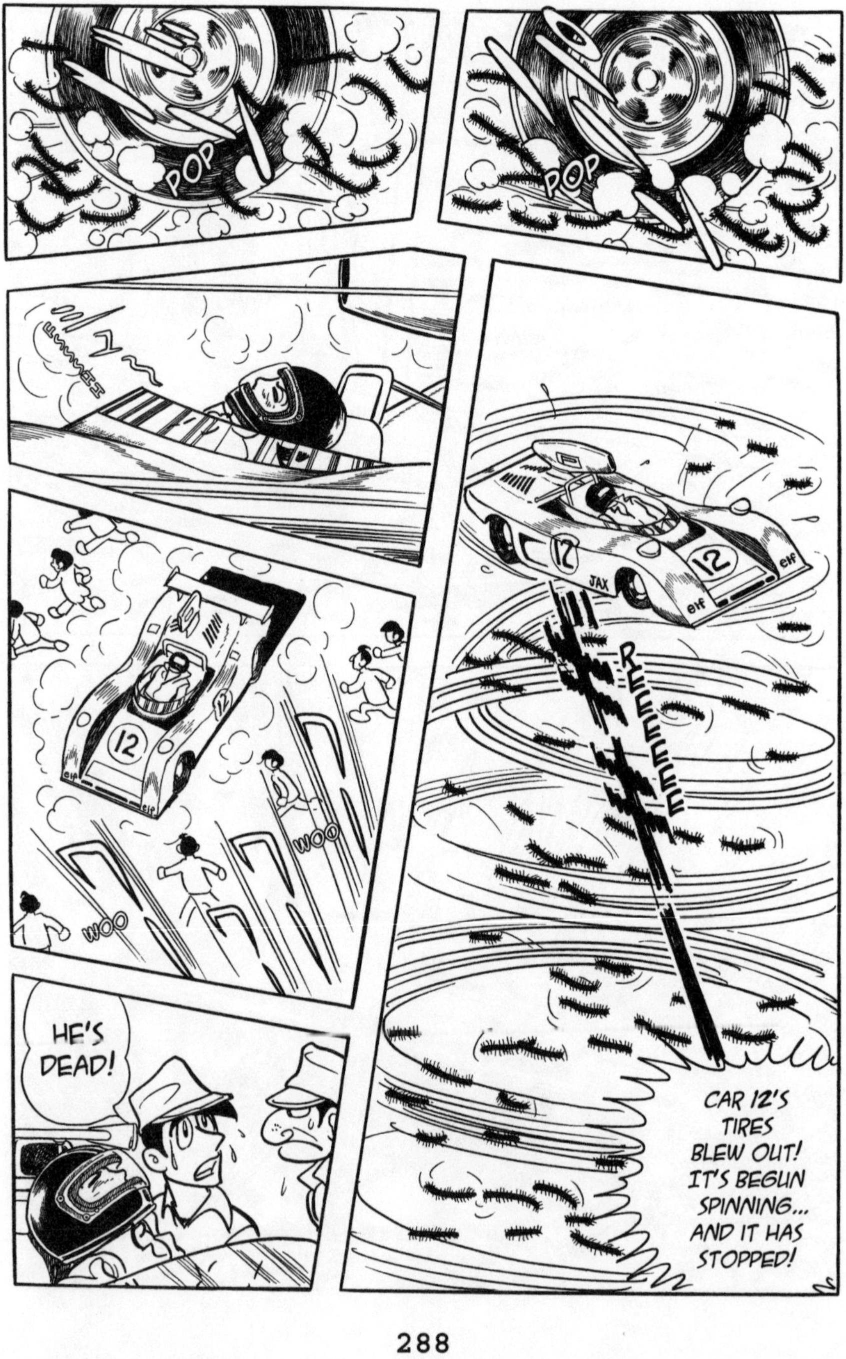
POP
POP
12
JAX
elf
REEEEEE
CAR 12'S TIRES BLEW OUT! IT'S BEGUN SPINNING... AND IT HAS STOPPED!
12
WOO
WOO
HE'S DEAD!

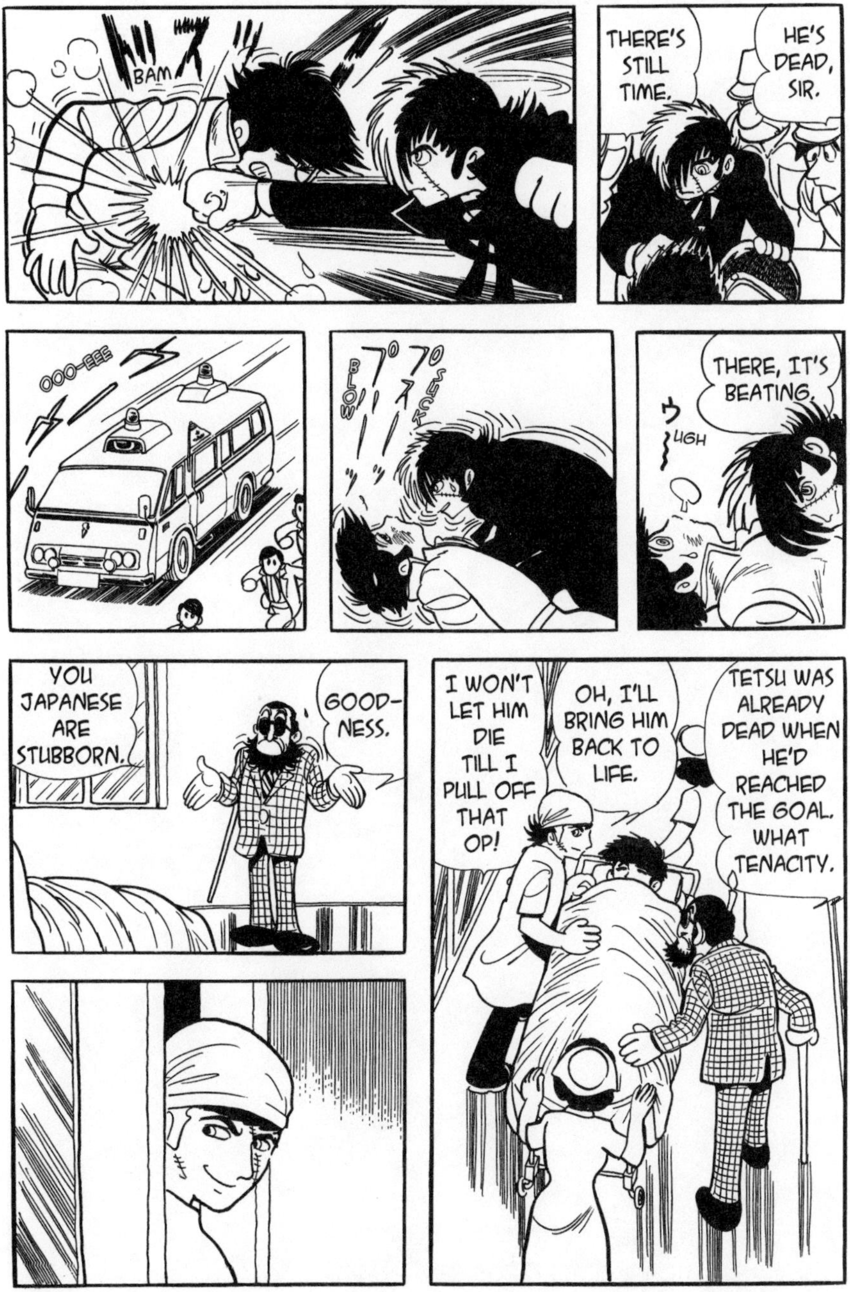
HE'S DEAD, SIR.
THERE'S STILL TIME.
BAM
THERE, IT'S BEATING.
UGH
SUCK
BLOW
OOO-EEE
TETSU WAS ALREADY DEAD WHEN HE'D REACHED THE GOAL. WHAT TENACITY.
OH, I'LL BRING HIM BACK TO LIFE.
I WON'T LET HIM DIE TILL I PULL OFF THAT OP!
GOOD-NESS.
YOU JAPANESE ARE STUBBORN.

GUINEA PIG

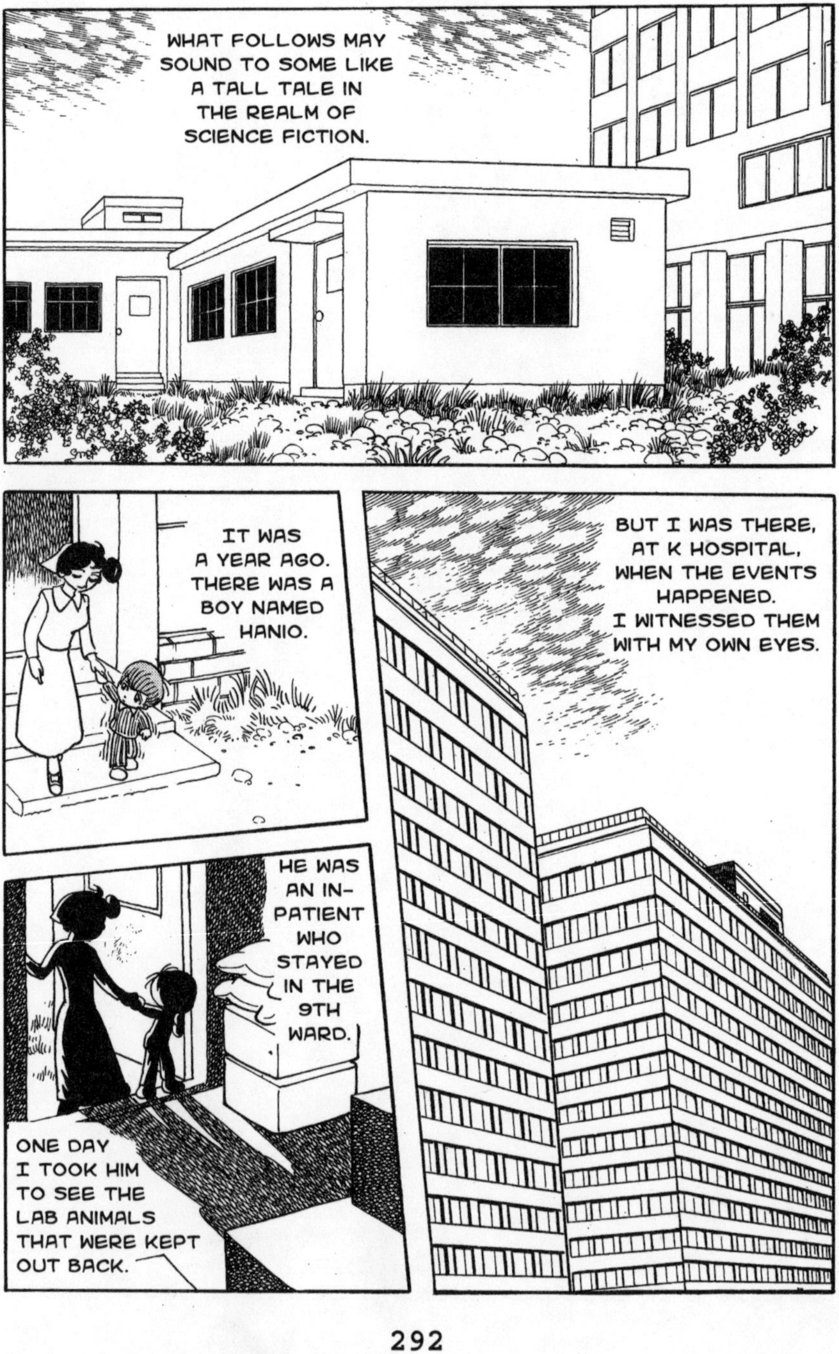

WHAT FOLLOWS MAY SOUND TO SOME LIKE A TALL TALE IN THE REALM OF SCIENCE FICTION.
BUT I WAS THERE, AT K HOSPITAL, WHEN THE EVENTS HAPPENED. I WITNESSED THEM WITH MY OWN EYES.
IT WAS A YEAR AGO. THERE WAS A BOY NAMED HANIO.
HE WAS AN IN-PATIENT WHO STAYED IN THE 9TH WARD.
ONE DAY I TOOK HIM TO SEE THE LAB ANIMALS THAT WERE KEPT OUT BACK.

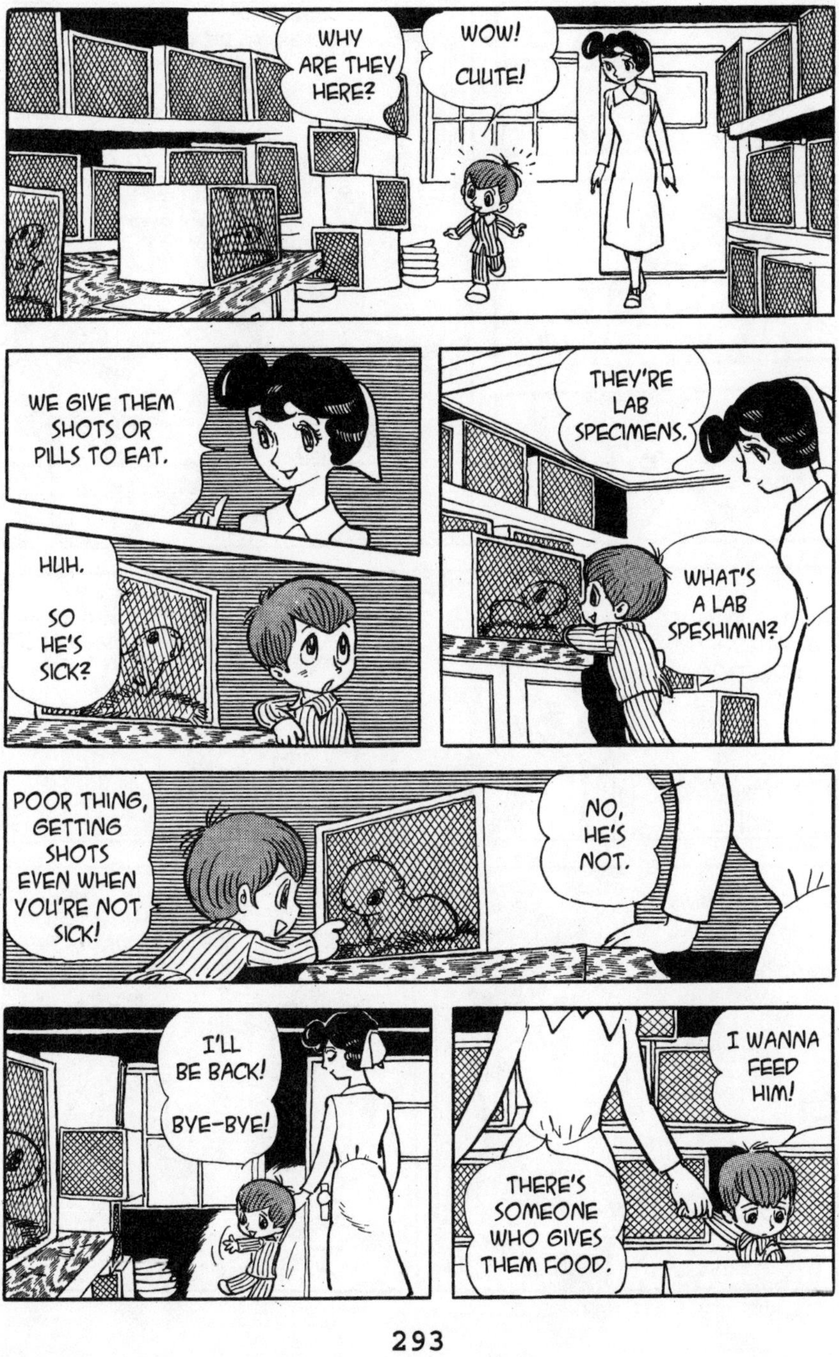
WOW!
CUUTE!
WHY ARE THEY HERE?
THEY'RE LAB SPECIMENS.
WHAT'S A LAB SPESHIMIN?
WE GIVE THEM SHOTS OR PILLS TO EAT.
HUH.
SO HE'S SICK?
NO, HE'S NOT.
POOR THING, GETTING SHOTS EVEN WHEN YOU'RE NOT SICK!
I WANNA FEED HIM!
THERE'S SOMEONE WHO GIVES THEM FOOD.
I'LL BE BACK!
BYE-BYE!

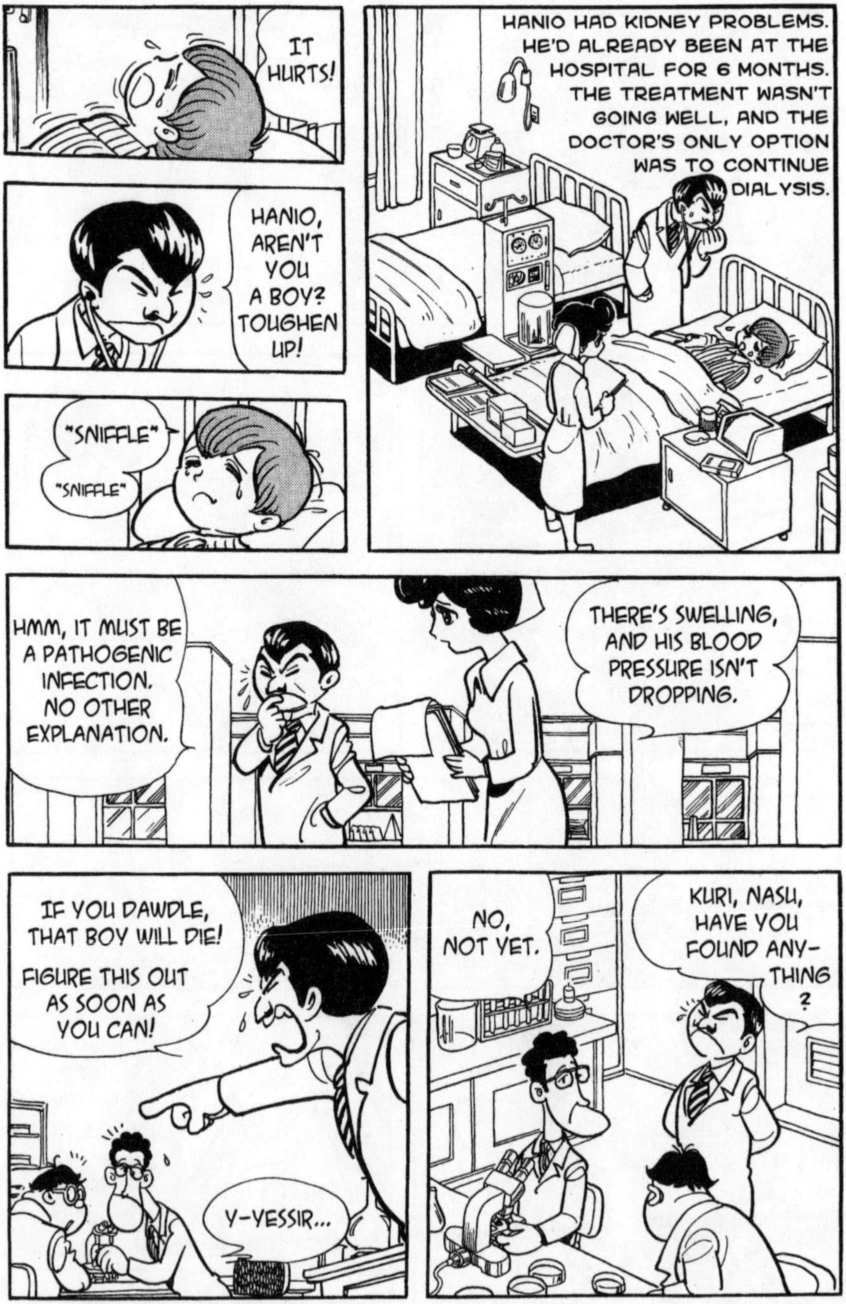
HANIO HAD KIDNEY PROBLEMS. HE'D ALREADY BEEN AT THE HOSPITAL FOR 6 MONTHS. THE TREATMENT WASN'T GOING WELL, AND THE DOCTOR'S ONLY OPTION WAS TO CONTINUE DIALYSIS.
IT HURTS!
HANIO, AREN'T YOU A BOY? TOUGHEN UP!
"SNIFFLE"
"SNIFFLE"
THERE'S SWELLING, AND HIS BLOOD PRESSURE ISN'T DROPPING.
HMM, IT MUST BE A PATHOGENIC INFECTION. NO OTHER EXPLANATION.
KURI, NASU, HAVE YOU FOUND ANY-THING ?
NO, NOT YET.
IF YOU DAWDLE, THAT BOY WILL DIE!
FIGURE THIS OUT AS SOON AS YOU CAN!
Y-YESSIR...

NOTE: KURI = CHESTNUT; NASU = EGGPLANT

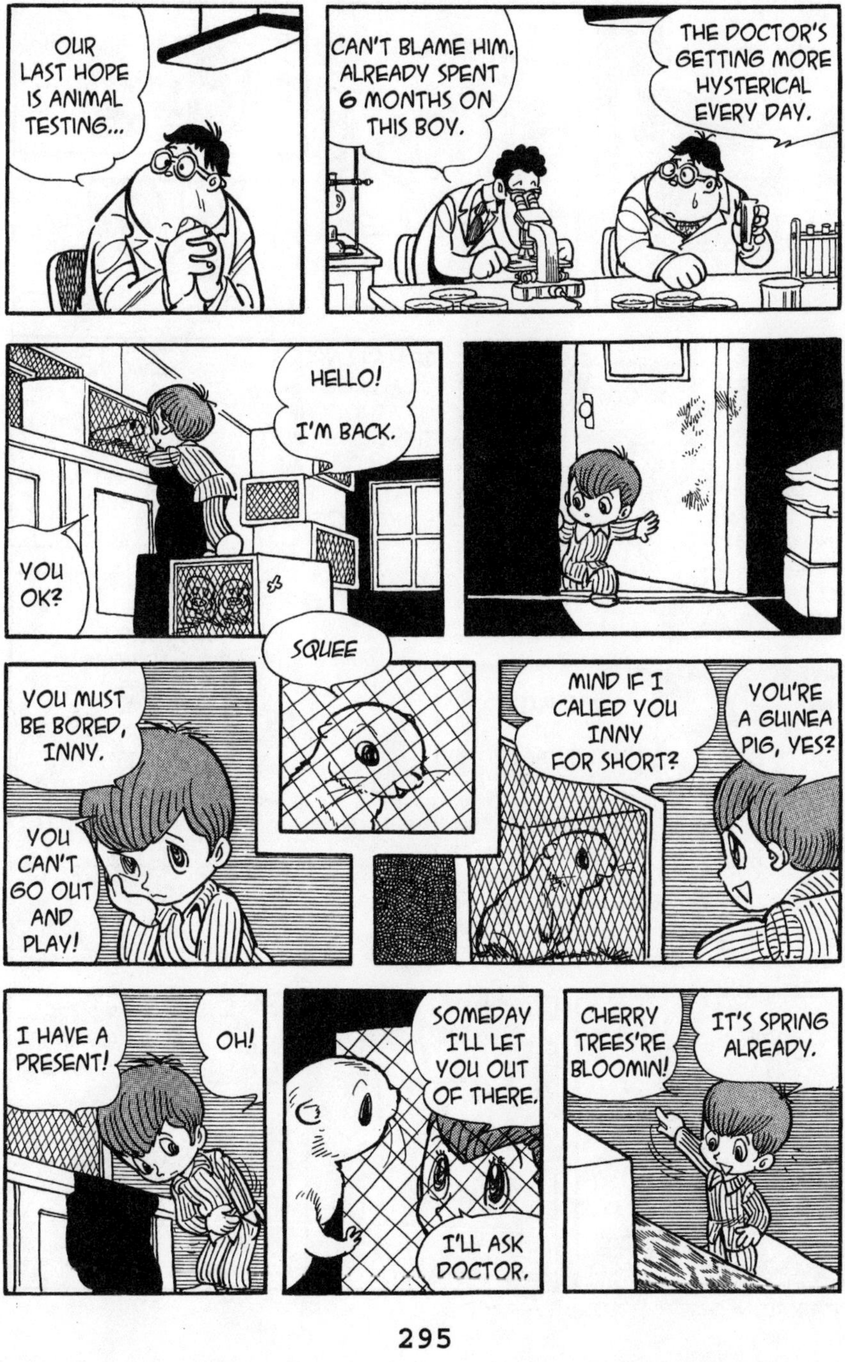
THE DOCTOR'S GETTING MORE HYSTERICAL EVERY DAY.
CAN'T BLAME HIM. ALREADY SPENT 6 MONTHS ON THIS BOY.
OUR LAST HOPE IS ANIMAL TESTING...
HELLO!
I'M BACK.
YOU OK?
YOU'RE A GUINEA PIG, YES?
MIND IF I CALLED YOU INNY FOR SHORT?
SQUEE
YOU MUST BE BORED, INNY.
YOU CAN'T GO OUT AND PLAY!
IT'S SPRING ALREADY.
CHERRY TREES'RE BLOOMIN!
SOMEDAY I'LL LET YOU OUT OF THERE.
I'LL ASK DOCTOR.
OH!
I HAVE A PRESENT!

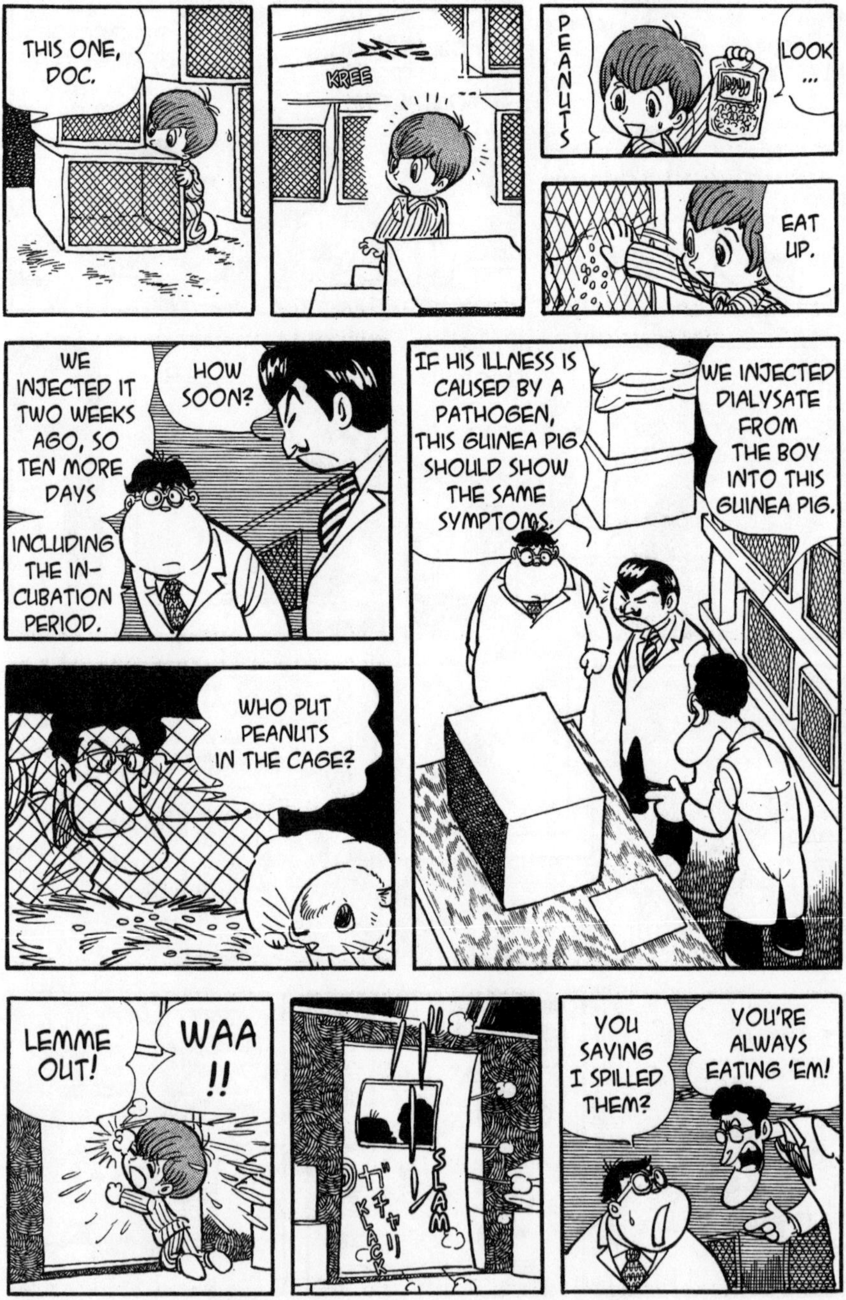
LOOK ...
PEANUTS
EAT UP.
KREE
THIS ONE, DOC.
WE INJECTED DIALYSATE FROM THE BOY INTO THIS GUINEA PIG.
IF HIS ILLNESS IS CAUSED BY A PATHOGEN, THIS GUINEA PIG SHOULD SHOW THE SAME SYMPTOMS.
HOW SOON?
WE INJECTED IT TWO WEEKS AGO, SO TEN MORE DAYS
INCLUDING THE IN-CUBATION PERIOD.
WHO PUT PEANUTS IN THE CAGE?
YOU'RE ALWAYS EATING 'EM!
YOU SAYING I SPILLED THEM?
SLAM
ガチャリ
KLACK
WAA !!
LEMME OUT!

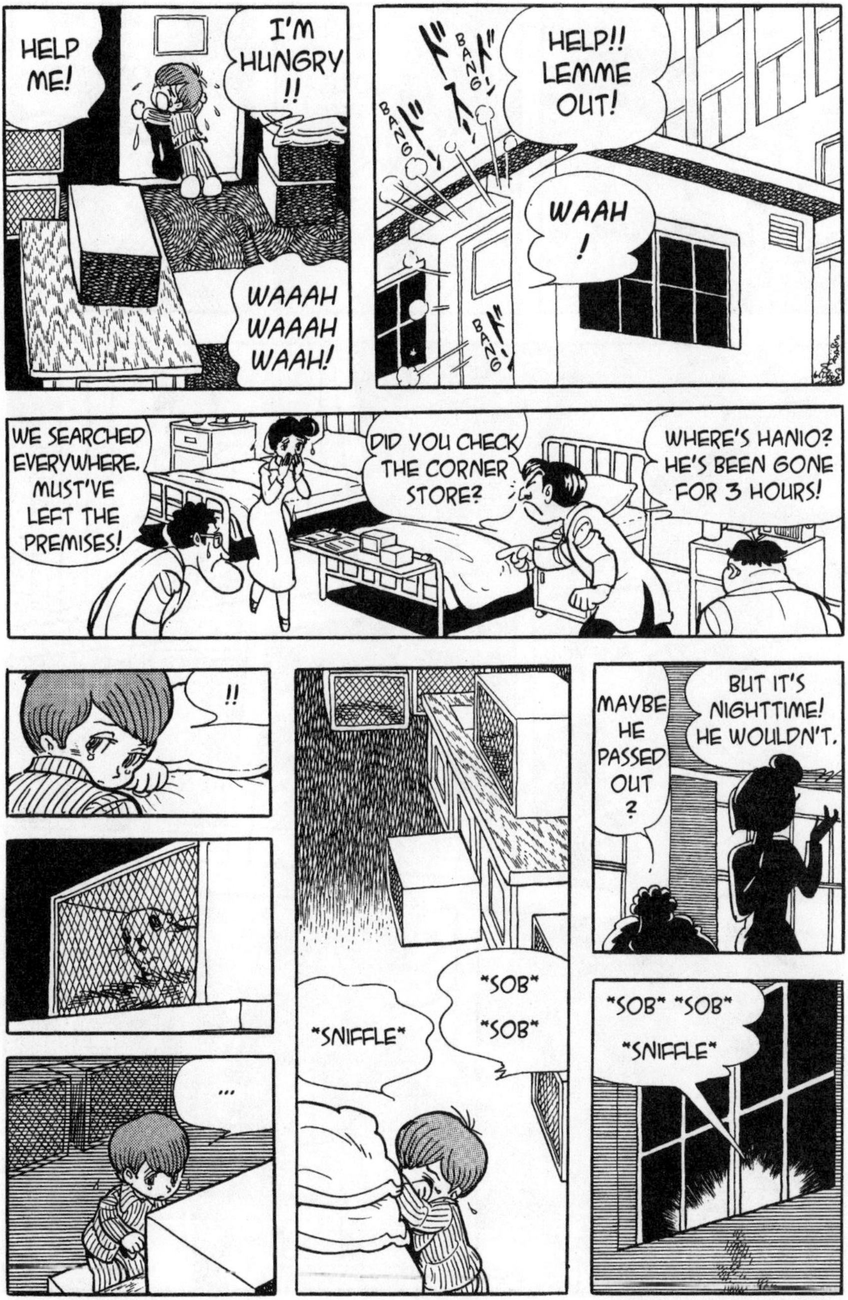
HELP!! LEMME OUT!
BANG
BANG
WAAH !
BANG
I'M HUNGRY !!
HELP ME!
WAAAH WAAAH WAAH!
WHERE'S HANIO? HE'S BEEN GONE FOR 3 HOURS!
DID YOU CHECK THE CORNER STORE?
WE SEARCHED EVERYWHERE. MUST'VE LEFT THE PREMISES!
BUT IT'S NIGHTTIME! HE WOULDN'T.
MAYBE HE PASSED OUT ?
SOB *SOB*
SNIFFLE
SOB
SOB
SNIFFLE
!!
...

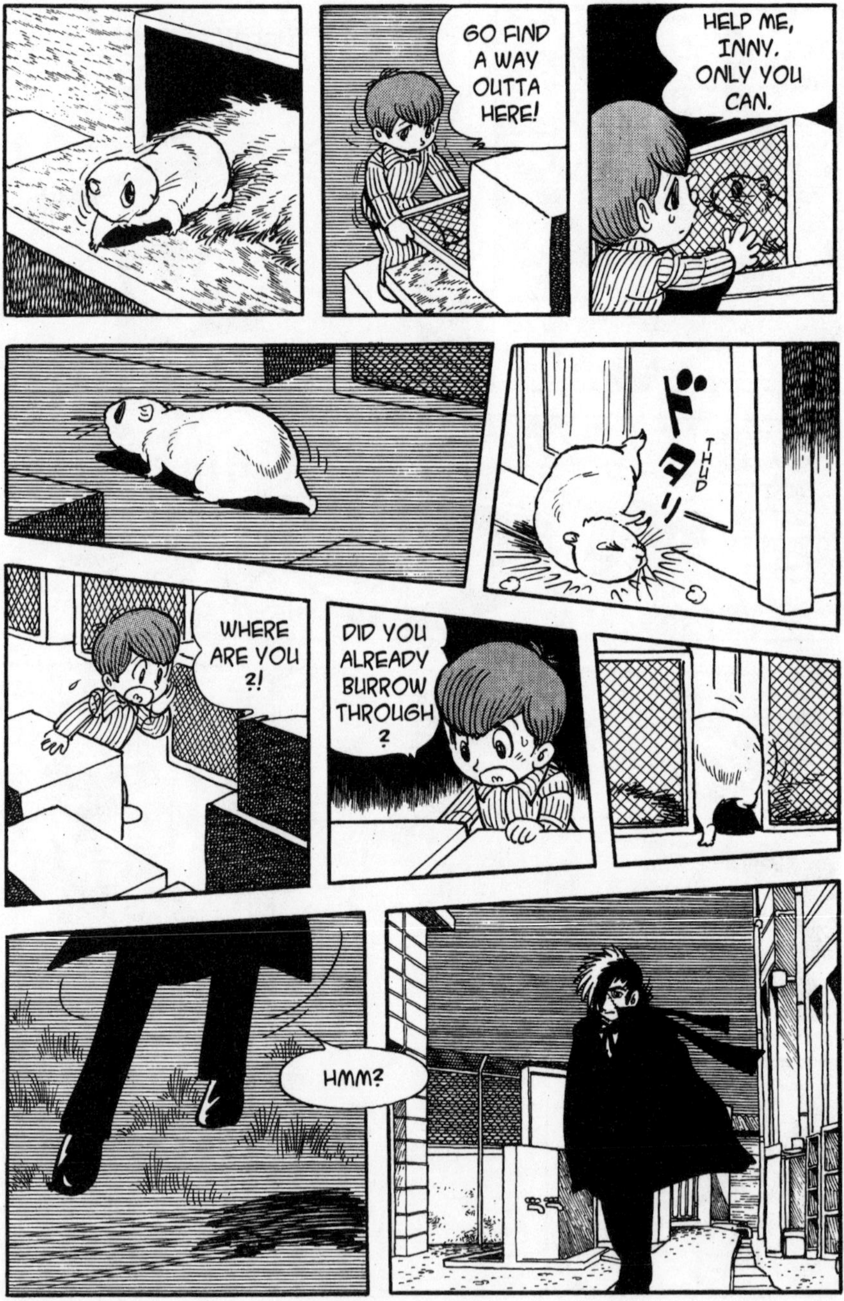
HELP ME, INNY. ONLY YOU CAN.
GO FIND A WAY OUTTA HERE!
ドタリ
THUD
DID YOU ALREADY BURROW THROUGH?
WHERE ARE YOU?!
HMM?

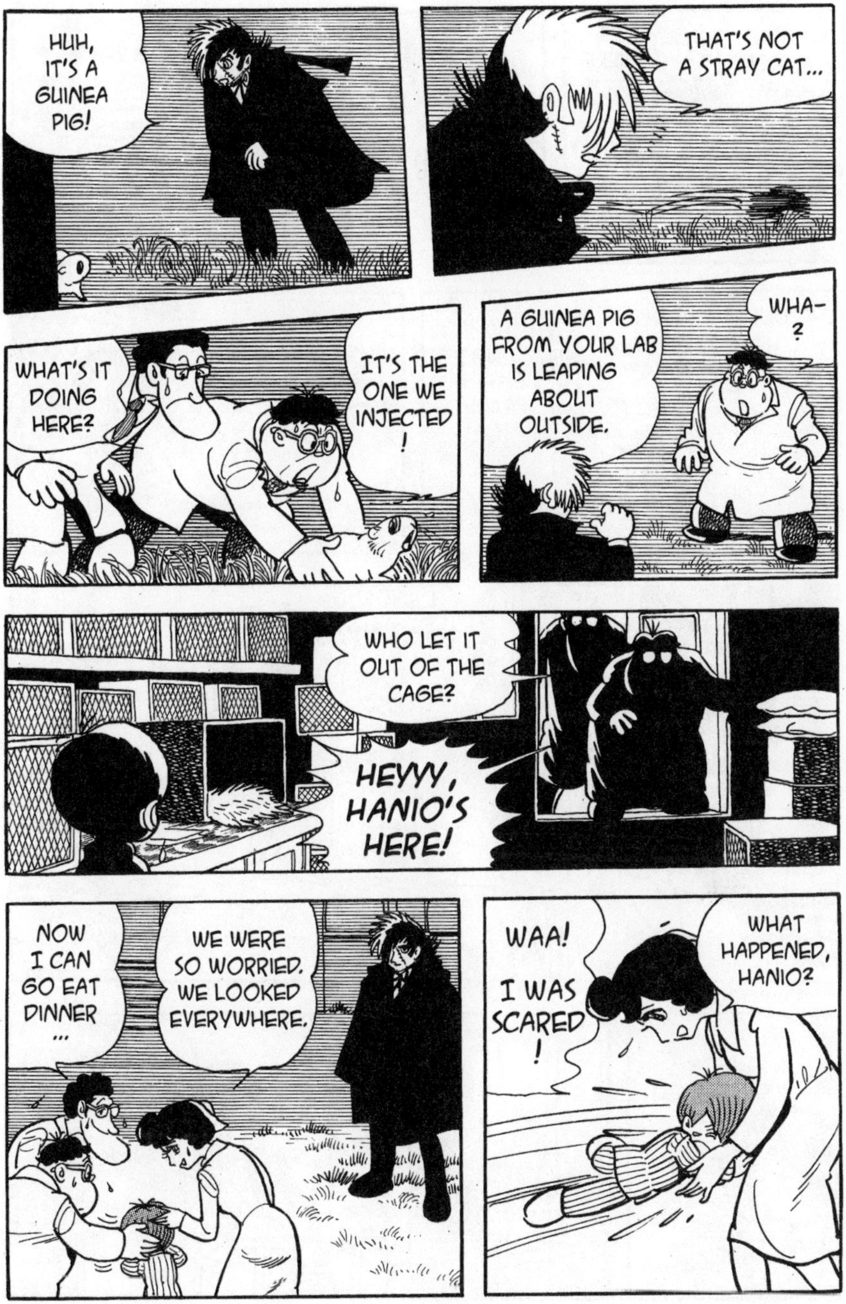
THAT'S NOT A STRAY CAT...
HUH, IT'S A GUINEA PIG!
WHA-?
A GUINEA PIG FROM YOUR LAB IS LEAPING ABOUT OUTSIDE.
IT'S THE ONE WE INJECTED!
WHAT'S IT DOING HERE?
WHO LET IT OUT OF THE CAGE?
HEYYY, HANIO'S HERE!
WHAT HAPPENED, HANIO?
WAA! I WAS SCARED!
WE WERE SO WORRIED. WE LOOKED EVERYWHERE.
NOW I CAN GO EAT DINNER...

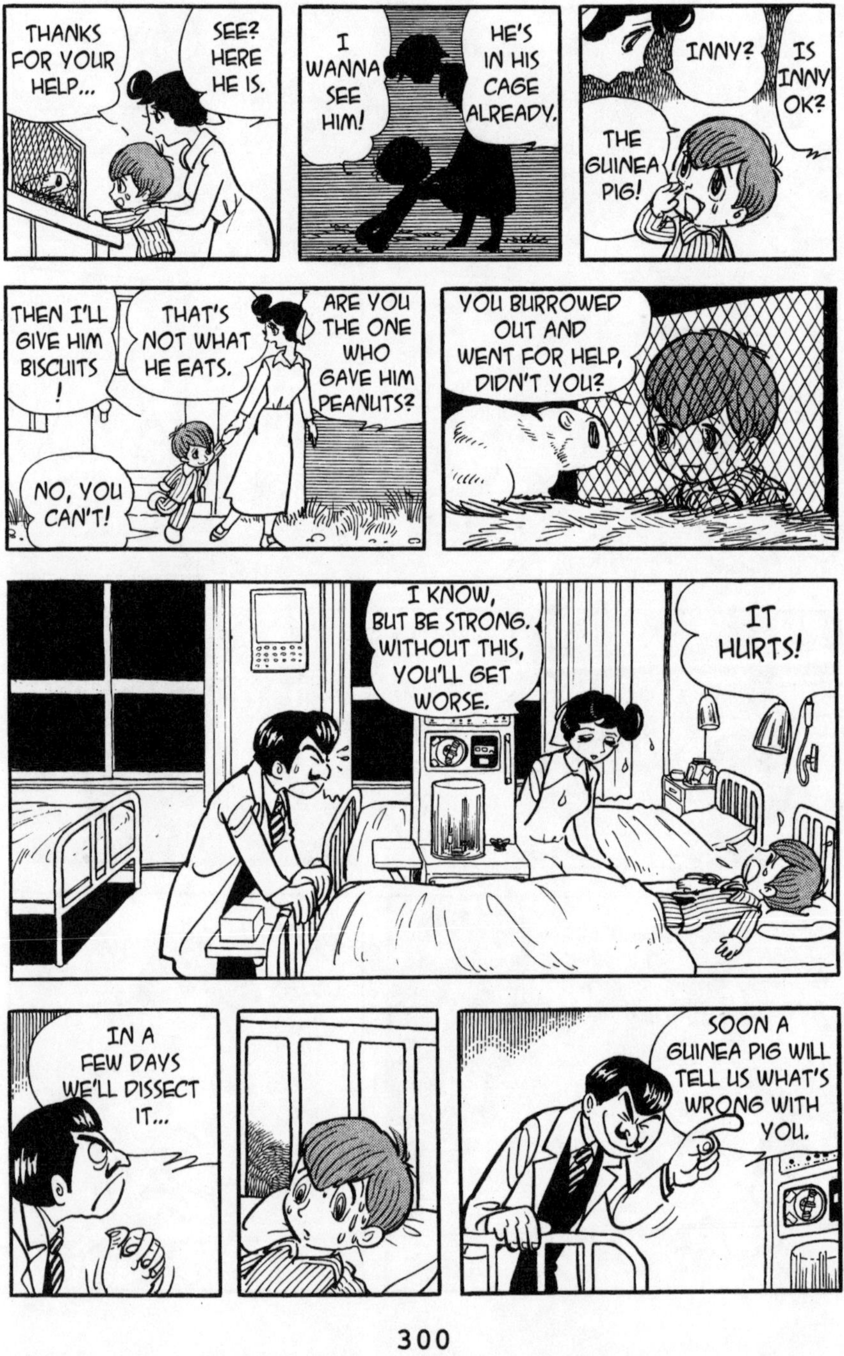
IS INNY OK?
INNY?
THE GUINEA PIG!
HE'S IN HIS CAGE ALREADY.
I WANNA SEE HIM!
SEE? HERE HE IS.
THANKS FOR YOUR HELP...
YOU BURROWED OUT AND WENT FOR HELP, DIDN'T YOU?
ARE YOU THE ONE WHO GAVE HIM PEANUTS?
THAT'S NOT WHAT HE EATS.
THEN I'LL GIVE HIM BISCUITS!
NO, YOU CAN'T!
IT HURTS!
I KNOW, BUT BE STRONG. WITHOUT THIS, YOU'LL GET WORSE.
SOON A GUINEA PIG WILL TELL US WHAT'S WRONG WITH YOU.
IN A FEW DAYS WE'LL DISSECT IT...

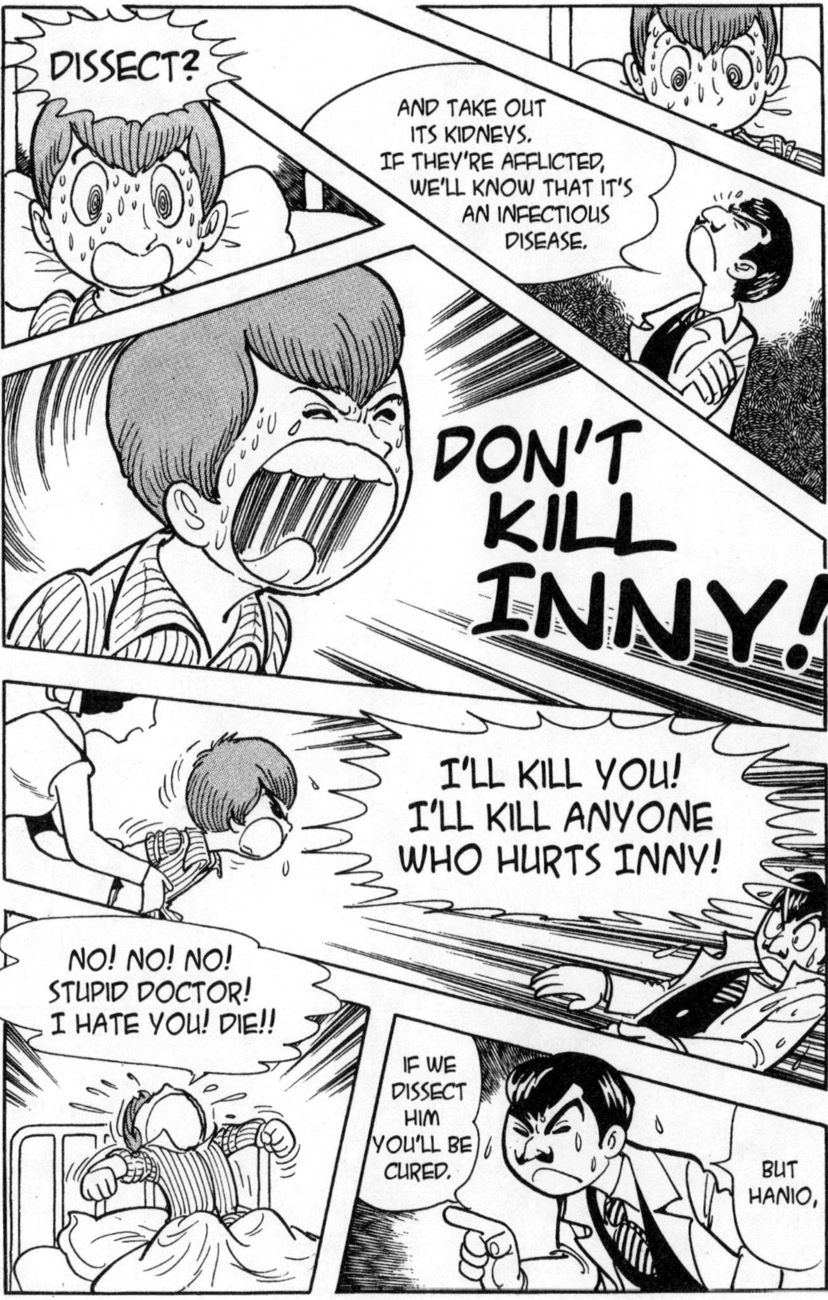
DISSECT?
AND TAKE OUT ITS KIDNEYS. IF THEY'RE AFFLICTED, WE'LL KNOW THAT IT'S AN INFECTIOUS DISEASE.
DON'T KILL INNY!
I'LL KILL YOU! I'LL KILL ANYONE WHO HURTS INNY!
BUT HANIO,
IF WE DISSECT HIM YOU'LL BE CURED.
NO! NO! NO! STUPID DOCTOR! I HATE YOU! DIE!!

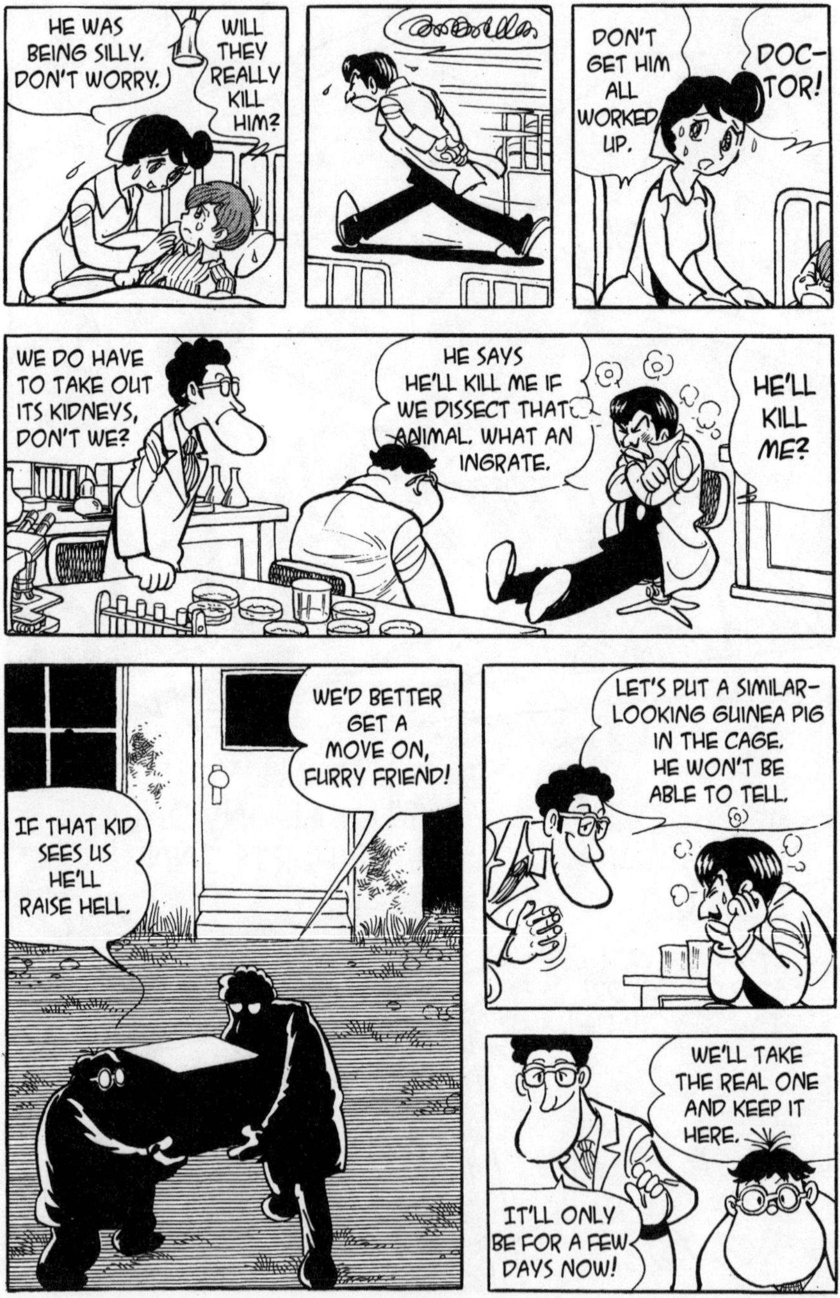
DOC-
TOR!
DON'T GET HIM ALL WORKED UP.
WILL THEY REALLY KILL HIM?
HE WAS BEING SILLY. DON'T WORRY.
HE'LL KILL ME?
HE SAYS HE'LL KILL ME IF WE DISSECT THAT ANIMAL. WHAT AN INGRATE.
WE DO HAVE TO TAKE OUT ITS KIDNEYS, DON'T WE?
LET'S PUT A SIMILAR-LOOKING GUINEA PIG IN THE CAGE. HE WON'T BE ABLE TO TELL.
WE'LL TAKE THE REAL ONE AND KEEP IT HERE.
IT'LL ONLY BE FOR A FEW DAYS NOW!
WE'D BETTER GET A MOVE ON, FURRY FRIEND!
IF THAT KID SEES US HE'LL RAISE HELL.

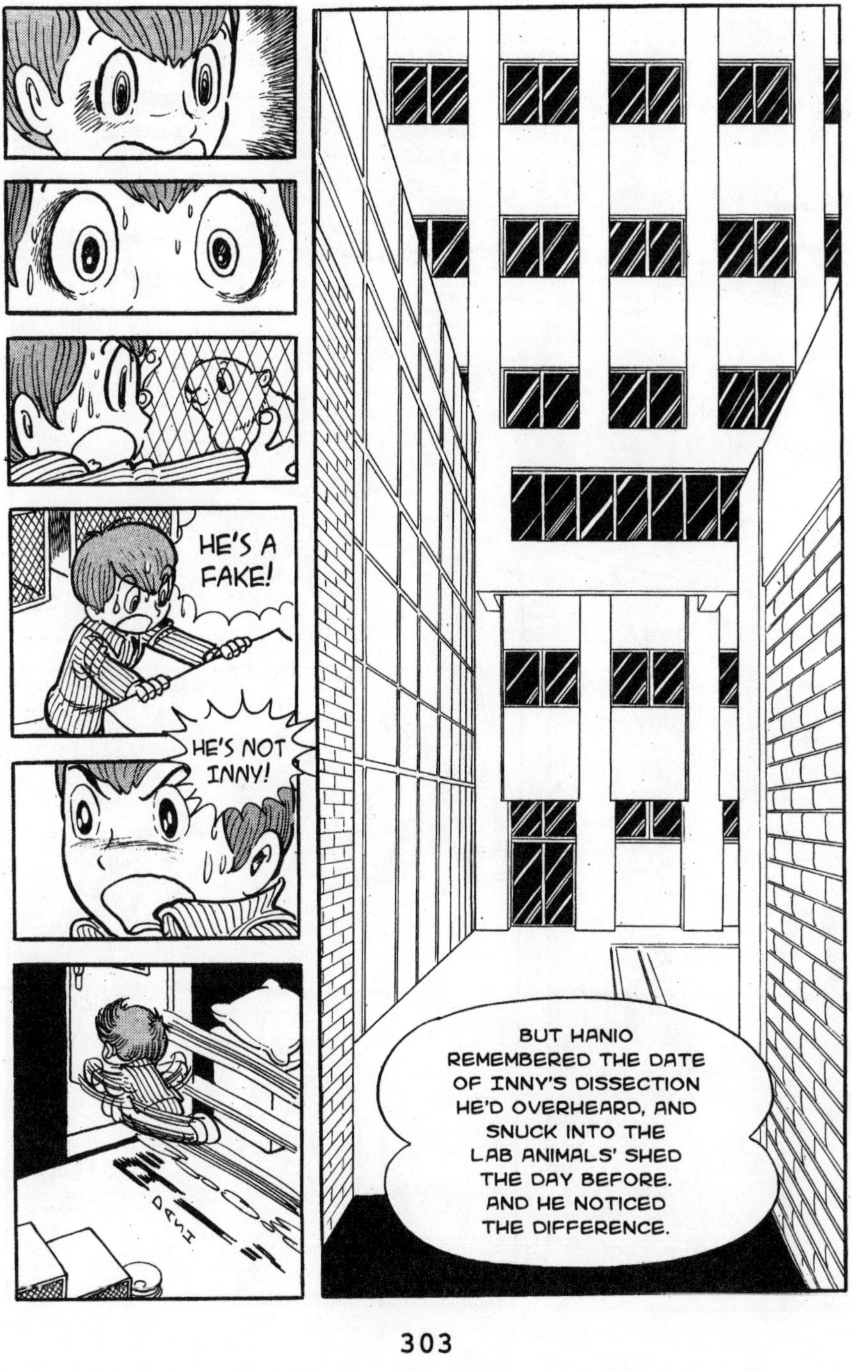
BUT HANIO REMEMBERED THE DATE OF INNY'S DISSECTION HE'D OVERHEARD, AND SNUCK INTO THE LAB ANIMALS' SHED THE DAY BEFORE. AND HE NOTICED THE DIFFERENCE.
HE'S A FAKE!
HE'S NOT INNY!

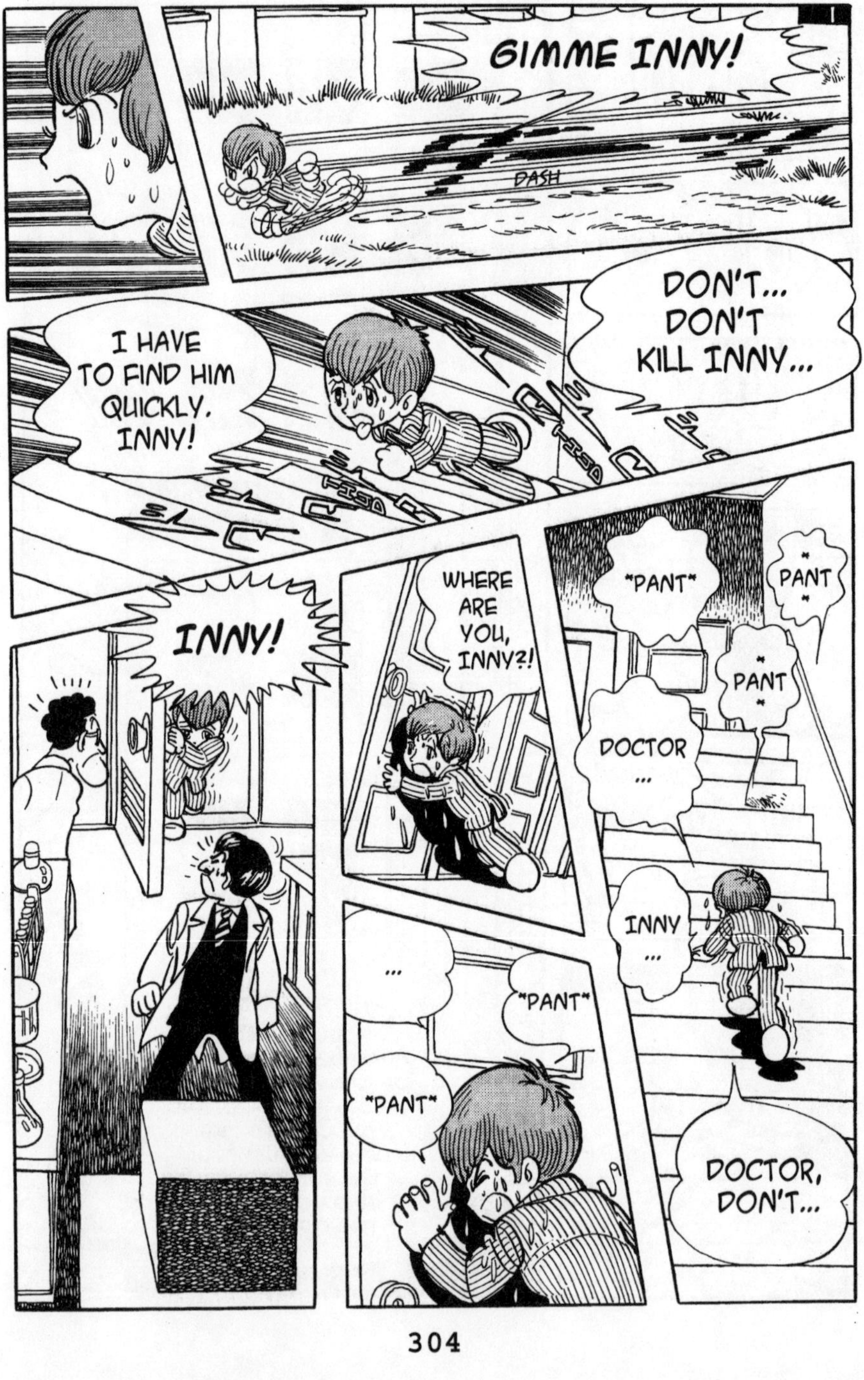
GIMME INNY!
DASH
DON'T... DON'T KILL INNY...
I HAVE TO FIND HIM QUICKLY. INNY!
PANT
PANT
PANT
DOCTOR ...
INNY ...
DOCTOR, DON'T...
WHERE ARE YOU, INNY?!
PANT
...
PANT
INNY!

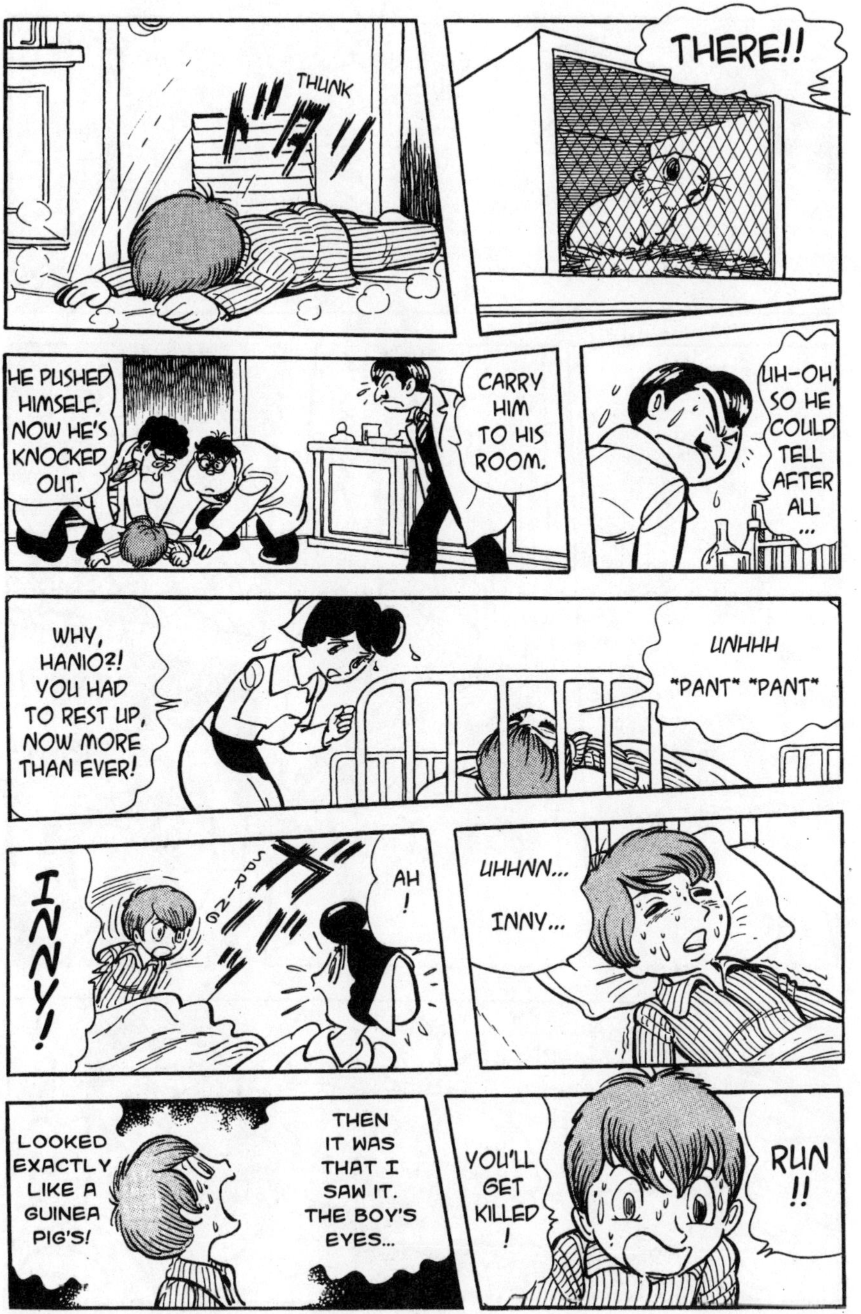
THERE!!
THUNK
UH-OH, SO HE COULD TELL AFTER ALL ...
CARRY HIM TO HIS ROOM.
HE PUSHED HIMSELF. NOW HE'S KNOCKED OUT.
UNHHH *PANT* *PANT*
WHY, HANIO?! YOU HAD TO REST UP, NOW MORE THAN EVER!
UHHNN... INNY...
AH!
SPRING
INNY!
RUN!!
YOU'LL GET KILLED!
THEN IT WAS THAT I SAW IT. THE BOY'S EYES...
LOOKED EXACTLY LIKE A GUINEA PIG'S!

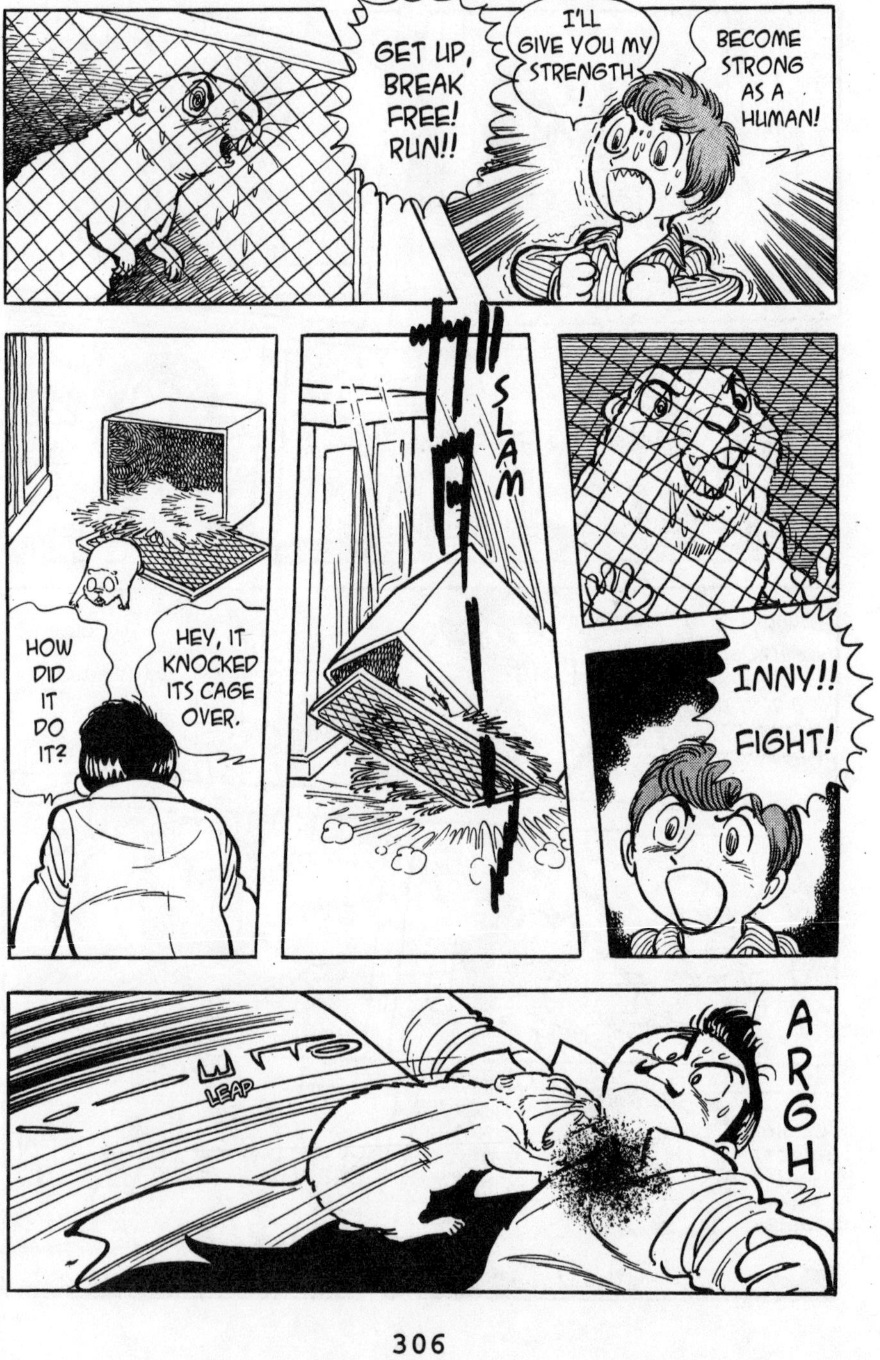
BECOME STRONG AS A HUMAN!
I'LL GIVE YOU MY STRENGTH!
GET UP, BREAK FREE! RUN!!
INNY!!
FIGHT!
SLAM
HEY, IT KNOCKED ITS CAGE OVER.
HOW DID IT DO IT?
ARGH
LEAP

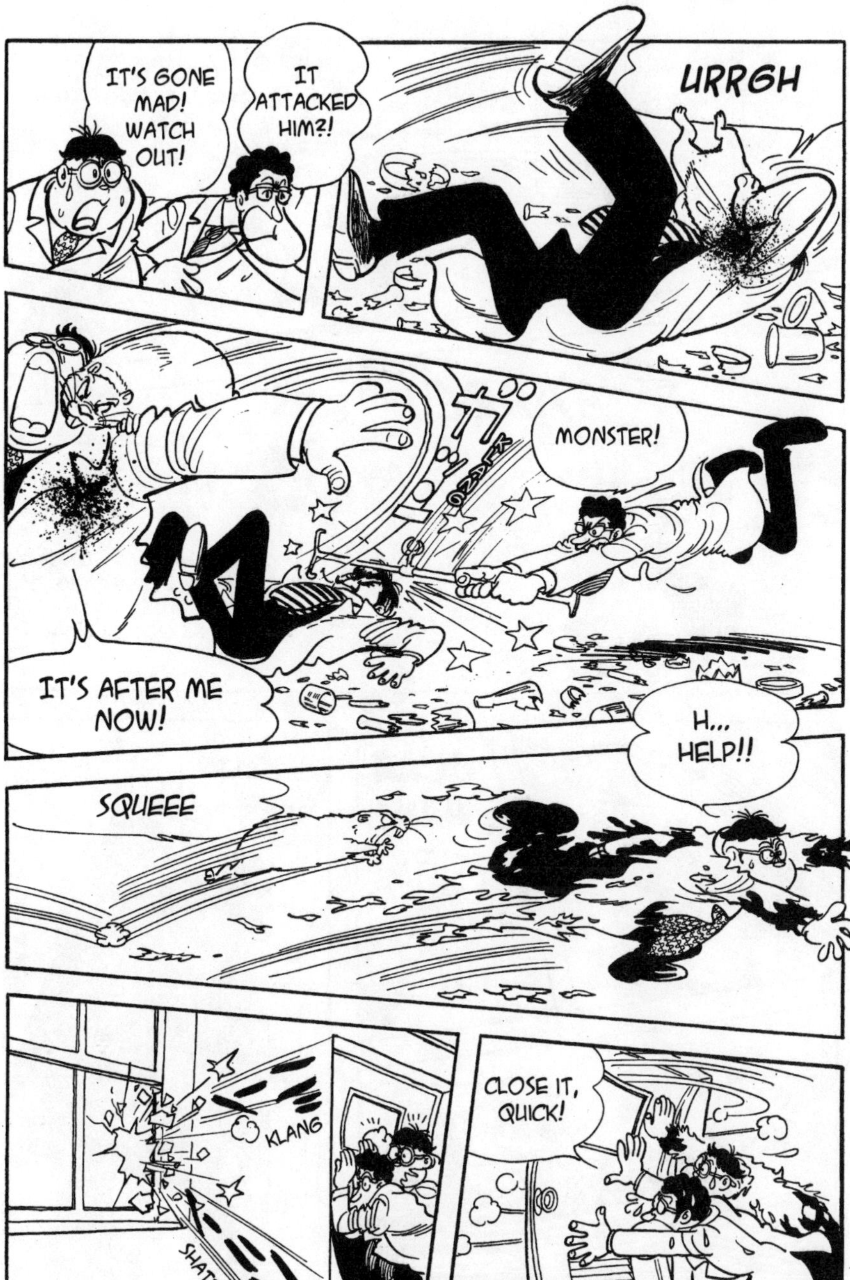
URRGH
IT ATTACKED HIM?!
IT'S GONE MAD! WATCH OUT!
MONSTER!
GZALK
IT'S AFTER ME NOW!
H... HELP!!
SQUEEE
CLOSE IT, QUICK!
KLANG
SHATTER

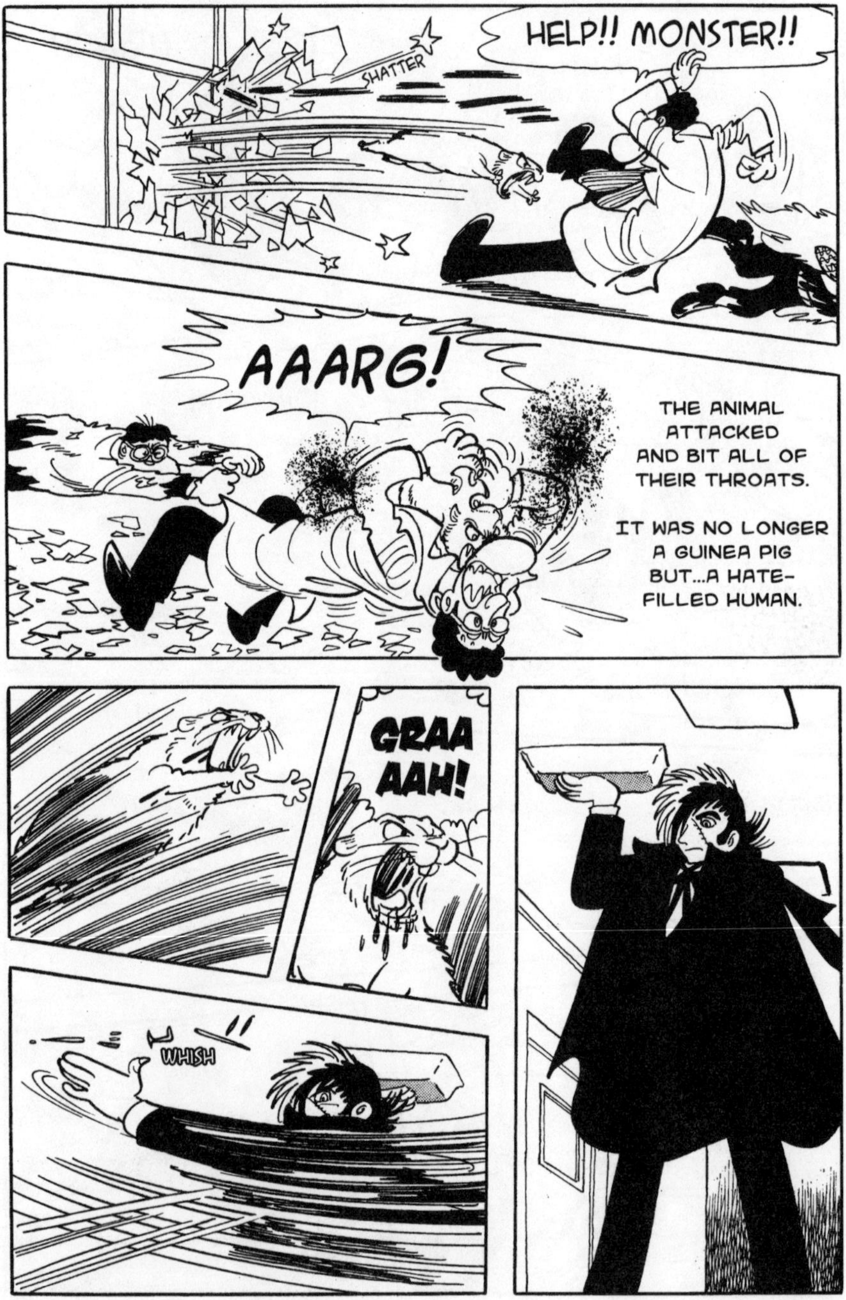
HELP!! MONSTER!!
SHATTER
AAARG!
THE ANIMAL ATTACKED AND BIT ALL OF THEIR THROATS.
IT WAS NO LONGER A GUINEA PIG BUT...A HATE-FILLED HUMAN.
GRAA AAH!
WHISH

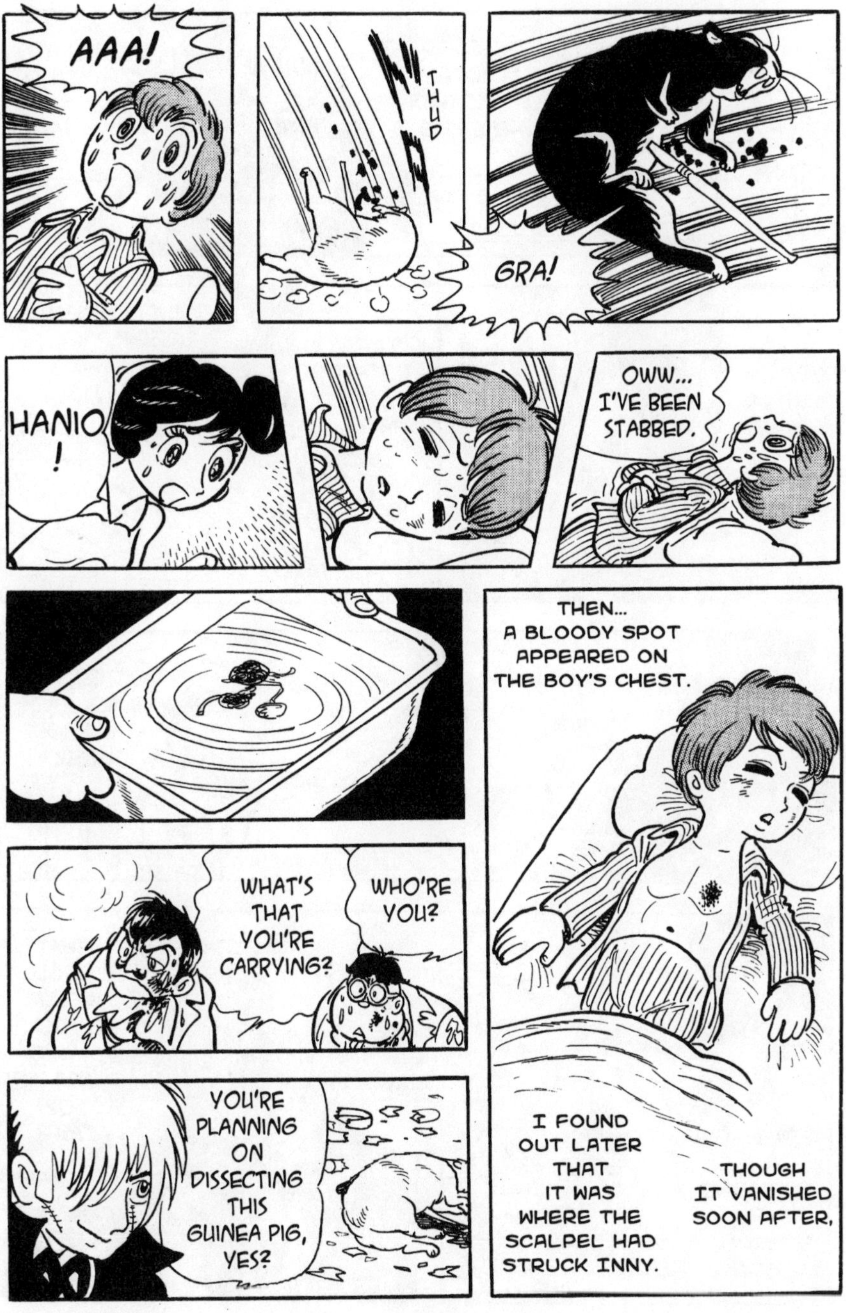
GRA!
THUD
AAA!
OWW... I'VE BEEN STABBED.
HANIO !
THEN... A BLOODY SPOT APPEARED ON THE BOY'S CHEST.
THOUGH IT VANISHED SOON AFTER,
I FOUND OUT LATER THAT IT WAS WHERE THE SCALPEL HAD STRUCK INNY.
WHO'RE YOU?
WHAT'S THAT YOU'RE CARRYING?
YOU'RE PLANNING ON DISSECTING THIS GUINEA PIG, YES?

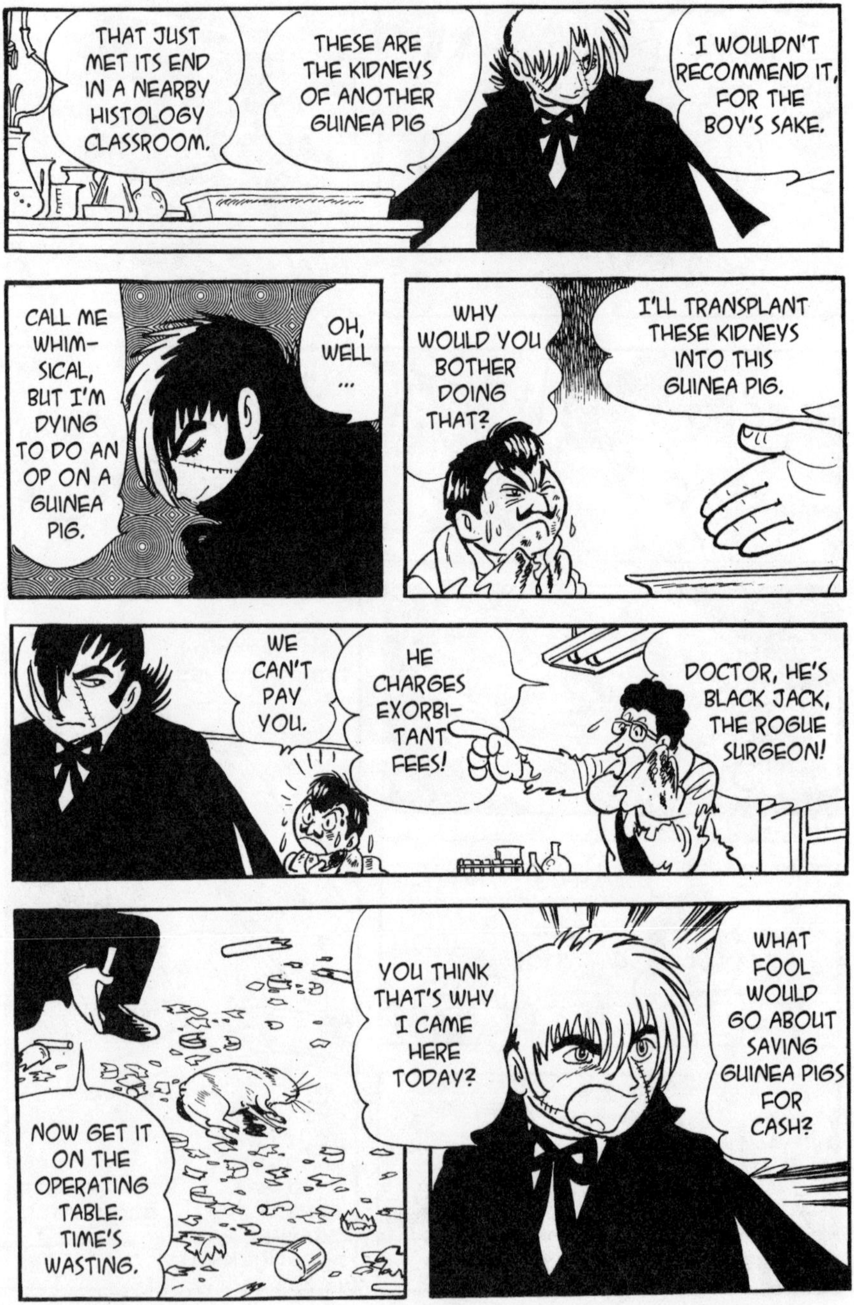
I WOULDN'T RECOMMEND IT, FOR THE BOY'S SAKE.
THESE ARE THE KIDNEYS OF ANOTHER GUINEA PIG
THAT JUST MET ITS END IN A NEARBY HISTOLOGY CLASSROOM.
I'LL TRANSPLANT THESE KIDNEYS INTO THIS GUINEA PIG.
WHY WOULD YOU BOTHER DOING THAT?
OH, WELL ...
CALL ME WHIM-SICAL, BUT I'M DYING TO DO AN OP ON A GUINEA PIG.
DOCTOR, HE'S BLACK JACK, THE ROGUE SURGEON!
HE CHARGES EXORBI-TANT FEES!
WE CAN'T PAY YOU.
WHAT FOOL WOULD GO ABOUT SAVING GUINEA PIGS FOR CASH?
YOU THINK THAT'S WHY I CAME HERE TODAY?
NOW GET IT ON THE OPERATING TABLE. TIME'S WASTING.

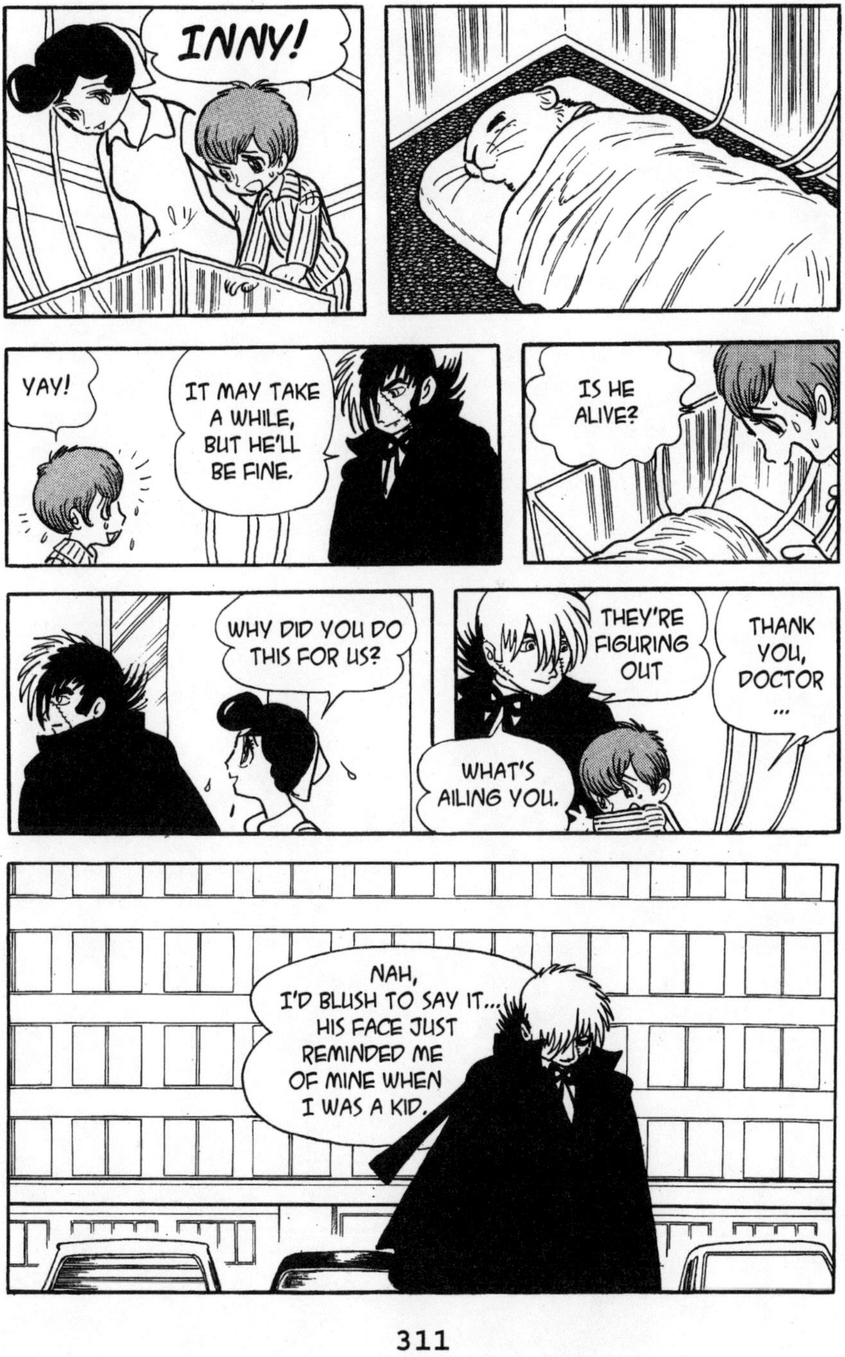
INNY!
IS HE ALIVE?
IT MAY TAKE A WHILE, BUT HE'LL BE FINE.
YAY!
THANK YOU, DOCTOR ...
THEY'RE FIGURING OUT
WHAT'S AILING YOU.
WHY DID YOU DO THIS FOR US?
NAH, I'D BLUSH TO SAY IT... HIS FACE JUST REMINDED ME OF MINE WHEN I WAS A KID.

SPECIAL EXCERPT

ODE TO KIRIHITO

A FEW YEARS BEFORE *BLACK JACK*, Tezuka had produced another masterpiece of medical manga, the thriller *Ode to Kirihito*. Unlike *Black Jack*, which appeared in a shonen or boys' magazine, *Ode* ran in a seinen or young men's periodical and accordingly treated adult themes in a more direct fashion, among other differences. While the much-lauded original Vertical edition has sold out, we'll be reissuing the translation in a new two-volume format in March 2010. We urge *Black Jack* fans above the age of sixteen who have yet to experience the narrative maelstrom that is *Ode* to plunge into it.

Note that *Ode to Kirihito* is printed Western style, or left to right. Please flip to the end of this volume to begin reading the excerpt that follows.

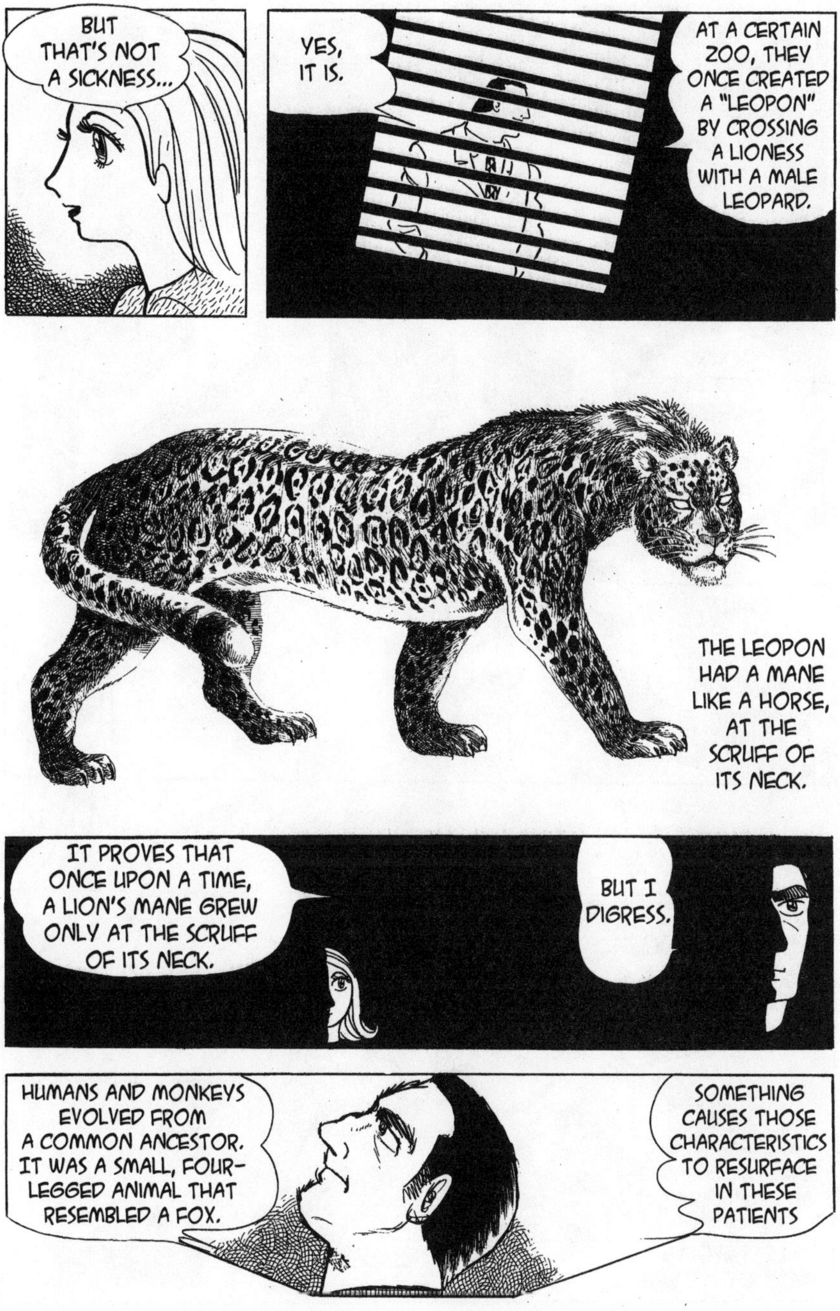
BUT THAT'S NOT A SICKNESS...
YES, IT IS.
AT A CERTAIN ZOO, THEY ONCE CREATED A "LEOPON" BY CROSSING A LIONESS WITH A MALE LEOPARD.
THE LEOPON HAD A MANE LIKE A HORSE, AT THE SCRUFF OF ITS NECK.
IT PROVES THAT ONCE UPON A TIME, A LION'S MANE GREW ONLY AT THE SCRUFF OF ITS NECK.
BUT I DIGRESS.
HUMANS AND MONKEYS EVOLVED FROM A COMMON ANCESTOR. IT WAS A SMALL, FOUR-LEGGED ANIMAL THAT RESEMBLED A FOX.
SOMETHING CAUSES THOSE CHARACTERISTICS TO RESURFACE IN THESE PATIENTS

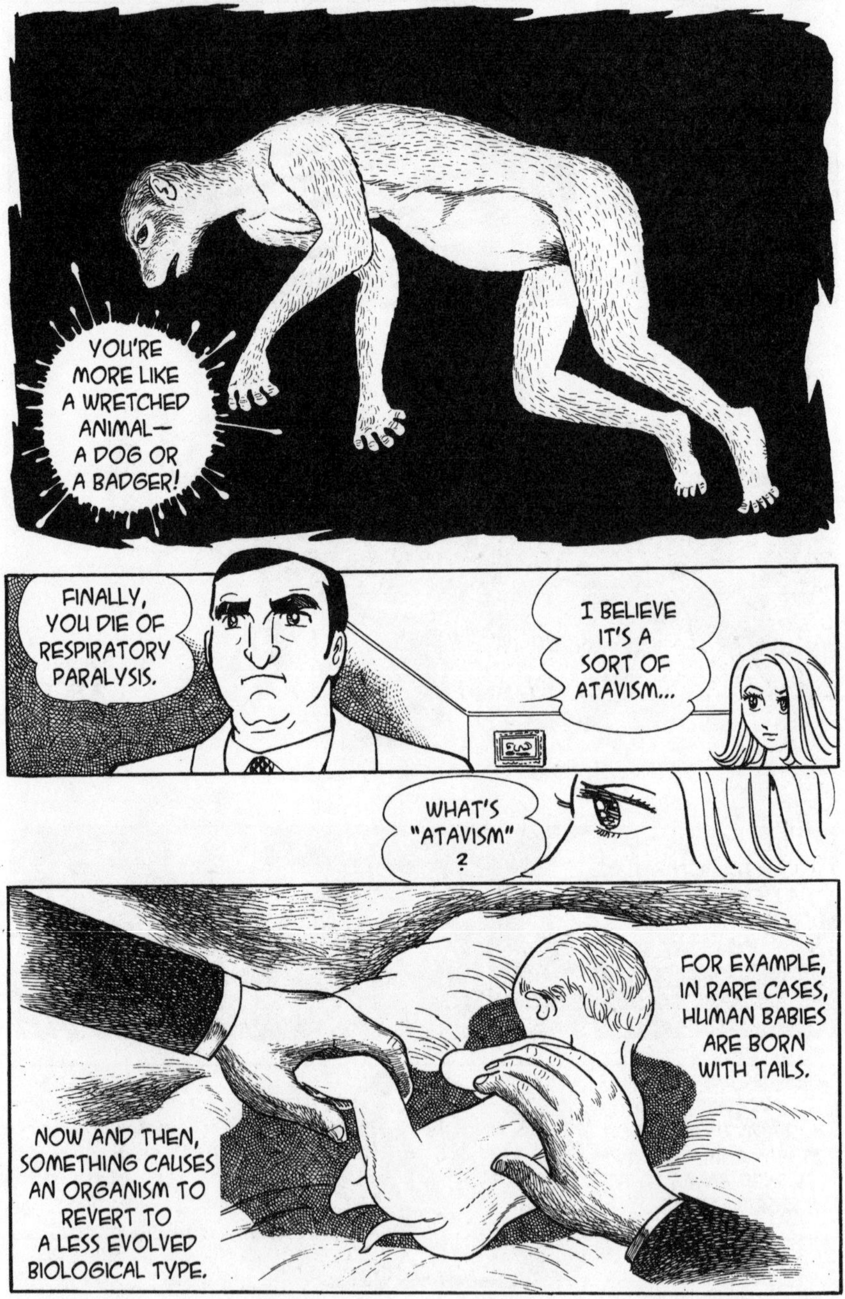
YOU'RE MORE LIKE A WRETCHED ANIMAL— A DOG OR A BADGER!
FINALLY, YOU DIE OF RESPIRATORY PARALYSIS.
I BELIEVE IT'S A SORT OF ATAVISM...
WHAT'S "ATAVISM"?
NOW AND THEN, SOMETHING CAUSES AN ORGANISM TO REVERT TO A LESS EVOLVED BIOLOGICAL TYPE.
FOR EXAMPLE, IN RARE CASES, HUMAN BABIES ARE BORN WITH TAILS.

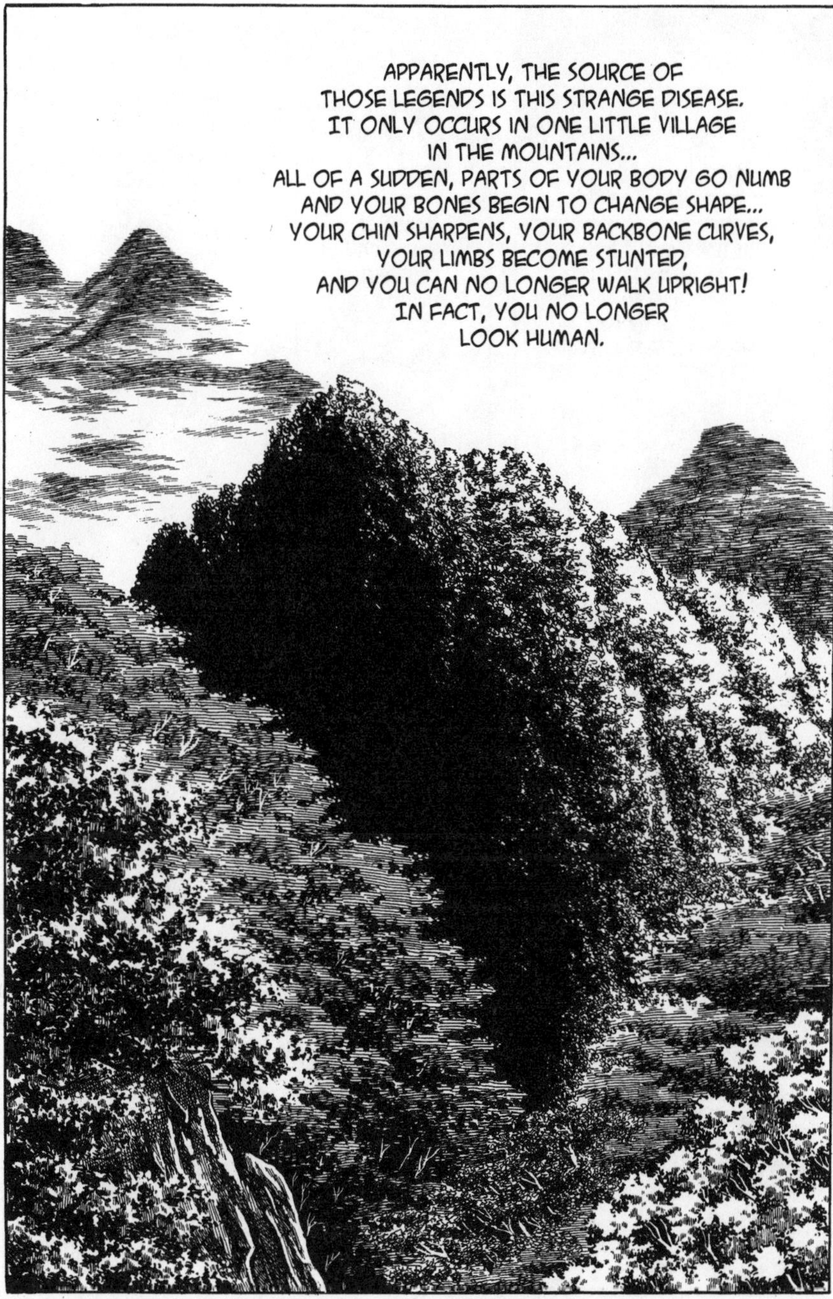
APPARENTLY, THE SOURCE OF THOSE LEGENDS IS THIS STRANGE DISEASE. IT ONLY OCCURS IN ONE LITTLE VILLAGE IN THE MOUNTAINS... ALL OF A SUDDEN, PARTS OF YOUR BODY GO NUMB AND YOUR BONES BEGIN TO CHANGE SHAPE... YOUR CHIN SHARPENS, YOUR BACKBONE CURVES, YOUR LIMBS BECOME STUNTED, AND YOU CAN NO LONGER WALK UPRIGHT! IN FACT, YOU NO LONGER LOOK HUMAN.

COME, NOW, YOU KNOW WHY. THE PATIENT IN ROOM 66 HAS A VERY RARE AND MYSTERIOUS ENDEMIC CONDITION CALLED MONMOW DISEASE. I'M COMPILING DATA ON IT. I'LL COMPLETE MY REPORT BY THE END OF THE YEAR AND PRESENT IT AT THE MEDICAL CONFERENCE.

IT'S JUST UNTIL THE END OF THE YEAR. THAT'S NOT SO LONG FROM NOW.

WHAT IS MONMOW DISEASE, ANYWAY?

SINCE LONG AGO...

A CERTAIN REGION OF SHIKOKU ISLAND HAS HAD LEGENDS OF DOG SPIRITS AND MAGICAL BADGERS... YOU'VE HEARD OF THEM?

NO! NO! NO! I WANT TO GET MARRIED RIGHT NOW!

I'M AFRAID I MIGHT STRAY!

STRAY?

WITH WHOM?

THAT DR. URABE...

HE LOOKS AT ME ALL FUNNY...

URABE ?!

I DON'T LIKE HIM ONE BIT. BUT HE COMES ON SO FORCEFULLY...

AND YOU'RE SO COOL TOWARDS ME...

HAS HE TRIED ANYTHING WITH YOU ?

NO. BUT THE WAY HE LOOKS AT ME...

WHY CAN'T WE JUST GET MARRIED SOONER?